Date Due

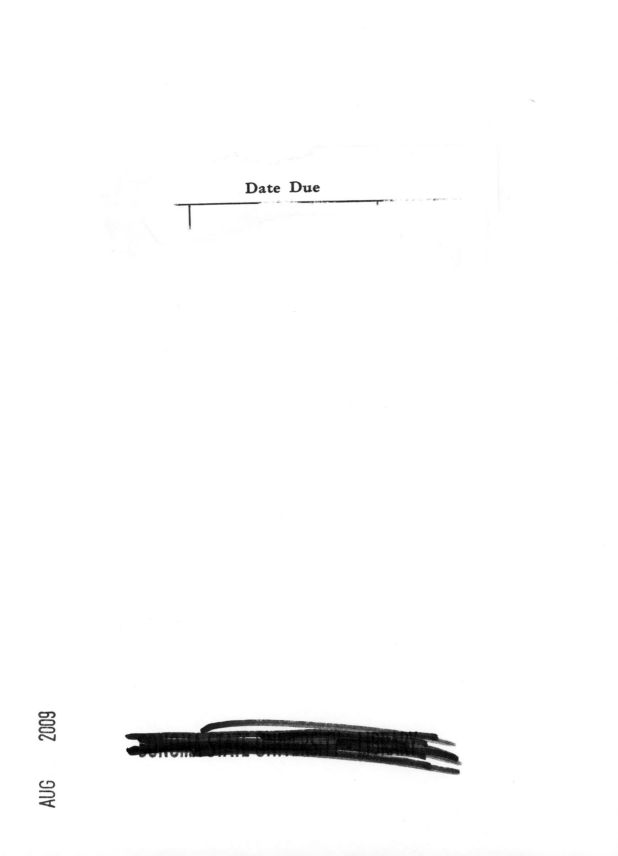

THE PRO/AM BOOK OF MUSIC AND MYTHOLOGY

Compiled, Edited &

with Commentaries by

THOMAS P. LEWIS

Volume 2: Supplements

Index

Pro/Am Music Resources, Inc.
White Plains, New York 10606

Postage stamp illustrations depicting musical themes courtesy Leonard Gilman Collection.

Every effort has been made to trace the ownership of all copyrighted material and to secure necessary permissions to reprint selections from these works. In the event of any question arising as to the use of any material, the editor/publisher, while expressing regret for any inadvertant error, will be happy to make the necessary corrections in future printings. The generosity of both publishers and authors in making portions of their work available for inclusion in these volumes is acknowledged with heartfelt gratitude. NOTE— please see the "List of Sources" at the end of Volume 2, pages 1341-1360, for a complete bibliography of these titles.

FIRST EDITION

Published in the United States of America by

PRO/AM MUSIC RESOURCES, INC.

63 Prospect Street, White Plains, New York 10606

SCHOOL & LIBRARY DISTRIBUTION

PRO/AM MUSIC RESOURCES, INC.

TRADE DISTRIBUTION

THE BOLD STRUMMER, LTD.

20 Turkey Hill Circle — Box 2037

Westport CT 06880

VOLUME 1   ISBN 0-912483-51-2
VOLUME 2   ISBN 0-912483-82-2
VOLUME 3   ISBN 0-912483-83-0

For
DAVID GOLDSTEIN

and in loving memory of my brother
JOHN PARKER MURDOCK
to whom music meant so much

CONTENTS

VOLUME 1

PART ONE: MUSIC IN MYTHOLOGY
*A Reference Guide with Readings on the Roles Played by Music
    in World Mythology, Religion and Folklore, Arranged Alpha-
    betically by Topic*

VOLUME 2

VOLUME 3

PRINCIPAL TOPIC HEADINGS FOR VOLUMES 1 & 2

FOREWORD

Research for *The Pro/Am Book of Music and Mythology* commenced in 1987 and has continued through 1992. Since the bulk of the main Reference and Text Readings portion (Part One) was completed in 1989, two Supplements have been added, in 1990 and 1991 respectively. I had also planned to write a brief concluding Essay expressing some more general aspects of mythology than those having to do with music alone — work on this began in 1989. This material was subsequently rewritten, and was expanded several times. It is now planned for publication (as an entirely separate Part Two) in 1993.

Selections from more than 250 sources have been made for the Reference/Text Readings portion, in addition to which another 200 or so titles are mentioned in the Essay portion. Thus, more than 450 book and other publications have been consulted in preparing the work as a whole.

SUMMARY OF CENTRAL IDEAS EXPRESSED IN THE WORK

Volumes 1 and 2 support the hypothesis that the principal role played by music in world mythology is as mediator between man and the divine (or supra-natural). An essay on the functions of music generally introduces Volume 1, while Volume 2 concludes with a detailed List of Sources, and a 101-page General Index.

Volume 3 consists of an original essay by the Editor which develops the following themes:

(1) "Reality" is that which obtains with respect to "being", and can be regarded as a kind of *perspective* from which the being of any being might be considered.

(2) Stories told about being itself, by beings who are themselves said to exist, may be called "reality parables", in that (in keeping with the present notion of reality) they suggest a perspective on the being of such a being. Reality parables dramatize the question, "how can a being take its own measure?"

(3) A "myth" is — in essence — a reality parable, in the author's view.

(4) These and related themes are explored with demonstrations and illustrations in fields such as art, philosophy, psychology, anthropology, linguistics, religion, and the natural sciences.

AFRICAN MYTHS — PRACTICES/BELIEFS. *(See pp.816, 911.)*

§6.15 Southern Bantu legends excerpted from *Indaba My Children: African Tribal History, Legends, Customs and Relgious Beliefs* by Vusamazulu Credo Mutwa (1985).

"MARIMBA. The hunting parties had all returned safely and the great gate was securely shut. The Wakambi were in tense readiness as they scanned the forests below for the first sign of the oncoming enemy. Night was falling fast and the land was once more shrouded in mystery.

"On the high palisades warriors stood to arms — hard-eyed and tense in every muscle — waiting for the Masai to come storming up the slopes of the ancient hill on which the First Village stood. As the night crept across the land with its sombre mantle, people became touchy and easily irritated, but they remained hard of eye and grim of face. The First Village ever built in the land was under the shadow of suspense and was firmly gripped in the cruel claws of the vulture of fear. Then the people heard a strange sound: a sound that was not of this world, that flowed through the silent dusk like a silver river through dark forests.

"It was a sound such as no human ears have ever heard before. It penetrated the very depths of the soul like cool water down a thirsty throat — like oil, soothing oil killing a cruel pain. Men stared at each other with incredulous wonder. Others groaned, and wept, blatantly and without shame.

"It was a sound of unearthly beauty, and to the surprise of everybody it came from the throat of the Princess *Marimba*, Chieftainess of the Wakambi tribe.

"She had taken the deadly bow of the captive Masai and had fitted a gourd to the middle of the bow itself, transforming the deadly weapon of war thus into the first *makweyana* bow-harp the world had ever seen. Not only had *Marimba* invented the first musical instrument,[1] but she was singing the world's first song as well:

O, little star so far above —
Oh, smiling moon up yonder;
You who on these fruitful vales
Shed, aye, your heatless light.

Carry my song on the wings of your
light —
Bear my refrains to the ends of the
world;
Carry my voice to the Land of the
Gods
Beyond the plains of Tura-ya-Moya.

Tell the Great Ones that live there
forever —
Tell those that rule all the stars up
above —
Tell the mother of all the seas and the
earth
Beyond the plains of Tura-ya-Moya:

Tell them that though the hyaenas of
death
Prowl without my kraal tonight —
Tell them that all these perils I'll face
And that I'll never cringe nor cower.

Tell them that I, their humble servant
maid,
Shrink not from the scowl of a foe —
For they who have the Great God as
ally

---

1   See Thompson Motifs A520.4 (Culture hero as poet [musician]), A1460 (Acquisition of arts), **FOLKLORE AND FOLKTALES — TYPOLOGY***, above. (Ed.)

Are twice the victors in war!

Tell them their servant implores them
For strength and their guidance true;
Mad is he who through Life's swamp-
    lands goes
Without the guides from Tura-ya-
    Moya!

"The Wakambi gathered in awe around their princess, their eyes wide open like so many astonished children. They had never heard a human being sing before. Never before had they heard sounds like those that streamed forth from the bow-harp as the princess gracefully struck the string with a short length of cane. They joined her as the magic of the song overwhelmed them then, and soon the whole settlement was singing.

"Their voices, most discordant from lack of experience, rang out across the startled heavens and the sleeping forests echoed and re-echoed to the heavenly strains of Tura-ya-Moya.

"And the vast Masai armies advancing through the forests upon the Wakambi settlement paused in bewildered confusion as that unearthly melody reached their ears faintly across the dark distance.

" 'Nangai of the Mountains, save us!'

"Like a deadly flower growing in a meadow of green grass, another strange idea was born in the brain of the princess arimba as she sang. This idea had nothing to do with music; it had a lot to do with death — soon to be meted out to the advancing Masai!

"She promptly ordered her warriors to cut broad, long strips of strong kudu hide while she organised the women into gathering piles of round stones in strategic positions behind the palisades. This done, the princess called her commanders together and explained to them the use of

the slings of hide with the stone shot. The men listened in blank amazement as the incredible woman explained the use of this simple and yet deadly weapon that she had just invented....

* * *

"The young prince Kahawa [son of Marimba and of the hunter Zumangwe, who had been trampled to death by a rogue elephant,] half-drew his bone dagger from its sheath. Into his eyes there came a look that [his friend] Mpushu [the hippopotamus] could not at first explain. It was the look that comes into the eyes of one who has just had a shattering inspiration, one who has suddenly found the answer to a problem that had been gnawing at the back of his mind with the persistence of a rat. Mpushu saw his friend direct a stare of unspeakable contempt at the god Nangai[2] floating on his throne in empty air. Then the young Kahawa sneered right into the god's face, sneered as one sneers at a human enemy whom one holds beneath contempt.

"Suddenly the eyes of the god blazed with cold, murderous fury. He realised that a dead Kahawa was more unlikely to speak than a live Kahawa. He made a snap signal to the nearest Night Howler,[3] who promptly snatched up Kahawa and held him aloft in one vulture-like claw.

" 'Now, mortal, speak or you shall die!'

"Kahawa began to laugh, a harsh, contemptuous and insulting laugh. The Night Howlers stared first at him and then at Nangai in great puzzlement and even the human beings huddled together looking at the son of arimba in blank amazement.

" 'Under the sun that shines in the skies above,' Kahawa said at last, 'there is nothing more tragic, more pathetic, than a creature once great and powerful, still clinging

---

2   An evil outcast god, who had enslaved the souls of the Massai and ordered them to attack the people of Marimba.
3   A huge hell-monster.

with stubborn tenacity to the tattered shreds of his vanished power. There is nothing more tragic than the sight of this creature trying to deceive itself and others into thinking that it still holds the power it held in the past. You are such, *Nangai,* you are no longer a god. You are nothing but a slightly higher form of common demon. When *Mulungu* drove you from the golden valleys of Tura-ya-Moya like a wounded and beaten cur he also stripped you of your immortal powers. You use force, *Nangai,* you torture like a common human thug. You used to have powers with which, if you had retained them, you could have learnt the whereabouts of my mother by simply reading my mind. Using force is an admission of failure. You are a failure, a pathetic fetish that-once-was and the Masai are your dupes. You send them in force to attack the whole settlement when all you [need] have done was to render yourself invisible, enter our village unseen and carry my mother away. You had to have help — on a large scale at that — you wretchen fallen fetish...'

" 'Silence, mortal dog! When I wish to hear your raving and idiotic prattling I'll ask for it! Where is your mother?'

" 'Find her yourself... use your godly powers...'

"*Nangai* gave a brisk command to the Night Howler, who slowly started sinking his talons into the flesh of *Kahawa.*

"It was just then that a miracle happened — a miracle in the form of a song that came floating through the night air like a ghost of pure mercy and deliverance. This song had a magic spell about it.[4] It stunned the fiendish Night Howlers. There was a musical instrument in the singer's hands which in future years became known as the *karimba* or *kalimba.* This unearthly music sent a haunting melody through the night and wove a mighty spell around the squatting Night Howlers. It paralysed them — destroyed them.

"They let out a mighty roar in unison and, as though they had all become victims of an alien virulent leprosy, their scaly flesh began to slough off their skeletons and to flow sluggishly down the slope of the clearing in the ruined village. Wisps of reeking steam erupted from their distended slime-green bellies as their foul bowels burst with sounds terrible to hear, and from these wisps floated the ghosts of the people they had already devoured.

"These ghosts were happy — happy to escape and float away to the land of Forever-Night, there to await their reincarnation.

"But first they joined in the song sung by the woman with the *kalimba.* They soared and dived and soared again. They danced and weaved and leaped in the dark night, and a regiment of them capsized the evil *Nangai's* throne and he fell like a lump of cow dung into the reeking, oozing slime that had been the flesh of the Night Howlers. All the people who had been herded together became caught in the webs of the Song of the *Kalimba.* They tore off their soiled loinskins, skirts and ornaments, flung them aside, and raised their arms in thanksgiving to the High Gods for their deliverance, after which they too joined in the sacred Song of the *Kalimba.*[5]

"Dead and living joined in and the very stars rejoiced. The gods wept crystal tears and bowed their heads in tribute and acclaim. *Marimba* led the hosts of dead and living with her song and the eastern sky

---

4   See Thompson Motif D1275 (Magic song), **FOLKLORE AND FOLKTALES — TYPOLOGY***, above. (Ed.)

5   Such a rich confluence of themes, here: music as a magical instrument, music as an instrument of the gods, music as communication between living and dead, music as communication between agents of civilization and primeval representatives of untamed nature, music as promoting Dionsyian frenzy, music as promoting ecstatic "heavenly" or otherwordly bliss... etc. (Ed.)

greyed with the first promise of coming dawn....

* * *

"*Marimba* looked down at the ugly snare that [the evil boy] *Malinge* had invented, [which was a particularly vicious and cowardly snare with which to catch young antelope, which had no purpose but to cause the animals to suffer], and shuddered. There was no mistaking it — the thing was deadly and only a madman, a monster of cruelty, could have invented this sort of thing. No wonder the old men [the judges] had... thrown *Malinge* to the crocodiles just before daybreak.

"Then *Marimba* got down on her knees and began to work. She dismantled the long trapdoor consisting of oblong flat pieces of wood tied together with buckskin thongs and gut. She made small alterations to the pieces of wood so that they were no longer of the same length and thickness. She ordered her handmaidens to bring her a number of *cusana* gourds of different sizes and to open each end, making a big hole in the one end and a small one in the side. Her next order was equally peculiar: the gourds were to be put in a large clay bowl at the gate of the village and word spread that all the old women of the village were to pass their morning water into the big bowl for three successive days. This, explained the great princess, was not only to place a permanent blessing upon the instrument; it would also make the gourds resilient and durable.

"Afterwards the gourds were boiled in animal fat to make them more resilient and waterproof. With her own delicate hands *Marimba* assembled the instrument while vast crowds of Wakambi men and women watched in awe and astonishment. She first assembled the hardwood frame with four carved legs, and along a flat piece of wood that connected the two ends of the oblong frame she stuck the gourds by their mouths firmly with tree resin.

"She then covered each of the holes in the sides of the gourds with silky laminæ which she obtained from the nests of the *munyovu* wasp, also stuck firmly with tree resin. The gourds were arranged under the central plank in gradually diminishing size. Then came the pieces of wood that formed the trapdoor, also arranged in the same order according to size, each piece directly across a corresponding gourd resonator. The strips of wood were suspended above their resonators by two lengths of thong.

"Thus the xylophone — the *marimba* — was born. Soon this melodious companion of the feast and the dance was sending its notes through the festive air, each note as gentle as a maiden's promise. The xylophone is a living instrument which can bend its notes to fit the blood-warming melody of a wedding song or harshen its voice and convey to the human mind the clamor and dark horrors of war — or the thrilling excitement and suspense of the hunt. Even without the accompaniment of a human voice one can tell a whole story with the xylophone alone. One can use the voice of this holy instrument to create various moods in one's audience. While other instruments speak to the ears, the xylophone speaks to the heart and the soul. Indeed it is an instrument worthy of bearing the name of the Goddess of Music.

The xylophone *(marimba)* — a sacred instrument —

MARIMBA XYLOPHONE

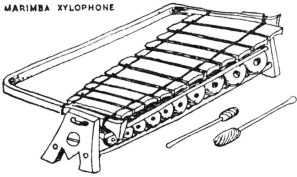

MARIMBA'S ORIGINAL DRUM

MADE OF FIRE-HOLLOWED
ROUGHLY TRIMMED LOG

* * *

" 'Marimba is indeed the mother of wisdom,' whispered the fat cook, *Mandingwe*.

" 'Nobody is the parent of wisdom in this world, *Mandingwe* [*Marimba* said]. I am nothing but a puppet serving the will of Those-we-do-not-see, and I try to serve as best I can. Now bring me the skin of a newly killed wildebeest, and also send *Kamago* the woodcarver to me.'

" 'As you say, Oh *Marimba*, said the cook respectfully, falling on her face in obeisance and then crawling backwards out of the Royal Hut.

"*Marimba* turned the old nut-grinding mortar into the first drum the world had ever seen and for the first time since the dawn of creation the forests shook to the pulsing beat of a drum. The instrument became so popular with the Wakambi that almost everybody wanted to have a drum in his own hut. The woodcarvers were very busy indeed. The princess *Marimba* made them of different sizes, each with a different quality of sound, from the loud hollow boom to the gentle pow-wow. The big ones were known as the 'male drums'; smaller ones were 'female drums', and the very small ones that children could carry around were known as 'sparrow drums'.

"The largest drums she ordered to be reserved for purposes of worship only[6] and these had the symbol of the River of Eternity carved into them in a continuous pattern all round, and on many of these drums were also carved symbols representing passages from the great poems of creation and sacred symbols of Spiritual Secret Knowledge. This she did to preserve the knowledge of the Wakambi for all time. Men were elected to look after these drums and this became their sole duty in life. These 'Drummers of High Honor' had to daub the instruments periodically with animal fat to preserve both the wood and the skin.... When a drum deteriorated beyond repair it was the duty of the oldest woodcarver to carve a new one—an exact replica in every detail, and

---

6   Which is especially appropriate if it is assumed that the instruments of which the largest are perhaps the best representatives were given to man by the gods or demigods or culture hero, or, on behalf of the gods or demigods, in the first place. In using such instruments for worship man is simply using the gods' own inventions to address these same gods back. Put a little differently, insofar as music itself or a musical instrument or song etc. is held to be an invention or an instrument of the gods, then it can also be regarded as an *extension* of these gods; thus it stands to reason that a suitable way of approaching or communicating with divine being is through or by means of such instruments—even becoming "at one" with them, so to speak, in one's singing and dancing and making of music... becoming "at one" with these extensions of divine being, with these incidents of the divine presence. (Ed.)

the old one was buried with the full burial honors with which a chief is buried....

"With the birth of the drum came the birth of new dances in the land of the Wakambi—dances like the *bupiro-mukiti*, or the dances of life, performed by both male and female dancers, or the *chukuza ya sandanda*, the dance of the baboon, which is performed by male dancers only. This is the most muscle-punishing dance that can ever be performed. All these dances were invented for one reason only—expression of tribal religion and the release of that beneficial life-force dormant in every human being, but which, when released, makes one feel closer in the 'arms of Eternity'.

"Also some of the dances performed by young people, like the famous 'love dance' of the Kavirondo, and the *gqashiya* of the Nguni, were invented so that the young people might find an opportunity to use up their excess energy.[7]"—Mutwa, pp. 15-17, 22-23, 34-37

§6.16 "HEVIOSSO (XEVIOSO)(God of thunder in Dahomey, associated with *Legba*.) In ancient times Heviosso was offered human sacrifices, but after the arrival of the Europeans a bull was used instead. The animal had its throat cut very slowly, the object being to draw off as much of the living blood as possible, for living blood is the true life-force. When the god accepts the sacrifice bells are run and the thunder chant, Ho Ho Ho, is shouted by all the priests and worshippers. The sacrifice is followed by eight days of dancing....

"The dances for Heviosso represent copulation with the earth; other dances are dramatic representations of the character of the thunder god. The dancers work themselves into a frenzy and rush about destroying plants and huts and attacking the bystanders. They sometimes go as far as to wreck the shrine of the god."—Carlyon, p.10.

AZTECS PRACTICES AND BELIEFS. *(See also pp.71, 943.)*

§31.4 "COYOLXAUHQUI ('Golden Bells'; moon goddess). The Earth Mother became pregnant and her children, the stars, were horrified. They felt it was a shameful state of affairs and plotted to kill her before she could bear the new child. Coyolxauhqui got to hear of the plot and ran ahead of the assassins to warn her mother. She reached the cave where the Earth Mother was confined just ahead of her furious siblings. As she arrived outside the cave the baby was born. He was *Huitzilpochtli* (an aspect of *Tezcatlipoca**) and had emerged fully-grown and armed ready for battle. Hearing the approaching mob he stepped calmly out of the cave and started to shoot. He killed everyone he saw, including the unfortunate Coyolxauhqui. Too late he was informed of his sister's fidelity. In order to make amends he cut off her head and tossed it up into the sky, where it became the moon. Golden bells can still be seen on the cheeks of the moon—the golden bells from which she derived her name."—Carlyon, p.46.

BAGPIPES. *(See also pp.75, 946).*

§34.3 "[THE WHITE GANDER (Irish).] There was a widow there one time and she lived somewhere near Dunmore. She had

---

7   In many cultures there is an identification between religious ecstasy and sexual joy or liberation. After all, it is essential to regenerate life—perpetuate one's species—which equally is to *serve* some governing divinity, and to *enlist such (a) divinity's blessing, or good offices.* To put it bluntly—however obviously—making love itself can and perhaps ought to be regarded as a religious or spiritual act. (Ed.)

only one son and he was a kind of a fool. Faith, he learned to play the bag-pipes a little, all the same, but the only tune he could play was the Rógaire Dubh (Black Rogue). The young fellows in the place used to invite him to play here and there for the fun of it, and he would earn a little money in that way, for people had pity for him.

"One Hallowe'en he was invited to play his pipes in a house two or three miles away. He went, of course, for he thought that there wasn't a better piper in Ireland than himself. When he was returning home late that night, he sat down on the parapet of a small bridge along the road, took up his pipes and started to play. Before long he saw the Pooka[8] behind him, with his pair of long horns. The Pooka jabbed his backside with his horns and threw him on to the road.

" 'Bad cess to you!' said the piper. 'Why did you do that to me? All I have is a little tenpenny piece to buy snuff for my mother with.'

" 'Never mind your mother or her snuff!' said the Pooka. 'Play the tune of the White Gander for me.'

" 'That's a tune that I can't play,' said the piper.

" 'I'll teach it to you,' said the Pooka.

"The Pooka gave him another jab with his horns and lifted him up on to the parapet of the bridge where he had been before.

" 'Now will you play it?' asked the Pooka.

"The piper took hold of his pipes again and began to play what he thought was the finest music he had ever knocked out of the pipes.

" 'You'll do what I need,' said the Pooka. 'The fairy* host sent me out tonight to search for a musician. You'll have to come with me to the house of the fairy woman on the top of Croagh Patrick and play music for them until morning.'

" 'That's good stroke of luck for me,' said the piper. 'When I was at Confession this year, Father Doncha put a penance on me

that I'd have to make a pilgrimage to Croagh Patrick on account of stealing a white gander from him. 'Twill be easier for me to go there along with you than any other way!'

" 'I promise you that you'll be well paid for your night's music,' said the Pooka.

"The Pooka then put his horns under the piper and lifted him on to his back. Off he went faster than the wind, through bogs and mountains and fields, through rough land and smooth land, through woods and scrub and bushes and briars, and past harbours. The devil a finer ride had the piper ever got before than he did that night! It didn't take them long to reach the top of Croagh Patrick. They were barely there when the Pooka put his horns under a rock that was there and threw it aside to show a fine, wide opening beneath it. The pair of them went in and came to a fine door. The Pooka struck it with one of his horns and opened it. In they went to a beautiful room with grand furniture. About a hundred old women were seated at a large table in the middle of the floor. They all stood up and had a thousand welcomes for the Pooka.

" 'Who is this that's with you?' they all asked together.

" 'He's the finest piper in Ireland. I met him and brought him here to ye tonight.'

" 'You're my thousand loves!' said one of them. 'We haven't had a dance as long as we can remember, for want of a musician.'

"They joyfully took hold of the piper and carried him around the big room, and gave him the finest drink of brandy that he had ever got in his ilfe. Then one of the old women tapped with her foot against the bottom of the wall, and a large door opened there. What came out through the door but the white gander he had stolen from the priest the previous summer! One of the old women ordered the gander to remove the table, as they wanted to dance. When the poor gander had done that, he was ordered to bring in the music chair for

---

8   Púca, supernatural animal like a horse.

the piper. When the chair was brought in, the piper sat on it, and the gander pricked him on the backside.

" 'You'll play the tune I'll make for you, you black rogue!' said the gander.

"The gander started to scream and squawk, and the piper began to play. The devil such fine music as he knocked out of the pipes nobody had ever heard before! All the old women went out dancing, and you may call it fine dancing! When they were tired, the gander pricked a hole in the bag of the pipes and the music stopped. At the end of the dance, all the old women had become young girls!

" 'Only for the gander pricking the hole in your bag,' said one of them to the piper, 'you'd keep on playing till we'd all draw our last breath!'

"They couldn't stop dancing while the music went on.[9] They were all very grateful to the piper, and they ordered the gander to get another set of pipes for him quickly. The gander did this, and all the girls gave the piper a golden guinea each for the night's music. They also gave him the gift of being the best piper in Ireland. He said goodbye to them then, and the Pooka came and took him on his back.

" 'I promised you that you'd be well paid for the night,' said the Pooka, 'and now you have three gifts. You have sense and gold and the gift of music from this night on.'

"Off they went back the way they had come until they reached the little bridge near Dunmore. They were there just as the cock was crowing in the morning. The Pooka said goodbye to him then, and the piper went home to his mother. They lived in love and comfort from that time on. They had plenty, and to spare. That's the story of the White Gander." —O'Sullivan, pp.76-78. For an alternative version of this story, see Douglas Hyde telling of "The Piper and the Puca", §34.6, p.948 below.

BURMESE MONK'S TALES.

§49A.1 See **INDO-CHINESE MYTHS AND LEGENDS***.

§49A.2 **"THE MONK WHO HATED MUSIC** [from the stories of the Thingazar Sayadaw (1815-86), themselves modeled on traditional Burmese folk tales]. *Prologue:* When the Thingazar Sayadaw was visiting Rangoon a man came up to him and said, 'My lord, the younger monks of Rangoon have banded themselves into a new sect known as the Junior Sect. They are determined to introduce reforms in the order. They refuse to attend any religious ceremony if an orchestra or a dancing troupe is present. To listen to music or to watch a dance is strictly against the rules of the order, and surely my lord will exhort the older monks of the city not to attend any religious ceremony where dancers or musicians are present?'[10] The Sayadaw smiled and commented, 'I am afraid that the Junior Monks hate music and dancing in the same way as the Monk Puppet Showman hated music and dancing.'

"A puppet showman, famous for his music and song, suddenly retired from his profession and became a monk. But people could not forget his fame as a puppet showman, and called him Monk Puppet Showman.

"Monk Puppet Showman did not become very learned in the scriptures nor did he practice any special austerity. In other words, he was a very ordinary monk. However, he refused to attend any religious ceremony where there was any dancing or music. 'I hate the very sound of music,' he declared again and again.

"In a few weeks this particular abstinence of Monk Puppet Showman won for him many admirers. 'Even great abbots do not

---

9   See also theme of **DANCING TO DEATH (OR INSANITY)***. (Ed.)
10   See footnotes to **FIDDLERS*** entry, below. (Ed.)

abstain from going to religious ceremonies where musicians and dancers perform,' people commented. After a few months a rich villager built and donated a special monastery for the Monk. Some years passed and the Monastery-Donor wanted to hold the initiation ceremony of his only son in pomp and splendor. By common custom, Monk Puppet Showman was invited to preside over the ceremony. As usual, the Monk insisted that he hated the very sound of music, and accepted the invitation to be present at the ceremony on the distinct understanding that there was to be no music or song or dance. The appointed day arrived, and everything was now ready for the initiation ceremony. The young men of the village, however, were in a mutinous mood, for, they asked, 'Whoever heard of an initiation ceremony without dance or song?' They became so persistent with their protests that the Monastery-Donor finally agreed to engage a drummer who would play a mere 'slow march' on the long drum.

"There was no time to inform Monk Puppet Showman of the new arrangement; moreover, the Monastery-Donor thought that there could not be any objection on the part of the Monk against the presence of a single drummer. Monk Puppet Showman soon arrived leading a procession of monks, walking slowly and sedately, and with downcast eyes. The drummer started to play the drum, and Monk Puppet Showman, on hearing the sound of the drum, exclaimed, 'The reason why I hate the sound of music is because it incites me to dance. But the harm is now done. So, drummer, stop your royal march and play a jig.' The drummer did as told, and Monk Puppet Showman, gathering up his robes, danced his way into the almsgiving hall."[11] — Htin Aung, pp.130-31.

CADMUS AND HARMONIA (WEDDING OF) (Greek).

§49A.1 "Cadmus is a name much celebrated by antiquity. According to Fabricius there were three persons so called, who flourished at very different periods. The eldest, and the most renowned, is Cadmus, the son of Agenor, king of Phoenicia; who

---

11   In addition to a traditional conflict between the perils and attractions of "profane" and "sacred" music, it sometimes happens that battlelines are drawn between younger and older generations, the former eager to dance and to take a wild" or indeed "Dionysian" pleasure in music, the latter enjoining a sort of emasculation of any such musical fervor. The reason — is it not? — is that in such cases music is seen as a sort of talisman through the powers of which a succeeding, freshly procreative generation is destined to destroy and to replace its no longer potent predecessors: this is the theme of ritual regicide and killing of the **TREE SPIRIT***, also annual rending by Titans of **DIONYSUS*** , the cycle of the seasons, etc.. (Ed.)

eldest, and the most renowned, is Cadmus, the son of Agenor, king of Phoenicia; who being sent by his father into Greece, in search of his sister Europa, whom Jupiter had stolen away, brought with him sixteen letters, and the art of making brass. Archbishop Usher, the authors of the *Universal History,* and Dr. Blair, agree in placing this event in the time of Joshua, that is, 1450 years before Christ; though Sir Isaac Newton and Dr. Priestly allow Cadmus to have flourished but 1045 years before the Christian Æra. Sir Isaac imagines that the emigration of the Phoenicians and Syrians was occasioned by the conquests of David. 'These people,' said he, 'fleeing from Sidon and from David, come under the conduct of Cadmus and other captains, into Asia Minor, Crete, Greece, and Lybia, and introduce letters, music, poetry, metals, and their fabrication, and other arts, sciences, and customs of the Phoenicians. This happened about one hundred and forty years before the Trojan War.[12] It was about the sixteenth year of David's reign that Cadmus fled from Sidon. At his first coming into Greece, he sailed to Rhodes, and thence to Samothrace, an island near Thrace, on the north side of Lemnos, and there married Harmonia, the sister of Iasius and Dardanus, which gave occasion to the Samothracian mysteries.'

"I shall not enter upon a long discussion concerning Harmonia, of whom, though many ancient authors make her a princess, of divine origin,[13] there is a passage in Athenæus from Euhemerus the Vanini of his time, which tells us, that she was by profession, *a player on the flute,* and in the service of the prince of Sidon, previous to her departure with Cadmus. This circumstance, however, might encourage a belief, that, as Cadmus brought letters into Greece, his wife brought *Harmony* thither, as the word [Greek term], *Harmonia,* has been said to have no other derivation than from her name; which makes it very difficult to ascertain the sense annexed to it by the Greeks in their music; for it has no roots by which it can be decompounded, in order to deduce it from its etymology.

"This derivation is given by some to Plato, in whose works, however, I have not been able to find it; but there is a passage in the Phoedon of that author, in which he evidently gives his sanction to the common etymology of the word, that is given by lexicographers, and generally adopted by the learned; who deduce it from [Greek term], which is derived from the old verb, [Greek term], to *fit,* to *join.* And yet, as the flute upon which Harmonia played was a single instrument, capable of *melody only,* and as she was said to be the first who performed upon that instrument in Greece, the inhabitants of that country perhaps called by her name the art which she had introduced among them, as the metal which her husband invented received his name [*Cadmia,* a name for copper ore]. Agenor, the father of Cadmus, was an Egyptian; and Cadmus is said by many ancient writers to have received his education in Egypt. Harmonia may likewise

---

12   Lest this chronology totally confuse, let me substitute some dates which, while not necessarily accurate, appear to be more commonly accepted today: Abraham leaves Ur in Chaldea, c.2100; Mycenaeans enter Greece, 2000-1700; invasion of Crete by Mycenaeans? — destruction of palaces and fall of Minoan civilization, c.1400; the Israelites under Moses leave Egypt, c.1250; invasion of Canaan by Hebrews: seige of Jericho, c.1220 (or later); Trojan War, c.1210 (or later); Philistines conquer Israel, 1050; David succeeds Saul as king of Judah, 1000; founding of Carthage by Phoeniceans, c.814; Homer, c.775; traditional date of founding of Rome by Romulus and Remus, 753. (Ed.)

13   According to Diod. Sic. 1.5, she was daughter of Jupiter and Electra, and grand-daughter of Atlas.

have come from that country; however, her wild flute has never been said to have furnished the Greeks with their musical scale; but there is nothing more extraordinary in a barbarous people having music *without a gamut,* than language *without an alphabet.*

"Diodorus Siculus has given a very circumstantial account of the wedding of Cadmus and Harmonia in Samothrace, at which all the Pagan divinities were present; and tells us, that this was the first hymenæal festival which the Gods deigned to honour with their presence. 'Ceres, who was tenderly attached to Jasion, the brother of the bride, presented corn to the new married couple; Mercury, brought his lyre; Minerva, her famous buckler, her veil, and her flute; Electra, the mother of the bride, celebrated there the mysteries of Cybele, the mother of the Gods, and had the orgies danced to the sounds of drums and cymbals. Apollo afterwards played on the lyre, the Muses accompanied him with their flutes, and all the other divinities ratified their nuptials with acclamations of joy.' This seems to be the outline of a dramatic representation, which was perhaps exhibited by the priests at some festival, or mystical celebration, in order to commemorate the wedding of Cadmus and Harmonia." —Birney, I, pp.218-19.

CHINESE PRACTICES AND BELIEFS—MYTHS AND LEGENDS. *(See also pp.133, 973.)*

§64.10 "THE TWO BELLS*. Formerly the big bell of the temple on the Southern Mountain and the big bell from the K'ai-yüan temple used to fly out to meet each other every day at midnight, one being a male and the other a female. One morning the bell from the K'ai-yüan temple was flying home when it saw a woman washing bed-sheets in the stream. It fell down into the water and cried: 'If you want to lift me out again, you must find ten women with ten sons to do it.' The women were found, but just as they were lifting the bell on to the bank, a bystander shouted out: 'One of the ten sons is a bastard,' at which the bell slipped back into the water and remains to this day buried in the sand, no more to be seen." —Eberhard, p.154.

§64.11 "TIEN-WANG (MO-LI)(The Heavenly Kings). These were four brothers, Buddhist gods whose duty was to guard doors. They were guardians of the Four Directions. Originally from India, their names were Vaisravana, Virudharka, Virupasa and Dhrtarastra. Each carried an object which, when mortals, they had used to control the elements. These objects were a sword, a guitar*, an umbrella and a marten (the animal). The sword raised tempests, the guitar governed the winds, the umbrella controlled the light of the sun and the marten killed and consumed malicious spirits. Because of their potency and aggressive energy the Mo-Li were ideal sentries." —Carlyon, pp.91-92.

CHIRON (SCHOOL OF)(Greek).

§64A.1 "Chiron is styled by Plutarch, in his *Dialogue upon Music,* the *wise Centaur.* Sir Isaac Newton places his birth in the first age after Deucalion's deluge, commonly called the Golden Age; and adds, that he formed the constellations for the use of the Argonauts, when he was eighty-eight years old, for he was a practical astronomer, as well as his daughter Hippo:[14] he may therefore be said to have flourished in the earliest ages of Greece, as he preceded the conquest of the Golden Fleece, and the Trojan war.

---

14 *Chron.* 25.

"He is generally called the son of Saturn and Philyra, and is said to have been born in Thessaly among the Centaurs, who were the first Greeks that had acquired the art of breaking and riding horses; whence the poets, painters, and sculptors, have described and represented them as a compound of man and horse; and perhaps it was imagined by the Greeks, as well as the Americans, when they first saw cavalry, that the horse and the rider constituted one and the same animal.

"Chiron was regarded by the ancients as one of the first inventors of medicine, botany, and *chirurgery* ; a word which some etymologists have derived from his name. He inhabited a grotto, or cave, at the foot of mount Pelion, which from his wisdom, and great knowledge of all kinds, became the most famous and frequented school throughout Greece. Almost all the heroes of his time were ambitious of receiving his instructions: and Xenophon, who enumerates them, names the following illustrious personages among his disciples: Cephalus, Esculapius, Melanion, Nestor, Amphiaraus, Peleus, Telamon, Meleager, Theseus, Hypolitus, Palamedes, Ulysses, Mnestheus, Diomedes, Castor and Pollux, Machaon and Podalirius, Antilochus, Æneas, and Achilles. From this catalogue it appears, that Chiron frequently instructed both fathers and sons; and Xenophon has given a short eulogium upon each, which may be read in his works, and which redounds to the honour of the preceptor. The Greek historian, however, has omitted naming several of his scholars, such as Bacchus*, Phoenix, Cocytus, AristÑus, Jason, and his son Medus, Ajax, and Protesilaus. It is not my intention to characterize these; I shall only mention such as interest Chiron more particularly.

"It is pretended that the Grecian Bacchus was the favourite scholar of the Centaur, and that he learned of this master the revels, orgies, Bacchanalia, and other ceremonies of his worship.

"According to Plutarch, it was likewise at the school of Chiron that Hercules studied music, medicine, and justice; though Diodorus Siculus tells us that Linus* was the music-maker of this hero. These are points which it is now not easy to settle; nor are they of any other consequence to our enquiries, than serving as proofs, that ancient authors all agreed in thinking it natural and necessary for heroes to have been instructed in music. *Nec fides didicit, nec natare,* was, in antiquity, a reproach to every man above the rank of a plebian.

"But among all the heroes who have been disciples of this Centaur, no one reflected so much honour upon him as Achilles, whose renown he in some measure shared, and to whose education he in a particular manner attended, being his grandfather by the mother's side. Apollodorus tells us that the study of music employed a considerable part of the time which he bestowed upon his young pupil, as an incitement to virtuous actions, and a bridle to the impetuosity of his temper. One of the best remains of antique painting now subsisting, is a picture upon this subject, dug out of Herculaneum,[15] in which Chiron is teaching the young Achilles to play on the lyre.

"The death of this philosophical musician was occasioned, at an extreme old age, by an accidental wound in the knee with a poisoned arrow, shot by his scholar, Hercules, at another.[16] He was placed after his death by Musæus among the constellations, (as Sagittarius) through respect for his virtues, and in gratitude for the.great services which he had rendered the people of Greece." — Burney, I, pp.257-58.

---

15   That is, from the remains of the town after the eruption of Vesuvius? (Ed.)

16   Hercules (Heracles) is also charged with the death of **LINUS***. See above. (Ed.)

CRETAN PRACTICES AND BELIEFS.

§70A.1 "According to Homer*'s description, Achilles' shield was decorated with a scene of youths and maidens dancing on 'a dancing floor, like the one that Daedalus designed in the spacious town of Knossos for Ariadne of the lovely locks.... Here they ran lightly round... and there they ran in lines to meet each other. A large crowd stood round... with a minstrel among them singing divinely to the lyre*, while a couple of acrobats [kept] time with his music... in and out among the people.' Theatre areas similar to such a dancing floor have been excavated beside the palaces of Knossos and Phaistos — oblong paved areas, bordered by shallow stone steps on which an audience could sit or stand. With Minos and his court in attendance, these theatres were probably used for a religious performance of some kind, most likely a sacred dance to summon the mother goddess. The Cretans customarily danced for this purpose in front of a sacred grove, pillar, or tree, as well as in theatre areas, and dances such as these may have been a source from which later Greek dramatic performances developed.[17] It was a female deity who was honored by these dances,[18] and women played an important role in the ceremonies, as they did in the bull games. Then they wore simply a loincloth; but for ritual dancing they often attired themselves in full court costume, with flounced skirt and tight bodice, their hair elaborately curled and their bosoms bare. Men adorned themselves fancifully as women did at the court of Minos. Both sexes wore bracelets and necklaces. Women twined gold filigree through their hair; men secured their long curls with strings of beads. They wore anklets about their legs and, invariably, a seal stone attached to a cord around their wrists. As early as the age of ten, boys and girls began to bind themselves with tight belts, probably made of metal and designed to keep their waists extremely slim." — Horizon, pp.270-71.

DANCE. (See also pp.161, 981.)

§74.4 "DANCE, MYTH AND RITUAL. Peoples in a more or less undeveloped state of culture very frequently express the rites or ceremonies of their faith in the dance. Such ceremonies as the making of rain or the magical quickening of the crops are carried out by imitating the actions through which 'the gods' or spirits of nature bring about the fall of rain or the growth of grain. In short, a pantomime or imitation of these magical processes is engaged in by the dancers, and this is regarded by them either as a strong hint to the gods to take the necessary magical action to ensure rain or growth, or as assisting them in the process....

"Dancing is a natural means of inducing religious or prophetic excitement. In Southern India the caste known as the 'Devil Dancers' rotate and leap furiously until they attain that degree of inspiration which they consider essential to the practice of healing among the populace. The same thing takes place among the shamans of Mongolia. Most readers will be aware that many strange Asiatic cults and numerous savage ones achieve the condi-

---

17 As can be seen elsewhere (**EGYPTIAN PRACTICES AND BELIEFS***, below), Burney (1789) emphasized an Egyptian paternity for many Greek musical instruments and practices, which may also include Greek theater generally; but clearly Minoan civilization also antedates so-called "Greek" (i.e. mainland) culture. (Ed.)

18 Sometimes called The Lady of Beasts, and frequently depicted with serpents entwined around each arm; an earth goddess, or mother earth. (Ed.)

tion of religious hysteria necessary to the performance of their ritual acts chiefly through the instrumentality of dancing. The late Sir R.R. Marett was of opinion that primitive religion was essentially something 'to be danced out'. Rhythmic motion, indeed, appears to be inalienable from the fervour of primitive religious excitement. From the swaying movements of the body which accompany prayer in primitive and even in some modern religious castes it is, in more senses than one, merely a step to the general movement of the entire body in the dance. Fertility dances in particular are nearly always attended with a singular degree of delirium on the part of the ritual dancers who engage in them. The spirit which inspires the idea that the performers are taking part in a process which will quicken cereal or vegetable growth appears to induce something akin to frenzy, and in this connection one need refer only to the temporary insanity of the dance-ritual of the Bacchic or Dionysiac* rites, with their outbursts of savage violence, symbolic of that wild fury which was thought to reside in nature, and which must be successfully imitated were the supernatural powers of production and increase to be awakened in their full potency." — Spence, pp.2,7.

* * *

"[THE DANCE OF LIFE.] The significance of dancing, in the wide sense, lies in the fact that it is simply an intimate concrete appeal of a general rhythm, that general rhythm which marks, not life only, but the universe, if one may still be allowed to so name the sum of the cosmic influences that reach us. We need not, indeed, go so far as the planets or the stars and outline their ethereal dances. We have but to stand on the seashore and watch the waves that beat at our feet, to observe that at nearly regular intervals this seemingly monotonous rhythm is accentuated for several beats, so that the waves are really dancing the measure of a tune. It need

surprise us not at all that rhythm, ever tending to be moulded into a tune, should mark all the physical and spiritual manifestations of life. Dancing is the primitive expression alike of religion and of love — of religion from the earliest human times we know of and of love from a period long anterior to the coming of man. The art of dancing, moreover, is intimately entwined with all human tradition of war, of labour, of pleasure, of education, while some of the wisest philosophers and the most ancient civilisations have regarded the dance as the pattern in accordance with which the moral life of men must be woven. To realise, therefore, what dancing means for mankind — the poignancy and the many-sidedness of its appeal — we must survey the whole sweep of human life, both at its highest and at its deepest moments.

" 'What do you dance?' When a man belonging to one branch of the great Bantu division of mankind met a member of another, said Livingstone, that was the question he asked. What a man danced, that was his tribe, his social customs, his religion; for, as an anthropologist has put it, 'a savage does not preach his religion, he dances it.'

"There are peoples in the world who have no secular dances, only religious dances; and some investigators believe with Gerland that every dance was of religious origin. That view may seem too extreme, even if we admit that some even of our modern dances, like the waltz, may ' have been originally religious. Even still (as Skene has shown among the Arabs and Swahili of Africa) so various are dances and their functions among some peoples that they cover the larger part of life. Yet we have to remember that for primitive man there is no such thing as religion apart from life, for religion covers everything. Dancing is a magical operation for the attainment of real and important ends of every kind. It was clearly of immense benefit to the individual and to society, by imparting strength and adding organised harmony. It seemed reasonable to suppose that it attained other beneficial ends, that were incalculable, for calling down blessings or warding off misfortunes. We may conclude, with Wundt, that the dance was, in the beginning, the expression of the whole man, for the whole man was religious.

"Thus, among primitive peoples, religion being so large a part of life, the dance inevitably becomes of supreme religious importance. To dance was at once both to worship and to pray. Just as we still find in our Prayer Books that there are divine services for all the great fundamental acts of life, — for birth, for marriage, for death, — as well as for the cosmic procession of the world as marked by ecclesiastical festivals, and for the great catastrophes of nature, such as droughts, so also it has ever been among primitive peoples. For all the solemn occasions of life, for bridals and for funerals, for seed-time and for harvest, for war and for peace, for all these things there were fitting dances. To-day we find religious people who in church pray for rain or for the restoration of their friends to health. Their forefathers also desired these things, but, instead of praying for them, they danced for them the fitting dance which tradition had handed down, and which the chief or the medicine-man solemnly conducted. The gods themselves danced, as the stars dance in the sky — so at least the Mexicans, and we may be sure many other peoples, have held; and to dance is therefore to imitate the gods, to work with them, perhaps to persuade them to work in the direction of our own desires. 'Work for us!' is the song-refrain, expressed or implied, of every religious dance. In the worship of solar deities in various countries, it was customary to dance round the altar, as the stars dance round the sun. Even in Europe the popular belief that the sun dances on Easter Sun-

day has perhaps scarcely yet died out. To dance is to take part in the cosmic control of the world. Every sacred dionysian* dance is an imitation of the divine dance.

"All religions, and not merely those of primitive character, have been at the outset, and sometimes throughout, in some measure saltatory. That was recognised even in the ancient world by acute observers, like Lucian, who remarks in his essay on dancing that 'you cannot find a single ancient mystery in which there is no dancing; in fact most people say of the devotees of the Mysteries that "they dance them out." ' This is so all over the world. It is not more pronounced in early Christianity, and among the ancient Hebrews who danced before the ark, than among the Australian aborigines* whose great corroborees are religious dances conducted by the medicine-men with their sacred staves in their hands. Every American Indian tribe[19] seems to have had its own religious dances, varied and elaborate, often with a richness of meaning which the patient study of modern investigators has but slowly revealed. The Shamans* in the remote steppes of Northern Siberia have their ecstatic religious dances, and in modern Europe the Turkish dervishes — perhaps of related stock — still dance in their cloisters similar ecstatic dances, combined with song and prayer, as a regular part of devotional service.

"These religious dances, it may be observed, are sometimes ecstatic, sometimes pantomimic. It is natural that this should be so. By each road it is possible to penetrate towards the divine mystery of the world. The auto-intoxication of rapturous movement brings the devotees, for a while at least, into that self-forgetful union with the not-self which the mystic ever seeks. The ecstatic Hindu* dance in honour of the pre-Aryan hill god, afterwards Siva [Shiva*], became in time a great

---

19 See **INDIAN (NORTH AMERICAN, SOUTH AMERICAN) MYTHS —
PRACTICES AND BELIEFS***, above. (Ed.)

symbol, 'the clearest image of the *activity* of God,' it has been called, 'which any art or religion can boast of.' Pantomimic dances, on the other hand, with their effort to heighten natural expression and to imitate natural process, bring the dancers into the divine sphere of creation and enable them to assist vicariously in the energy of the gods. The dance thus becomes the presentation of a divine drama, the vital reënactment of a sacred history, in which the worshipper is enabled to play a real part. In this way ritual arises.

"It is in this sphere — highly primitive as it is — of pantomimic dancing crystallised in ritual, rather than in the sphere of ecstatic dancing, that we may to-day in civilisation witness the survivals of the dance in religion. The divine services of the American Indian, said Lewis Morgan, took the form of 'set dances, each with its own name, songs, steps, and costume.' At this point the early Christian, worshipping the Divine Body, was able to join in spiritual communion with the ancient Egyptian or the later Japanese or the modern American Indian. They are all alike privileged to enter, each in his own way, a sacred mystery, and to participate in the sacrifice of a heavenly Mass*.

"What by some is considered to be the earliest known Christian ritual — the 'Hymn of Jesus' assigned to the second century — is nothing but a sacred dance. Eusebius in the third century stated that Philo's description of the worship of the Therapeuts agreed at all points with Christian custom, and that meant the prominence of dancing, to which indeed Eusebius often refers in connection with Christian worship. It has been supposed by some that the Christian Church was originally a theatre, the choir being the raised stage, even the word 'choir', it is argued, meaning an enclosed space for dancing. It is certain that at the Eucharist the faithful gesticulated with their hands, danced with their feet, flung their bodies about. Chrysostom, who referred to this behaviour round the Holy Table at Antioch, only objected to drunken excesses in connection with it; the custom itself he evidently regarded as traditional and right.

"While the central function of Christian worship is a sacred drama, a divine pantomime, the associations of Christianity and dancing are by no means confined to the ritual of the Mass and its later more attenuated transformations. The very idea of dancing had a sacred and mystic meaning to the early Christians, who had meditated profoundly on the text, 'We have piped unto you and ye have not danced.' Origen prayed that above all things there may be made operative in us the mystery 'of the stars dancing in Heaven for the salvation of the Universe.' So that the monks of the Cistercian Order, who in a later age worked for the world more especially by praying for it (*'orare est laborare'*), were engaged in the same task on earth as the stars in Heaven; dancing and praying are the same thing. St. Basil, who was so enamoured of natural things, described the angels dancing in Heaven, and later the author of the *'Dieta Salutis'* (said to have been St. Bonaventura), which is supposed to have influenced Dante in assigning so large a place to dancing in the 'Paradiso', described dancing as the occupation of the inmates of Heaven, and Christ as the leader of the dance. Even in more modern times an ancient Cornish carol sang of the life of Jesus as a dance, and represented him as declaring that he died in order than man 'may come unto the general dance.'[20]

"This attitude could not fail to be reflected in practice. Genuine dancing, not merely formalised and unrecognisable dancing, such as the traditionalised Mass, must have been frequently introduced

---

20   I owe some of these facts to an interesting article by G.R. Mead, "The Sacred Dance of Jesus", *The Quest,* October, 1910.

into Christian worship in early times. Until a few centuries ago it remained not uncommon, and it even still persists in remote corners of the Christian world. In English cathedrals dancing went on until the fourteenth century. At Paris, Limoges, and elsewhere in France, the priests danced in the choir at Easter up to the seventeenth century, in Roussillon up to the eighteenth century. Roussillon is a Catalan province with Spanish traditions, and it is in Spain, where dancing is a deeper and more passionate impulse than elsewhere in Europe, that religious dancing took firmest root and flourished longest. In the cathedrals of Seville, Toledo, Valencia, and Jeres there was formerly dancing, though it now only survives at a few special festivals in the first. At Alaro in Mallorca, also at the present day [1923], a dancing company called Els Cosiers, on the festival of St. Roch, the patron saint of the place, dance in the church in fanciful costumes with tambourines*, up to the steps of the high altar, immediately after Mass, and then dance out of the church. In another part of the Christian world, in the Abyssinian Church—an offshoot of the Eastern Church—dancing is also said still to form part of the worship.

"Dancing, we may see throughout the world, has been so essential, so fundamental, a part of all vital and undegenerate religion, that, whenever a new religion appears, a religion of the spirit and not merely an anaemic religion of the intellect, we should still have to ask of it the question of the Bantu: 'What do you dance?'

"Dancing is not only intimately associated with religion, it has an equally intimate association with love. Here, indeed, the relationship is even more primitive, for it is far older than man. Dancing, said Lucian, is as old as love. Among insects and among birds it may be said that dancing is often an essential part of love. In courtship the male dances, sometimes in rivalry with other males, in order to charm the female; then, after a short or long interval, the female is aroused to share his ardour and join in the dance; the final climax of the dance is the union of the lovers.... It is the more primitive love-dance of insects and birds that seems to reappear among human savages in various parts of the world, notably in Africa, and in a conventionalised and symbolised form it is still danced in civilisation to-day. Indeed, it is in this aspect that dancing has so often aroused reprobation, from the days of early Christianity until the present, among those for whom the dance has merely been, in the words of a seventeenth-century writer, a series of 'immodest and dissolute movements by which the cupidity of the flesh is aroused.' "[21] —Ellis, in Steinberg, pp.238-44.

* * *

"[THE WORLD AS BALLET.] The abstract thinker, to whom the question of practical morality is indifferent, has always loved dancing, as naturally as the moralist has hated it. The Puritan, from his own point of view, is always right, though it suits us, often enough, for wider reasons, to deny his logic. The dance is life, animal life, having its own way passionately. Part of that natural madness which men were once wise enough to include in religion, it began with the worship of the disturbing deities, the gods of ecstasy, for whom wantonness, and wine, and all things in which energy passes into an ideal excess, were sacred. It was cast out of religion when religion cast out nature: for, like nature it-

---

21 In fact, I should think that the associations of dance (and indeed music generally) with religion and with love are frequently merged; in dance one may worship, and one may pray; does one not, also, make love (of a sort) to or with some deity, or supposed natural or supernatural power? (Ed.)

self, it is a thing of evil to those who renounced instincts. From the first it has always mimed the instincts. It can render birth and death, and it is always going over and over the eternal pantomime of love; it can be all the passions, and all the languors; but it idealises these mere acts, gracious or brutal, into more than a picture; for it is more than a beautiful reflection, it has in it life itself, as it shadows life; and it is farther from life than a picture. Humanity, youth, beauty, playing the part of itself, and consciously, in a travesty, more natural than nature, more artificial than art: but we lose ourselves in the boundless bewilderments of its contradictions.

"The dance, then, is art because it is doubly nature: and if nature, as we are told, is sinful, it is doubly sinful. A waltz, in a drawing-room, takes us suddenly out of all that convention, away from those guardians of our order who sit around the walls, approvingly, unconsciously; in its winding motion it raises an invisible wall about us, shutting us off from the whole world, in with ourselves; in its fatal rhythm, never either beginning or ending, slow, insinuating, gathering impetus which must be held back, which must rise into the blood, it tells us that life flows even as that, so passionately and so easily and so inevitably; and it is possession and abandonment, the very pattern and symbol of earthly love. Here is nature (to be renounced, to be at least restrained) hurried violently, deliberately, to boiling point. And now look at the dance, on the stage, a mere spectator. Here are all these young bodies, made more alluring by an artificial heightening of whites and reds on the face, displaying, employing, all their natural beauty, themselves full of the sense of joy in motion, or affecting that enjoyment, offered to our eyes like a bouquet of flowers, a bouquet of living flowers, which have all the glitter of artificial ones. As they dance, under the changing lights, so human, so remote, so desirable, so evasive, coming and going to the sound of

a thin, heady music which marks the rhythm of their movements like a kind of clinging drapery, they seem to sum up in themselves the appeal of everything in the world that is passing, and coloured, and to be enjoyed; everything that bids us take no thought for the morrow, and dissolve the will into slumber, and give way luxuriously to the delightful present.

"How fitly then, in its very essence, does the art of dancing symbolise life; with so faithful a rendering of its actual instincts! And to the abstract thinker, as to the artist, all this really primitive feeling, all this acceptance of the instincts which it idealises, and out of which it makes its own beauty, is precisely what gives dancing its preeminence among the more than imitative arts. The artist, it is indeed true, is never quite satisfied with his statue which remains cold, does not come to life. In every art men are pressing forward, more and more eagerly, farther and farther beyond the limits of their art, in the desire to do the impossible: to create life. Realising all humanity to be but a masque of shadows, and this solid world an impromptu stage as temporary as they, it is with a pathetic desire of some last illusion, which shall deceive even ourselves, that we are consumed with this hunger to create, to make something for ourselves, of at least the same shadowy reality as that about us. The art of the ballet awaits us, with its shadowy and real life, its power of letting humanity drift into a rhythm so much of its own, and with ornament so much more generous than its wont.

"And something in the particular elegance of the dance, the scenery; the avoidance of emphasis, the evasive, winding turn of things; and, above all, the intellectual as well as sensuous appeal of a living symbol, which can but reach the brain through the eyes, in the visual, concrete, imaginative way; has seemed to make the ballet concentrate in itself a good deal of the modern ideal in matters of artistic expression. Nothing is stated, there is no intrusion of words used for the irrelevant purpose of describing; a world rises before one, the picture lasts only long enough to have been there; and the dancer, with her gesture, all pure-symbol, evokes, from her mere beautiful motion, idea, sensation, all that one need ever know of event. There, before you, she exists, in harmonious life; and her rhythm reveals to you the soul of her imagined being." — Symons, in Steinberg, pp.346-48.

* * *

"[RELIGIOUS DANCES.] All the mystery festivals which were celebrated in the Mediterranean lands, in antiquity and during the early post-Christian era must without exception have been combined with dancing. For example, a part of the Sabazios cult was a mad, whirling, round dance on the hill tops; in the Kybele-Attis cult it was a danced executed 'with winged dancing steps' (Casel). The Eleusis Mysteries in their later stages, which undoubtedly presented a conception of death and resurrection, and a picture too of the life of the blessed, were combined with a ring-dance which appears to have begun when the spirit emerged from its symbolic underworld journey and reached the splendid fields of the blessed (Casel, Czerwinski, Quasten). [A painting of an initiation dance of the Dionysian cult], from Casa Item in Pompeii, pictures a mystery induction ritual dance (Weege), apparently a slow, solemn dance, principally of twists and turns of the body. Bonnet mentions that in the Roman cult the dances consisted of backward and forward movements in cadence round the free-standing altar. In other cases the ring-dance took place around the tripod on which the oracle was introduced or the sacrifice made. The processional dances were executed with cadenced steps. Eitrem points out the common custom of performing the cult dance three times round the

altar: the symbol of perfection. This circling of the altar signified partly a purification and partly a defence. A magic and protective ring was thereby formed around the altar and all who stood before it.

"In Greece and Italy, as in Egypt, dances of various kinds were customary on the burial of the dead. The purpose of these dances appears to have been to gladden the dead, but still more to exorcise and expel the evil demons which wait for them[22] (Franz). In Greece and Italy the dead were comforted by boys and girls bearing wreaths and cypress branches, who executed solemn funeral dances with choral song. Immediately after the dancers came the priests. Cahusac reproduces a description from Plato's book on law (Book 12) in which he describes the burial of an Athenian king: the bier was preceded by a host of youths and girls, who carried wreaths and branches; they danced slowly and solemnly to musical accompaniment. After them came priests from various temples, clothed in their different robes. Franz reminds us of the antique Roman burial tablets, which reveal that dances were performed in the presence of the bier. Similar customs existed in Greece and Asia Minor. In this connection one should also bear in mind the funeral contests which took place in Greece from the earliest time; here, as also to some extent in Egypt, these contests in the presence of the god of the dead, were meant to illustrate the struggle in and after death with the enemy and the demons, and demonstrate also a victory over evil and death. Brede Kristensen holds that the dead were supposed to wage war on the arch-fiend in the kingdom of the dead and to win a victory for life. The contests at the graveside represent and manifest this idea. Similar was the Trojan contest, which was carried on by armed, mounted men, executing complicated manoeuvres in larger and smaller

---

22   A common function of music, generally. (Ed.)

circles, to and from, but all in a pattern which reproduced the labyrinth of Crete—the symbol of the underworld. That was a dance, not so much, however, in honour of the dead as seeking their aid and succour in the battle with the powers of the underworld.

"When Christianity appeared it was in a world in which a dance cult had existed as something obvious, right and necessary for the proper celebration of, or resistance to, powers which are not of the visible world. But something similar is true in respect of the power attributed to the dance in bringing healing to disease—a corollary, one might say, to its power to expel demons. The dance assists the living in their relations with the gods, but it also assists against the demons which cause disease. *The dance has its significance for life, death and disease.*

"As early as the fifth century BC there existed in Greece the so-called orpheotelestae, a kind of itinerant healers, who offered to dance around the sick, not infrequently in the form of a ring-dance. They pretended that thus they could cure all diseases, even mental disease (Baas).

"Only a few instances of similar dance customs in more modern times will be given here. In Bulgaria a dance for the healing of the sick has been discovered among the Kalin tribes: a ring-dance is performed, slowly at first, around the sick person, to a musical accompaniment which determines the pace at which the ring dancers approach or recede from the patient (Lübeck). The inhabitants of Naples perform a very similar dance around a severely afflicted person (Andrews), while in the little village of Pratteln, near Bâle, as late as the middle of the eighteenth century, ring-dances were performed at cross-roads as soon as any pestilential disease broke out (Bloch). Something similar is told of the people of Wertheim, who, during the plague of 1349, believed that they had found a cure by executing a ring-dance round a pine tree (Böhme). During the Middle Ages, according to a fourteenth-

century manuscript, there existed a dance with flaming torches around a new-born child; it was supposed to protect the child against evil spirits, especially against maladies which were thought to be induced by demoniac possession (Bloch)....

"In a commentary on the Gospel of St. Matthew, St. Chrysostom says of Salome's dance: 'For where there is a dance, there also is the Devil. For God has not given us our feet to use in a shameful way but in order that we may walk in decency, not that we should dance like camels (for even dancing camels make an unpleasant spectacle, much more than women), but in order to dance ring-dances with the angels. For it is shameful for the body to behave thus, the more so is it for the spirit to do so. Thus dance the demons and thus dance the servants of the demons.'

"It is easy to see that St. Chrysostom's condemnation is directed only at lascivious and indecent dances. He approves the dance of angels; we have been given our feet in order to dance with the angels, and certainly not only after death. The dance in the choir of the church, combined with the holy ritual, was... a dance with and in imitation of the invisible angels....

"From the fourth century [AD], and probably earlier, the idea prevailed in Christian circles that the holy spirits and God's forces danced in God's Paradise (Hermas, *The Shepherd*). In the latter part of that century the heavenly dance appears as a dance of the angels, in which the righteous take part. These dances of the angels belong to the mysteries of the Word (Clement). The ring-dances of the angels and of the Blessed are a part of bliss in Paradise; they are a reverent adoration of God, and of these the church dances are an imitation (Basileios). The former is connected with the mysteries of the Resurrection (Ambrose), and we must assume the same for the latter. The blessed and the righteous who, immediately after death, enter Paradise, therefore immediately take part in the dance of the Angels. If a blessed martyr reveals himself to those who venerate him, he does so dancing (Augustine). Some day all of us will perform ring-dances with the Angels in Paradise (Chrysostom).

"From about the year 150 it may be that a kind of boys' choir appeared, which played music, sang and danced during divine service (Justin). In the latter part of that century church dances appear to have become a part of the divine service (Clement). At the close of prayers hands were raised above the head to the accompaniment of a brief tramping or stamping dance (Clement), which was intended to show the desire, through prayer, to lift the body above the earth. In the fourth century the solemn church dance is said to have accorded with the revealed mysteries of the Resurrection (Ambrose).... It is possible that those about to be baptized approached the font dancing (Ambrose) in order to indicate resurrection from a sinful life to a righteous life after death by baptism. The church dance must be performed in the same manner as David danced before the Ark and this signifies a re-animation of the person for whom the dance is performed. It signifies a grateful approach to God through rapid rotations in the manner of the mysteries (Gregory of Nazianzus); it is closely allied to faith and in honour of grace (Ambrose).... At the beginning of the [fourth] century the church dance was performed in order, at the moment of triumph, to come into closer contact with God (Eusebius), and during the first part of the fifth century in order to proclaim in churches and chapels the victory and triumph of the Church (Theodoretus). From the beginning of the seventh century there begins to appear the curious parody church dance which later develops into the so-called fools' festival (Isidore). During the twelfth century there became linked with the church dance a number of ideas of the symbolic connexion between the details of the dance and the order of nature and of an original or res-

tored harmony, thus reviving similar ideas in the ritual dances of antiquity and in the dance symbolism of Christian gnosticism (Honorius)....

"Side by side with the sacral church dances there existed church dances of a purely popular character, i.e., dances in which only members of the congregation took part. The distinction, however, is not particularly sharp, for the Church, at least locally, permitted these dances and the priests were present; indeed it frequently happened that these popular dances were organized as part, and even as an essential part, of the Church festivals.... "[For example] in certain congregations in the district of Nules, Castellón de la Plana, on the east coast of Spain, north of the Valencia district, Christmas Eve was celebrated by throngs around a fire which was kindled in the market place outside the church. These throngs sang and danced. Some parishs in Mallorca celebrate St. John the Baptist on Midsummer Eve. Men and women dance through the streets to the music of a shawm, played by a man in clothes of grass representing St. John the Baptist (Capmány).

"It was especially the festival of Corpus Christi which in Spain was associated with religious dances, and there was not a single Corpus Christi procession but was accompanied by dancing. This dance is said to symbolize the triumphs which, according to sacred legend and biblical texts, were once celebrated, though occasionally we must admit that there were other symbolical notions....

"[In England] in the sixteenth century, during the reign of Queen Elizabeth, men and women danced to the music of pipes and drums both inside and outside churches, and in churchyards (Chambers). In the seventeenth century students and servants in York were even obliged to dance in the nave of the cathedral on Shrove Tuesday (Anonymous, 1871). In the whole of the county of Yorkshire it was also usual at Christmas to dance in country churches to the cry of 'Yole, Yole' (Christmas: Yule) (Gougaud). In England, however, dancing in churches was on various occasions forbidden. In Wiltshire there was another ancient custom, according to which the inhabitants of Wishford and Batford met every year and danced in Salisbury Cathedral (Anonymous, 1871)....

"The dance and the dead.[23] There is in Europe a very old and widespread idea that the dead are ill-natured beings who wish to injure the living. Numerous magical means have therefore been employed to prevent them from walking again. The dead desire the living (Kleinpaul) and thirst for their blood; they drag the living to them; they appear as vampires, werewolves, and ghosts, etc. The dead kill! Every dead person, says Kleinpaul, stretches up a hand from the grave in order to drag down a living person. Such ideas are to be found not only among the Germanic peoples, but also the Slavonic and Romanic (Krauss).... Only at one point in the year do people think that the dead are better disposed to the living: at Christmas. Hyltén-Cavallius tells of a dance of the angels at Finveden which was danced on Christmas Eve to the singing of Christmas psalms. It was a kind of sacrificial dance which was performed towards the end of the eighteenth century for the so-called dead. It was believed that the angels, that is to say, in this case, the spirits of the dead, participated in the dance. From Sydösterbotten in Finland there are similar reports that on Christmas Eve a visit was expected from the dead (Tegengren). In Germany also it was believed that at this time the spirits of the dead paid a visit (Reichhardt).

"Everywhere the most varied methods have been employed to prevent the dead from walking the earth again, from returning and creating misfortune or sickness. In her work *When Death Calls*, Louise Hag-

berg gives us an excellent and comprehensive survey of many such customs: needles were stuck into the skin or the feet of the dead; nails were driven into their feet, firmly securing the dead to their coffins; their legs were bound together, as also their feet and big toes; the arms were bound together; the body was enmeshed in a fishing net; seed, usually of flax, was strewn behind the dead when they were taken away from their homes; there were numerous ceremonies when the dead body was stood upright in the cottage room and when it was taken away, etc. These customs are well known in the Northern countries and in Germany (Franz), in England (Clemen), etc. In Lincolnshire the custom of binding together the feet of the dead was practised as late as 1916 (Clemen).

"However, all these magic rites to protect the living against the dead were insufficient. It was necessary to perform other rites for and against the dead during the time in which they were above ground after death. One was a part of the so-called death watch. Also we now encounter the dance as a means both of satisying and fending off the dead....

"Louise Hagberg and V. Backman give very much the same account of the conduct of the dance of death in Bjuráker [in Sweden]. Here there is a wall from the church to the shore at Norra Dellen which is called the *leckvallen*. Until the 1840s the dance of death was performed there. The dead body had previously been conveyed there either by rowing boat across the lake, or in winter by sledge across the ice. The dance took place immediately on arrival. The mourners held each other by the hand in pairs facing each other and these pairs formed up side by side in a large circle around the coffin. Then a kind of slow ring-dance was danced to the left. A special fiddler provided the music. The dance

---

23   See also **DEATH DANCE***, preceding and below. (Ed.)

was performed on Saturday evening, the day before the burial....

"In Germany people assembled around the dead; beer, bread and brandy were offered; cards were played and stories told. There were dancing, games and noise around the dead until lately (Sartori, Reichhardt).

"What is the real meaning of such jesting and merriment, music and dancing, at the death-watch? It has always been believed that music exorcized the dead, forced them into compliance at being taken to the grave and prevented them from walking the earth again. It was only later that the belief arose that music protected the dead from the demons and put the latter to flight (Quasten). Music thus acquired a significance very similar to that of the bells*. Quasten relates that in antiquity the hearse and the corpse were furnished with small bells, the sound of which drove the demons away, and that in the Christian world small bells might be laid beside the body in the coffin. Durandus, in the thirteenth century, declared with great emphasis that church bells expelled demons; bell-ringing at a burial formerly had precisely this significance of keeping the demons away. The Fathers of the Church were also not unfamiliar with the thought that music in the churchyard might reach the dead (Tertullian).

"So much may be regarded as certain: music for the dead served both to drive the demons away and to protect the dead; it could also be heard by the dead. The purpose of the death watch was evidently to comfort the dead and to make them happy on their last night on earth. I interpret the dance round the dead as a continuation and development of the early Christian churchyard dance for the martyrs....

"The dance for the martyrs was a dance of the angels and for that reason at the same time a dance of resurrection. For that reason it was comforting and consoling to the dead. It was for their refreshment. But at the same time it had the power to ward off demons, and was thus in agreement with the old Christian belief that the dance of the angels was a mystery associated with the resurrection, that is to say with the triumph over the forces of death....

"The struggle of the Church *against* religious dances in churches, chapels and churchyards began as early as the fourth century with Epiphanios and Basileios. At first the Fathers of the Church were cautious and hesitating. For example, even when it seemed that St. Augustine would have liked to forbid and condemn every form of church dance, he finally gave way when confronted with the often quoted biblical commands in the gospels of Matthew and Luke that whoever wishes to dance may dance. But neither is there any doubt that the opposition of the Church [at that time on the grounds, chiefly, that such dances were survivals of pagan custom] had already begun....

"From the fourth to the end of the eighteenth century ecclesiastical and lay authorities issued one prohibition after another against dancing in churches and church porches, in churchyards and for the dead. Every century, without exception, has such prohibitions: by Fathers of the Church, popes, archbishops, bishops, missionaries, councils, synods and state authorities. They were most frequent at the end of the Middle Ages and the beginning of modern times. They are directed mainly against the debasement of the dance, against the participation of women and against crude magical churchyard dances. But the desire to dance was strong and the dance ritual was supported by the books of the Bible, by the Evangelists and the writings of the Fathers of the Church. So the prohibitions had little success and the Church hastened to bring the religious dance under its protective wing....

"The religious Church dances still exist extensively today [1948]. As late as the first World War the hopping dance of the saints continued in Echternach in Luxembourg, so did Church dances in honour of the Virgin Mary in the Basque provinces. There

are also various dances, mainly processional dances, in association with Church
festivals in Spain and South American
republics; and there is a comprehensive
ceremony in the Coptic Christian Church
in Abyssinia. There are relics of the Church
dance in the Greek Orthodox Church, too;
these religious dances are performed in
honour of God and Christ, for the
glorification of Mary and the consolation
of the saints and martyrs, in honour of the
angels and the comfort and joy of the
dead." — Backman, pp.3-6,32,37-
38,95,97,108,132-36,154,331,334.

* * *

"The necessity to contact the spirits, to
appease them or to influence their will is
regarded by some scholars as the beginning of religion as distinct from magic, the
latter dealing with straightforward actions
in reaching the desired practical aim, for
example, the higher one jumps the higher
the flax will grow. According to Frazer, for
example, religion is 'a propitiation or conciliation of powers superior to man which
are believed to direct and control the
course of nature and of human life.'[24] But
one has to point out that some magic deal-
ings are concerned with spirits too, and in
many religious rites the magic element is
present. It is difficult to know where the
diving line is. For this reason, some
authors prefer to define them together as
a 'magico-religious' complex....[25]

"The functional characteristics of the
dance culture among traditional Central
and Eastern European peasants have so
many connections with old magical practices that they sound amazingly similar to
those practised in a 'primitive' community.
The 'Christian' façade is very thin, and
without much difficulty one can trace the
attempts of the Church to assimilate the

dance ritual into its own practices by superimposing new names and contents.

"Good examples of this are the dances of
the 'nestinari' in the Balkan area, or the fire
dances of the Anastenarides (Greek Orthodox sect) performed annually in Northern Greece. The dancers hold icons in their
hands, and the ceremony is connected
with the killing of a consecrated lamb. It is
executed to honour St. Helena. In reality,
it is presumably a Christianised Dionysian
ritual. Only recently (1972) the Bishop
Spyridon denounced it as a diabolical orgy
savouring of black magic. The unusual
feats [of these dancers] are explainable by
the fact that people who achieve a state of
dance-ecstasy are able to do things normally impossible, as for example, to walk
on fire without being hurt. This is known
among many different cultures, for instance in the Philippines and with the
Dyak tribes in Borneo.

"There are also still in existence ecstatic
dancing practices in the Mediterranean
basin which are connected with healing,
e.g. tarantism and related patterns in
Apulia, Sardinia, Spain and Provence; the
zar cult of North East Africa; the stambuli
or bori cults of Tunisia, Algeria and Morocco. Not only is the bite of the poisonous
spider tarantula healed by the dance that
eventually leads to exhaustion, but also
emotional and pscyhosomatic disturban-
ces are similarly dealt with.

"There have actually been Christian sects
who incorporated ecstatic group dances
into parts of their worship, for instance the
Shakers, in the United States in the
nineteenth century; converts to Christian
Churches in the West Indies — receiving
the Holy Spirit in the tradition of
Methodism; Spiritual Baptists in Trinidad
and on the island of St. Vincent, Jamaica,
Haiti, (known also as 'Shakers'); American
Indian Christian Churches of the
Northwestern United States.

---

24   *The Golden Bough* (1922), Chapter 4, "Magic and Religion", p.72.
25   M. Eliade, *Patterns in Comparative Religion.*

"There have been several Messianic movements, as for example in the late nineteenth century, the 'Ghost Dance Movement' which incorporated Western Indian Tribes of the United States. In achieving hypnotic states, visions were perceived. The people believed that they came into contact with dead relatives and received messages about the nearing end of the world. This combination of old Indian beliefs and Christian ideas was instrumental in the outburst of the tragic Indian uprising of 1890.[26]

"Similarly the 'Hallelujah Movement' of the South American Indians uses dance to achieve trance (Brazil, Amazon Basin and the Guianas). The motive of their search is a land without evil, without death.

"There are also other religions which use dance ecstasy as an element of their worship. A good example may be provided by the religious Muslim sect of 'the Whirling Dervishes', the Mevlevi dervishes of Konya (Anatolia). They have a very wide distribution| — from the Atlantic coast of North Africa to Malaysia and Indonesia. The origin of their dance ritual may actually have connections with an ancient Greek ritual (Konya was the home of the Phyrgian Dionysus*). Similarly the Hassidim (Jews of Eastern Europe) used ecstatic type of dance in their rituals to heighten the mystical powers of the divine.

"From [all of this] it becomes evident that there are deep-rooted connections between art (especially dance as the primary art form), magic and religion, owing to [a] unity they shared at the beginning of human history." —Lange, pp.65,71-73.

§74.5 "THE GRASS DANCE (Canadian/Blackfoot Indian).] At the tribal council Chief Long Knife says to Big Wolf, 'Two months have passed since the last hunt. The drying huts are empty, and our people are hungry for red meat. When the owls and the prairie dogs have gone to sleep, you will go in search of buffalo and come back to tell me where they can be found.'

"All day long Big Wolf walks from hill to hill, from butte to butte. On top of every rise he gazes out over the prairie, taking great care not to frighten any animals that might be nearby. Just as the sun is about to enter his teepee of stone, high up in the mountains, he sees what he is looking for: a large herd asleep in a ravine. He counts the animals ten times on his fingers and checks his bearings.

"Now he heads back to camp. His moccasins drag a little through the grass because he is quite tired, but when night falls he hears strange sounds. They are not the same as the music of the Blackfoot flutes — they are softer, and the beat is steadier. Big Wolf looks in the direction from which the music comes and thinks he sees a crowd of people far away by the edge of a pond, all dancing in time.

"Men who dance without the war drum are not dangerous, thinks Big Wolf.

"As he approaches the pond, the sounds and the movement of the group become more distinct. Big Wolf begins to mark time with them, then, caught up in the rhythm, starts dancing himself.

"He forgets the group, which continues its dance three arrow shots away. On a strip of prairie where the grass has been eaten away by the thin-lipped antelope, he spins around as if performing one of his tribe's ceremonial dances, keeping time with the strange music, which first slows him down, then makes him leap like a deer surprised by the hunter.

"Big Wolf dances far into the night and falls exhausted to the ground. The burning sun on his eyelids wakes him. He looks around. The strangers have gone. Nothing remains except the softly swaying rushes. Big Wolf searches in vain for traces of the dancers' moccasins where their feet have trampled down the grass. He finds noth-

---

26   J. Mooney, *The Ghost Dance Religion and the Sioux Outbreak of 1890.*

ing. But the breeze that comes along and stirs the tall grass carries the same music to his ears he heard the night before. Then he understands what has happened.

"He isn't too disappointed, because the new dance he brings back to the camp will earn him a lot of prestige." — Mélançon, pp.76-78.

§74.6 "[THE SHROVE TUESDAY VISITOR (French Canadian).] In olden times in Canada, Shrove Tuesday, the day before the beginning of Lent, was more strictly observed than it is to-day. The night was always one of great merriment and feasting. Boys and girls of the villages and country places gathered there for the last time before the long period of quiet. They danced until midnight, but the youth or maiden who dared to dance after the hour of twelve was henceforth followed with little luck. This rule was not often broken, for when it was broken the Spirits of Evil always walked the earth and brought disaster to the youthful dancers.

"In a remote village on the banks of a great river there dwelt in the seventeenth century a French peasant, a kind and devout old man. He had but one child, a daughter. She was a handsome girl, and naturally enough she had many suitors among the young men of the place. One of these she prized above all the others, and she had promised to become his wife. On the evening of the Shrove Tuesday before the date set for the wedding, as was the custom the young people of the village gathered at her home. It was a simple but joyous gathering, the last which the girl could attend before her marriage. Right merrily the dance went on, and all the guests were in high spirits. Soon after eleven o'clock a sleigh drawn by a great coal-black horse stopped at the door. It contained but one man. Without knocking at the door, the newcomer entered. The rooms were crowded, but the rumor soon spread whisperingly around that a new presence had appeared, and the simple villagers strove to get a look at the tall figure

in fine clothes. The old man of the house received the stranger kindly and offered him the best he had in his home, for such was the custom in the old days. One thing the gathering particularly noted — the stranger kept his fur cap on his head, and he did not remove his gloves; but as the night was cold this caused but little wonder.

"After the silence caused by the stranger's entrance the music swelled, and again the dance went on. The newcomer chose the old man's daughter as his partner. He came to her and said, 'My pretty lass, I hope you will dance with me tonight, and more than once, too.' 'Certainly,' replied the girl, well pleased with the honor, and knowing that her friends would envy her. During the remainder of the evening the stranger never left her side, and dance after dance they had together. From a corner of the room the girl's lover watched the pair in silence and anger.

"In a small room opening from that in which the dancers were gathered was an old and pious woman seated on a chest at the foot of a bed, praying fervently. She was the girl's aunt. In one hand she held her beads, with the other she beckoned her niece to come to her.

" 'It is very wrong of you,' she said, 'to forsake your lover for this stranger; his manner is not pleasing to me. Each time I utter the name of the Saviour or the Virgin Mary as he passes the door, he turns from me with a look of anger.' But the girl paid no heed to her aunt's advice.

"At last it was midnight, and Lent had come. The old man gave the signal for the dance to cease. 'Let us have one more dance,' said the stranger. 'Just one more,' pleaded the girl; 'my last dance, before my marriage.' And the old man wishing to please his only child, — for he loved her well, — consented, and although it was already Ash Wednesday the dance went on. The stranger again danced with the girl. 'You have been mine all the evening,' he whispered; 'why should you not be mine for ever?' But the girl laughed at his question. 'I am a strange fellow,' said the stranger, 'and when I will do a thing it must be done. Only say yes, and nothing can ever separate us.' The girl cast a glance towards her dejected lover in the corner of the room. 'I understand,' said the stranger. 'I am too late; you love him.'

" 'Yes,' answered the girl, 'I love him, or rather I did love him once,' for the girl's head had been turned by the attentions of the stranger.

" 'That is well,' said the stranger; 'I will arrange all, and overcome all difficulties. Give me your hand to seal our plight.'

"She placed her hand in his, but at once she withdrew it with a low cry of pain. She had felt in her flesh the point of some sharp instrument as if the stranger held a knife in his hand. In great terror she fainted and was carried to a couch. At once the dance was stopped and the dancers gathered around her, wondering at the sudden happenings. At the same time two villagers came in and called the old man to the door to see a strange sight without. The deep snow for many yards around the stranger's horse and sleigh had melted in the hour since his arrival, and a large patch of bare ground was now showing. Terror soon spread among the guests; they spoke in whispers of fear, and shrank from the centre of the room to the walls as if eager to escape; but the old man begged them not to leave him. The stranger looked with a cold smile upon the dread of the company. He kept close to the couch where the girl was slowly coming back to life. He took from his pocket a beautiful necklace, and said to her, 'Take off the glass beads you wear, and for my sake take this beautiful necklace.' But to her glass beads was attached a little cross which she did not want to part with, and she refused to take his gift.

"Meanwhile, in the home of the priest, some distance away, there was a strange happening. While he prayed for his flock the old priest had fallen asleep. He saw in his slumber a vision of the old man's home

and what was happening there. He started quickly from his sleep and called his servant and told him to harness his horse at once, for not far away a soul was in danger of eternal death. He hurried to the old man's home. When he reached there, the stranger had already unfastened the beads from the girl's neck and was about to place his own necklace upon her and to seize her in his arms. But the old priest was too quick for him. He passed his sacred stole around the girl's neck and drew her towards him, and turning to the stranger he said, 'What art thou, Evil One, doing among Christians?' At this remark terror was renewed among the guests; some fell to their knees in prayer; all were weeping, for they knew now that the stranger with the stately presence and the velvet clothes was the Spirit of Evil and Death. And the stranger answered, 'I do not know as Christians those who forget their faith by dancing on holy days. This fair girl has chosen to be mine. With the blood that flowed from her hand she sealed the compact which binds her to me for ever.'

"In answer, the old curé struck the stranger hard across the face with his stole, and repeated some Latin words which none of the guests understood. There was a great crash, as if it thundered, and in a moment amid the noise the stranger disappeared; with his horse and sleigh he had vanished as mysteriously and quickly as he had come.

"The guests were long in recovering from their fear, and all night they prayed with the curé that their evil deeds might be forgiven. That she might be cleansed from her sins and that her promise to the stranger might be rightly broken, the girl entered a convent to pass the remainder of her life. A few years later she died. And since that day in her little village on the banks of the great river, the Shrove Tuesday dancers have always stopped their dance at midnight; for youths and maidens still keep in mind the strange dancer in the fine clothes who wooed the peasant's only daughter and almost carried her off."[27] — Macmillan, in Clarkson & Cross, 214-17.

DANCING TO DEATH (OR INSANITY). *(See also pp. 175, 994.)*

§77.5 "LITTLE FREDDIE WITH HIS FIDDLE (Norwegian). [In his travels the boy Freddie befriended a strange being in need, for which he was granted three wishes. One of these wishes was that, because he loved to hear the fiddle play, and see people so merry and glad that they danced, he should have a fiddle that everything alive must dance to it. Another thing he wished for was, that no one might refuse him the first thing that he asked for. And so it was done. Now, one day he became the victim of a mean sheriff, who meant to cheat him....]

"[But] Little Freddie started playing his fiddle, and the sheriff began to dance so the thorns tore at him; and the boy played and the sheriff danced and cried and pleaded until the rags flew off him, and he had hardly a thread left on his back....

"When Little Freddie came to town, he went to an inn. He played on his fiddle, and everyone who came there started dancing, and he lived both merrily and well; he had no sorrows for no one could say 'No' to what he asked for.

"But one day, when the merrymaking was at its liveliest, the watch came to arrest the boy and drag him to the town hall; for the sheriff had complained about him, and said that he had both assaulted and robbed him, and nearly taken his life. And now he should be hanged, there was no way out.

"But Little Freddie had a way out of everything, and that was the fiddle. He started to play, and the watch had to dance until they fell down gasping. Then they sent for soldiers and guards, but they fared no better. As soon as Little Freddie took to playing his fiddle, they had to dance as long as he was able to make a sound; but they were worn out long before that.

"But finally they sneaked in on him and took him when he was asleep at night, and when they had him, he was sentenced to be hanged right away, and it was off to the gallows at once. A large crowd had come to witness this rare spectacle. And the sheriff was there, too, and he was so overjoyed because he would be repaid for his torn skin, and see that they hanged the boy.

"But it didn't go quickly, for Little Freddie was a feeble walker, and he made himself even feebler; [his] fiddle and musket he carried along, too, for nobody could get them away from him. And when he came to the gallows, and was going to climb, he rested on every rung of the ladder. On the topmost rung he sat down, and asked if they could refuse him one wish: that he might be allowed to do one thing. He would so like to play just one little tune on his fiddle before they hanged him.

" 'It would be both a sin and a shame to refuse him that,' they said. They couldn't say 'No' to what he asked for. But the sheriff begged, in heaven's name, not to let him pluck on a string, or it would be the end of them all. As for himself, they must *tie* him to the birch tree which stood there, should the boy start playing.

"It didn't take Little Freddie long to get the fiddle to sound, and everyone there started to dance, both those on two legs and those on four: both deacon and parson, and clerk and bailiff, and sheriff and the hangman, and dogs and pigs. They danced and laughed and shrieked all at the same time; some danced until they lay

---

27   See Thompson Motifs C631.6 (Tabu: Playing music on the Sabbath), G303.10.4.5 (Devil dances with maid and puts his claws through her hands), Q223.6.4(B) (Punishment for dancing on Sunday) and Q386.1 (Devil punishes girl who loves to dance), **FOLKLORE AND FOLKTALES — TYPOLOGY***, above. (Ed.)

stretched out as though dead; some danced until they fainted. They all faired pretty badly, but it went worst with the sheriff, for he stood tied to the birch, and danced and rubbed big patches of skin off his back. But no one thought of doing anything to Little Freddie, and he could go wherever he wished with his fiddle and musket. And he lived happily the rest of his days, for there was no one who could say 'No' to the first thing he asked for." — Asbjørnsen, pp.65-66.

DAPHNIS (Greek).

§80A.1 "(A) A son of Hermes* by a Sicilian nymph. The infant was exposed to the elements and left to die, but he was found and reared by shepherds, and educated by nymphs. Pan* taught him to play the flute* and sing; the Muses* inspired him with a love of poetry; and he is said to have invented pastoral song and story. He fell in love with Piplea and tried to win her from her master Lityerses by defeating him in a reaping contest; when he was on the verge of losing, Heracles* killed Lityerses. Daphnis was extremely fond of hunting; and when five of his dogs died he refused food and died also. (B) A shepherd on Mount Ida turned to stone by a jealous nymph. (C) A son of Paris and Oenone." — Zimmerman, p.81.

DEATH DANCE. (See pp.178, 995.)

§83.2 "[THE DANCE OF THE DEAD (Irish).] For a long time I have been listening to the old people telling about the man who was going to the fair at Ballydehob long ago to buy a cow. He didn't know what time it was when he was leaving the house, because a fox had taken off a fine March cock that they had a short while before. It was a fine, starry night, with no moon.

"He was alone, and he had about fifteen or sixteen miles of a journey ahead of him. He went on about ten or twelve miles where he was a stranger and didn't know anyone who lived there. As he was passing a house by the side of the road, he heard very fine, sweet music being played inside. He stopped to listen. He saw light in the house, and he could hear a lot of people dancing on the floor. The dance and music attracted him, for he had a light heart. He went to the door and knocked. It was opened for him and he went in. There was a fine, large kitchen, bursting with people, young men and women dancing. A fairly elderly man was sitting by the fire playing a fiddle for them.[28]

"This man who was going to the fair was a very fine dancer himself. He couldn't keep his feet from moving, so he took a quiet, graceful girl who was seated near the door by the hand and took her out on the floor. After the dance he bowed and thanked her and took her back to her seat. He drew himself aside, for there was a huge crowd dancing together on the floor.

28　Up to this point, the story resembles traditional tales about **FAIR**Y* dancers, fiddlers, pipers and the like. See §109.9 below, for example. In all of these cases music/dance appears to give talismanic control over nature (over life and death itself perhaps) to the dancer or player. Concepts of *death* and *devil* are also associated, suggesting that death is construed by some as a consequence of Satan's fall from grace: that is, of his expulsion from heaven, which is to say from "eternal life". Conversely, a sort of reawakening from death (or symbolic return to life?) seems to be made possible, at least temporarily, by e.g. fiddling, piping and dancing. For music as a magic restorative see e.g. **DRUM***, §93.10, below. (Ed.)

He was wondering where they had all come from. He stood watching the dance. He had never seen anything like it or heard such fine music. When he got a chance after a while, he gave a groat to the fiddler, and when the next dance started, he slipped out by the door. He said to himself, as he left, that he would try to find out more about these people when he would be on his way back from the fair in daylight. He didn't forget to put a mark opposite the house on the other side of the road, so that he would find the house on his return.

"Off he went then to the fair and bought a cow. He then ate his breakfast to face the road home. He left Ballydehob at ten o'clock in the morning, driving the cow before him. He kept an eye on the places he passed through. The houses were few and far between. He asked everyone he met had any of them been at the dance last night in a certain house in such a place. He asked them who was the fiddler. But none of them knew anything about such a dance, and there hadn't been a fiddler in the district for many years. He was told, however, that the old people had heard of a great fiddler who was there long ago, who used to play music in a dancing-school in a house by the side of the road. But he had been dead for forty years or more, and a new house had been built on the site of the dancing-school; a married couple lived there now.

"That's what the people he met along the road on his way home told him. At last he reached the house where he had seen the dance the previous night, and he recognised it easily. The door was wide open. He left the cow to graze along the road and went in. The woman of the house was within. She asked him about the fair, and then he asked her about the dance and the dancers she had the night before. He also enquired about the fiddler and where he lived. The woman didn't reply for a while, for she thought that he had either 'a drop taken' or else was a bit 'off his head'.

" ' 'Tis a long time since there has been a dance in this house,' said she. 'There used to be a dancing-school long ago where this is standing now; that's over forty years ago. The old people, who used to dance there when they were young men and women, say that there was no beating the fiddler who used to play for them.'

"He listened to her till she had finished.

" 'Come outside a minute with me,' said he to her.

"She followed him out, and he led her across the road. He put his hand into a hole in the fence and pulled out two socks.

" 'Do you see those two socks?' he asked.

" 'I do.'

"He then told her the whole story about the dance in her house the night before and how he had put his two socks into the hole in the fence so that he would know the house again on his way home. He told her about the dancers and how he had given a groat to the great fiddler they had.

" 'Now what do you think of all that?' he asked.

" 'The greatest surprise of all that I got,' said she, 'was when I found a groat on the chair near the fire when I was 'reddening' it this morning. I was the first up in the house, and it was I who took the bolt off the door and opened it. When I asked my husband had he left the coin on the chair, he said that someone had been playing a trick on me.'

" 'Now you know how the groat came to be on the chair,' said he.

" 'I have ever been hearing that 'they' are there,' said she." — O'Sullivan, pp.60-62.

DRUM. *(See also pp. 188, 996.)*

§93.10 [THE MAGIC DRUM (Eskimo*).] An old married couple had a daughter who did not want to marry. It was not that she lacked suitors; young men who were good hunters had come from great distances to take her for their wife. But she had refused all proposals. She had said no to all. To all, that is, but the last two brothers who had come.

"These brothers arrived with the same intentions as the others. When first they entered the igloo the girl took them to be men just like their predecessors. However, though they had neither said nor done anything extraordinary, the girl became attracted to them.

"She followed them outside the igloo. Scarcely were they outside when the two brothers reclothed themselves in the skins which they had left at the door. The young woman then recognized them for what they were — white bears.

"They took her away over the ice and forced her to descend into the water through a hole in the ice. For some time she was dragged along through the water, only to be abandoned when the bears came to another opening through which they disappeared.

"Left on her own, the girl sank to the floor of the ocean. When her feet touched bottom she was able to look about her. One side of the ocean appeared to be darker, the opposite side seemed brighter. She reasoned that the dark side must lie to the north so she began to walk toward the south where the light was brighter.

"While she was walking tiny sea animals surrounded her. They bit into her body, tearing away strips of flesh. Little by little her body was devoured. Eventually only her bones remained. Then she noticed an unusually bright area which led her to think that she was about to find a place where she could climb up to the land. She was nothing but a skeleton but resolutely she advanced toward the light. She found a crevasse in the ice and was able to climb up onto the ice surface.

"Having come this far she began to reflect on her past. In her mind's eye she saw her parents with their well-filled storeroom and she asked herself what she must do to have the same. While pondering this problem she took some snow and made a small igloo, one that resembled that of her

father. She also built a small platform as a storage place.

"When she had finished, she thought out loud: 'I have nothing warm in which to sleep. I need a sleeping bag, some skins and some furs.' With these thoughts she fell asleep.

"On awakening, the woman was surprised to see a big igloo, exactly like her father's, in front of her own. Near it lay a freshly killed caribou. Her dreams had been realized! She dried the caribou hide and made herself a sleeping bag. The meat she prepared for storage on the platform.

"From that time on, each night before going to sleep, she would think of what she needed, knowing that when she awoke the next day everything would be provided. In this manner she soon had all she required, except her own flesh. What the sea animals had eaten could not be replaced. She remained a walking skeleton.

"Each day she spent long periods of time on the ice. On one such occasion she happened to see hunters coming down to the sea ice to hunt seals. The young woman wanted to meet these people and talk to them. But when she approached them the hunters fled in fear. Disappointed, the girl watched them disappear into the distance. Then she returned to her igloo thinking: 'I would like to have met them, but I frightened them. It is I who prevented them from coming. I am but a skeleton and my bones clatter when I walk. No doubt they were afraid of me; that is why they ran.' She was sad and began to torment herself because she had been unable to get close to the hunters.

"The father of these hunters was an old man, and when his sons had gone to hunt at the sea he had been left behind. They had made him stay in his igloo; he was no longer capable of hunting and could not provide himself with anything to eat.

"Upon his sons' return they told their father: 'Yesterday we saw a woman who was nothing but a skeleton. She came to meet us, but we were afraid. We fled and did not see her again.'

" 'Ah, well,' replied the old man, 'I don't have much longer to live. I shall go and meet her tomorrow.'

"The next morning the old man went to find the girl and found her sitting in the entrance of her igloo. She did not move towards him, but when he arrived she invited him to enter the igloo. The interior was bright with the light from the stone lamps. They ate and then went to sleep.

"When morning came, the girl who had been reduced to a skeleton spoke to the old man who was no longer able to hunt.

" 'Make me a drum,' she said. 'Make me a very small drum.' The old man immediately went to work to satisfy her desire. When he finished he gave her the instrument. The woman blew out the lamps, took the drum and began to dance. She beat the drum with a stick while repeating a magic incantation.[29] The drum grew larger and the sound of the beat swelled and seemed to fill the air. The dance finished, the lamps were relit and the old man was once more able to see the girl. To his amazement the skeleton had gone; instead a pretty yound girl, dressed in superb clothing, appeared before him.

"The girl took the drum again, blew out the lamps, and began to dance. After a while she asked her visitor, 'Are you all right like that?' With his affirmative reply she relit the lamps. It was no longer an old man who appeared before her, but rather a handsome young man. The magic rhythm of the drum had given him back his youth.

"This is how the girl who had not wanted to marry and who had been eaten by the beasts of the sea found a husband.

"When they returned to the old man's family no one recognized him. His own sons said, 'Our father, who is very old has travelled north toward the sea and has not returned.'

" 'I am your father,' replied the man. 'I was once old and this woman was but a skeleton. However, we have both become young and handsome and now she is my wife.' " —Metayer, pp.14-18.

EGYPTIAN PRACTICES AND BELIEFS. *(See also pp.208, 1016.)*

§99.8 "[Diodorus Siculus] not only tells us that music, and musical instruments, were invented by the Egyptian deities, Osiris, Isis*, Orus,[30] and Hermes*; but that Orpheus* had from Egypt the fable of his descent into hell, and the power of music over the infernals; and enumerates all the great poets and musicians of Greece who had visited that country, in order to improve themselves in the arts. Herodotus too, who travelled into Egypt more than three hundred years before Diodorus, and a hundred before Plato, is so far from mentioning any prohibition against the pratice of music there, that he gives several instances of its use in their festivals, and religious ceremonies.

" 'The Egyptians,' says he,[31] 'were the first inventors of festivals, ceremonies, and transactions with the Gods, by the mediation of others. It is not thought sufficient in Egypt,' continues this father of history, 'to celebrate the festivals of the Gods once every year, but they have many times appointed to that end: particular in the city of *Bubastis*, where they assemble to worship Diana, with great devotion. The manner observed in these festivals at Bubastis is this: men and women embark promiscuously, in great numbers; and, during the voyage, some of the women beat upon a tabor, while part of the men play on the

---

29   See also references to **SHAMANS & SHAMANISM***. (Ed.)
30   Horus. (Ed.)
31   *Euterp.*

pipe; the rest, of both sexes, singing, and clapping their hands together at the same time. At every city they find in their passage, they haul in the vessel, and some of the women continue their music.'

"In the same book, he tells us, that in the processions of Osiris or Bacchus*, the Egyptian women carry the images, *singing the praises of the god, preceded by a flute.* And afterwards, in speaking of funeral ceremonies, he has the following remarkable passage: 'Among other memorable customs, the Egyptians sing the song of Linus*, like that which is sung by the Phoenicians, Cyprians, and other nations, who vary the name according to the different languages they speak. But the person they honour in this song, is evidently the same that the Grecians celebrate: and as I confess my surprize at many things I found among the Egyptians, so I more particularly wonder whence they had this knowledge of Linus, because they seem to have celebrated him from time immemorial. The Egyptians call him by the name of *Maneros*, and say he was the only son of the first of their kings, but dying an untimely death, in the flower of his age, he is lamented by the Egyptians in this mourning song, which is the only composition of the kind used in Egypt.'

"Strabo says, that the children of the Egyptians were taught letters, the Songs appointed by law, and a certain species of Music established by government, exclusive of all others.

"Indeed the Greeks, who lost no merit by neglecting to claim it, unanimously confess, that most of their ancient musical instruments were of Egyptian invention; as the triangular Lyre, the Monaulos, or single Flute; the Symbal, or Kettle-drum;

and the Sistrum, an instrument of sacrifice, which was so multiplied by the priests in religious ceremonies, and in such great favour with the Egyptians in general, that Egypt was often called, in derision, the *country of Sistrums* ; as Greece has been said to be governed by the Lyre....

"The Egyptian mythology, as well as the Grecian, is so much connected with the first attempts at music, and so many of the Pagan divinities have been said to be its first cultivators, that some slight mention of them is unavoidable.

"The sun, moon, and stars seem to have struck all mankind with wonder, awe, and reverence; and to have impressed them with the first idea of religious veneration. To the adoration of these succeeded hero-worship, in the deification of dead kings and legislators. This was the course of idolatry every where, as well as in Egypt: indeed the inhabitants of this country seem, from their early civilization, conquests, and power, to have spread their religious principles over the whole habitable earth; as it is easy to trace all the Pagan mythology of other countries, in the first ages of the world of which we have any account, from Egypt; and Isis and Osiris may be proved to have been the prototypes of almost every other God and Goddess of antiquity. For the *Moon*, or Luna, under the name of *Isis*, means all the most ancient female divinities of Paganism; as the *Sun*, under that of *Osiris*, does the male. Diodorus Siculus confesses, that there was ever a great confusion of sentiments concerning Isis and Osiris. The former is called Ceres, Thesmophora, or Juno, Hecate, Proserpine, and Luna; Osiris has been likewise called Serapis,

Dionysius,[32] Helios, Pluto, Ammon, Jupiter, and Pan.

"However, the history of these does not so immediately concern the present enquiries, as that of Mercury or Hermes, one of the *secondary Gods* of Egypt, who received divine honours on account of his useful and extraordinary talents.[33] This God must therefore be taken out of his niche, and examined.

"There is no personage in all antiquity more renowned that the Egyptian Mercury, who was surnamed Trismegistus, *or thrice illustrious.*[34] He was the soul of Osiris's counsel and government and is called by sir Isaac Newton, his secretary; 'Osiris,' says he, 'using the advice of his secretary Thoth, distributes Egypt into thirty-six *nomes;*[35] and in every *nome* erects a temple, and appoints the several Gods, festivals, and religions of the several *nomes.* The temples were the sepulchres of his great men, where they were to be buried and worshipped after death, each in his own temple, with ceremonies and festivals appointed by him; while he and his queen, by the names of Osiris and Isis, were to be worshipped in all Egypt; these were the temples seen and described by Lucian, who was himself an Egyptian, eleven hundred years after, to be of one and the same age: and this was the original of the several *nomes* of Egypt, and of the several Gods and several religions of those *nomes.*'[36] And Diodorus Siculus tells us, that Mercury was honoured by Osiris, and

afterwards worshipped by the Egyptians, as a person endowed with extraordinary talents for every thing that was conducive to the good of society. He was the first who, out of the coarse and rude dialects of his time, formed a regular language, and gave appellatives to the most useful things: he likewise invented the first characters or letters, and even regulated the harmony of words and phrases: he instituted several rites and ceremonies relative to the worship of the Gods, and communicated to mankind the first principles of astronomy. He afterwards suggested to them, as amusements, wrestling, and dancing, and invented the lyre, to which he gave three strings, an allusion to the seasons of the year: for these three strings producing three different sounds, the grave, the mean, and the acute; the grave answered to winter, the mean to spring, and the acute to summer.[37]

"Among the various opinions of the several ancient writers who have mentioned this circumstance, and confined the invention to the Egyptian Mercury, that of Apollodorus is the most intelligible and probable. 'The Nile,' says this writer,[38] 'after having overflowed the whole country of Egypt, when it returned within its natural bounds, left on the shore a great number of dead animals of various kinds, and, among the rest, a tortoise, the flesh of which being dried and wasted by the sun, nothing was left within the shell, but nerves and cartileges, and these being braced

---

32 *Sic*? I.e. Dionysus. (Ed.)

33 By *secondary divinities* is here meant such princes, heroes, and legislators, as were deified after death, for the benefits they had conferred on mankind when living, in distinction to the *heavenly luminaries,* or sun, moon, and stars, which were the first divinities of paganism.

34 See also **HERMES TRISMEGISTUS***, above. (Ed.)

35 Districts, or provinces.

36 *Chronology of Ancient Kingdoms,* 22.

37 Not only the Egyptians, but the ancient Greeks, divided their year into no more than three seasons, spring, summer, and winter, which were called [Greek term] or *hours* ; Hesiod (*Theogony*) [also] speaks of no more.

38 *Biblioth., lib.* ii.

and contracted by dessication, were rendered sonorous; Mercury, in walking along the banks of the Nile, happening to strike his foot against the shell of this tortoise, was so pleased with the sound it produced, that it suggested to him the first idea of a lyre, which he afterwards constructed in the form of a tortoise, and strung it with the dried sinews of dead animals.'

"It is generally imagined that there were two Thoths, or Mercuries, in Egypt, who lived at very remote periods, but both persons of great abilities. For the small number of strings in this lyre, it is reasonable to suppose that the invention of it was due to the *first* Egyptian Mercury: for that attributed to the Grecian had more strings, as will be shewn [in another place]. Most of the writers on music among the ancients have supposed, that the three sounds of this *primitive lyre* were E, F, G; though Boethius, who makes the number of strings four, says they were tuned thus: E, A, B, e; but this tuning, if not invented by Pythagoras, was at least first brought into Greece by that philosopher.

"No less than forty-two works are attributed to the Egyptian Hermes by ancient writers;[39] of these the learned and exact Fabricius has collected all the titles.[40] It was usual for the Egyptians, who had the highest veneration for this personage, after his apotheosis, to have his works, which they regarded as their Bible, carried about in processions with great pomp and ceremony: and the first that appeared in these solemnities was the Chanter, who had two of them in his hands, while others bore symbols of the musical art. It was the business of the *Chanters* to be particularly versed in the first two books of Mercury, one of which contained the hymns to the Gods, and the other maxims of government: thirty-six of these books comprehended a complete system of Egyptian philosophy: the rest were chiefly upon the subjects of medicine and anatomy.[41]

"These books upon theology and medicine are ascribed by Marsham[42] to the second Mercury, the son of Vulcan, who, according to Eusebius,[43] lived a little after Moses; and this author, upon the authority of Manetho, cited by Syncellus, regarded the second Mercury as the Hermes, sur-

---

39   *Clem. Alex. Strom., lib.* vi.
40   *Bib. Græc.* tom. i.
41   Several of these works, however, if we may judge by their titles, seems to have been upon the subject of music and poetry.
42   *Chro. Sæc.* I.
43   *In Chron.*

named Trismegistus. Enough has been said, however, to prove that the Egyptian Mercuries, both as to the time when they flourished, and their attributes, were widely different from the Grecian Hermes, the son of Jupiter and Maia.

"Though so ancient and honourable an origin has been assigned to the *Dichord* and *Trichord*, which can both be fairly traced from Egypt, yet the single flute, or *Monaulos*, is said by several writers not only to be a native of that country, and of much higher antiquity than the lyre, but, according to Anthenæus, from Juba's *Theatrical History*, to have been invented by Osiris himself.[44] The Egyptians called it *Photinx*, or crooked flute;[45] its shape was that of a bull's horn, as may be seen in many gems, medals, and remains of ancient sculpture. Not only the form of this instrument, but the manner of holding it, is described by Apuleius, in speaking of the mysteries of Isis: 'Afterwards,' says this author, 'came the flute players, consecrated to the great Serapis, often repeat-

ing upon the *crooked flute* turned towards the right ear, the airs commonly used in the temple.' All the representations which I have seen of this instrument, have so much the appearance of *real horns*, that they encourage a belief of its great antiquity; and that the first instruments in use of this kind, were not only suggested by the horns of dead animals, but that the horns themselves were long used as musical instruments, at least those sounded by the Hebrew priests at the siege of Jericho, we are repeatedly told, were *trumpets made of ram's horns.*[46]

"Before the invention of the flute, music could have been little more than metrical, as no other instruments, except those of percussion, were known; and when the art was first discovered of refining and sustaining tones, the power of music over mankind was probably irresistible, from the agreeable surprize, which soft and lengthened sounds must have occasioned. But proofs can be given of the Egyptians having had musical instruments in use

---

44   However, Plutarch says, that Apollo was not only the inventor of the *Cithara* but likewise of the flute. Indeed it was a very common practice with antiquity, to attribute to the Gods all the discoveries and inventions to which there were no lawful claimants among mortals. And though we may now venture to doubt of all the *marvellous* facts, which have been so seriously related by the most respectable historians of Greece and Rome, yet we must allow that the giving the invention of music, and musical instruments to the Gods, proves them to have been of the most remote antiquity, and held in the highest estimation by such as bestowed upon them so honourable an origin.

45   The Photinx was not a crooked flute, but the name given by the Greeks of Alexandria to the transverse flute. It is not to be confused with the Plaiaulos, which was held transversely, but was played by means of a reed mouthpiece. (Mercer, 1935)

46   Joshua, chap. vi.

among them, capable of much greater variety and perfection than those hitherto mentioned, at a time when all the rest of the known world was in a state of the utmost barbarism." — Burney, I, 168-69,172-75.

§99.9 "BES (A guardian god).[47]

"Bes chased away demons of the night[48] and guarded men from dangerous animals. His image was carved on bedposts, bringing a touch of coarse geniality into the boudoir.[49] He eventually became a protector of the dead and, amazingly, competed with even the refined and magnificent god *Osiris* for the attentions of men.

"Bes' only clothing appears to have been a leopard skin tied round his shoulders and an ostrich feather stuck in his uncombed hair." — Carlyon, p.273.

"[Bes was also a popular god worshipped in Canaan and Carthage: he was] a professional buffoon, fond of melodramatic dancing, risqué songs and mock-heroic posturing. He afforded the other gods much superior amusement. Originally a proletarian god, his sense of

fun gained him many converts among the merchant class. Bes is a beautiful joke played upon the inadequate by a mocking Fate. What makes him really attractive is that he doesn't try to win our sympathies by any of the insincere attitudes of sadness and mental agony shown by modern clowns. He is a bloated, randy, drunken, pompous, honest to goodness old-style knockabout comic." — Carlyon, p.310.

"HOTH (Tehuti, Thout, Djehuti, Zehuti; Great god of wisdom, magic, music, medicine, astronomy, geometry, surveying, drawing and writing.[50] Thoth's name means 'he of Ejehut', which was a province in Lower Egypt. His cult center was at Hermopolis (Ashmunen). He was depicted as an ibis-headed man or as an ibis- or dog-headed ape; on his head he wore the combined lunar disc and crescent. His priests claimed that he was the true universal demiurge who created everything by sound.

"Thoth, despite all attempts to find him parents in the mainstream of the gods, remains outside the Osirian family. His achievements are great. He helped to revive the dismembered *Osiris*, he

---

47 [See also pp.101, 212, 1016. (Ed.)] A god of a far different order from the serene and poised figures of the official pantheon. He was a plump, bandy-legged, hairy, rude dwarf with a wicked gleam in his pop-eyes, his tongue resolutely stuck out at the follies of mankind. Bes was a foreign god, an import from the land of Punt (Libya). He was a swaggering, jolly, mock-gallant pygmy, fond of music and clumsy, inelegant dancing. He was a popular proletarian god who was adopted by the middle classes; he was considered a tutelary god of childbirth and, strangely enough, of cosmetics and female adornments.

48 A traditional function of (some) music and musical instruments. See theme **T4a** (Music as magical weapon against evil spirits, means for combatting, routing, expelling evil spirits), *Introductory Remarks,* Vol I above. (Ed.)

49 Underscoring, however mildly, an association of music and dancing with lovemaking and procreating. See our theme **T2d** (Music as promoter of fertility), *Introductory Remarks,* Vol I above. (Ed.)

50 A fascinating list: one notes with interest the association of music with *magic* and *medicine* (i.e. with healing and curing, suggesting efforts to affect and possibly propitiate certain forces in nature); of music with *writing* and *drawing* (which could be regarded as having magical instrumentality — as belonging to the equipment of a professional priest or shaman); of music with *cosmology, science, surveying, numerology* — knowledge of the structure (the geography) of being. All of this, in turn, might be identified with the attaining of *wisdom.* (Ed.)

defended *Horus* and cured him from scorpion poison, he adjudicated in the dispute and afterwards cured the wounds which gods Horus and *Set* had inflicted on each other. He invented all the arts and sciences. His followers said that Thoth had certain books which contained all magic and all knowledge. He had locked them up in a crypt, and his priests claimed that they alone had access to them. Not without reason was Thoth called 'Thrice Greatest'.

"After spending a busy time on earth Thoth became overseer of the moon. He was responsible for measuring time (the first month of the year was named after him); he was in charge of all calculations, archives, inventories of treasure and loot. He was historian, scribe, herald and divine judge. Thoth was called *Hermes** by the Greeks[51] and is the original of Hermes Trismegistus* ('thrice greatest Hermes'), the mystical figure behind many an arcane school of celestial philosophy; and for those who know, the god was the originator of the Four Laws of Magic. (D.W.K.S.)." — Carlyon, pp.296-97.

ETRUSCAN PRACTICES AND BELIEFS.

§107A.1 "The Etruscans danced in order to appeal to their deities, to elicit the favor of the gods of war or expiate the sins that had brought down plague upon them. At festivals and religious ceremonies, and at funeral games as well, both male and female members of the guilds of dancers performed to the sound of stringed instruments and the shrill notes of the double flute. The flute* was the characteristic musical instrument in Etruria; it was also played as accompaniment to ordinary acts of daily life, such as baking bread and hunting game. The Etruscan word for dancer was *hister*, from which our word

histrionic comes; the Romans borrowed the word from Tuscan dancers, who were the first performers seen in Rome. Throughout the ancient world the Etruscans were renowned for their devotion to music. The Greeks attributed to them the invention of the trumpet*, an instrument that was probably exported from Etruria to the other Mediterranean lands.....

"Music and the dance played a prominent role in Etruscan life. Aristotle is claimed to have said that the Tyrrhenians fought, kneaded dough, and beat their slaves to the sound of the flute. Other ancient writers tell us that music provided an inevitable accompaniment to sacrifices, banquets, boxing matches, and solemn ceremonies, and that the Etruscans even used music to aid them in snaring wild pigs and stags. Their painted tomb scenes of dancing to music have an abandon and frenetic ecstasy never approached in either Greek or Roman art. As D.H. Lawrence expressed it: 'This sense of vigorous, strong-bodied liveliness is characteristic of the Etruscans, and is somehow beyond art. You cannot think of art, but only of life itself, as if this were the very life of the Etruscans, dancing in their coloured wraps with massive yet exuberant naked limbs, ruddy from the air and the sea-light, dancing and fluting along through the little olive-trees, out in the fresh day.' " — Horizon, pp.339, 330.

FAIRIES. *(See also pp.223, 1018).*

§109.9 "**FAIRY MUSIC (Scottish Highlands).** Although they often got mortals to play the pipes [bagpipes*] for them, the 'sith' were reputed to have great musical skill of their own, and when men and women of human race were stolen and taken into their dwellings, one of the

---

51   Hermes's associations with music are, of course, numerous. (Ed.)

greatest inducements to stay was the allurement of the fairy music.

"Of Fairy Music, James Stephens writes—

> From the darkness there came... a low, sweet sound; thrilling joyous, thrillingly low; so low the ear could scarcely note it, so sweet the ear wished to catch nothing else and would strive to hear it rather than all sounds that may be heard by man: the music of another world! the unearthly dear melody of the 'sith'! So sweet it was that the sense strained to hear it, and having reached must follow drowsily in its wake, and would merge in it, and could not return to its own place until that strange harmony was finished and the ear restored to freedom.

"One story tells how a brother and sister went on a starry night to Kennavarra Hill, to examine a bird snare they had set in a hollow near a stream. As they climbed down into the hollow they heard beautiful music coming from beneath their feet. Terror-stricken, they fled home. This tale was often related by the girl when an old woman.

"Near Portree in Skye there is a hillock called 'Sìthean Beinne Bhòdhich' (the fairy dwelling of the pretty hill). Those who pass it at night have heard the most beautiful music coming from under the ground; but have been unable to trace the exact spot from which it emanates.

"Curious plaintive music, said to be the fairy organ, is frequently heard from under the arches of Fraisgall Cave, in Sutherland; and strange singing blends with the melodies, as if pleading with the listener to come away to the Land Under the Waves where the sea-fairies have their dwelling.

"Strains of exquisite melody, as if played by a piper marching at the head of a procession, are to be heard going underground from the Harp Hillock to the Dun of Cas-lais, in Tiree; and many a wayfarer is said to have been lured into the knoll—never to be seen again.

" 'Cnocan nam Ban' (The Women's Hillock) in Barr Glen, West Kintyre, and 'Cnocan na Cainntearachd' (Hillock of Discourse), in the same district, are two fairy hills—famous for music and eloquence.

"On the high ground above Kyle Rhea, near the present boundary between Ross-shire and Inverness-shire, stands a cairn of stones known as 'Carn Clann Mhic Cruimein' (Cairn of the Clan Mac-Crimmon), marking the spot where a number of the MacCrimmons of Glen Elg were slaughtered by a band of Mathesons from Loch Alsh. The sweetest fairy music 'in all Scotland' is said to have been heard coming from this old cairn." — Robertson (Macdonald), pp.3-4.

"**THE DANCING FISHERMEN OF IONA (Scottish Highlands).** Once upon a time in Iona, a fisherman was under the spell of the fairy folk for a whole year and a day.

"According to the story, two fishermen were returning from the fishing vessel when they heard spirited music coming from a *brugh* (fairy dwelling), and observed several of the 'wee folk' dancing. One of the men joined the dancers without even waiting to lay down his catch of fish; but the other, remembering that a piece of metal acted as a protective charm against fairy spells, prudently stuck a fish hook into the door of the *brugh* before entering. He was thus free to leave when he wished; but his unfortunate companion was forced to remain—and was found by his friend when the year had gone—still dancing!

"He was trailed outside the fairy dwelling, still carrying his string of fish. By some strange magical coincidence they had remained fresh all the time he had been in the *brugh*; but now they fell rotten from the string." — Robertson (Macdonald), p.5.

"THE FIDDLERS* OF TOM-NAHURICH (Scottish Highlands). Long ago, when the only bridge over the River Ness was an old oak one crumbling with age, two fiddlers, Farquhar Grant and Thomas Cumming, came from Strathspey to Inverness in the hope of making some money and played in the streets. They reached Inverness on a winter evening, when snow lay on the ground and the air was keen with frost. They began to play their favourite airs; but few paid any attention to them and none thought of offering any reward.

"Despondently, they were making their way as dusk fell towards the river bank, when they saw a solitary figure coming to meet them — an old man with a white beard, wearing a green cloak and a curious red peaked cap. To the surprise of the fiddlers, he addressed them by name, and offered them a large fee if they would come and play for him and his friends.

"He led them at a headlong pace across the bridge and over the rough moorland towards the low hill of Tomnahurich, which rises abruptly from the level ground like a great up-turned boat. Half way up the hill, the old man stamped on the ground three times with his right foot. A door opened and the fiddlers followed their guide into a lofty hall, ablaze with lights. All round the walls were tables laden with food and wine; and the room was filled with a gay company of 'little people', dressed in green.

"After they had eaten and drunk, the fiddlers began to play reels and strathspeys, filling the room with their merry music. Untiringly they played, and as untiringly the company danced, until the little old man reappeared and told the two men that morning had come and the ball was over.

He led them to the door on the hill and gave them gold for their services. The men had never seen so much wealth before, and Thomas Cumming in his gratitude cried, 'May God bless you and your people!' As he uttered the name of the Deity, the little old man vanished; and when they looked at where the door had been they saw only the bare hillside.

"Marvelling greatly, they made their way to town, to find it changed. Instead of the old oak bridge across the river there was a stone one with seven arches. The buildings were not the same; the people wore clothes of a different pattern, and spoke English. They were laughed at because of the stupid questions they asked; so they made their way back to Strathspey. Here they gazed with wonder on the inscriptions on the tombstones in the churchyard. Their own names were there, along with those of friends and contemporaries!

"Together they entered the church, just as the minister was prouncing the benediction. As soon as he uttered the name of God, the two fiddlers crumbled into dust before the eys of the astonished congregation. The fairy gold they carried fell on the floor as a heap of withered leaves.

"It was not one night they had spent in the Fairy Hill of Tomnahurich, but a hundred years!"[52] — Robertson (Macdonald), pp.9-10.

"THE DANCER OF ETIVE (Scottish Highlands). More than two generations ago, two farmers of Druimechothais in Glen Etive went one Hogmanay to Kingshouse to fetch whisky. When they were between Dalness and Ionmhareuthuilain on the way home, they passed a *Sithean beag, cruinn, dubh* (a little round, blunt fairy hill). Night had fallen by

---

52 This marvelous story (and many others like it) brings to mind also the tale of Rip Van Winkle. If they bowled instead of danced, still the mysterious little men of the Catskills are cousins to Britain's elves and fairies. Indeed, when Rip went home at last, it was to find his Dutch neighbors gone, with English spoken in their place. (Ed.)

this time, and through an open door on the hill, they saw a light and heard sweet music issuing from it, and the sound of a great company dancing. One of the farmers said: — 'Let us enter and see what is going on here,' but the other refused.

"The first man entered the hill with his cask of whisky on his back, and the door closed behind him.

"When an hour had passed and there was no sign of him, his friend became afraid, and went home and related what had happened. No one would believe him and he was accused of having murdered his companion. He was tried at court, but adhered always to the same story.

"Eventually he was sent to Inveraray prison, and tried before the judges there; but they could make nothing of him, for still 'Bhadaonnan an t–aon rud aige' (he always kept to the same statement).

"Unable to find out any more than they knew when they arrested him, they let him go home. It was then October of the same year in which his companion had disappeared.

"On Hallowe'en night, a number of men in the district were engaged in the dubious practice of 'burning the rivers' between Ben Etive and Linge na Leuthchriege. To assist them in their night-work, they took a torch of withered pine and a great three-pronged 'morghath' (fishing fork) carried by the man who had lost his friend.

"Glancing in the direction of the hill, he saw a light issuing from it as before, and calling out to the others — 'If you will not believe me, believe your own eyes; let us go and see what it is.'

"They made their way to the 'Sithean', where they saw a great door standing wide open, and the sound of music and dancing within. The man with the fishing fork leapt forward and thrust it into the lintel above the door. The cold iron acted as a powerful 'sìan' (charm). He entered the hill unmolested, and finding his companion still dancing with the cask of whisky on his back, seized him by the neck and dragged him to the door.

" 'Let me stay till I dance this reel,' he pleaded. 'It is not a minute since I came in.' He was quite unaware that the reel had lasted from Hogmanay to Hallowe'en!

"The man was taken home and returned to his family." —Robertson (Macdonald), pp.14-15.

In this last, longer story, it is the Devil himself that plays the fairy part; appropriately, since the Devil (in certain of his aspects), elves and fairies, water-sprites* and so on belong to a common family. In fact, it is the music-making itself, among several things, which makes them members of this clan. (Ed.)

"LURE OF THE PIPES (Scottish Highlands). The scene was the heart of Diebidale deer forest in Ross-shire, the time was nearing midnight in the late December long ago, when the 'Wee People' danced on the top of the bogs that even a wild duck could not cross without breaking the surface. Halfway up one of the hills, known as Corrie Glas, stood Big John Clach-na-Harnich, and beside him were his two famous black dogs—a dog and a bitch. Big John was the head stalker on Diebidale, and he had been out all day and most of the night after the hinds, which they were shooting off. It had turned out to be a wild night, with a half moon; and John had taken shelter for a while against the buffettings of the storm.

"At last the night cleared a bit and he started for home. As it was late, he decided to go round the side of the hill and take a short cut home. He had been that road often before, and knew every step of it, and he could also jump the Poacher's Pool at Allt a'choin (The Dog's Burn) and still cut a few more miles off his road.

"If there was one thing on earth Big John loved besides good whisky, it was the pipes, and as he came near Allt a'choin, he thought he heard bagpipe* music. He stopped and listened, and sure enough, there it was, away to his right; and that piper could play! He was playing 'Brahan Castle', and John never heard it played so well before. He could not resist the music and started to walk towards it. He wondered as he went along who the piper could be, and what possessed him to come there and play on a night like that. As he neared the place where the sounds came from, the moon went behind the clouds and it became very dark.

"Things seemed to become very still as he walked on, and the sound of the pipes grew louder. The piper was now playing a reel — the finest reel John ever heard; and through the music he thought he heard hooching. All of a sudden, he saw a light, and going nearer, he saw a fail-roofed house. John knew he was not very far by now from the Poacher's Pool and Rory-the-glen's 'Black bothy'; but he could not remember ever seeing this place before. The sound of the pipes drew him on however, and he went forward to the door. But here a queer thing happened — the black bitch which would tackle the biggest stag in Diebidale, would not go another step. John stopped, and tried to coax her on, but she would not move, and lay down. Then John remembered that a bitch would not follow her master if the Unknown was in front. He was shaken at this; but the lure of the pipes was too great, and he said, 'Very well, you can stay here; as long as I have Black Simon with me and Killsure (his gun) under my arm, I'll face anything.'

"The piper was now playing 'Tulloch Gorm', and what a piper — the time he kept! Just as John went up to the door, it opened, and an old woman said — 'Come in John, I'm sure you will be near starved to death with the cold.' John thanked her, and said he would come in for a minute or two and hear the pipes. As he entered the house he took off his bonnet, and the old woman made to take it from him; but Black Simon, snarling and growling, snatched the bonnet out of his hand and held it in his mouth. The old woman then opened the kitchen door; and the sight that met John, he'll never forget. The house was full of men and girls. They were the finest

looking girls he had ever seen. They were nearly all dressed the same, in long frocks of a queer bluish-red colour; the men had greenish-red clothes. John had ears only for the piper however; and he looked round to see where he was.

"There he stood, near to the bed-closet door, and behind the spinning wheel to give room to the dancers. John was stunned when he saw the piper. Of all the pipers he had ever seen or heard about, this one was the King. He had on the full Highland dress; but for the life of him John could not tell the tartan. And the pipes! what pipes! — solid gold mounted — and as he played the Reel-o'-Tulloch, John thought he could see the blue sparks flying from his fingers and smoke coming from the chanter.

"The music stopped, and the piper looked at John and smiled; but never spoke.

"The only one that spoke of the whole company was the old woman, who then asked John if he would take a dram. He said he would, and she gave him a glass of good stuff. If the music was good, the whisky was better. As soon as he took the first sip, he thought his whole body was on fire right to the soles of his feet.

"John drained the glass, and then the piper started to play again — a schottishe this time — and the best-looking of the girls came towards John holding out her hands, smiling at him and silently inviting him to dance. The whisky had done its work well; and John thought he could manage the dance fine, and was on the point of taking the girl in his arms, when Black Simon again jumped in front of him. John looked down at the dog, wondering what was wrong with him, and then he saw, peeping from below the girl's long frock, instead of dainty feet, two horses' hooves. He drew back frightened out of his wits; and then looking towards the closet door where the piper stood, he saw a long red streak coming oozing out from below the door. He knew then the company he was in, and also that his end was near, and shouted

'God help me!' He could not have chosen better words; for all at once he saw the faces change, the piper's tartan turned to red, and over the blow-stock of the pipes, from which smoke and sparks emanated, he saw the face of Lucifer himself grinning at him.

"He took his only chance, and with one bound, reached the door and turned to call Black Simon, who had twice that night saved him, and was doing it a third time — for as John sprang for the door, the dog sprang at Nick; and as John turned, he saw Old Horny draw the dirk from its sheath (still wet with the blood of its last victim) and raise it to kill Black Simon.

"Quick as a flash, John's up with 'Killsure' and let drive with both barrels; but that was all the good it did, for John, who was hardly ever known to miss, saw the lead splash on the wall behind, after going harmlessly through Old Nick.

"John then bolted, and ran as hard as he could for the Poacher's Pool; but fast as he was, he found he was no match for the one who followed. Looking back, he saw the Monster, and on each side of him two of the girls, now howling fiends, with flames of fire streaming from their heads in place of the fair hair they had earlier. He could hear the clatter of their horses' hooves as they raced over the rocks and heather.

"John heard the gurgle of the water of the Poacher's Pool, and made a last supreme effort to reach it. Better to die in the cool water among the salmon, he thought, than be torn to bits by fingers of fire.

"Then just as Old Nick raised his bloody dirk to strike, across the water at Rory-the-Glen's a cock crew in the morning. John fell unconscious on the brink of the Pool, and it was hours after when he came to, to find his two dogs licking his face. 'Oh,' said he, 'Black Simon, I thought that your end came as the dirk fell'; but then Black Simon rolled over on his back, and John saw on the dog's breast four white hairs, and he knew that the Devil was powerless against the black dog as long as he had those hairs.

"And so to this day, if you listen at the Poacher's Pool, you will hear in the running water the sound of the pipes, on nights when the 'Wee People' dance on the bogs, and the wind blows round Corrie Glas." — Robertson (Macdonald), pp.196-200.

FIDDLERS. *(See also pp.245, 1025.)*

§110.10 "**THE SINFU' FIDDLE.** It is well known that formerly the Scotch Presbyterians did not approve musicians playing on the organ, which they said sounded 'mair like a penny wedding than a sermon,' or on any musical instrument whatsoever in their kirks. They called the Church of England at Glasgow 'the whistling kirk' from its possession and use of an organ. The minister at Arran was compelled to part with his piano in deference to the opinions of his parishioners. And across Kilbrannan Sound the people were equally determined that their spiritual pastors should not deteriorate in quality or efficiency through any sinful weakness for an instrument of music.

"There is a Cantire story told of a certain minister who was very fond of playing the violoncello, at which the elders and flock were so scandalized that they sent a deputation from the Kirk Session to wait on and remonstrate with him.

"They accordingly did so, and paid their visit late in the evening. The minister received them very cordially and prevailed on them to stay supper. After supper they talked of psalmody, and from that went on to converse about the national music of Scotland, more particularly of the beauty of one particular air, of which they were all fond.

"The violoncello was within reach, and the minister could not resist taking it and playing the air in question. The guests were delighted. 'Surely,' said the minister, who saw the opportunity of making the application of his tuneful discourse, 'surely there is no harm in that!'

" 'Oh, no, sir!' was the reply. 'It's no that wice-like [respectable-looking] thing, but it's the sma' sinfu' fiddle that we objec' till.' "[53] — Foster (Wit and Humor), p.132.

"FIDDLERS IN PARADISE. One day Saint Peter and Saint Paul had a quarrel at the gate of Paradise. They came to blows and fought like angry carters. The Prince of the Apostles, who was not himself at all that day, got the worst of it. In a fit of anger he seized the great heavy keys and hurled them with all his might right at Saint Paul. Fortunately the keys did not reach the mark but fell at the feet of Saint Paul, who picked them up and declared that henceforth he and not Saint Peter would open and close the gates of Heaven.

"This idea was abhorrent to Saint Peter. He begged his colleague to pardon the thoughtless gesture of a moment and give him back the keys. But this appeal fell on deaf ears. Then he threatened to take the matter to the Lord himself. But this threat brought forth nothing but a scornful smile, for Saint Paul knew Saint Peter had no appetite for the scolding the Lord would certainly give him for losing that temper of his again.

"As all of the fine points of the job of keeping the gates were not known by Saint Paul, he admitted many a soul who had no right to cross the sacred threshold. It was not long before the Devil himself came to the gate and reproached him for letting in arrant sinners. With a hurt expression on his grimy face the Devil said he never thought he would see a saint stoop to cheating a former archangel. He even talked of reporting the Saint's conduct to the Lord, but this menace did not frighten Saint Paul. He knew the Devil could not get into Paradise.

"Among the persons the Saint let slip into the dwelling place of the blessed were three fiddlers. Instead of behaving in a manner suitable to the place they had fraudulently entered, they began to play dance tunes that would have made a deacon with rheumatic legs dance the tarantella. Soon these musicians were surrounded by young male and female saints who quickly chose partners and began to dance, much to the indignation of the patriarchs and strict old saints. These went to the Lord and described the scandalous and unrestrained goings-on in Paradise.

"Many blamed Saint Paul for this disorder, and the Lord summoned him. 'The keys must be given back to Saint Peter, from whom they should never have been taken and to whom they rightfully belong,' said He. Then the Lord reprimanded the Prince of the Apostles for losing his temper, but the joy of regaining possession of the keys made him almost insensible to this rebuke. As for Saint Paul, he received orders to cast out of Paradise the three fiddlers who had slipped in because he did not know his job.

"Saint Paul found a secluded corner and sat down to think over his problem. He could hardly use brute force to throw them out since it was a rule that once inside the pearly gates, a soul, although it could leave of its own free will, could not be forced to depart. Now those fiddlers never left off fiddling, and the disorder in Heaven continued. They played so much that they wore out violin strings very rapidly. Their

---

53 Premise: the Devil invented the fiddle, and it is his instrument. This story illustrates a paradigmatic conflict in Christian Europe: music generally is believed to have supernatural power, for good *or* evil — a musical instrument is an instrument (talisman) for exercising, or in some way influencing an exercise of, such power. Supposedly, music can e.g. both summon *and* exorcise evil spirits, thus music is, respectively, bad *and* good; i.e., it can protect or destroy. Equally: people rejoice in music (life) — and, appear to be afraid of it! (Ed.)

bows were becoming terribly frayed. When Saint Paul understood that before long the fiddlers would have to have a new supply of strings and bows or be compelled to stop fiddling, he thought he saw a way of getting rid of the intruders. He summoned a town crier and placing him a little way outside the Heavenly gates, ordered him to beat on a drum and announce that he had for sale three fine fiddles, a good supply of strings, two dozen bows and a big stock of rosin. He was to invite those who would like to buy to come out to where he was, and he was to tell everyone that the prices were most reasonable.

"When they heard this announcement, the fiddlers leaped with joy. They rushed out of the gates to buy those new fiddles and the accessories. There was no haggling over prices; they bought up everything in sight. But when they tried to re-enter Paradise, Saint Peter slammed the gates in their faces. He turned a deaf ear to both the fiddlers and the crowd of young saints who begged him to let the joyous musicians enter Heaven again."[54] — Foster (Wit and Humor), pp.150-52.

§110.11 GYPSY FOLK TALES.[55]

"THE GYPSIES' FIDDLE (Sweden). The origin of Gypsy violinists, whose music banishes both unhappiness and strife, is explained in this tale told by the famous Swedish storyteller Johan Dimitri Taikon (1879-1950), who is also known by his Romani name, Milos, who said, 'Perhaps I should not tell it to you, for part of it is very sad — how little a daughter thought of her parents and brothers and how she was punished for it. But all stories have things that are good and things that are not good. And this one also has something so good that Gypsies all over the world know it and tell it.'

"In the days when the Gypsies had no fiddle on which to play, there lived a very beautiful girl who was a little bewitched. She was silly and did all kinds of foolish things.

"For that reason, even though she was very beautiful and very rich, no young man would look at her or marry her.

"Now, there was a young fellow, the son of a man who lived next to them, with whom she was in love. He was handsome and strong, and he was a good worker. But he would have nothing to do with the girl. He would hardly speak to her, and he never invited her to a dance, and that made her very unhappy.

"One day she was walking in the woods, singing and weeping at the same time. She was thinking of her love and how unhappy she was. Suddenly there was a man walking by her side. She didn't know how he came, for she had not seen him or heard his steps. He was dressed all in green, and he had burning black eyes. From the black hair on his head stuck out two little horns, and one of his feet looked like a goat's hoof. You can guess who that was. The Evil One himself.

" 'I see you are crying,' he said to the girl. 'You are in love with the son of the man who lives next to you, and he does not love you. But if you are willing to do a little

---

54 Among some people — ancient **CHINESE*** and **GREEKS***, for example — music symbolizes and is an expression of fundamental order and harmony. But among some Christians music is said to promote disharmony and disorder. However the Christians' mistrust of music also conceals a love of music, and lingering belief that one's "profane" or "animal" passions are natural after all; thus the younger male and female saints in Paradise are shown to have a marvelously good time dancing to tunes "that would make a deacon with rheumatic legs dance the tarantella," and they earnestly desire the "joyous" musicians to be readmitted to Heaven. (Ed.)

55 See also **GYPSY TALES AND BELIEFS***, below. (Ed.)

thing for me, and do what I tell you, he will love you more than life and marry you quickly.'

" 'I will do anything in the world for him to love me,' the girl said.

" 'Then just make me a present of your father and mother and your four brothers, and in return I will give you an instrument and teach you how to play it. When he hears you play he will love you with a love that has no end, and he will do everything in the world for you.'

"And the silly girl said, 'You can have my father and mother and brothers, you can have everything, so long as my love will marry me.'

"Goat's-Foot changed the father of that girl into a fiddle, her mother he changed into a bow, and out of her white hair he made the bowstrings. The four brothers he changed into four fiddle strings. Then he sat down with the girl and taught her how to play the violin. Soon she played so sweetly the insects stopped flying to listen and the boughs of the trees began twisting and dancing. It was music that went into the heart and brought tears to the eyes.

"No music like it had ever been played before. When the young man she loved heard it, he forgot home and hearth and work and dance. He married her at once, and they were very happy together for many years. No sadness ever came to their home, because the silvery music of the fid-dle worked a spell that drove all unhappiness away, even as it does to this day.

"One summer day the two were in the woods. After playing tunes on the fiddle that melted the heart, they went to look for berries, leaving the fiddle behind. When they came back in the twilight to look for it, they could not find it. All the looking in the world was of no use, because Old Nick with the horns had hidden it from their eyes. As the two walked home without the fiddle, he came with a carriage and four black horses and whisked them away, and they were never seen again.

"For years and years the fiddle lay in the woods, hidden under moss and leaves. How long it lay there I don't know, so I can't tell you.

"One day some Gypsies camped in that forest. One of the Gypsy boys went out to gather sticks for the fire and came to the place where the fiddle lay and by accident hit one of the strings with a piece of wood. There was a sound more beautiful than any he had ever heard, and he was frightened and ran off. But he couldn't forget the magic sound, and so he came back and got the violin and bow out from under the moss and the leaves. As he began moving the bow on the strings, rich and exciting sounds poured forth. He kept on moving that bow, making up music, which Gypsies always do to this day. The birds stopped singing and the wind stopped

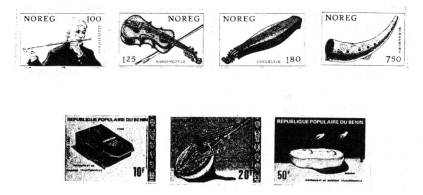

blowing just to listen to him. He ran back to camp and played the fiddle for his tribe. Never before had they heard such melodies, and it worked a spell on them. When the tune was sad, they were sad; when the music was wild, they felt wild.

"Quickly the other Gypsies learned how to play the fiddle, and they made other fiddles and taught other Gypsies how to play. So now nearly all Gypsies can play it, and they play the most heavenly melodies in the world. For only such melodies can come from that instrument.

"That is how the Gypsies got their fiddle, and it has been their instrument ever since, the instrument they love most." [56] — Tong, pp.45-47.

"HOW THE GYPSIES BECAME MUSICIANS (Yugoslavia). There have always been many extraordinarily talented Gypsy musicians, many of them violinists, and this fact has inspired several folktales. This short Yugoslav story is one example.

"Once upon a time God placed a fiddle on St. Peter's shoulders.

"Not knowing that there was a fiddle on his shoulders, St. Peter went into an inn where there were many jolly people.

"When they saw St. Peter with the fiddle, they called out, 'Play! Play!' But he was frightened at their shouting and began to run away.

"At the door the fiddle fell from his shoulders. He picked it up and went straight to God and asked him, 'What does this mean, God?'

" 'I made it for you,' answered God, 'so that you might play to people when they were lively and keep them in a good humor and prevent them from picking quarrels.'

" 'If that is so, let there be more musicians.'

" 'But who could there be?' asked God.

" 'Let there be the Gypsies,' answered St. Peter. 'Let them amuse people so that they may not shed blood when they drink and make merry.'

" 'Let it be so,' said God.

"And so it was." — Tong, pp.102-03.

FINNO-UDRIC PRACTICES AND BELIEFS. *(See pp.255,1028.)*

§111.5 See **KALEVALA***.

§111.6 **"ANTERO VIPUNEN.** A mythical Finnish giant who slept in the earth with trees growing on him. He had the magic songs which the great *Vainamoinen* needed to complete his ship. Antero Vipunen only

---

56 Among several considerations, this story establishes a link, not in legendary times but in something of a more recent and therefore "actual" past, between real, ordinary people (the Gypsies, who of course are real people), and a world of magic and the supernatural (a world of gods, insofar as the Evil One can be thought a divine being). The link is, of course... music. The ambivalence human beings apparently feel with respect to addressing the gods at all (for eternal life, help in love, in producing children, rescue from draught or the plague of one's enemies, etc.) is expressed in associating music (a magical instrument) with sin (the Evil One); indeed, in some religious communities, e.g. Moslem, music continues to be an object of mistrust. (The present story offers a possible variant of Thompson Motifs A1460.1, *Arts taught man by angel*, A1461.1, *Origin of violin*, and D1355.1.1, *Love-producing song*. Perhaps the following category should also be added to the Thompson index — unless, that is to say, one already exists and I have overlooked it: under G303: *Devil instructs mortal in playing the fiddle. Exacts terrible price.* See **FOLKLORE AND FOLKTALES — TYPOLOGY***, above and following entry.) (Ed.)

parted with the songs after cruel punishment from the eager hero-god." – Carlyon, p.257.

"HIISI (Finnish god of evil). Hiisi's songs and spells were sung by *tjetajat* or wizards. Finland has long had a reputation as a land of skilled sorcerers and necromancers. Their particular style of working is closely allied to the shamanism of the north, the use of sacred drums and the habitual trance-like states induced by monotonous chanting. Hiisi joined with other evil spirits to direct *Vainamoinen's* axe against himself; Hiisi being responsible for making the axe slice through the hero-god's veins." – Carlyon, p.257.

FOLKLORE AND FOLKTALES – TYPOLOGY. *(See also p.275.)*

§114.1 (Addendum)

"G303.6.2.1. *Devil appears invisible among dancers.* Canada, U.S.: *Baughman; Finnish-Swedish: Wessman 10 No. 79; Icelandic: Boberg.

"G303.10.4. *Dancers as followers of the devil.*

"G303.10.4.0.1. *Devil haunts dance halls.* French Canadian: Sister Marie Ursule.

"G303.10.4.1. *Devil dances with a maid until she dies.* Finnish-Swedish: Wessman 10 No. 81; Lithuanian: Balys Index No. 3251, Legends Nos. 347,353f.

"G303.10.4.2. *Two devils teach a dance-loving maid to dance.* Finnish-Swedish: Wessman 10 No. 83.

"G303.10.4.4. *Devil appears to girl who wants an escort for a dance.* French Canadian: Sister Marie Ursule.

"G303.10.4.5. *Devil dances with maid and puts his claws through her hands.* French Canadian: Sister Marie Ursule.

¶Text reading 1: see DANCE* §74.6, above.

"G303.10.14. *The bagpipe is the devil's bellows.* Dh I 189.

GREEK PRACTICES AND BELIEFS. *(See also p.332.)*

§130.3 See PHOENICIAN PRACTICES AND BELIEFS*.

§130.4 "Cadmus* appears to have been cotemporary with the Cretan Jupiter, from the fable, which makes him carry away his sister Europa from Sidon, in the shape of a bull, by which the expounders of ancient mythology understand the ensign of the ship in which they sailed together. The Phoenicians*, upon their first coming into Greece, gave the name of *Jao-pater*, Jupiter, to every king, as every Egyptian monarch was called Pharaoh, and Roman emperor Cæsar; and thus both Minos and his father were Jupiters. But though Cadmus and his companions were called Idæi Dactyli, and Curetes [Kuretes*], they seem not to have been the first who came into Greece; for both Strabo and Diodorus Siculus tells us that 'the Curetes, who introduced music, poetry, dancing, and arts, and attended on the sacrifices, were no less active about religious institutions; and for their skill, knowledge, and mystical practices, were accounted wise men and conjurers by the vulgar; that these, when Jupiter was born, in Crete, were appointed by his mother Rhea, to the nursing and tuition of him in a cave of mount Ida, where they danced about him in armour, with great noise, that his father Saturn might not hear him cry. And when he was grown up, these assisted him in his conquests, were appointed his priests, and instituted mysteries, in memory of the share which they had in his education.'

"This wild story, collected from all the best prose writers of Greece, is told by Sir Isaac Newton in his *Chronology*. It served his purpose, in support of his chronological hypothesis; and it is quoted here, in order to shew the simple state which music was in at its first introduction into Greece. No instruments are mentioned to have been used by the Idæi Dactyli, who attended Jupiter in Crete, but drums and cymbals, instruments of percussion, which affording but one tone, require little art in the player, or knowledge in the hearer....

"Aristotle has thought it worth recording, that Archytas of Tarentum, the famous mathematician, invented a rattle for children; and Perrault says, if we consider the music of the ancients according to the idea which the early writers give us of it, we shall find it to have been a kind of noise suitable to the *infancy* of the world, as the first instruments were certainly little better than rattles, or corals, fit only for children.

"And, indeed, the Phoenicians may be said to have brought into Greece *Time*, rather than *Tune* : but *Rhythm* is of such consequence both to poetry and to music, that this was no inconsiderable present.

"As the first music mentioned in the Grecian history, is that of the *Idoei Dactyli*, after the birth of Jupiter, which consisted of a rhythmical clash of swords, as modern morice-dancers[57] delight in the clash of staves; it is not unnatural to suppose, when this prince was grown up, had conquered his enemies, and was peacably established on his throne, that arts and sciences were cultivated and rendered flourishing, particularly music, through the skill and influence of Apollo*, and his other sons; and this perhaps was found to be the most effectual means of taming and polishing a rude and savage people....[58]

"According to a passage given from Æschylus, by Eustathius, notwithstanding the multiplicity of the Grecian divinities, '*Death* was the only God who could neither be moved by offerings, nor conquered by sacrifices and oblations; and therefore he was the only one to whom no altar was erected, and *no hymns were sung.*" — Burney, I, pp.220-22,273.

GYPSY TALES AND BELIEFS.

§132A.1 See **FIDDLERS**.

§132A.2 **THE ROM IN THE PIANO** (Czechoslovakia). This delightful story, with its self-assured hero, was told to Milena Hübschmannová in 1967 by Jan Sivák, who was forty years old at the time. He is a scrap metal dealer and the father of six children. Born in East Slovakia, he has lived in Most in northern Bohemia since 1947.

"There was once a poor Rom who had seven children, and they were hungry day in and day out—that's the way things were in the old days. His wife went beg-

---

57 Morris dancers. (Ed.)

58 It is not clear, to me, in the preceding passage, whether Burney means to suggest that the Phoenician Curetes or *Idoei (Idæi dactyli)* who came to Crete are supposed to have brought music itself, or merely a more sophisticated (i.e. rhythmic) kind of music. Moreover, if the expression *Jao-pater* derives from a Phoenician term, nevertheless the reference is clearly to (Roman) Jupiter, and not to the earlier, Greek form of Zeus. I will venture the following. Supposing the various myths to be literally true, it may be that two "events" have been conflated into one: (event 1) the use of non-rhythmic music to protect the infant Zeus at Mount Ida on Crete from his terrible father (Cronos; Latin Saturn)—an allegory for the most primitive performances of music in the region; and (event 2) some later arrival of a more advanced, rhythmical kind of music, from Phoenicia, to the southeast: combined to make a *single* occurrence, namely, the supposed performance by Phoenician Curetes of a frenzied (both percussive *and* rhythmical) music, at the side of (Greek) Zeus, (Roman) Jupiter. Who knows! (Ed.)

ging and the children had nothing to eat but what she brought home.

"One day a beggar came to them and said politely, 'God bless your evening, Rom.'

" 'May he also bless your evening, beggar,' replied the Rom. 'Where are you traveling, where are you wandering?'

" 'As a poor man from village to village. You know yourself how that is. Wherever God wills, there I spend the night. Listen, Rom, would you be willing to put me up for a night?'

"The Rom had no objection. 'You are poor and so am I. You can sleep here.'

"[The beggar sleeps at the Rom's house for the night, but the Rom's wife complains that they already have seven children and only one bed. Still the Rom persists and, next day, the couple discover that the beggar has left gold pieces behind. The beggar was none other than God.]

"When evening came [a second time], God returned. As before, he was dressed as a beggar, but this time he was carrying an old violin case.

" 'It's good that you came back!' the Rom rejoiced. 'You can't imagine how much I missed you.' He led him back into their hut.

" 'Watch out you don't break my violin!' yelled God.

"The Rom fixed God up nicely with his only bed. He ordered his wife, 'Wash him and give him food.'

" 'Listen, Rom,' said God, 'take the violin out of the case, but don't play it till tomorrow after I leave.'

"The violin—the Rom didn't know this yet—was made in such a way that whoever heard it play absolutely had to

dance.[59] But God felt too old to jump around like a fool, so at dawn the next morning he set out on his way.

"The Rom couldn't understand why God had given him the violin. Then he thought, *Wait, I want to try it out.* No sooner had he touched the strings than his seven children began to dance. He had to laugh at the way they hopped around so early in the morning. The Rom played on, so beautifully! And soon his wife was dancing too, until she was out of breath.

" 'Stop playing, husband,' she begged. 'I can't stand it anymore.'

"Now that the Rom understood what kind of violin God had given him, he got dressed and went to the village. Soon a baron came by. 'Baron,' asked the Rom, 'do you have a cigarette?'

" 'I spit on you, dirty Gypsy.'

"Just then a king went by. 'King, will you give me a cigarette?'

" 'Never in my life will I take out my golden cigarette case for a stinking Gypsy.'

"Then an innkeeper came along. For the third time the Rom asked, 'Dear innkeeper, give me a cigarette. Everything hurts when I can't smoke.'

" 'Beat it, you miserable Gypsy!'

"So the Rom took the violin and set the bow in motion. As he hit the first note, a dance of dances started. My God, how those three danced! The baron, the king, and the innkeeper waltzed and hopped like crazy, yelling again and again, 'Stop playing! Stop playing!'

"Nearby was a carpenter who had been watching the whole thing. 'Listen, Rom,' he suggested, 'you are a good violin player, I am a good carpenter. I'll build a

---

59 See Thompson Motif D1415.2.5 (Magic fiddle causes dancing) and as a cousin to D2061.1.2 (Persons magically caused to dance selves to death), **FOLKLORE AND FOLKTALES—TYPOLOGY***, above. See also **DANCING TO DEATH (OR INSANITY)***, above, and **(THE) WILIS***, below. Also, as remarked before (**FIDDLERS***, Supplement §110.11), a story of this kind can be said to represent an attempt to adapt the traditional or "legendary" theme of e.g. "*music as magical instrument through which contact is made between divine and mortal beings*" to a modern setting; to bring it into "actual" or "historical" times. (Ed.)

piano that you can fit into to play your violin. Then I'll got to market and sell the piano. Just wait and see how much money I'll sell you for! I'll live well, and so will you.'

"[The Rom agrees and the carpenter builds the piano. It fit the Rom like a glove, and he could play his violin in it comfortably. The king's daughter heard how beautiful the piano played, and saw the people dancing like fools. She must have the piano for her own. Helpless to disappoint her, the king gave the carpenter two bags of ducats. The piano is taken to her room, and the princess dances herself to exhaustion. She throws herself on her bed, and falls asleep at once.]

"The princess lay in her bed, only half covered. *How beautiful she is,* thought the Rom. He ate what little was left over [from her dinner], drank a sip, and hurry, back into the piano!

"The next morning, when the princess had gotten up, he played a little for her and stopped. After a while, he played once more and stopped again. The princess enjoyed the dancing, and both of them felt good. But the Rom kept dreaming that he would sleep in the bed of the king's daughter.

"[Once again he has only left-over crumbs to eat. But he felt sorry for the princess, who lay alone in the bed without a lover. He wished he could give the princess a nice gift. Then he left her a silver bow as a present, tied to her foot as she slept.

"Meanwhile, the king writes to all of the other kingdoms, bragging that no one else has such a wonderful piano as his. He even has this letter of his read on televsion, and printed in the newspapers.

"The Rom leaves the princess another present—a golden bow. Then he gives her another present—himself! He lies down beside her, in her bed.

"They become lovers. Meanwhile people come to see the piano with their own eyes. As soon as the piano begins playing, they all dance like fools.

"The Rom mixes with the guests. 'Where do you come from?' asks the king. 'Oh, I come from far away,' says the Rom.

"The foreign kings praise the piano beyond all measure. The only thing that displeases them is, that they do not have such an instrument for themselves. They decide to declare war on the king, and take his piano.

"The Rom knows what to do. 'Call in those kings who've challenged you to go to war,' he says. This is done.

"The Rom explains that it is he who has made the miraculous music.]

" 'There's no reason to have a war over this,' said the Rom. 'You certainly have Romani musicians in your lands too. Just give them each two bags of ducats and then you can put them in your pianos.'

" 'That's true!' shouted all the kings, as if with one voice.

" 'And now we will have a feast,' said the princess, inviting her guests to the table.

"All the kings dined more happily than ever because they would not have to go to war. But the Rom left the princess and returned to his wife, and if they haven't died, they are still living today."[60] —Tong, pp.216-22.

---

60 So much for the silliness of royalty. And the Rom—who had been kind to God—was no longer poor; and he had had a good time, too. (Ed.)

HARP. *(See also pp.340, 1083.)*

§137.6 "[IRISH.] There was a chieftain who lived near the sea long ago, himself and his wife, and she was very fond of singing and music. One day a dead whale was washed ashore by the tide, and the carcase remained on the shore until it rotted away and nothing was left but the skeleton.

"When the wind used to blow through the skeleton of the whale, it made lovely music. And the chieftain's wife made an instrument with strings out of the whale. Thus the harp was invented."[61] — O'-Sullivan, p.41.

HINDU PRACTICES AND BELIEFS. *(See also pp.364, 1093.)*

§149.8 "INDRA (Hindu god of war and fertility). His celestial abode on Mount Meru was full of dancers and musicians. Indra was capable of reviving those slain in battle, and with his arrows and thunderbolts he could tear open the clouds to make rain. Some claim that he was the twin of *Agni*, the god of fire. His wife is sometimes Indrani and sometimes Urvara, the fertile land." — Carlyon, pp.125-26.

"SHIVA (God of the cosmic dance; member of the supreme Hindu triad, along with *Brahma* and *Vishnu*).*[62] As Nataraja (dance-king), Shiva fills the whole cosmos with his joyful dance called *tandava*. He dances and dances until the cosmos is brought to the point of annihilation; it has to be destroyed in order to be reintegrated into the absolute. Shiva's intoxicating and revelatory dance was often the cause of conversion of heretics and enemies. It is finally creative, for it expresses the otherwise inexpressible....

"Shiva, locked in a trance, is often unapproachable, and so his active force, *shakti*, is personified in the goddesses, *Parvati*, *Uma, Durga* or *Kali*. As Uma, Parvati ('she

---

61   For references to the making of the harp in imitation of the whale's skeleton, see Irish Texts Society, *Lebor Gabála Érenn*, I, 89, 159; MacCulloch, *Mythology of All Races*, III, 137 [excerpted above as §137.5 (Ed.)]; Ossianic Society Transactions, V, 97 ff.; Wood-Martin, *Traces of the Elder Faiths in Ireland*, 180 f.

62   See also fuller entry, p.699 above. (Ed.)

of the mountains') was responsible for opening Shiva's third eye. Their physical union was a symbol of spiritual wholeness and forms the basic approach of the Tantric cult, which utlizes controlled sexuality to achive ecstatic insights."[63] — Carlyon, pp.137-38.

ICELANDIC FOLKTALES AND MYTHS. *(See also p.373.)*

§160.2 "THE OLD ICELANDIC AL-LEGORY OF THE CHURCH MODES.[64] Relatively little attention has been paid on the part of specialists in Old Icelandic to its Christian literature, although that litera-ture is first in point of attestation.[65] For that reason such things as allegory and the adoption of the modes of thought of the medieval church have only recently begun to be investigated again. The manuals stress the pagan literature, or what is thought to be pagan, so that one will find little understanding for the sort of allegory practiced in the twelfth-century church. It is the same for music: if one searches through the literature of Old Icelandic music, one finds over and over the state-ment that nothing is known of early music.[66] This is, of course, true for the na-tive pagan music of the North (remember that Iceland was first settled by the Nor-semen about 870), but we have a good deal of information about church music in Iceland during the twelfth century.

"There are, besides the usual musical ar-tifacts and occasional iconographic repre-sentations, a number of literary passages where music is mentioned. The most inter-esting of these for the present discussion, i.e., the question of the adoption of the music of the medieval church by the Icelanders, is a report in the *Life of Jón of Hólar*, who founded one of the early schools in Iceland in the year 1107:

> He procured a Frenchman named Rikini, a fine priest and his chaplain,

---

63   An identification of music with fertility, procreation, sexuality is by now a familiar theme throughout the present volume. The word *ecstatic*, in turn, may be used to describe a state which is sometimes common to the practice (occurrence) of both. (Ed.)

64   As will be seen, the allegorizing of various musical elements described in this article recalls similar practices in other cultures; see e.g. **CHINESE PRACTICES AND BELIEFS***, **HARMONY OF THE SPHERES***, etc. (Ed.)

65   For a survey of the problem, see my article, 'The Old Icelandic *Joca Monachorum*', to appear in *Medieval Scandinavia*. Cf. Sigurdur Nordal, 'Time and Vellum', *Modern Humanities Research Association Annual Bulletin*, No. 24 (1952), p.17: 'Even if the Icelanders had produced nothing else in this period, these translations would afford a remarkable witness to their literary interest and activity.... Now they are thrown into the shadow by the sagas, so that they are neglected by most scholars and their significance, even their existence is often almost forgotten.'

66   P.G. Foote and D.M. Wilson, *The Viking Achievement* (New York, 1970), p.188: 'We know almost nothing about Norse music.' *Kulturhistorisk Leksikon for nordisk Middelader*, XII (Copenhagen, 1967), 27-30; Otto Anderson, *Musik och Musikinstrument*, Nordisk Kultur, XXV (1934), particularly the sections on 'Nordisk musikkultur i äldsta tider' and 'Sveriges, Norges och Danmarks kyrkomusik'. It is noteworthy that this book does not contain a section on church music in Iceland.

to teach singing and verse making. Rikini was a good cleric; he could both compose and versify well, and he was so wise in the knowledge of singing and had such a good memory that he knew without books all the songs of the liturgical year, both the day services and the hours, with confident tone placement and definition of sounds....[67]

The saga goes on to tell that the children of several well-to-do families studied music under Rikini, for the blessing of all.

"We know that church song was not unknown in Iceland during the course of the twelfth century, although most of our evidence is inferential. We even have a text, mostly taken from the *Gemma animae* of Honorius Augustodunensis, which tells the meaning of each part of the Mass, and which indicates several times that parts of the Mass were sung.[68] The Icelanders of the twelfth century were well educated and well traveled, in spite of the fact that we still think of them as Vikings, and several had studied on the continent.[69] Although we have no evidence of their musical training, it was to be assumed that this included at least a knowledge of the church modes, along with the musical notation which went with this. Since we have so little evidence for Icelandic music, it is all the more surprising that a fragment offering precious information on this subject has until recently escaped our attention.

"One of our earliest Icelandic manuscripts is the so-called *Old Icelandic Book of Homilies,* a collection of sermons and homilies containing the allegories and typologies characteristic of the genre: the eight ages of man, Christ as the bait on the hook of the cross, the four evangelists as the four rivers of paradise, man as the tenth choir of angels, etc.[70] The first piece in the manuscript is a fragment of an allegory of the eight church modes. Until recently almost nothing has been written about it, because no one could make any

---

67   'Jóns saga helga', *Byskupa sögur,* ed. Guoni Jónsson, II (Haukadal), 41f. All translations in this article are mine.

68   *Homiliu-Bók,* ed. Theodor Wisén (Lund, 1872), 121-27. It also mentions antiphons.

69   On the education of the Icelanders, see my article 'The Allegories in the Old Norse *Veraldarsaga,'* to appear in *Michigan Germanic Studies,* and Otto Springer, 'Medieval Pilgrim Routes from Scandinavia', *Medieval Studies,* XII (1950), 92-122.

70   Wisén, *op. cit.*

sense out of it, and because this type of literature has traditionally been neglected, in spite of its great importance. The credit for having discovered the key to the riddle goes to Róbert A. Ottósson, already known for his work on Icelandic hymns. The first allegory in the fragment is translated as follows:

> ...age of this world, God's friends were strong, as is fitting for retainers and friends of the king.[71] The second is called grave... because a graver punishment came in this age of the world than later, in the flood because of evil life,[71] of the tower because of pride.[72] The third is called hard

tempered tone, because God laid a harder trial of man or of love on Abraham than on other men, in the testing of his love for Him.[73] The fourth is called *uox adulationis* 'adulation tone', because in Moses' age God looked after his people and indulged them in more ways than before.[74] The fifth is called tone of love song, because God granted to David and to Solomon the greatest understanding of bride and bridegroom, that is, of Holy Church and God.[75] The sixth is called lacrymose tone, because during the time of grace is offered remission of sin, and comfort is promised.[76] The seventh is called

---

71. He is obviously speaking of the first tone, which most medieval theoreticians hold to be totally flexible and capable of any meaning; cf. Hermann Abert, *Die Musikanschauung des Mittelalters und ihre Grundlagen*, reprint of 1905 ed. (Tutzing, 1964), p.236. Aegidius Zamorensis (Martin Gerbert, *Scriptores ecclesiastici de musica sacra potissimum*, II, 387a): '*notandum, quod primus tonus est mobilis et habilis et ad omnes secundum affectus aptabilis.*'

72. Genesis, 6-8; 11: 1-9. The second tone was usually called the grave tone; cf. Abert, *op. cit.*, 236f., and Cotto (Gerbert, II, 251a), de Muris (Gerbert, III, 235b), and anonymous Carthusian (C.E.H. de Coussemaker, *Scriptorum de musica medii aevi nova series*, II, 448).

73. The severity of the third mode is stressed by medieval writers, cf. Abert, *op. cit.*, p.238; Cotto (Gerbert, II, 251a), Aegidius Zamorensis (Gerbert, II, 387a): '*notandum, quod tertius tonus est severus incitabilis...*'; anonymous Carthusian (Coussemaker, II, 448): '*...tertius tonus severus est et ad iram vel bella provocans.*'

74. Our manuscript has an error here and writes *epter melos* for *eptirmælistónn*, which is simply the Icelandic translation for the Latin gloss *uox adulationis*. This is the commonplace ethos of the fourth tone, see Abert, *op. cit.*, p.239f. and Cotto (Gerbert, II, 251a), Aegidius Zamorensis (Gerbert, II, 387a); and de Muris (Gerbert, III, 235b).

75. The fifth is the age of David; Solomon is mentioned because it is in the Song of Songs that, according to medieval thought, Holy Church and Christ are wedded. Hermannus Contractus calls this the *tonus voluptuosus*; cf. Abert, *op. cit.*, p.240.

76. The connection between the lacrymose tone, *grátstónn*, and grace seems to have been occasioned by the paronomasia of *grát* 'weeping' and *gratia* 'grace'; the medieval Icelanders were very fond of punning, even in serious matters. The

tone of harshness (*inmitis*), because in the leave-taking (dying) of every man there is distress and fear.[77] The eighth is called tone of joy (*uox letitiae*), because in eternal life there is true joy and happiness without end.[78]

It is obvious that what we have here is an equation of the eight church modes with the eight ages of the world. Throughout patristic exegesis, but particularly after Saint Augustine, it was a commonplace to use some number scheme in the Bible or in Christian religion to organize the course of history. The world created in six days, it would pass away in six ages; the seventh age, corresponding to the day of rest, was the time of waiting for doomsday, and the last age, the eighth, would be the time of eternal bliss.[79] To these eight ages were at-tached the names of the patriarchs and John: the first age was Adam, the second Noah, third Abraham, fourth Moses, fifth David, sixth John the Baptist, seventh judgment, eighth heaven. It was also the custom to attach various and sundry schemes and numbers to the church modes, as to everything else, for '*nihil vacuum et sine signo apud Deum.*' Thus the tones were connected with the seven planets and the zodiac, the eight waves of the sea, the eight winds, the eight parts of speech, etc. It would not then surprise us to see them equated with the eight ages of the world.[80] It is of interest to the history of musical aesthetics to note that our frag-ment agrees in general with medieval prac-tice, as outlined by Abert, although it shows some independence, for, as Guido

---

labeling of the sixth tone as lacrymose was a commonplace; cf. Abert, *op. cit.*, 240f., and Hermannus Contractus (Gerbert, II, 148a), Cotto (Gerbert, II, 251a), and Aegidius Zamorensis (Gerbert, II, 387).

77   This is not the usual 'meaning' of the seventh tone; our author may have misunderstood something like Cotto's *mimicos* (Gerbert, II, 251a), since he gives the Latin gloss *inmitis*, but note that this ethos agrees well with the rest of his allegory, in which the seventh age is the time of death, when all have died and are awaiting the final judgment. Cf. also the Renaissance meaning attached to the seventh mode: 'The seventh tredeth stoute...' (cited in John Hollander, *The Untuning of the Sky* [Princeton NJ, 1961], p.212), and Guido (cited in Abert, p. 242, note 8): '*Per tetrardum beautitudo exprimitur, sed quae adhuc carne gravatur.*'

78   Abert, *op. cit.*, pp.343f.; cf. Hermannus Contractus: '*hypomixolydius iucundus vel exsultans.*'

79   The best discussion of the theme is Roderich Schmidt, '*Aetates mundi: die Weltalter als Gliederunsprinzip der Geschichte*', *Zeitschrift für Kirchengeschichte*, LXVII (1955-56), 288-317. It is common in Old Icelandic; see *Homiliu-Bók*, p.55. The entire *Veraldarsaga* is based on the scheme of six ages of the world, see my article 'The Allegories of the Old Norse *Veraldarsaga*,' to appear in *Michigan Germanic Studies*.

80   Róbert A. Ottósson, '*Das musiktheoretische Textfragment im Stockholmer Homilienbuch,*' *Opuscula*, IX (1970), 173f., has cited another such equation, from the well-known Leipzig Mass book of the thirteenth century. The connection of the sixth age with John the Baptist, which worries him, is already found in Augustine; cf. his *In Joannis Evangelium tractatus*, 9.6 (J.P. Migne, *Patrologia latina*, 35.1461); Schmidt, *op. cit.*, pp.311f.

has told us: *'diversitas troporum diversitati mentium coaptatur.'*[81]

"The first allegory is followed by another, even more complicated:

These have the same tenor. First (Adam), fourth (Moses), sixth (John), because all the family of Adam is called to one grace before the law, and under the law (Moses) and during the time of grace (John).[82] The dominant which they have is the ninth note of the scale, because at any time during which these three lived there were many who are now invited to the nine choirs of angels. These are joined by a second tenor: third (Abraham), fifth (David), eighth (heaven), and they indicate eternal freedom. Abraham freed his relatives who had been captured, and David went alone against the enemy of the Jewish people and took shame and oppression away from the people of God.[83] Thus also the bliss of heaven is free for ignoring and overcoming the things of this world. The dominant which they have stands on the eleventh sound of the scale. The number eleven is the most incomparable relative to the other numbers, for it cannot be divided by two, three or four.[84] Thus eternal bliss has no comparison with any other joy at all. But the second (Noah) tone has the lowest position of its dominant because that tone symbolizes the age of Noah, when that punishment of sin occurred which is the greatest lowering of all ages, when everyone was drowned with the exception of eight persons.[85] Then God said that He was sorry that He had created man.[86] Its dominant stands on the seventh note, because that indicates the fear of this world because of the flood, and all the ages of man pass in seven days. The seventh mode has the highest dominant, because it symbolizes the joy which comes about in the

---

81 *Micrologus*, chap. 14 (Migne, *Patrologia latina*, 141.393).

82 It was a commonplace also to divide the history of the world into three ages: *ante legem, sube lege et sub gratia;* cf. Schmidt, *op. cit.*, pp.299f. I have translated *rauster hald* as 'tenor', since it is an obvious calque on Latin *tenor vocis*.

83 This refers to Abraham's freeing of Lot (Genesis 14:13-17) and to David's slaying of Goliath (1 Kings, 17).

84 I have accepted Jón Helgason's emendation (cf. Ottósson, *op. cit.*, p.170) of *samvirpilegost* 'most comparable' to *ósamvirpilegost* 'most incomparable' to make it agree with *enga samvirping* 'no comparison' in the next sentence.

85 The word *læging* 'lowering' offers a typical Icelandic paronomasia, since it means both 'lowering' in the sense of 'reducing' and in the sense of 'humiliation'.

86 Genesis 6:6.

death of a good man, for it is the highest joy in this world when the good man welcomes the angels at the hour of his death.[87] And its dominant stands on twelfh sound and notes it.

"Ottósson, being an expert in medieval church music, immediately saw that this is a sure indication that the so-called Guidonian scale was in use in Iceland at this time;[88] if we assign numbers to it, one can see this more clearly:

```
1  2  3  4  5  6  7  8  9  10 11 12
r  A  B  C  D  E  F  G  a  b  c  d
```

Our allegory, then, simply assigns to each church mode its tenor or dominant, according to the usual scheme: That is, the first, the fourth, and the sixth mode have one dominant, the ninth note in the Guidonian scale, a; the third, fifth and eighth modes also share a dominant, c, the eleventh note of the scale; and the second and the seventh modes have each a different dominant, the seventh and twelfth notes of the scale, respectively.

"Thus, we can read the following scheme in our fragment:

MODE	DOMINANT		ETHOS	AGE
Primus	a	(9)	strong	Adam
Secundus	F	(7)	grave	Noah
Tertius	c	(11)	hard tempered	Abraham
Quartus	a	(9)	adulation	Moses
Quintus	c	(11)	love song	David
Sextus	a	(9)	lacrymose	John
Septus	d	(12)	harsh	World Sabbath
Octavus	c	(11)	joyful	Heaven

"This unusual allegory of the dominant, in fact, our whole allegorical fragment, is of importance to the history of music as another example of that neglected field of musical allegory.[89] To understand the aesthetics of medieval man, it is necessary to understand allegory, and to understand the aesthetics of medieval music we must have more investigation of musical allegories.[90] From the Icelandic side this fragment is of extreme importance as one of the few indications we have of the concepts of church music in early Iceland, and as another of those indications, so frequently ignored, that medieval Iceland was indeed in the mainstream of Western thought." —Marchand, pp.553-59.

---

87 The seventh age, the 'world sabbath', could be taken *in bonam partem* and represent the joy in the death of a good man, and *in mallam partem* and represent the torment of the damned. This is good medieval exegesis; cf. Saint Augustine, *De doctrine christiana*, 3.25, where he explains that the lion may stand for both Christ and the devil.

88 Ottósson, *op. cit.*, pp.171f.

89 To appreciate the allegorical significances of musical elements in a given culture, it is perhaps necessary first to understand the place that music is supposed to have with respect to "nature" itself, including supernatural elements. The present volume is in fact an attempt to elucidate (or at least to explore) such significations generally. (Ed.)

90 On allegory as aesthetics, see Edgar de Bruyne, *Etudes d'ethétique médiévale* (Brugge, 1948), particularly chap. 5; D.W. Robertston, Jr., *A Preface to Chaucer* (Princeton NJ, 1962), pp.57f.; for a recent treatment of one example, David S. Chamberlain, 'Wolberto of Cologne (d.1167): A Zenith of Musical Imagery', *Medieval Studies*, XXXIII (1971), 114-26.

INDIAN (NORTH AMERICAN) MYTHS — PRACTICES AND BELIEFS. *(See also pp.387, 1139.)*

§162.14 "TIRAWA (Creator and sky god of the Pawnee Indians). Tirawa arranged the dwelling place of man in the shape of a circle, edged all round with sky. You may verify this by climbing to the top of the nearest mountain and taking a look. This fact is represented in the Hako ceremony where the priest draws circles in the sand with his toes.

"Tirawa lived in heaven with his wife Atira. He declared his intention of creating men and ordered the gods to help him, promising them each a portion of his power to enable them to do so. Shakuru the sun was placed to give light and heat, Pah the moon was assigned the night. The Evening Star was placed in the west and called the Mother of All Things. The Morning Star, a soldier god, was set to guard the east borders; Pole Star was sent north and Death Star south. Tirawa spaced four other stars between them as supports for the sky.

"Evening Star was ordered to send a thunder storm into the middle of which Tirawa cast a stone; it made a hole through which a huge ocean could be seen. Tirawa gave the four major stars clubs and told them to beat the ocean; they did so and the waves divided to reveal the land. The god then ordered the stars to sing creation songs; the songs caused another storm which broke up the earth into hills and valleys. Again they sang, and again a fresh storm broke out. After four such songs and four storms they had created plants and trees, streams and rivers, and the germination of seeds. Tirawa ordered the sun and the moon to copulate. They produced a son. The Evening Star and the Morning Star followed suit and brought forth a daughter....

"[Soon] the two children of the sky were old enough to be taught the ways of men — the skills of speech, clothing, fire-making, hunting, agriculture, body-painting and tobacco-smoking. The man was taught how to conduct religious rituals and sacrifices. In time other stars had children and sent them to earth where they formed a tribe with the first man as their chief. He passed on all his knowledge to the others. Life would have been perfect were it not for death." — Carlyon, pp.42-43.

MUSIC AS AN APPROACH TO GOD (Christian).

§263D.1 See **CHRISTIAN PRACTICES AND BELIEFS***.

§263D.2 *"Music as an Approach to God: A Theology of Aesthetic Experience* — article by Fr. Richard Viladesau, priest of the diocese of Rockville Centre NY and teacher of Theology at Fordham University.

" 'Music is a beautiful and lovely gift of God, a queen over every stirring of the human heart. Nothing on earth is more powerful than noble music in making the sad joyful, the arrogant discreet, the despondent valiant; in charming the haughty to humility, and in mitigating envy and hatred.

" 'I give *musica* the next place after *theologia*, and the highest honor.'

"So wrote Martin Luther concerning the place of music in Christian spirituality. A composer and lyricist himself, Luther highly valued the use of music both in the sacred and secular spheres. With his collaborator Johann Walter he established the cantorship in the reformed Church; he established congregational singing as an important part of worship; and he wrote religious songs for recreational use. In his view, music in the Church served as a *predicatio sonora* — a resounding sermon. It was to be valued not only as a vehicle for sacred texts, but as being in itself a mirror of God's beauty, and thus a means of reaching the soul directly with a message about God which is inexpressible in words.

"Although Luther greatly expanded the use of congregational singing in the vernacular, his essential ideas on music stem directly from the medieval Catholic tradition which he inherited. Despite some initial opposition and occasional reservations, music had come to play such a significant role in the Church's life that Christian worship could hardly be conceived without it. Once the associations of music with pagan worship were overcome or forgotten, the 'mainstream' of Christian thought and culture has universally embraced music not only as an embellishment of liturgical life but as a symbol of the divine itself. From the time of Boethius, earthly music had been regarded as an imperfect reflection of the 'music of the spheres',[91] the celestial harmony of the heavenly bodies moved in their orbits by the 'prime Mover', God. When Dante proclaims in the last lines of the *Paradiso* that his mind and will have been moved by the same love that moves the sun and all the heavenly bodies (*ma gia volgeva il mio disiro e il velle... l'amor che move il sole e l'altre stelle—Paradiso* XXXIII, 143-45), he is expressing the commonly-accpted theory of Aristotle, who taught that the stars and planets are moved in their spheres by heavenly intelligences which are caught up in the love of God. Thus for Aristotle God moves the universe as its beloved, its reason for being. From this, both ancient and medieval thinkers developed the notion that the beautiful and harmonious motion of creation, inspired by love, is the 'music' with which it praises its maker and goal. Nicholas Brady's ode, 'Hail! Bright Cecilia', set to music as the *Ode for St. Cecilia's Day, 1692* by Henry Purcell, gives poetic expression to the idea that music is the 'soul' of the world, since it gives form and unity to the whole creation:

> Soul of the World! inspir'd by thee,
> The jarring Seeds of Matter did agree,
> Thou dids't the scatter'd Atoms bind,
> Which, by thy laws of true proportion join'd,
> Made up of various Parts one perfect Harmony.
> Thou tun'st this World below, the Spheres above,
> Which in the Heavenly Round to their own music move.

Likewise it is music which will bring the world finally to its ordained end in God, as John Dryden proclaims in his 'Song for St. Cecilia's Day', set to music by G.F. Handel:

> As from the pow'r of sacred lays

---

91   See **HARMONY OF THE SPHERES***, above. (Ed.)

The spheres began to move,
And sung the great Creator's praise
To all the bless'd above;
So when the last and dreadful hour
This crumbling pageant shall devour;
The trumpet shall be heard on high,
The dead shall live, the living die.
And music shall untune the sky.

"Thus the positive evaluation of music in the Church was founded on the idea that the music that we hear on earth gives us a sensible taste of the spiritual order and finality of all being, and in its truest nature expresses the praise of and desire for God.[92] Luther's congregational singing and the etherial choral music of the Masses of Palestrina or Victoria are based upon the same idea: that music raises the mind to God because it reflects and expresses the beautiful order of creation itself.

"For most modern people, a cosmology based upon the 'music of the spheres' belongs to a world-view which is irretrievably mythological and which has been definitively surpassed by modern science. Yet even for us the medieval idea seems to give poetic form to a valid intuition. Music seems to have a spiritual dimension which goes beyond mere sensible pleasure, and which somehow reflects a deeper reality. Anthropology makes it clear that primitive religion is inseparable from music and dance; and even for the most modern of cultures, music retains a mystical fascination, not only when heard in church, but also in the concert hall. What is it that gives to music this spiritual quality? What allows it to convey meaning? What accounts for its continual association with the sacred, so much as to make it, in Luther's words, a 'sonorous preaching'

"On one level, of course, music is 'spiritual' as the bearer of sacred words and texts; it is used to solemnize, ritualize, make these words 'sacred' in the etymological sense of separate, apart from the normal mode of communication. But this function would hardly be possible if

---

92 I mean nothing disrespectful when I point out that these are, of course, *beliefs* concerning music, which may or may not be "true" in a determinably physical or scientific sense. However one's beliefs nevertheless constitute, with other views and observations, a structuring *of* one's world, and in this (phenomenological) sense at least do represent a true picture of such a "world". Put differently, if one chose to abandon the substance of one's beliefs (assumptions and suppositions) entirely, then he would be required to abandon language itself insofar as it is not possible to exclude either from a consideration of the other. However without e.g. "language", any given "world" would itself no longer be, then — at least no such world could be said then to be "experienced", "sensed", "known" etc. — If, on the other hand, one "steps back", metaphorically speaking, to suppose a world *in which (one's) knowledge of that world is also (already) included, as a part of such a world*, then it would be equally reasonable to suppose e.g. music as an essential element or component of such a world. This would be to give the notion of an e.g. teleological significance of music pseudo-scientific credibility. (Ed.)

there were not something in music itself which makes it an apt medium for sacred word and gesture; and history and experience testify that wordless music (or music whose text is in a dead or unknown language, as with the Latin Mass or Sanskrit chants of Hindu priests) can often be equally effective in conveying a sense of spiritual reality.[93] The key to music's possibility for sacred meaning, therefore, must first be sought in asking what makes it possible for musical sound to convey meaning at all.

"On this question Nicholas Brady's poem once again may give us poetic insight:

'Tis Nature's Voice, thro' all the
      moving Wood
Of Creatures understood:
The Universal Tongue to none
Of all her num'rous Race unknown!
From her it learn'd the mighty Art
To court the Ear and strike the Heart:
At once the passions to express and
      move;

We hear, and straight to grieve or
      hate, rejoice or love:
In unseen Chains it does the Fancy
      bind:
At once it charms the Sense and cap-
      tivates the Mind.

"Music, in short, is a kind of symbolic *language:* not merely sound, but also 'voice'. It does not merely 'charm the sense', but also 'captivates the mind' and 'strikes the heart'.[94] Unlike our spoken languages, however, music is a universal tongue, based not on conventions which arbitrarily attach meaning to certain sounds, but on a kind of natural symbolism inherent in the sounds themselves.[95] Music is 'a tonal analogue of emotive life'.[96] That is, it *directly* symbolizes certain feelings: 'We hear, and straight we grieve or hate, rejoice or love.' This symbolism seems to be governed by a complex series of associations of sounds and rhythms with our natural bodily functions (e.g. faster or slower heartbeat), the intrinsic limitations

---

93 Another instance of this occurs at the opera hosue, when music sung to possibly unintelligible words (as when they are delivered in a foreign tongue) unmistakably promotes the intended drama nonetheless. (Ed.)

94 Neither author nor poet seem to explain how music can, in fact, do this, or in what sense it might be able to do this; or, indeed, what a 'language' itself might be said to consist of which is not verbal; however, both are striving for what appears (to this reader at least) to be a thoroughly valid point, however difficult it may be to express it. My own view is that the question of what a particular language *is* (in what sense it happens to be a "language") is inseparable from the question of what the language in question *does*; see the present writer's "Introductory Remarks", above. (Ed.)

95 This proposition, too, seems debatable; still, it is useful to set out such hypotheses, if only as a stimulus for thinking through the problem. An interesting discussion of meanings of and in music occurs in Jos Kessels, "Is Music a Language of the Emotions? On the Analysis of Musical Meaning", in *The Music Review* 47:3 (1986-87). After a brief survey of terms such as signs, symbols, percepts and concepts, the author writes that "music, like language, is a special form of concept-processing.... [Both] develop in time, and both consist of easily manageable elements suitable for building complex structures." He asks if e.g. the first movement of the *Moonlight Sonata* is really an expression of Beethoven's gloomy mood at the time he composed it, and the second movement an indication of how he has cheered up afterwards, or are the two movements a sort of description of two states of minds he sometimes experienced? In sum: "is music properly speaking an expression *of* something or, rather, a story *about* something? Is it a set of signs or rather a set of symbols?" He

of our hearing (loud and soft, or frequencies which are easy or difficult to hear together) as well as a certain degree of association with human sounds (weeping, sighing, laughter) or those of nature (the waters, the wind, etc.).[97] Added to this 'natural language' would be certain culturally determined conventions of meaning or association. Musical sounds are thus associated with certain basic human feelings; and these feelings, in turn, evoke the contents or situations that produce them. Music therefore is able not only to charm the sense by pleasurable experience, but also to engage the 'heart' by analogously representing emotional states and to engage the mind by evoking the meanings associated with those states in the human mind.

"A similar theory is used by Rudolf Otto in his classic work *The Idea of the Holy* (Oxford University Press, 1969) to explain the specific connection of music and art with the experience of the sacred. Otto speaks

of this connection as a 'law of associations'. The experience which grounds religion— the experience of the 'holy', the *mysterium tremendum et fascinans* (the fearful and attractive mystery)—is for Otto *sui generis*: it cannot be reduced to moral or aesthetic or any other kind of experience. Nevertheless, the feelings produced by encounter with the Holy have analogies with similar feelings produced in other areas of human life by beauty, moral goodness, or truth. The presence of one set of feelings can stimulate the appearance in consciousness of its analogues. Thus music properly constitutes a world and language unto itself; the feelings and moods it produces are

concludes that, generally speaking, the latter interpretation is preferable to the former. "So a piece of music may be likened to a story. But how it is understood is quite another story yet." (For an interesting discussion on a related topic, see Lawrence Ferrara, "Phenomenology as a Tool for Musical Analysis", *The Musical Quarterly* LXX/3 [G. Schirmer, Summer 1984]. In this article the author raises the obviously important question of the role which a listener, himself, plays with respect to supposing various meanings, etc. conveyed by a given piece of music.) (Ed.)

96   Susanne K. Langer, *Feeling and Form* (Charles Scribner's Sons, 1953).

97   The 'naturalistic' theory of the mechanics of aesthetic experience is explained at length in George Santayana's classic study, *The Sense of Beauty* (Charles Scribner's Sons, 1896). The essential idea, however, that beauty is a matter of the correspondence of experience to the proportions inherent in our organs of sense is already found in Thomas Aquinas; see for example *Summa Theologica*, I, 5, 4 ad 1.

simply 'musical', and should not be con-fused with any non-musical experiences. At the same time, some of these feelings afford analogies to the ordinary emotions of life, and by association can call those emotions into the hearer's mind. (Thus, for example, the canons and fugues of J.S. Bach almost invariably evoke the analogy of logic or of mathematics; to hear them is to have an inner experience somehow similar to that of proceeding step by step through an elegant geometrical demonstration and feeling the satisfaction of arriving at an inescapable conclusion.)[98]

"Likewise, some properly musical 'vibrations of mood' are similar and analogous to those aroused by the encounter with the Holy, and can by association produce the latter in the hearer's consciousness. It is for this reason that some forms of music are more intrinsically suited to serve as the medium and expression of religious content than others, and why some styles or techniques in music are peculiarly apt to express sacred meaning. (So, for example, the supreme moment of transcendence is frequently expressed by extreme softness of sound or even stillness: the analogue of the silent awe experienced before the Transcendent).

"Otto's theory throws a great deal of light on relation of music to spirituality. It accounts for the difference between what is called 'serious' and what is called 'light' music, and shows why there is some sense to the idea of a sacred 'style': those forms of music which have emotional and intellectual associations of sufficient 'depth' to be appropriate carriers of sacred words or themes (while 'light' or frivolous forms of music, although perhaps pleasant in themselves, may betray a sacred message by inappropriate associations which trivialize it). It also explains why music can be seen in religion as the height of spiritual expression or, alternatively, as the epitome of sensual depravity.[99]

"At the same time, Otto's position raises a further question: is musical experience merely the emotional *analogue* of sacred experience, so that it works exclusively by association; or can music and art *in themselves* be an experience of the sacred? This question leads to a re-examination of Otto's basic premise: is the human encounter with the Holy a separate experience, *alongside* those of the beautiful, the good, etc. — or is it rather *identical* with those experiences when seen in their deepest reality, as their ground?

"Without denying the validity of Otto's notion of associations of feelings, operating on many different levels, it is perhaps

---

98 I wonder, too, if — together with logicians and mathematicians — Bach isn't also *inventing* what he is doing, as he goes along. We often write something down, precisely in order to learn what it was we may have been thinking. One might well define certain forms of logic, not only with reference to philosophers and mathematicians, but also *though* reference to composers of music — not only in Bach's seventeenth century, indeed, but surely in our own as well. For an additional discussion, though it ranges far beyond the present scope, see Douglas Hofstadter's unusual study of *Godel, Escher, Bach: An Eternal Golden Braid* (Basic Books, 1979). (Ed.)

99 One may wonder if by "sacred" the author is tempted to mean only "solemn". But, if so, since many scenes in *Tristan und Isolde* are solemn enough, are they also (therefore) sacred? Is *any* solemn music also (therefore) sacred music? Conversely, the solemn, sacred-sounding music of the ceremonial scenes in *Parsifal* are, equally... "theatrical". And what shall be said, generally, of joyful music? "Agitated" music? What of baroque "sacred" music which employs ornamentation to a degree that, today, we might call "excessive"? (Ed.)

possible to regard the religious not simply as a parallel experience, but more as a kind of *meta*-experience (in a way parallel to the experience of being in metaphysics). Its object — the *mysterium tremendum et fascinans*, the numinous — would then be ontologically identical with the ultimate object of aesthetic or moral or intellectual experience, and would ground the analogies that are in fact found in the human reaction to the beautiful, the good, the true, and the holy.

"In this perspective, the ultimate reason for the possibility of music to mediate the spiritual is not merely because it echoes emotions which are felt in religious experience, but also and more profoundly because its object is the beautiful, which itself is godly and thus leads toward God. There are, of course, different kinds of beauty, and these can ground the multiple and diverse 'associations' with the feelings connected with spirituality. Music which represents and/or produces feelings of peace, contentment, joy, unity, harmony — or, on the other hand, of striving, power, majesty, awe — may call to mind similar feelings which occur in religious states. There are also different *levels* of beauty: from mere prettiness or sensual enjoyment

to the deepest and most mysterious attraction, in which there may be experienced a painful tension in the call to self-transcendence. Beauty at its profoundest may call for purification, discipline and even renunciation. What unifies all of these kinds and levels in music is precisely the fact of their being experienced not simply as representations of the feelings of human existence, but as presenting these feelings as in some way *beautiful* — and as such, as revelatory of the transcendent.[100]

"Why, then, is the beautiful a revelation of God? An answer to this question depends upon a recognition of what constitutes the experience of beauty and makes it possible. A passage from the novel *Doctor Zhivago* succinctly summarizes the critical insight. Pasternak writes of his hero:

> ...he made a note reaffirming his belief that art always serves beauty, and beauty is delight in form, and form is the key to organic life, since no living thing can exist without it, so that every work of art, including tragedy, expresses the joy of existence.[101]

---

100 I for one would maintain that while the earliest and most primitive musicians known to human history could not, of course, describe the matter in terms such as these, they certainly must have *felt* something precisely on the order the author describes. One would also experience all this "pre-theologically", which leads to an intriguing possibility: do we, indeed, *invent* (some of) our gods (or some of the aspects or attributes of a given divinity) through e.g. music? Still, again, the linkage of *God* with e.g. the *beautiful* is a tremendously attractive idea. The next question would be: of what does "beauty" consist? and, through what means or faculty can the "beautiful", itself, be apprehended? To this issue, the author himself turns next. (Ed.)

101 Transl. Max Hayward and Manya Harari (New American Library, 1958), p.378.

"The experience of beauty is a kind of delight: a joy in the experience of 'form', the organizing principle which gives 'shape' to things and to our knowledge of them. What distinguishes music from noise is precisely its patterns, which create a unity out of disparate elements. Analogously, 'form' or organization is what makes biological life possible; and, on yet another level, 'form' is what makes any existing thing into an identity, a whole which is differentiated from others; and 'form' is what corresponds to the mind's quest for intelligibility.[102] In this sense, 'form' is the key to existence itself, and delight in form — what makes existence possible — is an implicit affirmation of the goodness and joy of existence, of being itself.[103]

"The apprehension of the joy of existence, however, can only take place in an intelligent and free being if existence is somehow — even if only implicitly — seen as worthwhile, as meaningful and having an ultimate intelligibility or purpose. To experience beauty is to experience a deep-seated 'yes' to being — even in its finitude and its moments of tragedy; and such an affirmation is possible only if being is grounded, borne by a Reality which is absolute in value and meaning. In short, the experience of finite beauty in a spiritual being implies the unavoidable (although perhaps also thematically unconscious) co-affirmation of an infinite Beauty: that reality which we call God.

"The fact that God is the 'horizon' of every experience of beauty explains why even the tragic emotions can be experienced in art as 'beautiful', and why there is at the heart of every deep aesthetic experience — and perhaps particularly in music — an intense feeling of striving toward something beyond the moment itself. In Peter Shaffer's *Amadeus* the aged Salieri says of Mozart's music: 'This was a music... filled with such longing, such unfulfillable longing, that it seemed to me that I was hearing the voice of God.' This longing is intrinsic to the experience of finite beauty; for the joy of existence in any finite being can never be complete or ultimate, but must point beyond itself to a final and infinite goal.[104] It is in this sense that philosophers from Plato onward have seen beauty as the manifestation of God to the senses, and have claimed that 'the beauty of anything created is nothing else than a similitude of divine beauty participated in by things.'[105] In music, because it is temporal and therefore intrinsically fleeting, the symbolism of dynamism to a whole which is beyond the moment is especially present.

"It now becomes clear that music can lead the mind to sacred experience in three different but interconnected ways: by being the bearer or accompaniment to sacred words, gestures, or motions; by association with emotions characteristic of religious psychological states; and by the

---

102 Cf. *Summa Theologica* 1a, q5, 4, 1m; *Commentarium in de Divinis Nominibus*, lect. VI.

103 Mustn't it be pointed out — at the same time — that any given 'form' in a sense is a symbolizing or allegorizing of 'existence' (or of some aspect of 'existence') — that even the act of creating a given form can be said to "stand for" something, in itself — and that, therefore, just as "form" in general would appear to be allegorical, so musical forms (actual musical compositions) must also be? The notion "existence", itself, in my view is (necessarily) metaphorical. (Ed.)

104 With this one can agree — and still be confused by playright Shaffer's sentence. Does he mean to say that the voice of God is one of longing? Or, that a voice of (artistic, psychological) longing (for beauty, etc.) is, at the same time, a longing for (or, to know) God? (Ed.)

105 *Ibid.*, lect. V.

manifestation of beauty as the sign of the transcendental goal of human spirit.

"A specific example of great sacred msuic will perhaps show how the working of these three levels together can constitute a 'sonorous preaching' of faith. The inter- play of text, association, and beauty is heard in a particularly elegant way in the opening chorale of J.S. Bach's cantata *'Liebster Gott, wenn werd'ich sterben?'* ('Dearest God, when shall I die'? — BWV 8). The work begins with the creation of a musical picture; the oboe play a round-like tune, symbolizing the ceaseless turning of the wheel of time; the *pizzicato* of the violins reminds us of a clock, ticking away our hours and minutes; at intervals the viola da gamba, joined by the organ, simu- lates the pealing of a great church bell, while the flute joins on a single repeated high note to imitate the small bell tolling. Then enter the voices of the choir, singing a sober meditation on human mortality:

Dearest God, when shall I die? My time is constantly running out, and

the descendants of ancient Adam — of whom I am one — have this for their inheritance; to be only a short while, poor and miserable upon the earth, and then to become earth themselves.

"Seldom can art have produced a more ef- fective *memento mori*. Hearing the words, I am explicitly reminded that I must die, while the music, whose very nature is to pass through time, makes me feel the present experience of time's inexorable passage, and anticipates the inevitable mo- ment when the funeral bells will toll for me. Yet what makes Bach's treatment more than a mere didactic exercise is the spirit in which the whole is presented, for the feel- ing of the chorale is anything but morbid. Rather, it conveys a sense of peace, joy, comfort, beauty, even in the face of death itself. As E. Power Biggs [the noted or- ganist] once remarked, Bach looks death in the face and writes cradle songs. Thus for one who hears and understands the text, the music is felt as a profound statement of faith — a positive assertion of hope and joy

even in the face of the inevitability of death. The grounds of that hope are made explicit in the remaining sections of the cantata, which meditate on Christ as savior. The believer thus finds here a powerful and moving reminder and reinforcement of the basic attitude of supreme confidence and abandonment to God.[106]

"But what of the non-believer? Clearly it is not necessary to have Christian faith to appreciate the skill and beauty of Bach's music, apart from its message, and it would be possible to appreciate such a cantata on one level by consciously abstracting from the text. But to do so would deprive the experience of a major part of its aesthetic power. If one is really to feel the beauty of the emotion Bach evokes, one must feel what he feels;[107] and one must therefore in some sense believe with him in the ultimate beauty he is presenting: the triumph of good over death, the existence of a final purpose to life, the comfort of confidence in a loving saviour. The unbeliev-

ing hearer of Bach's music will not, of course, personally affirm the faith that is presented in it, but must at least *vicariously* feel the attitude of faith. For the act of aesthetic appreciation to take place, there must be a willing, if only momentary, suspension of disbelief; a willingness to see life, at least for this moment, *as if* the hearer shared Bach's faith.[108] This aesthetic act is of course far from real assent; yet it is significant, for it involves a certain openness to faith as a genuine human possibility. If one can feel, even for a moment, the real human possibility of such an act of confidence in the face of death, one is at least faced with the further question: how is such an act possible? What is it in the human being—even in the unbeliever—which can not only intellectually acknowledge, but can existentially *feel* a fundamentally positive stance toward existence, even in the face of death? In this sense, Bach's music—like all great religious music—performs a kind of 'apologetic' function by evoking in the

---

106 The author opens—not closes—this valuable line of inquiry. For certainly the effect of (to give an example on the level of a Bach composition) the *Ninth Symphony* of Beethoven is equally an exression of, and experience of, faith of *some* kind; in elevation, redemption, brotherhood, etc. Yet the *Ninth Symphony* is surely very "secular" in its text, associations, and, perhaps, in its style of music (in its particular kind of beauty). The question is not a simple one, then. My own feeling is that certain kinds of (artistic or other) experience *are* religious experiences—but, with or without a particular notion of "God" or, indeed, any notion of what others may choose to call "God" at all. As we all have, I have heard musical performances which really and truly do "lift me up to heaven"—and yet, in fact, the notion of "heaven" itself, in any religious or philosophical sense, is quite foreign to my own beliefs. Our author anticipates the sense of the objection, at least, in his next, closing paragraphs. (Ed.)

107 A thoroughly debatable—if interesting—contention. (Ed.)

108 Where this argument seems rather clearly to break down, I think, is in the field of purely instrumental or "absolute" music. What did Beethoven (again) actually intend to convey by the second movement of his *Fourth Symphony*? The story is told of a cocktail party following the premiere of Rodgers' and Hammerstein's *South Pacific*. 'Don't you just love Richard Rodger's 'Some Enchanted Evening'?' gushed an enthusiast, of Mrs. Oscar Hammerstein. Replied the latter: 'My dear, you are speaking of Mr. *Hammerstein's* 'Some Enchanted Evening'. What Mr. Rodgers wrote was, da-dee-da'-d-daaa-da.' " (Ed.)

hearer a belief in the beautiful, a belief in life, and raising therefore the question of the grounds of such belief.

"If what we have said above about the nature of beauty is true, then this 'apologetic' function is not restricted to music which is explicity tied to relgiious texts or even to faith, but occurs wherever the spirit is moved to an affirmation of beauty and the meaningfulness of existence. In this sense even secular music may be a 'sonorous preaching', for it leads the spirit—perhaps more effectively than any argument or reasoning—through the experience of beauty and the affirmation of life to an implicit knowledge of its Maker and Goal.[109] Thus music does more than convey a message *about* God; in its highest forms, it brings the hearer face to face with the reality of God himself. The hearer of great music may make his own the words which the eminent scientist Albert Einstein once addressed, after a concert, to the young violinist Yehudi Menuhin: 'Thank you. You have once again proved to me that there is a God in heaven.' "[110]—Viladesau, pp.4-9.

MUSICAL REFERENCES IN IMAGINATIVE LITERATURE.

§267A. 1 The present volume is largely made up of references to music in various of the world's mythologies. In addition, there are many entries having to do with religious beliefs and practices, and many others having to do with folk legends and tales.

All of these could be placed at various points along the scale of "mythology" itself, insofar as they all deal in some way with what a scientist might be expected to call supernatural beings or occurrences or explanations for something. However religious, mythological and folk lore also have in common that they belong in a general way to the category of literature, by which I mean any given body of imaginative or creative writing which is devoted to a particular subject—which may but does not necessarily have to be written down. (Examples of "written down" religious, mythological and folk lore are the Bible, the *Odyssey*, and the tales of the Brothers Grimm. Of course it is also true that the written-down form of these materials can be literature in the most elevated sense—thus the Bible, *Odyssey* and Grimm fairy tales, for example, have not only assembled and recorded certain popular narratives and beliefs, they have also done so according to the highest standards of what has come to be called "art".)

What has been left out of all this, meanwhile, for the most part, are individual works by certifiably individual authors. Appropriately perhaps, insofar as the particular notions of a particular author cannot reliably be said to express "popularly"-held beliefs. It can also be assumed that the works of a particular author—however much enjoyed and respected they may be—are not to be approached with the same reverence and faith with which authentic folk beliefs and conceptions customarily are.

---

109 I would agree; but I also wonder if, in making this admission, one has in fact compromised the author's intended argument? Still it doesn't matter, much; his points seem well taken (to me), and only various restrictions of language (and, ultimately, of one's ability to know, itself) stand in the way of a clear resolution of all the arguments. (Ed.)

110 In the preceding essay by Fr. Viladesau, I have subjected the author's remarks to a running commentary of my own. Ideally, I should have liked to have given *him* an opportunity to respond to my responses, in turn; alas, the printed page is not an ideal forum for evenly-matched debate. (Ed.)

However, it ought to be remembered that even "anonymous" authors were, once, *authors*: whether or not the particular leader known as Moses also set down the first five books of the Bible (and whether or not it was actually a person called "Homer" who composed both the *Iliad* and the *Odyssey*), it is a fact nevertheless that *someone* did, after all; moreover, while folk stories are, perhaps by definition, the work of many hands, still each of the (however many) contributors who have come to make his or her own contribution to a particular result was of course an actual person.

Lastly: some writers of literature in the narrower sense of "particular works by particular authors" have also, in their writings, given shape to conceptions which do in fact reflect more or less popularly-held beliefs or assumptions (indeed, they may even derive from folklore itself); or, their fancies have proved to be so broadly popular that there does seem a sense in which the intuitions of the particular artist appear to reflect beliefs or attitudes held by a given community at large. For example, while the "Dum-Dum" ceremony, at which intelligent apes are reputed to play upon a drum which they have "built especially for this mad and intoxicating revel", is presumably the invention merely of Edgar Rice Burroughs for his *Tarzan of the Apes*, at the same time the associating of music in general and of drums in particular with so-to-speak "religious" ceremonies, and with ecstatic or intoxicating behavior, is a common theme in mythology.

The purpose of this entry, then, is to suggest at least the perhaps not-always-so-remote relationship which some authors, at least, do enjoy with broader mythological themes and stories. The examples given here are only representative of a much larger supply to be found throughout the near and far reaches of creative or imaginative literature, but they ought to serve the purpose. All have been excerpted from the quite marvelous and cleverly written compendium by Alberto Manguel & Gianni Guadalupi which is titled *THE DICTIONARY OF IMAGINARY PLACES, Expanded Edition*, published by Harcourt Brace Jovanovich in 1987. Manguel and Guadalupi's book—like so many others which are quoted in this dictionary—ought to be in every library dealing with mythological and related subjects. (Ed.)

"ANIMAS, MONTE DE LAS [MOUNTAIN OF THE SPIRITS], near Soria, Spain. The mountain used to belong to the Knights Templars, who had been invited by the King of Spain the protect the city of Soria after it was recaptured from the Arabs....

"Travelers are advised to visit the mountain on the night of All Saints, when a phantom bell is heard tolling in the foggy air. The ghosts of the dead come out of their tombs in torn and bloody shrouds and hunt phantom stags on phantom horses. The wolves howl in fear, the deer leep in terror, the snakes utter frightened, sibilant sounds and the whole mountain rings with the clatter of galloping hooves. (Gustavo Adolfo Becquer, 'El monate de las ánimas', in *Leyendas*, Madrid, 1871.)

"APE KINGDOM, in Africa, somewhere in the high tree-tops of the tropical jungle, inhabited by large apes or Mangani. This particular tribe of apes is famous for having brought up the young Lord Greystoke after slaughtering his father...

"Travelers are advised to attend the famous Dum-Dum ceremony. It takes place in a natural amphitheatre—a hollow among low hills—in the center of which is a drum built especially for this mad and intoxicating revel. Historians say that from this primitive ritual have risen, unquestionably, all the forms and ceremonials of the modern Church and State. (Edgar Rice Burroughs, *Tarzan of the Apes*, New York, 1912.)

"APHANIA, a kingdom in Central Europe. The country is renowned for its many bells and steeples, and for the statue of King

Rumti who was changed into stone by a good fairy because, in his absent-mindedness, he had forgotten to give alms to a beggar....

"Warfare is frowned upon but it exists, and because drum practice is noisy, a special district called Bootinter was set aside on the sea-coast for the training of the soldiery and the manufacture and trial of big drums. To the scientific traveler, Bootinter is a place of great interest and is invariably visited by all tourists of note who can obtain a pass from the War Department. Spectacular trials take place here: for example, the great contest of 'Drums *versus* Cotton Wool' which is particularly worth attending. (Tom Hood, *Petsetilla's Posy*, London, 1870.)

"ASH GROVE, CASTLE: see PERI KINGDOM.

"BANOIS EMPIRE, in the subterranean world of Pluto, in the center of the earth.... The language of the Banois appears to have been simplified over the centuries; visitors will find it can now be learned in a matter of weeks. However, the Banois sing instead of speaking. Even the children of the country hum as they cry; adults sing harmoniously every hour of the day. (Anonymous, *Voyage au centre de la terre*, Paris, 1821.)

"BASTIANI, a large fortress [which] guards the only pass between the Tartary Desert and the southern slopes of the steep and uninterrupted chain of mountains that marks the border between the northern and the southern States of an unnamed country....

"In military circles in the Southern State, the silvery trumpets of Bastiana are famous for their red silk cords and for the crystal clearness of their blare. (Dino Buzzati, *Il deserto dei Tartari*, Milan, 1940.)

"BEKLA, capital of the Beklan Empire, [which] stands on the slopes of Mount Crandor which dominates the surrounding Beklan Plain. The walls of the city are six miles in circumference and rise to the south to enclose the summit of Mount Crandor, crowned by a large citadel....

"The most beautiful sight in the Upper City is Leopard Hill, with its terrace of vines and flowers. Above the gardens rise the twenty round towers of the House of the Barons, with circular balconies projecting like the capitals of giant columns. The height and shape of the marble balconies are all the same, but each one is decorated differently, carved with low relief sculptures of leopards, lilies, birds or fish, and the towers are known by the name of the plant or animal portrayed. They all end in slender painted spires which house the copper bells that summon the citizens of Bekla to festivals. (Richard Adams, *Shardik*, London, 1974.)

"BENSALEM, an island in the south Pacific, in the region of the Solomon Islands.... Although long isolated from the world, Bensalem was well known in ancient times, when it was frequently visited by ships from Tyre, Carthage, China and Atlantis....

"The most important institution on Bensalem is the House of Solomon, founded by Solamona and dedicated to the works and creatures of God. The house is named after the Hebrew King and preserves in its library his *Natural History* (referred to in I Kings 4:33) which was long thought to have been lost.

"According to Solamona: 'The end of the foundation is the knowledge of causes and secret motions of things; and the enlarging of the bounds of human empire to the effecting of all things possible.' The House's scientific research has led to the development of submarines and flying machines. Streams, cataracts and windmills are used to provide energy. Caves deep beneath the buildings are used for the production and preservation of metals... 'Perspective' houses are devoted to experiments in optical science.... Acoustic experiments are carried out in the 'Sound' houses, which also manufacture musical instruments like the violin-piano and devices to reproduce natural sounds. (Francis Bacon, *New Atlantis*, London, 1627; Viscount Herbert Louis Samuel, *An Unknown Land*, London, 1942.)

"BURZEE, an ancient forest lying beyond the Deadly Desert that marks the western boundary of Oz, close to Noland. In the center of its giant oaks and firs, a fairy ring has been traced on the smooth, velvety grass by the feet of elves and fairies who come here to dance at the full moon. (L. Frank Baum, *Queen Zixi of Ix, or The Story of the Magic Cloak*, New York, 1907.)

"CALNOGOR, the capital city of Atvatabar, five hundred miles inland. It can be reached from the city of Kioram by a sacred railroad as well as an aerial ship....
"The Pantheon or Bormidophia [in this city] is a place of worship and the abode of Lady Lyone, Supreme Goddess of Atvatabar. It contains the most extraordinary object in all Atvatabar: the throne of the Goddess, which consists of a solid gold cone, shaped somewhat in the form of a heart, some one hundred feet high. The throne is divided into three parts corresponding to the various castes of gods and to symbols of science, art and spirituality.... The middle section is dedicated to art and its attributes. It is twenty-four feet high and sixty feet in diameter, divided into two sections: the upper, representing the gods of Poetry, Painting, Music, etc.: and the lower, showing the qualities of the soul developed by art, such as Imagination, Emotion, Tenderness. (William R. Bradshaw, *The Goddess of Atvatabar*, New York, 1892.)

"CELESTIAL CITY, beyond the Delectable Mountains, surrounded by the river known as the River of Death, in Christian's Country.....

"Travelers who overcome the dangers of the long journey from the City of Destruction to the river receive great rewards for the toils and sufferings they have undergone. They are welcomed by a blast of trumpets and the inhabitants of the Celestial City gather to watch them cross the river. (John Bunyan, *The Pilgrim's Progress*, London, 1684.)

"CHANCE, ISLAND OF, situated off the coast of the United States near the Island of Fortune, where earthquakes are not infrequent. Here all appears to be left to chance, and all kinds of monsters are produced by a nature which appears to be still in an infantile state of experimentation. On the Island of Chance people are born with horseshoes instead of hands; they are considered to be as stupid as horses and left in the fields to graze. On the other hand, horses are born with human hands and have established workshops and tailors' shops. They can also play musical instruments, chance having given them the limbs that in other countries have granted man superior status.[111] (Abbé Balthazard, *L'Isle des Philosophes et Plusiers Autres*, Chartres, 1790.)

"CLOUDS, MOUNTAIN OF, in a country six months by sea from Basra, Iraq, probably in the Indian Ocean. Travelers would be wise to bring along a Persian magician with a knowledge of alchemy, as these are the only people who can easily find their way to the Mountain of Clouds. However, as it is their custom to sacrifice their travelling companions to satisfy their alchemical needs, prudence is recommended....
"Once landed, travellers should leave the magican on his own at the foot of the mountain; he will proceed to unpack a copper kettledrum and a silk drumstick decorated in gold, with which he will beat

---

111 Music as a symbol and instrument of civilization, in contrast to uncivilized primeval "nature". (Ed.)

the kettledrum. A cloud of dust will rise from the ground, slowly taking the shape of three fine camels, one of which the traveler is advised to ride [in furtherance of his journey].[112] (Anonymous, *The Arabian Nights*, 14th-16th century AD.)

"COMMUTARIA, a village on the Portsmouth-Waterloo line in Southern England. Everything a commuter longs for can be found in this village. It was set up by a distant descendant of the English scientist Merlin, to reward tired commuters. [On approaching] the train stops quietly, not with a jerk but as if in slow motion. The doors open silently and soft music, reminiscent of third-rate romantic Sunday afternoon films, fills the air. Outside, each commuter finds [the object of] his secret craving. (Elspeth Ann Macey, 'Awayday', in *Absent Friends and Other Stories*, London, 1955.)

"CORADINE, a country somewhere in Northern Scotland. It consists of a valley among rolling hills beyond which, twenty or twenty-five miles away, rise the high mountains of Elf....
"Coradine is notable for its architecture. No roads or avenues lead to the different buildings, each of which stands isolated without gardens or hedges. A typical example is the House of the Harvest Melody.... All the buildings in Coradine are ancient and no new houses are built; the inhabitants compare them to the hills, 'whose origins,' they say, 'are lost in the mists of time.'...
"Coradine food is simple. Breakfast and lunch consist of a crust of brown bread, a handful of dried fruit, and milk. [The inhabitants] drink no alchohol, only fruit juices. The people of Coradine produce music through small revolving globes which emit sounds resembling human voices. Their songs, however, had no words. Money is unknown. Communal

bathing is a popular entertainment. Giving or taking gifts is a grave offence – soemthing must always be given in return. (W.H. Hudson, *A Crystal Age*, London, 1887.)

"DISAPPEARED, an enormous city somewhere under the ocean. From a distance the traveller can see only deep, windswept water, but if he dives beneath the surface he will behold a city made of bricks. Towers, bazaars, factories, arches and palaces which once vibrated with the sound of melodious lute music make Disappeared look like a hydra. In the parks, by the royal palace where the queens came to bathe in the nude, visitors can admire the wreck of an ancient cutter. (Victor Hugo, 'La Ville disparue', in *La Légende des siècles*, Paris, 1859.)

"EARTHSEA, an archipelago consisting of hundreds of islands....
"Earthsea includes a wide variety of cultures, ranging from the simplicity of the mountain people of Gont to the sophistication of the people of Havnor, not to mention the inhabitants of Roke, to whom magic is simply a part of daily life.... All the islands, with the exception of the Kargad Empire, celebrate the Long Dance, which is held on the shortest day of the year. On that night the people dance down the roads of their island to the sound of drums, pipes and flutes. As they return, only the flutes are heard. There are of course regional variations – the Raft Folk, for instance, who perform the ceremony on their rafts, do not use an instrumental accompaniment – but the dance itself is universal and, symbolically, it binds together the sea-divided lands. The festival of Sunreturn, held on the shortest day of the year, is also universally recognized. Usually it involves the singing of the ancient chants and epics in which so much of Earthsea's past is recorded. (Ursula K. Le Guin, *A Wizard of Earthsea*, New York, 1968; *The*

---

112 Drum as magical instrument. (Ed.)

Tombs of Atuan, London, 1972; *The Farthest Shore*, London, 1973.)

¶"LONG DUNE, a long, low island in the far south-west of the Earthsea Archipelago. The island is uninhabited, but is visited once a year by the Raft Folk (or Children of the Open Sea as they are sometimes called) who come here to cut wood to repair their large rafts....

"On the shortest night of the year, torches are lit on the rafts as [the Raft Folk] lie gathered once more in a great circle. They then celebrate the Long Dance, the one custom they have in common with the islanders of Earthsea. The dance has no musical accompaniment; it simply follows the rhythm of bare feet pounding the floor of the swaying rafts and the thin voices of the chanters. Their songs are not of the heroes of Earthsea, but of the albatross, the whale and the dolphin.

"ENTELECHY, an island kingdom of unknown location. The main port is Mataeotechny, or 'Home of Useless Knowledge'.

"Although the Queen of the island is commonly known as 'The Quintessence', her true name is Entelechy, like the island itself. The name was given her by Aristotle, her godfather. Travellers will see the queen as young, fair and delicately built, but in fact she is more than two thousand years old. The queen has the ability to cure all diseases simply by playing a tune chosen according to the nature of the complaint the patient is suffering from; she does not even have to touch the patient.[113] The instrument on which she plays her miraculous music is a curious object: its pipes are made of cassia sticks; its sounding board, of guaiacum; its stops, of rhubarb; its pedals, of tussock; and its keyboard, of scammony. A tune played on this instrument will immediately cure the

blind, the deaf, and the dumb,, the leper and the apoplectic.

"The queen herself only cures 'incurable' diseases; less serious complaints are dealt with by her officers... who cure by other means than music. (François Rabelais, *Le cinquiesme et dernier livre des faicts et dicts du bon Pantagruel*, Paris, 1564.)

¶"ORACLE OF THE BOTTLE, ISLAND OF THE, not far from Lanternland, where travellers can obtain knowledgeable Lanterns as guides....

"Anyone wishing to consult the oracle is led into [a] chapel by Bacbuc, priestess of the Oracle. The visitor is then told to kiss the edge of the fountain and to perform three Bacchis dances. He then sits down between two stools and sings an Athenian drinking song. After the song has been sung,the priestess throws something into the water, which immediately begins to boil fiercely. A cracking sound is heard and the Oracle will then answer whatever question the visitor has put to it.[114]

¶"RINGING ISLAND, four days' sail from Ganabin Island. It is immediately recognizable because as travellers approach it, the air is filled with the sound of ringing bells.

"The island is inhabited by the Siticines or Dirge-Singers, originally people who were all changed into birds. The only human resident on Ringing Island is the sacristan, Master Aeditus. The birds live in sumptuous cages, each with a bell above it. The birds themselves are as large as men and behave exactly like men. Some are white, some black, some grey, some black and white, others half white and half blue. A few are red. All are beautiful and sleek....

"The birds of Ringing Island do not work or cultivate the soil; their sole activity is singing. Their abundant food supplies are given to them by all the countries of the

---

113 Musical instrument as shaman's implement, used for curing. (Ed.)
114 Parody on music as magical instrumentality, importance in mystical rites, etc. (Ed.)

world, with the exception of certain kingdoms that lie under the North Wind.

"EREWHON, a kingdom probably in central or northern Australia, though its location has been deliberately concealed by travellers who have visited it....

"In Erewhon, the traveller will find much the same customs as in Europe. He will be struck, however, by the primitive character of the Erewhonian appliances; they seem five or six hundred years behind Europe in their inventions (but this is also the case of course in many European villages). A few things are unknown in Erewhon: gunpowder and matches, for instance....

"One interesting site, very near the river which gives access to Erewhon, is the Erewhonian Stonehenge. It consists of rude and barbaric figures with superhuman, malevolent expressions on their faces—a mixture of Egyptian, Assyrian and Japanese features. They are six or seven times larger than life and of great antiquity, worn and lichen-grown. Each statue is built out of four or five enormous blocks. In ancient times, the Erewhonians sacrificed the ugly and diseased to these statues, in order to avert such scourges from falling on their own people. When the wind blows through these statues, which are hollow, it produces a melody reminiscent of Handel:

"...The only musical instruments in the houses are a dozen large bronze gongs which are kept in the larger drawing room and which the ladies occasionally beat at random, producing a rather unpleasant sound.[115] This music is also used in all mercantile transactions, most of which take place in what is called the Musical Bank. The Erewhonian coinage is entirely silver—gold pieces are very rare—and there are two distinct currencies in Erewhon, each under the control of two different banks and mercantile codes, the exact functionings of which are extremely complicated. The Musical Bank is socially acceptable, but its currency is of no use in the outside world; the other bank is commonly used but not talked about. The main branch of the Musical Bank is on a large central piazza. [If the] outside is impressive, the inside is even more so. It is very lofty and divided into several parts by walls which rest on massive pillars. The windows are filled with stained glass depicting the principal commercial incidents of the bank over many ages.[116] In a

---

115 Perhaps intended as a parody on the European institution of drawing-room *musicales;* however, the gong has a rather exotic and fanciful connotation of its own, appropriate to a mysterious place like Erewhon. (Ed.)

116 Thus likening such a bank to a cathedral, with which music of course is generally associated. (Ed.)

remote part of the building the visitor may hear men and boys singing: this is the only disturbing feature, as the music is singularly hideous to European ears. (Samuel Butler, *Erewhon,* London, 1872; *Erewhon Revisited,* London, 1901.)

"ETIDORHPA'S COUNTRY, an underground region, reached through an entrance in the well-known cave systems of Kentucky, in the United States. Through an archway in a clif flows a stream which must be followed into a tunnel... Eventually a large cave is reached, with a path leading away from the stream.... Beyond this lies a deep chasm running for many miles....

"For those who falter on the subterranean journey there is a chamber called the Drunkards Den. Here live a race of tiny degenerate beings, once intelligent and now stupid, shrunken and mis-shapen, each with one gigantic hand, leg or forehead. They tempt newcomers, trying to bring them down to their level by inviting them to drink. On earth it is the mind of a drunkard that becomes abnormal; here it is the body. The den is a vast amphitheater, one thousand feet in diameter, with a stone rostrum in the center where liquor is fermented in huge bowls. The traveller should resist the pleas of the drunkards who will then disappear to be replaced by a group of beautiful women who come forward dancing to the sound of soft music.[117] The most beautiful of all is the maiden Etidorhpa. (John Uri Lloyd, *Etidorhpa or the End of the Earth,* Cincinnati, 1895.)

"EUPHONIA, a small city of some twelve thousand inhabitants, in the Harz Mountains, Germany, considered by some visitors to be a gigantic music conservatory because music is the sole activity of its people. All Euphonians—men, women and even children—do nothing but sing, play an instrument or practise some other activity connected with the musical arts. Some make instruments, others print music, yet others spend their time in acoustical research or studying physical phenomena related to sound.

"The city is divided into sections corresponding to the various musical activities. Each voice, each instrument has a street that carries its name and is inhabited only by those concerned with that specific talent....

"Euphonian education begins at a very tender age; children are taught all possible rhythmic combinations, then the study of the scales and an instrument of their choice, finally singing and harmony. Upon reaching puberty—that time of life when true passions begin to be felt—adolescents are taught expression and *bello stile.* Sincerity of expression—that rare quality so difficult to appreciate—is held in the highest regard by all Euphonians and is therefore carefully taught. Those individuals who cannot or will not learn true sincerity of expression are exiled from the city, even if their voices or instrumental skills are excellent; however, such renegades are sometimes allowed to live in the farthest houses, preparing skins for drums or stringing instruments.....

"The beginning and ending of the hours of work and rest are announced by sounding a gigantic organ on top of a tower that dominates the whole city. This five-century-old instrument works on steam and can be heard almost four leagues away. Instructions and general information are also conveyed by the organ, in a musical code that only Euphonians can understand.....

"The philosophy of music is an important science in Euphonia, and the inhabitants study the laws and historical precepts on which musical evolution is based. At cer-

---

117 Theme of dangerous enticements of music; see e.g. **WATER SPIRITS***, **WILIS***.
(Ed.)

tain times of the year, Euphonians are invited to listen to the monstrosities which the rest of the world has admired for centuries and whose defects Euphonians are strongly advised to avoid....

"It is almost impossible for uninvited travellers to enter Euphonia; they are required to have marvellous voices, to play practically every instrument, and to pass personality tests judged very harshly by Euphonian officials. (Hector Berlioz, *Euphonie, ou la ville musicale*, Paris, 1852.)

"FAIRYLAND, a country of changing locations....

"The white marble palace of Fairyland stands on the banks of a river. By night it shimmers softly in the moonlight which is not reflected in the windows.... The library contains books which so absorb the reader that he becomes the traveller in a travel book, the hero in a novel or play; as he reads on, the story becomes his own. Another hall, filled with subdued crimson light, is supported by slender black pillars that intersect against the ceiling, forming a black and white pattern like the skeleton of a leaf. The voice of anyone who is moved to sing here is astonishingly beautiful. Embroidered draperies conceal the entrance to yet another hall with a black ceiling and floor and dark red pillars. Here stand white statues on black pedestals, depicting various positions of a waltz, so that the visitor has the impression that the statues have just stopped dancing. (George Macdonald, *Phantastes*, London, 1858.)

"FUTURA, a kingdom of unknown location. Travellers are advised to visit the temple of the king's daughters, built high on a rock above the sea. The route is somewhat long and progress may be slow. On reaching the rock, the traveller must pass through seven doors, each made of a different metal, corresponding to the seven

planets. An eighth door, made of gold, is reserved for the king alone and must not be opened. The doors are defended by dragons, flames, giants, winged serpents, sirens and a phoenix.[118] (Marie Anne de Roumier Robert, *Les Ondins*, Paris and London, 1768.)

"GRAAL FLIBUSTE, COUNTRY OF THE, of unknown location, bordering Transarcidonia and not far from the famous Chichi Archipelago. The country has no roads, only a few meadow and forest paths.... Certain parts of the country are best avoided, like the Wind province, haunted by boring ghosts....

"In the mountains lives King Gnar, advised by an ancient serpent with dark imaginings. Next to the royal palace, in a black chapel, a solitary organist as crooked as a mandrake root repeats the same musical phrase over and over for the questionable entertainment of travellers. (Robert Pinget, *Graal Flibuste*, Paris, 1956.)

"HARMONIA, a group of colonies or phalanges founded in the mid-nineteenth century. Because its members are sworn to secrecy, the location of Harmonia is unknown, but there is some suspicion of it being located either in a valley near Brussels or in the outskirts of Lausanne.

"Each colony consists of 1,500 to 1,800 members who hold everything in common and who share a large dwelling called a phalanstery, which contains all that is needed for an enjoyable and fruitful life....

"Communitarian life in Harmonia is based on total lack of repression, and full freedom given to all human passions.

"Travellers will find that what is considered civility and good manners in their country is looked upon as abnormal or uncivil in Harmonia. For instance, children who enjoy revelling in dirt are seen as model citizens because they find enjoyment in the city's improper sanitary sys-

---

118 Siren theme — potentially dangerous to travellers. (Ed.)

tem. The children are classified into what is known as Small Orders and rampage around each colony on nimble ponies, dressed up as hussars, to the sound of trumpets, bells and cymbals, and other musical instruments....

"The basis of Harmonian society is the classification of all passions.... Visitors are submitted to a number of tests before being classified and allowed to enter one of the groups of Harmonia. (Charles Fourier, *Théorie des Quatres Mouvements*, Paris, 1808; *Traité de l'Association Domestique Agricole*, Paris, 1822; *Le Nouveau Monde Industriel et Sociétaire*, Paris, 1829; *Le Nouveau Monde Amoureux*, Paris, 1967.)

"HAT PINS, a small village in the west of Rootabaga Country, where all the hat-pins used in the country are made, the majority being sent to the village of Cream Puffs....

The village of Hat Pins is the home of a famous old lady known as Rag Bag Mammy.... Rag Bag Mammy wears aprons with big pockets in which she carries gifts for the boys and girls of the village. Although she never speaks to adults, she is very fond of children, especially those who say 'Gimme', 'Gimme, gimme' and 'Gimme, gimme, gimme.' Sometimes, if she comes across a child who is crying, she produces a doll no bigger than a child's hand that can recite the alphabet and sing little Chinese-Assyrian songs. (Carl Sandburg, *Rootabaga Stories*, New York, 1922.)

"HELIKONDA, one of the Isles of Wisdom, in the north Pacific. Helikonda is devoted to a philosophy acquired from the study of foreign books [which] might be described as 'art for art's sake'....

"All Helikonda's streets radiate from its centers: there are streets of composers, streets of poets, streets of painters and streets of sculptors. The more conservative artists live nearest to the [central] piazza [which is used for concerts and dramatic representations], the more radical and experimental ones live farthest out.

"The government of Helikonda is republican, and the chief officer is a prefect selected from the represenatives of the various arts. The prefect is usually a musician, as musicians outnumber the other arts....

"The art forms of the past are still retained, but largely for educational and historical reasons. Visitors will notice, for instance, that a magnificent performance of Mozart will not be greeted by applause; the music will be analyzed as a petrified vestige from the past, a fossil preserved for centuries. The sole purpose of the performance and the subsequent dissection is to throw into more vivid contrast the art of the present and its superiority to the work of the past. The art of the present includes futurist performances, in which a vioin solo is played by a man hanging by his teeth from a swing, or in which a rider on a galloping horse paints a cubist picture on a stationary canvas.[119]

"Travellers with an interest in the arts will wish to know that the three greatest artists of the moment are Kakordo (a composer famed for his logarithmic symphony and his astounding string quartet on the parallelogram of forces), the poet Dadalabra and the painter and sculptor Patzoka....

"One of the most amazing inventions of Helikonda is the *optophone*, which transmutes any object into its musical equivalent. (Philosophically-minded travellers will recall that, in England, Walter Pater suggested that all artistic objects aspire to become music which is pure form.) It can perform the reverse function as well, giving a visual representation, for instance, of Mendelssohn's *Fingal's Cave*. The perception of both the aural and visual

---

119 This author clearly has *not* had a compellingly absorbing experience of contemporary art! (Ed.)

images, however, requires very highly developed senses and it is unlikely that most visitors will see or hear anything. Musical instruments have largely been replaced by the transcendental tone producer, which can be used to conjure up all possible sounds. The instrument resembles a cross between an organ and a dynamo engine; actually a complex arrangement of telephone diaphragms produce the sound. The one disadvantage of the tone producer is that each performance is unique and can never be repeated.

"The stated ambition of the leading artists of Helikonda is the unification of all the arts into one, to be apprehended via the sense of smell. Kakordo is already working on his odoriferous symphony which, when completed, will render all existing arts superfluous. (Alexander Moszkowski, *Die Inseln der Weisheit*, Berlin, 1922.)

¶"SARRAGALLA, the most highly developed of all the Isles of Wisdom.

"The advanced industrial civilization of Sarragalla is based upon a constant increase in production and upon constant time-saving. The economy has now reached the point where a perfect balance has been achieved between supply and demand and where wage struggles and strikes have disappeared of their own accord. Work has become a source of pleasure rather than an imposition....

"As scientifically minded travellers will know, Sarragallas's industry is based upon the power unleashed by the splitting of the atom with the lambda radioactive particle....

"Basically, Sarragallas's success is due to its ability to transfer energy from non-productive to productive activities, and to its achievements in time-saving. Even language has been abbreviated to save energy: it has all been reduced to telegraphic-style abbreviations.... The same principles have been applied to the arts: plays have been compressed to the length of a sketch, without losing any of their impact. In music, the main achievement has been the abbreviated sonata, which avoids the repetition of phrases, notes and measures that is so characteristic of the old music. The only publication successfully imported from abroad is the *Reader's Digest*.

"IMAGINARY ISLAND, situated neither to the north nor to the south; of moderate climate or, to use the Italian phrase, *in mezzo tempo;* noted for its soft and deilghtful air. This natural paradise lacks a population to benefit from its beauties and riches....

"The fauna of Imaginary Island consists of sea-horses, whales, dolphins, naiads and beautifully singing memraids who live in the lakes and rivers.... Elephants, dromedaries and unicorns are common. In the evenings, the animals gather in the meadows and join the birds and the naiads in song. (Anne Marie Louise Henriette 'Orléans, Duchesse de Montpensier, *Rélation de L'Isle Imaginaire*, Paris, 1659.)

"KIRAN, a city on the banks of the Oukranos River than runs through part of Dreamworld into the Cerenerian Sea. Its jasper terraces slope down to the river's edge and lead to a lovely temple where the King of Ilek-Vad comes from his far realm once a year, in a golden palanquin, to pray to the god of Oukranos. The temple is all of jasper and covers a full acre of ground with its halls and courts, its seven pinnacle towers and its inner shrine where the river enters through hidden channels and where someone is heard singing softly in the night. Travellers have heard strange music as the moon shines on the temple, but no one except the King of Ilek-Vad can say what that music is, for only he is allowed to enter the temple. (Howard Phillips Lovecraft, 'The Dream-Quest of Unknown Kadath', in *Arkham Sampler*, Sauk CIty, 1948.)

"KOSEKIN COUNTRY, a country under Antarctica, described for the first time at the beginning of the nineteenth century, when Adam More of Cumberland visited the area and wrote a chronicle of his voyage, enclosing it in a copper cylinder and throwing it into the sea. His account was found on February 15, 1850, near Tenerife and was subsequently published....

"In Kosekin Country the paupers are the honored and envied class, but the children and aged are also esteemed. If a man and woman love each other, they separate. The sick are objects of the highest regard, especially if they are incurable, because they require constant nursing....

"Kosekin music is sad and haunting, played on square guitars with dozens of strings. [The inhabitants] like Celtic music, brought to them by Adam More, and have adopted songs like 'Auld Lang Syne' and 'The Last Rose of Summer', which they use at their sacrifices. (James DeMille, *A Strange Manuscript Found in a Copper Cylinder*, New York, 1883.)

"LIVING ISLAND, a country inhabited by mythical beasts and talking boats and clocks, cigar-smoking fireplaces and animated musical instruments. The mayor is a friendly dragon called H.R. Pufnstuf.

"Travellers can visit Witchiepoo Castle, once owned by a scientist of the same name, who accidentally blew herself up after an unsuccessful encounter with Jimmy, a small boy whose flute she had tried to steal. (*Pufnstuf*, directed by Hollingsworth Morse, USA, 1970.)

"LOTUS-EATERS ISLAND, set among the rolling waves of the Mediterranean. The coast of yellow sand is blown by a breeze reminiscent of the sighs of a weary dreamer, and the time of day seems to be a kind of eternal afternoon.

"The island is inhabited by natives who feed on the lotus blooms and so obtain oblivion from all mortal cares.... Should the unwary visitor taste of the lotus, all desire to return to his native country will vanish, and he will only be able to go if made to leave by force. Should he decide to share the lotus eaters' repast, he will find that the shore will grow distant, the voices of his companions will seem thin, as if coming from the grave, and although awake he will feel asleep. Stranger still, he will hear the sound of an unknown music and not know that it is his own heart, beating in his ears. (Homer, *The Odyssey*, 9th century (?BC; Alfred, Lord Tennyson, 'The Lotus-Eaters', in *Poems*, London, 1833.)

¶"SIREN ISLAND, in the Mediterranean, exact position unknown. Visitors are not advised to approach it because it is inhabited by a curious species of birds with women's faces, known as the Sirens (though some chroniclers have confused them with Mermaids—and also Mer-King's Kingdom—because their customs are similar, as in the case of the Mermaid Lorelei who lives on a large rock in the River Rhine, Germany). The Sirens attract sailors with their sweet songs. Unaware of the danger, the sailors find themselves shipwrecked on the rocky coast of the island. To avoid this unpleasant fate, travellers can take one of three classic preventive measures: either lash themselves to the ship's mast, fill their ears with wax, or find a lyre virtuoso who can distract them with his music. Legend has it that after being ignored by the King of Ithaca, one of the Sirens, Parthenope, drowned herself in annoyance and was washed ashore in the Bay of Naples, Italy, which originally bore her name.

"A different species of Siren lives in Dublin, Ireland, and takes the form of a sexy barmaid who sings over her Guinness. (Homer; Apollonius of Rhodes, *Argonautica*, 12th cent. BC; Heinrich Heine, 'Die Lorelei', in *Buch der Lieder*, Munich, 1827; James Joyce, *Ulysses*, Paris, 1922.)

"MIDDLE-EARTH lies on the eastern side of the Belegaer, the great sea which separates it from Aman in the north-west of the known world....

"According to the legends of Middle-earth, the world was created by the music of Eru or Ilúvatar, the source of all creation and the mightiest of all beings.[120] He possesses the Imperishable Flame which kindled the Ainur or Holy Ones, the first of his creations. They sang to Eru, at first individually, but eventually in unison and harmony. Eru revealed his magnificent theme to the Ainur, and told them to use their powers to develop ornaments for it. Their singing in response filled the void of the Timeless Halls with the beautiful sound of complex melodies. Discord was introduced into the music by the song of Melkor, greatest of the Ainur, who rebelled and wanted to create themes all of his own imagining. He had already sought the Imperishable Flame in vain and now tried to add his variations to Eru's music. As a result the music developed into two separate themes: one beautiful, grand and slow, the other loud and repetititous. The latter sought to dominate the former but its loud elements were simply incorporated into the swelling theme since no music can be greater than that of Eru, the source of all music. Gradually, the music they had helped create became visible to the Ainur and they saw the world in whose creation they had participated, in the void but not of it. They saw its history and its development as well as many things they had not imagined, such as the children of Ilúvatar, the elves and men conceived by Ilúvatar alone. They were part of the third theme he introduced; his children were not Ainur, but were loved by them as being different and free, and the Ainur desired that elves and men should truly *be,* and not exist only as thought. Melkor however was envious of the gifts promises to elves and men and already sought to subjugate them to his will and to destroy their freedom.

"The desire of the Ainur was so great that Ilúvatar pronounced that he would send the Imperishable Flame into the world and that the world would exist. He pronounced the word 'Eä!' ('Let it be!') and so Eä, the world as it is, came into existence. (J.R.R. Tolkien, *The Hobbit, or There and Back Again,* London, 1937; *The Fellowship of the Ring,* London, 1954; *The Two Towers,* London, 1954; *The Return of the King,* London, 1955; *The Silmarillion,* London, 1977.)

¶"MORIA, the greatest of all dwarf dwellings ever constructed in Middle-earth. Moria, which the dwarves themselves call Khazad-dûm (literally, the Mansion of the Khazad or dwarves), lies deep beneath the Misty Mountains....

"[A war occurred, in which the dwarves lost their old home.] Although they are now scattered about and effectively living in exile, the dwarves still retain their own culture and language. They continue to make musical instruments, including the exquisite golden harps, examples of which were found in Smaug's hoard under the Lonely Mountain, and to sing the songs that tell of their past.

"MOOMINLAND (or MOOMIN VALLEY), on the coast of the Finland, to the south of Daddy Jones' Kingdom....

"The valley takes its name from certain creatures that live here, the *Moomins* or *Moomintrolls* as they are sometimes known, small, white, hibernating animals with large snouts, short tails and smooth, hairless skin. They walk on their hind legs and caommunicate by whistling, because they cannot sing. The *Moomins* are polite, considerate creatures who never forget to whistle 'thank you' and who always greet one another with great courtesy....

"The few *Moomins* who do not hibernate during the winter light bonfires at moonrise on the night before the run returns to Moominland, and dance around the fire carrying torches and beating drums. This delightful tradition goes back over a thousand years. (Tove Jansson, *Muumpeik-*

---

120 Theme of music, dance or sound bringing the world into existence. (Ed.)

ko ja pyrstötähti, Helsinki, 1950, and other works.)

"MUSICAL ISLAND, chiefly noteworthy for its strange flora of archaic instruments which grow in plantations protected by Aeolian bamboo fences: *taroles, ravanstrons,* sambucas, *archilutes,* pandoras, *kins, tchés, turlurettes, magreplas* and *hydraules.* The steam-organ given to Pepin in 775 by Constantine Copronymus is preserved in a greenhouse; it was brought here by St. Corneille of Compiègne. One can still hear its *octavina,* counter-bassoon, *sarrusophone, binious, zampogna,* bagpipe, serpent, *coelophone,* saxhorn and *enclure.* All the plants come into flower when the sonority rises at the summer solstice.

"The atmospheric sonority of the island is controlled by consulting thermometers known as 'sirens'. At the winter solstice, it falls from the sound of the swearing of a cat to the buzzing of a wasp or the droning of a fly.

"The heavens also make music to delight visitors on the island.[121] At night, Saturn rattles a sistrum against its rings; at sunrise and sunset, the sun and moon clash like resounding cymbals.

"The Lord of the Island sits on a throne perfumed with harps, listening to a choir of thrones, dominations and powers singing 'Let us drink both night and day' and 'Let us always be in love'. His own refrain — and habitual way of greeting visitors — is the chant 'Happy the man who enjoys the sound of cymbals on the hill where he dwells; he wakes alone in bed, at peace, and swears that he will never reveal the secret source of his bliss to the vulgar.' (Alfred Jarry, *Gestes et Opinions du Docteur Faustroll, Paraphysicien,* Paris, 1911.)

"MUSICIANS' ISLAND and COMEDIANS' ISLAND, two neighboring islands near Tierra del Fuego. Not much is known about Comedians' Island, but Musicians's Island is known to be very pleasant. No sounds are heard here except the music of songs and instruments. The inhabitants talk in a singsong voice, as if they were speaking Swedish. Their houses and gardens are laid out in a pattern that resembles a sheet of music. The inhabitants of both islands must pay a regular tax to the government of Foollyk, or Poets' Island. (Abbé Pierre François Guyot Desfontaines, *Le nouveau Gulliver,* Paris, 1730.)

"NARNIA, a land that lies between mountain ranges (which separate it from Archenland to the south), and wastes and moorlands (its frontier to the north)....

"The land of Narnia was created — not founded — by Aslan, a great lion from a country beyond the end of the world. Aslan was the son of the Great-Emperor-Beyond-the-Sea, the mysterious and all-powerful overlord of Narnia. The privileged few who have actually seen Aslan have been impressed by his mane and his eyes, and the way in which he combines massive physical strength with great gentleness and wisdom. But most impressive of all is Aslan's wonderful voice, which which he created Narnia by singing, summoning it up out of nothing.[122] Legend has it that the song of creation had no words and hardly any tune, but that it was the most beautiful song ever heard, making stars, constellations and planets appear suddenly out of the darkness. As Aslan sang, the black sky turned grey and then changed from white to pink and from pink to gold, as does the rising sun. The valley of Narnia sprang from nowhere,

---

121 Theme of music of the spheres. (Ed.)
122 Theme of singing, dancing, etc. the world into being. (Ed.)

and as Aslan began to pace up and down, singing a new and more lilting song, grass rose from the earth and quickly clothed the valley and the hills above. Trees began to grow, the song became wilder, the grassy land began to bubble and swell into humps; the swellings became bigger and bigger and finally burst, and an animal emerged from each and every hump, fully formed and active.[123] The newly created creatures immediately went about their natural business: birds sang, bees fed on the pollen of flowers, frogs flopped into the river and panthers and leopards washed themselves and sharpened their claws on the tree trunks. And in the same manner, by the sound of his voice, Aslan created the wild people of the woods — the fauns, the satyrs, and the dwarves. During these first days of creation, everything in Narnia grew spontaneously; a piece of metal quickly grew into a lamp post, gold and silver coins into gold and silver trees....

"One of the most intriguing customs of Narnia is the annual Great Snow Dance, held on the first moonlit night when there is snow on the ground. The fauna and dryads perform a complex dance, surrounded by a ring of dwarves, all dressed in their best scarlet clothes with fur hoods and furry top-boots, who throw snowballs in time to the music. If all the dancers are perfectly in position, no one is hit. This is, however, a game as well as a dance, and from time to time, a dancer will get slight-ly out of step and will be hit by a snowball, much to the amusement of all concerned. A good team of dancers, musicians and dwarves can, if they wish, continue for hours without anyone ever being hit.

"The forest dwellers are also fond of mid-night dances, when the nymphs from the wells and the dryads from the trees join the fauns in their revels....

"The ceremonies of Cair Paravel [a castle which originally stood on a small hill rising from a plain between two streams, which erosion has turned into a small island] are noted for their splendor. Supper in the castle illustrates admirably the glory and courtesy of the Narnians at home in their own land. The Great Hall is decked with banners hanging from the roof; each course is ushered in to the loud sound of trumpets and kettledrums. After the meal, which consists of a bewildering variety of dishes and refreshments, the evening is spent in listening to poetry and story-telling.[124] (C.S. Lewis, *The Lion, the Witch and the Wardrobe*, London, 1950; *Prince Caspian*, London, 1951; *The Voyage of the 'Dawn Treader'*, London, 1952; *The Silver Chair*, London, 1953; *The Horse and His Boy*, London, 1954; *The Magician's Nephew*, London, 1955; *The Last Battle*, London, 1956.)

"OKLAHOMA, NATURE THEATER OF, in the United States. Not much is known of what takes place in the Theater. Members are engaged by means of a placard that an-

---

123   Interestingly, this account has the style of primitive creation stories such as are found in North American Indian, African and Australian Aboriginal mythologies. (Ed.)

124   Trumpets and kettledrums seem not only to serve the purpose of literally heralding the arrival of food, but, in so doing, to bring attention to the fact that, as evidenced by this very having of food, "civilization" has won out over "nature". Equally it could be said that the blowing on trumpets, and beating on drums, has the effect of thanking certain "powers" for having rewarded those who have thus employed the arts of civilization (through agriculture, for example), with this gift of food. (Ed.)

nounces that the theater can find employment for everyone. Applicants are asked to present themselves at a given racecourse (for instance, Clayton Racecourse in New York State) from six in the morning until midnight.

"Upon reaching the racecourse, applicants will be greated by a confused blare of trumpets; these seem to be blown regardless of each other, confirming that the Theater of Oklahoma is a great undertaking—only small enterprises can afford to be organized.[125]

"At the entrance of the racecourse a long low platform is set up, supporting hundreds of women dressed as angels in white robes and great wings, blowing on long trumpets that glitter like gold. THe women are actually standing on separate pedestals, but these cannot be seen since they are completely hidden by the long flowing draperies.... Toa void monotony, the pedastals are of all sizes: some of the women are quite low, others soar to such a height that visitors will feel that the slightest gust of wind could capsize them. Two hours after they have started, the women are relieved by men dressed as devils, half of them blowing trumpets as

poorly as the women, half beating drums. (Franz Kafka, *Amerika*, Munich, 1927.)

"ORACLE OF THE BOTTLE, ISLAND OF THE: see ENTELECHY

"PARADISE ISLAND, in the south Pacific, so called because of its agreeable qualities. A mountain range divides the island in two. On one side lies the inhabited area, colonized by a group of Europeans who were shipwrecked here at the beginning of the sixteenth century. On the other side live the natives—brown-skinned, tall, and well-proportioned. They hold everything but their wives in common and therefore have little cause for contention.

"European visitors are considered physically and morally inferior. For fear that they may contaminate the natives, they are put into quarantine for five months and made to bathe regularly in a forest pool.

"The natives are very fond of music, both vocal and instrumental. Even the birds join in the singing and have, through force of repetition, learned the words of the songs. A harmless kind of lion, with a huge head and mane, roams the island annd is trained like a dog.[126] (Ambrose Evans [?], *The Adventures, and Surpizing Deliverances,*

---

125 The discordancy or lack of harmony also could be said to symbolize, in the world of Kafka, either lack of harmony or failure to attain the "salvation" of being in harmony with e.g. the "universe" itself. What seems to be at work is a sort of *anti*-Harmony of the Spheres. (Ed.)

126 Theme of music identified with conceptions of paradise. It may also be observed that, just as music is sometimes identified with "civilization", in contradistinction to "nature" over which man is thought to earn some victory, it is also sometimes the case that music appears to be identified, not with "civilized" man, but with those who continue to live in a more "natural" state, i.e. with those who remain "uncorrupted" by—precisely—civilization (who in this sense inhabit "paradise"). On one level this appears to be a contradiction; however, perhaps it is not. Perhaps a truly "civilized" person is one who has learned to live—not in opposition to nature (for all his "victory" over forces which resist the impositions of civilization)—but, in harmony with it. In sum an apparent contradiction is resolved, and consistency is restored, if music is identified with (or as) harmony *of, within, and with respect to* nature. (Ed.)

of James Dubourdieu, and His Wife, London, 1719.)

"PEPPERLAND, a country eighteen thousand leagues beneath the Sea of Green, approached through the Sea of Holes. Travellers will immediately notice that the keynote of Pepperland is color; features of the landscape include hills of all colors, thick forests of painted trees where many-hued birds and butterflies abound, and rolling parkland. The inhabitants dress in bright colors and rainbows are frequent. There are no towns or cities in Pepperland, indeed few buildings of any sort; social life centers around the bandstand, for all Pepperlanders are players and lovers of music.

"Pepperland was originally colonized, four scores and thirty-two bars ago, by Sgt. Pepper and his Lonely Hearts Club Band, who arrived in a yellow submarine (which can be seen today set on top of a pyramid). The present ruler (called 'The Leader') is the Lord Mayor, a musician and conductor; he is assisted by Young Fred, a valiant Pepperlander.

"[When Pepperland was threatened by the Blue Meanies, who meant to turn it and its inhabitants blue and grey,] Young Fred was dispatched in the yellow submarine to Liverpool, England, to persuade a group of four musicians, known with nostalgic affection as The Beatles, to return to Pepperland. The Blue Meanies, overcome by the Beatles' music, were driven off to Argentina, and Pepperland was restored to its colorful self.[127] (*Yellow Submarine* directed by George Dunning, UK, 1968.)

"PERI KINGDOM, a deep valley in Persia surrounded by ice-capped mountains, but warm and fertile. Villas and gardens can be seen around the lake that lies at its center. There is one island in the lake, the abode of Queen Pehlevi. Although a representative of the most ancient race in all El-findom, the queen lives in a comparatively modest pavilion surrounded by flowering trees: quince, lilac, laburnum and magnolia....

"The queen is a plump Peri, white-skinned and with her face farded with white lead. She wears no ornaments except a diamond belly-jewel. Her crown is a tall cylindrical hat of black gauze stretched over a frame of whale-bone. Normally she dresses in a diaphonous white robe that floats over her breasts, belly and thighs like a thin veil. She lives surrounded by a large number of cats, and her main interests are chess and music—she is an accomplished player of the oboe and a considerable chess player. She is, however, intent only upon winning and is not above cheating if necessary; it is not advisable to beat her. (Sylvia Townsend Warner, *Kingdoms of Elfin,* London, 1972.)

¶"ASH GROVE, CASTLE, an ancient Elfin realm in a valley beneath Mynnydd Prescelly, the most westerly mountain in Wales.... The Elfins of Castle Ash Grove are famed for the matchless mead they brew and for their great traditions of singing. They are good neighbors and are usually tolerant of cows and human children who stray into their realm, contenting themselves with watching them from their trees.

"The greatest achievement of the inhabitants of this small thatched castle has been to make the mountain above their valley appear and disappear; sometimes it is there, and sometimes it is not....

"The Queens of Castle Ash Grove have always been called Morgan and their line includes the notorious Morgan le Fay. Perhaps the most famous singer ever produced by the kingdom was Morgan Breastknot of Music. Her successor was Morgan Spider, so-called because of her skill in spinning, under whose reign the Elfins adopted the custom of disguising

---

127 Themes of music as restorative, dispeller of evil spirits; association of music with idea of paradise or utopian state or realm. (Ed.)

themselves as mortals and going to Worcester to listen to organ recitals in the cathedral and, later, attending the Three Choirs Festival in that city.

"PONUKÉLE-DRELCHKAFF, a vast African empire bounded in the northwest by Dahomey, in the north by the Baoutchi Massif and in the south probably by the Congo River.... The empire is divided into two very different sections by the Tez River, at the mouth of which rises the capital, Ejur. To the north of Tez is the Ponukéle region; to the south Drelchkaff....

"The fauna of Ponukéle-Drelchkaff comprises a number of curious specimens, for instance a large carrion-eating bird with powerful wings, large feet like those of the wader, and round orifices on the beak. A squirrel-like rodent with a small black mane will draw the visitor's attention; the hairs of this mane emit two musical notes of equal sonority. In the heavy-water stream lives a corpulent and inoffensive worm, endowed with a musical sensitivity; to bring it to the surface visitors should play a soft tune on the banks and it will appear at once to listen to the music. In the sea off the coast live certain animals that have not yet been fully studied. They resemble flags, curtains, soap, plates of zinc, blocks of jelly and several other objects. In underwater caves live sponges that have the shape and the function of the human heart. (Raymond Roussel, *Impressions d'Afrique*, Paris, 1910; *L'Afrique des impressions*, Paris, 1967.

"PRESENT LAND, near the South Pole, first sighted by Mr. Arthur Gordon Pym of Nantucket in 1828 and further explored in 1928 by the French adventurer Adam Harcz. It can be reached by plane from Enderby Land....

"The natives are androgynous humanoids, semi-transparent, as though made from white jade. With the exception of the thumb, their fingers are webbed with an almost transparent membrane like the fins of a Japanese fish. They have large eyes, their heads are covered with soft, short hair, their teeth and nails are like mother of pearl, they have very slender hands and feet and well-muscled bodies. Their gestures are graceful and gentle and their favorite pastime is to swim and play in the pools. They produce no bodily secretions and have no needs; they never sleep and they live on air. They communicate in a soft musical language and they seem to have none of the vices known to men.[128] (Edgar Allan Poe, *The Narrative of Arthur Gordon Pym of Nantucket*, New York, 1838; Dominque André, *Conquête de l'Eternel*, Paris, 1947.)

"RAMPOLE ISLAND, in the South Atlantic; the nearest port is probably Bahia Blanca, Argentina. The island is fertile and rich in vegetation, but only two areas are inhabited. The best-known settlement is a village in a narrow gorge on the coast, a straggling collection of huts, each surrounded by a palisade of thorns. The gorge is about three miles long and never more than one hundred yards wide. Cascades at the landward end mark the frontier between this settlement and the next, which stands in a broader river valley beyond a bluff....

"The people of the gorge are cannibals. Their skin is a dusky buff color, their dark hair drawn tightly back. They wear tattoos and anoint their bodies with a rancid oil. Although a naturally sturdy people, they suffer from a wide variety of illnesses and infections, probably because of the filthy conditions in which they live....

"[These] people have a certain amount of trade with the tribe that lives farther inland; dried fish, oyster shells and shark skins are left on a series of flat stones by

---

128 Music as a secret "mystical" language or means of communication, potentially suitable as a means of addressing some divinity in places of worship. (Ed.)

the cascades in exchange for primitive pots, pieces of hardwood, fruit and a type of nut. Although there is a degree of mutual understanding, relations between the tribes are often hostile and sometimes erupt into warfare, usually over complaints about trade. When war breaks out everything in the village is painted red, and hysterical dancing takes place.[129] All the young men are initiated as warriors by having their ears clipped and then are tortured by their elders to harden them for battle. (H.G. Wells, *Mr. Blettsworthy on Rampole Island*, London, 1933.)

"RINGING ISLAND: see ENTELECHY

"ROMANCIA, a walled kingdom extending from the Troximania Mountains to the coast. There are various routes of access, all relatively easy, as passports and letters of privilege are never examined closely; by land via a subterranean passage entered through a cave in the mountains, descending directly from the moon or from the stars, or by sea. All the visitor has to do is set out and keep going until he arrives in Romancia. The wall around the kingdom has several gates; legend has it that travellers who enter by the Gate of Love leave by the Gate of Marriage....

"Woods of love, planted with myrtles, palms, orange trees and ground cover of roses and violets, enhanced with the songs of birds, are scattered throughout the land for the convenience of lovers; but woods of jealousy, quarrels and false declarations also exist. Musically inclined trees, eternally green, are the home of dryads and fauns, while flowers such as the lotus and moly are plentiful and spring from the footsteps of beautiful women, who create gardens wherever they walk.[130]

"The fauna of Romancia include talking lions, tigers and bears; flying horses and unicorns are common... *Hirocecervi* and chimeras are kept in menageries near a pit of fire filled with salamanders; a pleasant pool of water serves as a prison for sirens who have debauched heroes with their singing. (Giullaume H. Bougeant, *Voyages Merveilleux du Prince Fan-Férédin dans la Romancie*, Paris, 1735.)

"ROMAN STATE lies beneath Northern England, around a subterranean sea at least three hundred miles wide. Settlements are scattered along the western shore, or wherever fresh water can be found....

"The settlements and cities contain no houses in the accepted sense of the word, but simply enclosures surrounded by hedges and furnished with benches. The only substantial buildings are the bathhouses, which are walled but roofless....

"The Roman State is based upon the total submission of the individual to the State, a system which appears to have arisen from the people's fear of the surrounding darkness.... The majority of people have no volition other than that granted to them by the State which is controlled by the all-powerful Masters of Knowledge who can be recognized by their powerful hypnotic stare. The educational system is designed to produce this condition in the masses. The task of teachers is to destroy the vitality and intellectual curiosity of children, using low-pitched music and rhythmic dancing to produce an hypnotic state in which the individual will can be destroyed.[131] (Joseph O'Neill, *Land Under England*, London, 1935.)

"SARRAGALLA: see HELIKONDA

---

129 Theme of hysterical or frenzied dancing; dancing associated with frenzied or ecstatic state. (Ed.)

130 Association of music with utopian or paradisiacal realms or states of being. (Ed.)

131 Dark side of music as promoting state of ecstasy; theme of music as instrument for gaining control over beasts and men. (Ed.)

"SELENE, a vampire city north-north-west of Belgrade, Yugoslavia, formerly in Hungary. It can be reached from Semlin (today Zemun), either by horse or on foot, following the old Austro-Hungarian military road along the Danube, leading to Peterswarden (or Petervaradin). Certain equipment must be assembled in Zemun before the journey: a bag of coal; a small burner; a few flasks of smelling-salts and candles. A Magyar surgeon and a sharp iron stake are also necessary. It is best to leave Zemun towards ten in the morning.

"Some three-quarters of a mile along the road, the landscape changes abruptly. The oleander, the ferns and even the wheat start to fade. The ground, at first green and soft, becomes dull and dark as if a rain of ashes had fallen upon it. The sky turns grey and a melancholic cloud covers the sun. The traveller will feel weak in the knees, a dizziness in the head and a mysterious weight on his chest. Suddenly darkness surrounds him. A distant bell tolls twenty-three times. The darkness fades and Selene appears.

"The traveller will suddenly find himself in the very center of the city, in front of a large circular palace built in several different architectural styles.... The whole is a dazzling succession of columns large and small, of pinnacles, spires, abaci, epistyles and architraves, each part building up to a central pyramid shape, very like a pagoda. Upon one of the columns stands the statue of a tiger clawing at the heart of a terrified girl.....

"A crystal bell tolls the first of the twenty-four chimes in the last hour of the vampire day. The traveller should then run for his life. From all the doors [in the palace] will appear tall men, somewhat effeminate, and thin, pale women with yellowish eyes and dark lips. A blackbird will rise from the flames that have sprouted on top of the pagoda-like building and sing. A far-off drum will start to beat and the bell to toll again. The vampires will try to lay their hands on the traveller who, without fear, must sprinkle them with vampire's heart-ash; the vampires will then explode in a bluish flash. (Paul Féval, *Le Ville vampire*, Paris, 1875.)

"SIREN ISLAND: see LOTUS-EATERS IS-LAND.

"SOUND, VALLEY OF, north of Sight Forest in Wisdom Kingdom. The valley is ruled by the Soundkeeper, who lives in a stone fortress and has been appointed guardian of all sounds by the old King of Wisdom. For years she ruled wisely, releasing the day's sounds at daybreak and gathering in the old sounds at moonset to be filed in vaults (open to the public on Mondays). As the population increased, there was less and less time to listen and many sounds began to disappear, while the sounds made by people became uglier and uglier. A certain Kakofonous A. Dischord Doctor of Dissonance (the 'A' stands for 'As loud as possible') and his assistant, Dynne, appeared and promised to cure everyone of everything. Much to the annoyance of the Soundkeeper he cured them of everything but noise; in consequence, the Soundkeeper abolished sound in the valley. The result was thunderstorms without thunder and concerts without music. Some necessary sounds were ground three times into powder and then thrown into the air when needed. Music was woven into looms and the people could purchase carpets of symphonies and tapestries of concertos. However, travellers will be relieved to know that nowadays the usual sounds are again available. (Norton Juster, *The Phantom Tollbooth*, London, 1962.)

"SYMZONIA, an underground realm discovered in 1820 by the Antarctic expedition under the command of Captain Seabourn, who managed to penetrate the southern ices, thereby confirming the theory of concentric spheres. This theory had been put forward in 1818 by John Cleves Symmes, who with his colleague James McBride later published *Symmes' Theory of Concentric Spheres* in 1826.

"According to their theory, the earth is formed by a series of spheres like Chinese boxes or nesting Russian dolls, There are five such spheres, each separated from the others by a stratum of atmosphere and each inhabited on its surface. These five concentric bodies are connected by a gigantic tunnel which is entered via either the North Pole or the South Pole. Both apertures take in the waters of the oceans and any ship can enter them with ease....

"In Symzonia [named by Captain Seabourn for the brilliant theoretician Symmes] everything is as white as snow. The inhabitants have white skins and dress in white and communicate through a musical language. They live happily and despise all material riches. Thanks to their intelligence they have managed to illuminate their realm by refracting the sunlight and moonlight that penetrates through both polar apertures, using a system of mirrors. Visitors are not made particularly welcome.[132] (Captain Adam Seabourn, *Symzonia, A Voyage of Discovery*, New York, 1820.)

"TARTARUS, a gloomy region south of Lillar. Travellers can reach it after crossing the ruins of a castle and an orchard of sawn-down trees. A desolate waste leads to a black wall crowned with plaster heads. Behind the wall rises a tower with blind windows. Though the road runs around the wall without coming to a gate, entrance can be gained by treading on a certain stone that causes part of the wall to give way.

"Inside flows a dark river, on the banks of which grows a tangled wood.... A Moravian chruchyard, with a flowerless garden shadowed by weeping birches, can be seen beyond the wood. A stone staircase leads to damp catacombs in the walls of which a nun was immured....

"From here on the path is guarded by a skeleton with an Aeolian harp and travellers are not advised to attempt to explore any further. (Jean Paul [Johann Paul Friedrich Richter], *Titan* Berlin, 1800-03.)

"THERMOMETER ISLAND, somewhere in the Atlantic Ocean, so called because the laws of the country allow couples to sleep with each other only if the sexes of both husband and wife, measured with special thermometers, have reached the same temperature....

"The islanders are born with the visible signs of their vocation: in this way each one is what he should be. Those destined to the science of geometry are born with fingers in the former of a compass; someone who is to be an astronomer is born with eyes in the form of telescopes; geographers are born with heads like terrestrial globes; musicians with hornlike ears; hydraulic engineers with testicles like water pumps and they are capable from an early age of urinating in long jets. (Denis Diderot, *Les Bijoux indiscrets*, Paris, 1748.)

"TROLL KINGDOM, in the Dovre Fjell Mountains of central Norway. The area is the home of a wide variety of trolls, brownies and goblins. Probably the most bizarre inhabitant of the kingdom is the Great Boyg, a monstrous invisible troll without shape or form. The only tangible sign of its existence is the slime that appears around it and a general smell of mustiness it secretes. The Great Boyg does not fight, but triumphs over its enemies through gentleness, and dwindles away to nothingness at the sound of church bells.[133] Pig-headed trolls wearing white

---

132 Music as secret "mystical" language or means of communication (potentially suitable as means of addressing some divinity in a temple, or other place of worship); association of music with idea of paradise or utopian state or realm. (Ed.)

133 Theme of music (church bells) as dispeller of (protection against) evil or malignant spirits. (Ed.)

night-caps are quite common. Two-headed trolls are now rare and the three-headed variety would appear to be extinct.

"Though trolls see everything as it really is, travellers with normal sight will notice that in Troll Kingdom everything seems to have a double shape or quality. For example, travellers may see a beautiful harp-maiden as a cow strumming with its hoof on a string of gut, and the dance-maiden as a sow in short stockings, trying to dance but never succeeding. Everything appears simultaneously black and white, ugly and beautiful. The Troll king who formerly ruled the kingdom once offered to scratch out the left eye of a visitor, so that he would see everything perfectly and thereby become a real troll. (Henrik Ibsen, *Peer Gynt*, Kristiania, 1867.)" — Manguel & Guadalupi, pp.14, 16, 22, 34-35, 38, 41-42, 57, 61-62, 73-74, 80, 82, 85, 105, 112-13, 115, 117-20, 123, 138, 151, 161, 163, 177, 197, 201, 215, 219, 222, 241, 249, 251, 253-54, 256, 258, 260, 275-76, 278-79, 291, 299, 309, 311, 322, 327, 331-32, 343, 346-47, 354, 358, 366, 369, 373, 379-80, 429.

MUSICAL SETTINGS OF MYTHOLOGICAL THEMES.

(See also p.574.)

§268.1 (Addendum)
ADAM, ADOLPH & de SAINT-JULIEN: *La filleule des fées [The fairies' god-child]* (ballet, 1849) [Black Fairy, Pink Fairy, spirits, White Fairy]

ASAFIEV, B.V.: *Christmas Eve* (ballet, 1938) [the Devil, evil spirits, witches]

ATTERBERG, KURT: *Les vierges folles* (ballet-pantomime, 1920) [2 angels]

BAJETTI, N.: see PANIZZA, ETTORE

BEETHOVEN, LUDWIG VAN: *The Seventh Symphony* (choreographic symphony, 1938; bk. & choreogr. Leonide Massine) [the Gods, spirit of Creation]

BERNIERS, LORD: *The Triumph of Neptune* (ballet, 1926) [fairy queen, goddess, sylphs]

BOWLES, PAUL: *Pastorela* (opera-ballet, 1941; orch. by Blas Galindo) [Archangel St. Michael, Archangel Lucifer, 3 devils (Belzebu, Pecado, Satanaz)]

BRITTEN, BENJAMIN: *Noye's Fludde (The Chester Miracle Play)* (1958)[voice of God]

COHEN, F.A.: *A Spring Tale* (ballet, 1939) [leaf-maidens, storm witches, tree sprite, wood-witches]

COSTA, MICHAEL: see PANIZZA, ETTORE

FINE, VIVIAN: *Alcestis* (ballet, 1960)

GADE: see PAULLI, E. HELSTED

HERTEL: *Flik and Flok* (ballet, 1862) [Amphitrite, king of the gnomes & his daughter, sea-nymph, spirits]

MAHLER, GUSTAV: *Symphony 8* (1910) [angels]

MANZOTTI, LUIGI: *Amor* (ballet, 1886) [Love]

MEDINS, JĀNIS: *Le triomphe de l'amour* (ballet, 1935) [the Spirit of Evil]

MÉTRA, OLIVIER: *Yedda* (ballet, 1879) [spirits of the Night (Japan)]

PANIZZA, ETTORE; COSTA, MICHAEL; & BAJETTI, N.: *Faust* (ballet, 1848) [angels, Bambo (Queen of the Demons), evil spirits, Mephistopheles, spirits of the air]

PAULLI, E. HELSTED & GADE: *Napoli, or the fisherman and his bride* (ballet, 1842) [Golfo (sea-sprite), naiads (Argentina, Coralla)]

PUGNI, CESARE: *Coralia or the Inconstant Knight* (ballet, 1847) [Troisondin (King of the Waters) & his daughter Coralia]

----: *Fiorita et la reine des Elfrides* (ballet, 1848) [Hertha (Queen of the Elfrits or Evil Elves)]

RACHMANINOFF, SERGE: *Paganini* (ballet, 1939; bk. SR & Michel Fokine; choreogr. Fokine) [divine spirits, evil spirits, ghosts, Satan]

de SAINT-JEAN: see ADAM, ADOLPHE

SCHUBERT, FRANZ: *Labyrinth* (ballet after FS *Symphony 7*, 1941; bk. Salvador Dali, choreogr. Leonide Massine) [Castor, 3 Fates, Pollux, Theseus]

STARER, ROBERT: *Phaedra* (ballet, 1962)

WAGNER, RICHARD: *Bacchanale* (ballet, 1939; bk. Salvador Dali, choreogr. Leonide Massine) (cupids, fauns, the 3 Graces, nymphs, satyrs, Venus]

OCEANIA (MYTHS OF) — PRACTICES AND BELIEFS. *(See p. 1272.)*

§278A.1 See ABORIGINAL (AUSTRALIAN) PRACTICES AND BELIEFS*.
HAWAIIAN MYTHS*.
MAORI PRACTICES AND BELIEFS*.

§278A.2 "DARAMULUN (Australian sky god). The one-legged Daramulun had many aliases, and many versions of his adventures are extant. During ceremonies, men swung bull-roarers* to imitate the sound of his voice. Bull-roarers don't sound much like bulls; the noise they make is a deep, rather eerie buzz.[134] Models of Daramulun show him with his mouth filled with quartz and with an exaggerated phallus. Sometimes he carries a stone axe, a suitable thunder weapon for a sky god.-" — Carlyon, p.348.

"KUNAPIPI-KALWADI-KADJARA (An Australian ogress). Kunapipi used her daughters to ensnare young men whom she killed and consumed. She regurgitated them, but only bones appeared which meant they could not be revived. Regurgitation is usually a symbolic rebirth.

"The mass disappearances became a problem, so Eaglehawk (*Yalungur*) went out to investigate.[135] He caught Kunapipi and killed her. Kunapipi's dying shout entered every tree. Eaglehawk made a bull-roarer* and swung it, giving her back her shout in the sound 'Mumuna'; this became her secret name.

"In another myth Kunapipi was entrusted with nine children by some foolish person. She delightedly swallowed all nine whole and ran away. The men went out to search for her along the river bank. A certain murkiness in the water showed that she was there; then they saw her huge black eyes break the surface of the water. The man called Lefthand speared her legs, and the man called Righthand broke her neck with his club. Kunapipi was still alive when they dragged her on land; but they killed her, cut her open, and recovered the children.

"These stories are background to a revivication ceremony. Young men, trembling with fear, are taken to the ceremonial ground. They really believe that the Old Woman Kunapipi will swallow them up. They hear her voice, the bull-roarer, and are smeared with blood. After a symbolic swallowing they re-emerge and take their places in society as adults. [See also *Wawalug*, below.] " — Carlyon, p.359.

"NEVINBIMBAAU (A terrible Melanesian ogress, connected with *Ambat*, Melanesian hero-god who taught men pottery and ritual). During the initiation ceremonies of Nevinbimbaau's cult her voice could be heard in the bull-roarers*. Part of the ritual consisted of a sort of puppet show which included the ceremonial creation and sacrifice of Nevinbimbaau's son-in-law and two wives." — Carlyon, p.367.

---

134 It is even questionable that they can be called musical instruments. However, throughout the present volume, they are. (Ed.)

135 "Yalungur: also called Warana; a totem ancestor of Australia. Yalungur figures in several stories about the Dreamtime *(Ungud)*, that mythical era in which the primal beings shaped the earth and created the rituals that men inherited with it. He created female sexuality." — Carlyon, pp.386-87.

"TILITR (God of song on Ifaluk). Tilitr enters men and women, causing them to compose songs. In other parts of Oceania men go fishing for new songs. They throw their lines into the sea, and when they feel it moving they are inspired to chant the music." — Carlyon, p.379.

"WAWALUG (A pair of fertility goddesses of North Australia).[136] The Wawalug arrived from the south and were guilty, it was said, of incest. One had a child and the other was pregnant, soon giving birth to a baby girl. In error they set up their camp by a waterhole sacred to Yurlunggur, the *Great Rainbow Snake* [the life-giver; in the Dreamtime he shaped the waterways of the land, and regenerated the earth and all living things, including man].... One of the Wawalug then unwittingly profaned the waterhole with blood. The pool welled up into flood; rain cascaded down and the great snake of water advanced on them. The Wawalug kept the flood away by singing and dancing, but after many hours of this, and utterly exhausted, they fell asleep. [Together with their two children, the two sisters are swallowed and later regurgitated by the Great Rainbow Snake.] The Great Snake then swallowed and regurgitated the Wawalug several times, each time marking out a new sacred spot for future ceremonies.

"These ceremonies dramatize the acts of swallowing and regurgitation which symbolize the rebirth of children into adults. The Great Snake is linked to the Great Mother, whose voice is heard in the bull-roarer* and whose name is 'Mumuna'. [See also *Kunapipi*, above.]" — Carlyon, pp.385-86.

ROMAN PRACTICES AND BELIEFS.

§338A.1 See index (under "Rome").

§338A.2 "LEMURES (Ghosts of the dead). The Lemures returned to wreak mischief and terror among the living. The ghost of Remus returned, not unreasonably, to complain about having been murdered, so Romulus instituted a festival in his honor to pacify him. It was called the Remuria, later corrupted to Lemuria.

"The festival rites were performed by the father of each household. Barefooted, at midnight, he would snap his fingers, wash his hands, and fill his mouth with black beans. He would then toss the beans over his shoulder while chanting a banishing spell. After more ritual hand-washing, he would strike a brass gong* and command the spirits to depart." — Carlyon, p.191.

RUHA D'QUDSHA (Middle Eastern/Gnostic).

§341A.1 "Chief demonic goddess of the Mandean Gnostics. Ruha D'Qudsha was entirely evil. She gave birth to the planets and with their help set out to ensnare and degrade mankind, using sexual love and alcohol as her main weapons. Other forms of sensuality were also used; she is described as trying to entrap Adam with 'embracing', and with 'horns and flutes'. Gnosticism abhorred sexuality and all forms of sensual pleasure. Its aggressive, nearly paranoid, proto-Puritanism was allied with a cynical attitude of blasphemy,

---

136 See also **ABORIGINAL (AUSTRALIAN) PRACTICES AND BELIEFS***, pp.10 and 16, above. (Ed.)

for Ruha D'Qudsha really means 'holy spirit.' "[137] — Carlyon, p.342.

SLAVIC MYTHS AND LEGENDS. *(See also p.725.)*

§369.4 "YARILO (God of love). His name is derived from a word with the meaning 'passionate' or 'uncontrolled'. Yarilo, god of human generative power, is connected to spring-sown corn, for in summer there were funerary rites celebrating his death, or harvest. Those who have perused *The Golden Bough* will instantly recognize the threnody, the women intoxicated with sorrow loudly bewailing the death of the beautiful young god, symbolized among the Slavs by an effigy made of the new straw.[138] The cult of Yarilo caused the Orthodox Church no end of worry; it was too deeply rooted in the Slav consciousness to be easily ignored, a powerful expression of their sexuality. In spring the most beautiful girl of the village would play the part of Yarilo. She would be dressed in white and adorned with flowers; where possible she would be mounted on a white horse. Her accompanying handmaidens would wear flowers and dance over the newly sown fields, singing traditional chants about the fertile powers of the god.[139] Yarilo himself is described as being young, handsome, and dressed in white, He carries flowers and sheaves of corn, rides on a white horse and is always barefoot." — Carlyon, p.255.

TANNHÄUSER AND VENUS (Medieval German).[140]

§384A.1 "A French knight was riding over the beauteous meadows in the Hörsel vale on his way to Wartburg, where the Landgrave Hermann was holding a gathering of minstrels who were to contend in song for a prize.

"Tannhäuser was a famous minnesinger, and all his lays were of love and of women, for his heart was full of passion, and that

---

137 Here negatively — in other cultures positively, as celebration and commitment to rebirth and renewal of life — music is again identified with sensuality, sexuality, procreation. (Ed.)

138 Reference possibly to Adonis (Tammuz), regarded as a corn-spirit. Frazer mentions, for example, the Syrian festival of el-Bûgat, festival of the weeping women or Tâ-uz festival celebrated in honor of the god Tâ-uz (Tammuz). "The women bewail him, because his lord slew him so cruelly, ground his bones in a mill, and then scattered them to the wind. The women (during this festival) eat nothing which has been ground in a mill, but limit their diet to steeped wheat, sweet vetches, dates, raisins and the like." — 10th-century Arabic writer, quoted in Frazer 1-vol ed. p.393. One is also reminded of Greek Maenads, associated with Dionysus, a god of agriculture in general and of corn in particular. (Ed.)

139 Brief as it is, this reference to singing and dancing is nevertheless very important as it is central to the whole rite of communicating with those forces in nature on which one's prosperity depends. The Orthodox Church may have been troubled by the cult of Yarilo because of its obviously "pagan", i.e. non-Christian associations, however it is to be remarked that the custom of celebrating Christ's death and resurrection, itself, can be interpreted with respect to universal themes of agricultural (and other) periodicity. (Ed.)

140 Classic tale of sacred *vs.* profane love — each of which has its own musical associations. In this story being a musician is, itself, something of a metaphor for being a pilgrim, by whom there are choices to be made. (Ed.)

not of the purest and noblest description.

"It was toward dusk that he passed the cliff in which is the Hörselloch, and as he rode by, he saw a white glimmering figure of matchless beauty standing before him, and beckoning him to her. He knew her at once by her attributes and by her superhuman perfection to be none other than Venus. As she spoke to him, the sweetest strains of music floated in the air, a soft roseate light glowed around her, and nymphs of exquisite loveliness scattered roses at her feet. A thrill of passion ran through the veins of the minnesinger; and, leaving his horse, he followed the apparition. It led him up the mountain to the cave, and as it went flowers bloomed upon the soil, and a radiant track was left for Tannhäuser to follow. He entered the cavern and descended to the palace of Venus in the heart of the mountain.

"Seven years of revelry and debauch were passed, and the minstrel's heart began to feel a strange void. The beauty, the magnificence, the variety of the scenes in the pagan goddess's home, and all its heathenish pleasures palled upon him, and he yearned for the pure fresh breezes of earth, one look up at the dark night sky spangled with stars, one glimpse of simple mountain flowers, one tinkle of sheep bells. At the same time his conscience began to reproach him, and he longed to make his peace with God. In vain did he entreat Venus to permit him to depart, and it was only when, in the bitterness of his grief, he called upon the Virgin Mother, that a rift in the mountain side appeared to him, and he stood again above ground.

"How sweet was the morning air, balmy with the scent of hay, as it rolled up the mountain to him and fanned his haggard cheek! How delightful to him was the cushion of moss and scanty grass after the downy couches of the palace of revelry below! He plucked the little heather bells and held them before him; the tears rolled from his eyes and moistened his thin and wasted hands. He looked up at the soft blue sky and the newly risen sun, and his heart overflowed. What were the golden, jewel-incrusted, lamp-lit vaults beneath to that pure dome of God's buildings?

"The chime of a village church struck sweetly on his ear, satiated with Bacchanalian songs; and he hurried down the mountain to the church which called him. There he made his confession; but the priest, horror-struck at his recital, dared not give him absolution, but passed him on to another. And so he went from one to another till at last he was referred to the pope himself. To the pope he went. Urban IV (1261-4) then occupied the chair of St. Peter. To him Tannhäuser related the sickening story of his guilt and prayed for absolution. Urban was a hard and stern man, and shocked at the immensity of the sin, he thrust the penitent indignantly from him, exclaiming, 'Guilt such as thine can never, never be remitted. Sooner shall this staff in my hand grow green and blossom than that God should pardon thee!'

"Then Tannhäuser, full of despair, and with his soul darkened, went away, and returned to the only asylum open to him, the Venusberg [mo[43]ut lo! three days after he had gone, Urban discovered that his pastoral staff had put forth buds, and has burst into flower. Then he sent messengers after Tannhäuser, and they reached the Hörsel vale to hear that a wayworn man, with haggard brow and bowed head, had just entered the Hörselloch. Since then Tannhäuser has not been seen." —Foster (Folktales), pp.24-26.

Tannhäuser und der Sängerkrieg auf der Wartburg (Tannhäuser and the Singing Contest of the Wartburg) (1845-76 opera by Richard Wagner): "Tannhäuser, a Christian minstrel, has been seduced by the pagan goddess Venus; surfeited with pleasure he returns to his comrades and takes part in the minstrels' contest for the hand of Elisabeth. But the words of his song betray carnal experience, and he is ordered to make the pilgrimage to Rome, from which he returns unshriven. He is finally saved by the self-sacrifice of Elisabeth." —Orrey, p.341.

ABORIGINAL (AUSTRALIAN) PRACTICES /BELIEFS. *(See p.1.)*

§1.7 "THE DANCING OF PRIEPRIGGIE [The Leader is a Singer of Songs]. Like sparks from a burning branch when it is struck on the ground, so the stars flew aimlessly through the dark sky. In a little valley in Queensland [in the Dreamtime] men and women danced their nightly dance, led by Priepriggie, the singer of songs, the whirler of bullroarers*, the skilled huntsman, the wirinun [medicine man or priest] with the flying feet. They sang his songs and danced his songs, while the stars left fiery trails in the sky, in a confusion of light and bewildering chaos. Above there was no order or rhythm, but in the little valley the chanting and the dancing footsteps blended as Priepriggie's people followed him round the magic circle. Their hearts thumped in the rhythm, and when the singing was over and they sank exhausted to the ground, they murmured to each other, 'Great is Priepriggie! If he wished he could even make the stars dance to his songs!'

"Men and women who spend the long hours of the night dancing, and who sleep until dawn, need food to sustain their bodies. The women had their tasks, and the men were hunters; but of all who sought for food, Priepriggie was the most successfull. He was first up at dawn, and this morning he stole through the pearly grey mist by the river bank until he came to the huge tree where the flying foxes [apparently, bat-like creatures (Ed.)] hung from the branches. They had returned from their nightly flight, and were sound asleep.

"His footfall was as light as the glint of sunbeams on the grass, and not a twig stirred, not a drop of dew fell from the leaves as he made his way towards the tree. The flying foxes hung in clusters from the bare branches. There was little food for a man or woman in a flying fox, but their leader was many times the size of his followers, and it was the leader whom Priepriggie was seeking in order to provide his people with a meal that night.

"Closer still he moved, until at last he could see the huge body of the leader of the flying foxes, surrounded by his wives and attendants. Priepriggie fitted the butt of his spear into his woomera [throwing stick], and drew it back, inch by inch, until his arm was fully stretched behind him. Then, with one convulsive thrust, with every ounce of body and muscles behind it, the throwing stick swept forward and the spear sang through the air. It pierced the body of the great flying fox and pinned it to the tree trunk. A moment later there was a deafening roar as the flying foxes woke and spread their wings. They flew out of the tree like a cloud of smoke and circled round, waiting for their leader.

"He did not come. Presently they saw his body against the trunk, with the half of the spear still vibrating. With another circling of the tree they saw Priepriggie crouched on the ground, his woomera in front of him. Like a cloud of flies they descended on him, lifted him up and bore him away. Higher and higher they mounted until they disappeared from sight.

"That night men and women searched for the singer of songs, but they could not see him anywhere. Their bellies were empty, because their hunting had not been successful, and a sadness descended on them.

" 'Without Priepriggie we are helpless,'[1] they cried. 'If we dance his dance, perhaps he will come back to us. Perhaps he is lost, and is waiting to hear our songs.'

"They broke into a shuffling dance, but it had no life in it. Suddenly they stopped. They heard the sound of someone singing. It came from a long distance, and seemed to come from the stars.

" 'Listen! It is the voice of Priepriggie,' they said.

"The song grew louder; a compelling rhythm beat through their heads, and set their blood running faster.

" 'Look! The stars are dancing.'

"The random, dancing stars had arranged themselves in order, and were dancing to Priepriggie's song. The men and women joined in. Their feet flew over the ground, the song rose from deep in their bodies and burst out of their throats. The new dance of Priepriggie was danced on earth and in the sky.

"The song was over. The dance was finished. They lay back and stared in amazement. Right across the sky the stars were resting in a ribbon of light. The dancers of the heavens were lying where they had fallen when the corroboree of the skies ended.[2] Though men mourned the loss of Priepriggie, they rejoiced because the Milky Way was spread above them to remind them that Priepriggie could charm the stars of heaven as easily as the feet of men." — Reed, 94-95.[3]

AFRICAN MYTHS — PRACTICES AND BELIEFS.

(See also pp.21, 816.)

§6.17 See **DANCING TO DEATH (OR INSANITY)***.

§6.18 "**THE DANCING GANG.** A water carrier once went to the river to fetch water. She dipped in her calabash, and brought out a cray-fish. The cray-fish began beating his claws on the calabash,

---

1   See also **INDIAN (NORTH AMERICAN) MYTHS, §162.18, Taligvak** (Eskimo folklore). (Ed.)

2   *Corroborees:* roughly, ceremonial meeting places (such as waterholes), where the men of different tribes could gather (Ed., after Chatwin).

3   This simple story is among the most powerful of its kind I have ever read. One could not pretend to exhaust the meanings at which it hints, or brings to mind. If Priepriggie is only a human being, nevertheless as a musician he *(a)* corresponds to and with the beings and forces of nature and *(b)* has power over them — even to arranging the stars of heaven. But is he not also god-in-man, brought among us in the guise of — precisely — a master of music? Finally he seems equally the son (representative, surrogate) of man and of god — the one in whom god and man are one — the son of god (man) who, in a rough, frontier manner (there is no elaborate trial before Pontius Pilate, but only the hunting of bats in search of food) gives up his own life for us. The common thread to all these interpretations meanwhile is music/song/dance itself: the great mediator between civilized man and the impenetrable forces of nature which (nevertheless) are all around us, and perhaps within our very reach. The author/compiler A. W. Reed urges the reader to "see the [Australian] land through the eyes of the primitive, clever, imaginative [aboriginal] people who had to fight to gain their nourishment from Mother Earth.... They lived close to the soil, these children of nature. They were dependent on her for sustenance, and in the teeming animal life and in the barren places alike they found evidence of the work of a Creator Spirit, and promise of Bullima, the after-life, where game abounded, there was soft grass to lie on, refreshing streams, and soft breezes. From their physical needs a majestic conception of nature was evolved,

and played such a beautiful tune, that the girl began dancing, and could not stop.

"The driver of the gang wondered why she did not come, and sent another to see after her. When she came, she too began to dance. So the driver sent another, who also began to dance when she heard the music and the cray-fish singing—

Vaitsi, Vaitsi, O sulli Van.
Stay for us, stay for us, how long
　　will you stay for us?

"Then the driver sent another and another, till he had sent the whole gang.

"At last he went himself, and when he found the whole gang dancing, he too began to dance; and they all danced till night, when the cray-fish went back into the water; and if they haven't done dancing, they are dancing still." — Dasent, p.443.[4]

§6.19 "GAUNA. In the mythology of the Bushmen of southwestern Africa, the chief of the spirits of the dead and the arch-enemy of the creator god Kaang. Les powerful than Kaang, Gauna, also called Gawa or Gawama, nevertheless eternally seeks to overcome him and to bring discord to the human world. Communal rites, especially a dance of exorcism, are performed to ward him off...."[5]

"MOYNA. A legendary hero of the Dogon people of Mali [a republic of Africa, formerly part of French West Africa (Ed.)]. He invented the bull-roarer*, a wooden object that creates an unusual sound when whirled at the end of a rope. Apparently, Moyna began to whirl the bull-roarer at a masked dance, which women were forbidden to attend. However, several women secretly looked on, but twhen they heard the sound of the bull-roarer, ran away in terror.

"Moyna told them that the sound was the voice of the Great Mask and that women and children must stay indoors when it was communicating with men, or it would destroy them.[6] The secret of the bull-roarer was passed on to Moyna's sons. The hero told them to use it whenever an important person died because its sound was like that of the spirits of the dead. The bull-roarer is used in African secret societies and its sound frightens many people." — Cotterell (Macmillan Myths and Legends), pp.201, 223.

§6.20 "KULUILÉ, THE DANCING GIRL (Mogho [Upper Volta] folk tale). A long time ago there was a girl named Kuluilé. She was called Kuluilé because she was very pretty, small and dainty.

---

with beneficent spirit ancestors — and the corresponding spirits of evil that are inimical to mankind" (*Myths and Legends of Australia*, 9). (Ed.)

4　This West Indies version of an African folktale appears in the appendix to a volume of Norse folktales! See also **DANCING TO DEATH (OR INSANITY)***. (Ed.)

5　See our theme T42a (Music as magical weapon against evil spirits. Release or exorcism of the spirit or soul, incl. expulsion of devils, evil spirits), *Introductory Remarks* Vol I above. (Ed.)

6　See our theme T1c (Music as medium through which the spirit world [of divinities, supranatural beings] attempts to signal or attract man; music announces presence of a god or spirit), *Introductory Remarks*, Vol I above. (Ed.)

"She lived in a hut with a hunchbacked dwarf, who everyone thought was her father. One day the son of the king saw her and fell in love with her. When the time came for him to select a wife, he declared that he would marry no one but Kuluilé.

"The king became very angry. She was a commoner and her father was only an ugly hunchbacked dwarf. There were hundreds of rich and beautiful princesses who would be honored to marry his son.

"Besides, one of the king's counselors, a learned old man, had reported that Kuluilé was not fit to be a queen, for she had an uncontrollable passion for dancing. Whenever she heard the beat of a drum*, or even a single note of music, she was irresistibly drawn to the sound and could not rest until she had reached it. Then she danced and danced until she fell breathless to the ground. A devil possessed her. Certainly this would not do for a queen.[7]

" 'My love will cure her,' insisted the prince.

"[However, the king forbids the prince to marry Kuluilé. Before long the Prince of the North, Nabiga Panga, the most powerful of all the rulers, wages war on him. He rides a proud lion and his captains are mounted on elephants, rhinoceroses and horses. Nabinga Panga rides at the head of an army of hundreds of thousands, vastly outnumbering the forces of the king.]

"No matter how bravely they fought, the fate of the kingdom seemed sealed....

"One night when the full moon was shining in a pale-blue sky, Kuluilé sat on a rock dreaming of the prince. From afar, she heard the beat of a drum and the sound of music. The music was soft, with a strong rhythm. Kuluilé began to tremble and soon all her body vibrated to the distant drumbeat, strong and clear in the silence of the night.

"Suddenly, she got up and ran, ran, ran, ran into the blue moonlight through the dark bush toward the strange drums. The dwarf saw her go, but he did not try to stop her. Instead, he smiled to himself in a satisfied way, went to his room and, for the first time in many months, slept well.

"After running a long, long way, Kuluilé came to a glade in the middle of a forest, where she found a large group of people, all dressed in white. They were singing to the accompaniment of beating drums. In their midst, two couples danced continuously. When they tired, other couples replaced them. Kuluilé pulled her white scarf over her head and joined the dancers. She danced, danced, danced, danced furiously, first with one partner, then another and another and another, until she had danced with everyone. Then she danced again with her first partner. She was so tireless and her steps were so firm that the dancers, astounded by her strength, changed the words of their song. Now they sang:

Hei, you! Newcomer! Dance gently!
    Dance gently,
For termites have eaten our knees.
Fleshless bones are all we have left.

"The music was so enchanting that Kuluilé did not hear their warning. At last there was a momentary pause. Seated on the ground, head back and eyes closed, Kuluilé rested. Then she took a deep breath and cried, 'It was beautiful, beautiful, beautiful! Let's dance again! Come on, everybody!'

" 'It is not for you to give orders!' said a corn-crake voice.

---

7   See also **DANCING TO DEATH (OR INSANITY)***; also our theme T4 (Music as magical means by which spirits or other supernatural beings or forces take possession of human or other celebrant, priest, victim etc.), *Introductory Remarks,* Vol I above. (Ed.)

"Suprised, Kuluilé looked up. The dancers had formed a circle around her and were watching her. But, instead of eyes, they had deep, black holes in their bare, white skulls. Instead of lips, their teeth grinned strangely in the cold moonlight. Their jaws and their cheekbones were white, without flesh. Kuluilé gasped. 'You are not hu-hu-human!'

"A hundred corn-crake voices replied: 'We were once. We are the phantoms of the bald mountains. You joined in our dance, and now you must stay with us.'[8]

" 'Let me go home,' Kuluilé begged.

"That is impossible. We did not ask you to come. Now you must be one of us. We will keep you in that big baobab tree until you lose your flesh. It will take seven weeks, and then you will be as we are and you will dance with us forever.' The phantoms let their robes fall to the ground and their white skeletons glowed terrifyingly in the blue light of the moon. Kuluilé fainted. The phantoms carried her to the big baobab tree and placed her inside its hollow trunk. Dawn was approaching, and they fled back to the darkness of the forest before the daylight powdered their bones into white dust.

"[In the morning the dwarf runs to the palace to tell the prince that Kuluilé is in great danger—that unless she is saved by a man who loves her, she will die. The prince consults his wizard who tells him that Kuluilé is kept prisoner in a big baobab tree by the phantoms of the bald mountains. At night the phantoms keep watch. During the day Naba Singsangué, the demon, guards her. If she is not rescued in time, she is doomed to become a phantom. The prince leaves at once, to rescue Kuluilé. Angrily, the king cries out at his son's desertion, when every man is needed to defend their land against the invader Nabiga Panga.]

" 'I cannot let Kuluilé die at the hands of the phantoms,' said the prince and rushed out followed by the dwarf. He mounted his white horse, the dwarf jumped up behind him, and they galloped away toward the bald mountains.

"On their way, they met a *kinkirga*. He was suffering from an especially severe headache and was looking for someone to shave off his heavy hair and relieve him. It takes a long time to shave a *kinkirga*, and the prince was in a hurry. But the dwarf said, 'Shave it off for him. A good deed is never wasted!'

"It took half a day to shave the *kinkirga*, and in the meantime, hundreds of others arrived to be shaved. When the prince had shaved the last one, forty-nine days had passed. The *kinkirsi* danced joyfully in gratitude and presented the prince with two bags of powder, one red and one black, the powders of life and death. They also gave him a little drum and said, 'Whenever you need us, beat this drum.' The first *kingira* insisted that the prince accept his pet spider as well. Then amidst joy and laughter, they quickly disappeared.

"It was high noon when the prince came at last to the phantoms's glade. It was empty but for Naba Singsangué, who guarded the baobab tree. He was a frightening monster. He had the head of a lion, the neck of a giraffe, the body of an elephant, the tail of an alligator.... Each time he roared, flames from his mouth burned everything in reach....

" 'Let's use the powder of death!' said the dwarf. He took a handful of the black powder and threw it at the monster. There was a great explosion, and when the fire died out, there was nothing left of Naba Singsangué but bare bones. The explosion had also split open the baobab tree, revealing a small, white skeleton.

"The moon was rising and the glade was slowly filling with phantoms. Soon they were singing and dancing. That very midnight Kuluilé was to be initiated into her life as a phantom.

---

8   See also **DEATH DANCE***. (Ed.)

"While the prince and the dwarf hid, waiting for the right moment to act, the spider went to work. In no time, he had woven a huge web over and around the glade. When the time came for the ceremony, to their surprise the phantoms could not reach the baobab tree. They were caught in the spider's silken threads. At first the phantoms screamed in rage and then in fear, for in a few hours it would be dawn.

"The prince and the dwarf went swiftly to the baobab tree.

"The prince opened the bag of red powder and spread the powder over Kuluilé's skeleton. Little by little, the flesh returned — strong, healthy flesh, under a beautiful, shiny black skin. Soon the body of Kuluilé was as it had been, but as yet she showed no sign of life.... Then, the first ray of the sun sparkled in the east, lit the sky and fell on the nose of Kuluilé. She sneezed four times, opened her eyes and smiled.

"[The prince, the dwarf and Kuluilé return home to find that the kingdom has fallen to Nabiga Panga. The king and all his counselors have been imprisoned. However, the prince now knows the true story of Nabiga Panga, and of Kuluilé.]

"An evil warlock had wanted the throne of a king for his own son, who had no talent for witchcraft. And when the king's first child, a daughter, named Kuluilé was born, the warlock cast a spell over her. As she grew, she developed an uncontrollable passion for dancing. In time the king, Kuluilé's father, died of grief, and the son of the warlock became king in his place and called himself Nabiga Panga. The dead king's jester, the hunchbacked dwarf, fled with the little princess, for a good witch had foretold her future: Kuluilé would be captured by the phantoms of the bald mountains, but would be rescued through the love of a noble prince and regain her kingdom.

"It was noon when the prince, the dwarf and Kuluilé returned to the city and went to the palace. Nabiga Panga was celebrat-ing his triumph and was dining with his captains on whole roast lambs.

" 'Usurper,' cried the prince, 'this is your last day!'

" 'Ah! Ah! Ah!' laughed Nabiga Panga. 'Where is your army?' Then he shouted, 'Put these fools with the other prisoners. They shall all die in half an hour.'

"The soldiers rushed forward to arrest Kuluilé, the prince and the dwarf.... The dwarf began beating the little drum given to the prince by the *kinkirsi.*

"At once thousands of little *kinkirsi* appeared in the city, in the palace, everywhere. The little people overpowered Nabiga Panga, his warlock-father and their men, and drove them deep into the forest, and they were never heard from again.

"Her kingdom was restored to Kuluilé. She married the prince, and when his father died, their combined lands became a powerful and prosperous empire.

"But for many years, the old counselors of the king continued to discuss these strange events and to debate on women's passions and the power of love.

"And if they are alive, they are debating still, as old men do." — Guirma, pp.16-28.

§6.21 **THE SOUL OF THE BANTU.** "The [after world or world of the dead] of which the Bantu dream is not so highly idealised as that of ancient Egypt; but there, also, the herd-boy still herds his cattle, the women hoe their gardens, reap their crops, and pound their corn, the hunter hunts, the patriarch delights his eyes with the sleek coats of his beautiful black-and-white cattle, the villagers gather for gossip in the evening hours, the drums* are beaten and the dance proceeds. [Sir James] Fraser, speaking of the Tumbuka belief, says: 'The land of the dead is a good land where no hunger or sorrow touches them. But they live as young men and women, and grind their heavenly corn, and dance together, and have beautiful domestic fowls. Sometimes in the quiet of the night a sound will be heard in the wood like the beating of a distant drum, and the people say, "The spirits are dancing in their village." '...[9]

"Revelation by Ancestor-Spirits Through 'Possession'. Sheane describes the 'possession' of men and women by spirits of dead Awemba chiefs. 'The possessed person, while the spirit is in him, will prophesy as to future wars, and warn the people of approaching visitations by lions. During the period of possession he eats nothing cooked by fire, but only unfermented dough. The functions of *mufumu ya mipashi* (chiefs of the spirits) are usually performed by women. These women assert that they are possessed by the soul of some dead chief, and when they feel the 'divine afflatus', whiten their faces to attract attention, and anoint themselves with flour, which has a religious and sanctifying potency. One of their number beats a drum, and the others dance, singing at the same time a weird song, with curious intervals. Finally when they have arrived at the requisite stage of religious exaltation, the possessed woman falls to the ground, and bursts forth into a low and almost inarticulate chant, which has a most uncanny effect. All are silent at once, and the *bashing'anga* (medicine men) gather round to interpret the voice of the spirit. In the old time many men and women were denounced as *waloshi* (sorcerers) by these possessed women, whereupon the accused, unless protected by the king, or willing to undergo the ordeal, were instantly killed or mutilated.'

"Every Konde chief has an expert hierolatrist,[10] whom he sends daily with an offering to the grave of the last chief, and who accompanies him when he goes thither to pray. When the chief dies, this man 'is in great danger, for the spirits take possession of his person, a danger which can only be averted by a powerful medicine supplied by the doctor, and taken as soon as the chief has died. If this is not done, he becomes mad, lives in the bush, gibbering and naming all the dead chiefs of the past, including names known to no living person, but supposed to be those of long-dead chiefs, uttered by themselves through him.' These tribesmen think there are other spirits that sometimes take possession of people. 'If the possessed makes for water, it is known that a water spirit has entered into him; if he goes to the hills, it is a mountain spirit. In either case the patient is taken by the medicine man to a waterfall, "where God dwells", and given medicine to drink.... A bell* is rung; the doctor speaks, "We have found you. Come out of the man." Then he takes water in his mouth and squirts it on the breast and back of the afflicted person, striking him at the same time with the calabash with which he took the water, and holding it for a little over the patient's head.'

"Hobley states that at a private sacrifice in a Kamba village, in Kenya Colony, 'sometimes a woman who goes into a cataleptic condition,[11] which is known as being seized by *aïmu*' (ancestral spirits) 'will say that to obtain rain a beast of a particular colour must be sacrificed.' And again, 'It often happens that during a ceremony at an *ithembo*' (shrine of an ancestor-spirit in a Kamba village) 'a woman is seized or possessed, and passes into a condition of semi-trance in which she will prophesy either than the rains are coming or that they will fail, or, in former days,

---

9   See our theme **T6a** (Music as herald of otherworldly or supernatural being. Music, song and dance as practices of the dead), *Introductory Remarks* (Vol I, above). (Ed.)

10   Hierology, the sacred literature of a given people; hierolotry, the worship of saints or sacred things. (Ed.)

11   "Catalepsy: muscular rigidity, lack of awareness of environment and lack of response to external stimuli, often associated with epilepsy, schizophrenia, and hysteria." – *American Heritage Dictionary of the English Language* (1969). (Ed.)

that a Masai raid is imminent. I was told that the message came from the *imu* or spirit of the person of olden time to whom the *ithembo* was dedicated, but quite clearly, that the spirit was only an intermediary, the message really coming from the high god *Engai* or *Mulungu*.' The same writer says that there was an epidemic of infectious mania or possession among the Akamba in 1906, and another in 1911. Speaking of the latter, he says: 'The spirit of a girl who was said to have died mysteriously was supposed to enter into people in various parts of the district — generally old women — and speak. The whole district rapidly became disturbed; the spirit, through its oracles, demanded that bullocks should be slaughtered; the order was implicitly obeyed, for any one who refused was supposed to be doomed. As a result, several thousand bullocks were slaughtered and consumed in a week or two. Great dances, at which meat was eaten, were held. Very soon the oracles became seditious, and plans were being made for the abolition of European government and attack on the Government station. The whole thing was kept secret at first, but eventually it all came out and a company of troops had to be sent to the district to calm the excited people; the elders, who felt sore at the loss of so many cattle, rallied to the support of law and order and the country gradually regained a normal state.'

"What is the explanation of these phenomena? The Bantu explanation is simple enough, and convincing to people who know nothing of modern medicine. It is based on the testimony of the patient, who asserts that he has a *dimo* within him, and upon the ocular evidence of neighbors to whom it is obvious that the man is not himself. Everything is of course viewed through the mystical atmosphere in which both the patient and his neighbors live, and always have lived; but all these cases, however multiform they may be, must unquestionably be classed with insanity, epilepsy, monomania, melancholia, and other forms of neurotic and mental disorder. The 'possession' is temporary in some cases, and periodic in others, particularly with women; and wild dancing and music, still more a peculiar drum-beat, induce fresh outbreaks of frenzy in some who seemed to be on the mend. There is often a history of previous eccentricity in the patient; and the attack is not infrequently ushered in with loss of consciousness, or convulsions, or other epileptic symptoms....[12] 'A sign that a man or woman has this *motheke-theke* [extraordinary (devilish) posssion]' says a Mosuto correspondent, 'is when he or she has crying fits, and running away, and often falling down when running away.' 'To be possessed' is a literal translation of the commonest Secwana phrase for 'to be insane' (*go tsénwa*)....

"The cure for 'possession' falls in which what the exorcists conceive to be the source of the trouble. The Mosuto correspondent to whom I have more than once referred, disdainfully depicts exorcism as a crowd, daubed with red ochre

---

12 Although in this account music only *reinforces* the drama of "possession" by supposed representatives of the spirit world, nevertheless see our theme **T4** (Music as magical means by which spirits or other supernatural beings or forces take possession of human or other victim), also **T5** (Music as magical means of promoting or inducing state or condition of ecstasy, frenzy, madness, losing oneself etc), *Introductory Remarks*, Vol I, above. (Ed.)

and garbed grotesquely, dancing and singing around the 'possessed'.[13] A missionary among the Lumbu gives a more detailed description, in which the drums figure largely and weird rites, lasting from evening until daylight, are performed by the chief exorcist, including in one case, the spearing of the spirits who had been lured forth by the smell of the feast. Among a variety of ceremonies, eminently calculated to excite the imagination of the sufferer, which Junod describes, mention is made of 'songs of exorcism, performed with accompaniment of rattles*, big tins and drums, close to the ears of the pretended possessed, in order to induce the spirit to reveal its name and to "come out".' Discovering the name of the spirit is always important to the exorcist. Le Roy's experience of tribes that must have imbibed not a little Arab folklore during centuries of residence within the orbit of Zanzibar, led him to conclude that a 'possessing' spirit is sometimes thought to be a malevolent and perverse being of non-human origin, whose only feeling for man is jealousy, bitterness and hatred. But whether of human or non-human origin, 'possessing' spirits generally have names, and always need sacrifices; and so the first business of an exorcist is to discover the spirit's name, why it entered into that body, and what sacrifice will satisfy its demands. This is done by interrogating the patient; and when the sacrifice is slaughtered, it is she ('usually they are women' he says) who drink its warm, steaming blood....

Modes of Ancestor Worship: Shrines, Altars, Chapels, etc. An old mentor of mine, chief of a small section of the Bobidid who lived in what has since become known as the North-western Transvaal, dictated a state-

ment of which the following is a translation. 'When my grandfather was dead, the stump that he used as a seat was given to his eldest son. Ground was made ready in the middle of the courtyard, and this stump and a *legoma* bulb were placed in it, a little circle of beaten and smeared earth being prepared around them. Early in the spring of the year, Kafir-beer was cooked and poured as a libation on this circle; and all the children, both boys and girls, being gathered together, each one sucked up a mouthful of beer from the circle and, holding it in the mouth, went outside the village and squirted it upon the ground. This completed the ritual: its name is *Go thebola dithota gonwe medimo* ("To make an offering to the graves, or to the spirits of the dead"). And his praise song may be sung.' In the sacred huts of 'most tribes in the Northern Transvaal.... drums are regarded as the earthly shrine of the tutelary spirits of the clan.' " — Willoughby, pp.73, 108-12, 276.

§6.22 HORSES, MUSICIANS AND GODS: THE HAUSA CULT OF POSSESSION-TRANCE (extracts from an anthropological account).

"Horses, musicians, and gods: these are three of the essential elements of the Hausa cult of possession-trance. The horses are cult-adepts, so described because of the image they have of themselves as mounts for the spirits which possess them; the musicians are non-initiates, professionals, whose function it is to preserve much of the oral tradition of the cult and to invoke the spirits with special songs during possession-trance performances; the gods are the divine horsemen, the residents of the invisible city of Jangare, supernatural spirits who mark their victims with illness and misfortune and then provide the source for its remedy. The purpose of this study is

---

13 Theme **T4a** (Music as magical weapon against evil spirits, means for combatting, routing evil spirits. Release or exorcism of the spirit or soul, incl. expulsion of devils, evil spirits. Protection of the dead from evil or harmful spirits or forces; also, of the living from the dead), *Introductory Remarks*. (Ed.)

to reach an understanding of who or what each of these groups is, what they do, and how they are brought together in *bori* practice and ritual...

"In the ethnographic literature on bori frequent mention is made of 'trance' or 'spirit-possession' with little regard as to their distinction or meaning.[14] For the most part these terms have been avoided here and adepts' altered states of consciousness identified with the term 'possession-trance'. Following Bourguignon (1973), possession-trance is defined as an altered state of consciousness which is institutionalized and culturally patterned. It is a learned skill, and adepts who enter possession-trance are expected to behave in certain ways, following cult 'rules'. Dissociation is described by initiates as due to possession by supernatural spirits, involving the impersonation of their speech and behaviour, and is followed by amnesia. During possession-trance a medium's personality disappears, and his gestures and speech are interpreted as belonging to the possessing world.

"In the absence of an altered state cult mediums, adepts, or devotees are described with the concept of 'possession'. This includes the belief that the supernatural spirits present on a medium at his initiation (or curing) are for ever with him, it being impossible to exorcize them from their victim. Trance in the absence of possession does not occur among the Hausa, and when 'trance' is used it is a shortened form of 'possession-trance'.

"Mention should be made of the Hausa terms used to refer to supernatural spirits. Bori has both a general and a specific sense; it is used in this study to refer to the cult of possession-trance—its general meaning. The term is also used by informants to indicate 'supernatural spirit' or 'mediumship'. Thus, when it is said of someone, 'He is able to do bori' or 'He has

bori', this means that he is a competent medium. *Iska* (pl. *iskoki*) is the common term used to refer to a supernatural spirit, but its primary meaning is 'wind'. In urban Hausa settlements *aljan* or *aljani* (fem. *aljana'* pl. *aljanu*) which is derived from the Arabic *jinn* is a frequent substitute for iska or bori (supernatural spirit)....

"*Hausaland.* The northern part of the Federal Republic of Nigeria and the southern part of the Republic of Niger is known as Hausaland. The country ranges from the savannah of the south to the sahel of the extreme north....
"The Hausa social system is highly stratified, and while other criteria are used socially to place people in the system, for example ethnic membership, kinship, descent and lineage, and sex, the single most comprehensive ranking system is based on occupation. The hierarchical ranking of political offices is a part of theis primarily ascriptive system, the highest political and social position being held by the emir. No single hierarchy covers all Hausa traditional occupations, but whichever authority is taken musicians and praise-singers and -shouters are placed in the broadly lowest rank. Among these bori musicians are evaluated least favourably. Mediumship in the possession-trance cult is an achieved status, not an ascribed status. Cult-adepts are therefore not listed in the hierarchy *per se*, but their 'primary' occupations are.

"Except for the absence of bori performance during *Ramadan* (the Muslim month of the Great Fast preceding the Lesser Feast) cult activity is sustained for the first half of the dry season and gradually diminishes in anticipation of the rains. During the rains, except for initiations which are sometimes held during the planting and growing season, bori activity practically ceases. Periodic possession-trance performances are coincident with

---

14   See also **MUSIC AND TRANCE***, below. (Ed.)

the increase in wealth and the number of social events reaffirming old or creating new obligations following upon the harvesting of crops....

"As mentioned [above] occupational classification is the most important factor in the evaluation of social status. The Hausa define musicians' work as a craft (*sana'a*) called *roko* (lit. begging), and those engaged in it — instrumentalists, vocalists, praise-singers and -shouters — are called *maroka* (s. *maroki*) and ranked in the lowest social category. The essential aspect of roko is the type of service performed, that is, acclamation, and its social and economic circumstances. That instruments and music may be used in this service is irrelevant for the Hausa. This attitude is exemplified in the case of instrumentalists who play a certain type of royal drum* in the emir's court. *Tambari* (royal hemispherical drum) players are not classified as maroka (although music is as much part of their activity as it is for any professional drummer) but as *bayi* (s. *sawa;* slave), a designation which they are careful to em-

phasize to avoid being confused with low class maroka. As royal slaves the status placement of tambari drummers is higher than other instrumentalists, probably due to their affinity to the royal courts in which they serve.

"Musicians, praise-singers and -shouters — all of them professional maroka — can be divided into the following categories: (a) the musicians of craft groups; (b) musicians in political life; (c) musicians of recreational music; (d) musician-entertainers; (e) musicians for the bori cult. Those in the first category have patrons within craft groups, and much of their economic support comes from performing for them. As Ames notes, musicians tend to concentrate their activities on one or other of the categories, but overlapping can be found especially in the case of *kalangu* (double-membrane, hourglass-shaped, pressure drum) players. Usually associated with butchers, kalangu drummers also perform recreational music for social dancing at marriage and naming ceremonies....

"The fifth category of musicians surveyed by Ames consists of those who play for the bori cult of 'spirit-possession' or possession-trance. In many respects such professionals are regarded as a group to be the lowest placed musicians in the maroka class. As individuals they may achieve fame and recognition through their excellence as artists, but such cases are clearly the exception rather than the rule.

"The reasons for this extremely low evaluation of their status seem to fall in two main areas, and Ames has touched on one of them. He notes that officially, at least, music has no part in Islamic ritual, and musical instruments are not played in the mosque (Ames 1973). The only exceptions to this practice are the unaccompanied chanting of religious poems and Muslim hymns, and the playing of the *bandiri* (a set of two or more drums, one type of which is a single-membrane circular frame-drum with or without circular metal jingles, and a second type which is a single-membrane bowl-shaped drum). The view that Muslim scholars, teachers, or mosque heads take is that many kinds of Hausa music are evil. They single out goge (single-stringed, bowed lute*) music, describing it as music of the devil. Since one of the two main instruments used in the invocation of bori spirits is the goge, they are somewhat justified in their conclusion that to their way of thinking, bori spirits are devils. It is understandable, therefore, why goge players (bori musicians) are not received with much enthusiasm by devout Muslims.[15]

"The second area of criticism of bori musicians is the fact that Hausa society views them as keeping bad company. This is of course a restatement of the stereotype, layman opinion concerning anyone who participates in bori rituals and its other activities. Its members are treated as deviants, and the musicians who play for them must share its social stigma. In other words, it is bad enough to be a musician, but inexcusable to practice one's craft in support of this heathen cult....

"Cult musicians mostly confine their efforts to performing songs associated with individual spirits. This repertoire is con-

---

15 See (in the *Introductory Remarks,* Vol I above) our themes T4 (Music as magical means by which spirits or other supernatural beings or forces take possession of human or other celebrant, priest, victim etc — negatively, one is possessed by demons or evil forces); T4c (Music as magical means of attracting, seducing, etc. victim. Music as means for tempting subject to indulge in evil or carnal ways) — in a *positive* context, of course, this might be regarded as only promoting fertility or perpetuation of one's kind; T5 (Music as hypnotic force — as magical means of promoting or inducing state or condition of ecstasy, frenzy, madness, losing oneself), negatively, suggesting demonic possession as in T4, but could also (positively) suggest communion with or attainment of some earthly or heavenly paradise or blissful state; T5c (Identification of music with love, sex, lust, physical release or abandon etc.) — again, to be shunned officially by a Puritanical or psycho-sexually repressive society; and, possibly, theme T6a (Music, song and dance as practices of the dead) — thus, again, something to be feared. I think it is interesting to reflect that — by prohibiting musical performance — devout Muslims would in effect seem to betray therefore a certain *belief* regarding various powers of music, to which others throughout the world freely do admit, and indeed *encourage* — having in some cases a religious or psychological dependence, even, on certain types of musical performance. In this respect official Islam — far from putting certain folkloristic customs and "superstitions" if you will into disrepute — *may in effect give them additional credibility.* Indeed do not prohibitions generally *heighten* one's expectations — curiosity, at least — concerning the attractions or efficacy of the thing that is prohibited? (Ed.)

servative, consisting essentially of the same songs which were performed by cult musicians before them. There is no stigma attached to this and no cult musician feels inferior because of a lack of inventiveness in creating new songs. Deviation is avoided, primarily because it would result in 'meaningless' music. As the participants say, 'What would be the use of a cult song if it were not able to be heard by some spirit?' But if new composition is avoided great value is placed on 're-composition', i.e. embellishment and improvisation. Song texts and melodies, vocal and instrumental, are subject to re-composition, and by this means a performer is able to imprint a standard piece of music with a mark of his own individuality.

"Two kinds of music are distinguished for most bori spirits, one vocal and instrumental and the other purely instrumental. Each of these types implies a specific kind of activity or situation involving cult-adepts at a possession-trance event. Vocal music honours or calls a spirit, and informs or entertains the audience. Its content consists of kirari (descriptive praise-epithets or praise-words and -names) for spirits, anecdotes involving the spirit or ceremonies held in its name, and invitations to possess a particular devotee.

The first of these categories is rigidly set in the oral tradition of the cult and changes little from generation to generation. For example, an examination of the song texts recorded by Tremearne (1914) in North Africa at the turn of the century reveals an impressive continuity between what he heard and what is performed in Kano today for the same spirits. Anecdotes change from musician to musician but in fact constitute a small part of total song content. The content of the actual call for a spirit's presence which immediately precedes a cult-adept's altered state of consciousness depends heavily on the pace of the induction and the vocalist's style. It is not primarily the linguistic content of the call wherein its effectiveness lies; is its melodic and rhythmic accompaniment.

"Specific song texts are linked to specific melody, rhythmic, and structural complexes. It is an unusual spirit which has only one 'song' (vocal or instrumental); many of them have three or more. Whereas it is clear why certain texts should be associated with certain melodies and rhythms in so far as consideration of linguistic tone and vowel length is essential in Hausa, there appears to be no linguistic reason why one song should be sung by a soloist while another involves the par-

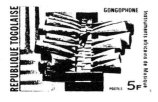

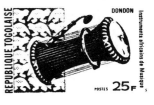

ticipation of a leader and chorus. In other words structural types do not vary directly with linguistic types.

"In addition to instrumentally accompanied songs for separate spirits one or more purely instrumental pieces are usually included. Described as *cashiya*, these have a faster tempo than vocal pieces and are intended for dancing. During a performance vocal usually precede, and sometimes also follow, instrumental pieces. The only time a cashiya-type rhythm is not initiated by a slow vocal form is when the 'trance sequence' of an event is under way and the instrumental piece is used to induce a reluctant devotee's dissociation state. A cashiya provides the opportunity for the instrumentalists to display their skill, but it is not performed for that reason alone. Consistent with the attitude that music must have a social or ritual use, musicians prefer to use a cashiya piece when a dancer requires it to demonstrate movements and gestures symbolically associated with a particular spirit or to fall into a trance state.[16]

"Part of the corporate, yet intangible, property of the cult of possession-trance is the music used to invoke spirits. Music is not owned by any individual and descendants may only lay claim to it if they meet certain other requirements. Where the membership core of a performing group consists of men who are patrilineally related it is tempting to assume that songs are inherited patrilineally. It is group membership, however, irrespective of how it is recruited, which describes specific lines of inheritance. Further, instrumentalists have a claim to the inheritance only of the music performed on the instruments which they themselves play. For example, goge-kwarya music is quite distinct from garaya-buta music, and musicians in one type or group would consider it inappropriate to claim or play the music of another.... The case for the transmission of vocal music is slightly different. Kirari epithets are a part of every cult-adept's vocabulary, and a vocalist may widen his collection with every opportunity he has for conversation." —Besmer, pp.1, 3-5, 31, 34, 58.[17]

---

16 Details of the actual *procedures*—musical and other—of spirit-invocation fall somewhat outside of the scope of the present work. The important point to stress here is simply that music is regarded as an essential medium for communication with "spirits"—i.e. gods or other-worldly beings which are imagined to affect human and earthly destinies in some fashion. It is true that "culturally advanced" societies might regard the "spirits" which are the objects of Hausa veneration as only "mythical" beings, and belief in them as essentially "superstitious"; however, in the churches, temples and synagogues of more "sophisticated" cultures, do we not similarly attempt to invoke and address our particular "gods" through music? In the end, Hausa practices may be viewed as local and particular instances of customs and beliefs which appear to be well-nigh universally held (in some form or degree or another), throughout the whole world and from one historical period to another. With respect to Hausa belief specifically, see in addition to themes mentioned previously **T1a** (Music as magical means of communication with god[s] or supreme being[s]) and **T1b** (Music gives magical power to musician; alternatively, musician as medium through which magical power is conveyed to a community or congregation)—*Introductory Remarks,* Vol I above. (Ed.)

17 For other stories and beliefs centering on the Hausa people, see §6.7 and §6.8, pp.28-30 above. (Ed.)

ANGELS AS MUSICIANS.

§12A.1 The following essay on musician angels as portrayed in art is excerpted from the wonderfully detailed, profusely illustrated volume *Music of the Spheres and the Dance of Death: Studies in Musical Iconology* by Kathi Meyer-Baer (1971) — to which readers interested in topics relating to the portrayal of music in the visual arts generally are warmly directed.

With respect to the conception of angels, in particular, I think it is relevant to point out that, traditionally, angels had come to represent a *medium*, if you will, between the spirit world (e.g. heaven, the hereafter, paradise etc) and the world of human beings. Thus art historian James Hall, in his *Dictionary of Subjects and Symbols in Art* (1974):

> **Angel** (Greek *angelos*, messenger). The messenger of the gods, the agent of divine will and its execution on earth, was found in the ancient religions of the east. In the Graeco-Roman pantheon Mercury was the messenger of Jupiter. Descriptions in prophetic and apocalyptic literature of the appearance of angles were a formative influence in medieval art: 'I saw the Lord seated on a throne... About him were attendant seraphim, and each had six wings; one pair covered his face and one pair his feet, and one pair was spread in flight' (Isaiah 6:1-2).... The Old Testament contains many references to beings whose function is to convey God's will to mankind. They act as annunciators (Abraham, the three angels), protectors of the righteous (Lot, the destruction of Sodom and Gomorrah), punishers of wrong-doers (Adam and Eve, the Expulsion), or may be the mystic personification of God himself (Jacob wrestling with the angel). Guar-

dian angels, whose cult was to become popular in the 16th and 17th centuries, appear in the Old Testament, among them Raphael and Michael, the protector of the Israelites (Daniel 10:13, 11:1). In the New Testament Luke's gospel contains numerous references to angels: the Annunciation to the Virgin by the archangel Gabriel (who likewise foretold the birth of John the Baptist to Zacharias, and who also appeared in Joseph's dream); the Nativity, flight into Egypt, agony in the garden, and elsewhere.... In the 5th century [the angels'] various ranks were codified in a work that the Middle Ages attributed to Dionysius the Areopagite, the convert of St. Paul. This work, the *De Hierarchia Celesti*, divided angels into nine categories, or choirs, which were grouped in three hierarchies as follows: (1) Seraphim, Cherubim, Thrones; (2) Dominations, Virtues, Powers; (3) Princedoms, Archangels, Angels.[18] The first hierarchy surrounded God in perpetual adoration, the Thrones sustaining him; the second governed the stars and elements; of the third, the Princedoms protected the kingdoms of the earth, and Archangels and Angels were divine messengers. (pp.16-17)

Among the principal themes of the present work are, of course, **T1a** (Music as magical means of communication with [the] gods or supreme beings) and **T1c** (Music as medium through which the spirit world [of divinities, supranatural beings] attempts to signal or contact man; music announces the presence of a god or spirit) — for which see the *Introductory Remarks*, Vol. I above.

It would seem to be entirely plausible, then, to *link* these two concepts — of angels as divine messengers; and of music as a means of announcing or communicating

---

18   For a more detailed account of Dionysius's classification scheme, see **HARMONY OF THE SPHERES***, below. (Ed.)

with the gods or supreme beings — in the single notion of "musician-angel", and this is precisely what artists of the Middle Ages and Renaissance etc. *did* do, as outlined in the following account. (Ed.)

"The angel as a participant in the making of celestial music finally began to be a prevalent figure in works of art in the fourteenth century. Angels appeared first as dancers, joining the dance of the blessed in paradise, and as singers in the heavenly choirs. The angel instrument player, ultimately the most popular image, was the last to join the making of celestial harmony, though angel players had appeared earlier in a rather different role related to the Psalms. The various forms of this development, and possible reasons for its seeming tardiness, will be discussed in this chapter, with a final note on the question of whether or not the celestial concerts depicted can be interpreted as reflections of contemporary reality.

"*Dancing Angels and the Dance of the Blessed.* Figures of angels or blessed souls dancing a round became a new motif to denote paradise in Christian iconography beginning in the first half of the fourteenth century. The many earlier dancing figures connected with the Beatus manuscripts, the *jongleurs* and acrobats who appeared so often on Romanesque and Gothic capitals, usually did not represent heavenly dancers. One example... from the Romanesque period, the dancers on the capitals at Saint Pons de Thomières, provides a rare exception.[19] In the fourteenth century, however, the motif of a round danced by angels or the blessed became prevalent, and the site of their dancing was usually understood to be the highest heaven, Empyreum, or paradise. On the other hand, angels forming a circle or semi-circle are not always dancing; it is possible that they illustrate the Dionysiac idea of angels moving the spheres, or that they simply correspond to early representations of adorants approaching the Lord or the Virgin from both sides.[20]

"Dancers in a ring, dancing a round, however, began to be a regular feature of paradise. We see them in Andrea da Firenze's painting of the Last Judgment in the Spanish Chapel in Santa Maria Novella at Florence. On the upper left, Saint Peter is greeting pairs of dancing girls adorned with wreaths and letting them into paradise; on the lower right, four women are dancing in a ring to the accompaniment of a tambourine* and a vielle [fiddle].[21]

"A similar group appears in the picture of *The Good Government* by Ambrogio Lorenzetti in Sienna.[22] Here the round is used as a sign of the good and harmonious society, in an allegorical reflection of the state of bliss in heaven. The dancing girls, including, again, a group of four dancing to the accompaniment of a tambourine, look quite different from the very realistic merchants and officials of the Italian town in the rest of the painting. They clearly come from another world, that of heaven and of Dante's *Paradiso*. By the time this was painted, the symbolic meaning of figures dancing a round must have been generally understood; it is not likely that girls

---

19 P. Meslplé, *"Les chapitaux du cloître de Saint Pons de Thomières"*, *Revue des arts* (1960), p.111.
20 R. Hammerstein, *Die Musik der Engel* (1962), p.237 and Fig. 73, characterizes the two groups of angels in Giotto's fresco *The Lord in Glory* in the Padua Arena as dancing. I would prefer to define them as approaching adorants.
21 The author's original volume includes reproductions of this and other art works discussed in the text. (Ed.)
22 E. v. Marle, *The Development of the Italian School of Painting* (1923-28), I, 470ff.

were usually dancing in the streets, even if the city were well ruled.

"By the fifteenth century the figures of the dancing blessed and the dancing angels became quite common. From early in the century there are the delightful celestial rounds in Fra Angelico's two paintings of the Last Judgment and in his *Death and Assumption of the Virgin*. In the latter, the earliest of the three works, Mary is surrounded by angels on three levels. In the middle layer there are five angels on each side, and again they are dancing a round. Angels with musical instruments appear on the highest of the three levels [instruments portrayed in this work include tambourine, psaltery, vielle, lute, busine (?)]. In the earliest of the two *Last Judgments*, Christ as the highest judge is surrounded by three rows of angels. The mandorla [i.e. a panel or contour in the shape of an almond—also an almond-shaped *aureole*, or radiant light which appears around the head or the body of a sacred personage (Ed.)] is supported by cherubim and then by two rows representing the other orders. Then follow, on the right and left, the saints and the patriarchs, seated on two benches, one group headed by the Virgin, the other by Saint John the Baptist. In the group on the right, King David can be identified by his psaltery. Thus, Fra Angelico has arranged the saints in the same order as Dante did in his heavenly rose.[23] The orders of the angels also appear as in Dante, all stationed in the highest heaven. The cherubim, with bird-like wings, forming the group nearest to Christ, reflect the oldest tradition. Further down and off to the sides, there are scenes of the damned and the blessed. Fra Angelico presents paradise as a charming flower garden in which blessed souls and angels, alternating, are starting a round. At the point where the circle remains open, two clerics, one a Dominican and one a Franciscan, are walking and talking; and again we remember the canto from Dante's *Paradiso* where representatives of the monastic orders play important roles in one realm of heaven. If Fra Angelico did not have this detailed knowledge directly from having read the *Divine Comedy* himself, Dante's ideas must have been commonly known. This is, incidentally, one of Angelico's pictures without a heavenly orchestra.

"The *Last Judgment* of the later period... has a slightly different arrangement. Christ, in the upper middle, is directly surrounded by the three highest orders of the

---

23 *Paradiso*, XXXI, 100; XXXII, 1-39.

CORREOS DE EL SALVADOR, C.A.

10c.

PITOS DE CARRIZO

angels, with the cherubim forming the outer frame of the mandorla and the seraphim and the thrones supporting it. In the background the three middle orders appear in rich array, and the minor classes of angels are in the clouds below. On the left... the blessed move upward through a flower garden on a sort of mountain path, the mountain being formed by clouds. At the bottom of this left panel, angels with wings, and the blessed, without wings but with a faint halo, again alternate. Farther up there appear groups of three, two of the blessed led by an angel, and still farther up the blessed are forming a kind of procession, not a round but a winding line, as if they were dancing.

"In the second half of the fifteenth century such dances became a favorite motif in a variety of scenes and surroundings. Clouds under some of the groups indicate that the dances are supposed to take place in heaven. Only certain important ones shall be mentioned here. Botticelli has angels dance [around Dante and Beatrice] in the illustrations to Dante's *Paradiso*. Danc-ing youths appeared on the balconies for the singers in the Cathedral of Florence [see detail from the so-called Cantoria by Luca della Robbia in the Cathedral of Florence, showing wingless *putti*, dancing and singing].[24] They are less important in Della Robbia's work, though his singers and players will presently warrant discussion. In Botticelli's *Nativity* there is a round of angels alternating with blessed in the foreground, and above a charming round of angels.[25] In his *Coronation of the Virgin* the group of the Virgin and Christ is surrounded by a similar round of dancing angels. Outside Italy, there is a round of angels in Altdorfer's[26] painting, *Birth of the Virgin*, where the whole scene is set in a cathedral, the Ecclesia, and in this work the cathedral is raised to the heaven of bliss by a crown of dancing *putti*. Dancing angels are sculptured on the foot of the font in the Saint Anthony chapel of Seville's cathedral (*ca.* 1500). Angels dance and also play in a Siennese *Mary in Glory* from the same period and in the *Madonna with the Girdle* by Matteo di Giovanni.[27]

---

24   "*Putto* (Latin *putus*, a little man), or 'Amoretto' (Latin diminutive of *Amor*, love or Cupid). The winged infant commonly found in Renaissance and baroque art, and having the role either of angelic spirit or the harbinger of profane love, had its origin in Greek and Roman antiquity. The Greek *erotes*, winged spirits, the messengers of the gods, that accompanied a man through his life, were derived from Eros, the god of love. In his earlier manifestations Eros was a youth, or *ephebe*, but by Hellenistic times had grown younger and more child-like in appearance. This form eventually merged with the *genii* of Roman religion, similar guardian spirits that protected a man's soul during his life, and finally conducted it to heaven. Early Christians adopted this pagan image for the representation of angels in catacomb paintings and on sarcophagi. The Middle Ages however based its image of the angel on the full-grown Roman goddess, the winged Victory, and the infants of antiquity disappeared until the Renaissance. Henceforth *putti* feature both as angels in religious painting — a role that reached its zenith in the art of the Counter-Reformation — and as the attendants of Cupid, the ubiquitous messenger of profane love in secular themes." — Hall, *Dictionary of Subjects and Symbols in Art*, p.256. (Ed.)

25   London, National Gallery; K. Escher, *Malerei der Renaissance in Italien (Handbuch der Kunstwissenschaft*, 1922), p.164, Fig. 156.

26   E. Heidrich, *Die alt-deutsche Malerei* (Jena, 1909), Pl. 154.

27   Marle, *Italian Schools of Painting*, IV, 165.

"By the fifteenth century the motif had become so popular that it influenced the representation of other figures, such as the Muses*. In antiquity, these goddesses had usually been shown seated or standing; only rarely were they dancing. For example, on a vase from the fifth century BC, the Muses are seated or standing, five of them with musical instruments [instruments depicted on this vase include harp*, lyre*, *kithara, aulos*]. The classical musical activity of the Muses is singing in antiphonal chorus, as in Homer and later in Petrarch. Around 1400, however, the *Libellus de imaginibus deorum* mentions, among the attributes of Apollo*, the 'laurel tree... under which the Muses nine perform their round' and dance around Apollo singing their melodies. In an Italian [illuminated] manuscript of about 1420, nine dancers are shown performing a round beside [a seated] Apollo. The text says that Apollo holds a kithara in his hand, but in the drawing his instrument is a rebec. According to the text, the muses dance around Apollo, but in the illumination they dance at his feet. Raphael followed the tradition of antiquity in his *Parnassus*, but Mantegna and Guilio Romano [in *Il Ballo d'Apollo con le Muse*] let the Muses perform a round.[28]

"*Singing Angels.* Representations of singing angels were initially less important th–those of other musical angels, and there appear to be reasons for their relative neglect. There are figures of angels holding scrolls with a text inscribed, a way of expressing singing, as well as telling or saying. However, depicting the act of singing itself, the opened mouth, might make an unfortunate impression, especially in sculpture. Indeed, in Romanesque sculpture this feature had a pejorative connotation. Puffed cheeks and lips were reserved for monsters, and especially for Satan. Perhaps this is why singing angels appear somewhat later than music-making or dancing angels. The earliest, so far, are the fourteenth-century angels found in Bohemia.[29] The singing angels by Gozzoli in the Riccardi Chapel are well known, as are the angels on Van Eyck's Ghent Altarpiece....[30] Mantegna included singing *putti* and angels on the tribunes in the Cathedral of Florence.

"Singing angels often appear in groups of three, sometimes among other groups playing on instruments but more frequently by themselves. In an illumination of the Adoration by Niccolo di Ser Sozzo Tegliacci,[31] we have two groups of angels, one with instruments and the other sing-

28   F. Knapp, *Andreas Mantegna (Klassiker der Kunst)* (1910), Pls. 59, 61, 62; E. v.d. Bercken, *Malerei der Renaissance in Italien (Handbuch du Kunstwissenschaft,* 1927), p.36, Fig. 32.

29   A. Friedle, *Mistr Karleniska Apokalypse* (Ivar, 1950), Pl. 2.

30   Marle, *Italian Schools of Painting,* XI; L. v. Puyvelde, *The Holy Lamb* (1947), pp.70, 81; E. Panofsky, *Early Netherlandish Painting* (1953), I, Pl. 150.

31   Bernath, *Die Malerei,* Fig. 424; Marle, *Italian Schools of Painting,* II, 601.

ing [the instruments shown include double end-blown flute, vielle, lute, psaltery]. In the *Mary in Glory* by Giovanni di Paolo, Mary appears in a mandorla formed by cherubim.[32] There is a whole orchestra of angels playing in her honor, and among them, on both sides, trios of singing angels. In the illumination for the Annunciation in the *Très riches Heures* at Chantilly, a trio of singing angels appears twice, once within the main picture and once in the margin at the bottom.[33] There are also angels playing on instruments in both locations, but they do not form groups. A group of three angels singing from a music book is to be found in the Nativity in the *Très riches Heures* at Chantilly, in the Madonna from the Saint Omer Altarpiece by Simon Marmion,[34] and in a Madonna from the Van Eyck school. Groups of three, singing from a scroll, appear in the Nativity pictures by the Master of Flémalle[35] and by Multscher,[36] in an Adoration scene from the Ortenberger Altar, in the *Madonna with Violets* by Lochner,[37] to mention only a few. This trio also appears in a number of later paintings, such as Borgognone's *Adoration of the Christ Child* and his *Madonna with the Saints*, where there are two trios of *putti* singing from books.[38] As late as the sixteenth and seventeenth centuries, singing angel trios appear in the Assumptions by Sabbatini and by Lanfranco, along with players of instruments in both instances.

They appear unaccompanied in Spada's *Vision of Saint Francis.*[39]

"The singing angels do not always seem to inhabit heaven, though sometimes they are in clouds. Often they appear to act as messengers from heaven. It is noteworthy that they are so often grouped in threes, a number which inevitably connotes the Holy Three, the Holy Trinity, though the choice of a trio may also have been due to the fact that this was the usual arrangement for the part songs of the fourteenth century.

"*Angel Orchestras.* The heavenly dancers and singing angels described above were eventually outnumbered by the representations of angels playing musical instruments. Indeed, these representations are so numerous that one can trace only some of the more important forms and traditions here, and touch only on the major problems involved. With few exceptions, all these representations of musician angels are meant to illustrate music and song in the praise of the Lord, of Christ, and of the Virgin in the highest heaven. There are a very few exceptions, where the angels appear as divine inspiration, as in the vaults of [Santa Maria della Bocca at] Offida and of Kampill near Bolzano.[40]II, 297, Fig. 245; A. Colasanti, 'Per la storia dell'arte nelle Marche', *L'Arte*, X (Rome, 1907). Here, the holy men are depicted in the act of writing their works. In Offida,

32   Marle, *Italian Schools of Painting*, IX, 456.

33   Panofsky, *Early Netherlandish Painting*, II, Pl. 36, Fig. 80.

34   G. Ring, *A Century of French Painting* (1949), Pl. 99, cat. no. 171, National Gallery, London.

35   Panofsky, *Early Netherlandish Painting*, II, Pls. 88-89. See also Fig. 233, Jacques Daret, *Nativity*.

36   Heidrich, *Die alt-deutsche Malerei;* Kaiser Friedrich Museum, Berlin.

37   Burger, *Die deutsche Malerei*, Cologne Museum.

38   Bercken, *Malerei der Renaissance*, p.54, Fig. 56.

39   C. Ricci, *Geschichte der Kunst in Nord-Italien* (1911), Fig. 754, Modena Gallery.

40   See Marle, *Italian Schools of Painting*, VIII, 359; for Kampill, see Burger, *Die deutsche Malerei*, SC

above each prophet an angel is playing on a musical instrument [including psaltery, positive organ, lute, bowed rebec, double flute, harp]. In Kampill, angels are kneeling and playing in front of the Church Fathers. Thus, angels have now taken over the role assigned to the Muses in pagan works.[41]

"The traditions of the angel orchestra range from representations based on the old, structured vision of the cosmos to those in which all divisions into spheres have been dissolved and angels fill the whole heaven. The structure of the cosmos may be clearly visible or it may be discernible through a more or less veiled division in several layers or groups. The groups may either represent all the nine orders or only sections; all the orders or only a selection may be recognized through their emblems, or sometimes the musician angels alone are distinguished by their instruments. The angels may just hold the instruments in their hands, or they may be represented performing, or dancing, as well as singing and playing. The figures of the angels may be differentiated from the crowds of the faithful and the blessed or they may be identified with them.

"However, apart from the exceptions where the music gives inspiration, the representations of musician angels can only be interpreted as expressing celestial music and harmony, and a state of bliss. They subscribe to the old Platonic tradition of identifying musical and cosmic harmony.[42] In the paintings after 1300 or so, the cosmos is not always represented in full, as nine spheres. To the contrary, all the orders of the angels are generally placed in the highest heaven, or paradise. In the earlier written sources, such as Capella, the pagan deities were the movers of the spheres.[43] Now the angels take their place, and at the same time are gathered in the highest sphere of heaven. Ultimately... the pagan deities and forces rejoined the music-makers, but for several centuries, until about 1500, the angels starred in this role.

"Starting in approximately the fourteenth century, angels became increasingly identified with the blessed, whereas in Dante's *Paradiso* they were still to be understood as separate entities. In earlier representations of the Last Judgment from the Romanesque period, the blessed were shown, to one side, as emerging from their graves and lifting the covers of the coffins. Mâle[44] and other scholars concluded, therefore, that the outlook of the twelfth and thirteenth centuries was more pessimistic, and that people then visualized the state in hell as more frightening, perhaps excluding any happier hereafter. But it seems to me that it was not that the state

---

41   E. R. Curtius, *Europäische Literatur und lateinisches Mittelalter* (1948), pp.233-50.

42   See also **HARMONY OF THE SPHERES***. See also our theme **T2** (The laws [structure] of music parallel the laws [structure] of nature or the universe, e.g. those having to do with the relation of heavenly bodies or other natural components to each other), *Introductory Remarks,* Vol. I above. (Ed.)

43   For a discussion of the widely influential *De Nuptiis Philologiae et Mercurii et de Septem Artibus Liberalibus Libri Novem* by Martianus Capella, writted c.500 AD, see **HARMONY OF THE SPHERES*** §136.9 below. (Ed.)

44   *L'art religieux du XIIIe siècle* (Paris, 1919); M. Meiss, *Painting in Florence* (1951); Panofsky, *Early Netherlandish Painting,* p.74.

of bliss was doubted, but simply that the painters and sculptors had not yet found a form for expressing the vision of paradise. In the literary sources, such as the writings of Saints Bernard, Bonaventure, and Thomas, one reads that light and music are the characteristics of the highest heaven. But how was music to be represented as long as the playing of instruments was considered sinful? Even Dante, in his grandiose vision, still mentions only singing and dancing, not instrumental music.[45] Heavenly music-makers with instruments had been shown in a few exceptional instances, such as the Beatus manuscripts. There they were a sign of the beauty of heaven, as also in the derived Romanesque sculptures. But it must be borne in mind that the new music, the *ars nova*, made its appearance in the thirteenth century, and that it was not until the fourteenth and fifteenth centuries that instrumental music came into its own as an art.[46] Attitudes toward instrumental music were changing, too, so that Johannes Tinctoris, who lived at the time of the flowering of the Burgundian court, could write in his *Complexus effectuum musicae (On the Effects of Music)*, 'If the painters want to picture the happiness of the blessed they paint angels with different musical instruments. This would not be permitted if the Church did not think that the happiness of the blessed was enriched by music.'[47] All these ideas and impressions are found integrated in the paintings from about 1300 on.

"Paradise is sometimes represented as part of the highest heaven, the Empyreum. It has been noted that in Fra Angelico's *Last Judgment*, paradise is a beautiful garden adjoining the highest heaven, where the celestial court sits, flanking Christ's mandorla. In Fra Angelico's painting, *Christ in Glory*, the scene is laid entirely in the highest heaven; the angels attending Christ are grouped as in the old frescoes, as if they were standing in different spheres, but the last scene shown is the Empyreum. In a later version of the Last Judgment, the construction of the hierarchy is more compact, and there is not the slightest doubt that the scene is the highest heaven; the other sections pale in comparison with the mandorla, which is flanked by the celestial court and the musician angels. This arrangement became typical for representations of the Coronation of the Virgin, where usually only the central scene is shown: Christ crowning the Virgin, surrounded by musician angels.

"The *Civitas Dei* also was adapted to this form.[48] For Augustine, the City of God was a spiritual community of the faithful; by the time in question it had become a celestial city, the heavenly Jerusalem, surrounded by walls like a medieval town. A very early representation occurs in a twelfth-century manuscript of the Canterbury school [illumination, The Lord in Glory in the Celestial Jerusalem, from Saint Augustine's *Civitas Dei*; instruments depicted include oval and guitar-fiddles, bowed rebec]. The walls form the frame of the illumination, with four high columns or towers. In four layers, the apostles and saints attend the heavenly court. On the highest tier, the Lord, in a mandorla, is flanked by six angels playing instruments: three string instruments with bows on the right and on the left, a wind instrument, a

---

45   Dante mentions musical instruments only as comparison, *Paradiso*, XII, 118; XIV, 118; XX, 24.

46   J. Wolf, *Geschichte der Mensural-Notation* (1904); G. Reese, *Music in the Middle Ages* (1940), pp.202f. and 324f. with rich bibliography.

47   E. de Coussemaker, *Scriptores de musica* (1867), II, 504.

48   A. de Laborde, *Les manuscrits à peinture de la Cité de Dieu* (Société des bibliophiles français, Paris, 1909).

dulcimer, and a harp. This motif was especially popular in the illuminations of the French manuscripts of the *Civitas Dei* [see e.g. 15th-century illumination The Lord in Glory in the Celestial Jerusalem; instruments depicted include shawms, lutes, harps]. Usually the Lord was placed in the center, flanked by the celestial court, surrounded by walls; musician angels appear above in the clouds or, more often, in the framework and margin borders. The scene is the highest heaven, Dante's Empyreum.

"A number of representations, however, adhere more to the older tradition that distinguished separate spheres. In an Italian manuscript from about 1400, the illumination to the text *Santa Trinità* [The Lord in Glory; instruments shown include psaltery, bowed fiddle or vielle] shows one arc with stars, denoting the dome of heaven or the firmament. Above is the figure of Christ. Two angels stand where the arc meets the border of the illumination; they are playing on a psaltery and a bowed instrument. These figures are tall compared with the arc, and it may be that the illuminator was inspired by a model in a church where an arch was flanked by the figures of two angels. The *Mary in Glory* by Geertgen or his school shows Mary surrounded by three circles of angels; however, the place of the scene is the highest heaven. In representations of the Adoration of the Lamb, the influence of the old tradition is even stronger, for a division into the parts of the cosmos, sometimes as on a chart, prevails. The Ghent Altarpiece divides scenes into distinct panels where the musician angels have their definite place.

"It has been mentioned that in the Beatus manuscripts, where the musician angels appear for the first time, they stand side-by-side with the musician Elders; yet at first it was the Elders who carried on the tradition, the angels as musicians being a later development. Where the angels ap-

peared beside the Elders, the latter were often placed in a group and played on musical instruments, while the angels showed the emblems of their orders but did not make music. For this combination we have a good and elaborate example on the Royal Portal at Chartres.[49] Fortunately, there is one work in which the two sections of the heavenly orchestra, the Elders and the angels, meet; and both are included as musicians in the hierarchy of the highest heaven. It is a fourteenth-century fresco, a Coronation [of the Virgin], in the Cathedral of Venzone in northern Italy [instruments shown include 3 psalteries, 2 lutes, 2 tambourines, portative organ; 2 busines, lute, vielle, drum (?) nakers, portative organ; 2 guitars*, fiddles, tambourine, psaltery, bowed rebec]. In the center, Christ is crowning Mary; above them there are angels with wind instruments, and Christ and Mary are flanked by rows of angels, with those in the front row carrying musical instruments. On the left of the center section there are three angels with lute, psaltery, and a wind instrument; on the right, three angels with a wind instrument, a portable organ, and a double drum. Above the group of Christ and Mary, and above the musician angels on top, there are angels, elderly men (perhaps the apostles), and youthful figures, all without music. On the farther sides, in separate sections, appear the Elders, identified by their crowns and beards, and they make music. The left-hand group has two tambourines, a portable organ, two lutes, and three psalteries; the right-hand group has what might be identified as a tambourine, a psaltery, three bowed instruments of different sizes (one with a curved neck), a harp, and a portable organ. This fresco is the only example I have been able to find which combines the tradition of both groups working together as musicians.

---

49   Et. Houvet, *Cathédrale de Chartres* (1926).

"When angels alone are the music-makers, the duty of playing on instruments is sometimes assigned to only one of the orders, sometimes to several; yet there are instances in which all of the angels play music. When only one order is playing, the instruments are usually given to the group placed lowest or farthest from the center. The Mary in Glory in the illumination by Niccolo di Ser Sozzo Tegliacci from a [fourteenth-century] Sienese manuscript [called Caleffo dell'Assunta, mentioned previously,] is an early example. The Virgin in the mandorla is supported by the inner circle of the angels; the orders of the cherubim and seraphim form two rows on top. Then follow, in descending order on each side, groups of adoring figures, singing angels, and, finally, angels with musical instruments (psaltery, lute, vielle, and flute).

"This arrangement, with the music-making assigned to the lowest order of angels, appears in numerous representations. In the *Assunta* by Masolino, the Virgin is in a mandorla formed by cherubim and seraphim. Both orders are shaped like swallows, with human heads with halos. An outer circle is formed by the other orders, with the angels carrying the emblems of their status — shields, orbs, lances, sceptres — the Virtues holding banners inscribed *virtues;* and at the bottom, there are four angels with psaltery, lute, vielle, and portable organ. In the Coronation by Leonardo da Biscussio, in a mandorla, Christ is crowning the Virgin and they are being blessed by the Lord. The angels frame the mandorla in a broad band. The corners, outside of this frame, are filled by groups of the saints, patriarchs, and donors. The angels themselves are divided into distinct groups. The innermost bands are formed by cherubim and seraphim. The outer circle has an arrangement different

from the Sienese and Masolino pictures: the angels are divided into four sections, and their position follows the line of the mandorlas so that the upper group forms a kind of steeple and has a counterpart of two groups of angels at the bottom. The groups at both top and bottom carry palm branches or fold their hands in prayer. The two middle sections of angels are musicians, with the singers in the higher rows and the angels playing on instruments in the lower row; the lower orders are on the sides....

"Most of the representations of musician angels originated in Italy. Neither in France nor in the northern countries is their appearance so general. Yet some specific traits of the French conception are worth mentioning. French works tend to show the Empyreum not as a dome of clouds but as similar to real cathedrals and cities. It has been noted that the *Civitas Dei* in French manuscripts has the form of a walled city.[50] The different approach of the French masters may be illustrated with an illumination from Fouquet's *Chevalier Hours* [Etienne Chevalier adoring the Virgin, from the *Heures d'Etienne Chevalier;* instruments shown include 2 recorders, cornette or *Rauschpfeife*, psaltery, vielle, lute].[51] Here, in the *Madonna in the Church*, Mary is seated in a cathedral portal or arched niche which has three voussoirs[52] of adoring angels. She is attended by angels in the position and costumes of choir boys. The illumination of the Holy Trinity from the same Book of Hours also sets the scene in the interior of a cathedral. Twelve circles of angels surround the Trinity. Cherubim and seraphim, the former characterized by six feathered wings, the latter by the color red, as of fire, form two circles around the Trinity. Rows of figures follow, like the voussoirs of a portal, starting at the bottom with saints and patriarchs and the like, and

50   Laborde, *Les manuscrits à peinture de la Cité de Dieu*, Pl. 127.
51   K. Perls, *Jean Fouquet* (1940), p.57, Fig. 25, and plate between pp.56 and 57.
52   *Voussoir*, one of the tapering or wedge-shaped pieces forming an arch or vault. (Ed.)

changing to angels in adoring postures as the row rises. Neither illumination suggests an outdoor image of the highest heaven so much as the interior of a cathedral.

"The work of the French masters also differs from the Italians in that the French angels are busier with practical duties as servants and pages, such as carrying the crown and the train of the Virgin's mantle, as shown, for example, in the Coronation illumination of the *Berry Hours*.[53] In Fouquet's *Chevalier Hours*, angels serve Saint Michael like pages, and one is supporting his wings while he is fighting the dragon.[54] A third characteristic of the French is that they often place musician angels in the arches of buildings. Thus, two angels with bowed instruments (mandorla [*sic?*] and vielle), appear in the frame of the Bargello Diptych (French, *ca.* 1390),[55] on the upper left part of the architecture. Musician angels appear in the architectural border of a drawing of Saint Jerome in his study by Pol de Limbourg, where they must be understood as signs of inspiration [illumination of Saint Jerome in his study by Pol de Limbourg, which appears in a fragmentary manuscript of the *Bible moralisée*; instruments shown include transverse flute, harp, nakers, lute, vielle, portative organ].

"One further French illumination worth noting is from the fourteenth-century manuscript of Dionysius [*De Hierarchia*] in the Bibliothèque Nationale [instruments depicted include vielle, shawms, 2 portative organs, 2 guitars].[56] At the bottom, Saint Denis is shown writing his book. Above him, in nine arcs, appear the nine orders of the angels, three angels on each side.[57] In three of these nine rows or arcs, the angels have musical instruments. The instruments are identical on both left and right sides of the arcs. In the lowest circle, each trio has a plucked instrument, a wind instrument, and a percussion instrument; in the fifth circle, a psaltery, an organ, and a tambourine; and in the ninth circle, cymbals, shawms, and vielles. In the arc second from the bottom, there are two cymbal players on each side, in addition to an angel with censers. The rest of the angels either hold censers or crowns, or they are adorants. This is the old tradition of the structure of the heavens in nine spheres with Dionysius's nine orders of the angels, but the orders have not the usual emblems and, contrary to the theory of the hierarchy, three of the orders are musicians.

"When discussing singing angels, we noted the frequent appearance of a trio of singers as messengers or as a sign from heaven. Groups of three music-making angels occur in all kinds of scenes, but they may always be regrded as messengers from heaven, whether they appear in clouds or on earth. For example a group appears in the clouds in the Saint Omer Altarpiece[58] by Marmion. Such a group is built into the hierarchy of Bosch's *Seven Cardinal Sins* [in which the instruments depicted include psaltery, busine, harp]. Christ enthroned is flanked by adoring angels, and four adoring angels kneel before Him while saints look on from the right. On the left, the

---

53   *Les belles heures de Jean de France,* ed. Jean Porcher (1953), Pl. xxx, fol. 30.
54   Perls, *Jean Fouquet*, p.73, Fig. 41.
55   Ring, *A Century of French Painters*, Pl. I.
56   H. Martin, *Légende de Saint-Denis* (1908).
57   For list of the nine orders, see James Hall quotation at the head of this entry. (Ed.)
58   Ring, *A Century of French Painting.*

blessed are seen entering paradise through a door, where they are received by Saint Peter and defended against Satan by Saint Michael. In the center foreground, three angels are making music on a psaltery, a wind instrument, and a harp. In Cranach's *Flight into Egypt,* two angels are playing on pipes beside the Christ-child, and there are similar angel musicians in the Adoration of the Child on the Ortenberg Altar [wherein are depicted harp and lute]. Four music-making angels are leaning against a column, playing and singing, in Bramantino's *Nativity;*[59] a similar group appears beside the Christ-child in Piero della Francesca's *Nativity.*[60]

"In the course of the sixteenth century, the image of a structure of heaven gradually dissolved. In Signorelli's painting in the cathedral at Orvieto, the elects upon entering heaven are greeted by musician angels on clouds, playing tambourines, lutes, a guitar, a harp, and a vielle.[61] In pictures of the Assumption, a theme now more popular than the Coronation, Mary is seen soaring or flying upward into the clouds, sometimes greeted or supported by angels. Relatively few of these angels are musicians. Thus, in Titian's *Assumption,*[62] one of the *putti* holds a tambourine and one a small pipe; in Sabbatini's *Assumption,*[63] a group of angels seems to be singing, one with a harp, another a plucked instrument (only partially shown). In the *Assumption* by Lanfranco, three angels are singing and one has a lyra da braccio. In the *Assumption* of Annibale Carracci, one

angel has a pipe and a viola da braccio. The orchestration is comparatively elaborate in a painting, *Paradise,* by Lodovico Carracci in San Paolo, Bologna, where angels in several groups are playing on wind, string, and percussion instruments; there is also a chorus singing in the background and one angel conducting. In the lower left of the picture are saints and, above, one angel is swinging a censer; yet no distinct layers are discernible. Indeed, in none of these paintings is there any suggestion of a systematic structure of spheres or orders....

"*Angels of the Psalter.* A final general category of representations of musician angels is formed by those related to the Psalms. The boundaries of this group may seem arbitrary in specific instances, but there is nonetheless a useful distinction to be drawn between the angel musicians of heavenly bliss discussed above and those related to the Psalms. The latter fill an essentially different role, that of replacing or representing the faithful in praising the Lord, and have relatively slight connections with the concepts of music of the spheres.

"The Psalms played an important part in Christian liturgy from the very beginning, and today about nine-tenths of the liturgy is drawn from the Psalter, not so much in the form of whole psalms as in isolated verses. The texts of the Psalms were thus ever present to the clergy and the community, and singing and praising the Lord with music are constantly mentioned in the

---

59 A. Venturi, *North Italian Drawings of the Quatrocento,* Vol. I (1930), Pl. 34; Suardi called Bramantino, Ambrosiana, Milan.

60 K. Clark, *Piero della Francesca* (1951), Pls. 125-28.

61 R. Hamann, *Die Frührenaissance der italienischen Malerei* (1909), Pl. 87.

62 H. Tietze, *Titian* (1950), Pl. 35.

63 Ricci, *Geschichte der Kunst,* p.387, Fig. 739; Accademia, Bologna.

Psalms.[64] Singing and playing on psaltery and harp are mentioned with greatest frequency, and the last Psalm (150) gives a detailed list of the instruments to be used to praise the Lord: trumpet, psaltery, harp, timbrel, stringed instruments, organs, and cymbals. Of course, it is not known exactly what most of the terms originally meant. 'Organ' is certain not an accurate translation, because there were no organs used by the Biblical peoples. And different translations name quite different instruments.

"In the Psalms it is not the angels specifically who are said to be singing and playing, but the multitude of the faithful that is called upon to sing the praise of the Lord. It may be recalled that one of the Gnostic books attributed singing to the angels only during the night.[65] The duty of singing during the day was to be performed by the faithful. Thus, in the earliest illuminations to the Psalter (the Utrecht Psalter, ninth century), it is not angels but the companions of David who play instruments. In the visions of the Lord in the Utrecht Psalter, adoring angels stand beside Him, while in the lower strata humans play instruments [the instruments depicted include lyres, krotalon, organ (operated with a sort of bellows), horns or oliphants].

"Later, musician angels began to appear in conjunction with the faithful in Psalter illustrations, and it might be noted that while this development is analogous to the angels' joining the dance of the blessed in paradise, it seems to have started somewhat earlier. The earliest example I have found is in the Majestas illumination of a Psalter manuscript supposed to have come from Gloucester in the thirteenth century. Here, in the border, there are six musician angels who seem to be more or less integrated into a kind of hierarchy. On the highest level, there are two with bowed instruments, plus two singers. In the lower stratum there are four harp players.

"The illuminations of the Queen Mary Psalter[66] are full of musicians, both angels and mortals. The angels are shown both in celestial scenes and in events taking place on earth. In the illumination of the Lord in Glory, four pairs of angels flank the mandorla. Three of these pairs play instruments, as follows: harp and psaltery, two stringed instruments, one with a bow, and two wind instruments. All the illuminations show the instruments being played, not just held, and one can tell that the artist must have known how these instruments were used.

"Single musician angels also seem to antedate grouped heavenly musicians in works of art in churches. Individual musician angels began to appear in windows and sculpture in the fifteenth century, often as a series either in lunettes on the same window or separate small windows, or spread out on the bosses. No specific number of musicians seems to have prevailed in this kind of presentation; their quantity evidently depended on the number of places they were intended to decorate.

"This type of angel is to be found in England, France, and Germany. One of the earliest specimens is the 'choir of angels' in the north transept of Westminster Abbey, dating from about 1250 [King David is shown with his harp and angel musicians]. There is a total of twenty-four angels, of which eleven carry objects used in the liturgy and the rest play musical instruments. As far as the instruments can be

64 E. Nikel, *Geschichte der katholischen Kirchenmusik* (1908), pp.88ff., with quotations from Saint Augustine on Psalms 42, 70, and 150; B. Finesinger, 'Musical Instruments in the Old Testament', *Hebrew College Annual*, III, (1926), with quotations from Jerome, Isidor, and Chrysostome.

65 Utrech Psalter in the Library of Utrecht University; facsimile, London, 1875.

66 British Museum, Royal MS, 2B VII; facsimile edition by G. F. Warner, 1912.

recognized, there are five strings, two winds, and five percussion instruments. The stringed instruments can be designated, though some of them seem rather fictional, as a lyre, a cithera (plucked and played with a plectrum), a viol with bow, a psaltery, and a harp. The wind instruments are a single and a triple kind of pipe; the percussion instruments are cymbals and tambourines. From a somewhat later date (fourteenth century) are the single angels with musical instruments (including a portable organ) at Saint Edmunds-Saint Mary and Exeter [wherein instruments shown include vielle, recorder (?), lute, bagpipe, harp]. At Gloucester, single angels appear on the bosses, some with the instruments of the Passion, and six with musical instruments: bagpipe, portable organ, harp, trombone (busine), vielle, and shawm. In the Lincoln Cathedral (second half of the thirteenth century), a choir is decorated with angels, including a number of musicians. Some are shown to be singers by their scrolls. The instruments used are several harps, a stringed instrument with a bow and one to be plucked, winds, among them a double aulos, and one percussion instrument. In the middle is a winged King David with harp and crown. In Germany there are a number of fourteenth-century musician angels in glass paintings; there are five angels (dating from 1335) at the Cisterciensi monastery in Bebenhausen, in stained glass lunettes in the refectory, who are playing a harp, a double aulos, a vielle, a plucked instrument (similar in form to the one in the Westminster cycle), and another bowed instrument. Glass lunettes in one Eustachius window in the dome at Erfurt show angels playing against a patterned background. In France, the appearance of such musician angels in glass windows is so frequent that Mâle speaks of hundreds

of them.[67] Like the few examples given here, they support the generalization that all kinds of instruments are played by this type of angel and that the instruments shown are of the period in which the work in question was executed....

"A link to the Psalms is perhaps more definite where musician angels decorate the balconies for choirs or for the organ. Among the most famous examples are the figures in the Exeter Cathedral,[68] (1951); K. Voll, *Memling (Klassiker der Kunst)* (1909), Pls. 120-22. Memling's paintings for an organ setting [featuring Christ and angel musicians], and [two] works of Donatello and Luca della Robbia. The decoration of the singers' balcony in Exeter Cathedral is dated about 1350; it consists of twelve angels standing in Gothic niches with the following musical instruments: lute, bagpipe, recorder, vielle, harp, pan's pipe, herald trumpet, portable organ, guitar, shawm, tambourine, and cymbals. The musician angels of Memling's organ decoration are placed in the clouds, in heaven, and beside the figure of Christ as Pantocrator, who is also flanked by three singing angels on each side. The composition is divided into panels. The side panels show groups of five angels, one group with psaltery, tromba marina, lute, trombone, and recorder; another with herald trumpet, trombone, portative organ, harp, and vielle.

"Both Della Robbia's and Donatello's panels were planned for the same place, the Cathedral of Florence, and at approximately the same time, around 1430-35. Della Robbia divided his balcony with ten panels. For the front, there are four panels in the upper row and four beneath the columns; then there are two for the sides. If there were any doubt that these groups are related to the Psalms, it would be cleared by the inscription on the border of the balcony, which cites the opening

67   Mâle, *L'art religieux de la fin du moyen-âge en France*, p.477.
68   Exeter, see C. J. Cave, *Medieval Carvings in Exeter* (1953); Gardner, *English Medieval Sculpture* .

phrase of the last five Psalms: *Laudate Dominum*. The two side panels show five and seven singers, and it may be that these numbers have allegorical meaning. The five singers would correspond to the five sacred tones (the notes do, re, mi, fa, sol) of the Magnificat; the seven to the movers and singers of the seven spheres. Though the figures have no wings, they might be presumed to represent angels, as they are standing on clouds. The four panels in the upper front row show a combination of playing and dancing figures. The order of the instruments follows the list in the 150th Psalm. Beneath we read the inscriptions: *tuba, psalterium et cithara, corda, tympanum, organum, cimbali benesonantes*, and *cimbali iubilationis*. There are 76 musicians, dancers, singers, and players. All the instruments were in use in the fifteenth century.

"Donatello decorated the counterpart to Della Robbia's balcony. He made the upper row a continuous round of dancing and singing *putti* with wings. On one panel of the lower row, two *putti* play the tambourine and cymbals. Donatello used similar motifs in three other works: two *putti* on the baptismal font at Siena play tambourine and horns; a round of dancing and singing *putti* with tambourine and cymbals appear on his outside pulpit at Prato; and his twelve panels for the altar in the Santo at Padua have singing and playing *putti*. At Padua, two panels show pairs of *putti* singing from books; the instruments are three stringed instruments (one of them a little viol with bow, a pochette, and a lute and a harp), percussion instruments (tambourine and cymbals), and wind instruments (twice the double aulos, and thrice recorders).

"The number of the performing angels in the works I regard as inspired by the text of the Psalms is not uniform; the figures are not always portrayed as angels. The maidens and youths of Della Robbia's balcony might equally well belong to a work on a secular theme. The musician *putti*, too, look as if they were taken from a joyful piece of pagan sculpture and were, rather, *eroti* or *amoretti*. In the English works and on the German glass windows, however, the musicians are definitely angels; here they have taken over the role of the faithful from the texts of the Psalms. With a few exceptions the background does not show any sign of cosmic spheres. That the place where the music is performed is heaven is sometimes suggested by the clouds on which the dancers and musicians are standing, and once by clouds and stars in the background. Thus there is occasionally a weak reflection of the traditional structure of heavenly music.

"The angel musicians deriving from the Psalms have the loosest connection with the cosmic spheres. Yet it is possible... that such sculpture and painting might have been seen by Dante, who integrated these figures into his vision of paradise which, in turn, influenced later representations. From the fourteenth century on, musician angels are regularly seen surrounding the Virgin, and this form became so prevalent that the Assumption paintings by Tintoretto and Gaudenzio Ferrari have survived under the title *Paradiso*.

"Angels' Instruments — Real or Imaginary? The painters of celestial concerts were free to assemble all the instruments they wanted, and it is obvious that very often the artists did not intend to depict reality. Therefore, the questions generally asked by musicologists — are the instruments which we see real ones, is this a real orchestra — are too simply formulated. Real instruments can be shown side by side with invented ones. Realism, illusion, and symbolism can be interwoven.

"This field as a whole is tangential to the main topic of this study, since it is properly part of *musica instrumentalis* and not of *musica mundana* or *musica humana*; but a few points are worth touching on here. A study of two ninth- and tenth-century manuscripts indicates a mixture of sources for the instruments. In the Beatus illustrations, the instruments seem to show some forms drawn after reality and some forms apparently in imitation of classical models. In the Utrecht Psalter there is also a mixture of contemporary and antique instruments, with the latter predominating. Of course, from the representations of contemporary instruments conclusions may be drawn concerning the practice of music-making at the time. However, one must be very careful. The problem is that one must know beforehand what to expect.[69] The knowledge to be drawn from the picture has to be supplemented by the text if a text accompanies the illustration, and has to be further combined with the information that can be gathered from reports of performances of the time. Then only can one apply the findings from what is observed in the paintings.

"The same problem exists for representations both of single instruments and of ensembles. Can one speak of angel orchestras if this term is understood in the modern sense? For instance, I am convinced that an illustration such as the one for the 150th Psalm in the Utrecht Psalter is not an image of actual music-making of the ninth or tenth century, when only music in unison was known. Even the Beatus ensembles, where all players have exactly the same instruments, are unlikely to represent reality when there are as many as twenty-four persons. In Gaudenzio Ferrari's ensemble [in his ceiling decoration *Assumption of the Virgin*] one can count more than seventy instruments, some of them completely imaginary. Shall we consider this a picture of music-making in the sixteenth century?

"As related to reality, I would like to point out several characteristics which can often be observed in the representations of angel orchestras. First, there is the trio combination of harp, lute, and a bowed instrument. These are the types that appeared, though usually separately, in the Beatus manuscripts. This trio is found in a number of other works, including one in which David and his companions are performers. The latter is a twelfth-century sculpture in the baptistry at Parma, a work attributed to Antelami, a sculptor probably apprenticed in Provence. This would help to confirm the theory that instrumental music wandered from Spain and Provence to the northern countries, northern France, and northern Italy. The second point is that often in the two groups framing the figure of the Virgin the lute appears on one side, and on the other there is a bowed instrument or a portative (which came into use about 1200).[70] Thus, this pairs an instrument which carries the tune with an instrument to provide chords in accompaniment. Both the combination of the trio and the pair in question can be imagined as ensembles of the *ars nova*. A third scene which seems a plausible reflection of actual music-making is one in which one type of instrument appears in different sizes. This sort of ensemble playing is known to have been popular far into the seventeenth century and still exists today in our quartet. There are such sets of instruments in the frame of the Landino il-

---

69 For example, the instrument of one of the elders at Fenouillard (tenth century) has open or drone strings, and similar strings appear on the viola da braccio of Raphael's Apollo (sixteenth century). To rely on observation alone can lead to major blunders in interpretation. One specialist on the history of instruments, C. Sachs, mistook the rod which David carries in the Utrech Psalter (Psalm 108) for the bow of a stringed instrument, and a Cretan goddess's snake for a lyre.

70 H. Hickmann, *Das Portativ* (1936).

lumination of the *Squarcialupi Codex*.[71] Another example is the famous painting of the angel concert from Matthias Grünewald's Isenheimer Altar. (This provides, incidentally, an interesting case of a complex relationship; one's first impression is that of a huge orchestra, yet there are actually only three viol players.)

"For the problem of reality versus illusion in orchestras, there is the excellent material E. Bowles has assembled, especially in his article on musical instruments in civic processions during the Middle Ages. Bowles collected descriptions from the fourteenth century onward, and especially from the fifteenth century. He quotes from poetic works and chronicles. The poets mention many instruments without specifying whether they were played simultaneously. In the reports contained in the chronicles, we read of a few musicians accompanying the king or prince, or, if the scribe mentions many instruments, he adds that they are sounding from all over the town, from all the towers and gates, or that the procession passes a number of places where different groups of musicians are set up. According to these accounts, groups of singers and instrumentalists performed on floats in processions, or passed before balconies and stages erected for the occasion on which certain scenes were represented. Sometimes figures from classic myths are mentioned, but more often we hear of our old acquaintances, the angels and the Elders. Such scenes are also included in some of the mystery plays. In a miracle play of the Incarnation, given at Rouen in 1474, the real musicians played from behind the figures of angels. In 1485, at the entry of Charles VIII into Rouen, figures representing the twenty-four Elders, in white brocade with crowns, held different instruments, while the town musicians stood behind them and played the music. In 1461, Louis IX, on his way from Reims to Paris, passed tableaux on erected scaffolds. On one, three sirens sang motets and bergerettes, while musicians beside them played 'grandes mélodies'. One of the reports mentioned by Bowles provides an interesting account of a scene of the twenty-four musician Elders; the Elders are described as having all kinds of instruments, but the actual music was made by musicians stanidng behind the group in the scene.[72]

"Thus there are instances both in paintings and in the reports in the chronicles where reflections and descriptions of actual music-making are discernible. And, admittedly, something can be learned from them concerning both single instruments and ensembles. But in the main, the question of whether or not these are representations of real performances seems put in the wrong way. It is perfectly possible that the representations were not so much imitations of an existing reality as the inspiration which led the composers to create the reality. In his cupola painting, Ferrari depicts real instruments and imagined forms. Some groups of his orchestra seem to represent real ensembles, combinations of instruments for which we have reports by several chroniclers. We see also some groups in which instruments of the same kind but in different sizes are shown. Such ensembles are documented

---

71   The *Squarcialupi Codex*, Pal. 87, Bibl. Laurenziana, Florence, fol. 121v, ed. Joh. Wolf (St. Louis, 1957), p.197; M. Agricola, *Musica instrumentalis deudsch* (1529); S. Virdung, *Musica getutscht* (1511).

72   E. Bowles, 'Musical Instruments in Civic Processions', *Acta Musicologica* (1961); L. Traube, *Vorlesungen und Abhandlungen*, Vol. 3 (1920), p.302. Also, there is a little-known miracle play, still annually enacted in Spain, in which children dressed as angels take part, singing. A set of the stage directions has survived from the fourteenth century.

in the contemporary treatises on musical instruments. From the fifteenth century we have numerous descriptions of actual ensemble performances and descriptions in which the instruments are listed. In the sixteenth century, small orchestras are mentioned for the accompaniment *in intermedii* of a group of comedians from Padua in Ferrara and in Florence in 1560. Two famous orchestras existed in Ferrara in the sixteenth century, one at the court and one in the convent of St. Vito. Of the latter we have enthusiastic reports by Artusi, Guarini, and Bottrigari. They mention that a nun conducted from a gravicembalo, list the many instruments, and emphasize the effect of the harmonious playing together. Later follow the reports by Pietro della Valle about the orchestras used by the Camerata in Florence about 1600. In the seventeenth century the famous orchestra, often regarded as the first modern institution of its kind, was the *Vingt-quatre Violons du Roi*, the string ensemble under Lully. And I wonder whether the number twenty-four is not a last reminder of the musician Elders." — Meyer-Baer, pp.130-32, 134, 136-39, 141-45, 147-51, 154, 156, 158, 161-63, 173-87.

ASIAN PRACTICES AND BELIEFS. *(See also p.66.)*

§24.4 KHMER MYTHOLOGY (Indo-China/Cambodia). "Of the thirty-two hells of Angkor Vat, a certain number are described in the *Trai Phum*. [Independently of these] there is a hell only peopled with phantoms, spirits, wandering souls.... 'It is the hell of deep night, intense cold, absolute silence, and continuing hunger.' The rays of the Sun never penetrate here. Ghosts or spirits (*pretas* or *khmoch* in Cambodian) in popular belief are moderately tall, always famished, with enormous bellies, but all the rest of their frames incredibly emaciated; they feed only on filth or excrement, without ever

being satisfied. Some have pigs' masks for faces, others vomit fire that burns them away, others cut and slash their flesh with their own nails.

"The *kmoch pray* are ghosts of women dead in childbirth and of stillborn babes... The *daerechhan* are beings that have been condemned to be born again in the shape of beasts without reason....

"Beside these animals there are a great number of a fantastic character, which figure very frequently in the tales and legends of the country: their reproduction in Cambodian drawings, sculptures, paintings, and jewels is often the basis of superb decorative motives. Among them I will cite the Reachea-Sey, a lion that has the power of leaping and flying through the air. The architecture of Angkor multiplied the representations of this animal (*Seng*) on the projections of the temple stairways.

"The Kruth (Garuda) is a bird with a human bust, with monstrous clawed feet, which in ancient as well as modern Cambodian art is more extensively found than in any other country.... This is the mythical bird, the serpents' foe, which in the Brahman religion is the god Vishnu's mount....

"Then come other creatures, Kenor, or Kenarey, akin to the Gandharvas* of India through their musical talents, with bird's wings and feet and a human bust. Modern Cambodian drawings often give very graceful conventionaliztions of these strange creatures (see illustration following page)....

"A myth particularly dear to the Khmer decorators must be told: it is that of the churning of the sea of milk, which at Angkor Vat extends over a length of some fifty yards.

"At Vishnu's suggestion the gods made a pack with the Asuras (demons) with the object of bringing out the *amrita*, the liquor of immortality, by churning the ocean of milk. The churn-staff is Mount Mandara, around which is coiled the serpent Ananta, to serve as a rope; Vishnu in the shape of a tortoise supports the mountain used

KENAREY
From a modern document.
Drawing by Mlle Sappho Marchal.

as a churn-staff. This god takes an active part in the churning in other ways: after seeing him as a resting-point for the churn-staff we see him half-way up in human shape brandishing discus and sword, and on the top of the mountain animating and superintending the action; Devas and Asuras pull alternately. The gods have been placed at the tail end of the serpent to leave the disadvantage with the demons, when the reptiles's jaws belch out poisonous flames, while the clouds, driven away from the opposite side, refresh the gods with beneficient rains.

"The sea of milk is churned in this way for more than a thousand years, and from it there start up in succession all kinds of fantastic creatures, until the moment when the poison let loose threatens to over-whelm the world and cause it to perish under sulphurous vapours; at Brahma's re-quest the god Shiva* [in Hindu mythology the arch-ascetic, the Divine Yogi — master of the cosmic dance; as Nataraja (dance king), Shiva fills the whole cosmos with his joyful dance called *tandava* (Ed.)] swallows the poison, which stays in his throat, whence he has his surname of Nilakantha (blue throat). At length appears the goblet of *amrita*, the liquor so greatly desired; from the tossing waves emerges likewise the Goddess of Beauty, Lakshmi: at sight of her the whole world is charmed. The sages sing her praises, the celestial musicians play their sweetest melodies for her, and the Apsarases, also born from the sea of milk, dance for her. Two elephants dip up water from a golden vase, to pour it over the head of the goddess. Before this charming welcome Lakshmi smiles at the gods and throws herself on Vishnu's breast; the Asuras, jealous at this preference, seize the cup of *amrita*, but Vishnu, in a female shape, distracts their attention, cheating them, so that he is able to retore the liquor to the gods. The vexed demons flee away and return to the nether realms of Patala." — Marchal, in Hackin, pp.200, 203, 219-20, 222.

AZTEC PRACTICES AND BELIEFS. *(See also pp.71, 821.)*

§31.4 XOCHIPILLI AND MACUIL-XÓCHITL — PATRONS OF DANCE.
"Xochipilli, 'the prince of flowers', the patron of dances, games, and love, and symbol of summer, was intimately connect with Centéotl. He is sometimes thought to be related to the Red Tezcatlipoca*, although the latter was more of a solar deity. His symbol, the *tonallo*, is formed by four points signifying the heat of the sun. Xochipilli is pictured adorned with flowers and butterflies, and he carries a staff, the *yolotopilli*, on which a human heart is impaled. A deity so similar to him that perhaps it is only his calendar name was 'Five Flower', Macuilxóchitl, also the patron of games, dances, and sports. His wife Xochiquetzal, 'the flower of the rich plume', was the personification of beauty and love. She was the goddess of flowers and the patroness of domestic work, but she was also the patroness of courtesans, the *auianime* or *maqui*, who lived with the bachelor warriors, because she had been kidnapped by the young Texcatlipoca, the

warrior from the North. She is characterized by two large, erect panaches [bunch of feathers or a plume, especially on a helmet (Ed.)] made from the feathers of the quetzal bird and by her richly embroidered garments.

"Xochipilli and Xochiquetzal were worshipped principally by the Indians of the *chinampas*, or floating gardens. They were the Xochimilcans, who then, as now, grew on their floating gardens flowers used by the temples and palaces of Tenochtitlán." — Caso, p.47.

§31.5 "To the Aztecs in Mexico and their neighbors to the South, the Mayans, the world is suffused with an almost supernatural quality of aliveness. Colors, flowers, wind, water — even the silence between the stars — are seen as symbols of the workings of the universe and of our place within it. The Aztecs believed in a complex system of gods, who personified many of the forces of nature. The sun itself was a god who lived in a house in the sky where there was much singing and dancing. Another god, Tezcatlipoca*, like many Aztec gods, took on different forms, but most often represented night. It was Tezcatlipoca who asked Quetzalcoatl — an important Aztec god who represented the spirit and the wind — to journey to the sun and bring the musicians there back to earth.

"[My book for children, *All of You Was Singing* — which is based on materials published in Irene Nicholson's *Mexican and Central American Mythology*, excerpted below[73] —] is a retelling of this myth about how music came to Earth. As with all myths, many meanings can be read into it. My own sense of this myth is the profound importance of music to the well-being of life. To sing is an affirmation of the melody and rhythm of life. And such singing continues, as in this Aztec song, even after us:

---

73 For complementary accounts, see also §31.2, p.71 above. See also **ORIGINS OF MUSIC***. (Ed.)

My flowers shall not perish
Nor shall my chants cease
They spread, they scatter."

— Lewis, preface to
All of You Was Singing.

"HOW MUSIC WAS MADE. Tezcat-lipoca [matter] besought Quetzalcoatl [spirit[74]] that he should make the journey to the House of the Sun,[74] comes. He gave Quetzalcoatl specific instructions: that when he reached the seashore he must en-list the help of Tezcatlipoca's three ser-vants who were called Cane and Conch, Water Woman, and Water Monster. Quet-zalcoatl was to order these three entwined together to form a bridge over which he could pass to reach the Sun. On arriving at the Sun he was to ask for musicians, and was to bring them back to earth to delight the souls of men.

"Quetzalcoatl did as he was told, and when the Sun saw him approaching he warned his musicians not to utter a word. Any who opened his mouth would have to return to earth with the wind god. The musicians, clad in white, red, yellow, and green, resisted the temptation to unloose their tongues; but at last one of them relented, gave voice, and descended with Quetzalcoatl to earth where he was able to give mankind the pleasure of music.

"In a sixteenth-century Nahua manu-script there is a poem describing this inci-dent:

Texcatlipoca — god of heaven
and of the four quarters of the
  heavens —
came to earth and was sad.
He cried from the uttermost depths
  of the four quarters:
  'Come, O wind!

Come, O wind!
Come, O wind!
Come, O wind!'
The querulous wind, scattered over
  earth's sad bosom,
rose higher than all things made;
and, whipping the waters of the
  oceans
and the manes of the trees,
arrived at the feet of the god of
  heaven.
There he rested his black wings
and laid aside his endless sorrow.
Then spoke Tezcatlipoca:
  'Wind, the earth is sick from
    silence.
  Though we possess light and
    colour and fruit, yet we have no
    music.
  We must bestow music upon all
    creation.
  To the awakening dawn,
  to the dreaming man,
  to the waiting mother,
  to the passing water and the flying
    bird,
  life should be all music!
  Go then through the boundless
    sadness
  between the blue smoke and the
    spaces to the high House of the
    Sun.
  There the father Sun is
    surrounded by makers of music
  who blow their flutes sweetly
  and, with their burning choir,
  scatter light abroad.
  Go, bring back to earth a cluster
    — the most flowering —
  of those musicians and singers.'
Wind traversed the earth that was
  plunged in silence
and trod with his strength of breath
  pursued,
till he reached the heavenly roof of
  the World

---

74 The bringer of wisdom, whose many manifestations included that of the wind god Ehecatl, who brought love to the human race when he bestirred the maiden Mayahuel.

where all melodies lived in a nest of
light.
The Sun's musicians were clad in
four colours.
White were those of the cradle
songs;
red those of the epics of love and of
war;
sky blue the troubadours of
wandering cloud;
yellow the flute players enjoying
gold
milled by the Sun from the peaks of
the World.
There were no musicians the colour
of darkness.
All shone translucent and happy,
their gaze turned forward.
When the sun saw the wind
approaching, he told hi
musicians:
'Here comes the bothersome
wind of earth:
Stay your music!
Cease your singing!
Answer him not!
Whoever does so
will have to follow him
back down there into silence.'
From the stairways of light
of the House of the Sun,
Wind with his dark voice shouted,
'Come, O musicians!'
None replied.
The clawing wind raised his voice
and cried:
'Musicians, singers!
The supreme Lord of the World is
calling you...!'
Now the musicians were silent
colours;
they were a circling dance held fast
in the blinding flame of the Sun.
Then the god — he of the heaven's
four quarters —
waxed wroth.
From the remotest places,
whipped by his lightning lash
flocks of cloud whose blackened
wombs
were stabbed and torn by lightning

assembled to besiege the House of
the Sun.
His bottomless throat let loose the
thunder's roar
Everything seemed to fall flat in a
circle
beneath the World's mad roof, in
whose breast
the Sun like a red beast drowned.
Spurred on by fear,
the musicians and singers then ran
for shelter
to the wind's lap.
Bearing them gently
lest he should harm their tender
melodies,
the wind with that tumult of
happiness in his arms
set out on his downward journey,
generous and contented,
Below, earth raised its wide dark
eye to heaven
and its great face shone, and it
smiled.
As the arms of the trees were
uplifted,
there greeted the wind's wanderers
the awakened voice of its people,
the wings of the quetzal birds,
the face of the flowers
and the cheeks of the fruit.
When all that flutter of happiness
landed on earth,
and the Sun's musicians spread to
the four quarters,
then Wind ceased his complaining
and sang,
caressing the valleys, the forests and
seas.
Thus was music born on the bosom
of earth.
Thus did all things learn to sing:
the awakening dawn,
the dreaming man,
the awaiting mother,
the passing water and the flying
bird.
Life was all music from that time
on.

"Throughout this myth, we notice that matter, the noumenal world [e.g. Tezcatlipoca], and spirit, the phenomenal [e.g. Quetzalcoatl], must always be closely intertwined. [Although it appears that in some cases the noumenal world rules over the phenomenal] and Tezcatlipoca has the right to give orders to Quetzalcoatl, there is really no vertical hierarchy here, but only a godly kind of peaceful coexistence, or rather a mutual self-help society in which the noumenal and the phenomenal exchange strength and music, to form the miracle of spirit incarnate." — Nicholson, pp.31-34.

Ed. note: Apart from its detail alone, this account is particularly distinctive in that it is one of the very few creation myths of which I am aware which include in such a prominent, central position the bringing of music down to the earth, in order to gladden the heart of man. In my view, as a fundamental concept this myth complements e.g. **PYTHAGOREAN*** and **CHINESE*** views of music as a reflection/symbol of the harmonious structure of the universe itself (see e.g. **HARMONY (HARMONIA) OF THE SPHERES***, and e.g. the **ORPHEUS*** and **VAINAMOINEN** — legends [Greek and Finnish respectively] which depict the musician as spiritual physician / tamer of the wilderness / soother of savage breasts — i.e. as a promoter of civilization or culture). For other important stories which also relate music in some important respect to the *sun god,* see **APOLLO*** (Greek) and **AMÉ-NO-UZUMÉ*** (Japanese).

§31.6 **AZTEC DRUMS ETC.** "Some beautiful wooden drums*, undoubtedly made for ceremonial use, have been preserved. Wooden drums were of two kinds. One was the *huéhuetl,* a vertical drum over the top of which a skin was stretched. It was played with the palms and fingers like an Afro-Cuban bongo drum. The other, the *teponaztli,* was a horizontal cylinder in the top of which one or two tongues of wood

were carved. These tongues were struck with sticks, the points of which were covered with rubber. The different lengths of the tongues produced different sonorous and penetrating sounds. Some of these were beautifully carved with religious motifs and were probably sacred instruments. Small drums made of pottery are also known. Music was also made by striking a turtle shell with splinters of deer bone. Rattles*, copper bells*, bone rasps, conch shell trumpets*, pan pipes*, whistles, and *ocarinas,* along with various kinds of simple and composite flutes*, were all utilized in honoring the gods. Music was probably not used for aesthetic enjoyment; rather, it constituted one of the emotional props in religious fanaticism. No funeral procession, ritual, or warfare took place without its appropriate musical setting." — Weaver, pp.251, 254.

§31.7 **"COYOLXAUHQUI ["Golden Bells"].** The ancient Aztec goddess of the moon. Her name means 'golden bells'*. She was killed by her brother Huitzilopochtli when he emerged from the womb of their mother, the earth goddess Coatlicue. Huitzilopochtli cut of Coyolxauhqui's head and threw it into the heavens to become the moon, aglow with the golden hue of her bells." — Cotterell (Macmillan Myths and Legends), p.193.

BAGPIPES. *(See also pp.75, 821.)*

§34.4 **HUNGARIAN FOLK BELIEF.** "A special place is held in the folk beliefs of Hungary by men who displayed unusual skills and prowess in handling animals. [For example, there have been many tales about the cunning shepherd, clever beekeepers etc.]

"It is held that under the hand of the cunning shepherd the livestock will multiply, and the animals will cease to stray and to graze on forbidden pastures. They will pass along the narrow path between the cornfields without doing any damage to the crop; sometimes the shepherd's crook alone or his dog will watch over the flock whilst the shepherd himself is having a good time in the tavern. He is sometimes said to have a set of bagpipes which ring out even when the owner is nowhere in sight. Such pipes cannot be stolen, and can be sold only if a number of conditions are all fulfilled." – Domotor, p.141.

§34.5 "HOW A BAGPIPE DREW HUNTERS FROM THE OUTSKIRTS (Caribou Eskimo Folktale). If a shaman* gets mad, he might not do anything right away. But he'll look mad. He might say, 'I'm angry.' Then people know it. And they have to wait. They wait to see what the shaman will do. They might have to wait a long time. But something will happen.

"Now, not so long ago a bagpipe washed up. A man from a village found it. He ran in hollering, 'A witch is here!' So a number of men went to the bayshore to harpoon the witch. But after they harpooned it, instead of dying it sang! 'It's not a witch, then,' the harpooner said.

" 'I agree!' 'I agree!' 'I agree!' the others said.

"Through the harpoon holes, the thing wheezed. Its arms were stiff and waving.

"Then the poorest man in the village slung it over his shoulder and carried it home. There he set it on a rack to smoke-dry.

" 'He can no longer be called the poorest man in our village,' his wife announced.

"It was true, not with the bagpipe in his possession.

"On the rack, in the smoke, it stopped singing. It had sung over the poor man's shoulder all the way home, with people following behind. But in the smoke it didn't cough. It just stopped singing. Smoke came out of holes in its arms.

" 'It's dead,' the wife said.

" 'No,' the man said, 'it's just not singing. Burp it like a baby and it will sing.'

" 'It's dead,' the wife cried.

"Just then the shaman from Padlei arrived. 'Is my magical instrument here yet?' he said. 'A man I hated used to own it. He made me angry a long time ago. I waited. He was out in the bay on a boat. Has my magical instrument washed in yet?'

" 'No,' said the wife. 'No – there's no such thing here.'

"With that, she wrapped up the bagpipe all hidden in a blanket at her breast.

" 'Hey – what's *that?*' the shaman said, pointing at the bundle.

" 'It's my son,' she said.

" 'Let's hear him cry,' the shaman said.

"With this, the men of the village sprang for their knives.

" 'I ask to hear a baby cry and you men all spring for your knives,' the shaman said. 'Secrets are being kept from me!'

"People were afraid now. They recalled past times when the shaman was angry. It wasn't good. The shaman held grudges.

"In the morning the best hunters went out after seals.

"The shaman appeared. 'I'm angry,' he said. 'Here is what I'll do.'

"The shaman stepped forward, lifted up the blanket, and blew into the baby's hollow foot. The baby let loose a horrendous wail, a cry, a howl, a wheeze, then did those things a second time. Then a third.

"Soon the first of the great hunters apepared at the village-edge. He was empty-handed. 'I heard our village cry for help,' he said, 'so I returned.'

"In a while all the hunters had been drawn in from the outskirts, from seal-haunts far away.

" 'We're starving,' the wife said. 'Where's seal to eat?'

" 'We returned without any,' the greatest hunter said. 'We were almost upon some seals when we all heard a cry for help. We returned for this reason.'

" 'Yes, we fear what was going on here,' yet another hunter said,

" 'What is crying under the blanket?' the shaman demanded to know.

"The wife pulled the blanket away and revealed the secret.

" 'All right, all right,' the shaman said. 'Give it to me. Now — I have it. Now — all the seals will wait for you. Go out for them.'

"That night, while people feasted on seals, the shaman played his magical instrument. The music was strange. Everyone listened. But they were happy when it ended and the shaman let people be.

" 'I'm pleased,' the shaman said, leaving.

"We say this: what pleases a shaman is unpredictable." — Norman, pp.189-91.

§34.6 **THE POOKA (Irish).** "The Pooka, recté Púca, seems essentially an animal spirit. Some derive his name from poc, a he-goat; and speculative persons consider him the forefather of Shakespeare's 'Puck'. On solitary mountains and among old ruins he lives, 'grown monstrous with much solitude', and is of the race of the nightmare. 'In the MS. story called "Mac-na-Michomhairle", of uncertain authorship,' writes me Mr. Douglas Hyde, 'we read that "out of a certain hill in Leinster, there used to emerge as far as his middle, a plump, sleek, terrible steed, and speak in human voice to each person about November-day, and he was accustomed to give intelligent and proper answers to such as consulted him concerning all that would befall them until the November of next year. And the people used to leave gifts and presents at the hill until the coming of Patrick and the holy clergy." This tradition appears to be a cognate one with that of the Púca.' Yes! unless it were merely an aughishka [each-uisgé], or Waterhorse. For these, we are told, were common once, and used to come out of the water to gallop on the sands and in the fields, and people would often go between them and the marge and bridle them, and they would

make the finest of horses if only you could keep them away from sight of the water; but if once they saw a glimpse of the water, they would plunge in with their rider, and tear him to pieces at the bottom. It being a November spirit, however, tells in favor of the Pooka, for November-day is sacred to the Pooka. It is hard to realize that wild, staring phantom grown sleek and civil.

"He has many shapes — is now a horse, now an ass, now a bull, now a goat, now an eagle. Like all spirits, he is only half in the world of form.

"*The Piper and the Pooka* (translated literally from the Irish of the *Leabhar Sgeulaigheachia*). In the old times, there was a half fool living in Dunmore, in the county Galway, and although he was excessively fond of music, he was unable to learn more than one tune, and that was the 'Black Rogue'. He used to get a good deal of money from the gentlemen, for they used to get sport out of him. One night the piper was coming home from a house where there had been a dance, and he half drunk. When he came to a little bridge that was up by his mother's house, he squeezed the pipes on, and began playing the 'Black Rogue' (an rógair dubh). The Púca came behind him, and flung him up on his own back. There were long horns on the Púca, and the piper got a good grip on them, and then he said —

" 'Destruction on you, you nasty beast, let me home. I have a ten-penny piece in my pocket for my mother, and she wants snuff.'

" 'Never mind your mother,' said the Púca, 'but keep your hold. If you fall, you will break your neck and your pipes.' Then the Púca said to him, 'Play for me the "Shan Van Vocht" (an t-seann-bhean bhocht).'

" 'I don't know it,' said the piper.

" 'Never mind whether you do or you don't,' said the Púca . 'Play up, and I'll make you know.'

"The piper put wind in his bag, and he played such music as made himself wonder.

" 'Upon my word, you're a fine music-master,' says the piper then; 'but tell me where you're for bringing me.'

" 'There's a great feast in the house of the Banshee,[75] on the top of Croagh Patric to-night,' says the Púca , 'and I'm for bring-ing you there to play music, and, take my word, you'll get the price of your trouble.'

" 'By my word, you'll save me a journey, then,' says the piper, 'for Father William put a journey to Croagh Patric on me, be-cause I stole the white gander from him last Martinmas.'[76]

"The Púca rushed him across hills and bogs and rough places, till he brought him to the top of Croagh Patric. Then the Púca struck three blows with his foot, and a great door opened, and they passed in together, into a fine room.

"The piper saw a golden table in the mid-dle of the room, and hundreds of old women (cailleacha) sitting round about it. The old women rose up, and said, 'A hundred thousand welcomes to you, you

Púca of November (na Samhna). Who is this you have with you?'

" 'The best piper in Ireland,' says the Púca.

"One of the old women struck a blow on the ground, and a door opened in the side of the wall, and what should the piper see coming out but the white gander which he had stolen from Father William.

" 'By my conscience, then,' says the piper, 'myself and my mother ate every taste of that gander, only one wing, and I gave that to Moy-rua (Red Mary), and it's she told the priest I stole the gander.'

"The gander cleaned the table, and car-ried it away, and the Púca said, 'Play up music for these ladies.'

"The piper played up, and the old women began dancing, and they were dancing till they were tired. Then the Púca said to pay the piper, and every old woman drew out a gold piece, and gave it to him.

" 'By the tooth of Patric,' said he, 'I'm as rich as the son of a lord.'

" 'Come with me,' says the Púca, 'and I'll bring you home.'

"They went out then, and just as he was going to ride on the Púca, the gander came up to him, and gave him a new set of pipes. The Púca was not long until he brought

---

75 "**Banshee.** The English name for Bean Sidhe, the Irish fairy. The banshee descends from old Celtic gods who have gone underground. In country districts the wailing of the fairy is said to foretell the approach of death." — Cotterell, *The Macmillan Il-lustrated Encyclopedia of Myths and Legends*, p.188. (Ed.)

76 " 'The *Banshee* [of Ireland],' says Mr. McAnally, 'is really a disembodied soul, that of one who in life was strongly attached to the family, or who had good reason to hate all its members. Thus, in different instances, the *Banshee's* song may be inspired by different motives. When the *Banshee* loves those she calls, the song is a low, soft chant giving notice, indeed, of the close proximity of the angel of death, but with a tenderness of tone that reassures the one destined to die and comforts the sur-vivors; rather a welcome than a warning, and having in its tones a thrill of exulta-tion, as though the messenger spirit were bringing glad tidings to him summoned to join the waiting throng of his ancestors.' To a doomed member of the family of the O'Reardons the *Banshee* generally appears in the form of a beautiful woman, 'and sings a song so sweetly solemn as to reconcile him to his approaching fate.' But if, during his lifetime, the *Banshee* was an enemy of the family, the cry is the scream of a fiend, howling with demoniac delight over the coming death agony of another of his foes." — Spence [Occultism], p.63. (Ed.)

him to Dunmore, and he threw the piper off at the little bridge, and then he told him to go home, and says to him, 'You'll have two things now that you never had before—you have sense and music' (ciall agus ceól).

"The piper went home, and he knocked at his mother's door, saying, 'Let me in, I'm as rich as a lord, and I'm the best piper in Ireland.'

" 'You're drunk,' said the mother.

" 'No, indeed,' says the piper, 'I haven't drunk a drop.'

"The mother let him in, and he gave her the gold pieces, and, 'Wait now,' says he, 'till you hear the music I'll play.'

"He buckled on the pipes, but instead of music, there came a sound as if all the geese and ganders in Ireland were screeching together. He wakened the neighbors, and they were all mocking him, until he put on the old pipes, and then he played melodious music for them; and after that he told them all he had gone through that night.

"The next morning, when his mother went to look at the gold pieces, there was nothing there but the leaves of a plant.

"The piper went to the priest, and told him his story but the priest would not believe a word from him, until he put the pipes on him, and then the screeching of the ganders and the geese began.

" 'Leave my sight, you thief,' says the priest.

"But nothing would do the piper till he would put the old pipes on to show the priest that his story was true.

"He buckled on the old pipes, and he played melodious music, and from that day till the day of his death, there was never a piper in the county Galway was as good as he was." —Hyde, in Yeats, pp.100-03.[77]

---

77   For another version see *The White Gander,* §34.3, pp.821-23 above. It seems to me that the present story also displays the principal features of a paradigmatic "shamanic session", described as follows by Mircea Eliade: "first, an appeal to the auxiliary spirits, which, more often than not, are those of animals, and a dialogue with them in a *secret language;* secondly, drum-playing and a dance [or e.g. playing of the pipes? (Ed.)], preparatory to the mystic journey; and thirdly, the trance (real or simulated) during which the shaman's soul is believed to have left his body [for has not our piper—in truth—only become en-tranced?]. The objective of every shamanic session is to obtain the ecstasy, for it is only in ecstasy that the shaman can *fly* through the air or *descend into Hell,* that is, fulfil his mission of curing illness and shepherding souls" (see **DRUM*** entry, §93.13 below). The present story is also somewhat akin in spirit to **THE SINGING BONE***, pp.719*ff,* Aarne-Thompson folktale type 780 (p.315 above). See also Thompson folktale motifs E489.5 (Dancing in afterworld), F261 (Fairies dance—akin to F455.3.2, Trolls dance, F470.2, Night-spirits dance, F482.5, Brownies dance), **FOLKLORE AND FOLKTALES—TYPOLOGY***; and also our themes **T4b** (Music as appeasement of good, evil, or indifferent gods or forces) and **T6** (Music as mediator between world of nature and world of man [culture]), *Introductory Remarks* (Vol I, above). The playing of pipes is a special skill which enables our piper to communicate with members of the spirit-world; in the story he also *learns* from the Púca, which suggests I should think a kind of initiation into certain "mysteries" if you will, of which the agency is music—finally, one senses that the playing of music is a somewhat *dangerous* undertaking (for which see the fate of poor humpback Jack Madden, in the **FAIRIES*** story, §109.12 below), and so he had better keep his wits about him, and do it well! (Ed.)

BELLS. *(See also p.78.)*

§40.13 "BELL. Its sound is a symbol of crea-tive power.[78] Since it is in a hanging posi-tion, it partakes of the mystic significance of all objects which are suspended be-tween heaven and earth. It is related, by its shape, to the vault and, consequently, to the heavens." — Cirlot, 24.

§40.14 **RUSSIAN FOLK BELIEF.** "Since, to the folk imagination, the devil was ubiqui-tous, it was necessary to be on constant guard and to protect oneself in every pos-sible way, especially at night. The rooster was considered a powerful enemy of the unclean force, and many stories of demons end successfully for the peasant simply be-cause the rooster crows, signaling the ap-proach of day. Other means of protection included prayers, church bells, holy candles, holy water, incense, the use of a yoke or halter, and various plants thought repulsive or prophylacic to demons (thistle, juniper)." — Ivanits, p.42.

§40.15 **BRITISH FOLKLORE.** Materials in this section from Katherine M. Briggs, *A Dictionary of British Folk-Tales in the English Language; Incorporating the F. J. Norton Col-lection* (1971).

"THE BELLS OF BRINKBURN. Cen-turies ago one of the priors of Brinkburn presented the bells of that building to the Priory of Durham. They had been the pride of the secluded sanctuary on the Co-quet [river], for their tones were possessed of great power combined with sweetness, and many tempting offers had Durham made to secure them, but hitherto to no purpose. But she prevailed at length, and the bells so coveted were removed from the tower and dispatched on horseback on their way to Durham under the care of some monks. They journeyed till they reached the River Font, which, owing to a

quantity of rain having fallen, was much swelled. However, they prepared to ford it; but when the horses reached the middle of the stream the bells by some means fell, or, according to the popular belief, were removed from the backs of the horses by miraculous interposition, and sank to the bottom. Owing either to the dangerous state of the stream or from the bells being unwilling to be removed, the exertions of the monks to recover them proved un-availing; so they returned to Brinkburn and reported the disaster. But the Brinkburn prior, determined not to be baf-fled, sent forthwith a messenger to Dur-ham to request the presence of his brother prior, and both ecclesiastics proceeded with full attendance to liberate the im-prisoned bells; and lo! the superior abilities of high church functionaries over humble monks was manifest to everyone; for they had no sooner ridden into the stream than the bells were lifted with ease; and being conveyed to Durham, were lodged there in safety. To this day it is a saying in Coquetdale that 'Brinkburn bells are heard in Durham'; and Wallis, in his *History of Northumberland*, assures us that the bells of Brinkburn were removed to the Cathedral on the banks of the Wear. Still, there are doubters. Walter White in 1859 says 'the deep pool where the bells were lost is still to be seen in the river' [Coquet]; and Mr Wilson is positive that some years ago 'a fragment of the bell was found buried at the root of a tree on the hill on the opposite side of the river'.

"Of the bells, William Howitt, in his *Visit to Remarkable Places*, etc., p.526, note, says: 'The Bell Tower looks down upon the Bell Pool, a very deep part of the Coquet, lying concealed beneath the thick foliage of the native trees that jut out from the interstices of the lofty, craggy heights, impending over either side. Tradition says that into this pool the bells were thrown in a time of danger in order to place them beyond the

---

78   See Harold Bayley, *The Lost Language of Symbolism* (London, 1912; reprint 1951).

reach of the invading Scots. It is still a favourite amusement among the young swimmers of the neighbourhood to dive for the bells of Brinkburn, and then it is generally believed that when the bells are found other treasures will be recovered with them.[79]

"KENTSHAM BELL. Great Tom of Kentsham was the greatest bell ever brought to England, but it never reached Kentsham safely, nor hung in any English tower. Where Kentsham is I cannot tell you, but, long, long ago the good folk of the place determined to have a larger and finer bell in their steeple than any other parish could boast.

"At that time there was a famous bell-foundry abroad where all the greatest bells were cast, and thither too sent many others who wanted greater bells than could be cast in England. And so it came to pass at length that Great Tom of Lincoln, and Great Tom of York and Great Tom of Christchurch and Great Tom of Kentsham were all founded at the same time, and all embarked on board the same vessel, and carried safely to the shore of dear old England. Then they set about landing them, and this was anxious work, but little by little it was done, and Tom of Lincoln, Tom of York, Tom of Christchurch were safely laid on English ground. And then came the turn of Tom of Kentsham, which was the greatest Tom of all.

"Little by little they raised him, and prepared to draw him to the shore; but just in the middle of the work, the captain grew so anxious and excited that he swore an oath. That very moment the rope which held the bell snapped in two, and Great Tom of Kentsham slid over the ship's side into the water, and rolled away to the bottom of the sea.

"Then the people went to the cunning man and asked him what they should do. And he said: 'Take six yoke of white milch-kine which have never borne the yoke, and take fresh withy bands which have never been used before, and let no man speak a word either good or bad till the bell is at the top of the hill.'

"So they took six yoke of white milch-kine which had never borne the yoke, and harnessed them with fresh withy bands, which had never been used, and bound these to the bell as it lay in the shallow water, and long it was ere they could move it. But still the kine struggled and pulled and the withy bands held firm, and at last the bell was on dry ground. Slowly, slowly they drew it up the hill, moaning and groaning with unearthly sounds as it went; slowly, slowly, and no one spoke, and they nearly reached the top of the hill. Now the captain had been wild with grief when he saw that he had caused his precious freight to be lost in the waters just as they had reached the shore; and when he beheld it recovered again and so nearly placed in safety, he could not contain his joy, but sang out merrily:

In spite of all the devils in hell,
We have got to land old Kentsham bell.

Instantly the withy bands broke in the midst and the bell bounded back again

---

79 [Source:] *Denham Tracts*, II, p.132. [Aarne/Thompson Folktale Type] ML7070 (Legends about church bells). [Thompson] Motifs: V115.1 (Church bells sunk in river); V115.1.2 (Raising sunken church bell). [See **FOLKLORE AND FOLK-TALES – TYPOLOGY*** (Ed.)]

down the sloping hillside, rolling over and over, faster and faster, with unearthly clanging, till it sank far away in the very depths of the sea. And no man has ever seen it since, but many have heard it tolling beneath the waves, and if you go there you may hear it too.[80]

"WHITBY BELLS. A favourite story told in connection with the abbey is one concerning its bells. It runs thus: The magnificent peal excited the cupidity of some sea-roving freebooter, and, landing with a sufficient force, he extracted the bells from the sacred building and conveyed them on board his vessel.

"This desecration was, however, not suffered to go unpunished, for ere the vessel had gone many miles she struck and foundered a short distance from a projecting ridge of rock called the 'Black Nab'. As a fitting conclusion to this, we are told, that he who dares on Hallowe'en to spend some time on the rock, and call his sweetheart's name, will hear it echoed by the breeze, accompanied with the ringing of marriage bells from the sunken chime."[81] – Briggs (Dictionary), Part B (*Folk Legends*), vol 2 pp.158-59, 241-42, 389.

§40.16 "At Cudworth [in England] a new bell, inscribed '*Sancta Maria Virgo, intercede pro toto mundo*' was presented to the church by a traveller who had lost his way in the Forest of Arden and found the village by following the sound of a small bell. He vowed, we are told, to give a large bell which would be even more effective. One of the bells at Whitnash was taken down

to be recast. On its way back to the church it was brought to a well between Whitnash and Radford – the source of Whitnash brook – to be re-consecrated. Perhaps it is surprising that such a place was chosen for the ritual, but a great many wells and springs which had been revered in pagan times were christianised and continued to be venerated. Unfortunately, the bell somehow fell into the well during the ceremony. It disappeared, and could not be recovered. But it was still able to toll, and when the country people wished to know the future they dropped stones into the well at night. The bell answered their questions eventually by ringing the following morning. One ring meant yes; two rings, no. The well no longer exists, but there is still a little stream, believed to possess healing powers."[82] – Palmer, p.39.

§40.17 "THE BELLS OF MUGEN [Japanese folklore]. In one of his works, *Kwaidan*, which was published in 1904, Lafcadio Hearn dates the legend of the bell of Mugen to 'eight centuries ago'. It was and is not unusual for bronze mirrors to be given to temples for making bells or images. Hearn writes of seeing a collection of such mirrors which had been contributed so that a bronze statue of Amida might be cast. In Mugenyama (*yama* means mountain) at the time of which Hearn wrote, a collection of mirrors was made for a temple bell. One woman gave her mirror which she had inherited from her mother, who had in turn inherited it from her mother. Apart from being an heirloom, the mirror was important to the woman because of

---

80 [Source:] Hartland, *English Fairy and Folk-Tales*, pp. 204-5. [Aarne/Thompson Folktale] Type ML7070 (Legends about church bells). [Thompson Folktale] Motifs C494 (Tabu: cursing); C401.4 (Tabu: speaking while raising sunken church bell); V115.1.3.2 (Church bell cannot be raised because person blasphemes); F993 (Sunken bell sounds).

81 [Source:] Gutch, *Country Folk-Lore*, II, *North Riding of Yorkshire*, pp.39-40.

82 See Aarne/Thompson Folktale Type ML7070 (Legends about church bells); Thompson Folklore Motif F993 (Sunken bell sounds) – FOLKLORE AND FOLK-TALES – TYPOLOGY*. (Ed.)

the design of lucky emblems engraved on its back: the pine, the bamboo, and the plum. She regretted having given it away, and she feared for the truth of the proverb of the mirror being the soul of a woman. When the time came for the great bell to be cast, the mirror given by the woman would not melt. As the villagers knew who had donated it, her shame was great. Her heart was revealed to all as being hard, as hard as the metal of her gift. She had given her heirloom with reluctance and, further, had regretted the giving. So the metal remain solid when the other mirrors, given in a different spirit, melted under heat.

"Eventually her bitterness of spirit, growing like a cancer, became so overpowering that she killed herself in anger, leaving a note to the effect that after her death, the mirror she had given would melt and that great wealth would come to whoever managed to break the bell incorporating the metal. This note was in fact a curse and the woman's spirit was a vengeful one, dying as she did in a state of bitter anger.

"After the bell was cast, it was beaten constantly by those who tried to break it and obtain the promised worldly wealth. The resulting incessant bell-clanging for this impious reason and, one would imagine, the noise, finally prompted the priests to roll the large temple bell down the hill below and push it into the swamp at the bottom, leaving only the legend behind." — Piggott (Japanese), pp.42-43.

§40.18 "THE PHEASANTS AND THE BELL [Korean folklore]. Once upon a time there lived a woodcutter. One day he went into the mountains to cut firewood, and there he saw two pheasants flying up and down in a distracted manner. When he came nearer he saw a snake on the point of devouring their eggs, which were lying under a bush. So he took the stick that supported his pack-carrier and beat the snake to death with it.

"Some ten years afterwards he went on a journey to Yongwol in the Province of Gangwon. One night he lost his way in a forest and at last came upon a house with a light in the window. He thought that perhaps he might stay the night there, and so he went and knocked at the door. A young girl came out and received him kindly, and took him in and gave him a good supper.

"After a little while the woodcutter asked, 'Are you living here alone, or are you expecting the rest of your family to return?' As he said this the girl changed colour and snarled viciously at him, 'Ten years ago you killed a snake with your stick. I am that snake. I bid you welcome, my enemy! Now I shall savour my revenge to the full. I am going to eat you up!'

"The woodcutter was very frightened at her menacing words, and begged her to spare his life. 'You were trying to eat the pheasants' egg,' he pleaded, 'I took pity on them and so I made up my mind to save them. So I beat you with my stick, but I did not mean to kill you. If I did kill you, it was quite by accident, and I apologize most humbly for my deed. Do spare my life, I beseech you!'

"The girl considered for a moment and replied, 'If you wish to live, there is one thing you must do for me. Near the summit of this mountain there stands an old deserted temple, and in it hangs a great bell. If you can sit here in this room and make that bell ring, then I shall let you go free and unharmed. Can you do that for me?'

"The woodcutter answered in great embarrassment, 'How can I ring that bell if I am sitting here? It is quite impossible. You are just toying with me, are you not?'

" 'You mean you cannot do it?' said the girl. 'Then you shall die this very minute.'

"So the girl transformed herself into a big snake to kill him, but no sooner had she done so than the solemn boom of the bell came clearly to their ears through the night. The snake immediately became a girl again, and sighed, 'You must be under Heaven's protection. I cannot hurt you now.' With these words she vanished.

"In the morning the woodcutter climbed to the top of the mountain. There he found the temple standing desolate. Under the great bell he found two pheasants lying dead, their heads battered and their wings broken, and on the surface of the bell itself were great dark stains of blood. He realized then that the two pheasants he had helped so long ago had sacrificed their lives to repay his kindness. They had dashed their heads against the bell, so that its sound might save their benefactor." — In-Sob (from *Ondoru Yawa,* told by Yi Hon-Gu; Myongczon, 1925), pp.96-96.

§40.19 **BELLS AROUND THE WORLD.** The following passages have been extracted from one of the best volumes on bells and bell-lore published to date — *Bells and Man* by Percival Price (Oxford University Press, 1983).

"**Decoration.** The bell is not only an object to be heard. It is also one to be seen. This is obvious from man's treatment of its surface from most ancient times. This treatment accords with three aspects of his regard for the bell: (1) as a magico-sacred object, (2) as an ornamental object, and (3) as a monumental object. As a magico-sacred object he has placed symbols and pictures on its surface for the purpose of attracting the attention of divine beings and causing them to act in his favour. As an ornamental object he has added decorations and otherwise treated it aesthetically so as to appear most pleasing to both gods and men. And as a monumental object he has put information on the bell, mostly in writing, which he wishes to be preserved for posterity.

"All three aspects are expressed in low reliefs (very rarely incisions) on the surface of the bell: mostly on the outer surface, but in a few examples on the inner surface also. They are seldom all found expressed on one bell. For example, the devout Hindu does not need script on his temple bell because portraits and symbols will suffice for its magico-sacred and ornamental aspects;

and if the name of the donor should be written on the bell it is not there to inform posterity, but so that the gods will benefit him for it. On Korean Buddhist bells divine spirits of the air are shown ready to go to the believer's aid when he rings the bell. Even Islam, which shuns portraiture but uses talismans, puts a crescent moon on camel bells to protect the animal while in the service of its master.

"The first subject of portraiture in widespread use on Christian bells was the Madonna. In the twelfth century she was depicted in line-relief made by etching in the mould, and later by the use of stamps or wax forms (*cire perdue*) to give a full low relief. In the fourteenth century the Crucifix became another popular subject, followed by certain saints, depicted in ever more stylized fashion to assure recognition. By the seventeenth century religious art on western European bells begins to lose its inner meaning and secular portraits begin to appear. On Eastern European bells the signs of devotion continued longer, although the art on some bells there may be cruder. On a few bells a medallion of a saint or a frieze of cherubs' heads is brought out with silver or, more rarely, gold paint. Many bells in various parts of the world would have been painted all over to aid their decoration, if it had not been discovered (as in Latin America) that paint had a bad effect on the tone of a bell....

"**Africa (excluding Egypt).** The three main uses of all sorts of bells in Africa have been for magic, music, and the protection and location of cattle. This last has been least affected by modern changes, and where the people are herdsmen, the tinkling of both wooden and iron bells may be heard over great stretches of countryside, especially in eastern Africa....

"In some places small open-mouth bells are preferred to large ones for working miracles, although their sounds, like that of the crotal, is relatively feeble. This may be due to associating faint sounds with the esoteric, as part of man's general belief that what is whispered is more important than what is said aloud. A tribe in Uganda considers the sound of handbells and ankle bells strong enough to disperse thunderstorms. Quite sensibly, it is not directed against the physical phenomenon, but against the storm fiend who causes it. This follows the concept which even became transferred to Christianity in Europe, that bell sounds frighten away demons. It is with this intent that both medicine men and laity employ bells to cure illnesses. In some places in Africa the medicine man wears an iron bell suspended on an iron chain, or brings a small bell in his hand and rings it from time to time in treating the sick. Sometimes bells are not used until it is felt certain that the demon has left the sick persn's body: then the bells are attached to it so that the fiend will not re-enter it. In some places people ring little bells while they are drinking, to keep evil spirits from entering their bodies; in others they hang them over their doorways to keep ghosts from entering their houses.[83]

"In Africa as elsewhere there are contrasts and paradoxes in the religious uses of bells. Medicine men may ring them to attract spirits to do their bidding for either good or ill. Although in some situations a faint bell tone is considered sufficient to cause a miracle, in others it must be as loud as possible and part of a sound battery making the most terrific din. Women do much magical bell ringing, yet with certain rites their mere presence profanes bell sounds.

"Bells are also rung simply to call the attention of spirits or men to an occasion. For this the priest in some tribes carried iron 'magic bells' in procession. In eastern Africa, when a magician tells of good luck he rings a bell so that the spirits will hear it; when a father has twins he puts little bells on his ankle to give notice to his neighbours of his fecundity. The practical development of this is telegraphy. African telegraphy rests on a tone-language structure, and employs, besides bells and drums*, one or two other percussion instruments, wind instruments, and the human voice....

"**Bali.** On the island of Bali there was an ingenious use of bells to get evil spirits out of the air. Small crotals (*gonsèng*) were attached to the tail and feet of birds, and as they flew or reeled in flocks the bells sounded....[84]

"**China.** The ancient Chinese wrote about the tone qualities of their bells, and ascribed marvelous powers to them, based on their theories of the essence of sound as a transcendental power. But we lack valid evidence of how far back in history were the bells referred to, and exactly what they were like....

"*Chou period.* About 1030 BC the Chou dynasty succeeded the Shang. Around this time a new type of bell appeared, called *chung*. After this, *chung* becomes the generic term for bell, and is used in compound words....

"The Chinese probably did not sound the earliest *chung* simply as a convenient in-

---

83 See our themes **T2b** (Music has magical effect upon orderly process of nature), **T2c** (It can effect specifically crops, animals, the weather etc), **T4a** (Music as magical weapon against evil spirits, means for combatting, routing evil spirits), **T4b** (Music as magical restorative. Music [or musician] blesses one's fields, household, family etc as a result of communication with gods or spirit beings), **T1b** (Music gives magical power to musician [e.g. shaman, doctor, priest]), *Introductory Remarks* Vol I above. (Ed.)

84 See our theme **T4a** (Music as magical weapon [for] expulsion of devils, evil spirits), *Introductory Remarks,* Vol I above. (Ed.)

strument for signals or a pleasurable one for tone. With their belief that sound was a manifestation of universal essence, they probably used them to help sustain Universal Harmony. However, as improper use could also destroy Universal Harmony, the bell had to be protected by magic symbols. Thus we find dragons (not necessarily unbenevolent) twisting in low relief on its sides, tigers projecting as fins from its flanks, and phoenix heads rising in bold relief above its crown. Sometimes on the flat top, the *t'ao-t'ieh* mask of the *nao* was also present. If the resultant unevenness of the bell's surface made its tone less pleasant (at least, judged by our hearing), that seemed to be of no account. It was what spiritual beings heard that mattered.

"One motif of bold relief, the *nai tou* or nipple, was employed more than all the others. It is still cast on many East Asiatic bells today. In origin it is probably a fertility symbol, although it has also been considered to be a symbol of the *lü*, a tube through which the mystic essence of music is drawn off. (Some *nao* bells have pairs of low swellings on their sides such as would suggest eyes, but their different shapes and treatment from the *nai tou* makes them seem unrelated.) There may also have been some foundry-practice reason, such as aiding gases to escape through the mould. At any rate, it seems first to have been a short sharp spike; then a longer one; then a shorter, thicker, blunter projection; and finally a low, round knob or cabochon [a polished gem or bead, cut in convex form but not faceted (Ed.)]. In the simplest examples, this was plain; in the most elaborate it was shaped into a coiled serpent with a feline head. Nipples were never placed singly. On bells of the Chou period there were always thirty-six. On the oldest *chung* they were distributed evenly around most of the side, as on a *chung* of the tenth century BC in the Museum of Chinese History, Peking. On later ones they were grouped into four panels of nine. Gradually these were placed higher up on the bell, where actual-ly they have less adverse effect on the tone, although the intention was more likely to leave space for other visual material below.

"This change marked the transition from the magico-sacred to the ornamental. Animistic forms remained, sometimes couched between the nipples; but gradually decoration in the form of delicate floral designs wound itself over all the bell except the nipples. The next transition occurred quickly. Short texts were introduced to fill plain spaces between the nipple panels. Then, as soon as the monumental aspect of the bell became fully realized, writing spilled over into every plain space, as in the treatment of other bronze sacerdotal vessels. As on these, the writing eulogized important people and events.

"Bells such as the *nao* and *chung* which we have been referring to were no common objects, but the rare properties of emperors, kings, and high noblemen. This is substantiated in the texts inscribed on them, and by the places where they have been found, namely in royal tombs. Perhaps because they were among the finest examples of a well developed bronze artificer's art, their tone (whatever we may think of it) was considered the proper sound for affecting the supernatural. As rarities, they were treasured. This eventually comes out in the legends. A seventh-century bell is inscribed 'We shall everlastingly prize this bell.' On a bell of the fourth or third century is written 'For a myriad years may it ever be treasured and used.' Such bells were prized as spoils of war, and used as bribes.

"There is, unfortunately, very little record of their acoustical use before the development of Confucian ritual in the fifth century BC. Authorities agree that they were rung to call the ancestral shades to the offerings set out for them, and sounded in ceremonies designed to contol the weather. They were one of the instruments whose tone aided crops. An anonymous author credited to the seventh century BC wrote:

Sonorous are the bells and drums.
Brightly sound the ringing-stones and
flutes.
　　They bring down with them blessings—rich, rich the growth of grain.
　　They bring down with them blessings—abundance, the abundance....

"Buddhism went so far as to give verbal
meanings to the sounds of its bells. Wind
bells proclaimed the holy Word of Buddha
with every passing breeze. Temple bells
periodically diffused the greeting, 'Na-o-
mi-to-fah!', O Buddha, hail! The sound of
the bell was in this case apotropaic
[designed to avert or turn aside evil] because the holy Word was apotropaic. The
chung bell seems to have been introduced
as soon as Buddhism began to flourish in
China, and there is early reference to its ef-
ficaciousness....

"In small bells, the *to* with handle was
replaced by an import from India somewhat resembling a Western handbell. It
was called a *ghanta*. Buddhism placed great
significance on both the visual and acoustical aspects of this small bell. In proper
hands it could be powerful; in improper
ones, dangerous. Its sound, a clear high
note to mortal ears, contained a mystical
quality which attracted the attention of
deities.[85] Therefore, the person who rang
it, the times when it was rung, and how
loud and how long, were rigidly fixed in
the liturgy. At some places there were different *ghanta* for different deities....

"Whatever mystic powers may have been
considered inherent in the sound of all
large temple bells, that of large Buddhist
bells had one that was unique. It
awakened a state known as the Call of
Buddha in men. Here we find the bridge
between ringing the consecrated bell to affect the gods and to inform mortals. Just as
the bigger and heavier the bell the farther
its sound diffuses, so for a Buddhist bell

the greater the area over which it awakens
the call....

"**Christian.** The employment of the bell
as an instrument of magico-sacred power
which we found to be almost universal in
other religions is so far removed from
modern Christian thinking that it comes as
a surprise to learn that this was its first use
in Christianity also. It was almost bound to
happen, because the reality of demons in
the culture in which Christianity was born
was accepted by its founder. Jesus cast out
devils and gave his disciples power over
unclean spirits without the use of any talismanic objects such as bells. But the
evidence is rather against his early followers having been without them. Bells
have been found in the Roman catacombs
where the early Christians were buried.
These were either for the departed to use
as protection in the darker passages of the
after life leading to the brighter realms
beyond (just as Christ descended into hell
before he rose on the third day), or they
were for the living who visited these secret
places to sound as a protection from those
souls who had not yet set out on this journey....

"In the use of bells in congregational rites
Christianity first adopted some of the uses
of small bells in pagan cults. This is not
surprising, for no new religion takes root
without absorbing some customs from its
soil, even though it may discard them later.
The pagan cults of the Roman empire consisted largely of sets of acts to be carried
out in a particular way on particular occasions with little theological explanation
of why they were performed, and some of
these employed bells. Thus the continuity
of the use of the crotal [a small spherical
rattle, as on a harness] from pagan into
Christian cults can be traced in late
Graeco-Roman evidence around almost all
the Mediterranean. The sistrum* or

85　See our theme **T1a** (Music summons the gods or divine beings), *Introductory Remarks*
　　Vol I above. (Ed.)

trimble, a small frame with crotals and tinkling discs which was held in the hand and shaken, was used in various pagan cults before it was taken into Greek, Syrian, Armenian, and Egyptian church rites. Excavations reveal that there was no break in the religious use of small open-mouth bells in Egypt, but only in the iconography on them. For a time they were cast plain because the pagan symbols had become distasteful and the Christian ones had not yet become fully accepted. The use of the handbell in Coptic ritual is considered by some to be a carry-over from the Isis cult, as also the crotals on the chains of the censer. A pre-Christian origin is ascribed to the little bells at the corners of the veil which covers the elements in the Coptic Mass, and to those on the flabellum [ceremonial fan used in religious ceremonies] or fan used in Syrian, Maronite, and Armenian services....

"*Clogga and campana.* Even before the 'freedom of the church', the early Christian hermits did not always live in isolation. Sometimes they visited cities and helped their fellow Christians. With the granting of church freedom came public preaching, and the handbell which drove away demons in the desert could be used to attract potential converts in the market place. Great churchmen preached far and wide. St Athanasius, friend of St Anthony of Egypt and successor to the deposed Arius as bishop of Alexandria, preached in Rome about the year 340 and then went on to Gaul. Other Egyptian clerics, who fled rather than renounce the doctrines of Arius, skirted Gaul to evangelize the Celts of Brittany, Cornwall, and Ireland. Irish disciples took this early form of Christianity on to Iceland and back over the continent from the Baltic to the Mediterranean.

"These men carried handbells with them, and made others where they established churches. In this way the peoples of northwestern Europe were first made aware of Christianity not by the sound of a semantron[86] but of a handbell. The Irish called it *clagan* or *clocca*. It was of small size and light weight, and was not cast but forged, usually being made by bending and annealing or riveting plates of iron into the shape of a bell with a handle, and suspending a clapper inside. A few were of hammered copper....

"The *clogga* served the missionary monk as an instrument of signal, a talisman, and a weapon. It was run to attract a gathering much as the Salvation Army uses handbells today. It kept away evil spirits. It made curses stick. Apparently these northern holy fathers were not always of a placid temper, for we read that St Rundbom and a bishop with him, on having their wills crossed by an Irish king, 'took the bells that were with them and cursed the king and the place'. According to the account the curse immediately took effect. A similar instance is recorded in the life of St Columba (died 597), who brought Christianity to Scotland. People took oaths on these portable bells with more fear of swearing falsely by them than on the gospels. The bell was carried into battle, to work a miracle. Like the king's sword, it was passed on as an investiture....

"Around the year 515, or about a quarter of a century after St Patrick was laid to rest with his bell beside him (a burial custom we have noted in various non-Christian cultures) a cleric named Ferrandus wrote from Carthage to Eugippius, Abbot of Lucullano, near Naples:

You can and must expose the Deity at all the hours appointed for prayer. And you do not do this alone; but you

---

86   "A wooden plank or an iron bar that gives a sound like a gong when struck with a mallet and that takes the place of a bell in Eastern Orthodox churches." — *Webster's Third New International Dictionary.* (Ed.)

call in many others to take part in this good practice, in connection with which a sonorous bell will serve your purpose, as the holy custom of the blessed monks has established it. We have sent you such a one, suitable for your purpose.

This is a long step from Carthaginian women driving away eclipses of the moon by ringing a bell, and it may have evolved from the use of a small bell at the door of a pagan temple to announce times when the people would be admitted.

"Nevertheless, we learn from this that the 'holy custom' of ringing a bell to summon to a Christian service had already been established in Africa. Here the bell is not called a *clogga* but a *campana*, a word which is to become the commonest medieval Latin word for 'bell', giving such derivates as *campanarius*, 'bell-ringer', *campanile*, 'bell tower', and *campanology* [the science of making bells; the art of bell ringing], the subject of this whole study. It comes from the geographical name, Campania, the province around Naples, which was famous from very ancient times for its bronze casting. An *aes Campanum* was a fine bronze casting from this region, and a *campana* was once used to produce a sound, but we have no proof that in pre-Christian times it was in the form of a bell. In AD 636 St Isidore of Seville called bells *vasi Campani* (Campania vessels). This gave rise to the pseudonymn *vas* for 'bell', as seen in *Hoc vas*, 'This bell', at the beginning of dedicatory inscriptions on bells, and *vasi sacri*, 'sacred bells', in church inventories of the Middle Ages....

"*Early monastic bells.* The evolution of the church bell from a small instrument held in the hand to a large one fastened at the top of a building took place in monasteries. Monks had the greatest need of bells because of their ordered routine; they had access to knowledge of how to make them through the widespread connections of their orders; and they had facilities for casting them in their equipment for making furnishings for their monasteries. Under these conditions it was natural that the Christian bell passed from being the personal chattel of an ecclesiastic to the corporate property of a religious institution....

"*The church's uses of bells: ringing for religious services.* We may now examine in more detail the uses to which the church put its ever-increasing number of bells. In the eighteenth century Remondini, an Italian ecclesiastic, listed seven occasions for ringing them in Roman Catholic church towers:

1. To gather the people to the sacred functions of the church.
2. To signify and distinguish its festivals.
3. To rouse the souls of the faithful to render devout thanks to the Highest for benefits received.
4. To implore divine help against the tempests of the air and the ferocity of the spirits of hell.
5. To decorate the solemn entry of princes and prelates.
6. To increase the happiness and gaiety of public processions, and in songs of praise to the Lord.
7. To make fervid the piety of the faithful in relation to the dead.

"Remondini, of course, was writing nothing new, but summing up a thousand years of the church's use of bells — specifically of those whose sounds went out into the open air. The earliest of these was to call to divine services, announce deaths, and mark the church seasons. When the clergy realized how well a bell on top of a church served to alert the laity they rang it for more occasions, increased it in size and numbers, and emphasized its importance. Church bells, they said, were the messengers of God's word; their sounds were comparable to the voices of the prophets of old. Some went so far as to inscribe *Vox Domini* — Voice of the Lord — on certain bells. Sanction for this was found in Psalm

29 (Vulgate 28), verse 4: *Vox Domini in virtute, vox Domini in magnificentia* — 'The voice of the Lord is powerful' (or 'in power'), 'the voice of the Lord is full of majesty' (or 'in majesty')....

"*Ringing for private rites.* At the approach of death there was the 'passing bell'. This custom, which seems to hark back to primitive Christianity with the use of small bells, was observed with a far-sounding bell when St Hilda lay dying at Whitby Abbey in 680. It was rung in the belief that evil spirits, ever waiting to seize a departing soul, were driven off in terror at its sound.[87] The 'passing bell' — sometimes rung on a small bell in the tower, sometimes on a handbell — might break in on anyone's activities, day or night, and when people heard it they stopped their work to pray for the soul of the one whose passing it signalled....

"*Ringing to drive away evil.* [By 789, during the reign of Charlemagne,] the church had to recognize two kinds of miracle-working bells: baptized ones and blessed ones. Baptized bells had more miracle-working power, and remained in the hands of the church. Blessed bells were limited to warding off evil, and could be owned by the laity. Housewives brought their small bells to be blessed so that they would continue to protect their home, and farmers their animal bells so that they would protect their cows, sheep, and pigs. In the twelfth century the Antonius cult, which was devoted to healing the sick, raised many pigs, and they placed a special value on the bells they hung on them. From ancient times the pig had been associated with earth fruitfulness because of its rooting in the ground. But it was a devil which St Anthony of Egypt made harmless through the power of his miracle-working bell. His followers claimed that their pigs could unearth bells which protected against weather and fire.

"Around this time there developed quite a commerce in blessed Christian bells. They were sold especially at shrines as an amulet for the general protection of the person and the home. Having been blessed at the relic of a saint they were regarded as carrying some of his power with them....

"One reason why the houses of European medieval towns were built close together around a church was so as to place its people and property under the protective umbrage of the sound of its bells. A statement attributed to St Thomas Aquinas (died 1274) pointed this out:

> The atmosphere is a battlefield between angels and devils... The aspiring steeples around which cluster the low dwellings of men are to be likened, when the bells in them are ringing, to the hen spreading its protective wings over its chickens; for the tones of the consecrated metal repel the demons and arrest storms and lightning.

"Thus the church bells, in addition to all their routine functions, were rung to dispel storms, quench fires, ward off human enemies, and stop disease. These, the four main disrupters of man's well-being, were caused by demons, who hovered just above the rooftops when not performing their nefarious acts on the ground below. So real were they to medieval man that he

---

87   One might also conjecture that the "passing bell" is meant to protect the living from these same evil spirits; as, indeed, from death itself, which has come to receive or take away the departed soul. Similarly, the habit of crossing oneself on such an occasion might signify both "blessing" the departed (wishing the departed well in the after-life), and the manipulating of a kind of surrogate talisman in order to protect oneself as well. See our theme **T4a** (Music [performed for] protection of dead from evil or harmful spirits or forces; also, of the living from the dead), *Introductory Remarks*, Vol I above. (Ed.)

portrayed their appearance in the gargoyles on his towers. Being immortal they could not be eliminated, only warded off. The sound of the bell which had received Christian baptism, the Vox Domini — Voice of the Lord — terrified them and put them to flight. Around 1330 the Abbot Farinator of St Florian, Austria, stated it quite simply: 'When clouds threaten damage one should produce noise with church bells, and they will go away.' In 1493 the publisher, Wynken de Worde, put it more wordily:

It is said that evil spirytes, that been in the regyon of thayre, doubte moche when they hear the bells rongen: and this is the same why the bells rongen when it thondreth and when grete tempeste and outrages of wether happen, to the end that fiends and wycked spirytes should be abashed and flee, and cease the movynge of the tempeste....

"This ringing did more than put to flight evil spirits who hovered just above the rooftops or performed malicious deeds on the ground below. Bells in a tower sound not only out and down, but upwards also. The upward-rising sounds acted as prayers ascending to the saints, the Blessed Virgin, and to all those who from their position in heaven (not far above the highest steeple) were constantly looking down upon, and ready to care for, the faithful on earth below.[88]

"The Christian hosts above not only heard the church bells, but saw them. In fact they could view them much better than mortals who had to climb up to them: only a hovering angel could observe close at hand that part of a bell facing outward, high in a bellchamber arch. The realization of this caused men to give much attention to the visual aspect of the bell, a concern which eventually produced graphic art to be hidden from men's eyes as fine as that made for their viewing. But first it brought about the placing of symbols and words on the bells which would spur divine beings to act. This type of inscription began to appear in the eleventh century perhaps in connection with the Pax Dei. The Pax Dei, or Peace of God, was a truce of one or two days a week which was promulgated as a means of diminishing, if not ending, the many private wars that kept breaking out in various parts of Europe and causing devastation and suffering to innocent people. In 1083 Archbishop Sigiwin of Cologne stated that, just as the *Dona nobis pacem* ('Grant us peace') had been inserted into the Agnus Dei of the Mass as a prayer for general peace desired by all, so *O Rex Gloriae veni cum pace* ('O King of Glory, bring peace') was inscribed on bells to petition for the Pax Dei.

"The concept of the sound of a church bell carrying prayers to heaven was not in conflict with its role as the Voice of the Lord speaking to the people.[89] Thus on some bells, instead of the petition, 'O King of Glory, bring peace', there was inscribed the response: *Christus Rex venit in pace* ('Christ the King brings peace'). These two formulae, never both on the same bell and seldom in the same region, were placed on bells from Italy to Scandinavia and Spain to Hungary as the two most popular inscriptions on western European church bells during the Middle Ages.

"In this era, when much reliance was placed on the power of both written wrods and symbols, the latter were also placed on bells to increase their potency. The power

---

88 See our theme **T1a** (Music as conveyor of praise, supplication [prayer] etc), *Introductory Remarks,* Vol I above. (Ed.)

89 See our theme **T1c** (Music as medium through which the spirit world [of divinities, supranatural beings] attempts to signal or contact man), *Introductory Remarks* Vol I above. (Ed.)

of the written word went out with the sound of the bell, but the symbol acted also while it was at rest, and protected it from demons who might get into the bellchamber and try to do it harm....

"The Eastern churches also rang bells to avert calamities, natural and otherwise. We know that around 1700 the bells of St Basil's Church in Moscow were rung to ward off demons and their evil influences, and that at various times all the church bells in that city were rung in connection with processions of penitents to end epidemics. The Russian Orthodox Church taught that the sound of the consecrated church bell acted on storms and other catastrophes through the union of its sound with the prayers of the people. At all times it gave a blessing, and the pious Russian crossed himself when he heard it. Inscriptions such as 'I drive away the cloud' on modern bells imply a recent use to affect the weather, and a special bell for this has been testified to by emigrants from Orthodox countries....

"Egypt. Both open-mouth bells and crotals were sometimes buried with the dead, both adult and chlidren, which reveals a belief in their efficacy in the after life. This implies that they were also worn by the living for protection on earth. Their use would be especially valued for defenceless persons such as children, and for those whose pursuits entailed hazards. This last would include those in priestly pursuits,

as we have seen in the reference to bells in Exodus....[90]

"Throughout the whole Pharaonic period (until 332 BC) most bells must have had some connection with temple life. Those in the hands of laymen might be instruments of supernatural power obtained at the temple and brought home. Those which remained in the temple could be *ex voto* gifts brought to the temple. In religious rites bell sounds would have a threefold function: keeping evil spirits away, gaining the attention of the deity, and shielding the officiant from the power of the deity. When a bell so used was not in service it was probably kept under a cloth to insulate its power from people....

"**Ancient Greece and Rome.** The earliest known bells in the region we poetically call the cradle of Western civilization come from the palace of the half-legendary King Minos on the island of Crete. They are not metal but clay objects, dated between 2000 and 1850 BC, a period when the Minoans, although already casting flatware, had not yet developed sufficient skill in pouring hollow objects to cast bronze bells. They have oval rims, suggesting sheep bells, and seem related to early clay bells both in western Asia and in Eastern Europe near the Black Sea....

"They were probably wind-bells, and originally had clappers of some perishable material, perhaps wood, which were blown by the wind. Their use differed

---

90 "The Book of Exodus, in chapter 28, verses 33 to 35, states a command of the Lord to Moses to place bells, alternately with pomegranates, beneath the hem (skirt) of the ephod, a priest's garment. That the purpose of these was the apotropaic power of their sound is shown in verse 35: 'And it [the ephod] shall be upon Aaron to minister: and his sound shall be heard when he goeth into the holy place before the Lord, and when he cometh out, that he die not.' From our modern viewpoint this seems not very different from the ancient Hindu concept that a mortal must ring a bell before he enters into the presence of a deity to worship. Exodus 39, verses 25 and 26, reports that the command was carried out: 'And they made bells of pure gold, and put the bells between the pomegranates... a bell and a pomegranate, a bell and a pomegranate, round about the hem of the robe to minister in; as the Lord commanded Moses'."

from that of Chinese wind-bells in that their sound was not to drive away an evil spirit but to attract a beneficent one. To this end they were hung up at shrines on the boughs of sacred trees as votive offerings....

"Customs using bells in relation to the dead and the dying seem to last longer and travel farther than other bell usages. When Ovid, who lived at the time of Christ, mentions ringing bells to drive away shades and spectres, we are reminded of Egypt and Alexander's sarcophagus. When Pliny, who lived a little later, tells us of wind-bells protecting a mausoleum in Tuscany we sense a link in the use of bells in the cult of the dead which extends east all the way to ancient China.

"The truly Roman use of the bell, however, was more for the living. People rang bells in the celebrations of imperial triumphs; they employed both open-mouth bells and crotals, solo and with other instruments, to mark the rhythms of dances at festivals. They opened and closed the games with a bell. Small bells were also sounded with sexual connotations: while female dancers used them in orgiastic dances for the entertainment of soldiers in lonely outposts, in Rome, wives suspected of infidelity were forced to wear them as they were jolted through the streets on donkeys as a public mockery....

"**India — Early and Hindu.** No doubt the bell was in use in India as long ago as in China, or as in Egypt or Iran, the only other regions which might lay claim to as ancient a use....

"[In the popular tradition] some of [the] Hindu deities carried crotals (*singita*), others open-mouth bells (*ghanti* or *ghantika*). Ganusha shook a garland of crotals in order to terrify people; Krishna wore a waistband of them to inform of his presence. Indra hung open-mouth bells on the sides of his sacred elephants, and Shiva* wore a small one on his left leg when as Nataraja, Lord of the Dance, he performed his miracle-working steps. His consort Durga, in her form as Parvati, held a bell of divine potency in her left hand. It was prayed to thus:

OM to the bell striking terror to our
enemies by thy world-wide sound!
Drive out from us all our iniquities.
Defend and bless us, O Lord.

"Here the bell is synonymous with a divinity. 'By thy world-wide sound' denotes the concept that what the ear hears is but a local physical manifestation of a world-pervading spiritual force which issues forth when it is struck. We shall find this concept recurring elsewhere. Here it should be noted that the Hindu rite which uses a bell in one hand and a sword in the other is probably derived from Hindu mythology, as also the bow with bells, and the stick with bells.

"If the divine uses of the bell were accounted for in Hindu iconography, its sacred form was derived from the abstract symbols of Brahmanism. In these, the universe is represented by a circle, and the universe of pure form by a hemisphere. Out of this hemisphere the world-lotus, womb of the created universe, emerges, and from it issue the hosts of the created world. The Hindu bell as a sacred symbol, actual or depicted, was composed of these three symbols: the circle, which is the loop by which it is held; the hemisphere, which is its crown or top; and the lotus, which is stylized in its sides flaring to a circular rim. The top and sides are separated by a flange, which may vary from a heavy moulding to a bead-line. As the world-lotus is incorruptible, so its symbolic colour is gold, and this is frequently made apparent on the bell by casting it in brass rather than bronze, to give it a golden sheen.

"It is noteworthy that this symbolism took a form which is acoustically good, and that it was chosen for Hindu bells because of its religious significance nearly two thousand years before it became the standard shape of Christian bells for acoustical reasons.[91] The oldest known bells of this form in India come from burial mounds dated around the sixth and fifth centuries BC. They are about nine centimetres high, and are cast. Long before the Christian era such bells were rung in Hindu temples to drive out evil spirits. They were also depicted on walls so that their mere appearance would keep demons away.

"Not all ancient Indian bells were of this lotus shape. Some, of a plain cylindrical form, have been found at the same sites. They are of wrought copper, which made them cheaper to produce and therefore more widely available. They resemble one type of bell used on animals in India today, and were doubtless used on animals then. In this usage they must have had a religious significance as well as a practical one, for the Hindu did not separate the religious from the secular. From the tradition that Krishna was once a cowherd came the regard for the cow—in south India, the buffalo—as sacred. Not all cows were equally sacred; those having the greatest economic value were the most sacred, and would have preference in wearing bells. The distinction probably arose in Vedic times (roughly 1500 to 500 BC) when the basic religious rite was sacrifice, and involved the slaughtering of animals. Gradually attitudes changed (as expressed in the slogan, 'Do not kill the guiltless cow!') and brought about the substitution of images. Sacred cows and buf-

faloes were allowed a life of freedom outside the temple. However, in some places at least, the bell which marked the most sacred animal of the herd was worn by it for a few days only, and chiefly at its dedication. This was because the bell itself came to be venerated as a god, a bell-god (*hiriadeva*). Most of the time it was kept out of sight in the priest's house or in a niche in the temple, where it was worshipped.

"There arose related customs. In the cult of Krishna garlands of bells (*gantamala*) were hung on cows and calves. In the cult of Shiva a bell was hung on his sacred bull. In the cult of Indra bells were hung from sacred elephants.

"With the substitution of images the forms of devotion changed from sacrifice to worship. The image (*arca*) by transubstantiation through special rites became a god. It was given a home, the temple, where it was not only worshipped but treated as an honoured guest. The air around it was kept free from little demons by incense from burners ringed with tiny lotus-bells. Every morning it was awakened ceremonially with the ringing of handbells and other musical sounds. Its attention was drawn to offered food by the priest ringing a handbell (*ghanti*). In Brahmanic rites the lamp was used along with the bell, to awaken the god from sleep so that it might consume the offering. In some temples it was left sleeping and worshipped in its mythical slumber. In these there was silence—no bells—as at The Temple of Sun Sleeping, at Sirigam.

"The god was adored. When, in the rites of worship, the priest recited sacred texts before it, he marked their pace with a handbell so that they would be uttered at a tempo conducive to their greatest spiritual effect. He also rang it to help the meditator withdraw into his mind so as to hear the inward sounds of Hindu mys-

---

91 However, it should *also* be noted that religious/mythological explanations can equally be invented to account for (rationalize) something which has already been shown to have a certain practical basis. (Ed.)

ticism. He rang it to call upon the god to give his blessing. In some temples devotees took part in climaxes in the ceremonies by ringing small bells on their persons as expressions of joy. They kept special bells in their homes for use in household worship. The priest's handbell remained on the lowest step of the altar before the god.

"As the use of the handbell in the worship of a god developed, so its handle became altered from a ring or circle, abstract symbol of the universe, to a figurine of a god — Shiva, Ganusha, Visnu, Hanuman, or another, according to the worship. This likeness of the god in the hand of the priest greatly added to the power and efficacy of the sound of the bell when it was rung before him. In some cults this power was realized in a handle formed into a coiled cobra with three, seven, or eleven hoods.

"The god was entertained. Out of this grew the great temple rituals employing music and dancing. These used handbells in an orchestra, and crotals (*kinkini*) on dancers' feet. These oldest of ritual bells became the symbol of the dance, a religious expression for which the devout dancer selected well tuned crotals, knowing that once she put them on after they had been blessed she could never renounce her profession of temple dancer. Before each ceremony she pressed them to her forehead and eyes and said a prayer. As she was not only a dancer but a singer, she also entwined their rhythms with her devotional song.

"The god received visitors in his earthly home. (In most Hindu cults the temple was, and is, primarily the home of a god, and not a place of congregational assembly. Thus worshippers are constantly coming and going.) These, his devotees, announced their arrival by ringing an attached bell (*ghanta*), suspended from a beam or a crossbar in the temple porch. How far back the use of such large bells as there are today (20 to 60 cm in diameter) goes, it is impossible to say. Before the eleventh or twelfth centuries there were

gongs* in some Hindu temples, and large bells may have come into them only after they disappeared from Buddhist use with the extinction of Buddhism. Sweetness of tone seems not to have been required of these bells; their symbolic form was more important. Prominent temples would have several bells in front of the room where the god dwelt.

"By ringing such a bell the worshipper not only announced his presence; he invited the gods and dispersed the devils. At its sound the lesser devas had to come. Therefore the first act of the worshipper on arriving at the temple was to pay homage to the bell, for this showed his obeisance to the god it would summon. After this he took the rope attached to the clapper and gave the bell a few vigorous strokes. At the same time he usually recited a formula such as the following:

> I bring out the sounds of the bell,
> which stand as a symbol for the evocation of the Divine Presence.

"When he had finished his devotions, which might include offering a gift and asking a boon, he would give the bell a single, milder stroke, to indicate to the god that he was leaving.

"These uses of bells in temple and home continue to the present day, and help to sustain the vitality of Hindu life. To them should be added the uses of bells in religious festivals. Many of these are local, and they occur more in the south than in the north. They vary from a single priest wearing bells on his legs while performing a simple rite, as in the Festival of Fire in the Nilgiri Hills, to a platoon of men ringing bells in a vast procession, as is done ahead of the two-storey car which is rolled through the streets of Mysore in the Festival of Juggernaut, Lord of the World. In festivals in Turipati in Madras State many bells are rung to create an intense emotional atmosphere. At Palni and other places in the same state dancers ring bells on semicircular frames like those once used by jongleurs in Europe as they sing and dance near the temple in festivities for Subrahmanya....

"Buddhist and post-Buddhist India. Around the fourth century BC Buddhism and Jainism were established as reforms of Hinduism. But as they developed separate rituals they put the bell to new uses. Jainism employed the bell less than Buddhism, and its effect on the history of the bell is negligible. Buddhism made transformations on its appearance and meaning which altered the history of the bell throughout much of Asia, as we have already seen in China.

"Buddhism based its ritual on one of the oldest forms of worship, the cult of *caityas* or sacred spots. It retained wind bells at these sites and recognized that their ringing drove away demons. But in addition to this it maintained that their sounds were a manifestation of the music of the heavenly spheres [see **HARMONY OF THE SPHERES***−(Ed.)] transmuted into a form which could be heard by human ears. We find an allusion to this heavenly music in one of the most poetic descriptions of bell sounds ever given. It was related by Gautama the Buddha to his disciple, Ananda, when the Buddha's life on earth was nearing its end. Describing the heavenly city of Kasavati, he said:

The Palace of Righteousness, Ananda, was hung round with two networks of bells. One network of bells was of gold, and one was of silver. The golden network had bells of silver and the silver network had bells of gold.

And when those networks of bells, Ananda, were shaken by the wind there arose a sound sweet, and pleasant, and charming, and intoxicating.

Just, Ananda, as when the seven kinds of instruments yield, when well played upon, to the skillful man a sound sweet, and pleasant, and charming, and intoxicating−just even so, Ananda, when those networks of bells

were shaken by the wind there arose a sound sweet, and pleasant, and charming, and intoxicating.....

"Besides wind-bells [the monasteries] must have taken over the handbell from earlier faiths. One or two Buddhist handbells said to have been made in India around the beginning of our era are preserved in Japan. Buddhism placed this bell in the grasp of at least two of its gods, and emphasized its miraculous power. This last was particularly true with the rise of *Vajrayana*, The Vehicle of the Thunderbolt, which appeared in India in the seventh century of our era.

"The Vehicle of the Thunderbolt stressed the acquisition of supernormal power, so that the gods should be compelled rather than persuaded. *Vajra*, this supernormal power, was symbolized in a bronze shaft long enough to be clasped in the hand and terminated at each end with claw-like prongs that joined at the tips. It was held in the hand during certain parts of the ritual. The *vajra* was kept at the altar along with the handbell (*ghanti*). This was also given a *vajra* handle, that is, the end which was not joined to the bell was terminated with prongs. On the top of the bell were cast arcane symbols of sounds which had mystical power. One or two of these might also be raised on the inside surface. The rest of the bell was left plain except for conventional borders at the shoulder and rim related to its lotus meaning.

"With the *vajra* in one hand and the *vajra*-bell in the other, the priest had two very strong symbols. The *vajra* represented the adamantine [rigidly firm − made of or having the quality of adamant, i.e., an imaginary stone of impenetrable hardness (Ed.)], the thunderbolt, the universal male sex principle. The bell, symbol of the lotus, represented the female sex principle. The combination formed intuition and compassion, also awakening and illumination, the world of appearance. The world of appearance is passing and deceptive, like the sounds of a bell.

"With this strong symbolism the sound of the *Vajrayana ghanti* not only drove away evil spirits and aroused the attention of the deity; it became an integral part of the ritual. This made the bell exceedingly powerful in proper hands, and very dangerous in improper ones because, in addition to the combined potencies in its visual aspect, its sound, except when occurring at the right places in the liturgy and produced by a priest, was blasphemy....

"**Japan.** The oldest bells found in Japan are among the most extraordinary anywhere. They are called *dokatu*, and belong to the Yayoi culture, which flourished from about 250 BC to AD 250. Their form is an oval conoid, about one-and-a-half times as high as wide, and slightly resembles that of certain early *nao* bells. But they differ in two features: they have a straight as opposed to an indented rim, and they have a flange which extends up from the rim on one side, over the top, and down to the rim on the other side. In the part of the flange above the top [of the bell] there is a hole, suggesting that this part of the flange might serve as a handle. There are also two smaller holes on either side of the upper half of the bell, and two notches in the rim on either side. The flange increases the apparent size of the bell, while the holes and the flange give the object a strangely anthropomorphic appearance, as if it were the abode of a spirit which looked out through the holes and moved its feet in the notches....

"*Dotaku* have been buried at numerous places along south-central Japan: on hilltops, in some places near crossroads, and always at sites naturally favourable for the veneration of the gods. Like certain bells in Korea [see below] they have been deliberately interred there, most of them singly, but in some places two to fourteen laid in straight rows, 'head to foot'. In the Middle Yayoi period (first centuries BC and AD) weapons were found with them.

"There is little doubt that the *dotaku* were sacred objects, and that their burial was related to an agrarian society's concept of the powers of nature and of its expectations from them. We [will note in the next section, on Korean bells,] the concern for sending the sound of a bell down into the earth in the later Buddhist period in Korea. This may well have been an earlier but similar concept, namely, that the sound was proof of a spiritual essence in the bell, and that planting it put this essence into the earth. To our ears their sound is a dull thud, no better or worse than that found in the earliest bells on the nearer Asiatic mainland, but this may have been all that was wanted....

"**Korea.** Some bells had a non-military use, for we are told that in the first century BC people in Korea hung bells and drums on a great pole for the service of the heavenly spirits. We know nothing of the size of these bells, and it is possible that they were wind-bells [see *China, India* etc above], the drums also being sounded by the wind, or by spirits riding on the air, to a people who believed that the natural phenomenon of wind was caused by the movement of unseen spirits....

"After about 670, when the native Silla dynasty gained control of all Korea, and Buddhism flourished as the state religion, the typical Korean large hanging temple bell, known as the *chong*, was evolved. It soon took on distinctive features which made it recognizably different from either Chinese or Japanese temple bells....

"On top [of one type of Korean temple bell] there is a suspension loop in the form of a single-headed dragon with its body coiled around the most uniquely Korean feature of all: a pipe which extends over 20 cm above the top, and is open at both ends. It is part of the same casting as the bell.

"This pipe, Koreans say, is necessary to let the sound out of the bell; but the explanation is not so simple as this. It seems to be a carry-over from a pre-Buddhist magico-sacred use of bells, and a substitute for holes in the sides of much earlier small bells. We have met the concept of the sound of the bell as a physical manifestation of a spiritual essence, and, in very early times in China, the ringing of bells to make the earth yield abundantly. In Buddhism the use of this essence was transferred from benefitting the harvest to benefitting the souls of the ancestors who dwell in the earth, which act would, in return, benefit those on earth both in this life and the hereafter. But some of this essence must also come out into the upper world; and for this purpose the pipe is placed on top to allow a portion of it to go upwards. Above ground it also diffuses many times farther than the audible sound of the bell.

"Related to this is the position of the large Korean Buddhist bell when suspended. The Chinese Buddhist bell was hung a storey above the ground, so that its emanations would come down on to a deity, exemplified by a statue, who would know how to distribute it. The Korean bell was hung close to the ground, only about thirty centimetres above it in some cases, and the ground hollowed out underneath and kept clear of earth so as to facilitate the entry of its emanations into the earth. In earlier times large pots were buried in these hollow places so as to echo the sound back into the bell and complete the tonal link with the earth.

"As it was believed that the ringing of the bell sent these spiritual emanations out to the ends of the world as well as down into the earth, so it was held that by making the bell larger, and thus increasing the power of its tone and the length of time it continued, the spiritual emanations would be stronger at distant points. The most effective bell would be the largest it would be possible to cast....

"**Tibet.** Both shamans and lamas use the handbell, the Tantric Buddhist *ghanta*. It is usually more profusely ornamented than its Chinese counterpart [see above], and particularly than its Japanese. The or-

namentation is highly symbolic, and includes symbols for sounds, not words, with occult power. It is kept in the hall of worship on a table beside other sacred objects (censers with small bells, candles and offerings), and is rung to attract the divinity's attention....

"The *drilbu*-type bell is employed at both simple and elaborate services apart from its use with the thunderbolt symbol (*vajra* or *rdo-rje*) at the altar. It may signal a choir to sing, instrumentalists to sound drums, cymbals, conch shells, trumpets, and clarinet- and trombone-like instruments, and actors to begin a mystery play. It may signal to stop all of this, or indicate changes in the ritual. In its great variety of uses it has been carried far beyond central Asia. Several examples related to the worship of Garuda, a Mongolian divinity, have been found on the North American side of the Bering Strait.

"Less widely used, but more constantly rung, is the wind-bell or spirit bell. Tibetans string these along with prayer flags on the rooftops both of temples and of lesser buildings as a means of perpetual guardianship. Where the wind-bell originated is not known. It may have evolved from an ancient Siberian custom of hanging both open-mouth bells and crotals as votive offerings on sacred trees. It seems particularly appropriate to the semi-barren central Asian plateau, where almost everything visible is motionless and silent, and only the invisible air moves and makes a sound. Sven Hedin describes the acoustical effect when many bells are rung by the wind at a large Tibetan monastery:

The strokes of the thousand temple bells blended into one clang, which filled the air and seemed to rise like a hymn to the dwellings of the gods; for at all corners, projections, and cornices are hung brazen bells with clappers attached to a spring, so that a very light breeze is sufficient to produce a sound. It is very pleasant to listen to this great carillon played by the wind as one wanders through the maze of Tashi-lunpo.

"T. Y. Pemba points out how the combined sounds of prayer flags and wind-bells dominate a Tibetan town in a river valley: 'at Pipithang one heard only the roar of the river close by, and the wind of the roof tops blowing the prayer flags, and the tinkling of bells.'

"There is a good reason for setting out wind-bells and prayer flags together in the wind. The written prayers manifest right thinking, and the sound of the bells brings this to the attention of divinities. We shall find a counterpart to this in medieval Christianity, in which it was believed that prayers cast on a bell were brought to the attention of the Christian divinity to whom the bell was dedicated, each time it rang. Christianity never made the process perepetual, as did Lamaism. This was done by utilizing water power to turn a wheel constantly (as at Himis monasery near Ladakh, Kashmir), the wheel moving prayer flags attached to it, and at each rotation ringing a bell....

"The large bell common to orthodox Buddhism is also found in Lamaist temples. The Chinese shape as exemplified in the great bell of the Mongolian Lamasery in Peking has been adopted westward across Mongolia and into northern Sin-kiang. But from there southwards the southern Asiatic shape, with its heavy 'collar', predominates. The bell is rung for its spiritual power, not as an accommodation to men." — Price, pp.xvi-xvii, 3-4, 9-11, 21, 23-26, 31, 35-36, 39-40, 54-55, 59, 64, 67-69, 73-74, 76, 78-79, 83-86, 107, 111-12, 122, 124, 127, 129

BIRDS (SONG OF). *(See p. 102.)*

§44.2 BLACKBIRD (British folklore).[92] "The blackbird has ever been one of Britain's most melodious songsters and this is doubtless why the Birds of Rhiannon [daughter of Hefaidd Hen, Lord of the Underworld] are said to be three blackbirds: they sing on the branch of the everylasting otherworldly tree which grows in the centre of the earthly paradise. Their singing entranced the hearer, ushering him or her into the Otherworld. They sing for Bran [Bran the Blessed or Bendigeid Fran — titanic legendary hero of Wales] and the Company of the Noble Head, in their feasting between the worlds." — Matthews and Matthews, p.33.

§44.3 "THE PRIEST WHO HAD ONE SMALL GLIMPSE OF GLORY [Mexican folktale]. In a church there was a priest who was very good, and one day, when he was already in his vestments and about to go say mass, he said, 'Oh, my Lord! Allow me just one small glimpse of your glory!'

"When he went out to the altar, he heard a little bird sing, but in such a marvelous way that he stopped, and raised his eyes looking for the bird. When he came to, he

---

92 Birdsong is not customarily included in the present work, however the present entry suggests a capacity as genuinely musical as it is (merely) animal... See also e.g. SIRENS. (Ed.)

hurried toward the altar to say mass, but he saw that the church was in ruins. There was no altar or anything any more.

"So he asked some people who were going by, 'What happened to the church?'

" 'But father, don't you know that a long, long time ago there was a priest who was going to say mass, and as he left the sacristy he heard a little bird sing, and none of his parishioners ever saw him again? No priest had ever asked us that question; you must be that priest without a doubt.'

"Then he, as well as the villagers, understood what had happened. And if because of one little glimpse of glory, he was in ecstasy for so many years, what would it be like if he saw God's glory in all its splendor?"[93] — Paredes, pp.122-123.

BUDDHA.

§48A.1 "A little over five hundred years before the birth of Christ there was born in India, near Benares, a prince who was named Gotama. His father was Suddhodana, king of the Sakya clan, and his mother Queen Maha-Maya, daughter of the king of a neighbouring clan.

"The story is told in the scriptures... of the young prince's luxurious boyhood, his decision to leave it all and search for enlightenment in regard to the miseries of life, and his long ministry as the Buddha, or the Enlightened One.[94]

"There was a widespread belief that one was continually reborn, each time reaping the results of what he had done in a former life, and that the highest happiness one could attain was a life with the gods. But Gotama Buddha decided that one can live so as never to have to be born again as a separate person, but rather so as to achieve Nirvana, the perfect peace that is without desires and without personal existence at all.

"The Buddha's teachings differed in many other ways from the older Hindu fatih: the gods were not a part of his plan of salvation; he disregarded castes; he discarded extreme fasting and other ascetic practices, which many Hindus had believed in, and taught that men should live moderately.

"Disciples flocked to him by the hundreds. He formed them into an Order of monks, who are sometimes called 'bhikkhus' or brethren.

"The stories and teachings [by and about him] are a mixture of accurate facts and legends which grew up around those facts.... Since the time of his death, many schools or movements have changed or expanded what he taught, and Buddhism, like Christianity, has become different things to different people....

"[From the literature of Buddhism:] **Heavenly music at the death of the Buddha.** And the Exalted One proceeded with a great company of the brethren to the Sala Grove of the Mallas, the Upavattana of Kusinara, on the farther side of the river Hiranyavati: and when he had come there he addressed the venerable Ananda [his disciple], and said: 'Spread over for me, I pray you, Ananda, the couch with its head

---

93   This story of music (birdsong) as a key to heaven (mediation with the supernatural) also includes the common secondary theme of music as an ecstatic or ecstasy-inducing experience. See also stories of fairies who cast their spells through music — so that what appears to be a night spent fiddling and dancing is — in truth — a passing of many years (e.g. tale of **THE TWO FIDDLERS***, p.250 above). The story includes Thompson Folktale Motifs B172.2 (Magic bird's song brings joy and oblivion for many years) and D2011.1 (Years seem moments while man listens to song of bird). (Ed.)

94   See index for other references throughout this text. (Ed.)

to the north, between the twin sala trees. I am weary, Ananda, and would lie down.'

" 'Even so, lord!' said the venerable Ananda, in assent, to the Exalted One. And he spread a covering over the couch with its head to the north, between the twin sala trees. And the Exalted One laid himself down on his right side, with one leg resting on the other; and he was mindful and self-possessed.

"Now at that time the twin sala trees were all one mass of bloom with flowers out of season; and all over the body of the Tathagata [name for the Buddha (Ed.)] these dropped and sprinkled and scattered themselves, out of reverence for the successors of the Buddhas of old. And heavenly Mandarava flowers, too, and heavenly sandalwood powder came falling from the sky, and all over the body of the Tathagata they descended and sprinkled and scattered themselves, out of reverence for the successor of the Buddhas of old. And heavenly music was sounded in the sky, out of reverence for the successor of the Buddhas of old. And heavenly songs came wafted from the skies, out of reverenece for the successor of the Buddhas of old!

"Then the Exalted One addressed the venerable Ananda and said: 'The twin sala trees are all one mass of bloom with flowers out of season; all over the body of the Tathagata these drop and sprinkle and scatter themselves, out of reverence for the successor of the Buddhas of old. And heavenly music sounds in the sky, out of reverence for the successor of the Buddhas of old!

" 'Now it is not thus, Ananda, that the Tathagata is righly honoured, reverenced, venerated, held sacred, or revered. But the brother or the sister, the devout man or the devout woman, who continually fulfills all the greater and the lesser duties, who is correct in life, walking according to the precepts—it is he who righly honours, reveres, venerates, holds sacred, and reveres the Tathagata with the worthiest homage. Therefore, O Ananda, be ye constant in the fulfilment of the greater and of the lesser duties, and be ye correct in life, walking according to the precepts; and thus, Ananda, should it be taught.'...

"Then the Exalted One addressed the brethren, and said: 'Behold now, brethren, I exhort you, saying: *Decay is inherent in all component things! Work out your salvation with diligence!*"

"This was the last word of the Tathagata." — Smith (Tree of Life), pp.117-18, 153-55.

CHANTING.

§59A.1 "The rhythmic repetition of words or phrases, usually done in conjunction with dancing, drumming, rattling and hand-clapping, is a primitive way to alter consciousness and raise power. The chants, along with the dancing, drumming, hand-clapping or other accompaniment, are gradually speeded up in tempo until a peak state is reached.

'Since ancient times around the world, chanting has been part of religious, ceremonial and magical rites. In ancient Greece, female sorcerers were said to howl their magical chants. Early and medieval sorcerers and magicians also chanted their incantations in howls and forceful voices, a practice carried over into the 20th century by magicians such as Aleister Crowley, who believed that the sound of words profoundly affects both man and universe. Modern witches and neo-pagans chant to raise power for magical spells (see WITCHCRAFT* — Cone of Power). The chants may be names of the goddess or horned god, rhymes, alliterative phrases or charms. Charms to chant may be obtained from books on folk and ceremonial magic; many witches create their own charms to suit the purpose at hand. Chanting usually is done in conjunction with a ring dance around the magic circle, or while working with cords. The Witches' Rune, composed by English witch Doreen

Valiente, is a common power-raising chant, the refrain of which is:

Eko Eko Azarak
Eko Eko Zomelak
Eko EKo Cernunnos
Eko Eko Aradia

"Shamans* chant power songs that follow rhythms and melodies that have been passed down through generations. The words vary according to the individual. Power songs help a shaman achieve an altered state of consciousness for healing or divining. The chanted songs are monotonous, short refrains and have different purposes. Every shaman has at least one chant to summon his power animal or guardian spirit, which provide the source of his shamanic powers.

"Native American Indians have chants for the undertaking of many activities, such as hunts, battles and weather control, and for the rites of funerals and initiations. Curing chants are important in Navaho ceremonies. The chants are long texts in which are entwined myths about how the chants were performed for the first time by deities or supernatural beings. The chanters must chant the texts perfectly, or else the cures will be nullified. Incorrectly rendered chants also will strike the chanter with the illness they are supposed to cure. The chants may go on for many days and nights. A chanter is assisted by helpers, all of whom are paid for their work. If a chanter of great repute does not err yet fails to cure an illness, he usually blames witchcraft as the reason. If sickness has been caused by a witch's spell, only Evil Way chants will be effective. Navajo chanters take care not to perform the same chant more than three times a year, lest they suffer the illness they cure." — Guiley, pp.55-56.

CHINESE PRACTICES AND BELIEFS — MYTHS AND LEGENDS. (See also pp.133, 826.)

§64.12 "[DIAMOND KINGS OF HEAVEN: MO-LI HAI (whose attribute is a guitar).] On the right and left sides of the entrance hall of Buddhist temples, two on each side, are the gigantic figures of the four great *Ssu Ta Chin-kang* or *T'ien-wang*, the Diamond Kings of Heaven, protectors or governors of the continents lying in the direction of the four cardinal points from Mount Sumêru, the centre of the world. They are four brothers named respectively Mo-li Ch'ing (Pure), or Teêng Chang, Mo-li Hung (Vast), or Kuang Mu, Mo-li Hai (Sea), or To Wên, and Mo-li Shou (Age), or Ch'ih Kuo. The *Chin kuang ming* states that they bestow all kinds of happiness on those who honor the Three Treasures, Buddha, the Law, and the Priesthood....

"*Mo-li Hai* holds a four-stringed guitar, the twanging of which supernaturally affects the earth, water, fire, or wind. When it is played all the world listens, and the camps of the enemy take fire." — Werner [China], pp.120-21.

§64.13 [MO-LI HAI (Dhritarashtra) — continued.] "[In the course of the last few centuries the two mythical heroes, Kin-kang (Vajra) and Li-shï (Balin), guardians of the doors of the temples — who were not Buddhist but popular in origin — were] gradually replaced by the Four Celestial Kings, T'ien-wang. These are four well-known Buddhist gods: Vaisramana for the North, holding a banner in his right hand and in his left a *stupa* [reliquary chamber], Dhritarashtra for the East, carrying a species of guitar; Virudhaka for the South, trampling a demon under his feet, and Virupaksha for the West, holding in his left hand a jewel in the form of a reliquary and a serpent in his right. The wholly Chinese custom of placing them at the entrance of temples as guardians hardly seems to go back further than Ming times; before that they were arranged at the four points of the compass round a *stupa*, or else they surrounded a group of statues, but no one thought of collecting them in this way in the first building. To-day this arrangement is almost universal, and the ancient guardians have nearly everywhere had to give way to them; but their name Kin-kang-li-shï (Vajrabalin) has to some extent remained attached to the function, and the Four Celestial Kings are often called by the title of the Four (Bearers) of the Thunder-bolts, Sï Kin-kang. The Taoists have borrowed these colossal figures, giving them the purely Chinese names of Li, Ma, Chao, and Wên, and they place them sometimes at the entrance to their temples in a position similar to that in the Buddhist temples. As for the popular religion, it has adopted one of them, Vaisramana, under his Taoist name of Li; this is Li Tower-bearer, Li T'o-t'a. But the group of four divinities would be completely forgotten if the *Tale of the Investiture of the Gods* had not saved it by adopting it in a travestied form. They are the four Mo-li brothers (Mara, but the word is taken as a family name, and not as meaning demon), supporters of the Shang, who were vanquished and slain after various mighty exploits. The eldest, Mo-li Ts'ing, was armed with a sabre that produced devastating whirlwinds and waterspouts. The second, Mo-li Hung, carried a closed parasol; when he opened it the sun and moon were hidden, and the earth was plunged in darkness, and the rain came down. The third, Mo-li Hai, had a guitar whose sounds, in exact accord with the elements, ruled the winds. (We know that in Chinese philosophy the Five Sounds, the Five Savours, the Five Cardinal Points, etc., are brought into relation with the Five Elements, so that to act upon one group reacts upon the others also.)[95] Lastly, the fourth, Mo-li Shou, carried a bag containing the monster Striped Marten, *hua-hu-tiao*, which when let loose devoured men. After their death and the final victory of the King of Chou they received the divine offices of protectors of the pagodas and regulators of wind and rain. It seems that the author of the *Tale of the Investiture of the Gods* drew from the folklore of his own time these popular interpretations of the attributes of the Four Kings: we find the guitar of Dhritarashtra unchanged in the hands of Mo-li Hai, and Mo-li Hung's parasol seems to me a bad and ignorant interpretation of Vaisramana's furled standard; but the other two are not so easy to determine. The author's part consisted less in the invention of the personages themselves than in the fantastic use he made of them in his account of the war between the Shang and the Chou." — Maspero, in Hacklin, pp.307-09.

§64.14 TIEN-WANG (MO-LI), The Heavenly Kings (continued). "These were four brothers, Buddhist gods whose duty

---

95 See our theme T2 (The laws [structure] of music parallel the laws [structure] of nature or the universe, e.g. those having to do with the relation of heavenly bodies or other natural components to each other, or with the conduct of such bodies or components with respect to each other), *Introductory Remarks*, Vol I, above. With respect to the figure of the guitar-bearing Mo-li Hai in particular, I should think that each of the following themes has some relevance: T2b (Music has magical effect upon orderly process of nature or life cycle.... Music can promote or retard the health of an individual or community), T1c perhaps (Music as medium through which the spirit world [divinities, supranatural beings] attemt to signal or contact man), and T5 (Music... can suggest attainment of peace or harmony with the universe or being). (Ed.)

was to guard doors. They were guardians of the Four Directions. Originally from India, their names were Vaisravana, Virudharka, Virupasa and Dhrtarastra. Each carried an object which, when mortals, they had used to control the elements. These objects were a sword, a guitar, an umbrella and a marten (the animal). The sword raised tempests, the guitar governed the winds, the umbrella controlled the light of the sun and the marten killed and consumed malicious spirits. Because of their potency and aggressive energy the Mo-Li were ideal sentries." — Carlyon, pp.91-92.

§64.15 CONFUCIUS.[96] Confucius (c.500 BCE) and his disciples edited much of the old Chinese history, teachings, and poetry; after his death, some of his followers wrote more books in which they recorded many of the words and acts of their teacher.

"[From THE BOOK OF CEREMONIAL RITES:] How Music Reflects What Is Within. When the mind is moved to sorrow, the sound is sharp and fading away; when it is moved to pleasure, the sound is slow and gentle; when it is moved to joy, the sound is exclamatory and soon disappears; when it is move to anger, the sound is coarse and fierce; when it is moved to reverence, the sound is straightforward, with an indication of humility; when it is moved to love, the sound is harmonious and soft. These six peculiarities of sound are not the nature of the voice; they indicate the impressions produced by external things. On this account the ancient kings were watchful in regard to the things by which the mind was affected." — Smith (Tree of Life), p.162.

"[From THE WAYS OF CONFUCIUS.] The Master said, 'Do you think, my disciples, that I have any concealments? I con- ceal nothing from you. There is nothing which I do that is not shown to you, my disciples; that is my way.'

"There were four things which the Master taught: letters, ethics, devotion of soul, and truthfulness.

"The Master said, 'I am fortunate! If I have any errors, people are sure to know them.'

"When the Master was in company with a person who was singing, if he sang well, he would make him repeat the song while he accompanied it with his own voice.

"The Master said, 'In letters I am perhaps equal to other men, but the character of the superior man, carrying out in his conduct what he professes, is what I have not yet attained to.' " — Smith (Tree of Life), p.176.

§64.16 **"Folk Tales from China: Stories of the Beginnings of Things.** *The Birth of the Flute* and the Lute**. In times long past, when the world was young, there were no musical instruments of any kind in the Flowery Kingdom. The Emperor Huang-ti, the 'Yellow Emperor' [see also p.138 (Ed.)], pondered the matter and said to himself, 'I will have a flute made for my good people that they may play on it; thus will I know of their joys and sorrows.'

"So he commanded his minister, Ling Lun: 'Do you go to the sacred K'un-lun Mountain in the West where Hsi-wang-mu, the Fairy Queen, abides. On its green southern slope there grows a wondrous bamboo that will make the instrument I desire. Betake you there in haste, and tarry not...'

"So Ling Lun started on his long journey to the green mountains in the far, far West. By day he traveled, following the course of the sun in the sky; and at night he rested under the stars. After many months he at last came to the foot of the green K'un-lun Mountain.

"Ling-Lun began his search for that wonderful bamboo his sovereign had told

---

96 See index for other entries.

him to obtain, and at last he found it—the Melodious Bamboo!

"With his sharp knife he cut off a small section of it. When, lo and behold two birds with resplendent plumage of all the colors of the rainbow flew and alighted on a tree nearby, to watch Ling Lun at his task. One of them was a male bird, and his companion a female.

"Soon the flute was fashioned, and Ling Lun blew on it, a single note flew out, sailing in the air like a silver arrow. The original Chinese musical note!

"Immediately the male bird began singing a scale of six sweet notes and then stopped. The female bird picked it up and sang another six notes, higher than the male's.

"Ling Lun memorized them all, and proceeded to reproduce them on his flute by cutting extra holes in it. Soon he was able to blow all twelve of the sweet notes which the birds had taught him.

"Thus was the first Chinese flute made during the august reign of Huang-ti (2697-2596 BC) and thus were the twelve basic Chinese musical notes received by the Chinese race from two wondrous birds one sunny day in the green K'un-lun Mountain, long, long ago.

"And now it was time for man to make a musical instrument delicate enough to speak the thoughts in his heart. Lo, the time had come for man to make his first lute.

"It was in the golden reign of Fu-hsi (2852-2736 BC) [see also pp.139, 512, 514, 687 (Ed.)], and one day the good Emperor noticed that over a certain green-barked tree in the imperial park hovered a magic radiance like that of a star. 'What wondrous fairy tree could that be?' said he.

"And the wise men of his court told the Emperor that it was the rare *wu-tung* tree, the chosen perch and bower of the sacred Phoenix Bird. 'Hai!' exclaimed the joyful Emperor, 'then a magical power must dwell in its wood. Of it I shall make a musical instrumet with tones sweet and sensitive enough to arrest the very clouds sailing in the sky.'

"Then, burning some incense as an offering, he had the tree cut down. Three equal sections he ordered made of the trunk. The first section proved too light; and the third too heavy. So he selected the middle section.

"This he first had soaked in the living water of a brook for two and seventy days, after which it was left to dry by itself in the cooling velvety shadow of a bamboo clump.

"Then Fu-hsi commanded the kingdom's master craftsman to appear before him, and to the man he handed the piece of seasoned wood, saying, 'Now of this make me the most wonderful lute.'

"And the craftsman put his heart and soul into the task. And one day, behold, the lute was made!

"The instrument measured a little over three feet six inches in length; and was eight inches wide at one end, and four inches at the other end. Five parallel strings

were attached to it, which gave out a descending scale of delicate magic tones. In later times, two more strings were added, thus giving it its name of 'The Seven-Stringed Lute'.

"And the heart of Fu-hsi sang for joy. 'Now,' he spake, 'with this lute mankind can sing the joys and sorrows in his innermost heart.'...[97]

"The Legend of the Big Bell. In the ancient city of Peking stands the famous Big Bell*, many times a man's height, cast during the glorious reign of the Emperor Yung-lo [see also BELLS*, p.82 (Ed.)]. Of this most wonderful bell the following tale is told:

"When the great Emperor Yung-lo had finished building the finest city in all Asia, Old Peking, he said, 'Now let there be cast a huge bell whose sweet voice shall float across the blue hills for a hundred *li*, north, south, east, and west.'

"And so he summoned the master bell-maker, the one and ony Kwan Yu. To him the Emperor said, 'Make me this great bell without regard to its cost. Let it be said that it is the greatest and noblest under heaven.'[98]

"So Kwan Yu started on his great work. Day and night he toiled unceasingly. For such a perfect bell he used the yellowest of gold, the whitest of silver, and the purest of iron that could be obtained from the body of Mother Earth. It would be his masterpiece.

"The metal was melted in the roaring furnace and was cast in a great mold. But, alas, when it was taken out of it, many a crack appeared on its surface.

"The great Kwan Yu started the work all over again: but a second time the bell came out imperfect. The gods must be displeased...

"When the Emperor heard that the casting of his big bell had failed a second time, great was his impatience. Kwan Yu was summoned into his presence and bluntly told: 'If you fail a third time, your head shall fall!' The heart of old Kwan Yu was sorely troubled, for he was afraid the third bell would turn out badly.

"Now, Kwan Yu had a daughter, the beautiful Ko Ngai, who saw the anxiety eating her old sire's heart. She must do something to help him. That night she secretly stole to the shadow of the city-wall and there consulted an old soothsayer.

"Said the soothsayer to the girl, 'Your father's bell to be perfect must have the blood of a virgin mixed into the metal...'

" 'The blood of a virgin... the blood of a virgin...' repeated the girl as she walked home. The dutiful Ko Ngai had already decided how to save her dear father.

"In the morning the third bell was to be cast, and her father was trembling in body and limb, fearing the uncertain outcome. But the smiling face of his beautiful

---

97   Is music divinely inspired — a gift or presentation of the gods, or divine beings — or do music and musical instruments only derive from, and, to a degree, imitate, nature itself? Consistent with the inclinations of Chinese mythology generally, which tends to identify the "gods" with legendary or semi-historical figures (important sages and emperors in particular), this tale takes the latter, essentially secular view. However, the context for discovering or "inventing" music itself is magical, and both the earth and all its creatures seem possessed by a kind of magical spirit to which music seems to point, and of which music seems an expression. Moreover, musical instruments are magical implements, in a way: that is, they seem to invoke the music (magical spirit) of nature itself... and — as if by magic — they disclose the very "joys and sorrows" (i.e. secrets or true feelings) of one's innermost heart. (Ed.)

98   For a detailed account of the sacred/mythological importance of bells in Chinese culture, see article by Percival Price under BELLS*, §40.19 above. (Ed.)

daughter, standing by his side, seemed to lend him a certain courage.

"The yellow flames of the furnace leapt and roared as if already mocking the old man with his failure. Suddenly a maiden's voice cut the silence: 'For thy sake, O my father!' and the brave little Ko Ngai leapt into the boiling mass of metal.

"Ko Ngai's maid-servant had tried to stop her, but only succeeded in pulling away from the determined maiden one lone embroidered shoe of hers. O supreme sacrifice!...

"When the bell was tried, hark! its sweet, mellow voice floated over the blue hills for a full hundred *li*, for the sacred blood of a dutiful daughter had made it perfect.

"In the olden days, when the Big Bell was struck in the cool evenings, the mellow tone would die among the distant hills of Peiping with a lingering *h-s-i-e-h*... note.

" 'Hark!' said the mothers telling the legend to the young ones, 'Little Ko Ngai is crying for her shoe.'...

"**Fairy Tales of Long Ago.** *The Broken Harp**. This is one of the most beautiful of the Chinese tales which have come down to us through twenty-five centuries.

"Once upon a time Yu Pe-ya, a minister of the state of Tsin, was sent on a friendly mission to the state of Ch'u. One night when the boat on which he was traveling was anchored in the river, Pe-ya ordered his servant to bring forth his harp that he might play a tune or two under the beautiful autumn moon.

"He played a sweet melody, and suddenly one of the strings of the harp snapped. Now, in those times there was a belief that the presence of an unsympathetic listener nearby would cause the string of a musical instrument to break. Therefore Pe-ya calmly ordered his servant to go ashore and find out if he could see anybody.

" 'Your Highness need not trouble,' said a voice from the bank. 'It is no unsympathetic listener that has been enjoying your sweet music.'

" 'Is it possible that on this wild hillside there should be a lover of music?' asked Pe-ya.

"Out of the night the answer came instantly. 'As possible, Sir, as that at the foot of this wild hillside there should be such a noble musician.'

"Pe-ya was pleased with the witty answer. He then said, 'Can my Brother then tell me what melody I was playing?'

"The invisible man on the bank replied, 'That was an old favorite song of Confucius bewailing the death of his favorite disciple, Yen Hui:

Alas, Yen Hui, so soon to die!
My hair with grief is turned to gray.
The frugal joys, thy humble home —

" 'At this point your string snapped, but the fourth line is

Shall charm the ages yet to come!'

"Pe-ya was convinced that the man standing on the bank was a cultured person, and invited him to step on board.

"Lo! a humble woodcutter in simple cotton clothes came to the boat. But Pe-ya instantly commanded wine and food to be served the guest. He soon learned that the woodcutter's name was Tzu-ch'i.

"Throughout the long night the two conversed till dawn had broken in the east. Each poured out his heart to the other, and they did not part till they had taken the oath of 'sworn brothers'. They promised each other to meet again at the same spot a year thence on the evening of the Mid-Autumn Festival.

"The year sped by. Pe-ya excitedly tied his boat at the same place where he had met his friend, the woodcutter, a year before. Tonight he would again meet his 'sworn brother' Tzu-ch'i, his 'heart interpreter' as he called him.

"The silver moon rose slowly in the sky, and again he took out his harp to play. He played on, and on. Tzu-ch'i did not come. Could he have forgotten? Pe-ya stepped ashore to find out. Alas, his friend had died!

"From Tzu-chi's father, Pe-ya learned that his friend's last wish had been to be buried near the spot where they had promised to meet.

"To the grave Pe-ya hurred with a weeping heart. He wept, and tuning his harp he sang:

I sing to thee, my last song, my last!

and with a knife he slashed the strings, and holding the harp high above his head, he shattered it into a hundred pieces on the grave-stone.

"And from that day on he took care of the aged parents of the dead Tzu-ch'i as if they had been his own." — Sian-tek, pp.69-73, 76-79, 107-09.

COLOR AND MUSIC.

§69A.1 See CORRESPONDENCES*.

§69A.2 "Colour symbolism is one of the most universal of all types of symbolism, and has been consciously used in the liturgy, in heraldry, alchemy, art and literature. [Mention may be made of] the superficial classification suggested by optics and experimental psychology. The first group embraces warm 'advancing' colours, corresponding to processes of assimilation, activity and intensity (red, orange, yellow and, by extension, white), and the second covers cold, 'retreating' colours, corresponding to processes of dissimilation, passivity and debilitation (blue, indigo, violet and, by extension, black), green being an intermediate, transitional colour spanning the two groups.... The serial order of the colour-range is basic, comprising as it does (though in a somewhat abstract sense) a kind of limited set of definitive, distinct and ordered colours.

The formal affinity between, on the one hand, this series of six or seven shades of colour — for sometimes it is difficult to tell blue from indigo, or azure from ultamarine — and, on the other hand, the vowel-series — there being seven vowels in Greek — as well as the notes of the musical scale, points to a basic analogy between these three scales and also between them and the division of the heavens, according to ancient astrobiological thought, into seven parts (although in fact there were sometimes said to be nine).... Ély Star and others maintain that the seven colours are severally analagous to the seven faculties of the soul, to the seven virtues (from a positive point of view), to the seven vices (from a negative viewpoint), to the geometric forms, the days of the week and the seven planets.[99] Actually this is a concept which pertains more to the 'theory of correspondences'* than to the symbolism of colour proper." — Cirlot, pp.52-53.

CORRESPONDENCES.

§70B.1 See **COLOR AND MUSIC*.**
HARMONY OF THE
SPHERES*.
ICELANDIC FOLKTALES
AND MYTHS*.
MUSIC — SYMBOLISM*.
NUMBERS*.

§70B.2 *Ed. note:* Although this article does not focus on music *per se*, any consideration of interlocking symbolisms eventually includes music within the general compass. "The theory of 'correspondences' is basic to symbolist tradition. The implications and scope of this theory are beyond measure, and any valid study into the ultimate nature of the universe must take it into account. But here we can give little more than a brief idea of its scope, with some particular instances. It is founded upon the assumption that all cosmic phenemena are limited and serial and that

---

99 See Ély Star, *Les Mystères du verbe* (Paris, 1908).

they appear as scales or series on separate planes; but this condition is neither chaotic nor neutral, for the components of one series are linked with those of another in their essence and in their ultimate significance. It is possible to marshall correspondences by forcing the components of any given scale or scales into a common numerical pattern: for example, it is not difficult to adapt the colour-scale from seven to eight colours, should one wish to equate it with the scale of temperaments laid down by modern character-study, or, for that matter, to reduce it from seven to six colours for some other comparable reason. But it is always preferable to make sure of the correspondences which exist (apparently) only in part between different patterns, rather than to force them into unnatural moulds. The attributes of the ancient gods were really nothing less than unformulated correspondences: Venus, for example, was felt to correspond with the rose, the shell, the dove, the apple, the girdle and the myrtle. There is also a psychological basis for the theory of correspondences, related to synaesthesia. Louis-Claude de St. Martin comments in his L'Homme du désir: 'Things were not as they are in our gloomy dwelling, where sounds can be likened only to other sounds, colours to other colours, one substance to another; there everything was of a kind. Light gave out sounds, melody brought forth light, colours had movement because they were alive; objects were at once sonorous, diaphonous and mobile enough to intermix and flow in a line through all space.'[100] In Schneider's view, the key to all systems of correspondences is music. He points to a treatise by Sarngadeva in the Indian Samgita Ratnakara (I, iii, 48) of the 13th century which expounds the mystic relationship between music and animals. He comments that nothing similar is to be found in the West, although he suggests that the capitals of San Cugat del Vallés and those at Gerona (of the 12th century) portray a series of animals which, being disposed in a kind of scale, are somewhat comparable. He points likewise to Jakob Böhme and Athanasius Kircher, both of whom sought to incorporate all these ideas into their systems of mystic correspondences (Musurgia universalis).[101] Ély Star offers a somewhat crude explanation of correspondences: 'Each of the colours of the prism is analogous to one of the seven faculties of the human soul, to the seven virtues and the seven vices, to geometric forms and to the planets, etc.'[102] Clearly there are certain correspondences of meaning and situation in the physical world itself. For example, sound is the more shrill (or higher) the faster it moves, and vice versa; hence, speed corresponds to height and slowness to lowness, within a binary system. If cold colours are retrogressive, then coldness corresponds to distance, and warmth to nearness; here, then, we have another scientifically demonstrable correspondence. Taking the septenary system, Star suggests some correspondences between colours and musical notes, which we find exact enough: violet (the leading-note); red (the tonic); orange (the super-tonic); yellow (the mediant); green (the sub-dominant); blue (the dominant); indigo (the sub-median).[103] The Greeks, the Cabbalists and the Gnostics founded a great deal of their philosophy upon the theory of correspondences. Porphyry mentions the following, between the Greek vowels and the planets: alpha corresponding to the moon; epsilon to Mercury; eta to Venus; iota to

---

100 See Gaston Bachelard, L'Air et les Songes (Paris, 1943).

101 See Marius Schneider, El origen musical de los animales-simbolos en la mitologia y la escultura antiguas (Barcelona, 1946).

102 See Ély Star, Les Mystères du verbe (Paris, 1908).

103 See Ély Star, Les Mystè de l'Etre (Paris, 1902).

the sun; omicron to Mars; upsilon to Jupiter; and omega to Saturn.... Among the most important of systems of correspondences is the Zodiac: corresponding to the twelve signs of the Zodiac, one finds the months of the year, the tribes of Israel, the labours of Hercules, and the colour-scale adapted to include twelve colours." — Cirlot, pp.62-63.

DANCE. *(See also pp.161, 828.)*

§74.7 "Rhythmic bodily movements, often accompanied by music, chanting, and clapping, which — from an occult point of view — may result in an altered state of consciousness or trance state, especially when performed in a ritual setting. Dance has this function in many forms of primitive worship, and is a characteristic of fertility rites, and the ceremonies of the dervishes, voodoo, and witchcraft*." — Drury, p.55.

§74.8 "The corporeal image of a given process, or of becoming, or of the passage of time. In Hindu doctrine, the dance of Shiva* in his role as Nataraja (the King of the Cosmic Dance, symbolizing the union of space and time within evolution) clearly has this meaning.[104] There is a universal belief that, in so far as it is a rhythmic art-form, it is a symbol of the act of creation.[105] This is why the dance is one of the most ancient forms of magic. Every dance is a pantomime of metamorphosis (and so calls for a mask to facilitate and conceal the transformation), which seeks to change the dancer into a god, a demon or some other chosen form of existence. Its function is, in consequence, cosmogonic. The dance is the incarnation of eternal energy:

this is the meaning of the circle of flames, surrounding the 'dancing Shiva'.[106] Dances performed by people with linked arms symbolize cosmic matrimony, or the union of heaven and earth — the chain-symbol — and in this way they facilitate the union of man and wife.[107]" — Cirlot, p.76.

DANCE AND RELIGION.

§74A.1 See **DANCE***— Religious dances (p.834).

§74A.2 From Judith Lynne Hanna essay in Mircea Eliade (Editor in Chief), *The Encyclopedia of Religion* (1987). There is always some question of the degree to which "dance" also is or involves "music". I have included dance references throughout the present work because it so often does imply some musical accompaniment, and in that sense suggests an extension or part of a musical performance itself. What, then, of dancing *without* sound (or where sound accompaniment is, at best, minimal)? But even this, I should suppose, is at the very least *musical* — insofar as some rhythm, gradations of intensity (simulating crescendos and decrescendos), and a sort of melodic "shape" is expressed and presented, e.g. by physical patterns and gestures. (In this latter sense, other visual and plastic arts — painting and sculpture, for example — could be held to be at least partly "musical", as well.) In addition, all too frequently overlooked, I believe, is a common *musical impulse*, which is to say, one begins perhaps with an *urge to express oneself musically* — after which one chooses this or that particular mode of expression, such as singing, dancing, playing an instrument, or conducting (all of which — be

---

104 See Luc Benoist, *Art du monde*, (Paris, 1941).

105 See Ania Teillard, *Il Simbolismo del Sogni* (Milan, 1951).

106 See Heinrich Zimmer, *Myths and Symbols in Indian Art and Civilization* (New York, 1946).

107 See Marius Schneider, *La danza de espadas y la tarantela* (Barcelona, 1946).

it noted—alike involve physical activity). In this sense singing, playing, conducting and dancing are related, not merely to each other, but, more fundamentally still, to a common (musical) parentage. Dance is perhaps also musical at a symbolic or metaphorical level; its functions in a religious or mythical context, at least—such as mediation between human and divine, between nature and the supernatural—so often parallel functions of music generally. Indeed, is it not fair to regard e.g. the sacred dancing of a Native American as kind of chanting—or even singing—with certain portions of one's body? (Ed.)

"Dance is part of many systems of belief about the universe that deal with the nature and mystery of human existence and involve feelings, thoughts, and actions. Why, how, and to what ends do humans dance in religious practice?

"From a comparative worldwide perspective, dance may be seen as human behavior composed—from the dancer's point of view—of purposeful, intentionally rhythmical, and culturally patterned sequences of nonverbal body movements. These are different from ordinary motor activities; they have inherent and 'aesthetic' value, that is, appropriateness and competency. According to historical and anthropological research, people dance in order to fulfill a range of intentions and functions that change over time. They dance to explain religion, create and recreate social roles, to worship or honor, conduct supernatural beneficence, effect change, embody or merge with the supernatural through inner or external transformations, and reveal divinity through dance creation.

"The power of dance in religious practice lies in its multisensory, emotional, and symbolic capacity to communicate. It can create moods and a sense of situation in attention-riveting patterns by framing, prolonging, or discontinuing communication. Dance is a vehicle that incorporates inchoate ideas in visible human form and modifies inner experience as well as social action. The efficacy of dance in contributing to the construction of a worldview and affecting human behavior depends upon the beliefs of the participants (performers and spectators), particularly their faith in their ability to affect the world around them.

"Dance may also be meaningful in itself in terms of sensory sensitivity and perception: the sight of performers moving in time and space, the sounds of physical movements, the odors of physical exertion, the feeling of kinesthetic activity of empathy, and the sensations of contact with other bodies or the dancer's environment. Meaning may also lie in the expectation that within a particular dance style a particular dance element—rhythm, effort, spatial pattern, or use of the body—will be recognized, repeated, or followed by a different element at some specified point in the dance. Alternatively, meaning may be found in novelty, surprise, incongruity, ambiguity, and altered states of consciousness.

"More like poetry than prose, dance may also have cognitive, languagelike references beyond the dance form itself. Meaning may be conveyed through various devices such as metaphor (a dance in place of another expression that it resembles to suggest a likeness between the two), metonym (a dance connected with a larger whole), concretization (mimetic presentation), stylization (somewhat arbitrary religious gestures or movements that are the result of convention), and icon (a dancer enacting some of a god's characteristics and being regarded or treated as that god). Meaning may also be in the spheres of the dance event that include nondance activity: the human body in special action, the whole dance performance, performance segments as they unfold as in a narrative, specific movements or style reflecting religious values, the intermeshing of dance with other communication media such as music, the presence of a dancer conveying a supernatural aura or energy.

"We have no way of knowing the origins of religious dance. Rock art verifies its antiquity, however, and many peoples have explanatory myths. The Dogon of Mali, for example, says that God's son the jackal danced and traced out the world and its future; the first attested dance was one of divination that told secrets in dust. A spirit later taught people to dance. Hindus of India believe that Shiva* danced the world into being and later conveyed the art of dancing to humans.

"A popularly held psychological and theological theory found in numerous histories of dance suggests that dance evolved instrumentally to cope with unknown happenings in the human environment. Spontaneous movement — an outlet for the emotional tension endemic in the perpetual struggle for existence in a baffling environment — developed into patterned, symbolic movements for the individual and group. When a desired situation occurred folowing an instrumentally intended dance (for example, rain followed a danced request), the dance was assumed to have causative power and sacred association. Over time, style, structure, and meaning in dance changed through the perception of supernatural revelation, individual or group initiative, and contacts with other people.

"**Acceptance of Dance as Religious Practice.** Views of mind and body, especially concerning emotion and sexuality, affect dance in religion (as well as in other aspects of life). Whereas various arts use the body as an accessory to create sounds or visual objects, dance is manifest directly through the body and evokes bodily associations. Christian, Muslim, and Hindu beliefs and practices illustrate significantly different perspectives about dance and religion.

"Christianity's love-hate relationship with the body and acceptance of a mind/body dichotomy — which the rationalism of sixteenth-century Europe intensified — has led to both positive and negative attitudes toward dance. Recognizing Christ as fleshly, Christianity views the human body as a temple housing the Holy Spirit, and it calls its church the 'body of Christ'. Paul said, 'Glorify Christ in your bodies.' From the second century, Christians (e.g. Theodoret of Cyrrhus, Clement of Alexandria[108]) described dance as an imitation of the perpetual dance of angels, the blessed and righteous expressing physically their desire to enter heaven. Christianity built upon the Hebrew tradition of demonstrating through pious dance that no part of the individual was unaffected by the love of God. Yet Christianity also scorned flesh as a root of evil to be transcended, even mortified. Misunderstanding Paul's view of flesh, by which he meant to refer to the individual acting selfishly, led to negative attitudes toward the body in general that he did not share. Christianity's rejection of the body reflects an inability to come to terms with the passing of time and with death.

"Although the Greeks, Hebrews, and Christians took part in ancient fertility and sustenance dances, some of these dances took the form of unrestrained, sensual rites. This perceived debasement of religion led to the periodic proscription of dance and penalties against dancers. Legends of Salome's sensuous dance, for which she received John the Baptist's head in reward (she either obeyed her revengeful mother in requesting this or expressed her anger about John's not reciprocating her sexual interest in him), have kept alive negative associations with dance. Some Christians hold any glorification of the body, including dancing, anathema: outspoken enemies of physicality with an ascetic dislike of eroticism, which could undermine faith and unsettle the hierarchic

---

108 For whose views on the relation between Orpheus and Christ see **ORPHEUS***, below. (Ed.)

status quo, they preach the ideal of the Virgin. Western philosophy and Victorian prudishness have not, however, affected the Eastern Orthodox church to the extent of eliminating dance in worship.

"Because the nineteenth- and twentieth-century European industrializing nations that imperialistically dominated the world economy were largely Christian, this religion has had a worldwide stifling impact on dance. Europeans recognized that non-European dance intertwined with indigenous religions and moralities. Even though these dances often had themes and origins comparable to those of European folk dances, colonialists considered indigenous dances to be the manifestation of savage heathenism and thus antagonistic to the 'true faith'; therefore they frequently sought to eliminate them. The British influence, for example, contributed to the demise of Hindu temple dancing without succeeding in spreading Christianity. However, even when proscribed or out of fashion, dance rises phoenixlike in new religious transformation. Black slaves in the United States, members of Nigerian Yoruba Assemblies of God, and a number of white Christian groups have all included in their worship what appears to be dance—but under a different name, such as 'play', 'the shout', or 'feeling the Lord'.

"As former European colonies in Africa, Latin America, and Asia regained independence, they frequently reevaluated and renewed their devalued dances. Moreover, counterreactions in the twentieth-century West to claims of the separation of mind from body have led to a renaissance of dance as religious practice in that cultural milieu, too. When Westerners developed more accepting attitudes about the body, and biblical scholarship on dance increased after the 1960s, a sacred dance movement gave impetus to the reappearance of Christian congregational, choir, and solo dancing.

"Islam generally disapproves of dancing as a frivolous distraction from contemplating the wisdom of the prophet. Its religious leaders look upon dancing with contempt.

"The sacred and secular, the ritualistic and playful, and the spiritual and sexual do not everywhere have the dichotomous character so common in Muslim and in industrial societies where specialization and separation are hallmarks. For example Hinduism generally merges the sacred and the sexual in a felicitous union. As religion is about mystery, potential danger, hope of heaven, and ecstasy, so too are sexual love and its ramifications. Rather than considering carnal love a phenomenon to be 'overcome' as in some Christian denominations, a strand of Hinduism accepts sexual congress as a phase of the soul's migration. Through the path of devotion (*bhakti*), a surrender to the erotic self-oblivion of becoming one, a man and a woman momentarily glimpse spiritually and symbolically the desired absolute union with divinity. This is a microcosm of divine creation that reveals the hidden truth of the universe. The dance conveys this vision of life in telling the stories of the anthropomorphic gods. Hinduism has a pantheon of deities and is really a medley of hundreds of belief systems that share commonalities, as do Christian denominations. The supreme, all-powerful God is manifest in a trio of divinities: Brahma, Vishnu (who appears in the incarnation of Krishna, of amorous nature and exploits), and Shiva (Lord of the Dance, who created the universe which he destroys and regenerates through dance). Shiva's rhythms determine those of the world. The classic Indian sacred treatise on dance, the *Natya Sastra*, describes dance as an offering and demonstration of love to God, a cleansing of sin, a path of salvation, a partaking of the cosmic control of the world, and an expression of God within oneself.[109]

"Typology of Sacred Dance Practice. Dance is frequently an element of the process by which meanings are exchanged through symbols related to the supernatural world of ancestors, spirits, and gods. In this respect, from the perspectives of various religions and the functionalist, structuralist, and feminist theories that view religion as part of the larger social system, there appear to be nine categories of dance, neither exhaustive nor mutually exclusive. The specific dances referred to in the discussion below are from different times and cultures, removed from their rich historical and social contexts; they are chosen to illustrate kinds, or classes, of beliefs and acts.

"Explaining religion. Dance is part of ritual constructions of reality communicated to people so that they may understand the world and operate in it. The lore of sacred and profane belief, often intertwined, is told and retold in dance.

"In Early Christendom, dancing began as metaphor and metonym for the mysteries of faith. During the first part of the Middle Ages, dancing accompanied Christian church festivals and processionals in which relics of saints or martyrs were carried to call attention to their life histories. Later, in the twelfth, thirteenth, and fourteenth centuries, dance was an accepted liturgical art form in mystery and miracle plays. Elaborate dramatic presentations flourished in the Renaissance, but then printed tracts, pamphlets and books, and other promotions of the ascendance of the mind began to erode the importance of dance as a medium of religious expression. The Jesuits sponsored ballet as honorable relaxation in the seventeenth and eighteenth centuries until its suppression for being veiled political commentary.

"The Spanish Franciscans used dance dramas, especially those depicting the struggle of the church against its foes, to explain the Christian faith to the illiterate New World Indians they hoped to convert. Pageants of Moors and Christians were common. Appropriating indigenous Indian dances, the Franciscans suffused them with Christian meaning. Similarly, Muslims in East Africa at the end of the nineteenth century used indigenous attachment to the old Yao initiation dances to gradually introduce another dance that was regarded as an initiation into Islam.

"Contemporary Western theatrical dance performances in churches, public theaters, film, and television perpetuate the tradition of dance explaining religion. Choreographers present biblical scenes, incidents, and concepts in addition to religious philosophy, characters, events, and processes. Of course, all religious dance may have an entertaining element.

"Creating and re-creating social roles. Often used as a means to legitimize social organization, religion may employ dance as its agent to convey attitudes about the conduct of social life at the same time that it fulfills other purposes and functions. An example comes from Hinduism, which has a rich ancient history in the arts and religion. Although both male and female royalty in early India may have been well versed in dancing, the *Natya Sastra* is the scripture of a male sage, Bharata Muni, who upon receiving instruction from the gods later handed it down through his sons. He thought danced enactments of myths and legends would give people guidance in their lives. His treatise says that dancing is symbolic.

"Male brahmans (members of the priestly class) taught dance to males who performed only as young boys (*gotipuas*), to males who performed in all-male companies (*kathakali*), and to women dedicated to serving in the temples (*devadasis**). A dancer usually performs both male and female roles and movement styles for the

---

109 See also **HINDU PRACTICES AND BELIEFS*** §149.9, below. (Ed.)

deities in private devotions and at religious festivals involving the larger community.

"Some common religious dance themes are about male-female relations. In the allegories of Radha (loveliest of the milkmaids) and Krishna (the eternal lover dancing in the heart of every man), for example, their illicit love becomes a spiritual freedom, a type of salvation, and a surrender of all that the strict Indian social conventional world values.

"Human analogies explain Hindu divinity; conversely, the tales of the gods — more powerful versions of men and women, with the same virtues and vices — provide sanctified models for human actions as well as fantasies with vicarious thrills related to cultural sexual taboos. Danced enactments of legends send messages that it is acceptable for men to lustfully wander outside of marriage, whereas, in contrast women are supposed to be faithful to their husbands, forgive them, and bear their children in spite of the pain, risk of death, and agony from high infant mortality.

"In the West Sepik District of Papua New Guinea, the Umeda people convey gender status through the annual Ida dance, a ritual for sago palm fertility and a celebration of survival in the face of physical and mystical dangers. Although the sexual division of labor is supposedly complementary, in this dance cultural creativity of men is pitted against the biological creativity of women, and female culture is opposed and ultimately conquered by male culture.

"The myths and metaphors of religious codes present basic propositions concerning expected behavior between leaders and followers besides relations between the sexes. Such codes are danced for all to see. The Indian *kathakali* (in which feminine-looking boys learn to dance female roles) draws upon the physical training techniques from Kerala's military tradition. This powerful and spectacular drama staged as a public ritual for the entire community has been claimed to be a reaction to foreign aggression and a reaffirmation of the priestly and warrior social status, as well as an affirmation of masculine pride in martrilinear and matrilocal society.

"Dance in pre-Conquest Mexico was devoted to deities and agricultural success; its performance, as well as its representation in artifacts, appears to have served contemporary sociopolitical organization encompassing diverse, geographically dispersed ethnic groups. Nobles, priests, and commoners, old and young, male and female, each had distinct dances and spatial levels for performing at the pyramid temple.

"*Worship or honor.* At regularly scheduled seasonal times, at critical junctures, or just spontaneously, dances are part of rituals that revere; that greet as a token of fellowship, hospitality, and respect; that thank, entreat, placate, or offer penitence to deities, ancestors, and other supernatural entities. Not only may dance be a remedial vehicle to propitiate or beseech, it may also be prophylactic — gods may be honored to preclude disaster.[110]

"Dance is a means of religious concentration as well as of corporeal merging with the infinite God. The Jews dance to praise their God in sublime adoration and to express joy for his beneficence. The Hebrew scriptures refer to 'rejoicing with the

---

110 Lest one is tempted to take functions such as these for granted, with respect to music and dancing, one need only pause to think of other activities of a similar nature: in short, they are few enough. Few other arts (literature, painting, drama) or physical activities (sports) have quite so obvious a religious or sacred significance or connotation. Indeed, possibly the only activity with a *stronger*, more *direct* religious significance or intention would be — prayer itself. (Ed.)

whole being' as well as to specific dances performed for traditional festivals. The God-given mind and body are returned to God through dance. As a result of the destruction of the Temple in 70 CE, Jews generally eliminated dance and song from regular worship until such a time as they could return from the Diaspora and rebuild the Temple. The Talmud, ancient rabbinical writings that constitute religious authority for traditional Judaism, describes dancing as the principal function of the angels and commands dancing at weddings for brides, grooms, and their wedding guests. Procreation is God's will, weddings a step toward its fulfillment, and dancing a thanksgiving symbolizing fruitfulness. Even in exile there could be dancing, because out of the wedding might be born the Messiah who would restore the people to the Land of Israel.

"In Christianity the Catholic church allowed dances created for special occasions such as the canonization of cardinals or commemoration of their birthdays. Throughout Latin America devotional dances are part of a pilgrimage and processional fiesta system that fuses Indian and Catholic tenets. The dance training and production preparation are often undertaken as part of a religious vow to a powerful saint, the Virgin, or a Christ figure. The Mormons believe that when engaged in by the pure of heart, dance (excluding the embracing-couple position of Western social dance) prepares the individual and community for prayer meetings or other religious activity; devotion and recreation unite the individual with God. Brigham Young, who led the Mormon migration from Illinois to Utah, discovered that dance was a means to strengthen group morale and solidarity through providing emotional and physical release from hardship.

"In Orissa, India, the custom of small boys dancing dressed as girls has coexisted with a female dance tradition since the fifteenth century. The *sakhi-bhava* cult believes that since Krishna is male, the most effective way of showing devotion is a female, like the milkmaids (*gopis*) who dance their love for Krishna.

"The Gogo of Tanzania dance the Cidwanga as a sign of reverence in the annual ritual for good rains and fertility. Groups in Nigeria provide many illustrations. The Kalabari believe that human beings make the gods great. Fervent worship adds to a deity's capacity to aid the worshipers, and just as surely, the cutting off of worship will render them impotent or at the least cause them to break off contact with erstwhile worshipers. Among the Efik, the worshipers of the sea deity Ndem briskly dance in a circle at the deity's shrine to express metaphorically the affective intensity of a wish, for example, a wish for a child or a safe journey. The brisker the dance, the more likely Ndem is to grant requests.

"Because among the Ubakala dance honors and propitiates the respected living, it is not surprising that the spirits of the departed and other supernatural entities are also honored in this way. Some deities, such as the Yoruba Sango, love to be entertained and can best be placated with good dancing. Like the human creatures they basically are, the ancestors of the Fon of Dahomey [in Africa] (or the other spiritual entities who are given anthroposocial attributes) are believed to love display and ceremony. Thus both living and spiritual entities are believed to watch a dance performance, and both categories of spectators may even join the dancers, the latter often doing so through possession. Supernatural beings are sometimes honored to ensure that they do not mar festivals.

"*Conducting supernatural beneficence.* Dance may be the vehicle through which an individual, as self or other (masked or possessed), becomes a conduit of extraordinary power. Among the Ganda of central Uganda, parents of twins, having demonstrated their extraordinary fertility and the direct intervention of the god Mukasa, would dance in the gardens of their friends to transmit human fertility supernaturally to the vegetation. Yoruba mothers of twins dance with their offspring and promise to bless all those who are generous with alms. Here, the motional, dynamic rhyth, and spatial patterns of dance transfer desired qualities to objects or individuals.

"The men and women of Tanzania's Sandawe people dance by moonlight in the erotic Phek'umo rites to promote fertility. Identifying with the moon, a supreme being believed to be both beneficial and destructive, they adopt stylized signs or moon stances; they also embrace tightly and mimic the act of sexual intercourse. The dance, metaphorically at least, conducts supernatural beneficence.

"Because dance movement is metonymical with life movement, dance parody of sorcerer-caused disease and death affects the ascendance of life spirits and health forces. Thus the Tiv of Nigeria [see **AFRICAN MYTHS—PRACTICES AND BELIEFS***, pp. 31*ff.* (Ed.)] parody dropsy and elephantiasis through dance.

"The Sun Dance of the hunting peoples of the Great Plains of North America was an elaborate annual pageant performed during full summer when scattered tribal bands could unite in a season of plenty. Representatives danced to renew the earth, pray for fertility or revenge for a murdered relative, and transfer medicine. The typical Sun Dance involved a week of intense activity culminating in dramatic climactic rites. Male dancers participated in accord with personal vows made previously for success in warfare or healing of a loved one. Each dancer strove to attain personal power. Dancers were pierced through the breast or shoulder muscles and tethered with thongs to the central pole of a ceremonial lodge altar. Staring at the sun, they danced without pause, pulling back until the flesh gave way.

"Effecting change. Dance may be used as a medium to reverse a debilitating condition caused by the supernatural or to prepare an individual or group to reach a religiously defined ideal state. This includes status transformation in rites of passage, death, curing, and prevention, as well as rites to reverse political domination.

"The United Society of Believers in Christ's Second Appearing, commonly called Shakers because of their dramatic practice of vigorous dancing, believed that the day of judgment was imminent. Numbering about six thousand members in nineteen communities at its peak, the group held that salvation would come through confessing and forsaking fleshly practices. Notwithstanding their professed attitudes toward the body, the first adherents were seized by an involuntary ecstasy that led them to run about a meeting room, jump, shake, whirl, and reel in a spontaneous manner to shake off doubts, loosen sins and faults, and mortify lust in order to purify the spirit. In repentance they turned away from preoccupation with self to shake off their bondage to a troubled past. This permitted concentration on new feelings and intent.

"Dancing for the Shakers, who believed in the dualism of spirit versus body, appears to be a canalization of feeling in the context of men and women living together in celibacy, austerity, humility, and hard manual labor. Shaker dance involved a sequence of movements, designed to shake off sin, that paralleled the sexual experience of energy buildup to climax and then relaxation. Individualistic impulsive movements evolved into ordered, well-rehearsed patterns. Shaking the hand palm downward discarded the carnal; turning palms upward petitioned eternal life.

"For Buddhist Sherpa lamas, laymen, and young boys in Nepal, dancing is a means by which they resolve the necessity of simultaneously affirming and denying the value of worldly existence. The spring Dumje ceremony purges the forces of repression and guilt that oppose the erotic impulses so that life may continue. The young boys' highly lascivious *tek-tek* masked dances represent sexuality as well as the children who are its desired fruits.

"Dance mediates between childhood and adult status in the Chisungu, the girls' initiation ceremony of the Bemba of Zambia. The women conducting the ceremony believe that they are causing supernatural changes to take place as each initiate is 'danced' from one group with its status and roles to another. Among the Wan of the Ivory Coast, a man must dance a female initiate on his shoulders. During the initiation to an ancestral cult, the Fang of Gabon carry religious statues from their usual place and make them dance like puppets to vitalize them.

"Another form of status change occurs at death. The Ubakala of Nigeria perform the dance dramas Nkwa Uko and Nkwa Ese to escort a deceased aged and respected woman and man, respectively, to become ancestors residing among the spirits, later to return in a new incarnation. These forms are similar to the dances in the Christian tradition that enable one to enter heaven.

"Among the Dogon, death creates disorder. But through the symbolism and orderliness of dance, humans metaphorically restore order to the disordered world. Symbolically spatializing things never seen, the Dogon represent heaven on earth. So, too, at the time of death, the mask dance helps to mitigate the psychic distress and spiritual fear of the dead.

"The funeral dance of the Nyakyusa in Tanzania begins with a passionate expression of anger and grief and gradually becomes a fertility dance. In this way dancing mediates the passionate and quarrelsome emotions felt over a death and the acceptance of it.

"Dances related to death were common in medieval Europe, a largely preliterate society dominated by the Christian church. It interpreted an economically harsh and morally complex world that was fought over by God and the Devil. Part of a convivial attempt to deny the finality of death, dances also had other manifesta-

tions and functions. In the so-called Dance of Death [see Death Dance*], a performer would beckon people to the world beyond in a reaction to the epidemic Black Death (1347-1373), a bubonic plague outbreak in Italy, Spain, France, Germany, and England. Evolving with the image of the skeletal figure seen as our future self, the dance was a mockery of the pretenses of the rich and a vision of social equality. The dance emphasized the terrors of death to frighten sinners into repentance. Hallucinogenic and clonic cramp symptoms of bread and grain ergot poisoning, called Saint Anthony's Fire, led some of its sickly victims to move involuntarily in dancelike movements. Such people were believed to be possessed. Other victims sought relief from pain through ecstatic dancing, considered to be of curative value and efficacious in warding off death. Dances were also connected with wakes for the dead and the rebirth of the soul to everlasting life. Dancing at the graves of family, friends, and martyrs was believed to comfort the dead and encourage resurrection as well as protect against the dead as demons.

"Among the Gogo, dance metaphorically effects a supernatural change through role reversal in a curative and preventative rite. When men fail in their ritual responsibility for controlling human and animal fertility, disorder reigns. Then women become the only active agents in rituals addressed to righting the wrong. Dressed as men, they dance violently with spears to drive away contamination.

"The Hamadsha, a Moroccan Sufi brotherhood, performs the *hadrah,* an ecstatic dance, in order to cure an individual who has been struck or possessed by a devil. They seek a good relationship with a *jinni,* ('spirit'), usually 'A'ishah. In the course of the dance, people become entranced and slash at their heads in imitation of Sidi 'Ali's servant, who did so when he learned of his master's death. A flow of blood is believed to calm the spirit. The Hamadsha women fall into trance more readily and dance with more abandon than the men.

"Dance was an integral part of many American Indian religious revivals and reaffirmations in response to historical, economic, and political situations they wanted to change. The Northern Paiute and peoples of the northwest Plateau believed that ceremonies involving group dancing, a visible index of ethnic and political alliances and action, would bring about periodic world renewal. The Indians thought certain group dances had the power to end the deprivation that resulted from defeat at the hands of the whites and bring about the return of Indian prosperity. The Ghost Dance religion incorporated Christian teachings of the millennium and the second coming of Christ in order to attract acculturated Indians.

"The Mexican dance groups, known as *concheros, danza Chicimeca, danza Azteca,* and *danza de la conquista,* originated in the states of Querétaro and Guanajuato as a response to the Spanish Conquest in the sixteenth century. The groups may also be seen as 'crisis cults', syncretistic attempts to create prideful cultural identity and new forms of social integration. Participants at the low end of the socioeconomic scale and heavily represented in the laborer and shoeshine occupations, adopt the nomenclature of the Spanish military hierarchy and perform dances reenacting the Conquest that were derived from Spanish representations of the Moors and Christians. The warlike dances involve women, the aged, and children as well as [adult] men.

"*Embodying the supernatural in inner transformation: personal possession.* Dance may serve as an activating agent for giving oneself temporarily to a supernatural being or force. This process is usually accompanied by a devout state and is often aided by autosuggestion or autointoxication, further reinforced by audience encouragement. The dance itself is often characterized by a particular type of musical accompaniment and repetitive, rapid turning or frenzied movement. A possessed devotee may achieve a consciousness of identity or a ritual connection with the supernatural iconically, metonymically, metaphorically, or experientially and cross the threshhold into another order or existence.

"A supernatural possessor may manifest itself through the dancer's performance of identifiable and specific patterns and conventional signs. In this way it communicates to the entire group that it is present and enacting its particular supernatural role in the lives of humans. Thus fear of the supernatural entity's indifference is allayed. Possession may alter somatic states and cause a dancer's collapse. The specific characteristics of possession are culturally determined, and even children may play at possession.

"There are four types of personal possession. Diviners, cult members, medicine men, and shams are among those who participate in the first type, 'invited' spirit mediumship possession dances. Numerous African religions and their offshoots in Haitian Voodoo and Brazilian Macumba, as well as other faiths, involve the belief that humans can contact spiritual entities and influence them to act on a person's behalf. Thus the worshiper takes the initiative and lends his or her body to the tutelary spirit when there is an indication that the spirit wishes to communicate with the living or when the devotee desires a meeting. As a sensorimotor sign, the dance may indicate the deity's presence or a leader's legitimacy; as a signal, it may be a marker for specific activities; as a metonym, it may be part of the universe; and as a metaphor, it may refer to human self-extension or social conflict.

"The Kalabari believe a possessed dancer brings the god as guest into the village. Dancing the gods is considered an admirable achievement. Masquerade dancers may become possessed, and in some cases the performer is expected to await possession before dancing. In possession dances the ability of Water People gods to materialize as pythons is accented as they metamorphose from acting like men to writhing on the ground and slithering about the house rafters as the great snakes do. The *oru seki* ('spirit') dancing occurs in the ritual to solicit a special benefit or to appease a spirit whose rules for human behavior have been infringed. Possession of the invoker, an iconic sign in the midst of the congregation, assures the spirit's presence, power, and acceptance of the invocation and offerings.

"Among the Ga of Ghana, it is through a medium whose state of possession is induced by dance, that the god signifies its presence and delivers messages prophesying the coming year's events and suggesting how to cope with them. Possession legitimizes leadership among the Fanti of Ghana. Because the deities love to dance, the priests assemble drummers, become possessed, and then speak with the power and authority of the deities. The Koran shaman attains knowledge and power in the role of religious leader through trance possession induced by dancing.

"Possession may be a mechanism for individuals to transact social relationships more favorably. Healing practices often mediate the natural, social, and supernatural. In Sinhala healing rites, an exorcist attempts to sever the relationship between a patient and malign demons and ghosts. The exorcist's performance of various dance sequences progressively builds up emotional tension and generates power that can entrance both the healer and the patient. Their bodies become the demonic spirit's vehicle, constitute evidence of its control, and convince spectators of the need, as the healer prescribes, for a change in social relations that will exorcise the demonic spirit and transform the patient from illness to a state of health.

"A second kind of possession dance, known as 'invasion', also often a metaphor and signal of social pathology or personal maladjustment, indicates that a supernatural being has overwhelmed an individual, causing some form of malaise, ill-

ness, or personal or group misfortune. Dance becomes a medium to exorcise and appease the being, thus freeing the possessed individual and ameliorating his or her irksome ascribed status or difficult situation. Meeting the wishes of a spirit as part of exorcism frequently imposes obligations on those related to the possessed.

"The *vimbuza* healing dance of the Chewa and Tumbuka societies in Malawi is a socially sanctioned means of expressing those feelings and tensions that if otherwise broadcast would disrupt family or community relationships. The dance is medicine for the *vimbuza* disease; which causes terrifying dreams or visions, the eating of unusual meat, or the uttering of a specific groan.

"A third kind of possession, called 'consecration', involves initiation and the impersonation of a deity, during which time the dancer becomes deified. In India the audience worships the young performers in the Ramalilas who play Krishna, Raha, Rama, and other mythic heroes in the same way they would revere icons. Performers of the Tibetan sacred masked dance, or *'cham,* are viewed as sacred beings.

"Not only may individuals be possessed by supernatural entities but they may also experience 'essence possession', the fourth type, by a religious or supernatural potency, an impersonal supernatural. Among the Lango of Uganda, *jok* is liberated or generated in dancing. Similarly, among the !Kung San of Namibia, dance activates *n/um,* that potency from which medicine men derive their power to protect the people from sickness and death. The medicine dancer may go into trance and communicate with spirits without being possessed by them. The ceremonial curing dance may be called for in crisis situations, or the dance may occur spontaneously; it is redressive and prophylactic.

"*Merging with the supernatural toward enlightenment or self-detachment.* Illustrations of another form of inner transformation through dance come from Turkey or Tibet. In Turkey the followers of the thirteenth-century poet-philosopher Mawlana Jalal al-Din Rumi, founder of one of Islam's principal mystic orders, perform whirling dances. Men with immobile faces revolve in long white shirts with covered arms outstretched, slowly at first and then faster until they reach a spiritual trance. These men, the dervishes (the word refers to a person on the threshold of enlightenment), strive to detach themselves from earth and divest themselves of ties to self in order to unite with a nonpersonified God. This process occurs through revolving movement and repeated chanting that vibrates energy centers of the body in order to raise the individual to higher spheres.

"The Tibetan Buddhist dance ritual called Ling Dro Dechen Rolmo permits imaging the divine. The dancer's circular path and turning movement aid the participants toward enlightenment by providing a means to realize that the deity is a reflection of one's own mind.

"Embodying the supernatural in external transformation: the masquerade. Sacred masquerade dances, part of a people's intercourse with the spirit world, make social and personal contributions through symbolic actions that are similar to those made through dances that explain religion, create and re-create social roles, worship and honor, conduct supernatural beneficience, effect change, and involve possession. The Midimu masked dancing of the Yao, Makua, and Makonde of Tanzania and Mozambique helps to explain religion by marking the presence of the supernatural (dead ancestors) in the affairs of the living. In effect, ancestors return from the dead to rejoice on the occasion of an initiate's return from the training camp. The Dogon's masked-society dancing patterns depict their conception of the world, its progress and order, and its continuity and oneness with the total universe. Thus dance is here a model of the belief system. Participants in the Nyau society of Chewa-

speaking peoples dance a reenactment of the primal coexistence of men, animals, and spirits in friendship, and their subsequent division by fire. The people believe that underneath their masks the dancers have undergone transformation into spirits.

"Social roles are emphasized when the Yoruba's Gelede society masquerade figures appear annually at the start of the new agricultural year to dance in the marketplace and through the streets. They honor and propitiate the female *orisa* ('spirits') and their representatives, living and ancestral, for the mothers are the gods of society and their children its members. All animal life comes from a mother's body. Although both men and women belong to the Gelede cult (to seek protection and blessings and assuage their fear of death), only men dance, with masks portraying the appropriate sex roles of each character. Mothers have both positive (calm, creative, protective) and negative, or witch, dimensions (unmitigated evil affecting fertility, childbirth, and the functioning of men's sexual organs). The mothers possess powerful *ase* ('vital, mystical power'). A man can have *ase* most fully when he is spiritually united with an *orisa*. When men symbolically externalize the vital life forces in dance, they may be asserting their virility and freedom in the presence of the powerful mothers and, in addition, recognizing and honoring their powers in order to appease them to ensure that they utilize their *ase* for male benefit.

"Among the Nafana people of the Ivory Coast, masked dancing occurs almost nightly during the lunar month of the year. The dancing is intended to worship and to effect change. Living in the masks, the Bedu spirits bless and purify the village dwellings and their occupants and metaphorically absorb evil and misfortune, which they remove from the community so that the new year begins afresh.

"The masked (antelope headdress) dance of the Bamana of Mali represents Chi Wara, the god of agriculture, a supernatural being, half animal, half man, who first taught men how to cultivate the soil. Chi Wara's public presence is an invocation of its blessings. In a concretized form that makes appeals more understandable to the young, animal masked dancers remind humans that they have some animal characteristics as participants respond to the dancers positively and negatively. In this way the masked dancing presents human foibles at a distance for examination without threat to individuals, thus helping to effect change.

"Masked dancing can be a metaphor for both normative and innovative behavior. Under religious auspices the dancer is freed from the everyday restrictions on etiquette and thus able to present secular messages and critiques. Presented by the unmasked, these messages might produce social frictions or hostilities rather than positive change.

"Among the Nsukka Igbo of Nigeria, the council of elders employed masked dancers representing an *omabe* spirit cult whenever there was difficulty in enforcing law and order. In Zambia, Wiko Makishi masqueraders, believed to be resurrected ancestors and other supernatural beings, patrol the vicinities of the boys' initiation lodges to ward off intruders, women, and non-Wiko.

"A Chewa man residing with his wife and mother-in-law often resorts to the male masked Nyau dancer to mediate between himself and a mother-in-law whose constant demands on him he resents. When the dancer dons the mask of the Chirombo ('beast'), he directs obscene language against her. No action may be taken against him, for in his mask he enjoys the immunity of the Chirombo. Afterward the mother-in-law often reduces her demands.

"Socially sanctioned ritual abuse with ribald and lewd movements and gestures in a highly charged atmosphere is permitted in the Bedu masked dance mentioned above. There appear to be humor and an underlying feeling that these acts are socially acceptable and that through them participants will be purged of whatever negative emotions they may harbor.

"The masked dancer may be an iconic sign, revered and experienced as a veritable apparition of the being he represents, even when people know that a man made the mask and is wearing it. Because the Angolan Chokwe mask and its wearer are a spiritual whole, both in life and death, when a dancer dies, his mask is buried with him.

"*Revelation of divinity through dance creation.* Within a Protestant Christian view, artistic self-expression is analogized to the creative self-expression of God as creator. Dancing a set piece is considered a reflection of the unknowable God's immanence irrespective of the performer's intention. The dancer is to dance as God is to creation. The language of movement is God given, and both the progression of a dancer's training and the perfection of performance reveal God's achievement. Within the Franciscan view, God is present in good works and in the creative force of the arts. Through dance rituals in Latin America, performers become one with creation. When an individual dances with expertise — individuality, agility, and dexterity — the Gola of Liberia consider this to be a sign of a *jina's* gift of love given in a dream.

"Dance appears to be part of a cultural code or logical model enabling humans to order experience, account for its chaos, express isomorphic properties between opposing entities, and explain realities. Dance and religion merge in a configuration that encompasses sensory experience, cognition, diffused and focused emotions, and personal and social conflicts. People dance to explain religion, convey sanctified models for social organization, revere the divine, conduct supernatural beneficence, effect change, embody the supernatural through internal or external transformation, merge with the divine toward enlightenment, and reveal divinity through creating dance. Permeated with religious tradition, dance continually changes.

"In many parts of the world that have, to a large extent, become modernized and secularized, participants in nonsacred theatrical dance often choose to explain religion, create and re-create social roles, honor the divine, and infuse their dances with elements drawn from religions throughout the world. Many folk dances associated with religious holidays or events have been transformed into theatrical productions and into performances (by dancers other than the 'folk') for recreational purposes." — Hanna, in Eliade (vol. 4), pp.203-12.

Ed. note: To rest the overall religious or sacred significance of dance or music-making on the degree to which it may or may not be *efficacious* with regard to certain functions — e.g. to approve or denigrate dance as a spiritual medium depending on whether or not the rains come or the lame walk — seems (to me) roughly comparable to demanding of e.g. sporting events that they should be (genuinely) worth something! In fact, no "real" territory is commonly gained or lost in a sporting event, nor — apart from certain tokens and trophies (including, to be sure, cash awards in some cases — which may even be regarded as a corruption of sport) — is anything *else* substantially won or acquired as a condition of one's besting an opponent. However, sporting events have their own *raison d'être*, nonetheless. Similarly it may be asked what, precisely, is gained or *accomplished* by putting on a play, in the sense of "effectively" altering the order of the world? Nevertheless drama — too — has special significance... precisely as drama. In my view the marriage of music, dance and the sacred to which reference has been made in the preceding essays reveals — in certain respects — an essential *nature* of each.

DANCING.

§76.4 See HUNGARIAN FOLKTALES*.

DANCING TO DEATH (OR INSANITY). *(See also pp.175, 843.)*

§77.6 "THE MONKEY'S FIDDLE [African folktale]. Hunger and want forced Monkey one day to forsake his land and to seek elsewhere among strangers for much-needed work. Bulbs, earth beans, scorpions, insects, and such things were completely exhausted in his own land. But fortunately he received, for the time being, shelter with a great uncle of his, Orang Outang, who lived in another part of the country.

"When he had worked for quite a while he wanted to return home, and as recompense his great uncle gave him a fiddle and a bow and arrow and told him that with the bow and arrow he could hit and kill anything he desired, and with the fiddle he could force anything to dance.

"The first he met upon his return to his own land was Brer Wolf. This old fellow told him all the news and also that he had since early morning been attempting to stalk a deer, but all in vain.

"Then Monkey laid before him all the wonders of the bow and arrow that he carried on his back and assured him if he could but see the deer he would bring it down for him. When Wolf showed him the deer, Monkey was ready and down fell the deer.

"They made a good meal together, but instead of Wolf being thankful, jealouy overmastered him and he begged for the bow and arrow. When Monkey refused to give it to him, he thereupon began to threaten him with his greater strength, and so when Jackal passed by, Wolf told him that Monkey had stolen his bow and arrow. After Jackal had heard both of them, he declared himself unqualified to settle the case alone, and he proposed that they bring the matter to the court of Lion, Tiger, and the other animals. In the meantime he declared he would take possession of what had been the cause of their quarrel, so that it would be safe, as he said. But he immediately brought to earth all that was eatable, so there was a long time of slaughter before Monkey and Wolf agreed to have the affair in court.

"Monkey's evidence was weak, and to make it worse, Jackal's testimony was against him. Jackal thought that in this way it would be easier to obtain the bow and arrow from Wolf for himself.

"And so fell the sentence against Monkey. Theft was looked upon as a great wrong; he must hang.

"The fiddle was still at his side, and he received as a last favor from the court the right to play a tune on it.

"He was a master player of his time, and in addition to this came the wonderful power of his charmed fiddle. Thus, when he struck the first note of 'Cockcrow' upon it, the court began at once to show an unusual and spontaneous liveliness, and before he came to the first waltzing turn of the old tune the whole court was dancing like a whirlwind.

"Over and over, quicker and quicker, sounded the tune of 'Cockcrow' on the charmed fiddle, until some of the dancers, exhausted, fell down, although still keeping their feet in motion. But Monkey, musician as he was, heard and saw nothing of what had happened around him. With his head placed lovingly against the instrument, and his eyes half closed, he played on, keeping time ever with his foot.

"Wolf was the first to cry out in pleading tones breathlessly, 'Please stop, Cousin Monkey! For love's sake, please stop!'

"But Monkey did not even hear him. Over and over sounded the resistless waltz of 'Cockcrow'.

"After a while Lion showed signs of fatigue, and when he had gone the round once more with his young lion wife, he growled as he passed Monkey, 'My whole kingdom is yours, ape, if you just stop playing.'

" 'I do not want it,' answered Monkey, 'but withdraw the sentence and give me my bow and arrow, and you, Wolf, acknowledge that you stole it from me.'

" 'I acknowledge, I acknowledge!' cried Wolf, while Lion cried, at the same instant, that he withdrew the sentence.

"Monkey gave them just a few more turns of the 'Cockcrow', gathered up his bow and arrow, and seated himself high up in the nearest camel thorn tree.

"The court and other animals were so afraid that he might begin again that they hastily disbanded to new parts of the world."[111] – Honey, pp.14-18.

DANSE MACABRE. *(See p. 177.)*

§79.2 "DANCE OF DEATH. Popular theme in the Middle Ages, in which a skeleton led men and women to the grave – the final stage of life's journey. In the Spanish *danza macabra*, skeletons are shown carrying a scythe, a clock, and a banner; while in the medieval Tarot, the card Death shows a skeleton wielding his scythe through a field of bodies, leveling king and commoner alike." – Drury, p.55.

DEATH DANCE. *(See pp. 178, 844.)*

§83.3 "THE DANCE OF DEATH. I have just heard again the ghost story so often told by Mrs Thompson Hankey:

"Two beautiful but penniless sisters were taken out in London by an aunt. A young

---

111 Concerning the magical powers of instruments as an extension or heightening of characteristics inherent in music (and musical instruments) generally, see footnote to ORLANDO* entry, §286A.2, below. (Ed.)

gentleman from the North, of very good family and fortune, fell in love with one of them, and proposed to her, but she was with difficulty persuaded to accept him, and afterwards could never be induced to fix a date for their marriage. The young man, who was very much in love, urged and urged, but, on one excuse or another, he was always put off. Whilst things were in this unsettled state, the young lady was invited to a ball. Her lover implored her not to go to it, and when she insisted, he made her promise not to dance any round dances, saying that if she did, he should believe she had ceased to care for him.

"The young lady went to the ball, and, as usual, all the young men gathered round her, trying to persuade her to dance. She refused any but square dances. At last, however, as a delightful valse was being played, and she was standing looking longingly on, she suddenly felt herself seized round the waist, and hurried into the dance. Not till she reached the end of the room, very angry, did she succeed in seeing with whom she had been forced to dance: it was with her own betrothed.

"Furious, she said she should never forgive him. But, as she spoke, he disappeared. She begged several young men to look for him, but he could not be found anywhere, and, to her astonishment, everyone denied altogether having seen him. On reaching home, she found a telegram telling of his death, and when the hours were compared, he was found to have died at the very moment when he had seized her for the dance.

"Mrs Thompson Hankey knew all the persons involved.[112]—Briggs (Dictionary), Part B (*Folk Legends*), vol 1 pp.433-34.[113]

DRUM. *(See also pp. 188, 845.)*

§93.11 "A symbol of primordial sound, and a vehicle for the word, for tradition and for magic.[114] With the aid of drums, shamans* can induce a state of ecstasy. It is not only the rhythm and the timbre which are important in the symbolism of the primitive drum, but, since it is made of the wood of 'the Tree of the World', the mystic sense of the latter also adheres to it.[115] According to Schneider, the drum is, of all musical instruments, the most pregnant with mystic ideals: In Africa, it is associated with the heart. In the most primitive cultures, as in the most advanced, it is equated with the sacrificial altar and hence it acts as a mediator between heaven and earth. However, given its bowl-shape and its skin, it corresponds more properly to the symbolism of the Element of earth. A secondary meaning turns upon the shape of the instrument, and it should be noted that it is in this respect that there is most variation in significance. The three essential shapes are: the drum in the form of an hour-glass, symbolizing Inversion and the 'relationship between the two worlds' (the Upper and the Lower); the round drum, as

---

112 [Source:] Augustus Hare, *In My Solitary Life*, p.181. [Thompson Folklore] Motifs: E310 (Dead lover's friendly return); E421.1.1 (Ghost visible to one person alone); E493 (f)(Ghost dances with mortal)(Baughman). This ghost was perhaps rather a wraith than a ghost, since he appeared at the moment of his death.

113 For an African version of the dance of the dead, see **AFRICAN MYTHS — PRACTICES AND BELIEFS***, §6.20. (Ed.)

114 See Heinrich Zimmer, *Myths and Symbols in Indian Art and Civilization* (New York, 1946).

115 See Mircea Eliade, *Images et Symboles* (Paris, 1952).

an image of the world; and the barrel-shaped, associated with thunder and lightning.[116]" — Cirlot, 89.

§93.12 "THE SHAMANIC DRUM. The

drum has a role of the first importance in shamanic* ceremonies. Its symbolism is complex, its magical functions many and various. It is indispensable in conducting the shamanic séance, whether it carries the shaman to the 'Center of the World', or enables him to fly through the air, or summons and 'imprisons' the spirits, or, finally, if the drumming enables the shaman to concentrate and regain contact with the spiritual world through which he is preparing to travel.

"It will be remembered that several initiatory dreams of future shamans included a mystical journey to the 'Center of the World', to the seat of the Cosmic Tree and the Universal Lord. It is from a branch of this Tree, which the Lord causes to fall for the purpose, that the shaman makes the shell of his drum. The meaning of this symbolism seems sufficiently apparent from the complex of which it is a part: communication between sky and earth by means of the World Tree, that is, by the Axis that passes through the 'Center of the World'. *By the fact that the shell of his drum is derived from the actual wood of the Cosmic Tree, the shaman, through his drumming, is magically projected into the vicinity of the Tree;* he is projected to the 'Center of the World', and thus can ascend to the sky.

"Seen in this light, the drum can be assimilated to the shamanic tree with its notches, up which the shaman symbolically climbs to the sky. Climbing the birch or playing his drum, the shaman approaches the World Tree and then ascends it. The Siberian shamans also have their personal

trees, which are simply representatives of the Cosmic Tree; some shamans also use 'inverted trees',[117] that is, trees planted with their roots in the air, which, as is well known, are among the most archaic symbols of the World Tree. This whole series of facts, combined with the relations already noted between the shaman and the ceremonial birches, shows the intimate connection between the Cosmic Tree, the shaman's drum, and ascending to the sky.

"Even the choice of the wood from which the shaman will make the shell of his drum depends entirely on the 'spirits' or a transhuman will. The Ostyak-Samoyed shaman takes his ax and, closing his eyes, enters a forest and touches a tree at random; from this tree his comrades will take the wood for his drum on the following day. At the other end of Siberia, among the Altaians, the spirits themselves tell the shaman of the forest and the exact spot where the tree grows, and he sends his assistants to find it and cut the wood for his drum from it. In other regions the shaman himself gathers up all the splinters. Elsewhere sacrifices are offered to the tree by daubing it with blood and vodka. The next step is 'animating the drum' by sprinkling its shell with alcoholic spirits. Among the Yakut it is considered best to choose a tree that has been struck by lightning. All these ritual customs and precautions clearly show that the concrete tree has been transfigured by the superhuman revelation, that it has ceased to be a profane tree and represents the actual World Tree.

"The ceremony for 'animating the drum' is of the highest interest. When the Altaic shaman sprinkles it with beer, the shell of the drum 'comes to life' and, through the shaman, relates how the tree of which it was part grew in the forest, how it was cut,

---

116 See Marius Schneider, *El origen musical de los animales-simbolos en la mitologia y la escultura antiguas* (Barcelona, 1946).

117 Cf. *Finno-Ugric [and] Siberian [Mythology]*, pp.349 ff.; R. Karsten, *The Religion of the Samek*, p.48; A. Coomaraswamy, 'The Inverted Tree'; Eliade, *Patterns in Comparative Religion*, pp.294 ff.

brought to the village, and so on. The shaman then sprinkles the skin of the drum and, 'coming to life', it too narrates its past. Through the shaman's voice, the animal whose skin has been used for the drum tells of its birth, its parents, its childhood, and its whole life to the moment when it was brought down by the hunter. It ends by promising the shaman that it will perform many services for him. In one of the Altaic tribes, the Tubalares, the shaman imitates both the voice and behavior of the resuscitated animal.

"As both L. P. Potapov and G. Buddruss have shown,[118] the animal that the shaman 'reanimates' is his alter ego, his most powerful helping spirit; when it enters the shaman he changes into the mythical theriomorphic [having the form of a beast (Ed.)] ancestor. This makes it clearer why, during the 'animation' rite, the shaman has to relate the life-history of the drum-animal: he sings of his exemplary model, the primordial animal that is the origin of his tribe. In mythical times every member of the tribe could turn into an animal, that is, he was able to share in the condition of the ancestor.[119] In our day such intimate relations with mythical ancestors are the prerogative only of shamans.

"During the séance the shaman re-establishes, for himself alone, a situation that was once general. The deeper meaning of this recovery of the primordial human condition will become clearer after we have examined other examples. For the moment, it is enough to have shown that both the shell and the skin of the drum constitute magico-religious implements by virtue of which the shaman is able to undertake the ecstatic journey to the 'Center of the World'. In numerous traditions the mythical theriomorphic ancestor lives in the subterranean world, close to the root of the Cosmic Tree, whose top touches the sky. Separate but related ideas are present here. On the one hand, by drumming, the shaman flies away to the Cosmic Tree; we shall see in a moment that the drum harbors a large number of ascensional symbols. On the other hand, by virtue of his mystical relations with the 'reanimated' skin of the drum, the shaman is able to share in the nature of the theriomorphic ancestor; in other words, he can abolish time and re-establish the primordial condition of which the myths tell. In either case we are in the presence of a mystical experience that allows the shaman to transcend time and space. Both metamor-

---

118 Potapov, *Seremonia* and (with Menges) *Materialien zur Volkskunde der Tüurkölker der Altaj;* Buddruss, *Schamanengeschichten aus Sibirien,* pp.74 ff.

119 See also **INDIAN (NORTH AMERICAN) MYTHS — PRACTICES AND BELIEFS***, §162.16 (*Zuñi Tales and Beliefs*) — "the gods of Zuñi, like those of all primitive people, are the ancients of animals.... The world is a universe of animals.... The first-born [of the animals] are gods and are usually called the ancients, or the first ones; the later-born generations are descendants of the gods" etc. (Ed.)

phosis into the animal ancestor and the shaman's ascensional ecstasy represent different but homologizable expressions of one and the same experience – transcendence of the profane condition, re-establishment of a 'paradisal' existence lost in the depths of mythical time.[120]

"Usually the drum is oval in shape; its skin is of reindeer, elk, or horse hide. Among the Ostyak and the Samoyed of eastern Siberia, the outer surface bears no design. According to J. G. Georgi,[121] the Tungus drums are ornamented with representations of birds, snakes, and other animals. Shirokoroff thus describes the representations that he saw on the drums of the Transbaikal Tungus: the symbol of *terra firma* (for the shaman uses his drum as a boat to cross the sea, hence he indicates its shores); several groups of anthropomorphic figures, to left and right; and a number of animals. No image is painted in the center of the drum; the eight double lines drawn there symbolize the eight feet that hold the earth above the sea.[122] Among the Yakut there are mysterious signs painted in red and black and representing men and animals. Various images are also attested on the drums of the Yenisei Ostyak.

" 'At the back of the drum there is a vertical wooden and iron handle, which the shaman graps in his left hand. Horizontal wires or wooden wedges hold innumerable bits of tinkling metal, rattles, bells*, iron images representing spirits, various animals, etc., and frequently

weapons, such as an arrow, a bow, or a knife.'[123] Each of these magical objects has its own symbolism and plays its part in the shaman's preparing or performing his ecstatic journey or in his other mystical experiences.

"Designs ornamenting the skin of the drum are characteristic of all the Tatar tribes and the Lapps. Among the Lapps both faces of the skin are covered with images. They are of the greatest variety, although among them are always the most important symbols, as, for example, the World Tree, the sun and moon, the rainbow, and others. In short, the drums constitute a microcosm: a boundary line separates sky from earth, and, in some places, earth from the underworld. The World Tree (that is, the sacrificial birch climbed by the shaman), the horse, the sacrificed animal, the shaman's helping spirits, the sun and moon, which he reaches in the course of his celestial journey, the underworld of Erlik Khan (including the Seven Sons and Seven Daughters of the Lord of the Dead, etc.), into which he makes his way when he descends to the realm of the dead – all these elements, which in a manner summarize the shaman's itinerary and adventures, are found represented on his drum. We have not space to record all the signs and images and to comment on their symbolism. We will only note that the drum depicts a microcosm with its three zones – sky, earth, underworld – at the same time that it indicates the means by which the

---

120 In fact several common "mythological" aspects of music are present here, including music as conducive of ecstasy and of abandonment of "selfhood", music as giver of magical power, music as a transcending (numinous) instrumentality, music as a means of accessing the divine, music as mediation between human and divine (or between the natural and supernatural), music as a characteristic feature of earthly or heavenly paradise, music as magical restorative, etc. See *Introductory Remarks*, Vol. I, above. (Ed.)

121 *Bemerkungen auf einer Reise im russischen Reiche im Jahre 1771*, I, 28.

122 *Psychomental Complex*, p.197.

123 Donner, *La Sibérie*, p.230; cf. Harva, *Die religiösen Vorstellungen*, pp.527, 530; W. Schmidt, *Der Ursprung*, IX, 260, etc.

shaman accomplishes the break-through from plane to plane and establishes communication with the world above and the world below. For, as we have just seen, the iamge of the sacrificial birch (= World Tree) is not the only one. We also find the rainbow; the shaman mounts to the higher spheres by climbing it. We find, too, the image of the bridge, over which the shaman passes from one cosmic region to another.

"The iconography of the drums is dominated by the symbolism of the ecstatic journey, that is, by journeys that imply a break-through in plane and hence a 'Center of the World'. The drumming at the beginning of the séance, intended to summon the spirits and 'shut them up' in the shaman's drum, constitutes the preliminaries for the ecstatic journey. This is why the drum is called the 'shaman's horse' (Yakut, Buryat). The Altaic drum bears a representation of a horse; when the shaman drums, he is believed to go to the sky on his horse. Among the Buryat, too, the drum made with a horse's hide represents that animal. According to O. Mänchen-Helfen, the Soyot shaman's drum is regarded as a horse and is called khamu-at, literally 'shaman-horse'. Among certain Mongol tribes the shamanic drum is called the 'black stag'. Where the skin is from a roebuck, the drum is 'the shaman's roebuck' (Karagas, Soyot). Yakut legends tell in detail of the shaman flying through the seven skies with his drum. 'I am traveling with a wild roebuck!' the Kragas and Soyot shamans sing. And the stick with which the drum is beaten is called 'whip'

among the Altaians. Miraculous speed is one of the characteristics of the táltos, the Hungarian shaman. A táltos, 'put a reed between his legs and galloped away and was there before a man on horseback'.[124] All these beliefs, images, and symbols in relation to the 'flight', the 'riding', or the 'speed' of shamans are figurative expressions for ecstasy, that is, for mystical journeys undertaken by superhuman means and in regions inaccessible to mankind.

"The idea of the ecstatic journey is also found in the name that the shamans of the tundra Yurak give their drum: *bow* or *singing bow*. According to Lehtisalo as well as Harva,[125] the shamanic drum was originally used to drive away evil spirits, a result that could also be obtained by the use of a bow. It is quite true that the drum is sometimes employed to drive away evil spirits, but in such cases its special use is forgotten and we have an instance of the 'magic of noise' by which demons are expelled. Such examples of alteration in function are fairly frequent in the history of religions. But we do not believe that the original function of the drum was to drive away spirits. The shamanic drum is distinguished from all other instruments of the 'magic of noise' precisely by the fact that it makes possible an ecstatic experience. Whether this experience was prepared, in the beginning, by the charm of the sounds of the drum, a charm that was evaluated as 'voice of the spirits', or an ecstatic experience was attained through the extreme concentration provoked by a long period of drumming, is a problem that does not concern us at present. But one fact is certain: it was *musi-*

---

124 G. Róheim, 'Hungarian Shamanism', p.135.
125 *Die religiösen Vorstellungen*, p.538.

cal magic that determined the shamanic function of the drum, and not the antidemonic *magic of noise.*[126]

"The proof is that, even where the drum is replaced by a bow — as among the Lebed Tatars and certain Altaians — what we have is always an instrument of magical music, not an antidemonic weapon; there are no arrows,[127] and the bow is used as a one-stringed instrument. The Kirgiz *baqça* does not use the drum to prepare the trance, but the *kobuz*, which is a stringed instrument. And the trance, as among the Siberian shamans, is induced by dancing to the magical melody of the *kobuz*. The dance, as we shall see more fully later, reproduces the shaman's ecstatic journey to the sky. That is as much as to say that the magical music, like the symbolism of the shamanic drum and costume and the shaman's own dance, is one of many ways of undertaking the ecstatic journey or ensuring its success. The horse-headed sticks that the Buryat call 'horses' attest the same symbolism.

"Among the Ugrian peoples shamanic drums bear no decoration. On the other hand, the Lapp shamans ornament their drums even more freely than the Tatars. Manker's extensive study of the Lapp magical drum reproduces and analyzes a large number of designs. It is not always easy to identify the mythological figures and the meaning of all the images, which are sometimes quite mysterious. In general, the Lapp drums represent the three cosmic zones, separated by boundary lines. In the sky, the sun and moon are discernible, as are gods and goddesses (probably influenced by Scandinavian mythology), birds (swan, cuckoo, etc.), the drum, the sacrificial animals, and so forth; the Cosmic Tree, a number of mythical personages, boats, shamans, the god of the chase, horsemen, etc., people the intermediate space (the earth); the infernal gods, shamans and the dead, snakes and birds are found, with other images, in the lower zone.

"The Lapp shamans also use their drums in divination. This custom is unknown among the Turkic tribes.[128] The Tungus practice a sort of limited divination, which consists in throwing the shamanic

126 The two are sometimes combined; see e.g. **ORLANDO (Roland)***, below, and the effects of Astolpho's horn-blasts. (Ed.)
127 The arrow embodies a twofold magico-religious significance; on the one hand, it is an exemplary image of speed, of 'flight'; on the other, it is the magical weapon par excellence (the arrow kills at a distance). Used in purification ceremonies or ceremonies to eject demons, the arrow 'kills' as well as 'drives away' and 'expels' evil spirits. Cf. René de Nebesky-Wojkowitz, *Oracles and Demons of Tibet*, p.543.
128 With the possible exception of the Kumandin of the Altai. Cf. Buddruss, in Friedrich and Buddruss, *Schamanengeschichten*, p.82.

drumstick into the air; its position after falling answers the question asked.

"The problem of the origin and dissemination of the shamanic drum in North Asia is extremely complex and far from being solved. Several things point to its having been originally disseminated from South Asia. It is indubitable that the Lamaist drum influenced the shape not only of the Siberian but also of the Chukchee and Eskimo drums.[129] These facts are not without importance for the formation of present-day shamanism in Central Asia and Siberia, and we shall have to return to them when we attempt to sketch the evolution of Asiatic shamanism.

"*Ritual Costumes and Magical Drums Throughout the World.* We cannot possibly consider presenting a comparative picture of the costumes and drums or other ritual instruments employed by sorcerers, medicine men, and priests all over the world.[130] The subject pertains rather to ethnology and is only of subsidiary interest to the history of religions. Let us mention, however, that the same symbolism that we have deciphered in the costume of the Siberian shaman also appears elsewhere. We find masks (from the simplest to the most elaborate), animal skins and furs, and especially bird feathers, whose ascensional symbolism requires no stressing. We also find magical sticks, bells, and very many kinds of drums.

"H. Hoffmann has usefully studied the resemblances between the Bon priests' costume and drum and those of the Siberian shamans.[131] The costume of the Tibetan oracle-priests includes, among other things, eagle feathers, a helmet with broad ribbons of silk, a shield, and a lance.[132] V. Goloubew had already compared the bronze drums excavated at Dongson with the drums of the Mongol shamans. Recently H. G. Quaritch Wales has worked out the shamanic structure of the Dongson drums in greater detail; he compares the procession wearing feather headdresses in the ritual scene on the tympanum to the Sea Dyak shamans decorated with feathers and pretending to be birds.[133] Although today the drumming of the Indonesian shaman is given various interpretations, it sometimes signifies the celestial journey or is thought to prepare the shaman's ecstatic ascent. The Dusun (Borneo) sorcerer puts on some sacred ornaments and feathers when he undertakes a cure; the Mentaweian (Sumatra) shaman

---

129 Cf. Shirokogorff, *Psychomental Complex*, p.299.

130 Cf., for example, E. Crawley, *Dress, Drinks and Drums: Further Studies of Savages and Sex*, pp.159 ff., 233 ff.; J. L. Maddox, *The Medicine Man*, pp.95 ff.; H. Webster, *Magic*, pp.252 ff. On the drum among the Bhil, see Wilhelm Koppers, *Die Bhil in Zentralindien*, p.223; among the Jakun, Ivor H. N. Evans, *Studies in Religion*, p.265; among the Malays, W. W. Skeat, *Malay Magic*, pp.25 ff., 40 ff., 512 ff; in Africa, Heinz Wieschoff, *Die afrikanischen Trommeln und ihre ausserafrikanischen Beziehungen*; A. Friedrich, *Afrikanische Priestertümer*, pp.194 ff. 324. etc. Cf. also A. Schaefner, *Origine des instruments de musique*, pp.166 ff. (skin drum).

131 *Quellen zur Geschichte der tibetischen Bon-Religion*, pp. 201 ff.

132 Nebesky-Wojkowitz, *Oracles and Demons of Tibet*, pp. 410 ff. Cf. also Dominik Schröder, 'Zur Religion der Tujen des Sininggebietes (Kukunor)', last art., pp.235 ff., 243 ff.

133 *Prehistory and Religion in South-East Asia*, pp.82 ff.

uses a ceremonial costume that includes feathers and bells; the African sorcerers and healers cover themselves with the skins of wild beasts, with animal bones and teeth, and similar objects. Although the ritual costume is comparatively rare in tropical South America, some of the shaman's accessories take its place. Such, for example, is the *maraca*, or rattle, 'made from a gourd containing seeds or stones and fitted with a handle'. This instrument is considered sacred, and the Tupinamba even bring it offerings of food.[134] The Yaruro shamans perform on their rattles 'highly stylized representations of the chief divinities whom they visit during their trances'.[135]

"The North American shamans have a ceremonial costume that tends to be symbolic; it consists of eagle or other feathers, a sort of rattle or a drum, small bags with rock crystals, stones, and other magical objects. The eagle from which the feathers are taken is regarded as sacred and is left free.[136] The bag with the accessories never leaves the shaman; at night he hides it under his pillow or his bed. The Tlingit and the Haida use what can even be called a real ceremonial costume (a robe, a blanket, a hat, etc.), which the shaman makes for himself in accordance with the instructions of his tutelary spirit. Among the Apache, besides eagle feathers, the shaman has a rhomb, a magical cord (which makes him invulnerable and also enables him to foresee future events, etc.), and a ritual hat. Elswhere, as among the Sanpoil and the Nespelem, the magical power of the costume is embodied in a mere red cloth wound around the arm.

Eagle feathers are attested among all the North American tribes. In addition, they are used, fastened to sticks, in initiation ceremonies (for example, among the Maidu), and these sticks are placed on shamans' graves. This betokens the direction that the dead shaman's soul has taken.

"In North America, as in most other regions, the shaman uses a drum or a rattle. Where the ceremonial drum is missing, it is replaced by the gong or the shell (especially in Ceylon, South Asia, China, etc.). But there is always some instrument that, in one way or another, is able to establish contact with the 'world of the spirits'. This last expression must be taken in its broadest sense, embracing not only gods, spirits, and demons, but also the souls of ancestors, the dead, and mythical animals. This contact with the suprasensible world necessarily implies a previous concentration, facilitated by the shaman's or magician's 'entering' his ceremonial costume and hastened by ritual music.

"The same symbolism of the sacred costume surives in more developed regions: wolf or bear furs in China, the bird feathers of the Irish prophet,[137] and so on. We find the macrocosmic symbolism on the robes of the priests and sovereigns of the ancient Orient. This series of facts falls under a 'law' well known to the history of religons: *one becomes what one displays*. The wearers of masks *are* really the mythical ancestors portrayed by their masks.[138] But the same results — that is, total transformation of the individual into something *other* — are to be expected from the various signs and symbols that are sometimes merely indicated on the costume or directly on the body:

---

134 A. Métraux, *La Religion des Tupinamba et ses rapports avec celle des autres tribus Tupi-Guarani*, pp.72 ff.

135 Id., '*Le Shamanisme chez les Indiens de l'Amérique du Sud tropicale*,' p.218.

136 W. Z. Park, *Shamanism in Western North America*, p.34.

137 Cf. N. K. Chadwick, *Poetry and Prophecy*, p.58.

138 In my own general essay, below (Vol. III), I have stressed the point that one "is" the particular self or role which he creates in and for himself; indeed, such a pretense or assumption seems to me to be the source of *any* given "selfhood", at all. (Ed.)

one assumes the power of magical flight by wearing an eagle feather, or even a highly stylized drawing of such a feather; and so on. However, the use of drums and other instruments of magical music is not confined to séances. Many shamans also drum and sing for their own pleasure; yet the implications of these actions remain the same: that is, ascending to the sky or descending to the underworld to visit the dead. This 'autonomy' to which instruments of magico-religious music finally attain has led to the constitution of a music that, if not yet 'profane', is certainly freer and more vivid than a purely religious music. The same phenomenon is observable in connection with the shamanic songs that narrate ecstatic journeys to the sky and dangerous descents to the underworld. After a time adventures of this kind pass into the folklore of the respective peoples and enrich popular oral literature with new themes and characters....

* * *

"In passing, we may also cite the magical drum and its role in Indian magic.[139] Legend sometimes tells of the divine origin of the drum; one tradition records that a *naga*, (snake-spirit) teaches King Kaniska the efficacy of the *ghanta* (drum) in rain rites. Here we suspect the influence of the non-Aryan substratum — the more so since, in the magic of the aboriginal Indian peoples (a magic that, though not always shamanic in structure, is nevertheless on the border of shamanism) drums have a considerable place." — Eliade [Shamanism], pp.168-80, 420.

§93.13 SHAMANISM [continued]. "A shamanic session generally consists of the following items: first, an appeal to the auxiliary spirits, which, more often than not, are those of animals, and a dialogue with them in a *secret language;* secondly, drum-playing and a dance, preparatory to the mystic journey; and thirdly, the trance (real or simulated) during which the shaman's soul is believed to have left his body. The objective of every shamanic session is to obtain the ecstasy, for it is only in ecstasy that the shaman can *fly* through the air or *descend into Hell,* that is, fulfil his mission of curing illness and shepherding souls....[140]

"The symbolism of the ascension into heaven by means of a tree is... clearly il-

---

139 See E. Crawley, *Dress, Drinks and Drums: Further Studies of Savages and Sex*, pp.236 ff.; Claudie Marcel-Dubois, *Les Instruments de musique de l'Inde ancienne*, pp.33 ff. (bells), 41 ff. (frame drum), 46 ff. (two-headed round-bodied drum), 63 ff. (hour-glass drum). On the ritual role of the drum in the *asvamedha*, cf. P. É. Dumont, *L'-Asvanmedha*, pp.150 ff. J. Przyluski had already drawn attention to the non-Aryan origin of the Indian name of the drum, *damaru;* cf. 'Un Ancien Peuple du Punjab: les Udumbara', pp.34 ff. On the drum in the Vedic cult, cf. J. W. Hauer, *Der Vratya*, pp.282 ff.

140 It occurs to me that this structuring of a paradigmatic "shamanic session" is dramatized — however unwittingly — in some British and Celtic stories about fairies. See in particular discussion of "The Piper and the Puca" — entry for **BAGPIPES***, §34.6 above, footnote 77 (p.950). (Ed.)

lustrated by the ceremony of initiation of the Buriat shamans. The candidate climbs up a post in the middle of the yourt [or yurt — a large circular domed movable tent used by nomads of Siberia and Mongolia (Ed.)], reaches the summit and goes out by the smoke-hole. But we know that this opening, made to let out the smoke, is likened to the 'hole' made by the Pole Star in the vault of Heaven.... Thus, the ritual post set up in the middle of the yourt is an image of the Cosmic Tree which is found at the *Centre of the World*, with the Pole Star shining directly above it. By ascending it, the candidate enters into Heaven; which is why, as soon as he comes out of the smoke-hole of the tent he gives a loud cry, invoking the help of the gods: up there, he finds himself in their presence.

"A similar symbolism is the explanation of the important part played by the shamanic drum. Emsheimer has shown that the dreams or ecstasies that accompany the initiation of the future shamans include a mystical journey to the Cosmic Tree at the top of which is found the Lord of the World. It is from one of the branches of this Tree, which the Lord lets fall for the purpose, that the shaman fashions the barrel of his drum. But we know that the Cosmic Tree is supposed to be situated at the Centre of the World and that it connects Earth with Heaven: the frame of his drum beng made of the actual wood of the Cosmic Tree, the shaman's drumming transports him magically near to the Tree; that is, to the Centre of the World, the place where there is a possibility of passing from one cosmic level to another.[141]

"Thus, whether he is climbing up the seven or nine notches of the ceremonial birch-tree or is at work on his drum, the shaman is on a journey to Heaven. In the former case he is laboriously imitating the ascent of the Cosmic Tree; in the latter, he is *flying* around the Tree by the magic of his drum. The shaman's *flight*, moreover, takes place quite frequently; often it is confused with the ecstasy itself." — Eliade [Myths, Dreams], pp.61, 64-65.

§93.14 SHAMANISM [continued]. "Shaman. The word comes from the pastoral herding peoples of the Asian steppes, who use it to refer to those individuals in a tribe or community who are professional trance-travelers, handling the tribe's communication between this world and the spirit world. Shamans are healers, psychics, weatherworkers; they lobby the higher powers to assure a good hunt. In modern psychological terms, you could say they have mastered such nonordinary states of consciousness as lucid dreaming, clairvoyance, clairsentience, and out-of-body travel. They are also actors and actresses, dancing on the edge in full view of their community, their transformation a public performance.

"You don't just become a shaman. An initiation is required; a teacher is usually vital. The training is rigorous, often, in the classic shamanic cultures, to the point of near death. It is thought necessary to weaken the body almost to the point of extinction for the spirit world to establish a strong channel. Only after the spirits come, can a shaman leave his body and go adventuring up and down the World Tree. (The World Tree is the image the shamanic cultures give to the domain of experience that the occult tradition calls the Other World, and that some scientists of con-

---

141 In this connection see Thompson folktale motif F175 (Magic music lures to otherworld journey), FOLKLORE AND FOLKTALES — TYPOLOGY*; and our themes T1a (Music as magical means of communication with god[s] or supreme being[s]. Music as magical conveyance to territory of gods or spirit beings) and T6 (Music as a mediator between world of nature and world of man [culture]), *Introductory Remarks*, Vol I, above . (Ed.)

sciousness call the domain of nonordinary and transpersonal experience.)

"A shaman typically needs three things: power songs to summon his spirit allies, spirit allies to guide him to the World Tree, and a drum to ride there on.

Damaru. Before Buddhists came to Tibet, there were powerful shamans, a religion called Bon, which still exists in some areas. The practitioners of Bon have legends of drums coming from the gods, flying through the sky with drums, and so on. The Buddhists wanted to distinguish themselves from these shamans, and so they did their rituals without drums.

Later, a great teacher, Tsong Khapa, had a friend named Chumbu Neljar, who did many rituals for the god Mahakala, and he used the drum *damaru.* Mahakala would come down and rumble around; sometimes during the ritual, if Chumbu was tired, Mahakala himself would play the drum. Tsong Khapa asked Chumbu, 'Why do you use this drum? You know we don't use drums because that's the way of shamans.' Chumbu replied, 'I do it for Mahakala. He likes it.'

Tsong Khapa was not convinced. He said, 'Try not using it for a while, and see whether there's any difference. Personally, I think it's a superstition, and you don't really need it.'

So Chumbu stopped used the *damaru.* But he felt unhappy, and never saw a trace of Mahakala. Everybody was miserable. When Tsong Khapa returned he asked, 'Was there a difference?'

Chumbu replied, 'There was a great difference! Mahakala didn't like it, and I don't like it. So please, let's go back to using the drum again.'

Tsong Khapa then reinstituted the use of drums in ritual. They've been used ever since, and remain close to the heart of Mahakala and many other deities. Mahakala carries a skull

damaru himself. The skull is a symbol of the unity of Emptiness and Great Bliss: inside, colored blood red, symbolizes Great Bliss; outside, colored white, symbolizes Emptiness. It is also a person turned inside-out, so to speak—their skull becomes a vessel of their realization of Emptiness and Great Bliss. The rattling of the *damaru* impels the healer to dissolve their consciousness out of the coarse body of blood and limbs and flesh, and flow into their central nervous system, dissolving through inner heat into the inner channels and merging into realization of what is called 'Clear Light' or 'Translucent Light'. When you do these practices, and when you are initiated, you must have a *damaru*, and must always keep it with you. — TARTHANG TULKU.

"*Morgon-Kara, the First Shaman of Irkutsk.* The Buriat of Irkutsk (Siberia)... declare that Morgon-Kara, their first shaman, was so competent that he could bring back souls from the dead. And so the Lord of the Dead complained to the High God of Heaven, and God decided to pose the shaman a test. He got possession of the soul of a certain man and slipped it into a bottle, covering the opening with the ball of his thumb. The man grew ill, and his relatives sent for Morgon-Kara. The shaman looked everywhere for the missing soul. He searched the forest, the waters, the mountain gorges, the land of the dead, and at last mounted, sitting on his drum, to the world above, where again he was forced to search for a long time.

"Presently he observed that the High God of Heaven was keeping a bottle covered with the ball of his thumb and, studying the circumstance, perceived that inside the bottle was the very soul he had come to find. The wily shaman changed himself into a wasp. He flew at God and gave him such a hot sting on the forehead that the thumb jerked from the opening and the captive got away.

"Then the next thing God knew, there was this shaman, Morgon-Kara, sitting on his drum again, and going down to earth with the recovered soul. The flight in this case, however, was not entirely successful. Becoming terribly angry, God immediately diminished the power of the shaman forever by splitting his drum in two.

"And so that is why from that day to this, shaman drums, which originally were fitted with two heads of skin, have only one [i.e. have a skin covering on one side only, the other being left open (Ed.)].' — Hart, pp.20, 125, 127.

§93.15 **MORE DRUM LORE.** "*How Universe, the Supreme Being, Makes Rain* (Siberia — Koryak People). One time, when Big Raven was living on earth, it rained for so long that his underground house filled with water, and everything he owned got wet and began to rot.

" 'Universe must be doing something up there,' Big Raven said to his eldest son, Ememqut. 'Let's fly up and see.'

"They went outside, put on their raven coats and flew to Universe's place. As they got near, they could hear the sound of drumming. It was Universe who was drumming, with his wife, Rain Woman, at his side. Universe had cut off Rain Woman's vulva and hung it on his drum. He was using his own penis as a drumstick. Whenever he beat the drum, water poured from Rain Woman's vulva like rain.

"When Universe saw Big Raven, he quickly hid the drum and the rain stopped.

" 'The rain has stopped,' Big Raven said to Ememqut. 'We can leave.'

"As soon as they left, the drumming began again and the rain started to fall. So Big Raven and his son turned right around and went back, and as soon as Universe saw them he again hid the drum and the rain stopped. This time Big Raven whispered to his son, 'We'll pretend to go,

but instead we'll hide and see what they are doing.'

"Big Raven and his son disguised themselves as two reindeer hairs and lay on the floor and watched as Universe asked his wife for the drum which she took from the secret hiding place. As soon as Universe began to play it, it began to rain as hard as before.

"Big Raven said to Ememqut, 'I'm going to make them fall asleep. You watch where they put the drum and the stick.'

"He made a sleeping spell, and Universe and his wife fell into a deep sleep. Then Big Raven took the drum and the drumstick from their secret hiding places and roasted them over the fire until both were dry and crisp. Then he returned them and broke the sleeping spell. Immediately Universe picked up his drum and began to beat on it, only this time the more he beat it the finer the weather became, until there wasn't a cloud in the sky. Then Universe and his wife went to bed.

" 'Now,' Big Raven said to Ememqut, 'let us really go home.'

"The wonderful fine weather lasted for days, but the hunting was terrible. No one had any luck hunting reindeer or sea mammals. Everyone began to starve because Universe was asleep.

" 'I'm going up there to see what's going on,' Big Raven said. He put on his raven coat and flew up to Universe's place to talk with him. 'We're having very good weather,' he told Universe, 'but everybody's starving. We can't find any game.'

" 'That's because I'm not looking after my children,' Universe replied. 'Go back home. From now on you'll have good hunting.' So Big Raven left and when his sons next went hunting they found sea mammals and wild reindeer. And when Big Raven himself pulled from the ground the post to which his dogs were tied, out came a whole herd of reindeer. Many of these he sacrificed to Universe, and after that he had only good luck with his hunting....

"The Origin of the Wooden Drum (Africa— Dan People). God created the wooden drum.[142] It belonged to a large genie with one eye, one arm, and one leg, whose village was in a termite hill. This genie chopped down trees and cleared the brush, and in the center of this open space he set the wooden drum.

"One day an orphan left his village and went into the bush. Arriving at the genie's clearing he spotted the wooden drum. Two sticks were lying on it. The boy took the sticks and began to beat the wooden drum.

"A genie stuck his head out of the termite mound and said, 'Who told you to beat the wooden drum?'

" 'No one told me,' answered the boy.

" 'Since you have already started to beat the drum,' said the genie, 'continue so that I may dance. If I dance and my feet get tired, you can kill me. But if my feet don't tire and your hands do, then I'll kill you.'

"The young boy beat on the wooden drum. The genie danced. When he got tired he went on the other side of the termite mound and a fresh genie popped out and resumed dancing. Eventually the boy tired and the genie killed him.

"Now this boy, though an orphan, had a younger brother. For three days the boy waited in the village for his older brother to return. When he didn't, the younger boy decided to go look for him. When he arrived at the genie's clearing, he saw the wooden drum and beside it the severed head of his brother. 'What! Is this the head of my brother?' he said. 'And what's this wooden thing on the ground with the two pretty sticks on it?' The younger brother

picked up the sticks and began to beat on the drum.

"Immediately a genie appeared and said, 'Go ahead, beat on that drum while I dance. But if your hands get tired before my feet do, I will kill you.'

"The young man beat the drum; the genie danced and danced.

"But he did something his brother didn't do. Whenever the genie danced around to the other side of the termite mound, the boy went with him. They circled for a long time. Finally the genie said, 'My foot is tired. I'm going to dance with my shoulder.'

"The genie danced with his shoulder until that got tired. Then he danced with his neck. When that got tired he shook his arm. Then he said, 'This is the day when it will happen.'

" 'When what will happen?' asked the boy.

" 'I am tired all over, what more can I say?' said the genie.

"Then the boy said, 'The day has arrived for me to avenge the death of my older brother, whose head lies here in the dirt. I don't fear you.'

"He killed the genie. Then he went around to the other side of the termite hill and set it on fire. All the genies died.

"Picking up the wooden drum, the young man returned to his village....

"The Vision of Tailfeather Woman (North America—Sioux People). Here is the story of the beginning of the ceremonial powwow drum. It was the first time when the white soldiers massacred the Indians when this Sioux woman gave four sons of hers to fight for her people. But she lost her four sons in this massacre and ran away after she knew her people were losing the war. The soldiers were after her but she ran into a lake.... She went in the water and hid under the lily pads. While she was there,

---

142 See our theme **T1c** (Music sent [to man, animals] as gift of the gods or heavenly beings; music as invention of the gods), *Introductory Remarks*, Vol I above. (Ed.)

the Great Spirit came and spoke to her and told her, 'There is only one thing for you to do.'

"It took four days to tell her. It was windy and the wind flipped the lily pads so she could breathe and look to see if anyone was around. No—the sound was all that she made out, but from it she remembered all the Great Spirit told her. On the fourth day at noon she came out and went to her people to see what was left from the war.... The Great Spirit told her what to do: 'Tell your people, if there are any left [and he told her there were], you tell your people to make a drum and tell them what I told you.' The Great Spirit taught her also the songs she knew and she told the men folks how to sing the songs. 'It will be the only way you are going to stop the soldiers from killing your people.'

"So her people did what she said, and when the soldiers who were massacring the Indians heard the sound of the drum, they put down their arms, stood still, and stopped the killing, and to this day white people are always wanting to see a pow-wow.

"This powwow drum is called in English 'Sioux drum', in Ojibwa *bwaanidewe'igan*. It was put here on earth before peace terms were made with the whites. After the whites saw what the Indians were doing, how they were having a good time and had no time to fight, the white men didn't fight. After all this took place the whites made peace terms with the Indians. So the Indians kept on the powwow. It's because the Sioux woman lost her four sons in the war that the Great Spirit came upon her and told her to make the drum to show that the Indians had power too, which they keep secret....

Dharma Drum. The big drum, called *ngo*, is round to symbolize the universe, and empty within to symbolize the dharma (teaching). When we sound the drum it symbolizes spreading dharma throughout the universe. A dragon and a calf are painted on the frame of the drum. The dragon relates to the biggest sounds, thundering loudly all over the universe.

The music is to attract the attention of the deities, and to give them pleasure. Deities exist on a larger scale than humans, and we try to entertain them with appropriate music.

We always say it's like having an important guest in one's house, such as a king or nobleman. You greet them politely, give them a cool drink, offer some fruit, sit down for some food, and then provide music to entertain them. Only later do you ask for favors or assistance. Entertainment first.

The purpose of the rituals is to host the deities properly, to entice them into your house, entertain them, then finally to give them your prayerful message, and send them away on their mission—such as protecting all living beings, putting a stop to war, hunger, or similar beneficial action.— TARTHANG TULKU.

"Underneath the world's extraordinary musical diversity is another, deeper realm in which there is no better or worse, no modern or primitive, no art music versus folk music, no distinctions at all, but rather an almost organic compulsion to translate the emotional fact of being alive into sound, into rhythm, into something you can dance to."—Hart, pp.7, 23, 25, 29, 148.

§93.16 **AN AFRICAN (KRACHI FOLK-TALE.** "All the natives are fond of listening to and repeating stories classified by Mr. [Rudyard] Kipling as 'Just-So' stories, and in their mass of tales these figure to a great extent. One could without difficulty fill many volumes with them, but the following will suffice to illustrate the type and show the great simplicity of the native mind. At the same time the power of imagination seems pretty lively and the power of ingenuity extreme.

"A Krachi tale tells how Nyame [apparently a local king or chief (Ed.)] in the olden time had a cow. It was a wonderful cow of an immense size, and Nyame was very proud of this cow. He had told every one that this cow was to be kept until the time came when his mother-in-law should die and that then he would sacrifice it to her. But Anansi[143] heard this and he wanted badly to eat the cow himself. So he repaired one day to Nyame's house and after some talk mentioned the cow, and Nyame explained what he intended to do with it. Then Anansi said: 'Nyame, you have no respect for your mother-in-law. A cow is only a common thing and yet you want to offer it to her when she dies. That is wrong. Only a man would suffice, and you had better think the matter over.'

"Nyame was ashamed then and said that Anansi was right, but that he did not know where to find a man to sacrifice. Anansi at once offered himself[144] on the condition that Nyame would give him the cow. Nyame agreed, and Anansi went away with the cow which he at once killed and ate.

"Then Anansi began to realize that he had done a foolish thing and that Nyame would certainly ask for full payment when the old woman died. He therefore made his sons dig a great hole leading to Nyame's house and then covered the entrance. The hole led right up to the yard where Nyame was wont to hear complaints and other matters, but it did not pierce the surface.

"Shortly after the old woman died and the news came to Anansi. Quickly he ordered his sons to go down the hole and to take with them his talking drums. He had told them what to do. Then came the messengers from Nyame and took him away to Nyame's house.

"Nyame greeted him and told him the news and that he was now about to take the promised payment. At once the man who did the killing came forward and seized Anansi, who began to cry out. At the same time there sounded the drums, and everyone was astonished and asked what they were saying. And Nyame heard them and knew what they sang – how that Anansi was about to die but that he would not die alone, for as soon as he was dead Nyame's wife would die and accompany him, and then Nyame's son would follow, and last of all Nyame himself.

"This made Nyame afraid, and he called to his counsellors and asked if they too had heard the message of the drums. And they begged him and told him that they had heard. Then Nyame sent for Esono the Elephant who knew all about drumming and asked him to interpret the words of the drums. And the elephant interpreted. He said they sang that when Anansi died much sorrow would come to Nyame and that all would follow Anansi to the grave, even Nyame himself.

"Then Nyame released Anansi from his promise and the latter ran back to his house and called to his sons to come back with the drums. Just as they were coming out of the hole Cotere the House Lizard, who was the linguist to Nyame, came in and saw the deceit which had been practised. He was very angry and said he would go back at once and report to Nyame. But Anansi begged hard for his life.

"It was of no use, however; and when he had promised to go back to Nyame and tell all if the lizard would let him have one night more to allow him to make a big dance for his own funeral custom, the linguist agreed and sat down to watch the spider.

"Anansi himself made great preparations. He sent his wife out to get food and drink. He made his children clean up the yard

---

143 The trickster spider – widely popular figure in West African folklore; in some accounts (e.g. Bantu) associated with the sun, in others identified as a creator of the world (Gold Coast mythology). (Ed.)

144 A common enough practice formerly. Such men were known as 'King's souls'.

and then began to make himself ready in his best clothes. All this time the lizard sat quietly in the yard. Then Anansi said to him: 'Friend, this is my last night. You must rejoice with me. Let me help you to make ready.' And the lizard agreed, and then Anansi told him to open his mouth so that he could clean his teeth for him and scrape his tongue. The lizard agreed and immediately Anansi cut off his tongue.

"Then the lizard ran back to Nyame to tell him all that he knew but found he could not speak. All he could do was to nod his head. He still nods his head to this day." — Cardinall, pp.170-72.[145]

§93.17 From *Hamlet's Mill: An Essay on Myth and the Frame of Time* (de Santillana & von Dechend).

"But even apart from the celestial 'ladder', and the sky-travel of the shaman's soul, a close look at shamanistic items always discloses very ancient patterns. For instance, the *drum*, the most powerful device of the shaman, representing the Universe in a specific way, is the unmistakable grandchild of the bronze lilissu drum of the Mesopotamiam Kalu-priest (responsible for music, and serving the god Enki/Ea).[146] The *cover* of the lilissu drum must come from a black bull, 'which represents Taurus in heaven', says Thureau-Dangin.[147] Going further, W. F. Albright and P. É. Dumont[148] compared the sacrifice of the Mesopotamian bull, the hide of which was to cover the lilissu drum, with the Indian Ashvamedha, a huge horse sacrifice which only the most successful king (always a Kshatrya) could afford. They found that the Indian horse must have the Krittika, the Pleiades, on his forehead, and this too, according to Albright, is what the Akkadian text prescribes concerning the bull. This should be enough to indicate the *level* of phenomena brought into play.

"The striking of the drum covered with that specific bull hide was meant as a contact with heaven at its most significant point, and in the Age of Taurus (c.4000-2000 BC) this was also explicitly said to represent Anu, now casually identified as 'God of Heaven'. But Anu was a far more exact entity. In cuneiform script, Anu is written with one wedge, which stands for the number 1 and also for 60 in the

---

145 For another African (Hausa) story featuring Anansi — or Spider — see **AFRICAN MYTHS — PRACTICES AND BELIEFS*** §6.7, p.29 above. (Ed.)

146 See B. Meissner, *Babylonien und Assyrien* (1925), vol. 2, p.66.

147 *Rituels accadiens* (1921), p.2. See also E. Ebeling, *Tod und Leben nach den Vorstellungen der Babylonier* (1931), for a cuneiform text in which the hide is explicitly said to be Anu (p.29), and C. Bezold, *Babylonisch-Assyrisches Glossar* (1926), p.210 s.v. 'sugugalu, "the hide of the great bull", an emblem of Anu'. We might point, once more, to the figure of speech used by Petronius' Trimalchio, who, talking of the month of May, states: *'Totus coelus taurulus fiat'* ('the whole heaven turns into a little bull').

148 'A Parallel between Indian and Babylonian Sacrificial Ritual,' *JOAS 54* (1934), pp.107-28.

sexagesimal system (the Pythagoreans would have said, he stands for the One and the Decad). All this does not mean some symbolic or mystical, least of all magical quality or quantity, but the fundamental time measure of celestial events (that is, motions).[149] Striking the drum was to involve (this time, yes, magically) the essential Time and Place in heaven.

"It is not clear whether or not the Siberian shamans were still aware of this past. The amount of highly relevant star lore collected by Holmberg, and the innumerable figures of definitely astronomical character found on shamanistic drums could very well allow for much more insight than the ethnologists assume, but this is irrelevant at this point. What is plain and relevant is that the Siberian shamans did not *invent* the zodiac, and all that goes with it.

"There is no need for a detailed inspection of Chinese mythical drums, merely a few lines from an 'Ocean of Stories':

In the Eastern Sea, there is to be found an animal which looks like an ox. Its appearance is green, and it has no horns. It has one foot only. When it moves into the water or out of it, it causes wind or rain. Its shining is similar to that of the sun and the moon. The noise it makes is like the thunder. Its name is K'uei. The great Huang-ti, having captured it, made a drum out of its skin.[150]

"This looks prima facie like the description of an ancient case of delirium tremens, but the context makes it sober enough. This is a kind of Unnatural Natural History which has small regard for living species, but deals with events from another realm. The One-Legged Being, in particular, can be followed through many appearances beginning with the Hunrakán of the Mayas*, whose very name means 'one-leg'. From it comes our 'hurricane', so there is no wonder that he disposes of wind, rain, thunder and lightning in lavish

---

149 Compare the sexagesimal round of days in customary notation of the oracle bones of Shang China, 15th century BC, about which Needham states that it is 'probably an example of Babylonian influence on China' (*Science and Civilisation in China* [1962], vol. 4, Pt. 1, p.181.

150 M. Granet, *Danses et légendes de la Chine ancienne* (1959), p.509. Such imagery is by no means unique. E.g., the *Taittiriya Sanhita* says: 'The pressing stone [of the Soma-press] is the penis of the sacrificial horse, Soma is his seed; when he opens his mouth, he causes lightning, when he shivers, it thunders, when he urinates, it rains' (7.5.25.2 = *Shatapatha Brahmana* 10.6.4.1 = *Brihad Aranyaka Upanishad* 1.1; see R. Pischel and K. F. Geldner, *Vedische Studien*, vol. 1, p.86).

amounts. But he is not for all that a mere weather god, since he is one aspect of Tezcatlipoca* himself, and the true original One-Leg that looks down from the starry sky—but his name is not appropriate yet.

"And so back by unexpected ways to mythical drums and their conceivable use. A lot more might be found by exploring that incredible storehouse of archaic thought miraculously preserved among the Mande peoples of West Sudan.[151] In the large and complicated creation myth of the Mande, there are two drums. The first was brought down from heaven by the bardic ancestor,[152] shortly after the Ark (with the eight twin-ancestors) had landed on the primeval field. This drum was made from Faro's skull and was used for producing rain. (The experts style Faro usually 'le Moniteur', thus avoiding mislabeling him as culture hero, savior or god.)[153] The first sanctuary was built, and the 'First Word' revealed (30 words there were) to mankind through the mouth of one of the twin-ancestors, who 'talked the whole night, ceasing only when he saw the sun and Sirius rising at the same time'. When the 'Second Word' was to be revealed (consisting of 50 words this time), and again connected with the heliacal rising of Sirius, the ancestor 'decided to sacrifice in the sanctuary on the hill the first twins of mixed sex. He asked the bard to make an arm-drum with the skin of the twins.[154] The tree, from which he carved the drum, grew on the hill and symbolized Faro's only leg.[155]

"Here again are important one-legged characters, of whom there are a bewildering number with various functions all over the world. It is not necessary to enter that jungle, except to note that the temporary mock-king of Siam, who was set up for yearly expiatory ceremonies, also had to stand on one leg upon a golden dais during all the coronation ceremonies, and he had the fine-sounding title of 'Lord of the Celestial Armies'.[156] The Chinese K'uei is then no isolated character. The Chinese myth is more explicit than the others and becomes more understandable because the

---

151 In East Africa, the drum occupied the place that the Tabernacle had in the Old Testament, as Harald von Sicard has shown in *Ngoma Lungundu: Eine afrikanische Bundeslade* (1952).

152 In the **AZTEC*** creation myth quoted above (see §31.4), the god Quetzalcoatl *also* brings music down from heaven — the House of the Sun. (Ed.)

153 Cotterell, *A Dictionary of World Mythology:* "According to the Bambara peoples of the Niger River, the creation of the world is a continuous process. Pemba and Faro, they say, descended from the sky, but at first it was Pemba who sought to govern the world. He was a wood spirit, the maker of the first woman, and the king of trees. Musso-koroni, the first woman, planted Pemba in the soil and her human and animal offspring shed blood in sacrifice to his divinity. But she did not like Pemba's thorns, ceased to be his consort and instead, Musso-koroni wandered the world causing disorder and sadness. The water spirit Faro too disliked the growing power of Pemba and so he uprooted him. Thereafter, the Bambara assert, the harmony of daily life has depended on the creativity of Faro, and his spirits" (255-56). (Ed.)

154 It is an hourglass-shaped drum, with two skins, said 'to recall the two geographic areas, Kaba and Akka, and the narrow central part of the drum is the river itself [Niger] and hence Faro's journey'.

155 Germaine Dieterlen, 'The Mande Creation Story', *Africa* 27 (1957), pp.124-38; cf. JSA 25 (1955), pp.39-76. See also Marcel Griaule, *'Symbolisme des tambours soudanais'*, *Mélanges historiques offerts à M. Masson 1* (1955), pp.79-86; Griaule and Dieterlen, *Signes Graphiques Soudanais* (1951), p.19.

156 W. Deonna, *Un divertissement de table 'à cloche-pied'* (1959), p.33. See J. Frazer, *The Dying God* (Pt. III of *The Golden Bough*), pp.149f.

Chinese were extremely sky-conscious. Their sinful monsters are thrown into pits or banished to strange mountain regions for the sin of having upset the calendar.

"As for K'uei himself, engagingly introduced as a green oxlike creature of the Eastern Sea, he will grow more bewildering as his nature unfolds. Marcel Granet writes that the Emperor Shun made K'uei 'master of music' — actually ordered no less a power than the Sun (Chong-li) to fetch him from the bush and bring him to court, because K'uei alone had the talent to bring into harmony the six pipes and the seven modes, and Shun, who wanted to bring peace to the empire, stood by the opinion that 'music is the essence of heaven and earth'.[157] K'uei also could cause the 'hundred animals' to dance by touching the musical stone, and he helped Yü the Great, that indefatigable earth-mover among the Five First Emperors, to accomplish his labor of regulating the 'rivers'. And it turns out that he was not only Master of the Dance, but Master of the Forge as well. He must have been a remarkable companion for Yü the Great, whose dancing pattern (the Step of Yü) 'performed' the Big Dipper.[158]

"Enough of drums, and of their shamanic use. They have at least ceased to seem like tribal tom-toms. They are connected with time, rhythm and motion in heaven." — de Santillana and von Dechend, pp. 124-28.

Ed. note: The figure of K'uei is somewhat elusive. Kramer, *Mythologies of the Ancient World:*

[An] anecdote recorded in *Han Fei-tzu*, ch. 33, and *Lü-shih ch'un-ch'iu* XXII, 6; both iii cent. BC has to do with a curious being called K'uei. In the euhemerized histories he is the human Music Master of the sage ruler Shun (trad. xxiii cent. BC), but from other

scattered references we can see that he was actually a mythological creature having only one foot. In the story, the ruler of Confucius' native state of Lu is made to ask Confucius: 'I have heard that K'uei was one-footed [*yi tsu*]. Is this really so?' To which Confucius replies: 'K'uei was a man, so why should he have one foot?' Then he goes on to explain that because K'uei's royal master Shun was greatly pleased with K'uei's musical ability, he once exclaimed of him: 'As to K'uei, one (like him) is enough [*yi erh tsu*].' By later people, however, this saying came to be misconstrued as meaning that K'uei had but one foot (*yi tsu*)....

[Among Taoist writings there is also a reference] in the seventeenth chapter of the *Chuang-tzu* (iii cent. BC) [to a conversation] between a centipede and that same K'uei whom we have just encountered in Confucian dress. There is no doubt that Chuang Tzu's K'uei is a mythological creature, for he is made to complain to the centipede about his own difficulties in hopping around on one foot, and to ask the latter how he succeeds in controlling those many feet of his. The allegory's purpose, however, is not at all mythological but philosophical. From it we learn the Taoist moral that every creature should be satisfied with his own native endowment, but nothing whatsoever concerning the K'uei himself, other than the basic fact that he is one-footed. (374-76).

Leach, *Funk and Wagnalls Dictionary of Folklore, Mythology and Legend:*

Kuei. In Chinese folklore, a disembodied spirit; a ghost or demon; either the *p'o*, or physical soul, of a dead person which has escaped and become a demon, or the *hun*, or spirit-soul, of

---

157 Granet, *Danses et légendes*, pp.311, 505-508.
158 We are indebted for this last piece of information to Professor N. Sivin.

one dead, which for various reasons may be loose in the world. Both are kuei; both are regarded as malicious demons and are greatly feared. (593)

In his *Myths and Legends of China*, E. T. C. Werner mentions a K'uei or Chung K'uei who

ascended to Heaven and became arbiter of the destinies of men of letters. His abode was said to be the star K'uei, a name given by the Chinese to the sixteen stars of the constellation or 'mansion' of Andromeda and Pisces. The scholars quite soon began to worship K'uei as the God of Literature, and to represent it on a column in the temples. Then sacrifices were offered to it. This star or constellation was regarded as the palace of the god. (106)

Werner also notes that the Chinese character *kuei* commonly denoted a disembodied spirit, or ghost, or (as a plural) demons.

Consistent with this author's account of Chung K'uei, Raymond Deloy Jameson tells us (in Leach) that **Kuei Hsing** was

an ugly dwarf associated, along with Chu Yi, with Wen Ch'ang, the Chinese God of Literature. The legend is that he was a brilliant student and won the first prize in the Imperial examinations. But because of his ugliness the emperor refused to grant him the golden rose that should have been his award. Kuei Hsing threw himself into the ocean, was rescued by a sea monster (a dragon), and ascended into Heaven where he took up his residence on the star *kuei hsing*, now construed as being located in the square part of the constellation Ursa Major. He is popularly represented holding a writing brush in his right hand, a bushel measure in his left, and kicking up one leg behind him [again that famous leg? (Ed.)]. This twisted position is thought to suggest the

Chinese ideograph *kuei*. Wen Ch'ang also has his abode in the big square mansion in Ursa Major. (593).

Finally, in *Chinese Fairy Tales and Folk Tales*, Wolfram Eberhard relates the story "Why does Li T'ie-kuai have a Poisoned Leg?". One day the Immortal Li T'ie - kuai — who many people said had been an ordinary man once — bought some ordinary garlic in the street, and put it in his bag. Through a deception he contrived to trade bits of the garlic for some of the red pills of immortality that were being shared by the Immortals.

The Immortals were not annoyed at being deceived, but climbed on to a cloud and flew off to the Mountain of the Volcano, and having eaten the red pills [himself], Li T'ie-kuai was able to go with them. When they arrived at the Volcano, the Immortals flew very high; but Li being only a beginner could not reach great heights, and he lost one of his legs, which was burnt off in the fire. That is why he has a poisoned leg.

Other people say that, when he was young, he was very poor, and his mother ordered him to go into the hills every day to collect wood.... One day there was no wood in the house. His aunt cursed him: 'Lazy devil,' she said, 'to-day we will use your foot as fuel.' Now Li T'ie-kuai had already learnt some tricks from the Immortals in the hills, so he went to the fireplace, sat down, and stuck his foot into the fire, which blazed up much brighter than with wood. When his aunt saw him she shouted out: 'Are you mad? I was only joking when I said you ought to stoke the fire with your foot; I didn't mean it seriously,' and at the same time she pulled his foot out of the fire. But that was a grave mistake, because the bottom part of the leg fell off and naturally became poisoned. If his aunt had not pulled it out, he could have taken it out when the food was cooked and there would have been nothing to see. The aunt used the burnt-off leg to brush up the cinders. (226-27)

But, by this point we have long stopped talking about music at all...

EGYPTIAN PRACTICES AND BELIEFS. *(See also pp.208, 847).*

§99.10 "**BES.** Dwarf-god, grotesque in appearance, benign in nature.

"The Egyptians had a number of monstrously formed dwarf-deities for which the name Bes was employed. The god in a plumed crown was normally bearded with his broad face surrounded by a lion's mane and ears....

"He has his most crucial contribution to make to Egyptian life in his role as protector of childbirth in partnership with Taweret.... A spell survives for reciting four times over a clay dwarf placed on the crown of the head of a woman in labour where complications have arisen. In it Bes is addressed as 'great dwarf with a large head and short thighs' and as 'a monkey in old age' — the notion of ugliness as a deterrent to evil spirits is as strong in Ancient Egypt as the swords which Bes often brandishes.... It was thought that Bes brought good luck and prosperity to married couples and their children.... The aggression of knife-carrying Bes is directed at any threat to the family....

"His tutelary duties aside, Bes has a genial temperament which expresses itself through merrymaking and music. On furniture found in the tomb of Queen Tiye's parents (Dynasty XVIII) Bes strikes a tambourine*, an instrument which he can also be seen shaking over 1,000 years later on the walls of the Hathor temple on the island of Philae — there he plays the harp* as well. In this latter instance Bes performs the task of placating the goddess Hathor with music on her initially reluctantly un-

dertaken journey from Nubia to her sanctuary at Dendera. His popularity spread beyond the borders of Egypt: from Kition in Cyprus comes an ivory plaque of Bes (about 1200 BC). He was also used as a motif by Phoenician craftsmen in ivorywork which decorated the furniture and caskets of Nimrud in Assyria. Towards the end of Ancient Egyptian civilisation a new iconography reflected the adoption of Bes by the occupying Roman forces — statuettes of the god dressed as a legionary.

"**HATHOR.** Universal cow-goddess, symbolic mother of the pharaoh.... Hathor can also be represented as a lioness, as a snake 'who laughs with Wadjet' or a sycamore. The papyrus was a plant sacred to her since the habitat of wild cattle was in the swamps by the Nile. A ritual of plucking up papyrus stalks was performed in her honour.

"Her nature is predominantly benign but she does have a destructive streak which is best evidenced in the legend involving the narrowly-avoided annihilation of the human race by Hathor as the 'Eye of Re'....

"[She is also recognized as a funerary goddess.] This aspect of Hathor is especially prominent in western Thebes where the necropolis was under her safekeeping....

"Representation in tombs, such as that of Queen Nefertari (Dynasty XIX), and in the Book of the Dead show seven cows whose role is to determine the destiny of a child a birth. Each Hathor has her own name....

"[Goddess of love, music and dance.] Hathor is [also] the supreme goddess of sexual love in Ancient Egypt, immediately identified with Aphrodite by the Greeks when they came into contact with her cult. The turmoil or ecstasy which can result from physical desire are reflected in the conflicting forces of Hathor's personality as a goddess of destruction as 'Eye of Re' or a goddess of heavenly charm. In love poetry Hathor is called the 'golden' or 'lady of heaven'. Concommitant with her connection with love is her ability to encourage sensual joy by music and dancing. In fact the child of Hathor and Horus at the temple of Dendera is the god Ihy [see below] who really personifies musical jubilation. Dances in honour of Hathor are represented on the walls of couriers' tombs, and in the story of the return of Sinuhe to the Egyptian court after years abroad, the princesses perform an Hathoric dance to celebrate the occasion. In the myth of the contest for power between Horus and Seth it is the goddess herself, 'lady of the southern sycamore', who cures her father Re of a fit of sulking by dancing naked in front of him until he bursts into laughter.

"Music in the cult of Hathor was immensely important and there were two ritual instruments carried by her priestesses to express their joy in worshipping the goddess.

"(a) SISTRUM*. The bronze sacred rattle 'sesheshet' in Egyptian—popular into the Roman world—which was shaken in honour of Hathor, consisted of a column-handle with cow-eared Hathor at the top surmounted by a loop, across the width of which stretched three or four horizontal bars piercing small disks that would jangle. There was also the ceremonial sistum made of glazed composition terminating in a naos or shrine, which was meant to be a votive offering to the goddess.

"(b) MENAT. This is a necklace, thick with beads and a counterpoise long enough to be grasped in the hand, which was not worn but shaken by Hathor's priestesses.

"The crypts in the main cult centre of Hathor in Egypt at Dendera give, in superbly carved wall reliefs, an idea of the sacred musical instruments and ritual objects and statues of the goddess that were originally contained in them. Also at Dendera (Ancient Egyptian 'Yunet'), sacred to Hathor since at least the Old Kingdom, music accompanied the procession that brought the cult image of the goddess from the darkness of the sanctuary up onto the roof where a special chapel had been constructed for the ceremony of the union with the sun disk enabling Hathor to bathe in the rays of the sun-god.

"IHY. Young god personifying the jubilation emanating from the sacred rattle.

"The name of Ihy was interpreted by the Egyptians as 'sistrum-player' which was the raison d'être of this god. The sistrum was a cultic musical instrument used primarily (but not exclusively) in the worship of Hathor, mother of Ihy. At Dendera temple Ihy is the child of the union of Hathor and Horus and is depicted as a naked young boy wearing the sidelock of youth and with his finger to his mouth. He can hold the sacred rattle and necklace (menat).

"In the temple complex the birth house or 'mammisi' was a sanctuary where the mystery of the conception and birth of the divine child Ihy was celebrated. His name is rarely found outside the confines of Dendera temple—e.g. occasionally in spells in the Coffin Texts or Book of the Dead where he is called 'lord of bread... in charge of beer', a possible reference to the celebrations at Dendera deliberately requiring a state of intoxication on the part of the acolyte in order to communicate with Hathor."—Hart, pp.58-61, 76-81, 98.

§99.11 **Set Singing and Music Before Thy Face.** *Ed. note:* The following song has been found written in several tombs beside the picture of a harper. Music is mentioned only briefly (in one line), but, given the seriousness of the context—a carefully considered contemplation of the place of a person's life and being in the overall scheme of things—for music to be included at all would appear to be significant. It seems to me that the line could be interpreted in three ways. First and most obviously the living are urged to "seize the day"—to enjoy life's pleasures etc while one can. Among these pleasures, music is given a prominent place. Secondly, I would guess that along with other tokens of one's earthly life it could be that some sign of *music* or *musicians* is to placed in the tomb of the dead, in order to accompany the subject on his journey into the afterlife. Just as the urging to "clothe thee in fine linen" could easily mean to do so not only in life — but also to be so attired in the tomb — so the instruction to "set singing and music before thy face" could mean to do so not only in life, but also as one lies in his tomb, preparing to take up his place among the dead. I also feel that there is a third, poetic-philosophical sense to this line. Generations come and go, time moves on. To die is to quit the realm of actual, particularized, mortal being — it is to join the world of spirits. Do we not — then — put on music like a vestment (so to speak), as our eternal spirit assumes its new abode?

"It is well with this noble prince. The happy destiny hath come to pass.
"Generations pass away and others stand in their place since the time of them that were of old.
"Re getteth him up in the morning and Atum setteth in the west.
"Men beget, women conceive, and every nose draweth breath.
"But when day dawneth their children are come in their place.
"The gods that were aforetime rest in their pyramids, likewise the noble and the glorified, buried in their pyramids.
"They that built them castles, their places are no more. What hath become of them?
"I have heard the discourse of Imhotep and Harzozef with whose words men speak everywhere.
"Where are their places now? Their walls are destroyed, their habitations are destroyed as if they had never been.
"None cometh again from thence that he may tell us of their state, that he may recount to us their lot, that he may set our heart at rest until we also hasten away to the place whither they are gone.
"Rejoice, and let thy heart forget that day when they shall lay thee to rest.

"Cast all sorrow behind thee, and bethink thee of joy until there come that day of reaching port in the land that loveth silence.
"Follow thy desire as long as thou livest, put myrrh on thy head, clothe thee in fine linen.
"Set singing and music before thy face.
"Increase yet more the delights which thou hast, and let not thy heart grow faint. Follow thine inclination and thy profit. Do thy desires upon earth, and trouble not thine heart until that day of lamentation come to thee.
"Spend a happy day and weary not thereof. Lo, none may take his goods with him, and none that hath gone may come again." — Smith (Tree of Life), pp.236-37.

ETHOS (Greek). *(See also p.217).*

§107.2 See **HARMONY OF THE**
      SPHERES*.
      MUSIC AND TRANCE*
      (The Renaissance).

FAIRIES. *(See also pp.223, 853.)*

§109.10 British mythology. "This word derives from 'Fays' meaning the Fatae or Fates. Although latterly fairies have been understood as diminutive beings inhabiting flowers, etc., their true stature, both actual and mythical, is considerably greater. They are the British version of the Irish *Sidhe* dwellers, bestowing gifts of prophecy and music, living in bliss in their own fairy hills. According to oral tradition, they originate from the angels of the Fall or are children of Adam by Lilith, the elder brethren of humanity who are neither divine nor human, but none the less immortal." — Matthews and Matthews, pp.72-73.

§109.11 "There are numerous legends in which men and women who are helpful and polite to fairies are rewarded, while those who are rude, ungrateful or unkind are punished; this is also a constant theme in fictional fairytales.... They can bestow skills as well as gold, and these may become hereditary. One of the commonest is musical skill; in Scandinavian lore, the Näck* or Fossegrim who lives in waterfalls is a fine fiddler, and many human players have learnt the art from him, or memorized one of his tunes. The McCrimmons of Skye, the most famous family of pipers in Scotland, are said to have learnt their skill originally from the fairies. Long ago, there was a young McCrimmon whose older brothers would not let him learn the bagpipes* (or, in some versions, who was too stupid to learn); a fairy gave him pipes with a silver chanter and taught him a magnificent tune, 'The Finger Lock'." — Simpson [European], p.65.

§109.12 **Elves of the Northern countries.** "Beside the dwarfs there was another numerous class of tiny creatures called Lios-alfar, light or white elves, who inhabited the realms of air between heaven and earth, and were gently governed by the genial god Frey from his palace in Alfheim. They were lovely, beneficent beings, so pure and innocent that, according to some authorities, their name was derived from the same root as the Latin word 'white' *(albus)*, which, in a modified form, was given to the snow-covered Alps, and to Albion (England), because of her white chalk cliffs which could be seen afar.

"The elves were so small that they could flit about unseen while they tended the flowers, birds, and butterflies; and as they were passionately fond of dancing, they often glided down to earth on a moonbeam, to dance on the green. Holding one another by the hand, they would dance in circles, thereby making the 'fairy rings', which were to be discerned by the deeper green and greater luxuriance of the grass which their little feet had pressed.

Merry elves, their morice pacing
    To aërial minstrelsy,
Emerald rings on brown heath tracing,
    Trip it deft and merrily.
            — Sir Walter Scott.

"If any mortal stood in the middle of one of these fairy rings he could, according to the popular belief in England, see the fairies and enjoy their favour; but the Scandinavians and Teutons vowed that the unhappy man must die. In illustration of this superstition, a story is told of how Sir Olaf, riding off to his wedding, was enticed by the fairies into their ring. On the morrow, instead of a merry marriage, his friends witnessed a triple funeral, for his mother and bride also died when they beheld his lifeless corpse.

Master Olof rode forth ere dawn of the
        day
And came where the Elf-folk were
        dancing away.
    The dance is so merry,
So merry in the greenwood.

And on the next morn, ere the daylight
        was red,
In Master Olof's house lay three
        corpses dead.
    The dance is so merry,
So merry in the greenwood.

First Master Olof, and next his young
        bride,
And third his old mother — for sorrow
        she died.
    The dance is so merry,
So merry in the greenwood.
        — *Master Olof at the Elfin Dance*
                (Howitt's tr.)

The Elf Dance. These elves, who in England were called fairies or fays, were also enthusiastic musicians, and delighted especially in a certain air known as the elf-dance, which was so irresistible that no one who heard it could refrain from dancing. If a mortal, overhearing the air, ventured to reproduce it, he suddenly found himself incapable of stopping and was forced to play on and on until he died of exhaustion,[159] unless he were deft enough the play the tune backwards, or some one charitably cut the strings of his violin*. His hearers, who were forced to dance as long as the tones continued, could only stop when they ceased." — Guerber (Norsemen), pp.246-47.

§109.13 "THE LEGEND OF KNOCK-GRAFTON (Irish). There once was a poor man who lived in the fertile glen of Aherlow, at the foot of the gloomy Galtee mountains, and he had a great hump on his back: he looked just as if his body had been rolled up and placed upon his shoulders; and his head was pressed down with the weight so much that his chin, when he was sitting, used to rest upon his knees for support. The country people were rather shy of meeting him in any lonesome place, for though, poor creature, he was as harmless and as inoffensive as a new-born infant, yet his deformity was so great that he scarcely appeared to be a human creature, and some ill-minded persons had set strange stories about him afloat. He was said to have a great knowledge of herbs and charms; but certain it was that he had a mighty skilful hand in plaiting straws and rushes into hats and baskets, which was the way he made his livelihood.

"Lusmore, for that was the nickname put upon him by reason of his always wearing a sprig of the fairy cap, or lusmore (the foxglove), in his little straw hat, would ever get a higher penny for his plaited work than any one else, and perhaps that was the reason why some one, out of envy, had circulated the strange stories about him. Be that as it may, it happened that he was returning one evening from the pretty town of Cahir toward Cappagh, and as little Lusmore walked very slowly, on account of the great hump upon his back, it was quite dark when he came to the old moat of Knockgrafton, which stood on the right-hand side of his road.[160]

---

159 See also DANCING TO DEATH (OR INSANITY)*. (Ed.)

160 Moat does not mean a place with water, but a tumulus or barrow. [WBY]

"Tired and weary was he, and noways comfortable in his own mind at thinking how much farther he had to travel, and that he should be walking all the night; so he sat down under the moat to rest himself, and began looking mournfully enough upon the moon, which

Rising in clouded majesty, at length
Apparent Queen, unveil'd her peerless light,
And o'er the dark her silver mantle threw.

"Presently there rose a wild strain of unearthly melody upon the ear of little Lusmore; he listened, and he thought that he had never heard such ravishing music before. It was like the sound of many voices, each mingling and blending with the other so strangely that they seemed to be one, though all singing different strains, and the words of the song were these:

Da Luan, Da Mort, Da Luan, Da Mort,
Da Luan, Da Mort;

when there would be a moment's pause, and then the round of melody went on again.[161]

"Lusmore listened attentively, scarcely drawing his breath lest he might lose the slightest note. He now plainly perceived that the singing was within the moat; and though at first it had charmed him so much, he began to get tired of hearing the same round sung over and over so often without any change; so availing himself of the pause when *Da Luan, Da Mort*, had been sung three times, he took up the tune, and raised it with the words *augus Da Dardeen*, and he went on singing with the voices inside of the moat, *Da Luan, Da Mort*, finishing the melody, when the pause again came, with *augus Da Dardeen*.

"The fairies within Knockgrafton, for the song was a fairy melody, when they heard this addition to the tune, were so much delighted that, with instant resolve, it was determined to bring the mortal among them, whose musical skill so far exceeded theirs, and little Lusmore was conveyed into their company with the eddying speed of a whirlwind.

---

161 The words *La Luan Da Mort agus Da Dardeen* are Gaelic for 'Monday, Tuesday, and Wednesday too'. Da Eena is Thursday. Story-tellers, in telling this tale, says Croker, sing these words to the following music — according to Croker, music of very ancient kind:

Mr. Douglas Hyde has heard the story in Connaught, with the song of the fairy given as 'Peean Peean daw feean, Peean go leh agus leffin' [*pighin, pighin, da phighin, pighin go ieith agus leith phighin*], which in English means, 'a penny, a penny, twopence, a penny and a half, and a half-penny'. [WBY]

"Glorious to behold was the sight that burst upon him as he came down through the moat, twirling round and round, with the lightness of a straw, to the sweetest music that kept time to his motion. The greatest honor was then paid him, for he was put above all the musicians, and he had servants tending upon him, and everything to his heart's content, and a hearty welcome to all; and, in short, he was made as much of as if he had been the first man in the land.

"Presently Lusmore saw a great consultation going forward among the fairies, and, notwithstanding all their civility, he felt very much frightened, until one stepping out from the rest came up to him and said:

Lusmore! Lusmore!
Doubt not, nor deplore,
For the hump which you bore
On your back is no more;
Look down on the floor,
And view it, Lusmore!

"When these words were said, poor little Lusmore felt himself so light, and so happy, that he thought he could have bounded at one jump over the moon, like the cow in the history of the cat and the fiddle; and he saw, with inexpressible pleasure, his hump tumble down upon the ground from his shoulders.

[At last he fell into a sound sleep, and when he awoke discovered that he was lying just at the foot of the moat of Knockgrafton, with the cows and sheep grazing peaceably round about him. He also found himself in a full suit of new clothes, which he concluded the fairies had made for him.

[The story of Lusmore's hump got about, and a great wonder was made of it. It was the talk of everyone, high and low. One morning, as Lusmore was sitting contented at his cabin door, an old woman came to him asking for directions to Cappagh. It seemed that the son of a gossip of hers had a hump upon him that would be his death; could he not use the same charm

as Lusmore, so that the hump might be taken off him?

[Lusmore told his story so that the poor man—Jack Madden was his name—was brought across the country in a cart, and left under the old moat of Knockgrafton.]

"Jack Madden... had not been sitting there long when he heard the tune going on within the moat much sweeter than before; for the fairies were singing it the way Lusmore had settled their music for them, and the song was going on: *Da Luan, Da Mort, Da Luan, Da Mort, Da Luan, Da Mort, augus Da Dardeen,* without ever stopping. Jack Madden, who was in a great hurry to get quit of his hump, never thought of waiting until the fairies had done, or watching for a fit opportunity to raise the tune higher again than Lusmore had; so having heard them sing it over seven times without stopping, out he bawls, never minding the time or the humor of the tune, or how he could bring his words in properly, *augus Da Dardeen, augus Da Hena,* thinking that if one day was good, two were better; and that if Lusmore had one new suit of clothes given him, he should have two.

"No sooner had the words passed his lips than he was taken up and whisked into the moat with prodigious force; and the fairies came crowding round about him with great anger, screeching and screaming, and roaring out:

" 'Who spoiled our tune? Who spoiled our tune?' and one stepped up to him above all the rest, and said:

Jack Madden! Jack Madden!
Your words came so bad in
The tune we felt glad in; —
This castle you're had in.
That your life we may sadden;
Here's two humps for Jack Madden!

And twenty of the strongest fairies brought Lusmore's hump, and put it down upon poor Jack's back, over his own, where it became fixed as firmly as if it was nailed on with twelve-penny nails, by the best carpenter that ever drove one. Out of their castle they then kicked him; and in the morning, when Jack Madden's mother and her gossip came to look after their little man, they found him half dead, lying at the foot of the moat, with the other hump upon his back. Well to be sure, how they did look at each other! but they were afraid to say anything, lest a hump might be put upon their own shoulders. Home they brought the unlucky Jack Madden with them, as downcast in their hearts and their looks as ever two gossips were; and what through the weight of his other hump, and the long journey, he died soon after, leaving, they say, his heavy curse to any one who would go to listen to fairy tunes again." — Croker, in Yeats, pp.43-48. [162]

FAIRYTALES.

§109A.1 "[In fairytales] magic flutes, pipes, and fiddles indicate nothing about or attest

only indirectly to the beauty of music, but they indicate the direct power of its effect, forcing all who hear them to dance or come running—whether it be humans (KHM 110, AT 592)[163] or animals (sheep, goats, hares: AT 570, *The rabbit-herd*). Not infrequently mention is made of minstrels. In individual versions of *Faithful John*, it is believed that a story devised by a minstrel can be identified in the background. But even narrators who are themselves minstrels take very limited advantage of the opportunity to portray fairytale heroes or a supporting figure as minstrels. Jachen Filli from Guarda, an enthusiastic singer and clarinet player and the leader of a dance band, does indeed tell of the fiddler who plays and sings so beautifully before the statue of St. Cecilia that she tosses him one of her golden slippers (*St. Kümmernis* type, KHM 157 A), and he quite happily mentions the music and dancing at the festival closing the fairytale—but, unlike in the Grimms' version, he does not have Faithful John make music during the sea

---

162 I suppose that this tale may be interpreted in a number of ways; I would only suggest that, in this story, at the very least a musical performance (instrument, song, dance of a certain kind) is to be treated as a medium or talisman of an extremely *potent* kind, which must be employed with a very great care, and always at one's peril. For variously related themes see (in our *Introductory Remarks*, Vol I above) **T1a** (Music as magical means of communication with god[s] or supreme being[s]) — letting the fairies stand in here for such "gods" or "supreme beings" — **T4** (Music as magical means by which spirits of other supernatural beings or forces take possession of human or other victim), **T4b** (Music as magical restorative, of mental or physical health.... Music as instrument of enchantment), **T4c** (Music as magical means of attracting, seducing etc, victim) and — this being I should think of the greatest relevance here — **T6** (Music as a mediator between world of nature and world of man [culture]). See also Thompson folktale motifs E489.5 (Dancing in afterworld), F175 (Magic music lures to otherworld journey), F261 (Fairies dance — akin to F455.3.2, Trolls dance, F470.2, Night-spirits dance, F482.5, Brownies dance), **FOLKLORE AND FOLKTALES — TYPOLOGY***. (Ed.)

163 KHM number is according to Johannes Bolte and Georg Polívka, *Anmerkungen zu den Kinder- und Hausmärchen der Brüder Grimm* [Grimm Brothers' children's- and house-tales] (1913-32; reprint 1963), while the AT number refers to Antti Aarne and Stith Thompson's *The Types of the Folktale*, 2nd Ed. (Helsinki, 1963).

voyage.[164] These purely mood-setting touches are alien to the oral tradition of fairytale narration. Music and musical instruments are as a rule only mentioned when they have some function in advancing the plot. In the Finnish story in which the hero is supposed to fetch the emperor a 'living kantele', a sort of self-playing zither, both the expedition to the far-off country and the (continually interrupted) making of the instrument by otherworldly figures are painstakingly described — but whether the kantele then actually plays and how, we never learn.[165] Local legends and saint's legends show much more interest in things acoustic than the fairytale. The Kümmernis-Cecilia story is a religious fairytale; the *singing bone,** whose numerous versions almost all contain verses to be sung (the tunes have been noted down here and there), is a local legend fairytale. The real local legend tells not only with zest of things heard, but also of when otherworldly beings have bestowed on humans the art of singing, yodeling, or alphorn blowing. The saint's legend also has a sensitivity to smells — the corpses of saints give off a marvelous, pleasant scent. The Zurzach Book of Miracles tries to make the effect of music palpable using a taste simile: The singing of the angels 'was as sweet in the ears of the listeners as if honey between the teeth of those dining' ('*vox psallentium angelorum... tam dulcis in auribus audentium, velud mel est in dentibus manducantium*').[166]

"The power and beauty of sound naturally come into their own in another way in the fairytale insofar as a narration is an acoustic reality. The rhythm and melody of the voice of the male or female narrator are just as much a musical element as the imitations of the sounds of nature, alliterations, assonances, and verses. Leopold Schmidt correctly observes that musical instruments in the fairytale are 'played not for artistic reasons and not for entertainment,' that they serve more 'to foster a magical, conjuring effect in a story.'[167] This is also largely true of recited and sung verses in the fairytale; they are not 'lyrical interludes' but have 'a very direct function' (Karlinger),[168] one often magical: Otherworldly beings speak in another language, e.g. in verse ('The Frog King', KHM1; 'The Singing Bone', KHM 28, 'The Juniper Tree', KHM 47, etc.), and the sung verses are there to bring something about — in the *singing bone* fairytale type (AT 780), for example, it is the revenge of the murdered boy. The bone flute is a transformation of the boy; through it he comes back again — it is his epiphany. Nonetheless, although both the musical instruments and the verses almost always have an important plot function in the fairytale — especially in the European — a basic difference exists between them: One does not hear the musical instrument — perhaps it may not even be indicated whether it is actually played — but the melody of the sung verse is realized; the narrator sings it. To this degree the verses to be sung in the fairytale have an actual esthetic function, not only of a higher degree, but of a quite different sort from that

---

164 Leza Uffer, *La Tarablas da Guarda* (Basel, 1970).

165 August von Löwis of Menar, ed., *Finnische und estnische Volksmärchen* (1922; reprint 1962).

166 Latin text with German translation in Adolf Reinle, *Die Heilige Verena von Zurzach* (Basel, 1948), 61.

167 Leopold Schmidt, *Die Volkererzählung* (Berlin, 1963), 48.

168 Felix Karlinger, *Die Funktion des Liedes im Märchen* (Salzburg/Munich, 1968), 6.

of the instruments mentioned in the narratives. Above the level of the bare plot rises the level of speech (dialogs, monologs); above that, the level of spoken verse; and this last level is still transcended, exceeded by the verses sung."[169] — Lüthi, pp.27-28.

Ed. note: "[In fairytales] magic flutes, pipes, and fiddles indicate nothing about or attest only indirectly to the beauty of music, but they indicate the direct power of its effect," etc. To this analysis I am inclined to add that, not only in myth and fairytales but perhaps to some extent generally, such "magical" and other "powers" of music are — *themselves* — a part of the beauty, attractiveness, and indeed very *nature* of music. Again, whereas the author distinguishes between "musical" and various "magical" aspects of music and musical instruments — or, again, between using music to "foster a magical, conjuring effect" rather than for "artistic reasons and entertainment" alone — I wonder if gradually the point does not emerge that a part, at least, of what it is to be "musical" *is* to be "magical"? In fairytale and myth, at least, it is frequently the case that the "artistic", "entertainment"-providing aspects of music have, themselves, some magical or sacred or religious significance. The frequent use of (or merely reference to) singing and dancing and the employment of musical instruments as talisman or magic wand (i.e. as medium for summoning or celebrating, influencing or protecting oneself against or with respect to spirits in nature, including God or the devil) suggests I should think that, somehow, this *is* the sort of thing that music is, at least in part; is, at least in part, what it is for a thing to have a "musical" aspect. Similarly, it is not so much the case perhaps that music may be used as a language which is other than (more elevated than) spoken speech,

but, that music *is* a kind of language which — in some respects at least — seems e.g. more "elevated" than (because more ritualized and therefore more "magical" sounding than?) speech. In the present volume almost all references to folktales in which important parts of a given story or ritual are sung, chanted, or danced (as is usually the custom in North American Indian folk tales, for example) have been excluded, since to include all of these would amount to including most North American Indian folk tales (for example); it should be kept in mind, however, that merely *to* sing or chant or to "dance" a narrative or poetic text is — in making that performance or recital "musical" in this way — to make it "magical", then .

FIDDLERS. *(See also pp.245, 858.)*

§110.12 "THE FIDDLER IN HELL [Russian folktale]. Once there was a peasant who had three sons. He lived richly, gathered two potfuls of money, and buried one pot in the threshing barn and the other under the gate. This peasant died without having told anyone about his money. One day there was a holiday in the village; a fiddler was walking about leisurely, when suddenly he fell through the ground and found himself in hell, at the very spot where the rich peasant was being tormented. 'Good day, my friend,' said the fiddler. The peasant answered: 'You have fallen into the wrong place; this is hell, and I am in hell.' 'But, uncle, why were you sent here?' 'Because of my money. I had a great deal of it, but I never gave to the poor, and buried two pots of it in the ground. Now I will be tormented, struck with sticks, and lacerated with claws.' 'What shall I do? I might be tormented too.' 'Sit

---

169 Karlinger, *ibid.*, 9: "Singing and talking are... two different levels." Talking belongs to "everyday life", whereas singing is associated with "extraordinary situations and circumstances."

on the stove behind the chimney, do not eat for three years: thus you will be saved.'

"The fiddler hid behind the chimney; the devils came and began to beat the rich peasant, saying all the time: 'That's for you, rich man! You hoarded a great deal of money, and you did not know how to hide it; you buried it in such a place that we have a hard time guarding it. There is constant coming and going through the gate, the horses crush our heads with their hooves, and in the threshing barn we are thrashed with flails.'

"As soon as the devils left, the peasant said to the fiddler: 'If you ever get out of here, tell my children to take the money — one pot is buried under the gate and the other in the threshing barn — and tell them to give it to the poor.' Again a whole band of devils came rushing in and asked the rich peasant: 'Why is there a Russian smell here?' The peasant said: 'You have just been in Russia and you have the Russian smell in your nostrils.' 'Impossible!' They began to search, found the fiddler, and cried: 'Ha, ha, ha! A fiddler is here!' They dragged him down from the stove and forced him to play the fiddle. He played for three years but it seemed to him like three days; he got tired and said: 'How strange! Sometimes I played and tore all my strings in one evening, and now I've played for three days, and not one string has broken, blessed be the Lord!' He had no sooner said these words than all his strings snapped. 'Well, brothers,' he said, 'you can see for yourselves, my strings have broken, I have nothing to play on.' 'Just wait,' said one devil, 'I have two sets of strings and I'll bring them to you.' He ran away and came back with some strings; the fiddler took them, tightened them, and again said, 'Blessed be the Lord,' when the two sets of strings snapped. 'No, brothers,' he said, 'I cannot use your strings; I have some of my own at home; if you let me go, I'll bring them here.' The devils refused to let him go. 'You won't come back,' they said. 'If you don't trust me, send one of your num-

ber to escort me.' So the devils chose one of their company to go with the fiddler.

"He came to the village and heard a wedding being celebrated in the last house. 'Let's go to that wedding!' 'Let's!' They went into the house. Everyone recognized the fiddler and asked him: 'Where have you been for three years?" 'I was in the other world.' They regaled themselves, then the devil said to the fiddler: 'We must go now.' The fiddler said: 'Wait a little while; let me play my fiddle and amuse the young couple.' They stayed there until the cocks began to crow; then the devil vanished, and the fiddler said to the rich peasant's sons: 'Your father orders you to take his money: one pot is buried under the gate, and another in the threshing barn; and he said that you should give it all to the poor.' The sons dug up the two pots and began to distribute money to the poor; but the more they gave, the more there was in the pots.

"They put the pots on a crossroads; whoever passed by took out of them as many coins as his hand could clutch, and still the money in them did not decrease. A petition was sent to the tsar, saying that in a certain town there was a winding road about fifty versts long and that a straight road would reduce this distance to about five versts; and the tsar gave orders that a straight bridge be built. A bridge five versts long was erected and this used up all the money contained in the two pots. At that time a maiden gave birth to a son and abandoned him; this boy did not eat or drink for three years, and an angel of God always accompanied him. The boy came to the bridge and said: 'Ah, what a wonderful bridge! May God give the kingdom of heaven to him whose money built it!' The Lord heard that prayer and ordered his angels to release the rich peasant from the darkness of hell." — Afanas'ev, pp.180-182.

§110.13 "THE PEASANT AND HIS THREE SONS [German folklore]. A peasant had three sons. He loved and respected the two older ones, because they were skillful and clever. But the third one often was beaten for his clumsiness and stupidity. [One day a well-dressed gentleman offered each of the lads his choice between gold, silver, or to learn an art. The first two chose gold and silver respectively, which pleased their father tremendously. But the third replied, 'I should like to learn an art!']

" 'You shall be able to transform yourself into whatever you choose,' said the gentleman. 'If you want to be a golden pigeon, just spread your arms and move them as if you wanted to fly. If you want to be a golden fish, throw yourself into the water. And if you want to be a golden hare, run on all fours. If you do so, you will be able to surmount every obstacle!' After these words, the gentleman vanished.

"The boy went on and he met a few men who recruited soldiers for their king, for a war had broken out not long before. As the fellow did not want to go home, he cheerfully went with them. When they approached the enemy, the king suddenly despaired, because he had left at home some important papers. 'I'll give my daughter in marriage to the one who goes and fetches the papers within twenty-four hours; moreover, he will become my sucessor!' said the king.

" 'I shall do it,' said the simpleton. No sooner had he said so than he was running over the fields like a golden hare. He came to a great forest. In order to cross it more quickly, he changed into a pigeon and flew over it. [Then] he heard a woeful squeak, which came from a little mouse that was caught in a trap. 'Let me free, and I shall help you as well!' called the little mouse....

" 'All right!' said the fellow and opened the trap. Then he jumped into the water and swam away. [He came to the palace and the queen gave him the papers.] 'But how did you manage to get here in such a short time?' asked the queen. So the fellow told her of his good luck. And in order to prove his words, he transformed himself into a hare, into a pigeon, and into a fish before the queen. The queen wanted to keep a sign and tore out one of the hare's

golden tufts of fur, one of the pigeon's golden feathers, and one of the fish's golden scales. [She also made him a present of her] handkerchief that was richly embroidered with gold.

"[On his return journey to the king, the simpleton was killed by a robber as he slept by a lake.] The robber took the papers and hurried to the king. The king was very pleased to have the notes, and when the war was successfully finished, he kept his promise and wanted to give the robber his daughter in marriage. The wedding was to take place the following day.

"[Meanwhile the little mouse] found its saviour dead on the shore. It quickly took a flute* out of its wallet and began to play. The fellow opened his eyes, saw his little rescuer, and realized what had happened to him.

" 'Be quick and get ready,' said the little mouse. 'Tomorrow the wedding will be celebrated in the palace. If you hurry, you might be there in time. Here, take this fiddle. If you play it, everyone who hears it must dance.'

"The lad thanked his helper, jumped into the water, and hurried to the king's palace.

"He first went to the kitchen and played the fiddle that the little mouse had given him. Immediately, the cook and all the maids started dancing. The fellow played on and wept bitterly. The queen came to the kitchen and recognized the handkerchief with which the fellow dried his tears. Meanwhile, the king had joined them, and the fellow told them about his bad luck. He related how he had obtained the papers and how a robber had then killed him as he lay asleep by the lake and how this robber was now trying to get his reward as well. The queen asked him to transform himself before them. Then they might believe him. So the fellow transformed himself into a hare and Lo! the tuft that the queen had torn out before fitted exactly, and so did the feather and the scale. Now the king and the queen saw that they had almost given their daughter to an imposter. The robber was captured and hanged, whereas the simpleton married the daughter and became the successor of the king. For many years his subjects lived happily under his government." — Ranke, pp.112-15.

FINNO-UGRIC PRACTICES AND BELIEFS. *(See pp.255, 862.)*

§111.7 "NUM and VAINAMOINEN. [Num was] the sky [and thunder] god of the Samoyeds.[170] The heavens were supreme in Uralian cosmology, the Voguls even believed that their sky god Numitorem sent down animals to the forests and fish to the rivers. No representation of Num was fashioned by the Samoyeds, but a myth tells how he sent birds to explore the watery chaos at the beginning of the world, and made land from the mud that one of them brought back in its beak. In Finnish tradition an eagle flew over the limitless waters, searching for a dry spot to lay its eggs. Suddenly it caught sight of the knee of the sorcerer Vainamoinen [see also **KALEVALA***] protruding above the surface of the water. There the eagle made a nest and laid its egg. When the slumbering sorcerer felt some discomfort in his knee, he stirred, changed the position of his limbs, and inadvertently caused the egg to fall into the water. It broke at once: the yolk became the sun and moon, while the pieces of shell formed the earth and stars.

"Vainamoinen, the archetypal magician of the far North, was the son of Ilmatar, the air goddess. A cultural founder hero, he invented the zither and his playing of this ancient instrument filled the forests with delight. Wild animals grew tame and the turmoil of the elements ceased.

Vainamoinen also led an expedition to find the arcane *sampo,* which seems to have 'ground out' prosperity." — Cotterell, pp.171-172.

§111.8 "OVDA. [Contrasted with myths about the Lapp culture hero Leib-olmai, the literal meaning of which is 'alder man'. Leib-olmai was] the bear man, or bear god, honored by the Lapps: he it was who gave luck to the hunter, preventing injury in the skirmish with the bear. At bear feasts the hunters' faces were sprinkled with extract of alder bark, a ritual in honour of Leib-olmai.

"An unfriendly forest spirit, quite the opposite of the bear god, was Ovda, the assailant of Finnish woodsmen. Ovda wandered in the forest as a naked human being, but its feet were turned backwards. Sometimes it appeared as a man, sometimes as a woman. The method of destruction used by Ovda was ingenious: it enticed people to dance or wrestle, and then tickled or danced them to death."[171] — Cotterell, p.167.

FLUTE. *(See also p.259.)*

§112.13 "The basic meaning of the flute corresponds to erotic or funereal anguish. The complexity of its symbolism derives from the fact that, if, by virtue of its shape, it seems to have a phallic significance, its tone is nevertheless related to inner, feminine intuitive feeling (that is, to the [Jungian] anima).[172] It is also related to the cane and to water." — Cirlot, 110.

§112.14 "**THE KID AND THE FLUTE-PLAYING WOLF.** A kid wandered away

---

170 "A Uralic group of people, related to the Finno-Ugrians, living in the arctic and subarctic regions of Asia." — Jonas Balys, in Leach, ed., *Funk and Wagnalls Standard Dictionary of Folklore, Mythology and Legend,* 969.

171 See also **DANCING TO DEATH (OR INSANITY)***. (Ed.)

172 See Marius Schneider, *El origen musical de los animales-simbolos en la mitologia y la escultura antiguas* (Barcelona, 1946).

from his mother and into the forest, where he soon found himself being stalked by a wolf. He began to run, calling over his shoulder to the wolf: 'I know that I am destined to be your dinner, but before I die I would like you to do me a favor. Please play the flute, so that I may meet my end dancing.' The wolf decided to oblige the kid and began to play a flute, which he just happened to have with him. The sound of his playing attracted the attention of a pack of dogs, however, and when they saw the wolf they began to give chase. As he fled, the wolf called back to the kid: 'Well, it's all my own fault, for I am a butcher by trade, and had no business playing a flutist.' The moral of this fable is: Those whose behavior is not adapted to the particular circumstances in which they find themselves, may discover that they have lost something that seemed to be already within their grasp." -Aesop [Medici], p.117.

§112.15 "THE FISHERMAN WHO PLAYED THE FLUTE. There once was a fisherman who enjoyed playing the flute. One day, he went down to the sea carrying both his nets and his musical instrument. When he reached the shoreline, he sat down on a rock that jutted out over the sea and began to play the flute. He thought that the sweetness of his music would so beguile the fish that they would leap up onto the shore and become stranded. Things did not work out as he had hoped, however. After a long solo performance, he had not landed a single minnow. So he put his flute aside, picked up his nets, and began to fish in the conventional manner. He soon brought in a big haul and—as he

dragged the overflowing nets onto the sand—some of the fish leapt out onto the shore, Seeing them flail about on the ground, the fisherman remarked: 'Oh, what contrary creatures you are. When I played the flute for you, you wouldn't dance. Now that I've stopped playing, you're hopping about.' The moral of this fable is: When faced with adversity, there are those who can only wave their arms and shout—but to no avail." —Aesop [Medici], p.155.

§112.16 "THE CHARM OF THE FLUTE. The flute is often mentioned in history as being used for the purpose of charming animals and the serpent seems to have been peculiarly delighted with its music. It is said that adders will swell at the sound of the flute, raising themselves up, twisting about and keeping proper time.[173] A Spanish writer says that in India he had often seen the Gentiles leading about enchanted serpents, making them dance to the sound of a flute, putting them around their necks, and touching them without harm; and to this day a musical instrument of this nature is used by the snake-charmers of that country. In opposition to this, Hippocrates mentions a man, Nicanor, who fainted whenever he heard the sound of a flute." —Spence [Occultism], p.163.

§112.17 "THE THREE MUSICIANS (German folktale).[174] Once upon a time three musicians left their home and set out on their travels. They had all learnt music from the same master, and they determined to stick together and to seek their

---

173 See our themes T2b (Music has magical effect upon orderly process of nature) and T4b (Music as instrument of enchantment), *Introductory Remarks* Vol I above. In this case the effect of the instrument actually *is* hypnotic etc, however, this type of occurrence has also passed into legend: indeed, it might be said that actual properties or capabilities of music and musical instruments become the *basis* for supposing even more remarkable (i.e. magical) properties and capabilities. (Ed.)

174 Adapted from *Die drei Musikanten* in Ludwig Bechstein, *Das Deutsche Märchenbuch* (Leipzig, 1845).

fortune in foreign lands. They wandered merrily from place to place to play from fairs to festivals and made quite a good living, and were much appreciated by everyone who heard them play. One evening they came to a village where they delighted all the company with their beautiful music. At last they ceased playing, and began to eat and drink and listen to the talk that was going on around them. They heard all the gossip of the place, and many wonderful things were related and discussed. At last the conversation fell on a castle in the neighbourhood, about which many strange and marvelous things were told. One person said that hidden treasure was to be found there; another that the richest food was always to be had there, although the castle was uninhabited; and a third, that an evil spirit dwelt within the walls, so terrible, that anyone who forced his way into the castle came out of it more dead than alive.

"As soon as the three musicians were alone in their bedroom they agreed to go and examine the mysterious castle, and, if possible, to find and carry away the hidden treasure. They determined, too, to make the attempt separately, one after the other, according to age, and they settled that a whole day was to be given to each adventurer in which to try his luck.

"The fiddler* was the first to set out on his adventures, and did so in the best of spirits and full of courage. [Inside the castle the heavy front door shuts and is bolted behind him — though no one can be seen. Full of terror the fiddler wanders throughout the place, upstairs and downstairs, through lofty halls, splendid rooms, and lovely little boudoirs, everything beautifully arranged. But the silence of death reigns everywhere. In the kitchen he finds the most delicious food prepared, and a fire burning, and before he has time to think the fiddler is ushered into a little room by invisible hands, and there a table is spread for him with all the delicious food he had seen cooking in the kitchen.]

"The youth first seized his fiddle and played a beautiful air on it which echoed through the silent halls, and then he fell to and began to eat a hearty meal. Before long, however, the door opened and a tiny man stepped into the room, not more than three feet high, clothed in a dressing-gown, and with a small wrinkled face, and a grey beard which reached down to the silver buckles of his shoes. And the little man sat down beside the fiddler and shared his meal. When they got to the game course the fiddler handed the dwarf a knife and fork, and begged him to help himself first, and then to pass the dish on. The little creature nodded, but helped himself so clumsily that he dropped the piece of meat he had carved on the floor.

"The good-natured fiddler bent down to pick it up, but in the twinkling of an eye the little man had jumped on to his back, and beat him till he was black and blue all over his head and body. At last, when the fiddler was nearly dead, the little wretch left off, and shoved the poor fellow out of the iron gate which he had entered in such good spirits a few hours before. The fresh air revived him a little, and in a short time he was able to stagger with aching limbs back to the inn where his companions were staying. [In the morning in answer to his companions' questions, the fiddler replied:] 'Go there yourselves, and see what's to be seen! It's a ticklist matter, that I can assure you.'

"The second musician, who was a trumpeter*, now made his way to the castle, and everything happened to him exactly as it had to the fiddler. He was just as hospitably entertained at first, and then just as cruelly beaten and belaboured, so that next morning he too lay in his bed like a wounded hare, assuring his friends that everything had gone to a very queer tune in a key that he didn't like at all. Notwithstanding the warning of his companions, the third musician, who played the flute, was still determined to try his luck, and, full of courage and daring, he set out, resolved, if possible, to find and secure the hidden treasure. After all, he was the sharpest.

"[Things transpire as they had before. Then, at table as usual,] the little man let his piece [of game] fall on the ground. The flute-player was good-naturedly just going to pick it up, when he perceived that the little dwarf was in the act of springing on his back. Then he turned round sharply, and, seizing the little creature by his beard, he gave him such a shaking that he tore his beard right out, and the dwarf sank groaning to the ground.

"But as soon as the youth had the beard in his hands he felt so strong that he was fit for anything, and he perceived all sorts of things in the castle that he had not noticed before, but, on the other hand, all strength seemed to have gone from the little man. He whined and pleaded. 'Give me back my beard again. Give it back and I will instruct you in all the magic art that surrounds this castle, and will help you to carry off the hidden treasure, which will make you rich and happy for ever.'

"But the cunning flute-player replied: 'I will give you back your beard, but you must first help me as you have promised to do. TIll you have done so, I won't let your beard out of my hands.'

"[The old man leads the youth through dark secret passages, underground vaults, and grey rocks till at last they come to an open field, and after that a stream of rushing water. Then the little man draws out a wand and touches the waves, whereupon the waves part and the two cross the river with dry feet. The little man leads the youth to a castle far bigger and more splendid than the one they have left, to a room in the middle of which stands a bed hung all round with heavy curtains.]

"Over the bed hung a bird's cage, and the bird inside it was singing beautiful songs into the lonely silence. The little grey man lifted the curtains from the bed and beckoned the youth to approach. On the rich silk cushions embroidered with gold a lovely maiden lay sleeping. She was as beautiful as an angel, with golden hair which fell in curls over her marble shoulders, and a diamond crown sparkled on her forehead. But a sleep as of death held her in its spell, and no noise seemed able to waken the sleeper.

"[She is a mighty Princess, who has lain asleep with a magic sleep for hundreds of years, with only the dwarf to look over her. But now with the loss of his beard the little man has lost his power. He instructs the flute-playing youth what to do.]

" 'Take the bird which hangs over the Princess's head, and which by its song sang her into this enchanted sleep—a song which it has had to continue ever since; take it and kill it, and cut its little heart out and burn it to a powder, and then put it into the Princess's mouth; then she will instantly awaken, and will bestow on you her heart and hand, her kingdom and castle, and all her treasures.'

"[The youth does as he is bid, and the Princess awakens, and looking into the happy youth's face she kisses him tenderly, thanking him for freeing her from the magic sleep. She promises to be his wife. Then a troop of servants, male and female, flock into the apartments where the happy couple sit, and after wishing the Princess and her bridegroom joy, disperse all over the castle to their different occupations.]

"But the little grey dwarf began now to demand his beard again from the youth, for in his wicked heart he was determined to make an end of all their happiness; he knew that if only his beard were once more on his chin, he would be able to do what he liked with them all. But the clever flute-player was quite a match for the little man in cunning, and said: 'All right, you needn't be afraid—you shall get your beard back before we part; but you must allow my bride and me to accompany you a bit on your homeward way.'

"The dwarf could not refuse this request, and so they went together through the beautiful green paths and flowery meadows, and came at last to the river which flowed for miles round the Princess's land and formed the boundary of her kingdom. There was no bridge or ferry-boat to be seen anywhere, and it was impossible to get over to the other side, for the boldest swimmer would not have dared to brave the fierce current and roaring waters. Then the youth said to the dwarf: 'Give me your wand in order that I may part the waves.'

"And the dwarf was forced to do as he was told because the youth still kept his beard from him; but the wicked little creature chuckled with joy and thought to himself: 'The foolish youth will hand me my beard as soon as we have crossed the river, and then my power will return, and I will seize my wand and prevent them both ever returning to their beautiful country.'

"But the dwarf's wicked intentions were doomed to disappointment. The happy youth struck the water with his wand, and the waves at once parted and stood still, and the dwarf went on in front and crossed the stream. No sooner had he done so than the waters closed behind him, and the youth and his lovely bride stood safe on the other side. Then they threw his beard to the old man across the river, but they kept his wand, so that the wicked dwarf could never again enter their kingdom. So the happy couple returned to their castle, and lived there in peace and plenty for ever after. But the other two musicians waited in vain for the return of their companion; and when he never came they said: 'Ah, he's gone to play the flute', till the saying passed into a proverb, and was always said of anyone who set out to per-form a task from which he never returned." —Lang (Green), pp.286-93.

§112.18 RITUALS OF MANHOOD: MALE INITIATION IN PAPUA NEW GUINEA (SAMBIA).[175] "Initiation into male cults entails both secrecy from those who are excluded and the revelation of esoteric knowledge to initiates. The New Guinea cults develop this pattern in characteristic ways. First, because the path to manhood is a gradual process of creation, there is not simply a circle of the initiated into which novices are ritually inducted. Rather, the process typically covers a span of many months, often a number of years, as a boy is made into a man. The revelation of esoteric knowledge, induction into the mysteries, takes place step by step.... It is a graded progression to the manhood that must be created by acts of nurturance, ordeal, purification, and instruction. Initiates learn how to be men, how to protect themselves from dangers of pollution. Learning the exegetic keys to ritual symbolisms becomes (as among the Baktaman [Barth 1975] or Bimin-Kuskusmin [Pole, this volume]), not an end in itself, but a key to understanding—hence to being able to live—a male life. The ultimate revelations of mystery, the unmasking of the deception of sacred flute or bull-roarer*, serve to underline the collective responsibilities, and hence solidarity, of men. One of the striking parallels between men's cults in Amazonia and those in New Guinea is the use of sacred flutes and bull-roarers as symbols of male power (including, of

---

175 See also reference to flute symbolism in New Guinea pp.260, 262-63 above (Ed.)

course, phallic power; see Van Baal 1963 and Dundes 1976, as well as Herdt, this volume). Not only are the cult objects strikingly similar: the uses to which they are put, the threat of gang rape or death to women who see the deception,[176] and the myths in which men gain control of objects first controlled by women (Murphy 1959) show close parallels. The symbology of the cult objects is explored in several of the chapters that follow, most deeply by Herdt for the Sambia." — Keesing (in Herdt), p.9.

"Fetish and Fantasy in Sambia.[177] Central to the ethos of Sambia male initiations are secret bamboo flutes of great and mysterious power. Sambia men come to 'worship' those flutes with an ambivalent mixture of fear and affection. Perhaps we should expect this of a male cult whose ritual instruments personify a compelling need to separate boys from their mothers and reinforce masculine authority traumatically, therefore creating a hierarchy of dominators over underlings. Beyond these political facts, though, there is a paradoxical side of the flutes which is as puzzling with regard to Sambia as it is when found in other New Guinea societies: the conviction that these flutes — paramount symbols of maleness — are animated by an eroticized *female* spirit. Men's ritual attachment to this Janus-faced fetish and its relationship to a culturally constituted fantasy system is the key problem of this chapter....

"K. E. Read's landmark study (1952)... from the very start gave precedence to the sacred nama flutes as a dominant symbol of [the initiatory cult of the Gahuku-Gama tribe of the Eastern Highlands of New Guinea. It showed] how they always appeared in the three grandest pageants of masculine life — initiation rites, pig festivals, and intermittent 'fertility rites'; how they were linked to powerful, male-controlled, mystical spirits; how their sounds were meant to excite men and frighten women; and how, oddly enough, the material shell of a flute was not in itself sacred but was easily replaceable. Read never forgot these aspects of the nama cult, as his writings show (see 1951, 1952, 1954, 1955, 1956)....

"My [own] contention is that the efficacy of Sambia flute symbolism derives simultaneously from subjective meanings based on individual developmental experience and from the flutes' culturally constituted patterns of significance. To explicate this relationship between individual subjectivity and flute-oriented behavior requires concomitant studies of Sambia gender identity and eroticism. There are several reasons for this emphasis on sex and gender. First, the flutes are used as a political weapon vis-à-vis the social suppression and sexual repression of both women and boys. Second, the flutes' secret embodies the greatest of all mysteries of Sambia: the origins and divergence of maleness and femaleness. Third, the Sambia initiatory cult prescribes male homosexual activities

---

176 See also e.g. **INDIAN (SOUTH AMERICAN) MYTHS — PRACTICES AND BELIEFS* — §163.9, Kalapalo Myth and Ritual** (Ed.).
177 This chapter is based on 2-1/2 years of fieldwork, 1974-1976, 1979, funded by a Fulbright scholarship to Australia. The Sambia are a mountain-dwelling hunting and horticultural people who number some 2,000 persons and inhabit one of New Guinea's most rugged terrains. The population is dispersed through narrow river valleys over a widespread, thinly populated rain forest. Marriage is usually by sister exchange or infant bethrothal, although the latter form of prearranged marriage is culturally preferred.

that inform the ritual development cycle of all males. Fourth... Sambia men transmit to initiates a fantasy system concerning the flutes and their sounds, some of whose components are explicitly erotic. The Sambia flutes thus elucidate a pervasive symbolic complex known throughout Papua New Guinea, and one to which I shall later allude: namely, the identification of men with their masculinized ritual cults, flutes, and fantasy female beings....

"A first principle: The flutes are an imaginative and multivalent fetish. They constitute more than a material instrument, a collective representation, or a cultural symbol. The flutes are man-made ritual paraphernalia capable of creative evocative effects that become adored and feared. This religious power, associated with other societal phenomena like kinship affiliation or ethnic identity, we anthropologists know well enough. Nevertheless, there is that other dimension of the Sambia flutes, too: their capacity to ritually excite, to stir erotic interest, or to signify such subjective experiences or their opposite — repression....[178]

"A boy [is thought to have] female contaminants inside of him which not only retard physical development but, if not removed, debilitate him and eventually bring death. His body is male: his tingu contains no blood and will not activate. The achievement of puberty for boys requires semen. Breast milk 'nurtures the boy', and sweet potatoes or other 'female' foods provide 'stomach nourishment', but these substances become only feces, not semen. Women's own bodies internally produce the menarche, the hallmark of reproductive maturity. There is no comparable mechanism active in a boy, nothing that can stimulate his secondary sex traits. Only semen can do that; only men have semen; boys have none. What is left to do, then, except initiate and masculize boys into adulthood?

"*Ritual behavior.* The first sign that a collective initiation is approaching comes in the guise of piercing, melodious cries that appear mysteriously as if from nowhere but that children are told come from old female hamlet spirits (*aatmwog-wambu*). First from within the men's house, later near the emerging ritual cult house, and eventually at the edges of the forest, the haunting sounds demandingly increase in tempo. This signal alerts women of the coming ritual preparations. Boys, whose consternation may turn to curiosity or fear, are comforted or teased (according to the person and situation) with remarks like 'The female spirit wants to get you; she wants to kill and eat you.' Mother or father may smile or laugh or fall silent — responses that underscore the mounting tension that intrudes on the household of a boy whose time has come....

"THE FLUTES. In what follows, our primary interest shall be with ritual behavior focused on the flutes. This behavior encompasses two primary contexts: the penis and flute ceremony (hereafter referred to as the flute ceremony); and the new intitiates' first entrance into the cult house, an event that leads to erotic encounters with the bachelors on the same evening. The ritual significance of the

---

178 See also the present editor's thematic scheme regarding music and mythology in the *Introductory Remarks* (Vol I, above), in particular themes **T2d** (Identification of musical instruments with male and female sex characteristics, i.e. insofar as life cycle is affected. Magical effect of music as guarantor, restorative agent, promoter of fertility), and **T5c** (Identification of music with love, sex, lust, physical release or abandon, etc., e.g. Dionysian attributes). Music and musical instruments are identified equally with the phenomenon of procreation itself *and* with (male, female) instruments for achieving this. (Ed.)

flutes — as symbols and signs — stems from subjective, verbal and nonverbal, and situational dimensions of meaning (cf. Turner 1964) set within the naturalistic flow of the ceremonies. This perspective requires an aside about the flutes as physical objects.

"Sambia have several types of ritual flutes, but they lump them together under the category term *namboolu aambelu* ('frog female'). Each flute is made from newly cut bamboo left open at one end. The hollow tubes vary in length from one to three feet; they also vary in the thickness and species of the bamboo. Two types of flute are blown vertically from the mouth (like a jug pipe); another type is winded horizontally through a blowhole. They are always blown in pairs. Men tell women and children that the flute sounds are the wailful cries of the old female hamlet spirit who figures prominently in folklore. The bullroarer (*duka' yungalu*, 'bird's call'), by contrast, is far less secret than the flutes and is said to produce a sound akin to a powerful but not mystical bird (cf. what Gahuku-Gama and BenaBena say about their flutes; see Langness 1974; Read 1952). Like the various forms of making grass sporrans or like incorporeally owned ritual customs, ritual flutes — both their size and associated tunes — are identified with phratry [kinship group — an exogamous subdivision of the tribe, comprising two or more related clans (Ed.)] membership and political alliance among Sambia hamlets. The flutes are played frequently during all collective initiations; once during a clubhouse ceremony near the end of fourth-stage initiations; and during the funeral ceremonies of young adult men or bachelors only. (This implies that the flutes 'belong' to the bachelors, just as the youths 'belong' to the flutes.)

"The flutes are secretly guarded but played during ritual in pairs. They are hidden from women and children, who are said by the men to fear the sound. Punishment, even possible death, awaits those who might violate this code. (Men casual-

ly discuss this possibility; they take great care to conceal the flutes, and no infractions occurred during my stay.) The bamboo tubes themselves are of little intrinsic importance; they are easily made and discarded following the rituals. They are not stored or saved; they are not rubbed with semen, pig's grease, or blood nor are they stuffed with any material, such as pork (cf. Berndt 1962; Read 1952). The longer flutes are referred to as 'male' (*aatmwul*) and metaphorically as penes. The shorter and thinner flute is called a 'female' (*aambelu*) and is sometimes likened to the glans penis. The pairs of flutes, moreover, are said to be 'married' and are called 'spouses' (*kwolu-ammbelu*).

"*The initiatory events.* At the start of the initiation, boys are taken from their mothers, sometimes forcibly and sometimes not, but always in an atmosphere of great tension. They are placed in the men's house momentarily, and from there on, the boy's ritual sponsors (*nyetyangu*, also 'mother's brother') become their primary guardians until the conclusion of initiation....

"As the novices are led into the forest for the first ritual they leave behind their mothers, women, and playmates....

"On the third day of the intitiation the flutes are revealed, so boys learn of their secret significance; this revelation shall be our focus....

"The day opens with a male 'stretching rite', so called because switches are beaten against the boys to 'open the skin' and foster bodily growth (*perulyapi*). Several hours later the boys' noses are bled, a powerful and traumatic experience, according to the testimony of boys and men alike. Then follows another painful rite in which stinging nettles are employed to 'cleanse' the skin and 'stretch' it. Finally, some four hours later in the afternoon, men assemble the novices for ceremonial dressing and painting in warrior garb. This sets the stage for the flute ceremony; it is later followed by a ceremonial procession back to the dance ground, whereupon the boys enter the cult house for the first time.... As the decorating proceeds, the men quietly begin to make lewd jokes about the boys and their sponsors. The jokes are directed at the lads' emerging homosexual-fellator status. The tempo of jesting reaches a peak at the fastening of the novices new grass sporrans [among Scottish Highlanders, the leather or fur pouch worn at the front of the kilt (Ed.)]. This joking draws on the Sambia view that one's type of grass sporran (of men) or skirt (of women) signals erotic status and role. The attachment of that new sporran thus dramatically distinguishes novices from the category of 'neuter' children to which they formerly belonged....

"Next comes the flute ceremony itself, which begins in military silence as the forty-two novices [at a ceremony which I witnessed] are lined up, decked out in their stunning new attire, and made to await the surprises in store for them.

"Two groups, each composed of four bachelors playing flutes, arrive from the forest. They circle the boys. There is total silence but for their music. The flute players are paired; one man plays a short flute, and another blows a longer flute, their musical chords harmonizing. They continue to play for about five minutes. During this period, Karavundun, a married man, picks up a long bamboo containing a narrower flute within it. He passes down the line of novices, attempting to insert the tip of the smaller, contained flute into their mouths. Approximately half the boys refuse to suck the flute. Karavundun does not press them, and there is no angry scene such as there was at another flute ceremony, when a bachelor, Erujundei, threatened the reluctant boys with a machete. When a novice refuses, Karavundun simply smiles. Indeed, he jokes about those who react with displeasure. Some men nearby openly snigger at the recalcitrant novices. On the other hand, those who take to the act, 'correctly' sucking the flute, are lauded, and the surrounding spectators nod their heads in approval.

"Then, in visible anger at the defiant boys, Kokwai, a bachelor, unexpectedly enters the scene and strikes the novices with a long flute. Another man shouts, 'Hit them hard; it is not like you were fighting them to draw blood!'

"Another instructing elder, Merumei, then repeatedly intimidates the novices by drawing attention to the large assembled crowd of men: 'You uninitiated boys like to make jokes.... Now, make some jokes for the crowd of men here, we want to hear them!' He commands the boys: 'You kwulai'u—open your mouths for the flute, they will place it inside... to try it on you. All of you, look at the large group of men... this large group.... You novices put it [the flute] inside your mouths, try it!'

"The flutes are thus used for teaching about the mechanics of homosexual fellatio, and in the first references to it, the elder draws attention to the physical proof of the elders to verify his words. He does so, however, not by allusion to semen but instead by allusion to the penis...

"The elders now condemn the novices for their childish mimicking of the flute sounds. As they do so, the flute players again strike the boys' chests with the butts of the flutes.

"Mugindanbu begins, saying, 'When you were uninitiated, you all played a game of imitating this sound [i.e. of the flutes], "Um-huh, um-huh". Now tell us, does this sound come from your mouths?'

"Damei demands, 'You boys think fit to imitate the flute sounds, [so] now make this sound, show us how you produce it. Why should we elders show you how to make it!

" 'All of you boys look at this elder. What do you think he has done? Heard the teaching this moment and grown to be big. All of them [the men] 'ate' the penis... and grew big. All of them can copulate with you; all of you can eat penises. If you eat them, you will grow bigger rapidly.'

"The novices are enjoined to secrecy and then told of the fatal consequences of breaking this taboo: 'For if you do [reveal the secrets], they [unspecified] will kill and throw your body into the river. Sambia boys, you will be thrown away into the Sambia River.... Moonagu [phatry] boys, you will be killed and your bodies thrown into the lower Sambia River....'

"Two elders, Damei and Worangri, then spontaneously represent themselves as authorities.... 'We would not trick you. You must all sleep with the men. When you climb trees, your bones will ache. For that reason you must drink semen. Suppose you do not drink semen, you will not be able to climb trees to hunt possum; you will not be able to scale the top of the pandanus trees to gather nuts. You must drink semen... it can "strengthen" your bones.'

"In the next sequence of rhetoric, semen is likened to mother's milk. Boys are taught that they must continually consume it to grow....

"Another man shouts that unless the boys drink semen, they will fail to blow the flutes properly: 'If you do not think of this [fellatio] you will not play the flutes well. A boy who does not sleep with men plays the flute badly, for his mouth is blocked up.... If you sleep with men you shall play the flute well.'

"In the final sequence, the boys' old pubic aprons are dramatically cut with a machete by the elder Mugindanbu. The limp pubic coverings then become the focus of a castration threat aimed at the boys as a deadly warning against adultery. The flutes are played again for several minutes. Merumei then lectures and shouts at the boys: 'When you are grown you cannot become sexually excited over the attractive wife of another man. You can touch your own wife, that is all right. The flute wants to kill you, for if you steal a woman, she will cry out like the flute, and her man will kill you. If you touch another man's wife you will die quickly... they will kill you. We are trying you out now for the time later when you might steal another man's wife. Then we would not just cut your grass sporran. If your penis rises and you want to steal a woman, we will cut it

off.' The elder cuts the old pubic covering midway between the abdomen and the genitals. 'No one will help you, we will cut off your penis and kill you.' By this act, not only is homosexual fellatio enjoined, but premarital heterosexual activities are tabooed and condemned.

"Following the flute ceremony which lasts barely an hour, the boys are carefully lined up for a last inspection prior to their ceremonial parade back to the cult house. The large group of novices and older initiates file down the hillside to the dance ground, preceded by adult men who form phalanxes around the area, separating the boys from the throng of women and children who have assembled for a last view of them. For several minutes, led by a protecting shaman*, the novices are paraded around the decorated grounds. He then conducts them inside the new cult house for the first time....

"A while later something striking occurs, for as the boys entered the great cult house they heard the flutes being played within. The boys are again taunted. 'You can't go inside the moo-angu,' the men say. They shout, 'It's the menstrual hut of women.... women are giving birth to babies.... The babies are crying.' Then another man says, 'Look! an aatmogwambu [female hamlet spirit] is in the ritual house....' The boys are led into the cult sanctuary just the same, and not more than an hour later something even more remarkable happens.

"The novices are seated on the earthen floor of the cult house. It is dusk, and after going through days of initiation, on top of this particularly long and trying day, they look pretty worn out. The women and children outside have by now been chased off. A fire has been built (for the first time), and a smattering of men sit idly beside the hearth near the lads.

"Some bachelors unexpectedly tromp inside, playing flutes. There are two groups of four flute players each, as there were in the earlier flute ceremony, but they are disguised. There is silence again except for the flutes. A man says to the boys, 'An old woman spirit has come... she is cold, she wants to come sit by the fire....' The bachelors then squat to the floor, their hands and faces disguised by bark capes: the youths are impersonating female hamlet spirits. A young man says, 'She is an aat-mogwambu; she has come to cry for you.... Go away! Not good that she swallows her spit for you [a common metaphor for erotic desire]. You must help straighten her out [another common metaphor, this for sucking the bachelors' penis until ejaculation, which "slackens" the penis]...; if you feel sorry for her, you must help her out [an implicit statement that boys should serve as fellators to the bachelors].'

"The men then joke about this squeamishly. The flute plaers hobble around behind the tense boys, playing their flutes beneath their capes. The boys are again struck on their chests with the flutes. They are told not to reveal the flutes' secrets. An elder also comments, 'If you see the flutes in [your] dreams, it means that men will soon come to attack and kill you. You must think about this image....' The bachelors unmask themselves, and the novices are hit on the heads with the flutes, which are then thrown into the hearth fire; the lads are made to stand near the fire, warming themselves and 'strenghtening' their bodies with its heat. The 'formal' ceremony is over, but something else is to follow.'

"[There follows a good deal of outlandish exhibitionism on the part of the bachelors, who expose their naked buttock to the boys, and after that private homosexual intercourse outside on the darkened dance-ground area; all but a handful of novices serve as fellators, not once, but twice and more.]

"*Ritual experience*. The music of the flutes is awesome... It is plausible to assume that a boy comes to perceive the flutes as a real danger to both his mother and himself. This dangerous mystery is no doubt a source of the fearful and fascinating ambivalence of the flutes, which are finally revealed to the boys in the initiation ceremony....

"The flute-oriented behavior involves several interlocking fantasies of enigmatic significance in which the novices' later subjective experience is suspended. The principal drama occurs in the cult house on the evening of the flute ceremony. The flute-playing bachelors – the impersonators – present themselves to the novices as (1) old female hamlet spirits, (2) wailing for the boys, (3) having lots of 'water' (i.e. semen), and, men asserted, (4) if boys felt 'sorry' for those beings, (5) they ought to 'help them out' (i.e., relax the bachelors' penes by acting as their fellators), since, to take the native idiom, (6) the flutes (like helpless infants) are 'crying out for milk' (i.e., semen). This last point apparently concerns how the flute – as a fetish – bonds the flutist bachelor (who blows it) with the novice (who sucks it) and, specifically, links the penetrating penis with the cavity of the mouth. If this fantasy system, with its convoluted ins and outs of flute players and flute suckers, seems as baffling to the reader as it first appeared to me, then reconsider its consequences.

"The ritual behavior, first of all, imaginatively effects an identification between the impersonating bachelors and the female spirits. In the cult-house context, youths are dressing up as spirits. That masquerade is more than simply a metaphoric, 'cultural performance' (Wagner 1972); it is *also* a psychologically exciting disguise, a kind of pseudo-transvestite identity similar to that of female impersonators. Why initiation motivates the impersonation of specifically female cult spirits is not hard to understand, if we bear in mind the primordial traumatic act of maternal detachment and loss.

"Here is a hypothesis. The female hamlet spirits are thinly disguised surrogates for the mothers of boys, who have been 'lost' and left behind. The impersonating flute players thus become their substitutes.

"Remember, though, that it is the bachelors who dramatize and act out the figures of 'wailing spirits'. It is they who demand attention from the displaced boys by objectifying and then transferring back to the novices hostile images of loss and care following maternal separation. The flutes are rueful, then, because their spirits have 'lost their sons'. This is not, however, the most of what bachelors communicate; permeating that sarcastic melody is also an expression of erotic seduction: that the impersonators have 'lots of water'. (Do the speakers mean semen or mother's milk— or is the difference, at that moment, really important?) In other words, semen is contextually equated with breast milk as the bachelors' phallus is equated with the mother's breast. The ritual fantasy tries to transfer boys' attachments to their mothers into homosexual fellatio activities with bachelors.

"The ethnography of the flute ritual confirms that a fantasy isomorphism is created between the flute player and maternal figure and between the flute sucker and infant figure. This intersubjective fantasy postulates some kind of primary-process association linking the child's experience of suckling at his mother's breast with the novice's act of sucking the bachelor's penis. One element of this complex appears to be that the bachelor has a mature glans penis and semen; he can engage in sexual intercourse, whereas the novice cannot.

"At the bedrock of this extraordinary fantasy system, I think, is a piece of deep scripting: the ultimate complementary acts (and relationships, i.e., mother-son, husband-wife) are maternal breast-feeding (see Mead 1949) and fellatio intercourse. In the primordial mood associated with the flutes, one suspects the men are transferring a powerful metacommunication: 'Forget your mother and wanting to be like her; you'll soon have a penis that gives milk like we do.' To what extent is that conviction internalized among boys?

"Now we are in a better position to tease apart the mechanisms by which flute-oriented behavior radically alters the novice's maternal attachment relationship (Bowlby 1969). Culturally, the flute is ritually tendered and registered as a symbolic substitute for the boy's mother. Psychodynamically, in a context of traumatic maternal separation, Sambia ritual attempts to use the flute as a detachable phallus and a substitute for the female breast (cf. Bowlby 1973). The bachelors' impersonation of female hamlet spirits illustrates but one of various attempts to shift the boys' core gender identity (Stoller 1968). The flute-oriented behavior, releasing feelings of helplessness and fear, supplants the mother as the preferred attachment figure by offering the culturally valued penis and homosexual relationships as sensual substitutes for the mother's breast and for the mother as a whole person (cf. Bowlby 1973; Bateson 1972). In behavioral terms, ritual utilizes psychophysiological techniques of 'brainwashing' (Sargent 1957), such as extreme aggressive behavior, to redirect the child's attachment away from the preferred maternal figure and compel it toward male figures.

"Here is, in sum, a partial interpretation of the flutes' initial effects on masculine development. The secret of the flutes becomes an unspoken understanding between a boy and his father vis-à-vis his mother. It also becomes a bond among male peers in opposition to women. With the novice living under threat of castration and death, any heterosexual tendencies are blocked for years, and ritualized homosexuality becomes the royal road to unblocking them. A shame-provoking secret of male development is obviously that masculinization occurs under the hegemony of continual asymmetrical fellatio. Ritual secrecy—defended by the fearful flutes—prevents women from 'knowing' that homosexual relationships transform their fledgling sons into handsome youths (Herdt 1981). It is the flutes that become their other 'mothers' and 'wives'.

"It is likely, however, that the redirection of maternal attachment is never quite successful. Such bonds are, after all, the foundation of character structure; and while they may be modified, the underlying feelings of loss are perhaps handled as much by denial and repression as by anything else. Moreover, homosexual bonds are transient. It is essential to underline this viewpoint, for it helps to account for men's ambivalence towards the flutes and homosexual activity in general. Indeed, it is apparent that death threats are necessary for men to accomplish their task: maternal separation and ritualized masculinization are not actions that boys would themselves initiate....

"[I will propose that] the psychological distancing mechanisms present in Sambia ritual (e.g., female avoidance, secrecy, ritualized homosexuality) imply [a number of fundamental assumptions] about male identity and character structure. In all facets of one's existence, as the flutes reveal, the differences between maleness and femaleness are fetishized, exaggerated, and blown up. This symbol structure suggests that in male erotic life, constant hostility is often needed to create *enough* of a distance, separateness, and dehumanization of women to allow there to occur the *ritually structured* sexual excitement necessary for culturally tempered heterosexuality and the 'reproduction' of a society.

"The flutes provide that symbolic funnel of polarity. Melanesians, however, are not the only ones to have known that, for the magical flute is, after all, a very old human symbol.

"The ancient Greeks, in their own way, also 'worshipped' flutes, and the myth of the creation of their instruments seems timeless. Their maker was Pan* (see Bulfinch 1967), the god of flocks and shepherds, who was fond of music but whom the Greeks nevertheless dreaded by

association with the gloom and loneliness of his dark forests. He desired the beautiful and much-loved nymph Syrinx* and one day intercepted her as she returned from the hunt. Pan attempted to beseech her, but she became afraid:

> She ran away, without stopping to hear his compliments, and he pursued till she came to the bank of the river, where he overtook her, and she had only time to call for help on her friends the water nymphs. Pan threw his arms around what he supposed to be the form of the nymph, and found he embraced only a tuft of reeds! As he breathed a sigh, the air sounded through the reeds, and produced a plaintive melody. The god, charmed with the novelty and with the sweetness of the music, said: 'Thus, then, at least, you shall be mine.' And he took some of the reeds, and placing them together, of unequal lengths, side by side, made an instrument which he called the Syrinx, in honour of the nymph.

From this lovely tale the Greeks identified the origins of their flutes. Is it not oddly disconcerting, though, that among lonely travelers, 'sudden fright without any visible cause was ascribed to Pan, and called a Panic terror' (Bulfinch 1967)?

"Plaintive melody and Panic fear: even the ancient Greeks knew the Janus face of our flutes." — Herdt, pp.46-47, 49-50, 56-64, 66, 76-80, 91-92.

GILGAMESH (Epic of) (Babylonian). *(See also p.330.)*

§125.2 "[Among the stories of the adventures experienced by the hero Gilgamesh and his mighty friend, the wild-man Enkidu, one] relates how Gilgamesh assisted Inanna [goddess identified with the planet Venus] in felling a tree, guarded by a snake, a wind, and an eagle. From the sacred timber they made a magic drum and drumstick, which Gilgamesh accidentally let fall into the nether world. When Enkidu tried to recover them, he forgot to observe the special instructions given for his protection, and was trapped forever. Out of a hole, opened in the ground by Ea, the spirit of the dead hero issued 'like a puff of wind', and described 'the house of dust', where princes were servants and earthly rank offered no protection at all." – Cotterell, p.29.

The incident is also mentioned in G. S. Kirk, *Myth: Its Meaning and Functions in Ancient and Other Cultures:* "Inanna has found a tree floating in the Euphrates and plants it in her garden; enemies interfere with it (the *Imdugud*-bird nests at the top, a snake at its foot, and the vampire Lilith in the middle); Gilgamesh comes to the rescue, and in gratitude Inanna gives him a *pukku* and *mikku*, evidently a drum and drumstick with cultic or ritual meaning, that she had made out of her tree. Unfortunately Gilgamesh somehow lets these objects fall into the underworld. Enkidu offers to retrieve them, goes down to the nether world, and behaves so obstreperously there (in spite of Gilgamesh's warnings to the contrary) that Ereshkigal, queen of the dead, keeps him for good. In short, he dies. Gilgamesh, distraught, cannot win back his friend, but is granted a temporary visit from his spirit. Enkidu, or rather his ghost – and the comparison with the ghost of Patroclus in the twenty-third *Iliad* is, indeed, almost irresistible – gives a hair-raising account of conditions down below: vermin devour his body, and his fate is compared unfavourably, it seems, with that of those who have many sons to render them funerary offerings." – Kirk [Myth], p.108.

GONG. *(See also p.332.)*

§128.3 "Principal musical instrument of Asia, with religious and magical uses similar to those of bells* in the West; sounded to accompany religious ceremonies, to drive away evil spirits or to expel the demons of disease; drinking from one after taking an oath gives the oath a binding significance; gongs are male or female according to tone, and are sometimes given individual names." – Cavendish [Man, Myth and Magic], p.1135.

GREEK FOLKTALES.

§129A.1 **THE BLESSING INCARNATE.** In a story called "The Blessing Incarnate", the playing on a pipe* causes a castle to move – recalling other magical musical phenomena such as the destruction of the wall at Jericho; see also Thompson motifs D1224 (Magic pipe) and D2140 (Magic control of elements), **FOLKLORE AND FOLKTALES – TYPOLOGY***, pp.282, 290, above.

The relevant portion of this story is the following:

"The Blessing Incarnate.... So the king called for the vizier and ordered him that at once and without any delay and at his own expense everything must be provided for which the prince had asked. And the vizier, willy nilly and whether he had the money or hadn't – anyhow [he did as he was told]. And the prince took [the dresses for the princesses, and the ladder which had been provided,] and went to the castle and gave them to the princesses. The princesses... gave him the pipe for which he had asked, and when he was a long way off the castle he blew upon it, and the castle began to shake and to move and to go forward of itself at the sound of the pipe....

"When the castle began to shift and to move, the prince ran forward quickly to the king and asked him where he should bring the castle to a stop, the castle which had in it the Fair One of the World. And the king ordered him to bring it to a stop close to his palace. When the castle came to a stop, the king asked to go up into it, that he might see the Fair One of the World. But she refused to receive him [etc]." — Dawkins (More Greek Folktales), p.67.

"THE SIMPLETON BROTHER, OR THE INCENSE AND THE MAGIC PIPE.

Stories of a pair of brothers or of a family of brothers of which the youngest is a sort of clever buffoon are common enough everywhere, and there is no lack of them in Greece. Most of what is needed has been said by Halliday in his notes on *The mad brother*. Yet it is worth while to give an example of a rather special type of this story, of which I find four full examples: from Chios, Thrace, Epeiros, and Zákynthos; I have translated the version from Thrace. The special feature of this form of the story is that the fool brother, after being the death of his mother and doing a good deal more mischief, finds a great quantity of incense. This he takes, generally up a mountain, apparently to be nearer to God, and there offers it. He is rewarded by the gift of a magic pipe* to the sound of which everyone must dance,[179] and by this he makes his living. There is a version from Kárpathos, which has all the other episodes but not that of the incense, and a Cappadocian story from Malakopf has most of the story. Two other versions from Cappadocia, from Araván and Delmesó, are rather different; they begin with the two brothers dividing their animals according to whether they go into the old or the new stable: the clever brother knew that they would go into the stable to which they are accustomed. On the pipe to which everyone must dance a note is hardly needed; the reference in Stith Thompson's *Motif-Index*, D1415, may be consulted.[180] In conclusion., all these stories are often dished up with a certain amount of the scatological buffoonery fortunately rare in Greek stories.

"The Simpleton Brother, or The Incense and the Magic Pipe. Once upon a time there were three brothers and they had an old mother; also hens and an ox. The elder brothers worked hard and looked after their mother. One day they left their youngest brother, who was a simpleton, to look after their mother and to feed the fowls; to feed the ox too.

"The youngest brother fetched water for the fowls; as they drank they threw up their heads. Then said he: 'Don't be mocking God, you fowls.' The fowls went on drinking with their heads held high: 'Don't be mocking God, you fowls,' and he took up a stick and killed them. The ox was chewing, and the simpleton asked it for some mastich gum for himself to chew. Once he said it and twice he said it: 'Give me some mastich gum; mastich, mastich.' The third time he killed the ox and put its head on the pitchfork and set it up in the sheep-fold. Then he put water in the kettle and boiled it and gave his mother a wash, scalding her with the boiling water; so she died. Then he changed her clothes and combed her hair and set her up in the corner. He boiled an egg and peeled it and set it in her mouth; in front of her he put her distaff and her spindle, for her to spin wool.

"In the evening his brothers came and asked him where the fowls were. 'There they are: they mocked at God and I killed them.' 'Where is the ox?' 'He was chewing mastich; I asked him for some. "Give me some mastich." He wouldn't, and I killed him.' Then he showed them the ox's head, stuck on the pitchfork. 'Where is our

---

179 See also DANCING TO DEATH (OR INSANITY)*. (Ed.)

180 In fact D1415.2.4 (Magic pipe causes dancing); see FOLKLORE AND FOLK-TALES — TYPOLOGY*, p.285 above. (Ed.)

mother?' 'She is sitting in the house. I gave her a wash and combed her hair and put her to sit in the corner; I gave her her distaff and spindle to spin; then I boiled an egg and set in in her mouth.' The brothers went to find their mother and saw her there dead. They began to lament and left the house crying. The simpleton shouted out: 'Where are you going?' 'You shut the door and come with us.'

"The simpleton tore up the door and set it on his back. They went on and on and came to a high tree; they climbed up it to pass the night there. The simpleton too climbed up, carrying the door. In the morning the elder brothers went away; the simpleton stayed there up in the tree. In the evening the king came there with all his men; they sat there to rest and eat some bread. The simpleton up in the tree was hungry and from the bottle he had he rained a little water down on them to make the king go away. When he saw that the king did not move, he began to drum on the door with his feet as if it were thundering. The king was alarmed and with all his people went off; leaving behind them the food and the cauldrons. The simpleton climbed down and ate and ate. Then he found a sack of incense and this he burned to the honour of God. The angel of God descended and asked him: 'What reward would you choose to have for the good deed you have done me?' Then the simpleton asked for a pipe for him to play on, and all trees and all beasts and all men should dance to its music: with that pipe he made his living. God gave it to him because he had a simple soul." — Dawkins (Greek Folktales), pp.396-68.

"THE SUN RISES IN THE WEST [Six versions of this tale have appeared, from Smyrna, Thera, Chios, Mytilene, Macedonia, and Symi.]

"There was once a boy skilled in playing the flute*, and one day a snake heard him and was so much delighted that he gave him a present of money; and this several times. Finally the snake told the boy that

when he died he must bury him in his garden, and from the body would spring up a wonderful tree, a tree which, just as the snake, of which it was in a way an embodiment, changed its skin, in the same way would every year change its leaves. We may note that deciduous trees are not as common in the Levant as they are with us. The man could then challenge visitors to say what the tree was called: in one version we are told that it was a snake-cypress. With Greek self-confidence they would make their bets freely, and they would all get the name wrong, and by this kind of bet the man would make a lot of money. So he became very rich.

"But one day there came a cunning rascal, generally a Jew, and induced either his wife or his servant to betray the secret; so the man lost his bet and became very poor. In the Symi version, this part of the story is not well told; the man's fortune was money given him by the snake, and he lost it, not by betting on what he thought was a certainty but by ordinary card-playing.

"In the second part of the story we hear how he got his money back again. He went off to implore the help of the sun, and, just as he had become rich by betting, the sun told him he could regain his wealth by another bet; though bold it should be a certainty. For to help him the sun said that he would on the next day rise not in the east but in the west; on so incredible a happening the man would be able to place any bet he liked and so could regain his money. The Jew came again and in mockery accepted the new bet and so all was well again. In my *Leographía* paper I have suggested that a better title for the story would be *The two Bets*, or perhaps *The Biter bit*.

"So far we have a plain and neatly constructed story, but two variants, [those from Macedonia and Symi], present an interesting addition which we shall see has been grafted on to it from quite a different story. We are told that when the man was on his way to find the sun he met several characters, all of whom were in some sort of trouble and begged him to find out from the sun what they should do to find relief. In the Macedonian version, he met an apple-tree whose crop always failed, and a river the waters of which were sucked away into the ground. In the Symi story, he met a girl and her sister who could not find husbands, a fig-tree whose figs were always wormy, and two mountains tormented by perpetually clashing one against the other. This incident of the people asking for help belongs properly and regularly to the quite different story of the man who went out in search for his Luck, of which a version from Kos has been printed in *Forty-five Stories*, No. 35, with a long discussion on Luck and Fate as they appear in Greek stories. As we have in both stories a man in search of a remedy for his troubles, it was quite natural to graft this bit of the Luck story into the story of the Two Bets: in the search episode the two were running parallel....

"It has been suggested to me that the boy charming the snake by the music of his flute is very Indian in style.[181]

"From *The Sun Rises in the West* (Version A – from Thera). There once was a lazy fellow who spent his time playing the flute: he was so lazy that he lay down on his face when he played it. As he was playing in this way he noticed a snake, and the snake was so much pleased with the music that it brought him a hundred francs as a present. When he brought this money home to his wife, she asked him: 'And where did you steal it?' He answered: 'You just take the money and don't be uneasy.' Then again he went off and played the flute, and once more the snake gave him a hundred francs.

When for the third time he went to the same place and played, the snake said: 'I am sick and my end has come. You must dig here and you will find my body. And when you have found me, take me and bury me in your garden.' This the flute-player did, and in the place where he buried the snake there grew up a beautiful tree, which bore (according to his wish) fruit of two kinds, quinces and oranges....

"From *The Sun Rises in the West* (Version B – from Symi), Once upon a time there lived a fisherman with his wife and his son. One morning as the fisherman was getting ready his gear to go fishing, his wife said to him: 'Won't you take our son with you? All day he sits playing in the sun and I can do nothing with him.' 'I will,' said the fisherman, and went off with the boy.

"Before they got to the sea the boy stopped by a half-ruined tower which was by the path, and cut a reed and made a flute and began playing on it. 'I don't want to go with you, father,' said he to the fisherman. 'I'll stop here and play my flute and when you have done fishing come and take me home with you.' The fisherman had a very great weakness for his son and never opposed him, and so the boy went on playing all sorts of tunes on his flute. Some time went by, and suddenly out from a stone in the ruined tower there came a little snake with golden scales; it raised its head and began to dance to the music of the flute. For some time it went on dancing, and finally left the boy a gold coin and hid itself again in the wall. The boy picked up the coin; he was surprised by it, for he had never seen anything so bright; as bright as lightning. But his father, when he

---

181 See Thompson motifs D1223.1 (Magic flute) and D1442.13 (Magic musical instrument tames animals) – FOLKLORE AND FOLKTALES – TYPOLOGY*. We may also note symbolic (sexual and fertility etc) associations between snake and flute. The playing of the flute brings prosperity; in this respect, these folktales of a "civilized" country such as Greece also bear a close relation to the beliefs and fancies (mythologies) of "primitive" people who play on instruments (e.g. flute and drum) in order to win divine attention and favor and so encourage the general health and a good harvest. (Ed.)

came back with a few fish, could not believe his eyes. When they were back in the village they went to the best shop there and with the gold piece bought all sorts of fine things. 'God has had pity on us and has worked His wonders,' said the wife when she had heard the story. 'You must go to the same place tomorrow and again play your flute.'

"And this is what in fact he did. Every day the boy used to go to the ruined wall and play his flute, and when the snake had done dancing, it used to give him a gold coin.

"The years went by and gradually the fisherman's family became rich. They built a fine house and had servants, and when the boy grew up they bethrothed him to the most beautiful young lady of family in the village. The marriage soon took place with great rejoicing and festivities. But what with the preparations for the wedding and all the feasting, the boy never had time to go to visit his friend the snake and to play the flute to him. However, as soon as he was quiet again he took his wife and they went to the ruined tower. He sat down with her by the broken wall and began to play on his flute. He played and played but to no purpose: the snake did not show himself. Very much vexed, the boy took a pck-axe and began to break down the old wall. When he had broken it down he found that under the foundation there was an enormous cauldron full of gold coins, and above it there was the snake dead. He wept for the snake as if for his most loved friend and buried it in the garden of his house. With the money, which he conveyed to his house by night

so that no one should see him, he bought more fields and became the richest man in the village and in all the neighborhood. So he and his wife and their children, who had very soon been born, lived a life of great happiness...." — Dawkins (More Greek Folktales), pp.77-79, 81-82.

HARMONY (HARMONIA) OF THE SPHERES. (See also p.337.)

§136.6 See ETHOS (Greek)*.
MUSIC — SYMBOLISM*.

§136.7 "Music of the Spheres. Concept introduced by Pythagoras, who related the mathematical relationship between tones on the musical scale to the orbits of the planetary spheres. The symbolic links between celestial bodies and music also interested such Renaissance mystics as Marsilio Ficino, who sought to correlate the different stars and constellations with musical tones." — Drury, p.186.

§136.8 Music of the Spheres — from R. Murray Schafer, *The Tuning of the World* (1977).
"There are two basic ideas of what music is or ought to be. They may be seen most clearly in two Greek myths dealing with the origin of music. Pindar's twelfth Pythian Ode tells how the art of aulos* playing was invented by Athena* when, after the beheading of Medusa, she was touched by the heart-rending cries of Medusa's sisters and created a special *nomos** in their honor. In a Homeric hymn to Hermes* an alternative origin is mentioned. The lyre* is said to have been in-

vented by Hermes when he surmised that the shell of the turtle, if used as a body of resonance, could produce sound.[182]

"In the first of these myths music arises as subjective emotion; in the second it arises with the discovery of sonic properties in the materials of the universe. These are the cornerstones on which all subsequent theories of music are founded. Characteristically the lyre is the instrument of Apollo*, the aulos that of Dionysian* festivals. In the Dionysian myth, music is conceived as internal sound breaking forth from the human breast; in the Apollonian it is external sound, God-sent to remind us of the harmony of the universe.[183] In the Apollonian view music is exact, serene, mathematical, associated with transcendental visions of Utopia and the Harmony of the Spheres. It is also the *anahata* of Indian* theorists. It is the basis of Pythagoras*'s speculations and those of the medieval theoreticians (where music was taught as a subject of the quadrivium, along with arithmetic, geometry and astronomy), as well as of Schoenberg's twelve-note method of composition. Its methods of exposition are number theories. It seeks to harmonize the world through acoustic design. In the Dionysian view music is irrational and subjective. It employs expressive devices: tempo fluctuations, dynamic shadings, tonal color-

ings. It is the music of the operatic stage, of *bel canto,* and its reedy voice can also be heard in Bach's Passions. Above all, it is the musical expression of the romantic artist, prevailing throughout the nineteenth century and on into the expressionism of the twentieth century. It also directs the training of the musician today....

"Ears and Clairaudience. We will not argue for the priority of the ear. In the West the ear gave way to the eye as the most important gatherer of information about the time of the Renaissance, with the development of the printing press and perspective painting. One of the most evident testaments of this change is the way in which we have come to imagine God. It was not until the Renaissance that God became portraiture. Previously he had been conceived as sound or vibration. In the Zoroastrian* religion, the priest Srosh (representing the genius of hearing) stands between man and the pantheon of the gods, listening to the divine messages, which he transmits to humanity. *Sama* is the Sufi word for audition or listening. The followers of Jalal-ud-din Rumi worked themselves into a mystic trance by chanting and whirling in slow gyrations. Their dance is thought by some scholars to have represented the solar system, recalling also the deep-rooted mystical belief in an ex-

---

182 An Egyptian version is mentioned in Allen, *Philosophies of Music History* (1962), p.53 (Stafford, after Apollodorus): "The Nile having overflowed its banks, [among] the dead animals left on the shores [was] a tortoise.... Mercury, walking along the shore of the river, happened to strike his foot against this shell, and was so pleased with the sound produced that the idea of the lyre suggested itself to his imagination." See also **ORIGINS OF MUSIC***. (Ed.)

183 See our theme T1c (Music sent [to man, animals] as gift of the gods or heavenly beings; music as invention of the gods), *Introductory Remarks,* Vol I above. (Ed.)

traterrestrial music, a Music of the Spheres, which the attuned soul may at times hear.[184] But these exceptional powers of hearing, what I have called clairaudience, were not attained effortlessly. The poet Saadi says in one of his lyric poems:

I will not say, my brothers, what *sama* is
Before I know who the listener is.

"Before the days of writing, in the days of prophets and epics, the sense of hearing was more vital than the sense of sight. The word of God, the history of the tribe and all other important information was heard, not seen. In parts of the world, the aural sense still tends to predominate....

"*The Music Beyond*. Before man, before the invention of the ear, only the gods heard sounds. Music was then perfect. In both East and West arcane accounts hint at these times. In the *Sangita-makaranda* we learn that there are two forms of sound, the *anahata*, 'unstruck', and the *ahata*, 'struck', the first being a vibration of ether, which cannot be perceived by men but is the basis of all manifestation. 'It forms permanent numerical patterns which are the basis of the world's existence.'

"This is identical with the Western concept of the Music of the Spheres, that is, music as rational order, which goes back to the Greeks, particularly to the school of Pythagoras. Having discovered the mathematical correspondence between the ratios of the harmonics in a sounding string, and noting that the planets and stars also appeared to move with perfect regularity, Pythagoras united discovery with intuition and conjectured that the

two types of motion were both expressions of a perfect universal law, binding music and mathematics. Pythagoras is reported to have been able to hear the celestial music, though none of his disciples was able to do so. But the intuition persisted. Boethius (AD 480-524) also believed in the Music of the Spheres.

How indeed could the swift mechanism of the sky move silently in its course? And although this sound does not reach our ears (as must for many reasons be the case), the extremely rapid motion of such great bodies could not be altogether without sound, especially since the courses of the stars are joined together by such mutual adaptation that nothing more equally compacted or united could be imagined. For some are borne higher and others lower, and all are revolved with a just impulse, and from their different inequalities an established order of their courses may be deduced. For this reason an established order of modulation cannot be lacking in this celestial revolution.

"If one knew the mass and velocity of a spinning object, it would be possible theoretically to calculate its fundamental pitch. Johannes Kepler, who also believed in a perfect system binding music and astronomy, calculated the following pitches for each of the planets.

---

184 See also Hindu **SHIVA***, dancing the universe into being, and our theme T2 (Music identifies individuals and a people collectively with the physical and spiritual universe, or cosmos. Music [and/or dance] invokes or induces the world or cosmos itself *into being*. The laws [structure] of music parallel the laws [structure] of nature or the universe, e.g. those having to do with the relation of heavenly bodies or other natural components to each other, or with the conduct of such bodies or components with respect to each other) — *Introductory Remarks*, Vol I above. (Ed.)

In Kepler's notation, the pitches looked like this:

In modern notation, like this:

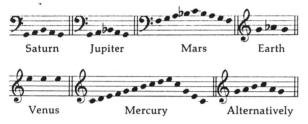

"The Music of the Spheres represents eternal perfection. If we do not hear it, it is because we are imperfect. Shakespeare puts it eloquently in *The Merchant of Venice* (V, i).

> Look, how the floor of heaven
> Is thick inlaid with patines of bright gold:
> There's not the smallest orb which thou behold'st
> But in his motion like an angel sings....
> Such harmony is in immortal souls;
> But whilst this muddy vesture of decay
> Doth grossly close it in, we cannot hear it.

"But our imperfection is not merely moral; it is physical also. For man, the perfectly pure and mathematically defined sound exists as a theoretical concept only. The French mathematician Fourier knew and stated this when he was developing his theory of harmonic analysis. Distortion results the moment a sound is produced for the sounding object first has to overcome its own inertia to be set in motion, and in doing this little imperfections creep into the transmitted sound. The same thing is true of our ears. For the ear to begin vibrating, it too has first to overcome its own inertia, and accordingly it too introduces more distortions.

"All the sounds we hear are imperfect. For a sound to be totally free of onset distortion, it would have to have been initiated before our lifetime. If it were also continued after our death so that we knew no interruption in it, then we could comprehend it as being perfect. But a sound initiated before our birth, continued unabated and unchanging throughout our lifetime and extended beyond our death, would be perceived by us as — *silence*.

"This is why... all research into sound must conclude with silence — not the silence of negative vacuum, but the positive silence of perfection and fulfillment. Thus, just as man strives for perfection, all sound aspires to the condition of silence, to the eternal life of the Music of the Spheres.

"Can silence be heard? Yes, if we could extend our consciousness outward to the universe and to eternity, we could hear silence. Through the practice of contemplation, little by little, the muscles and the mind relax and the whole body opens out to become an ear. When the Indian yogi attains a state of liberation from the senses, he hears the *anahata*, the 'unstruck' sound. Then perfection is achieved. The secret hieroglyph of the Universe is revealed. Number becomes audible and flows down filling the receiver with tones and light." — Schafer, pp.6, 10-11, 260-62.

§136.9 Selections from *Music of the Spheres and the Dance of Death: Studies in Musical Iconology* by Kathi Meyer-Baer (1971):

"The ideas of the musical cosmos and the angel* orders were woven into all the beliefs of the [post-Hellenic, post-Biblical] period, into Jewish, Pagan, and Christian thought; and the first five or six centuries of the Christian era saw the crystallization of systematic concepts in both fields, concepts which were to influence thought and art throughout the Middle Ages and beyond. The orders of angels were further elaborated by authors of different creeds, and the Christian version [of the nine orders of angels] was finally, in effect, codified in Dionysius's treatise, *The Celestial Hierarchy*. The idea of music in the cosmos underwent more or less parallel development, particularly by pagan authors, which may be said to have culminated in Martianus Capella's encyclopedic *De Nuptiis Philologiae et Mercurii et de Septem Artibus Liberalibus Libri Novem.*

"Non-Christian Theories. The *Talmud* celebrated classes of angels praising the Lord, and it, too, began by citing nine castes.[185] Among their names only 'cherubim' and 'seraphim' are used later in Dionysius the Areopagite's definitive hierarchy. Their number in the *Talmud* is a thousand times a thousand, alternately ten thousand times ten thousand, and later ninety thousand myriads. In one place it is said that the angels sing during the night only, to replace the Jewish community, which sings during the day. The *Talmud*'s angels understand and know only Hebrew. Seven spirits appear before the throne of the Lord, and there are seven heavens. The singing angels are located in the fifth heaven, Maon, and their choir is composed of 694 myriads of singers.[186] Here they sing 'from the rising sun till night "the name of His beautiful realm be praised," they answer each other and alternate in the hymns of praise.'

"One important feature of the *Talmud*'s account is the description of paradise. This is located in the heaven Arabo, the highest of the seven and the abode of Mechiza. Here stands the figure of the Lord, attended by the Just Ones and by angels, who are not identical with the blessed. There are two kinds of angels: the eternal ones, who are archangels, and those born anew every day out of a stream of fire[187] which is part of the Empyreum. The angels sing hymns of praise, the Just Ones perform a dance in which the Lord takes part; but the Just Ones also vie with the angels in singing the praise of the Lord. The angels and the Just Ones form concentric circles, an arrangement which recurs later in maps of the universe in the early manuscripts that show musician angels, as well as in Dante's *Paradise*. The red-colored angels of many later paintings are the fiery seraphim.

"The pagan authors of the early Christian era elaborated the idea of music in the cosmos. Poseidonius, Plotinus, and his followers Proclus and Porphyrius emphasized the connection between the Muses* and the spheres. The Muses sing while turning the spheres, and their song *is* the harmony of the universe. Whereas in Plato's *Republic* the sirens replaced the nine Muses, two Neoplatonic writers, Proclus and Lucian (second century), had the sirens sing in the island of bliss, Elysium, which has been transferred to the stars, while the souls of the blessed dance and sing, in an image similar to that in the poem about Jambulus. Porphyrius identified the society of Apollo* and the Muses with the harmony of the world. There are similar descriptions (omitting Apollo) by Chalcidius, Macrobius, Claudianus Mamertius, Fulgentius, and, last but not least, Martianus Capella, whose *De Nuptiis* will be analyszed in detail later. Jamblicus (fourth century) also described the dance of the blessed on an island. That the Muses move the nine spheres was mentioned by

---

185 Earlier versions of the *Talmud* mention three or seven classes of angels.
186 This number seems to have no symbolic explanation; the Revelation of Saint John tells of 144, that is, 12 x 12 singers.
187 Kohut, *Über die jüdische Angelologie*, p.9; his sources are Enoch and Midrasch Rabba.

Claudianus, Macrobius (fourth century), and Simplicius (sixth century), though Zeus (*Jovis custos*) is the moving force in the commentary to *Timaeus* by Chalcidius. The idea that each Muse corresponds to one sphere and to one musical tone, and that the harmony results from their music, was outlined by Sidonius Apollinaris, and again by Martianus Capella. From the Persian orbit there is the *Apocalypse* of Arda Viraf, where the soul travels through seven heavens; and Mani, the reformer of the *Avesta*, who is the link between Persian and Roman beliefs and one-time teacher of Saint Augustine, told of three heavens through which the soul had to pass.[188]

"One further idea found in these writings bears noting: the concept of the duality of gods or forces in the cosmos. This idea is not in itself directly related to music, but there is an analogy between this duality and the interplay of the macrocosmos and the microcosmos in the human soul, and hence a link to music as a means for establishing the harmonious correspondence of both. The important work in this context is the *Asclepius* attributed to Apuleius, a book based on the *Logia Chaldea*, which remained influential as late as the thirteenth century. Musical harmony was regarded as a simile for the harmony of soul with the universe by Plotinus, and this view was also expounded in detail by Saint Augustine in the sixth book of his *De Musica*. It was this relationship that Boethius (early sixth century) called *musica humana*. The validity of this correspondence is the basis for the double meaning of the term 'motion', used in music as well as for emotions in the human soul...."

"*Martianus Capella.* Pagan images of music in the cosmos were systematically articulated in Martianus Capella's long poem or treatise *De Nuptiis Philologiae et Mercurii et de Septem Artibus Liberalibus Libri Novem*. It was written about 500 in North Africa, supposedly as a textbook for his son. The book was widely read, as evidenced by numerous surviving manuscripts and frequent references to it, and was republished many times, well into the eighteenth century.

"*De Nuptiis* is cast as one of the tales of travel through the spheres that were popular in the first centuries BC and AD; it is also essentially a *summa* of all the pagan allegorical figures related to the arts. It is not a complete theory, but Capella succeeded in demonstrating the relationships and connections of these figures in a story which recounts Mercury's courtship of and marriage to Philologia. The couple travels up through the spheres, to the castle of Zeus, where the wedding takes place. As a wedding present, Zeus gives them the seven liberal arts. The story follows the journey through the heavens, which are identified with the gods of the planets. The guides on the trip are the Muses, who, for the first time, have individual character. They turn the spheres and make them emit different sounds. Urania, the leader, spins the outermost sphere of fixed stars, which revolves the fastest and has the highest pitch. Then come the other Muses and their spheres, in descending order:

URANIA	FIXED STARS
POLYHYMNIA	SATURN
EUTERPE	JUPITER
ERATO	MARS
MELPOMENE	SUN
TERPISCHORE	VENUS
CALLIOPE	MERCURY[189]
CLIO	MOON
THALIA	EARTH

---

188 Saint Augustine, *Contra Manichaeos*, *Patrol. lat.* 34, 219; s.a. *Patrol. lat.* 42; J. Lebreton, *Histoire de l'église* (1935).

189 (Capella calls this sphere Cyllenium)

Thalia is left to guard the vegegation, for the earth's sphere does not rotate and does not give a sound. It might be noted that nothing is said in this context about the distances between the planets.

"In the chapter on arithmetic, one of the liberal arts, ratios are explained by using the example of musical intervals; and though the connection with the spheres is not made here, the report of the journey relates the space between the spheres to musical intervals: the greater the interval, the wider the distance, the more fatiguing the journey. The consonance of the music is said to be perfect. The sphere of Jupiter follows the Doric scale and has the brightest light. It is called *pyrois*, the fiery one, or, in Latin, the Empyreum. During the procession and the ceremony, in Jupiter's castle at the sacred wedding, the chorus of the Muses sings with sweet sound. Their song is accompanied by various instruments — trumpets*, flutes*, and the organ*. This music is said to blend in perfect harmony, because the song follows the rules of the sacred numbers. In the castle, Philologia is dazzled by the shining light of seven candles. In addition to the chorus of the Muses, the bride is welcomed by the heroes, the 'rulers of the elements, the most beautiful multitude of angels...' and the souls of the blessed elders: Linus, Homer, Mantuanus (Virgil), Orpheus, and many of the philosophers. The story ends with a kind of prophecy: whosoever proceeds to the Empyreum will experience metaphysical bliss.

"Martianus, then, speaks of two perfect harmonies: one is the harmony of the spheres, and the other is the dulcet chorus of the Muses. The order of the Muses cor-responds to the order of the spheres, the liberal arts to the Muses. The harmonies are based on the order of the sacred numbers. It should also be noted that some of Capella's allegories were influenced by Christian ideology. The Empyreum was not known to pagan mythology as the highest heaven. Also, Capella has the angels, the elders, and the multitude — all inhabitants of the heaven of John's Revelation — living in complete harmony with the heroes of the Olympic heaven.

"Capella blended his parallel elements into a charming vision, into a cosmos where all work in harmony. He does not say whether the perfect harmonies of the spheres and of the Muses' song are the same. By touching on motifs only, he offers a solution that combines all the allegorical parallels. Yet he circumvents the problem of specifically identifying the nine Muses and the eight spheres and the seven liberal arts with exact musical intervals. Perhaps this is precisely the reason why his book was so influential.

"*The Church Fathers.* The writings of the Church Fathers reflect all the traditions mentioned so far: the sounding cosmos of pagan ideology, the manifold structure of the heavens from the Neoplatonists and the Gnostics, and the hosts and choirs of singing angels and the blessed from the Bible. Saint Ambrose,[190] quoting Origen, stated that through the motion of the stars, a marvelous sweet harmony is established and that Plato was its discoverer. Saint Augustine[191] noted that the cosmos 'in spiritual and intellectual vision' is composed of seven, eight, nine, or ten heavens. Clement of Alexandria[192] described the

---

190 Ambrose, *De Abraham, Patrol. lat.* 14, 480; Ambrose, *Enarrat. in XII psalmis Davidicis, Patrol. lat.* 14, 922.

191 *De Genesi, Patrol. lat.* 34, *cap.* 29.

192 Clement, *Eclogae prophetarum*, as quoted by Bousset, *'Die Himmelsreise'*, p.148; *Neutestamentliche Apokryphen*, p.424.

journey of the soul through seven heavens which represent steps of purification in a way similar to that recounted in the apocryphal *Apocalypse* of Abraham.[193] In Clement we find, too, reference to the apocryphal Acts of Saint John, which contained a hymn relevant to our topic:

> The Grace dances. I shall play the
>   aulos,
> The number eight dances with us
> The number twelve dances above
> The whole cosmos takes part in the
>   dance
> Whosoever does not take part in the
>   dance does not know what shall
>   come.

"All these remarks and texts show the survival of older ideas. It is not surprising that the Church Fathers, many of whom were brought up in the classic tradition, accepted them without debate, through they were strongly opposed to the pagan rites. Yet the text of the hymn also reflects change and transition. The Greek dancing Graces are replaced with a single dancing Grace; the harmony of the cosmos becomes the harmony which the blessed shall find in after life. In the highest heaven, the blessed souls are dancing. This hymn was apparently admitted to the early Christian liturgy, for in the fourth century Saint Augustine[194] mentions it and rejects it, significantly enough, for reasons of detail.

"In the early Church writings a decisive shift occurred toward greater emphasis on the elaboration of the angel orders. It appears that it was especially the Fathers of the Eastern Church who brought about this change.[195] In the third century, Hippolytos of Rome, the author of the *Canon*, wrote a commentary to the *Book of Daniel* in which he still identified the nine heavens with the nine Muses, and the Muses with the planets. But Cyril of Jerusalem (third century) mentions nine hosts of singing angels; and Ephrem of Edess (third century) has the seraphim sing and extol the Lord, while the cherubim have the duty of carrying the throne of God (a distinction mentioned also by Philo, who identified the throne with the chariot of the Lord).

"In the liturgy of the Eastern Church, Syrian as well as Byzantine, the nine hosts of angels were represented in processions.[196] The different castes are mentioned in the *Praefationes*, with the seraphim and the cherubim forming the rear of the procession. The Apostolic Constitutions list the nine orders in the seventh and ninth books and state that 'the holy seraphim and cherubim sing the song of victory and shout with never-ceasing voice, "Holy".' Basilius of Caesarea provides the text of this hymn. The choir sang: 'Taking mystically the part of the cherubim and singing the thrice Holy for the Trinity which grants us everlasting life, let us wait for the King of the Universe who is invisibly accompanied by the heavenly hosts.' The priest sang: 'You dwell on the throne of the cherubim, Master of the seraphim, because you are

---

193 M. R. James, *Testament of Abraham* (Texts and Studies), II (1892); the meaning of the term 'Testament' is identical with 'Apocalypse'.

194 Letter to Cerebrius, No. 237, *The Fathers of the Church: A New Translation* (New York, 1956), Vol. 32, p.182.

195 Justin, *Apologia pro Christianis, Patrol.* gr. 6, 336; G. Bareille, *'Le culte des anges à l'époque des pères de léglise,' Revue Thomiste,* Vol. 8 (1900) p.41.

196 W. Neuss, *'Das Buch Ezechiel', Beiträge zur Geschichte des alten Mönchstums,* Heft 1/2 (1912).

praised by the angels, archangels, and the crowns [thrones?], dominations, virtues, forces, powers, and the many-eyed cherubim. Around you in a circle stand the seraphim; with never-ceasing voice and never-ceasing praise they answer each other with the victory hymn, singing and shouting "Holy".'[197]

"This certainly is evidence that a cult of angels was incorporated into the liturgy of the Eastern Church of the fourth century. Opposition to this cult was reflected in the decisions of the Councils of Laodicea in 375 and 492.[198] It is understandable that adoration of angels would have been forbidden in the early Christian era, because the Fathers were afraid that the sirens and victories, *nikes,* invoked in pagan Greek and Oriental funeral rites, might have too much influence. After the fourth century, the restrictions were eased, and the castes of angels acquired special characteristics.

"The text of the hymn quoted above, from the apocryphal Acts of Saint John, does not refer to any place or particular heaven where this praising is performed, though angel choirs are assigned to specific locations in many later works of art. Choirs representing angels must have remained popular also in the liturgy of the Western Church. On this there are two interesting reports from the ninth century, one from the Saint Riquier monastery at Centula (France) and another from Corvey (Westphalia, Germany). The chroniclers speak of three groups of singers, including one composed of boys, forming a *chorus angelicus* which is said to sing the Gloria from the western gallery of the church.

"Dionysius's Angel Hierarchy. Dionysius's famous treatise, *The Celestial Hierarchy,* is regarded as the source of the vision of the nine classes of angels. This book, ascribed to Dionysius the Areopagite, was first mentioned at the Council of Constantinople in 533. The author wrote it as a secret treatise for an initiated group of clergy and did not intend it for the common reader. Indeed, its teaching is cloaked in mystic language to make it accessible only to the initiated. The philosophy propounded by Dionysius is based on a theory that a light mystically emanates from the Lord and is transmitted through the hierarchy, the holy order of the angels, to mankind. While this treatise on the hierarchy is accepted as the source of the many later descriptions and representations of musician angels and orchestras,[199] the text itself says nothing, or almost nothing, concerning music; its emphasis is on the other duties of the angels.

"Dionysius divides the celestial hierarchy into nine 'choruses', using the term not in its musical sense but to mean 'group' or 'class'. The nine orders are arranged in a scale. They are divided into three groups, each of which is subdivided into three classes. The author's terminology is full of symbolic meanings. The number nine, the result of multiplying 3 by 3, is clearly a symbol of the Trinity. The purposely obscure writing has necessitated many commentaries elaborating on the special tasks of the orders. The highest group is described as 'standing' around the Lord, and it is their duty to teach heavenly wisdom to the middle sections, who in turn must teach the lowest orders, until the heavenly wisdom reches some initiated

---

197 'The Liturgies of the Eastern Church', in I. F. Hapgood, *Servicebooks of the H. Orthodox Church* (2nd ed., 1922).

198 F. Lugt, 'Man and Angel', *Gazette des Beaux-Arts* (May 1944).

199 See **ANGELS AS MUSICIANS*** §12A.1 above. (Ed.)

members of mankind. This is their chief duty. In addition, all the orders must praise the Lord with the Thrice Holy, the number three again mystically referring to the Trinity. It should, however, be noted that the term used [Greek term] means spoken praise and acclamation, rather than singing, and that none of the angels' emblems refers to music. Another major characteristic of the angels is their shining appearance, and the higher the order, the greater the radiance. Their sense of hearing is explained as their faculty to accept heavenly spiritual inspiration. The following list of correspondences has been drawn from the commentaries:[200]

ANGELS WITH SIX WINGS, THE
    COUNSELLORS:

Seraphim	Flames	Love
Cherubim	Eyes	Knowledge
Thrones	Wheels	Devotion

ANGELS WITH FOUR WINGS, THE
    RULERS:

Dominations	Royal insignia	Nobility
Virtues	Scale	Calmness
Powers	Arms	Activity

ANGELS WITH TWO WINGS, THE
    SERVANTS:

Principalities	Sceptre	Law
Archangels	Crozier	Work
Angels	Censer	Prayer

"Although Dionysius's description of a celestial order of angels did not mention music, it influenced later visions in which music came to have a prominent place; and it seems probable that the very elaboration of a Christian angelic order more or less parallel to pagan concepts of cosmic order should be regarded as providing the vital link to the musical images that ultimately emerged.

"In Dionysius's treatise on the celestial hierarchy, the angels rotate in wheels unrelated to the circumference of the spheres. The cosmos is not constructed of spheres, and the wheels on which the angels move are fire. To the order of the seraphim, the highest and nearest to the Lord, belongs the emblem of flames, and their allegorical epithet is love. The cosmos as a whole is ruled by love, an especially happy formula for reconciling earlier concepts with Christian ethics[201] and the origin presumably of Dante's *amore che tutto nuove*, the force that moves the cosmos.[202]

"The treatise is one of the early attempts to combine Greek and Gnostic concepts with Christian ideology. In its original form, it has not much to contribute directly to this study's particular problem, that is, the integration of music into the vision of the Christian cosmos.

"By the eleventh century, the various traditions of cosmic and angelic orders had merged, and the vision had assumed an aspect familiar today: the blessed sing and dance in the highest heaven, be it Elysium or Empyreum. There are nine spheres or heavens and nine choirs of angels. The spheres are moved by angels or the Muses.

---

200 E. v. Drival, *'L'iconographie des anges'*, *Revue de l'art chrétien* X (1886), 272ff.; B. de Roffignac, *'Les anges moteurs et l'iconographie du moyen-âge'*, *Société des Antiquitaires du Centre, Mémoires* (1935).

201 Dionysius's idea that 'manifestation of the nature of God is a glorious hymn in which we celebrate his love' also occurs in pagan writings, including those of Aristoxenos, quoted by Cicero, *Tusc.,* 19 and 41; Nikomachus, *Arith.,* II; Philo, *De gigant.,* 3, 8; *De somniis,* I, 37; Plotinus, *Enn.,* II, 9.5 and V, 1.2; Proclus, *In Timaeum,* V, 320 A.

202 M. A. Gaetani di Semoneta, *La materia della 'Divina Commedia' ecc. in sei tavole* (1865); K. Vossler, *Die Göttlicher Komödie* (1907-19).

Their song results in the harmony of the universe, and this harmony can be transmitted, through music, to the human soul. The idea of correspondence of heavenly and human harmony through music was first formulated by St. Augustine, later by Boethius, and subsequently adopted by many poets and philosophers." — Meyer-Baer, pp.29-41.

§136.10 Selections from "The Music of the Spheres" in *Harmonies of Heaven and Earth* (1987) by Joscelyn Godwin:

"*Angelic Orders and Muses: the Great Chain of Being.* In the Renaissance it was recognized that the hierarchy of existence, the 'Great Chain of Being', has a subtle inner construction which, if one were to stretch the analogy, would appear as a series of loops or folds. Visually, the picture of such a chain becomes impossible, but music now fits the metaphor to perfection. The notes of music also form a hierarchy, from the lowest pitch to the highest, but within this scale there is an organizing factor at work that makes every eighth pitch the same, yet not the same: it is a repetition at a different octave.

"An anonymous twelfth-century poet was perhaps the first to anticipate this doctrine as applied to the planetary and angelic orders. In his poem which he sets to a kind of plainchant, he tells of how 'there is a concord of planets similar to that of notes', illustrating it with a diagram in which the scale of planets is continued upwards for a further octave to include seven of the traditional Nine Orders of Angels, as given by St Gregory the Great (*Hom.* 36,7). Here is [the] complete [scale]:

a	Seraphim
g	Cherubim
f	Thrones
e	Dominations
d	Principalities
c	Powers
b	Virtues
a	Fixed Stars
g	Saturn
f	Jupiter
e	Mars
d	Sun
c	Venus
B	Mercury
A	Moon[203]

"Two centuries later, Dante in the *Convivio* (c.1305) was to make explicit the correspondence of the lowest three spheres with the Angels, Archangels, and Thrones (following the peculiar ordering only found in this work), from which one can deduce a complete matching of spheres with their angelic governors:

Primum Mobile	Seraphim
Fixed Stars	Cherubim
Saturn	Powers
Jupiter	Principalities
Mars	Virtues
Sun	Dominations
Venus	Thrones
Mercury	Archangels
Moon	Angels

"Giorgio Anselmi, the early Renaissance astrologer and physician, returned in his *De musica* of 1434 to the Gregorian order and omitted the Primum Mobile (which might, after all, be thought to correspond to God, as it does in Aristotle) in order to incude the four elements at the lower end.

---

203 From Reinhold Hammerstein, *Diabolus in Musica*, Bern & Munich, Francke, 1974 [Godwin]. For comparison charts of various correspondences with musical elements, see also **INDIAN (ASIAN) MYTHS – PRACTICES AND BELIEFS***, §161.19 below. (Ed.)

Fixed Stars	Seraphim			
Saturn	Cherubim			
Jupiter	Thrones			
Mars	Dominations			
Sun	Principalities			
Venus	Powers			
Mercury	Virtues			
Moon	Archangels			
Elements	Angels[204]			

"In his *Musica practica* of 1482 Ramis de Pareja, an important Spanish theorist, again assigned notes to the hierarchy, but he gave them not as Angels but as the Nine Muses whom Martianus Capella had already distributed across the spheres.[205] Ramis, moreover, continued his diagram to cover a second octave to a', though without any additional correspondences beyond indicating with a kind of spiral the octave equivalences.

a'	*not assigned*	
g'	"	
f'	"	
e'	"	
d'	"	
b	"	
a	Fixed Stars	Urania
g	Saturn	Polyhymnia
f	Jupiter	Euterpe
e	Mars	Erato
d	Sun	Melpomene
c	Venus	Terpsichore
B	Mercury	Calliope

A (silent)	Moon Earth	Clio Thalia[206]

"This threefold scheme of notes, planets and Muses became a favourite. It was repeated by Franchinus Gaffurius (*De Harmonia Musicorum Instrumentorum Opus*, 1518), Henry Cornelius Agrippa (Book II of *De Occulta Philosophia*, 1533), Heinrich Glarean (*Dodecachordon*, 1547), and others. The Angels, it might seem, were usurped by the Muses in the humanistic enthusiasm of the time. But it is clear from their very first description in the *Theogony* of Hesiod (8th-7th centuries BC) that the Nine Muses are the very same beings as the Angels of monotheism. All that one has to understand — and for many it is unthinkable, admittedly — is that these beings actually exist and that they are knowable. To Hesiod they appear as messengers who accost chosen human beings such as poets, charging them with a divine mission (Greek *angeloi* = messengers), at the same time leading their own life a little below the summit of Olympus, i.e. just below the hierarchy of the Gods. The implication of the Muses' patronage of the arts, a theme so beloved in the Renaissance, is that the Arts in their essence are no human invention but a gift of superhuman origin and inspiration, reflecting some form of universal knowledge and wisdom; and that the route to this wisdom lies through mediation by a feminine principle.[207] At

---

204 Giorgio Anselmi, *De musica*, ed. G. Massera, Florence, Olschki, 1961.

205 Martianus Capella, *The Marriage of Mercury with Philosophy*, transl. by William Harris Stahl & Richard Johnson, with E. L. Burge, as Vol II of *Martianus Capella and the Seven Liberal Arts*, N.Y., Columbia University Press, 1977.

206 Bartolomeo Ramis de Pareja, *Musica practica*, Bologna, 1482, ed. J. Wolf, Wiesbaden, 1968.

207 It is interesting to compare differing cultural views of the relation of the arts (in particular, music) to the divine. In some cultures the gods or supranatural beings *invent* or *make a present* of the arts, generally for the sake of mankind; in other cultures (e.g. Vedic) music in particular (more generally: sound, *nada*) is a manifestation or emanation *of* the Cosmic or Life Force or Energy, and — as such — is to be enjoyed by the gods no less than by all other forms of being, both animate and inanimate. (Ed.)

the other extreme of Greek Antiquity, the Neoplatonist Proclus (AD 410-485) distinguishes the Muses from those other heavenly musicians, the Sirens,[208] by explaining that the gift bestowed by the Muses is an intellectual harmony, that of the Sirens a corporeal one — 'which is why the Muses are said to prevail over the Sirens and to be crowned with Sirens' feathers'. To the Christian division of the planetary from the angelic realms, then, we can equate the Classical distinction of Sirens from Muses.

"The Angels return again in the fullest scheme of all, described in a verse epic on the history and destiny of France: *La Galliade* (1578) by Guy Lefèvre de La Boderie. La Boderie was a student and translator of two of the most subtle and erudite of Renaissance philosophers, Pico della Mirandola and Francesco Giorgi. In the latter's *Harmonia Mundi* (1525), which he translated into French, La Boderie had immersed himself in a world-view governed by Platonic harmonies and Kabbalistic correspondences. Giorgi himself had never assigned pitches to the entities which he brought into relationship, but he had gone much further than most authors in giving correspondences to the planets and angels for the Sephiroth (Divine Emanations or aspects) and the Hebrew Names of God. The scheme developed by La Boderie (with some unaccountable variations from Giorgi) is as follows, embracing tones, Jesus and the Angelic Orders, the Names of God, the Sephiroth, the planets, elements, and the faculties of creatures. The Angelic Orders now appear in the ordering of Dionysius the Areopagite [see CHART I, below].[209]

"Ambitious as this scheme is, La Boderie does not exploit to the full the possibilities of musical symbolism. It was the English Hermeticist Robert Fludd (1574-1637), another close reader of Giorgi, who took the necessary step of extending the musical matrix beyond the two-octave gamut of Greek and medieval theory. Fludd's cos-

CHART I

a'	Jesus	Ehieh	Kether	Primum mobile	
g'	Seraphim	Iah	Binah	Ninth sphere	
f'	Cherubim	Iehovah	Chokhmah	Fixed Stars	
e'	Thrones	El	Chesed	Saturn	
d'	Dominations	Iehovah	Geburah	Jupiter	
c'	Virtues	Elohim	Tiphereth	Mars	
b	Powers	Iehovah zevaoth	Netzach	Sun	
a	Principalities	Elohim zevaoth	Hod	Venus	Knowledge
g	Archangels	El sadai	Yesod	Mercury	Honour of King
f	Angels		Malkuth	Moon	Fear of God
e				Fire	Intellect
d				Air	Reason
c				Water	Sense
B				Earth	Life
A				Earth's Centre	Being

---

208 *Commentary on the Republic*, transl. by A. -J. Festugière, Vol 3.
209 Guy Lefèvre de La Boderie, *La Galliade*, Paris, 1578.

mological system contained three worlds: the elemental, comprising Earth, Water, Air and Fire; the Ethereal, comprising the spheres of the planets anbd Fixed Stars; and the Supercelestial, imagined as a further series of spheres containing the Angelic Hierarchy. Therefore in its full development his musical gamut covers three octaves, assigning one to each world and thereby symbolizing the correspondences between them as of one octave to another. In one of his several schemata,[210] designed to illustrate the Incarnation of God through the form of Universal Man, each octave has seven notes, as one would expect, but this requires some compromise. Clearly the ninefold Angelic Hierarchy will not fit, so Fludd devotes the highest octave instead to the Holy Trinity and man's higher faculties. The Fixed Stars are omitted, and the four Elements are stretched to fill seven steps [see CHART II, below].

"In another chart which correlates man's Spirit and Soul with the spheres of the Universe, Fludd abandons the diatonic scale but retains the perfect intervals of octaves, fourths and fifths. He is therefore free to use all Nine Orders of Angels, to increase the number of celestial spheres to nine, and to reduce the elements to their proper four [facing page, CHART III].

"With these and the several other charts that appear in his book, Fludd makes it clear that there is no one fixed way of looking at things. This capacity to shift viewpoints is a virtue he shares with other Hermeticists, such as Agrippa, whose widely-read book on *Occult Philosophy* had proposed schemes of cosmic correspon-

CHART II

f	God the Father	
e	The Word	
d	Holy Spirit	*Supercelestial and*
c	Mind	*Spiritual Octave*
b	Intellect	
a	Reason	
g	Will	
f	Saturn	
e	Jupiter	
d	Mars	*Celestial and*
c	Sun	*Middle Octave*
b	Venus	
a	Mercury	
g	Moon	
f	Fire	
e	Higher region of Air	
d	Middle region of Air	*Elemental and*
c	Lower region of Air	*Corporeal Octave*
B	Fresh Water	
A	Salt Water	
G	Earth	

---

210 Robert Fludd, *Utriusque cosmi... historia*, Oppenheim, 1617-21.

dences based on all the numbers from one to ten, and twelve.

"Only with this ambiguity in mind can one unravel the beautiful but at first sight baffling engraving of the Cosmic Monochord that occupies two pages of Fludd's *Anatomiae Amphitheatrum* (written 1621, published 1623). At the head stand four statements expressive of Fludd's essential monism:

The Monad generates a monad and
reflects its ardour in itself.
The One is all things and all things are
the One.
GOD is all that there is; from him all
things proceed and to him all
things return again.
The infinite dimension of the
TETRAGRAMMATON: in and between
all things.

Next comes the dimension of duality, essential to cosmic manifestation. At the left-hand end, where the tuning-peg governs the whole monochord, is Alpha in a tri-angle, symbol of God as beginning: 'The central principle or Dark Aleph'. To this corresponds, on the right, the Omega, symbol of God as 'end and circumference'. Towards the upper corners are parallel statements: 'God is the beginning, and the beginning is the end'; 'God is the end, and the end is the beginning'. Another symbol of this reciprocity is the Tetragrammaton, spelled out in palindromic form: Iod, He, Vau, He, Iod. The scrolls read as follows:

God (alpha), or the Lesser Aleph of the
uncreated darkness, or potency,
reveals itself for the world's creation by changing to light, or act.
God (omega), or the Greater Aleph,
emerging from dark earth or the
created darkness, reveals itself to
men for the world's salvation.

The language of these statements must be understood in the context of Fludd's Kabbalistically derived doctrine of God's twin powers of non-acting and acting. The Lesser or Dark Aleph is the first emergence

CHART III

Seraphim	} Spiritual 4th	
Cherubim		
Thrones		
Dominations		
Principalities		SPIRITUAL OCTAVE
Powers	Spiritual 5th	
Virtues		
Archangels		
Angels		
Primum Mobile	} Middle 4th	
Fixed Stars		
Saturn		
Jupiter		
Mars		MIDDLE OCTAVE
Sun	Middle 5th	
Venus		
Mercury		
Moon		
Fire	} Material 4th	
Air		MATERIAL OCTAVE
Water	} Material 5th	
Earth		

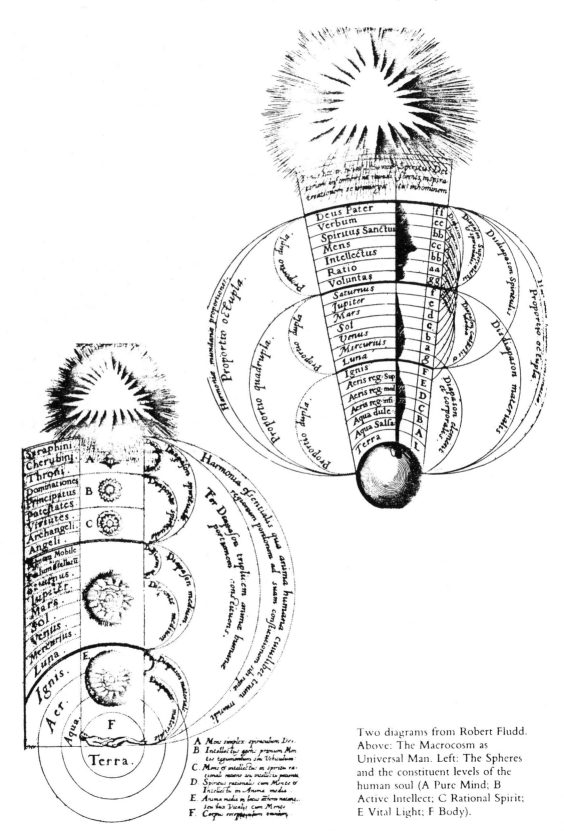

Two diagrams from Robert Fludd. Above: The Macrocosm as Universal Man. Left: The Spheres and the constituent levels of the human soul (A Pure Mind; B Active Intellect; C Rational Spirit; E Vital Light; F Body).

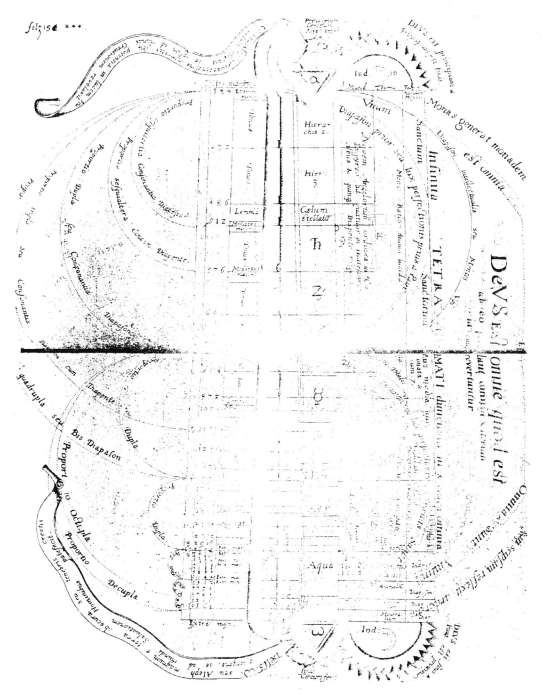

Robert Fludd's Cosmic
Monochord.

of a universe from non-manifestation; the Greater or Light Aleph is the completion of that universe, whether viewed as the end of time, as the final expansion of space (the circumference), or as the lowest point of the created hierarchy.

"Three different musical systems are overlaid in the chart. First, on the monochord itself are the notes of the diatonic scale for three octaves from C to c^3, and thereafter the octaves alone up to c^6. This is musically correct, as are the proportions of string-lengths and the intervals marked on the lower arcs. Between c^6 and the bridge at the Omega end, there is theoretically an indefinite series of higher octaves. Similarly, the numerals in the lowest column, which give the proportions of string-length for each scale-tone in the lowest possible whole numbers, could be continued up to infinity if space allowed. The intervals are named in the adjacent column. At the right-hand end of the uppermost section, some of these octaves are assigned to classes in the cosmic hierarchy: to the Minerals, Vegetables, Animals, and to Man. As far as the notes and numbers in the bottom section are concerned, this scheme illustrates the division of the World-Soul as described in Plato's *Timaeus* by means of the numbers 1, 2, 3, 4, 8, 9, 27, here given on the lowest line of all.

"Second, there is a system of three octaves similar to those diagrams of Fludd's previously described, each assigned to one of the three worlds. The words immediately above the planetary symbols read:

Nine orders of Angels in the Empyrean
   Heaven, corresponding to the four
   notes of the diatessaron [4th] and
   five of the diapent [5th].
Nine spheres of the Ethereal Heaven.
Nine regions of the Elemental World.

Corresponding to these in the Microcosm is the series of three octaves shown by the three diminishing unbroken arcs. These are the 'intellectual or mental', 'vital or

spiritual', and 'elemental or corporeal' ocrtaves, i.e. the three major divisions of Man into Intellect or Spirit (in the higher sense), Soul, and Body.

"Thirdly, there is a two-octave system, shown by the two equal arcs drawn in dotted lines:

First octave or light of perfection first
   emanating from the Father, viz.
   the Son.
Second octave or light of perfectio, viz.
   the Holy Spirit, from the Father
   and the Son.

The monochord thus becomes in its highest respect the symbol of divine emanation in the Holy Trinity, the equality of Persons being aptly reflected in the identical pitch of the two halves of a string when stopped in the middle.

"To the reader who has preferred not to follow these labyrinthine schemes, I owe a word of explanation as to why Robert Fludd, I, or anyone else considers them worthwhile. Fludd's deep and extensive learning had acquainted him with a number of disparate doctrines, each of which his natural ecumenicism recognized as containing a true insight into the nature of things. To name some of them: there was the mathematical description of Plato's *Timaeus;* the spatial system of the Ptolemaic cosmos, expanded by the addition of the Angelic Hierarchies; the Hermetic doctrine that Man the Microcosm reflects the structure of that Macrocosm; the evident hierarchy of states of consciousness, from the God-knowing Intellect down to the mineral realm. Finally, there was the inner organiztion of the Godhead itself into the three Persons of the Holy Trinity, into the fourfold Tetragrammaton I H V H, or into the duality of action and non-action. How is one to bring all these together? It is difficult to conceive of a more powerful application of *musica speculativa* — of music as mirror of reality — than Fludd's attempt to unify all these disparate truths through the symbol of the monochord and its scale....

"*Gurdjieff's Law of Octaves.* George Gurdjieff (1872 or 1877-1949), founder of the Institute for the Harmonious Development of Man, is reported by his sometime pupil P. D. Ouspensky as teaching that 'The seven-tone scale is the formula of a cosmic law which was worked out by ancient schools and applied to music.'[211] In Gurdjieff's own system the diatonic scale does not serve merely as an image of the septenary: its inner organization becomes of paramount importance. The scale he chooses from the many possible ones is the modern major, characterized by its sequence of two whole-tone intervals (C-D-E), a semitone (E-F), three whole tones (F-G-A-B), and, if transition to the next octave is included, a final semitone (B-C'). In exactly the same way, Gurdjieff explains, all human and natural developments take place not by an even progression but with two discontinuities in every phase or cycle. These occur in the scale as the two semitones mi-fa (E-F) and si-do (B-C')…. Progress through the whole-tones is plain sailing, but when the semitones are reached the whole development can be knocked off course, even reversed, unless extra energy is brought to bear. Gurdjieff calls this necessary energy the 'additional shock' that may be supplied from the resources of the developing thing or person, or may come deliberately or accidentally from outside. Ouspensky quotes the following explanation:

In an ascending octave the first [semitone] 'inverval' comes between mi and fa. If corresponding additional energy enters at this point the octave will develop without hindrance to si, but between si and do it needs a *much stronger additional* shock for its right

development than between mi and fa, because the vibrations of the octave at this point are of a considerably higher pitch.

"In Gurdjieff's system of work on oneself, the ascending scale is the model for one's deliberate growth, as one watches for the points which require an additional shock. But he also uses the scale as a symbol for the opposite process of emanation from above. Taken in the downward direction, it is the model for the descending levels of manifestation. God's work is not so difficult as our own, for (the quotation goes on) 'a descending octave develops much more easily than an ascending octave'. The first semitone occurs right away between do and si, and the 'material for filling it in is often found either in the do itself or in the lateral vibrations evoked by do'. The fa is not reached without incident, and the second semitone fa-mi crossed with a '*considerably* less strong' shock than the first.

"One cannot help wondering whether Gurdjieff would have invented a different scheme, had he lived in a culture and era when a different form of seven-note scale was the norm. For the semitones do not necessarily fall between the 3rd and 4th and the 7th and 8th steps. In the scale on D, for instance, they fall between steps 2 and 3, 6 and 7, whether one takes the scale up or down: D E F G A B C D' or D' C B A G F E D. As the Dorian or First Mode of the Middle Ages, and the diatonic Phrygian Mode of Ancient Greece, this D-mode with its perfect intervallic symmetry has a good claim for primacy. The modern major, however, is the inversion of the Greek diatonic Dorian (E D C B A G F E), the mode preferred by the Demiurge of Plato's *Timaeus* for the construction of the world; so, allowing for a reversal of up and down, it is also a strong contender. Such matters

---

211 P. D. Ouspensky, *In Search of the Miraculous*, N.Y., Harcourt Brace & World, 1949.

could be argued *ad nauseam*: every speculative musician has a favourite scale.

"We will not enter the intricacies of Gurdjieff's 'cosmic octave', which puzzled even his closest followers. But Ouspensky transmits a simplified scheme that is of great interest, covering as it does all the principal levels of being within the tones of a single octave. Like all earth-centered schemes, it gives the superficial impression that all of Creation is aimed towards our little world. But it is also true to our experience, as we have explained of geocentricity in general. We look through the pinhole of earthly, sensible existence to the ever expanding levels above us. And what is beneath the pinhole? Infinite contraction, according to this scheme, ending in a Nothingness that is paradoxically also the Absolute [see CHART IV, below].

"Herbert Whone suggests that these very meanings are concealed in the names given to the notes of the scale by Guido d'-Arezzo in the tenth century: Ut, Re, Mi, Fa, Sol, La. In the sixteenth century, with the change from hexachordal to heptachordal theory, the leading-tone B was also given a name, Si, and in some countries the Ut was renamed the more singable Do. Whone gives the following table (some Latin words corrected) [CHART V]:[212]

CHART IV

C′	The Absolute as All	} semitone requiring 'shock', supplied
B	All created worlds	} by the Will of the Absolute
A	Our galaxy, the Milky Way	
G	Our solar system; the Sun	
F	The planetary world	} semitone filled by organic life on
E	The Earth	} earth, receiving planetary influences
D	The Moon	
C	The Absolute as Nothing	

CHART V

DO	(Dominus)	God as creator
SI	(Sider)	Star systems
LA	(Lactea)	The Milky Way, Man's particular galaxy
SOL	(Sol)	The Sun
FA	(Fata)	Planets – the spoken word – a man's fate
MI	(Microcosmos)	The Earth – Man's role upon the earth
RE	(Regina Coeli)	The Moon [Queen of Heaven]

---

212 Herbert Whone, *The Hidden Face of Music*, London, Gollancz, 1974.

We can add that the orinal Latin word Ut was a better name, being a word that embraces a whole range of meanings referring to cause: the English 'thus', 'since', 'as', 'in order that', 'how', 'like', etc., and also linking etymologically with Thoth, Egyptian god of creative intelligence, and the Sanskrit *tat,* the indefinable 'that'.

"Gurdjieff's scale has more than a casual resemblance to the Great Monochord of Robert Fludd, described above, which is strung between the Light and Dark Alephs as twin faces of the Absolute. The late James Webb, friend of my youth and impartial student of Gurdjieff and Ouspensky, saw a similar connection between the Enneagram, another fundamental Gurdjieffian symbol, and a ninefold diagram in Athanasius Kircher's *Arithmologia.* Webb believed that 'in the *Arithmologia* Kircher was expressing a final synthesis of Renaissance mysticism and that Gurdjieff's cosmology somehow derives from it'.[213] The coincidences are striking, certainly, but not surprising when one remembers that all three philosophers were working (here, at any rate) within the same perennial tradition of Hermetic wisdom, with its significant numbers and its law of correspondence between the Above and the Below.

"Gurdjieff uses the seven-note scale to symbolize evolution on the one hand and hierarchy on the other. But the septenary is not bound to the hierarchical dimension which has been our authors' almost exclusive concern. The octave-space can be conceived equally well not as a ladder (Latin *scala*) but as a Pleroma: the fullness of manifestation on any or all levels into which flow the seven primal differentiations of God's power. In Theosophy (especially that of H. P. Blavatsky and Alice A. Bailey) much is taught about these 'Seven Rays'. A diagram will illustrate the essential difference between the two views of the septenary or of the seven notes [CHART VI].

CHART VI

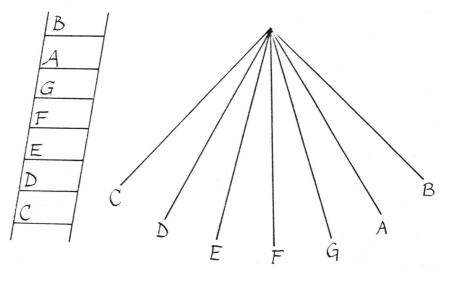

The Scale as ladder   The Scale as the Seven Rays

213 James Webb, *The Harmonious Circle,* London, Thames & Hudson, 1980.

"The second diagram answers to the fact that the notes of the scale are qualitatively different from one another, but such that a higher (or lower) pitch is not 'superior' to its neighbour, as the Seraphim may be to the Cherubim. Each has its own character and its part to play in the unfoldment of the musical Pleroma. Using a symbol in which there is even less suggestion of hierarchy, the ancient Gnostics made the seven tones of the Scale correspond to the seven Ionian vowels **SYMBOL HERE** . These in turn matched the seven planetary powers, which on their own level are not so much a hierarchy as a reflection, in appropriate mode, of the Seven Rays. In an anonymous Gnostic text, the Godhead is made to say:

> The seven vowels celebrate me, who am the imperishable God; indefatigable Father of all beings, I am the indestructible lyre* of the Universe; it is I who found out the harmonious concord of the heavenly whirlwind.

We will meet again this Creator, with his power to harmonize the rays that proceed from the Absolute. But in order to comprehend him, we must first turn to the symbolism of the harmonic series.

"The Harmonic Series and its Symbolism. In the early modern era it was not widely known that the harmonic series corresponds to the vibrations into which any musically resonant body tends to fall. But the sequence of intervals was familiar as the series of integral divisions of a string (1/2, 1/3, 1/4, 1/5...). Moreover, it was readily audible as the notes of the natural trumpet*, the valveless instrument for which

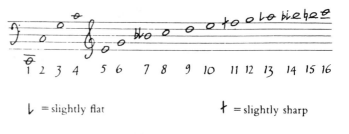

$\flat$ = slightly flat $\sharp$ = slightly sharp

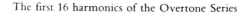

The first 16 harmonics of the Overtone Series

Bach and Handel wrote. The notes available on a natural trumpet in C are the first sixteen or so harmonics of its fundamental:

"This series of intervals is inexhaustible in its multifaceted symbolism. If the Angel's song is indeed one of knowledge, they could not choose a better theme on which to descant. Two simple interpretations of it were made by Andreas Werckmeister (1645-1706), a German provincial organist and theorist, who knew it as the 'trumpet scale'. The first of his schemes refers it to the Six Days of Creation, the second to the progressive revelation of God.

"In Werckmeister's creation scheme,[214] the first note or fundamental corresponds to the creation of light, first awakener of the senses. On the second day, the waters were separated from the dry land, and this is represented by the first differentiation of an octave (1-2) with a 'formless void' within it. On the third day, this space was filled with herbs and trees, like the 3 which appears in the next octave 2-4. On the fourth day, with the creation of the Sun and Moon, we enter the third octave of 4, 5, 6, 7, 8: 'a light by which we can glimpse a complete harmony' with the greater and lesser lights represented by the major and minor thirds (4-5, 5-6). The problematic seventh harmonic, an out-of-tune B-flat, 'shows how times are not always good, but sometimes a dissonance must be mingled

---

214 Andreas Werckmeister, *Musicae Mathematicae hodegus curiosus*, Frankfurt & Leipzig, 1687, reprinted Hildesheim, Olms, 1972.

in with this life'. The fifth day and fourth octave sees the creation of the animals in all their variety, including both good and bad sounding notes: hence there are animals both clean and unclean. Finally on the sixth day Man is created to rule over the whole earth, just as the musician must rule over and control all these numbers or notes.

"Werckmeister's second scheme arises from the symbolism of the triad. He would have read in the odler German theorists of the likeness of the Holy Trinity in the common chord or major triad (harmonics 4, 5, 6). Johannes Lippius, for example, had praised it in 1612 as the 'true and unitrisonic root of all the most perfect and most complete harmonies that can exist in the world... the image of that great mystery, the divine and solely adorable Unitrinity'. Now Werckmeister applies the four octaves of the trumpet's harmonics to the four successive periods of divine revelation. Octave I (harmonics 1, 2) now symbolizes God the Father as He was before Creation; II (harmonics 2, 3, 4) the time of the Old Testament, when the Trinity was concealed; III (harmonics 4, 5, 6, 8) the time of the New Testament, in which the Trinity was revealed; IV (harmonics 8, 9, 10, 12, 15, 16) the melody of the Christian life, in earth and heaven. With good symbolic reason, he here excludes the dissonant harmonics 7, 11, 13, 14 for they would represent sin.

"These dissonant harmonics are a problem, and not only for trumpet-players. The B-flats (7, 14) and A (13) that are rather too flat, and the F (11) that is not quite sharp are ironed out in practical music (with the striking exception of the horn-calls in Benjamin Britten's *Serenade*). But in theory they are all too present, and in symbolism they often serve the purpose not merely of representing but of explaining the evil in the world.

"A very explicit association of the first dissonant harmonic (the seventh) with evil comes in the first work of Louis-Claude de Saint-Martin (1743-1803). Published in 1775 under his pseudonym of 'The Unknown Philosopher', this large work, entitled *Des Erreurs et de la verité*, summarizes what Saint-Martin had learnt from his master the theosopher Martinès de Pasqually (1710-1744). This symbolism may therefore originate with the latter. Saint-Martin first explains the symbolism of the common chord (meaning harmonics 4, 5, 6, with the addition of 8). The major triad, he says, is the foundation of all music and an image of the Unity that encloses everything – or nearly everything.[215] The two different thirds that for Werckmeister expressed the double nature, divine and human, of God the Son take on a similar role here: they show that every being is under a double law, that of its own unitary Principle and that of the separate body it inhabits. But this duality, being the rule of all manifestation, is not itself evil. Ideally it is crowned and brought to completion by the addition of a new octave (8) above the triad: an image of the First Principle (the root of the triad, 4) in perfect concord with the original.

"Saint-Martin now transposes this symbol to the level of macrocosmic entities and to a time before the world began. In fact, he is describing the rebellion of Satan against God and the consequent origin of evil. But he does not use these names, speaking instead of First [God] and Second [Satan] Principles. The 'image of the Principle', he says, *should* be a perfect octave, but before the beginning of time it diverged, asserting its own will and separating itself from the First Principle to become the origin of all evil – which is likewise the forsaking of one's own Principle to run after an illusory separateness. He does not make it clear whether he un-

---

215 Louis-Claude de Saint-Martin, *Des Erreurs et de la Verité,* Edinburgh, 1775, reprinted n.p., Le Lis, 1979.

derstands this note to be the flattened seventh degree of the scale, or the over-flat seventh harmonic:

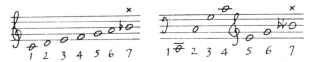

Flat seventh degree   Seventh harmonic

But he obviously has in mind the note which changes a perfect major chord into a 'dominant seventh', thereby disturbing its harmonic equalibrium and demanding a particular resolution:

Major chord changing to dominant seventh and resolving

Some theorists, attempting to explain the origin of this dominant seventh chord, which has been the mainspring of tonal harmony since the seventeeth century, have traced it directly to the harmonic series. They say that it is an image of the overtones 4, 5, 6 and 7, and should ideally be tuned like these harmonics, with an over-flat seventh, whenever it occurs. This has the symbolic advantage of making every note contain, in its 7th and other dissonant harmonics, its own dissatisfaction and yearning for resolution. To sound the seventh is simply to bring this tendency out into the open. Yet even when it is resolved, the resolution can never be final, for the chord to which it resolves will also contain its own seventh harmonic, its own discontent, like the seed of evil and disharmony present in every being. If we were to sound that note in the above resolution, it would be to insert an E-flat into the chord

on F, thereby requiring a further resolution to the chord a fifth lower, on B-flat. And so the process would continue indefinitely, spiralling without hope of redemption through an eternal geometric series of ever lower fifths, into a hellish realm of double flats where no musician likes to venture:

Endless progression of dominant sevenths

"But lest one should think the equation of this dissonance with the principle of evil too conclusive, or too facile, I turn to a person who recorded an entirely contrary opinion of the dominant seventh, Bettina Brentano von Arnim (1785-1859). In her youth, this brilliant woman had a correspondence with Goethe in which she aired her stream of consciousness — sometimes profound, often beautiful, occasionally scatter-brained. (One of her letters records the famous speech of Beethoven in which he says that 'music is a higher Revelation than all wisdom and philosophy', and much else on his art and mission). On 24 July, 1808, she writes to Goethe, who has been studying thoroughbass and feels like rejecting the flat seventh for its failure to fit in with the laws of harmony:

But, heathen, thou must become a Christian! The flat seventh does not harmonize certainly, and is without sensible basis; it is the divine leader, — the Mediator between sensual and heavenly Nature; it has assumed flesh and bone, to free the spirit to tone, and if *it* were not, all tones would remain in limbo... the flat seventh by its resolution leads all tones, whch pray to it for delivery, in a thousand different ways, to their source – divine spirit.[216]

– Godwin, pp.167-76, 180-87.

§136.11 Excerpts from *The Untuning of the Sky: Ideas of Music in English Poetry, 1500-1700* by John Hollander:

"*Harmony.* The Greek word *harmonia,* meaning originally a fitting or joining together of discrete and disparate entities, has a musical meaning that differs so subtly from the modern musical use of the word 'harmony' that many translations of Classical texts, overlooking the difference, give the derived word for the original. To any reader with a knowledge of music and its history, however, such a translation is not only wrong but fundamentally misleading. In the first place, our whole modern sense of 'harmony' and 'harmonious' is conditioned by our experience of polyphonic music, so that 'harmony' cannot help but suggest *the ordering of simultaneously sounding musical tones,* taken together as a 'package' or *gestalt.* In the abstract sense, 'harmonious' tends to carry over this suggestion of a chord, and events to which it is applied are so designated because they consist of discrete and dissimilar sub-entities which lose their individuality to the degree of being perfectly blended into a whole.

"Greek musical theory devoted little discussion to what we would call today 'harmonics'. The Greek *harmoniai* were scales, or melodic schemata; in general, *harmonia* is to be thought of as referring to *melody* rather than to vertical tonal aggregates. In the still more extended senses of the Platonic metaphors of the ordering of the cosmos and of the soul of man, the notion of a harmonious blending of opposite qualities is extremely easy for the modern reader (and has been for readers, actually, since about the tenth century) to misinterpret: a musical chord can be thought of as 'blending' and marrying dissimilar or even contrary elements. The notion is rather like that of *e pluribus unum.* But even a little exploration of extant musical and metamusical theory (for we should so distinguish between the writings of Aristoxenus, Aristides Quintilianus, pseudo-Plutarch, Ptolemy, etc., on the one hand, and the philosophical speculations of Plato in the *Republic, Laws,* and *Timaeus,* for example, or Aristotle in the *Politics,* on the other) will lead us to avoid such error.

"For the Greek notion of 'harmony' we should rather seek to understand an idea of relative proportion, of an order that consists in the ratios of quantities to each other, rather than of a notion of blending that depends on the *simultaneous* effects of separate or even warring elements. It is almost as if our modern architectural term 'scale' (referring to the *relative* sizes of portions of buildings) were to be interpreted as having derived from a purely musical sense. The disposition of musical intervals (considered merely as distances between successive scalar steps and leaps, rather than between simultaneously sounding tones) in terms of ordered ratios would then be seen as applicable to architecture, or even to all smoothly functioning systems: 'scale' would mean 'proportion' and 'just disposition of the relative role of parts in a whole'. This would be close to the Greek notion of *harmonia.*[217]

"An understanding of this notion will explain clearly the combined interests of the Pythagoreans in music and mathematics in

---

216 Bettina Brentano von Arnim, *Goethe's Correspondence with a Child,* 1839.

217 See R. G. Collingwood, *The Idea of Nature* (Oxford, 1945), pp.49-55, esp. 52 n; also, Robert S. Brumbaugh, *Plato's Mathematical Imagination* (Bloomington, Indiana, 1954), pp.85-87. Of general relevance to this discussion is the exposition of Greek musical thought in Julius Portnoy, *The Philosopher and Music* (New York, 1954), pp.4-44.

forming the basis of their cosmology. The Pythagorean experiments with the monochord showed that the intervals of the diatonic scales could all be produced, with reference to a given fundamental pitch, by successively dividing a string of a given length and observing the tone produced upon plucking the divided string. Certain intervals, such as the octave, fourth and fifth, were shown to result from dividing the string in the most 'perfect' ratios, such as 1/2, 2/3, etc., where the numerators and denominators of the fractions consisted of the smallest possible integers. Since these intervals *happened to play significant roles in the tonal systems of Greek music as it was already developing*, it was concluded that these 'consonant' intervals were most pleasing to the ear because they were most 'harmonious' or perfect, mathematically speaking. With reference to the idea of harmony as proportion outlined above, we might say that these intervals could be comprehended in terms of the simplest basic ratios, and therefore were most harmonious in the sense of being most perfectly rationalizable in terms of a system of such ratios. These intervals, to pursue our modern analogy, had the clearest and best 'scale' with respect to their fundamental pitch.

"The Pythagorean notion of the perfect consonances and their necessarily beautiful effects upon a hearer is an important one in Western history. Up through the Renaissance and even later, the harmony of the parts of the cosmos, on the one hand, and of the parts of the human psyche, on the other, were seen as the basic elements of the same universal order. In the Ptolemaic astronomy, for example, the universal proportions could be seen as realized in the ratios to each other of the diameters of the heavenly spheres. In terms of this 'harmony', the old myth of the music of the spheres as representing the sounds of heavenly perfection could be reinterpreted as a metaphysical notion, characterizing not only the order of the universe but the relation of human lives to this cosmological order.

"The music of the spheres becomes such a central image in Christian musical thought that we may usefully turn to it for a moment. In the *Repubic*, Book X, Socrates' relation of the myth of Er includes a mention of this Pythagorean myth; it describes the heavenly spheres bearing 'on the upper surface of each' a siren, 'who goes round with them, hymning a single tone or note. The eight together form one harmony'. It is not, of course, that we are to think of a *chord of eight tones;* here, rather, the 'harmony' is an ordered intervallic relationship among all of these tones, more in the manner of the intervals obtainable by step or skip in a scale. The singing siren that produces the tone on each sphere, of course, becomes beautifully adaptable, eventually, to membership in a Christian angelic choir. But the more common version of the myth, such as is put down elaborately by Aristotle in *De Caelo* (II, 11), maintained that it was the rubbing against each other of the supposedly hard, glassy celestial spheres that produced the sound. In answer to the objection that no mortal had ever heard that music, it was often retorted that the constant droning of that noise deadened the ears of earthly inhabitants by custom alone, and that because it was so constant, it was inaudible.

"The form in which the myth of the music of the spheres is handed down to the Middle Ages, however, may be seen in its treatment by Cicero in the *Somnium Scipionis* and in the someowhat Neoplatonized commentary upon the latter by the fourth-century writer Macrobius. The passage from Cicero desribing the heavenly music revealed in Scipio's dream might be considered the *locus classicus* of the heavenly music motif:

" 'What is this large and agreeable sound that fills my ears?'

" 'That is produced,' he replied, 'by the outward rush and motion of the spheres themselves; the intervals between them, though unequal, being exactly arranged in a fixed proportion, by an agreeable blending of high and low tones various harmonies are produced; for such mighty motions cannot be carried on so swiftly in silence; and Nature has provided that one extreme shall produce low tones while the other gives forth high. Therefore this uppermost sphere of heaven, which bears the stars, as it revolves more rapidly, produces a high, shrill tone, whereas the lowest revolving sphere, that of the moon, gives forth the lowest tone, for the earthly sphere, the ninth, remains ever motionless and stationary in its position in the centre of the universe. But the other eight spheres, two of which move with the same velocity, produce seven different sounds — a number which is the key of almost everything. Learned men, by imitating this harmony on stringed instruments and in song, have gained for themselves a return to this region' (tr. C. W. Keyes).

"It might be added that Cicero's seven tones constituted the seven discrete pitches of a *harmonia* or scale. The significance of the fact that stringed instruments specifically are mentioned here will be treated later. We might observe here that it is Macrobius' comment on this last sentence that lays the groundwork for eventual Renaissance expositions of the ethical character of man's relationship to the music of the spheres: 'Every soul in the world is allured by musical sounds so that not only those who are more refined in their habits, but all the barbarous people as well, have adopted songs by which they are inflamed with courage or wooed to pleasure; for the soul carries with it into the body a memory of the music which it knew in the sky, and is so captivated by its charm that there is no breast so cruel or savage as not to be gripped by the spell of such an appeal.'[218] Thus microcosmic man, imitating in his *musica instrumentalis* or practical music the ideal order of the *harmonia mundi*, can regain in some small way the *musica humana*, the ordering of his being, that characterizes the music of the spheres and the prior good state of his soul.

"The abstract harmony or proportioned order of the universe that was figured forth in a *musical* order (and we must recognize the metaphorical nature of such a notion, almost from the beginning), was itself applicable to the individual human soul, as well as to the *anima mundi*. The notion of the soul as a *harmonia* or proportionate distribution of unlike parts accommodated itself equally well to the musical metaphor and to the same kind of interpretation of it as was given in the myth of heavenly music. Treatments of the harmony of the soul as a 'blending' of opposites must, again, be understood not as the kind of blending of tonal elements into a chord, but rather as a division of a whole into parts in the ratio of two to three, three to four, etc. Boethius' *musica humana* is the result of the common utilization of the idea of harmony in connection with ethics and psychology.[219] Like the music of the spheres, the music of the individual soul (and the music of the harmonious *polis*, for that matter) was to undergo a kind of conceptual dislocation with the development of polyphonic music in the later Middle Ages: the concept of *harmony* as chordal blending would also color the interpretations of Classical psychology by later Medieval and Humanist writers.

"*Ethos*. The link between the music of universal order and the music of human composure lies in the identity of the kind

---

218 Macrobius, *Commentary on the Dream of Scipio*, tr. W. H. Stahl (New York, 1952), p.195.

219 Aristotle, *De Anima*, 407b-408a, calls the soul a 'kind of harmony' because a harmony is a *krasis kai synthesis*, a 'blending and combination' of opposites. The harmonious structure of the World Soul and of the human sould is elaborated in Plato's *Timaeus*.

of order imposed in both cases. In a more literally musical sense, the actual effects of musical sounds upon a listener were also elaborated by Greek theory. Now, it is not the Western classical world alone whose musical systems embody the notion of modal *ethos*. Aside from Judaeo-Arabic modal systems, and the Hindu *ragas*, which bear close affinities with Greek music, amazingly intricate sets of correspondences were maintained in ancient Chinese music between pitches, mystical numbers, physical elements, directions, seasons, constellations, divinational trigrams, and hexagrams, etc.[220] But the Greek theory of the character of each of the various music scales, and of the effects of these inherent characters upon any listener, remained always within the realm of the theory of practical music. As such, it became the interest of all manner of writers dealing with the most concrete musical subjects, and even of today those who would tend not to be concerned with Pythagorean and Neoplatonist ideas of world harmony.

"Literary history has preserved some familiarity with the names of the Greek scales, such as the Dorian, Lydian, Phrygian, Mixolydian, etc., and of the various moral characteristics conventionally associated with them. These characteristics are perhaps best known through the discussion in Plato's *Republic* of what scales (or keys)[221] ought to be allowed in the Just City. It was specifically in connection with melodies (and hence with scales or melodic species) that the various shades of psychic tension or laxity represented by the different sorts of *ethos* were supposed to operate; the precise explanation for the power of music to produce these effects in its melodic patterns, however, was usually rather obscure. It was felt that, to use a modern analogue, the 'sad' and 'joyful' characteristics of major and minor keys resided, somehow, in the tonal configurations themselves. One has only to imagine an elaborate set of keys, each with as firmly established a character as those of major and minor scales in Romantic music, in order to understsand the complete certainty of Ancient writers with respect to the modal *ethos*.

"The reason for the association of an attitude with a musical pattern, however,

---

220 See Kazu Nakaseko, 'Symbolism in Ancient Chinese Music Theory', *Journal of Musical Theory*, I (1957), pp.147-180. Also see Curt Sachs, *The Rise of Music in the Ancient World*, pp.105-113, 172-183 [Hollander]. See also **INDIAN (ASIAN) MYTHS — PRACTICES AND BELIEFS*** §161.19 below. (Ed.)

221 In this brief discussion, I have not differentiated between the *harmoniai* and the *tonoi* or transposing scales. For a clear exposition of the structure of the Greek modal system, see Sachs, *The Rise of Music in the Ancient World*, pp.216-238. Gustave Reese, *Music in the Middle Ages* (New York, 1940), pp.11-44, also provides an excellent discussion of this and other questions; considerably dated is the treatment of Henry S. Macran in his edition of *The Harmonics of Aristoxenus* (Oxford, 1902), pp.1-85.

would seem to be no great mystery. Let us examine for a moment the Dorian scale, whose character was 'manly' or 'calm and grave' or sometimes 'warlike, but not frenzied'.[222] Musically speaking, the so-called Dorian tetrachord upon which the scale is based was an historically important one and retained in Attic times in a chauvinistically tinged name. It lay at the center of the fully developed greater perfect system, and its specific tonal center coincided with that of the system itself (in it, the thetic and dynamic *mese* were identical). We may also assume that the texts sung to it, and the ceremonies and occasions upon which it was employed, all contributed to its ethical aura. To pursue a modern analogy, we might propound a fictional situation for nineteenth-century America in which all music was extremely formalized and regimented. Let us assume that only a few keys are in use, namely, C major, F major, and B-flat minor. Let us also imagine that all musical compositions were of one of three types: either military marches and patriotic songs accompanied by brass bands; or homely, sentimental songs to be accompanied by a guitar, banjo, or some other plucked string; or thick, impassioned string quartets without

texts at all, originally composed and usually played by foreign musicians with unpronounceable names. If these three sorts of composition were to be invariably written in C major, F major, and B-flat minor respectively, some sense of character might easily arise for these keys. The first, or 'American', key would have the advantages of 'simplicity and straightforwardness' (we must put aside here the problem of transposing brasses), in having no sharps or flats in its signature, and in being somehow appropriate for patriotic activities and sentiments. The second key would be 'milder, higher and thinner' than the first, and its *ethos* (might it be called the 'home' or 'mountain' mode?) would be more 'warm', 'relaxed', and 'fond'. The third key, on the other hand, would be 'wild and irrational', having a key signature cluttered with flats, no text upon which to depend for ethical clarification, a generally suspicious foreign air, etc. (it might be called the 'barbarous' mode). If this situation sounds strained and caricatured, it is really only a dramatically illuminated representation of the Dorian, Lydian, and Phrygian scales of the Greeks.[223]

---

222 It may strike some readers as curious that we should consider the topic of *ethos* in a work concerned with the relations between music and mythology; however, to attribute e.g. emotional or moral attributes or characteristics *to* an otherwise "neutral" musical element (such as the key, scale, mode of a particular composition) is, in a sense, to personify—and therefore to mythologize—the element in question. Ultimately it is to raise the question: what is it that an experience of music shares with our experience of other *fundamental* aspects of nature (including the divine—life force—cosmic energy etc) —including those of which even human beings, perhaps, continue to have an only limited knowledge, or less than complete understanding? (Ed.)

223 For other discussions of the troublesome problem of *ethos*, see Reese, *op. cit.*, pp.44-50; also, Sachs, *The Rise of Music*, pp. 248-252.

"Central to the notion of *ethos*, however, and as can be seen in the last key in our fictitious model, is the whole problem of text and melody. There was, by and large, a suspicious attitude toward textless, purely instrumental music on the part of Greek thinkers.[224] While it was guaranteed that *ethos* was a property of scales and melodies written in those scales (and not of the consonances, nor of the texts accompying the melodies),[225] it was nevertheless made quite clear that *rational* music needed the infusion of the tone by the word for its effects. Aristotle may be attempting to gloss over the need for a text here in his distinction in *De Anima* between two sorts of tone-producing vibrating air-columns: those possessing souls (such as human windpipes), and those without (such as wind instruments).[226] But it was primarily language that was of importance in this conection (Aristotle's 'rational' sound-producers, having souls, could also produce speech). One of the fundamental reasons for the disapproval of the music of the *aulos** or oboe involved the fact that the performer thereon cannot sing while he is playing, as in the case of the lyre, *kithara*, or other stringed instruments.

"It is instrumental music, devoid of words, that is the model of 'pure' music for the nineteenth- and twentieth-century listener, but it is only since the Renaissance that instruments have developed anything like their modern roles. In Classical antiquity, the task of the instrument was to accompany by doubling (or at best, heterophonically embroidering upon) the vocal line. Distinctions between winds and strings were made by philosophers on many bases, however, of which the ability to frame a singer's text was only one. The myth of Marsyas* tells how the goddess Athena* picked up an *aulos*, blew upon it, happened to catch sight of the dreadful grimace into which the exigencies of the embouchure had twisted her face, and cast the instrument aside as being unfit for dignified use. Marsyas, who picked it up, was later flayed by Apollo*, lord of the lyre, for his insolence and disobedience. The legend of Midas and his unwise choice of the Panic wind music over the sublime Apollonian string-produced sounds is a similar case in point. In general, the wind was deemed inferior to the string because of difficulties that attended its proper tuning (boring properly placed stopping holes in a conically pierced wind is always difficult). The well-tuned string was not only the Pythagorean model of the harmoniously proportioned sound producer, but the problem occasioned by various tunings of the lyre formed the basis of the whole ratioalized musical system in Attic times and after, and of the notational conventions as well.

"The polarity of string and wind, then, bore a long tradition of association with the antitheses of reason and uncontrolled

---

224 In traditional (e.g. Vedic) Indian music also, the meaning or significance of music in a sense *begins* with that of the text. (Ed.)

225 The pseudo-Aristotelian *Problems*, XIX, 27, treats of this in some detail. Also see Egon Wellesz, *A History of Byzantine Music and Hymnography* (Oxford, 1949), pp.44-52.

226 *De Anima*, 407b-408a.

passion.[227] Textless music, itself associated with wind instruments rather than with strings, constantly risked disapproval from technical and philosophical writers, and in general it was song that remained the pure type or model 'music' in Classical times. We must thus remember that, all theoretical disquisitions to the contrary, the whole notion of musical effect is intimately involved with the notion of the sense of a text, and, ultimately, of the meaning of words. There is thus no modern post-Romantic problem, in the case of Classical music, of the substitution of musical 'meaning' for that of language, and no concomitant mystique abut the 'musical' power of 'poetic language'. The one notable exception to this may have been the widespread ancient belief in the curative powers of music, where only the soothing, healing effects of certain modes (often the lower pitched, 'relaxed' scales were thus employed), completely independent of any sung text, were held to have therapeutic value.[228] But this belief in music's healing powers remains, on the whole, a distinct body of doctrine during the Classical period, and becomes associated with a general ideology of music and the human soul only in the Christian Middle Ages, when the ancient myths are accommodated to such Biblical events as David's soothing of Saul's madness, and when therapy can be considered, figuratively, as salvation....

"The Survival of Classic Doctrine. The transmission of scraps of ancient musical theory by Boethius, Cassiodorus, Isidore of Seville, and other writers provided the Medieval world with the basis for a rapidly proliferating body of *musica speculativa.* Radical changes in actual musical practice during the first millenium of the Christian era began to lay the groundwork for the eventual development of the full-blown polyphony that would come to characterize Western music. Concepts and terms that had been retained since the late Classical period either acquired confusing new meanings or lapsed into misunderstood use. The names of the Greek *harmoniai,* for example, became transferred to the tones or 'modes' of Gregorian chant in such a confusing way that Renaissance and post-Renaissance musicians would call 'Phrygian' the scale produced by running from *E* to *e* on the diatonic keyboard, for example, while it was that same scale which designated the Dorian tonality for the Greeks. The 'rhythmic modes' of twelfth-century polyphony took their names from the feet of Classical metrics (iambic, trochaic, dactylic, etc.). Most important of all, the consonant intervals of Greek harmonic theory were gradually reinterpreted in terms of the simultaneously sounded, chordal intervals of a polyphonic harmonic system. The very word 'harmony' began to change its meaning, and although the change was an ex-

---

227 See Kathleen Schlesinger, *The Greek Aulos* (London, 1939), pp.57-62. For a suggestion about the role of the *aulos* in the development of *ethos,* see pp.135-137. Aristotle, *Politics,* 1342b, remarks on the close connection between that instrument and the Phrygian tonality.

228 An excellent and compendious discussion of this is to be found in Bruno Meineck, 'Music and Medicine in Classical Antiquity', in *Music and Medicine,* ed. Dorothy M. Schullian and Max Schoen (New York, 1949), pp.47-95.

tremely subtle one, it allowed for great changes in the notion of *harmonia mundi*, for example. It is, I think, safe to suggest that writers of the twelfth century and thereafter, confronting the image of the music of the spheres, would 'hear' it as actual polyphony. As contrapuntal styles grow more complex and characteristic, even a particular set of musical conventions may have been called to mind. Surely a 'harmony of the spheres', with each angel-mounted sphere producing its own part in a heavenly consort, becomes more plausible, even to the untrained musical experience, with vocal polyphony as a model for all music.

"An amusing instance, actually, of an overly literal interpretation of the avowedly metaphorical music of the spheres is a rather well-known one of Johannes Kepler, in the early seventeenth century. The notion of an actually audible music, so roundly pooh-poohed by Aristotle, continued to survive in a figurative role, whether as an inaudible, ideal harmony (in the most general sense), or as an ancient error, committed not in total darkness.[229] Even figuratively considered, it was a notion supportable by the scheme of Ptolemaic cosmology. But with the rise of the new astronomy of Copernicus, Galileo, and Kepler, the very notion of a set of geocentric spheres, bearing along with them the heavenly bodies and all participating in one vast, harmonious dance, vanished once and for all. Yet the old myth and, particulary, the literally musical interpretation of the idea of abstract harmony, remained extremely strong. Thus Kepler, in his *Harmonices Mundi*, published in Linz in 1619, concluded his extremely Pythagorean discussion of mathematics and world order (including the geometric 'harmonies' of the regular polygons and solids, the psychology and metaphysics of acoustical harmony, etc.) with a remarkable version of the old story.

"After having completely dismissed not only the actuality of the heavenly spheres but the very circularity of the planetary orbits (his great contributions to astronomy lay in this latter demonstration), Kepler nevertheless went on to prove that there was a harmony to the cosmos. If the Ptolemaic system's demise no longer allowed the tones generated by the planets to be attributed to the ratios of the diameters of their orbits (these having been shown by Kepler to be elliptical), God had nevertheless seen fit, Kepler insisted, to arrange for a heavenly music, inaudible though it might be. Therefore, he argued, if one plots an average angular velocity for each planet, and then works out ratios of these to each other, one can discover that each planet does indeed produce music. Far from being simply a tone, as in the older theory, Kepler's heavenly bodies each produced a little melodic fragment. And, finally, he argued that there was no real harmony without an agreement between differing parts; he arranged to show that these fragments could be woven together in six-part modal counterpoint (Venus proved a disrupting influence and a dissonant one, when employed in the same texture as the earth). His comments indicate how completely he accepted the notion that the sixteenth-century polyphonic style of his younger days *was* harmony, pure and simple:

Accordingly the movements of the heavens are nothing except a certain

---

229 See the first part of the article by Eric Werner and Isaiah Sonne, 'The Philosophy and Theory of Music in Judaeo-Arabic Literature' *Hebrew Union College Annual*, XVI (1941), pp.288-292. For the survival of the notion in the sixteenth century, see, for example, Montaigne's 'Of Custome' in Florio's translation of the *Essayes* (1603), I, 22, in the reprint of the Tudor Translations (London, 1908), I, 114. Also, Barnabe Googe's translation of Palingenius' *The Zodiacke of Life* (1576), pp.212-213.

everlasting polyphony (intelligible, not audible) with dissonant tunings, like certain syncopations or cadences (wherewith men imitate these natural dissonances), which tend towards fixed and prescribed clauses—the single clauses having six terms (like voices)—and which marks out and distinguishes the immensity of time with those notes. Hence it is no longer a surprise that man, the ape of his Creator, should finally have discovered the art of singing polyphonically (per concentum), which was unknown to the ancients, namely in order that he might play the everlastingness of all created time in some short part of an hour by means of an artistic concord of many voices and that he might to some extent taste the satisfaction of God the Workman with his own works, in that very sweet source of delight elicited from the music which imitates God.[230]

"The *polyphonic interpretation* of the idea of abstract harmony, then, survived long after the original musical notion of proportion had been lost. It was probably only in the rediscovery of the proportions which generated the primary consonances by Renaissance architects that the notion of

strictly proportional harmony maintained itself. The musical consonances, interpreted in the old Pythagorean way as intervals produced by stopping the monochord, played an important role in sixteenth-century architectural theory and practice, as Rudolf Wittkower has so elegantly demonstrated.[231] But throughout the Middle Ages, speculative writers on all manner of subjects, and particularly theologians, could employ the figurative notion of *harmonia mundi*, embellishing the abstract idea with all sorts of literally musical correspondences, drawn either from the bits of Classical theory transmitted by Boethius or from the musical theory of their own day. This tradition extends even into the late Renaissance, when Classical models for speculation on many subjects were utterly commonplace and even outmoded.

"Thus, while John Scotus Erigena can propound a complicated theological dialectic of harmony and discord, at times reversing the natural abstract significance of the musical notions, Jean Bodin in the late sixteenth century can discuss at great length the harmonic proportions that govern the good commonwealth, reinforcing his conclusions about the harmonious music of monarchy with comparisons of

---

230 Johannes Kepler, *Harmonices Mundi*, V, vii, tr. Charles Glenn Wallis, in *Great Books of the Western World* (Chicago, 1952), XVI, 1048. See E. A. Burtt, *The Metaphysical Foundations of Modern Science* (New York, 1954), pp.52-71 [Hollander]. I might add that Kepler's notion of "to some extent tast[ing] the satisfaction of God the Workman with his own works" through the performance of music recalls our own themes **T1a** (Music as magical means of communication with god[s] or supreme being[s]) and **T1c** (Music as medium through which spirit world [of divinities, supranatural beings] attempts to signal or contact man), *Introductory Remarks*, Vol I above. (Ed.)

231 Rudolf Wittkower, *Architectural Principles in the Age of Humanism*, second editon (London, 1952), pp.103-135. Otto von Simson, in *The Gothic Cathedral* (New York, 1956), XX n., 21-58 and *passim*, attempts to demonstrate the prior use of the musical consonances in Medieval architectural proportions.

classes and levels of society to musical parts in a polyphonic texture.[232] But despite the wide range of musical speculation in the Medieval period, despite the survival in many weird and adapted forms of elements of the musical theories of Antiquity, it was only in the fifteenth century that the scattered and usually separated parts of *musica speculativa* began to come together in one more or less organic body of theory. It seems to have been Marsilio Ficino who for the first time brought together cosmological harmonic theories, Greek doctrines of *ethos*, later Neoplatonist psychology and metaphysics, and conclusons drawn not only from some knowledge of Classic music from ancient writers but from contemporary practical music as well. He was the first of a succession of comprehensive, almost encyclopedic musical theorists, such as Gioseffe Zarlino and Marin Mersenne (in the following century), to try to present as complete and fully rationalized as possible an account of the power of music to affect a listener. It is perhaps the unification of theories of *ethos* and of cosmological harmony, the comprehensive treatment of the connection between Boethius' *musica mundana* and *musica humana*, that, as one commentator has suggested,[233] is the most significant accomplishment of Ficino's comments on musical subjects. It is surely true that in such a combined view we can see an *account*, an *explanation* in the empirical sense, in its germinal form; even though the account given by Ficino is necessarily a metaphysical one, it is nevertheless cognizant of acoustical and musical fact, and aims at consistency and completeness.

"It was with the revival of Classical learning that a fully developed musical ideology finally emerged. The use of musical concepts and figures derived therefrom in the Christian Middle Ages had by and large operated in brillian flashes. A numerological symbol, a particular interpretation of harmonic unity, a sustained conceit here and there, illuminated points of metaphysical and cosmological doctrine. It is not surprising that the use of such figures flourished among mystical writers, in particular. Traditional word-plays helped to sustain and proliferate such images: a pun on *chorda* ('string') and *cor, cordis* ('heart'), possibly first introduced by Cassiodorus, became so deeply imbedded in habitual thinking that the very origins of the word 'concord' (in the latter, rather than in the former of the pair of words) often even today are mistaken for being musical.[234]

"But Renaissance thinkers united many themes: cosmology, physiology (correspondences between elements, humors, and musical modes were revived and made much of, as were those between the systole and diastole of the human heartbeat and the alternation of upbeat and downbeat in musical and prosodic rhythm), lore concerning the fabled effects of ancient music and myths of its heroes, old doctrines of music's powers of physical and psychic therapy, physical fact (the phenomenon of sympathetic vibration in two perfectly attuned strings became a commonplace image for the resonances of spiritual sympathy), and whatever could be accommodated of the practical music of the contempoary scene. Musical theorists in the proper sense employed this body of *musica*

---

232 Jean Bodin, *The Six Bookes of a Commonweale*, tr. Richard Knolles (London, 1606), III, viii, Prop. X, expounds this musical theory of the state at greater length, developing latent implications in some of Bodin's remarks.

233 See D. P. Walker, 'Ficino's *Spiritus* and Music', *Annales Musicologiques*, I (1953), pp.131-150.

234 See Leo Spitzer, 'Classical and Christian Ideas of World Harmony', *Traditio*, II (1944), 435-445.

speculativa for polemical or laudatory purposes more than in technical exposition. But as a subject of human knowledge, embraced by both Classic and Christian world views, the musical ideology of the Humanist epoch was as current among non-musical thinkers and writers as among technical theorists.

"To accommodate the myths and abstract schemes of *musica speculativa* to what was often the inflexible reality of practice, Renaissance musicians sought consciously to revolutionize that practice so as to make it conform more with Neoclassical ideals. But it is important to remember that much of the material of speculative music was actually much more *literary* than musical even throughout the Middle Ages; and this body of literary material created all the more conceptual and semantic confusion as it was more strongly heard.

"*The Musical Instrument in Image and Practice.* Perhaps in no area of musical concern does the literary ideal confront the hard actuality of practice [more than] in the case of instruments. Especially during the Renaissance, when instrumental music *per se* was beginning to emerge from its subservient role as a substitute or doubling voice in vocal polyphony, attempts to accommodate received doctrine concerning the use and nature of musical intruments to the instruments actually known and used in the music of the sixteenth century were widespread. Metaphors from Christian theologians, Classical attitudes toward the wind and stringed instru-

ments, emblematic uses of musical instruments in the graphic arts — all put on contemporary dress; and musical instruments of the Renaissance became figuratively associated with those of Biblical times or Greek Antiquity.

"By the simplest metonymy,[235] a musical instrument can be made to stand for the music itself which is produced upon it, and we have already remarked that the wind and string instruments came to represent for Greek writers two different musical traditions. Such strict figurative uses of the different species of instruments were by no means invariable, however. It was by and large most common to allow the strings to represent abstract 'harmony' and 'order' by typifying musical harmoniousness and ordered tuning. Thus the Platonic notion of the World-Soul (as well as the individual psyche) considered as a tuning, or *harmonia*, finds figurative expression in the image of the World-Lyre, or the stringed instrument of the human soul. One seldom sees, during the Medieval or Renaissance periods, any such figure employing a wind or percussive instrument (the eventual metaphorical treatment of the organ becomes an exception, particularly in the seventeenth century). But, on the other hand, [one frequently discovers] Roman or Medieval poets using the instruments' names indiscriminately;[236] and it is only in certain contexts that particular instruments retain or develop symbolic values.

"The use of musical instruments for poetic imagery thus has a long history, and

---

235 "A figure of speech in which an idea is evoked or named by means of a term designating some associated notion. The words *sword* and *sex* are metonymical designations for *military career* and *womankind* in the example 'He abandoned the sword and the sex together' (Sterne)." — *American Heritage Dictionary of the English Language* (1969). (Ed.)

236 See, for example, Horace, *Carmina* I, 12 'Quem virum aut heroa lyra vel acri tibia sumis celebrare, Clio?' but see also Epodes, 9, ll. 1-6, where there may be some irony expressed in the 'sonante mixtum tibiis carmen lyra, hac Dorium, illis Barbarum': the modes of peace and war, friend and enemy combine uneasily, even after a great victory.

popular figurative associations of certain instruments with others, with certain musical styles, activities, states of feeling, and abstract notions tend to reinforce the effectiveness of instrumental metaphors in sixteenth-century verse and prose alike. The translation of Classical instruments and theories about them into strictly contemporary terms was a convention of Renaissance thought; and while one could only condemn any nineteenth- or twentieth-century translator who rendered 'lute' for the Greek *kithara* or *lyra* (alas, a distressingly common practice, apparently based on the notion that any obsolete instrument is the equivalent of any other), one would have to treat the matter very differently in the case of an earlier translation. The 'lute-harp-lyre' constellation, uniting the contemporary string instrument with those of David and Orpheus, for example, represents no capricious substitution of one term for another. Rather, it depends upon a consistent habit of figurative association of the instruments and what they stand for.

"For example, we might turn for a moment to a popular sixteenth-century version of an ancient author's discussion of the Greek wind-string dichotomy, included in the biography of a popular historical figure. Thomas North's translation of Plutarch (1579) renders a particular passage from the life of Alcibiades as follows:

> Afterwards when he was put to schoole to learne,... he disdained to learne to playe of the flute or recorder: saying, that it was no gentlemanly qualitie. For, sayed he, to playe on the vyoll with a sticke, doth not alter mans favour, nor disgraceth any gentleman;

but otherwise, to play on the flute, his countenaunce altereth and chaungeth so ofte, that his familliar friends can scant knowe him. Moreover, the harpe or vyoll doth not let him that playeth on them, from speaking, or singing as he playeth: where he that playeth on the flute, holdeth his mouth so harde to it, that it taketh not only his wordes from him, but his voyce.[237]

Here, *lyra* ('lyre') is rendered as 'vyoll' (and *plektron* as 'stick'); on another occasion, 'harpe' is used. The almost universal translation 'flute' for the oboe-like *aulos* is of less interest or significance. What is important is that in this passage, representing a typical storehouse of general learned knowledge of an element of ancient musical doctrine, the contemporization of the instrument terms is almost automatic. Most often, the sixteenth-century translated version of the lyre or *kithara* (the smaller and larger forms of what is essentially the same instrument) will be the lute, the most important stringed instrument of the Renaissance. The lute was originally an Arabic importation into Europe; the fifteenth century saw its development along more characteristically Western lines and the eventual emergence of a standard tuning and stringing. In the following century, the lute's importance can be partially measured by the fact that it alone (aside from the keyboard instruments) possessed a unique kind of notational system (the various tablatures), while other instrumets were simply employed at will to play any unspecified vocal parts that might fall within their range.

"The significance of the lute as a Renaissance lyre, as opposed to the use of the

237 Plutarch, 'Life of Alcibiades', from *Lives, Englished by Thomas North* (1579), reprinted in the Tudor Translations (London, 1895), VIII, 91-92. Plutarch goes on to blame on Alcibiades' objections 'partly in sporte, and partly in good earnest', the fact that 'teaching to play of the flute was put out of the number of honest and liberall exercises, and the flute it selfe was thought a vile instrument, and of no reputation' (p.92).

harp in the same function, is an interesting question of iconography whose solution must depend upon further researches. In general, it might be remarked that the respective Biblical and Classical associations of the two instruments seem to be preserved quite clearly in sixteenth-century translation and graphic representation. A metonymic use of the lute (for the lyre) to represent poetry as well as music is a familiar one; occasionally a harp will be used in a similar context to refer to a religious muse. In England, in particular, there were specific regional associations for the bardic harp, which by the sixteenth century had already undergone considerable decline as a courtly and folk instrument. It was acknowledged to be an instrument common to Scotland, Ireland, and Wales;[238] in the latter case, along with the *crwyth* or *crowd*, it was occasionally mentioned in poetry in order to evoke the venerable Welsh origins of the paternal side of the Tudor line.

"A most instructive case of the figurative use of lute and harp in sixteenth-century popular imagery involves one more link in the speculative chain connecting *musica mundana* and *musica humana*. An intermediary stage between microcosm and macrocosm, between men, each 'a little world, made cunningly' and the widest universe of which they could conceive, was that of the body politic. The political aspects of Renaissance musical speculation involved certain elements of ancient political thought. Among these were the State treated as a harmonious organism (as we saw above in the case of Jean Bodin), music itself, in a political context, treated as if it were political or social ideology to

be carefully controlled (as in Plato's ideal city), or else a crucial discipline in the training of citizens (Aristotle). But it is more than just a conventional symbolic reference to abstract harmony that is intended by the political use of the lute as a sixteenth-century image. An important source of both visual and poetic imagery is the first of the Renaissance emblem books, Andrea Alciati's *Emblemata* (first published 1531); it includes in all of its editions the picture of a lute, represented in an engraving as lying on a bed or couch (in later editions, with an open book of lute-music beside it). The emblem's motto proclaims it to be a figure of Alliance *(Foedera)*, and an additional caption classifies the whole emblem under 'Fides', 'trust'. The Latin verses below the *impresa* are inscribed to the Duke of Tuscany, who, it is hoped, will unite all of Italy. In them, the lute is referred to as a 'cythara', and the Duke is begged to accept it as a gift when 'nova cum sociis foedera inire paras' ('ready to enter into a new treaty with his allies'). It continues:

> Difficle est, nisi docto homini, tot tendere
>   chordas,
> Unaque; si fuerit non bene tenta fides,Rup-
>   tave (quod facile est) perit omnis
>   gratia conchae.
> Illeque praecellens cantus, ineptus erit.[239]

(It is difficult, except for a learned man, to attune so many strings; and if one string be not well tuned, or broken [which is easy], all grace of the shell is destroyed, and that excellent music will be weak.)

"The political parable here is obvious, and the implicit pun in the very notion of

---

238 See John Seldon's gloss on Michael Drayton, *Poly-Olbion*, in *Works*, ed. J. W. Hebel (Oxford, 1933), IV, 121. The whole description of the musical contention between England and Wales is of great interest, particularly for its lists of instruments and for its comparison of instrumental techniques to modes of versification. See *Works*, IV, 78.

239 D. A. Alciati, *Emblemata* (Lyons, 1551), sig. A8v.

'concord' is somehow at work. Alciati's poem concludes with a repetition of a warning already made: '*At si aliquis desciscat (uti pleerunque viedmus) / In nihilum illa omnis solvitur harmonia*' ('But if anyone breaks aways [as we often observe], all that harmony falls apart into nothing').

"The emblem might well be taken for no more than a figurative treatment of *concord* in general (or more specifically, political treaties); but in the Hellenistic (?) *Hieroglyphics* of 'Horapollo' (first published in 1505), the lyre is treated as the symbol of a political leader, a man who 'binds together and unites his fellows', with the added explanation that 'the lyre preserves the purity of its sounds'.[240] While Alciati makes specific use of a polyphonically oriented notion of 'harmony' or 'concord' (a quasi-chordal 'harmony' is produced by all the strings of the instrument, provided it is in tune), it seems clear that the older source employs a more extended metaphor which involves the rational and well-tuned associations of the lyre in antiquity. Alciati himself, incidentally, uses an implied pun on *fides* ('trust') and *fides* ('stringed instrument'), a connection retained in the emblem literature of the following centuries,[241] and which attains the currency, if not the importance, of the other pun expounded in such devices as '*Chorda trahit corda*', and in the very notion of heart-strings.[242]

"To complete the picture, it should be observed that Alciati's emblem book, which went through 175 editions between 1531 and 1750 (or which 125 were before 1600), influenced directly and indirectly many other such books in many other languages. In one of the most beautiful of the English emblem books, an interesting version of Alciati's conceit appears; Henry Peacham's *Minerva Brittana* (1612) contains a cut of an Irish harp, labelled in Latin 'The Irish Republic to King James'. Beneath it are the following lines:

> While I lay bathed in my native blood,
> And yield nought save harsh & hellish
>> soundes:
> And save from Heauen, I had no hope
>> of good,
> Thou pittiedst (Dread Soveraigne) my
>> woundes,
>> Repairdst my ruine and with Ivorie
>> key,
>> Didst tune my stringes, that slackt or
>> broken lay.
>
> Now, since I breathed by the Royall
>> hand,
> And found my concord, by so smooth
>> a tuch,
> I giue the world abroade to vnderstand
> Ne'er was the musick of old Orpheus
>> such,
>> As that I make, by meane (Deare
>> Lord) of thee,

---

240 *The Hieroglyphics of Horapollo,* tr. George Boas (New York, 1950), p.111.

241 See for example Mario Praz, *Studies in Seventeenth Century Imagery* (London, 1939), I, 138; also Joannes Michael van der Kelten's iconographical handbook, *Apelles Symbolicus* (Amsterdam, 1699), pp.422-432, for a summary of emblems using stringed instruments.... An amusing sentimental and trivialized version of Alciati's lute device may be seen in the anonymous *Emblems for the Improvement and Entertainment of Youth* (London, 1769), p.11, where the lute lying on a book of music is called an emblem of 'True Alliance; teaching us to make proper Associations with such as are agreeable to our Humour, Ways and Manners; by whom we may profit, and receive Benefit'.

242 *Apelles Symbolicus,* p.427.

From discord drawne, to sweetest vnitie.[243]

Thus the instrument of state may be seen to take on a local character: the harp is at once the spirit of Ireland and the tuneable string instrument of Alciati and the ancient writers.

"The correspondences and divergences between Classical and Renaissance instruments were amazingly fertile in the way of producing poetic and graphic imagery, but it must be remembered that such images depended for their effect upon a more general context of received ideas about music, both speculative and practical. Lately we have come to think of imagery as the most important element of the poetry of the sixteenth and seventeenth centuries; and literary criticism today [1961], more than ever before, tends to trace the history of that poetry along lines of development of the increasing structural and functional complexity of its imagery. Even within the sixteenth century itself, a gradual change may be observed from the unadorned poetry of exposition (even in the case of lyrics), through the use of imagery to adorn statement, to the eventual usurpation of the role of exposition and statement by the imagery itself at the beginning of the following century. Musical ideas and images, then, may be seen to enter the corpus of narrative, reflective, lyric, and dramatic poetry in many ways; but whether as the subject of discourse, praise, blame, or explication, on the one hand, or as the material for amplifying imagery on the other, both speculative and practical music were likely to be confused, compared, and contrasted against a constantly deepening background of received ideas about the nature and effects of musical sound.

"A musical ideology, a set of almost automatic responses to questions about the ability of music to arouse feelings in a listener, seldom operates in a vacuum. In the foregoing remarks we have seen some of the ways in which the musical ideology of the Middle Ages and Renaissance was shaped by the operation of (practical) musical actualities upon historic speculative materials. But literary history constantly shows us how poetry always makes its own demands upon idea and climates of thought. The following chapters [omitted here (Ed.)] will attempt to follow the development of music's role in English poetry, both as subject matter and as image, with a view toward showing the changing nature of the relationship between poetry and doctrine in regard not only to the facts and mythology of music but with respect to some of the more general questions of metaphysics, cosmology, and psychology which the broad and rich area of speculative music so generously embraced." — Hollander, pp.26-51.

HARP. *(See also pp.340, 867.)*

§137.6a See **NORSE MYTHS AND LEGENDS***.

§137.7 "Musical instrument venerated in many societies and believed to keep evil forces at bay, as in the case of David* soothing Saul (I Samuel 16:23), though he may really have played a lyre*; in the tomb of Rameses III in Egypt priests are shown playing harps; in Western Europe the harp is associated with bards and fairies*; the belief that angels play harps in heaven probably stems from Revelation (14:2) in which harps are associated with the

---

243 Henry Peacham, *Minervae Brittana* (London, 1612), p.45; also reproduced as Plate V in *The Mirrour of Maiestie,* ed. Henry Green and James Croston (London, 1870).

redeemed on Mount Zion." — Cavendish [Man, Myth and Magic], p.1212.

§137.8 "Equated with the white horse[244] and the mystic ladder. It acts as a bridge between heaven and earth. This is why, in the Edda, heroes express their desire to have a harp buried with them in their grave, so as to facilitate their access to the other world. There is also a close connexion between the harp and the swan.[245] It might also be regarded as a symbol of the tension inherent in the strings with its striving towards love and the supernatural world, a situation of stress which crucifies man in every moment of the anguished expectation of his earthly life. This would explain the detail of Bosch's *Garden of Delights*, where a human figure hangs crucified on the strings of a harp. Music being a symbol of pure manifestation of the Will (Schopenhauer), the harp would seem to be a particularly intense and characteristic embodiment of sound* as the carrier of stress and suffering, of form and life-forces." — Cirlot, 139.

§137.9 **AOIBHELL** (Irish folklore). "A woman of the Sidhe [the Hollow Hills wherein lived the Aes Sidhe or Daonie Sidhe, the Irish equivalent of the fairies] at Craig Liath in Munster. She was the tutelary spirit of the O'Briens, thouh in later years she was considered to be more like a banshee since whoever hears the music of her magical harp does not long survive the experience. She was the mistress of Dubhlainn [who prophesied that he would die in battle unless he put on her cloak of invisibility]." — Matthews and Matthews, p. 24.

§137.10 **CORMAC COND LONGES** (Irish folklore). "The son of Conchobar mac Nessa. He was exiled because [of] his championship of Fergus mac Roigh [King of Ulster] at the treachery of Conchobar's slaying of the sons of Usna. As Conchobar lay dying, he asked his son to return and become king. Despite a prophecy warning of the possible outcome, Cormac went. During his stay at a hostel, *Craiftine* [below] played his harp so soothingly that Cormac slept and was overpowered by soldiers." — Matthews and Matthews, p. 51.

§137.11 **CRAIFTINE** (Irish folklore). "He was harper to Labraid Longseach [seducer and husband of Moriath, the daughter of Scoriath, King of Gaul; later King of Leinster in Ireland]. He gained his harp due to a peculiarity of his master's, for Labraid had horse-ears. This blemish was kept secret from everyone lest Labraid be deposed, but his barber knew and he was sworn to secrecy. However, he could not restrain himself from telling a tree. This was cut down and made into a harp for Craiftine but when it was played, it revealed the truth about the King.[246] Craiftine also harped the parents of Moriath to sleep so that Labraid could love her. Cormac Cond Longes [above] slept with Craiftine's wife, to revenge which, Craiftine was a party to Cormac's death, again by lulling him to sleep." — Matthews and Matthews, p. 52.

§137.12 **DAGDA** (Irish folklore). "One of the Tuatha de Danaan [the people of Danu or Danaan (Danann) — a figure so ancient that no stories about her have survived]. Bres mac Elatha [the son of Eriu, at one time elected a king of the Tuatha de Danaan, against whom they eventually arose, at which time he joined the ranks of their enemy — the Fomorians] ordered him to build forts but would give him little

---

244 See Harold Bayley, *The Lost Language of Symbolism* (London, 1912; reprint 1951).
245 See Marius Schneider, *El origen musical de los animales-simbolos en la mitologia y la escultura antiguas* (Barcelona, 1946).
246 See also **SINGING BONES***. (Ed.)

food. Together with Lugh and Ogma [warriors of the Tuatha de Danaan], he planned to attack the Fomorians. [Dagda] mated with the Morrighan [Morrigan, Great Queen—archetypal goddess of Ireland] over a river and she prophesied his success. Attired as a rustic fool, he entered the enemy stronghold where he discovered the disposition of the Fomorians. His harp was called 'the Oak of Two Greens' and 'the Four-Angled Music'. With it he was able to play three kinds of music: the sorrow-strain, the laugh-strain, and the sleep-strain. It was with the latter that he was able to subdue those Fomorians who had abducted his harper. He was the guardian of the cauldron which satisfied all hunger, brough from Murias [one of the four cities from which had come the Tuatha de Danaan to Ireland]. His name means 'Good God', but his other names or titles are Eochaid Ollathair (All-Father) and Ruad Rofessa (Lord of Great Knowledge) indicating his similarity to the Wild Herdsman [guardian of the beasts of the forest, a black giant who wields a club]."— Matthews and Matthews, p.58. [For additional background on the Celtic gods in Ireland, see **IRISH MYTHS AND FOLKTALES***, §170.9 below. (Ed.)]

§137.13 **MABON** (Welsh folklore). "The son of Modron [a mystery title which merely means "mother"]. He was one of the famous prisons of Britain according to the 'Triads'. The story of his loss and discovery is told in *Culhwch and Olwen* [a famous romance with Arthurian associations]. He was stolen from between his mother and the wall when he was three nights old. From the context of the story it is obvious that this happened at the beginning of time.... Mabon is the Wondrous Youth of Celtic tradition: like Merlin, he is the child of otherworld and earthly parents. His cult was widespread in north-west Britain, along Hadrian's wall. He shares many of the aspects of Greek Apollo*; as hunter and harper, he appears in many inscriptions on Romano-British dedications. Like

Angus [see **IRISH MYTHS AND LEGENDS***, below], he is the god of youth. His name merely means "son" and so is a mystery title which is ascribable to many suitable local deities."—Matthews and Matthews, p. 111.

§137.14 **MAG TURED, SECOND BATTLE OF** (epic battle of the Tuatha De Danann—including Lug, Dagda, Ogma—against the invadian Fomorians) (Irish folklore). "Now Lug and the Dagda and Ogma pursued the Fomorians, for they had carried off the Dagda's harper, whose name was Uaitne. Then they reached the banqueting-house in which were Bres son of Elotha and Elotha son of Delbaeth. There hung the harp on the wall. That is the harp in which the Dagda had bound the melodies so that they sounded not until by his call he summoned them forth; when he said this below:

> Come Daurdabla!
> Come Coir-cethar-chuir!
> Come summer, Come winter!
> Mouths of harps and bags and pipes!

"Now that harp had two names, Daur-da-bla 'Oak of two greens' and Coir-cethar-chuir 'Four-angled music'.

"Then the harp went forth from the wall, and killed nine men, and came to the Dagda. And he played for them the three things whereby harpers are distinguished, to wit, sleep-strain and smile-strain and wail-strain. He played wail-strain to them, so that their tearful women wept. He played smile-strain to them, so their women and children laughed. He played sleep-strain to them, and the company fell asleep. Through that sleep the three of them escaped unhurt from the Fomorians though these desired to slay them.

"Then the Dagda brought with him the heiffer which had been given to him for his labor. For when she called her calf all the cattle of Ireland which the Fomorians had taken as their tribute, grazed.

"Now after the battle was won and the corpses cleared away, the Morrigu [also Morrig(h)an — one of three war goddesses of Old Irish mythology (Ed.)], daughter of Ernmas, proceeded to proclaim that battle and the mighty victory which had taken place, to the royal heights of Ireland and to its fairy hosts and its chief waters and its river-mouths. And hence it is that Badb (*i.e.,* the Morrigu) also describes high deeds. 'Has thou any tale?' said everyone to her then. And she replied:

> Peace up to heaven,
> Heaven down to earth,
> Earth under heaven,
> Strength in every one, etc.

"Then, moreover, she was prophesying the end of the world, and foretelling every evil that would be therein, and every disease and every vengeance. Wherefore then she sang this lay below:

> I shall not see a world that will be dear
>   to me.
> Summer without flowers,
> Kine will be without milk,
> Women without modesty,
> Men without valor,
> Captures without a king....
> Woods without mast,
> Sea without produce....
> Wrong judgments of old men,
> False precedents of lawyers,
> Every man a betrayer,
> Every boy a reaver.
> Son will enter his father's bed,
> Father will enter his son's bed,
> Every one will be his brother's
>   brother-in-law....
> An evil time!
> Son will deceive his father,
> Daughter will deceive her mother."

— Cross and Slover, pp.47-48.

§137.15 "SAINT DAVID. Patron saint of Wales, actually a pagan god Christianized in the 11th century AD. He was the Welsh sea god worshiped as Dewi, from the Aryan *devi* or *deva*, 'deity'. Though he was called a 6th-century bishop, nothing was written of him until 1090, more than 500 years later....

"David's title, the Waterman, was explained by Christian scholars to mean he was a teetotaler. Welsh sailors knew better; their traditions placed him in the depths of the sea. They called him Davy Jones, who like the sea god Mananann kept the souls of drowned seamen in his 'locker'....

"Even in Christian disguise, David retained the sacred skills of a bard. It was claimed that his miraculous talent for harping and singing came from his lineal descent from the virgin Mary, of the ancient house of King David the Harpist, in the eighteenth generation. Mary was also identified with the Welsh sea-goddess Marian, Dewi's bride, receiver of the souls of the dead. Welsh bards called their death songs *marwysgafen*, the 'giving to Mary', sung to send the funeral boat to the Isles of the Dead." — Walker, pp.212-213.

§137.16 "SAINT BRIGID AND THE HARPS (Irish folklore). It was not in the nature of things that a Celtic saint should despise music or poetry. St. Brigid being once on a journey, sought hospitality for herself and her sisters in the *lios* of a petty king. This king and his chief officers, including his harpers, were absent, but some of his sons did all that religious reverence and a hospitable spirit could for the suitable reception of their honoured guests. After a frugal meal the hosts and guests continued an interesting conversation, during which Brigid, observing the harps suspended on the wall, requested the princes to favour her with some of the ancient melodies of the country. 'Alas, honoured lady!' said the eldest, 'our father and the bard are absent, as we have mentioned, and neither my brothers nor myself have practised the art. However, bless our fingers, and we will do all in our power to gratify you.' She touched their fingers with the tips of her own, saying some prayers in a low voice; and when the young men sat down to the instruments, they drew from them such sweet and powerful melody as never before was heard in that hall. So enthralling was the music that it seemed as if they never could tire of playing, nor their audience of listening. While the performance was still proceeding the king and his suite entered the large hall, and were amazed at hearing sweet and skilful strains from the untaught fingers of the princes. Recognising the saint and her daughters, their wonder ceased. The gift was not conferred for the occasion, for the princely performers retained their power over the harp-strings while they lived." — Kennedy, pp.334-35.

§137.17 "DAVID'S HARP [Jewish folktale — Palestine, 19th century]. Now King David had a wondrous, magic harp,[247] which he hung by the window of his bedroom chamber. And at midnight the North wind came and blew across its strings, and made wonderful music. That music gently woke King David and called him to take up his pen, and he wrote the psalms in a trance. The words rose up from within him effortlessly, and the Holy Spirit spoke through him as if he himself were a kind of harp. That is how the Psalms came to be written.

"Nor was this the only blessing brought by this magic harp. For the notes plucked by the fingers of the wind also carried King David into the future, even beyond the time of his death, so that he had a vision of the Temple in Jerusalem that his son Solomon would build in the days to come. But so too did he have a vision of the future days in which the Temple would be destroyed, and the people of Israel would be driven into exile into Babylon. That is when David wrote the words of this psalm:

By the rivers of Babylon,

there we sat down, yea, we wept,
when we remembered Zion.
We hung our harps upon the willows
    in the midst thereof.
For they that carried us away captive
required of us a song,
and they that wasted us
required of us mirth, saying
sing us one of the songs of Zion.

How shall we sing the Lord's song
in a strange land?

"Then the day arrived when the bleak exile of David's vision took place: the walls of the Temple were torn down and the people were driven into exile. It was a bitter time indeed. Yet the day also came when the Jews returned to the Holy Land and set about rebuilding Jerusalem. In those days there lived in Jerusalem an old man whose name was Shabbatai. And this old man had thought long and hard about the wonders of David's harp, for he himself was a maker of lutes and harps. Every time he carved and strung another harp, Shabbatai thought of the harp of David and wondered what had been its fate. For he knew well the tales of its wondrous ways, and the legend that its strings were made from the sinews of the ram which Abraham sacrificed instead of Isaac at Mount Moriah. The thought possessed him that if that harp could be found, perhaps the Holy Spirit could once again emerge and bless Jerusalem as it had in the days of King David.

"But where could David's harp be found? It had disappeared at the time of the Bayblonian exile. And the more the old man thought about this, the more certain he became that King David's harp had surely been among those hung in the willow trees in Babylon. For the people had no doubt recognized that David's prophecy in the psalm had come true, and

---

247 In many accounts, a lyre-like instrument. (Ed.)

to honor the prophecy they surely must have hung David's harp among their own.

"In this way, the notion of searching for David's harp in the willow trees by the rivers of Babylon took root in the old man's mind. He shared this thought with everyone he knew, but they all thought he had taken leave of his senses. Eventually the longing to search for the wondrous harp overwhelmed Shabbatai, and he decided to undertake the journey to Babylon no matter what the obstacles, and he made preparations for the journey.

"His wife and children tried to convince him to abandon the mad notion that King David's harp could still be found. Besides, he was an old man, how could he complete such a journey? But every night, Shabbatai dreamed he glimpsed David's golden harp hung in the branches of a willow, just beyond his reach. So one day he simply set out with no more than a waterbag, a pouch filled with dates and figs, and a staff which he had carved himself.

"Now it was a terrible wilderness the old man had to cross, and his journey was as difficult as that of the Children of Israel in their desert wanderings. Yet Shabbatai felt as if he were guided by the distant strains of David's harp, calling to him as it had to King David at midnight. In this way he was inspired to overcome every obstacle, and managed to cross mountains and valleys, rivers and streams, and the desert wilderness that seemed to stretch before him endlessly.

"This great effort took its toll on the old man, and left him worn and frail by the time he finally reached Babylon. There he searched along the shores of every river for the willow trees in which the harps might be hung. He looked among the branches of many a willow tree, but not one of them contained even a single harp. Yet, only when he was certain that he had searched beside every river in Babylon did Shabbatai become discouraged, and begin to fear that he had failed in his quest.

"With no one to turn to for help, the old man sought out the burial place of the righteous sages who had died in that land of exile, and he called upon the dead to come to him and reveal where the harp could be found. For a long time Shabbatai prayed before the tombs, but all he heard was the whispering of the wind.

"Then, all at once, Shabbatai saw a shadow cast from behind him, and when he turned around he saw an old man standing there who did not have the appearance of one of the living, but of one who had come from the Other World to greet him. The ghostlike figure spoke and said, 'What is it that you wish to know?' Shabbatai poured out his heart and pleaded to be guided to the willow tree in which King David's harp could be found.

"When the ancient sage heard this, he said, 'You are right to search for David's harp, but you are looking in the wrong place. For the psalm does not say that the harps were hung in Babylon, but in the willows of Zion, for the people hung them there before they departed, knowing from the first they could never sing the songs of the Lord in a strange land. It is in Zion that the harp can be found. Not in the land of our exile.' Then this the ghostly figure began to fade from view until he vanished from before Shabbatai's eyes. And although he had not dared to ask, Shabbatai was certain that the sage could have been none other than King David himself, who had come there to guide him. So that day he started back to the Holy Land. He was not discouraged that he had come all that distance in vain, because at the end of that journey he had learned a valuable secret. And the hope of finding David's harp still inspired him and served as his guide.

"So it was that the long journey back to the Holy Land seemed but a moment to the old man, who once again heard the distant calling of David's harp. And as he approached the boundaries of the Land of Israel, it seemed to Shabbatai that he could see a divine presence hovering above the trees and flowers, and he realized that the Holy Land had lost none of its holiness since the time of King David, but that it had been hidden from his sight and that of the other inhabitants. Now it had been revealed to Shabbatai's eyes at last.

"The old man's family was so overjoyed to see him again that they did not even ask about his mission, they just assumed he had failed. Nor did Shabbatai reveal all that had happened to him, for he had decided to say nothing about it until he had succeeded in finding the harp.

"But where was Shabbatai to seek the harp in the Holy Land? He could not look to the rivers of Babylon to lead him to the willows; in the Holy Land willow trees grew everywhere. Where was his search to begin? Shabbatai considered this question for the longest time, and one day the answer dawned on him as a great revelation. He took leave of his astonished family and set out once again, this time for Mount Zion. For although all of the Holy Land is called Zion, there is one specific mountain that bears that name.

"When he reached Mount Zion, old Shabbatai found that he was able to climb it as if he were a young man, so inspired was he there. He searched the mountain until he was familiar with every willow tree, but he did not find a single harp. This was more than the old man could bear. He had been so certain this time. He sat down in despair and put his head in his hands, and in that moment his heart almost broke. But just then the distant strains of a music more beautiful than anything he had ever heard reached his ears. And all at once a sense of peace came over the old man.

"Then he arose like one in a trance and followed the music. When he turned in the right direction, the music seemed to grow louder, and when he turned the wrong way it grew dim. In this way Shabbatai was led to a cave, whose entrance was hidden behind a willow tree. He entered the cave, and found it filled with a glowing light, and he passed through it, still led by the hypnotic strains of the wondrous music. At last he reached the other end of the cave and came out into a garden that seemed to be surrounded by an aura. He knew he had reached a very sacred place. When he looked up Shabbatai's breath was taken away—for there, in every tree, he saw a harp, its strings plucked by the wind. This was the unearthly music which had led him there. But most wonderful of all was a gleaming, golden object that Shabbatai saw in the upper branches of the finest willow tree of all, one which towered above all of the others. It was at that moment that the old man completed his quest, for he had found the harp of David he had sought for so long. He seated himself at the foot of that lofty willow, and listened to the very strains that had wakened King David himself on so many nights and inspired him to write the immortal psalms. And there, beneath that tree, the old man remained, and some say that he can be found there still, listening as the music of the Holy Spirit drifts across the Holy Land, far more beautiful than anyone can imagine." — Schwartz [Miriam], pp.163-67.

§137.18 THE *NGOMBI* HARP OF AFRICA.

"Meaning in harps, like all African instruments, may be signified externally by the presence of decoration or sculpture, or lie entirely in the internal domain of cultural understanding. Symbolism may inform the naming of parts of the harp, and supernatural power may be invested in its sound. In some cases, the concepts that connect the visual, aural, and social spheres of culture are so clearly expressed that the harp can be seen to represent both the macro- and microcosmos of a particular culture.

"The Bwiti *ngombi* is a case in point.[248] It represents both the microcosmic world of the living and the macrocosmic world of the gods and ancestors. The *ngombi* par-

---

248 James Fernandez has written much about the remarkable symbolism of the *ngombi*. My sources here are [his publications of] 1965, 1973, 1982 and 1986.

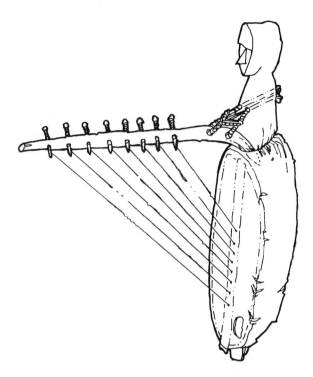

ticipates in Bwiti through the realm of its body (material aspects) and that of its voice (sound) (DeVale 1988). In both realms, it expresses the complementarity of female and male, a concept that informs Bwiti ritual; it is evident in the equal participation in Bwiti of men and women, and in the division of a Bwiti chapel, the sacred space where Bwiti ritual is centered, into male and female halves.

"On the microcosmic level, in the realm of the body, the harp's resonator symbolizes the stomach of the female principle, the source of all life, and its neck is the symbol of male potency. The juncture of the neck and resonator symbolizes sexual union. The painting of the sound table also has meaning; it is usually painted red (blood) on the left half and white (semen) on the right, corresponding to the female and male halves of a Bwiti chapel. In the realm of the voice, four strings are considered to be male and four female; they are said to intermingle harmoniously in music as humans do in Bwiti ritual and society.

"On the macrocosmic level, the harp symbolizes both the voice and body of *Nyingwan Mbege*, the Sister of God, to whose life-giving benevolence Bwiti members appeal. Each element of the harp represents a part of her body: her features are carved or sculpted on the shelf of the harp; the resonator is her stomach, her womb, the spiritual Source of Life; the neck and tuning pegs are her spine and ribs; and the strings, her tendons and sinews. Even the soundholes cut out of the sound table have meaning: the upper two are her breasts, the sources of her nurturance; and the lower soundhole is the birth hole. The music, the sound of the harp, is her voice, the female voice of pity and consolation, and with it comes her special powers to drive evil spirits out of the Bwiti chapel while inviting the ancestors in. The powers of the Sister of God work through the harpist, who is considered to be the guardian of the chapel,[249] and the spirits of ancestor harpists enter the body of the harp, as the rest of the ancestors enter the chapel.

"The *ngombi* is also a vehicle for communication between living Bwiti members and their gods and ancestors;[250] the eight strings, like the eight sacred trees, are locales for sending and receiving messages between them. Its sound is simultaneously the music played by the dead in the

---

249 See our themes **T1b** (Musician as medium through which magical power is conveyed to a community or congregation) and **T1c** (Music as medium through which spirit world [of divinities, supranatural beings] attempts to signal or contact man), *Introductory Remarks* Vol I above. (Ed.)

250 See our theme **T1a** (Music as magical means of communication with god[s] or supreme being[s]), *Introductory Remarks* Vol I above. (Ed.)

afterworld, or by the angels in heaven in the Christianized forms of Bwiti; it transmits their blessings to the living Bwiti as well as carries the Bwitis' prayers to the ancestors and gods.

"The harp is so highly respected by Bwiti members that it, in turn, is honored with ritual procedures. As the Sister of God, the *ngombi* is the power of the night, her symbol is the moon; she must not be exposed to the light of the male power of day, the sun. Thus, at the end of the all-night Bwiti ceremonies, four 'exit songs' are sung for the harp, and it is danced in procession from the chapel to its own special light-tight storage chamber at the end of the village.

"The *ngombi* is vital to the efficacy of Bwiti ritual. In its totality, through the realms of both its body and its voice, the harp unites both microcosm and macrocosm of Bwiti society and religion. Through the power of its music, the *ngombi* serves as the primary path of communication between the world of the living and that of the gods and ancestors, the seen and the unseen." — DeVale, in Brincard, p.59.

HARPIST.

§137A.1 "The symbolism of the harpist follows from that of the instrument. He frequently occurs in literature, one of the most famous examples being in Goethe's *Wilhelm Meister*. In a German poem — 'Die Krone' — Guinevere arouses her husband's jealousy by telling him of a knight who rides past every night, singing.... Celtic folklore tells how Yseult was abducted by a harp-player. [In a related context] the tale of the Pied Piper describes how the children follow him as he plays a tune on his pipe. All these figures are personifications of the fascination of death, that is,

Freud's death-wish. Also, in Greek mythology the psychopomp Hermes is the inventory of the lyre and the flute.[251"] — Cirlot, p.140.

HAWAIIAN MYTHS. *(See p.343.)*

§141.4 PE-LE, GODDESS OF VOLCANIC FIRE.[252] *Ed. note:* In this central Hawaiian legend Lo-hi-au — culture hero and leader of his people — wins the favor of the gods; dies; and is reborn; nature's deadly might is not tamed, but at least is accommodated; a "new" world begins for mankind. Through it all meanwhile there is music — the dancing of gods in the lehua groves... the hula... the rhythmic chanting, and the incantations... the steady beat of the drum — functioning as a medium through which the worlds of men and gods seem to overlap, and blend.

"Pe-le, the Goddess, came up out of her pit in Ki-lau-ea. No longer would she sit on the lava-hearth below, with skin rugged and blackened, with hair the colour of cinders, and with reddened eyes; no longer would she seem a hag whom no man would turn towards. She came up out of the pit a most lovely woman. Her many sisters were at her side, and each of them was only less lovely than was Pe-le upon that day. They stood each side of her because it was forbidden to come behind the Goddess or to lay a hand upon her burning back....

"[Pe-le and her sisters bathed and feasted, and sported themselves in the water and along the beach. Then Pe-le went into a cavern and laid herself down to sleep. As she slept] the youngest of her sisters, the little Hi-i-aka-of-the-fire-bloom, [went] to where the groves of lehua showed their scarlet blossoms. She was enchanted with the trees that she went amongst; she gathered the blossoms and wove them into

---

251 See A. H. Krappe, *La Genèse des mythes* (Paris, 1952).
252 For an alternative and fuller treatment, see pp. 343, 352, above.

wreaths. And then she saw another girl gathering blossoms and weaving them into wreaths, and she knew this other girl for the tree-spirit, Ho-po-e. And Ho-po-e, seeing Hi-i-aka, danced for her. These two became friends; they danced for each other, and they played together, and never had Hi-i-aka, the little sister of the dread Goddess, known a friend that was as dear and as lovely as Ho-po-e — Ho-po-e whose life was in the grove of the lehuas.

"As for Pe-le, the Goddess, she slept in the cavern, and in her sleep she heard the beating of a drum*. It sounded like a drum that announces a hula. Her spirit went from where she slept; her spirit-body followed the sound of that drum. Over the sea her spirit-body followed that sound. Her spirit-body went to the Island of Kauai. There she came to a hall sacred to Laka: a hula was being performed there. As a most lovely woman Pe-le entered that hall. All the people who were assembled for the hula turned to look upon her. And in that hall Pe-le saw Prince Lo-hi-au.

"The Prince was seated on a dais, and his musicians were beside him. [When he beheld Pe-le he could think of no one else.] She let him have kisses, but kisses only. [Then] she rose in her spirit-body, and floated away, leaving the house, leaving the island, crossing the sea, and coming back to where her body lay in the cavern in Puna.

"[Wildly Prince Lo-hi-au sought for the woman who had been with him, and when he could not find her he hung himself by his own loin-cloth. The people found their chieftain dead. Meanwhile Hi-i-aka, the sister of Pe-le, had fallen in love with Prince Lo-hi-au. She and Pe-le made a compact between them, that Lo-hi-au should be restored to life, that he would be the lover of Pe-le for five days and five nights, and after that he would be the lover of Hi-i-aka. Hi-i-aka agreed not to caress him or kiss him before this time — but only on the condition that Pe-le herself would not bring fire to the lehua groves of her friend, the tree-spirit Ho-po-e.

"[H-i-aka restored Lo-hi-au to life, through her incantations. But then, she could not resist kissing him. In consequence Pe-le sent fire, and blackened the earth — including the groves of Ho-po-e. Lava overtook Lo-hi-au also — and he died a second time.

"[At last the two sisters became reconciled. Kane-milo-hai — Pele's brother — was summoned, to restore the Prince to life a second time.]

"And Kane-milo-hai, coming over the waters in his shell-canoe, found Lo-hi-au's spirit, in the form of a bird, flitting over the waters. He took it, and he brought it to where Lo-hi-au lay. He broke up the lava in which the body was set, and he reformed the body out of the fragments, restoring to it the lineaments that Lo-hi-au had. Then he brought the spirit back into the body.

"And afterwards it happened that Hi-i-aka, wandering where the lehua groves were growing again, and knowing that after dire destruction a new world had come into existence, heard the chant:

Puna's plain takes the colour of
    scarlet —
Red as heart's blood the bloom of
lehua.
The nymphs of the Pit string hearts
    in a wreath:
O the pangs of the Pit, Ki-lau-ea!

Hi-a-ka went to where the chant came from; she discovered Lo-hi-au restored to life once more, With him she wandered through the land below Ki-lau-ea. Men and women were peopling the land, and the Gods of the Pit were not now so terror-inspiring." — Colum, pp.261-71.

HIAWATHA.

§146A.1 "The legendary sage of the Iroquois Indians of North America. He was an Onondaga chief who founded the League of Five Nations, also known as the Iroquis Confederacy, in the sixteenth century.

"At first, the shaman Atotarho opposed the league's formation and killed Hiawatha's wife and daughter. The bloodthirsty magician had snakes instead of hair, and misshapen hands and feet. But the singing of the great Iroquois chiefs calmed his mind and restored his body to normal. Then, Atotarho and Hiawatha were reconciled and the five peoples united. These comprised the Cayuga, the Mohawk, the Oneida, the Onondaga and the Seneca." — Cotterell (Macmillan Myths and Legends), p.206.[253]

HINDU PRACTICES AND BELIEFS. *(See also pp.364, 867.)*

§149.9 "SIKHISM — doctrine and practices of a Punjabi monotheistic Hindu religious sect founded and developed c. 1469-1708. "The focal point of Sikh life and worship is the Guru Granth Sahib [the sacred scriptures — also called *Adi Granth.* The *Guru Granth Sahib* includes religious teachings expressed in metrical form by six of the Gurus (the first and ninth), as well as verses by some Hindu and Muslim teachers with a similar religious outlook]. Sikh worship takes place in its presence and consists of the congregational singing of hymns from the scripture, led by musicians, and the reading and exposition of the scriptures by members of the congregation. The place where acts of worship are held is called a *gurdwara* (literally the door *[dwara]* of the guru), the abode of the guru. In fact this name may be applied to the room of a private house as well as to a place of public worship owned by the community, provided it contains a copy of the scripture.... Public worship *(diwan)* may take place on any day.... At the Golden Temple in Amritsar, the principal Sikh shrine on the site of a building originally constructed by Guru Arjan, the daily reading of the scripture begins before dawn and continues beyond sunset." — Cole, in Hinnells, p.251.

§149.10   **HINDU   DANCE   AND RELIGION.** "Bharata Natya Sastra. All Indian dancing claims as its origin the *Bharata Natya Sastra,* a canonical work *(sastra)* outlining the theories and practice of the art of the theatre and dance combined *(natya)* written by the sage Bharata. Attributed dates for the manuscript of this Sanskrit treatise vary from 3 BC to 5 AD, but it is apparent from the context that the inception of the work is of even greater antiquity than the earlier of these dates and is lost in mythology. The man Bharata figures in Hindu thought as a combined sage and patron saint of the dance. It is to him, it is said, the gods revealed the art of dance. He codified this knowledge and formulated its theories for the practice and study of succeeding generations. This sastra is also referred to as the Fifth Veda (Holy Book), so sacred is Bharata's relation to art, and so religious is the Hindu concept of dance. In the sastra, the entire gamut of theatrical experience, philosophy, theory, and practice is adumbrated. Its details reach extremes, notating even the exact measurements for three types of theatre houses and the numbers of possible movements of the human body in dance. The sastra does not stand alone. It

---

253 "Singing" in this case may be closer to rhythmic chant — as an invocation of spells etc — than to melodic song *per se.* Yet the connotation here as in other native American "song" is clearly contrasted to prose speech, is commonly (if not inevitably) associated with dance and some use of instruments, and may rightly be called, I should think, "musical". See also Biblical story of David's calming Saul; shamanism (under **DRUM***); our theme **T4b** (Music as magical restorative of mental or physical health), *Introductory Remarks* Vol I above. (Ed.)

has been followed by a considerable body of literature through the ages commenting on, annotating, and enlarging details of Bharata's original revelations.

"Among all Indian dance techniques, Bharata Natya (whose name derives from the sastra), as now practiced, mostly closely conforms in spirit and procedure to the clear outlines of the ancient canonical works. Bharata Natya enjoys therefore a double distinction. While being India's most brilliant dance, it is also the most classic....

"Religion. The connection between dance and religion is deep, particularly in Hinduism where Shiva* is supposed to have created the very world by setting its first rhythm in motion by dance. Mythology abounds in descriptions of the gods dancing under a variety of circumstances. Every evening Shiva dances with his son Ganesa on the peak of Mount Kailas in the Himalayas. Shiva dances in victory over conquered forces of evil. He even once curbed his wife's pride by a dance contest in which he immodestly lifted his leg into the air and left her a victim of embarrassment, unable to continue dancing. Shiva's consort, Parvati, is said to have originated Lasya, or soft style of dance. It is to this class that Bharata Natya, as it is primarily practiced in the South today, belongs. Shiva and Parvati are not the only dancers among the gods. There are few who do not have some kind of dance ascribed to them.

"Temple festivals were until recently inseparable from dance. Tamil [people of Tamil Nad in Southeast India] preoccupation with religion led the people to dot their checkered patches of growing paddy fields with ornate temples and gates (gopura). No temple is without sculptures of dancers both inside and outside. Some temples in Tamil Nad date from the sixth century, the beginning of Hindu architecture in stone. Many are dedicated to Shiva, the creator-destroyer and the source of all movement within the cosmos. The static deity of these temples is represented by the stone lingam (phallus); the dynamic deity is in bronze and of varied form and name. Sometimes the dynamic form worshipped is Shiva as Nataraja (King of the Dancers)....

"To the dancer, the four arms of the nataraja are a depiction of dance movement in an immovable and static medium. To the mystic, the arms and legs of the figure have a cosmological significance, as the dance is taken as merely a human representation of a cosmic fact. In the nataraja the frontal palm of the right hand which is lifted and slightly bent represents security (abhaya) to devotees, the left hand which is thrown across the body with fingers drooping down (kari-hasta) points to the feet of the Lord as the refuge of the devotee, the upraised left foot represents the blessing (anugraha) bestowed by the Lord. In one of the upper arms, Shiva carries a small drum representing the creative sound which began the universe, and in the other, fire which represents destruction. Under his right foot is a conquered demon signifying triumph over evil. Within these figures of the dancing king is expressed the entire function of the Lord Shiva, as creator, preserver from spiritual and material evil, and savior of mankind.

"In Chidambaram, one of Tamil Nad's holiest temples, Shiva as Nataraja is the central deity. Here at the theoretical center of the world (literally, chidambaram) the Lord who created the world by dancing is worshipped. The walls of the fourteenth-century gates are adorned with carved stone representations of temple dancers in 108 Bharata Natya poses. Some poses are gymnastic rather than artistic to modern ways of thinking, and are not performed by artists of today. Remaining poses in Chidambaram provide, however, a favorable similarity and comparison with modern Bharata Natya. The stone of the past lives, as it were, in the flesh of today.

"Gods and their dances are perpetuated in many temple stones and bronzes. The Belur and Halebid temples of Mysore, among the loveliest in all India, are mainly devoted to dance. They were built by the

Canarese Hoysala king, Bittiga, after his conversion from the Jain religion (a reformist Hinduism similar to Buddhism) to Vaishnavism (the worship of Vishnu as central deity), and commemorate his driving the Tamil Chola kings from Kannada in 1116 AD. The legend of many of these sculptures describes how Vishnu took the form of a ravishing female goddess, Mohini, and danced in order to bring about the defeat of the demon Bhasmasura. The demon had been given the power to kill anything over which he held his charmed hand. Intoxicated with his own magic he became obsteperous. Mohini lures him into a dance contest and strikes a pose in which she holds her hand over her head. In his abandon the evil giant follows suit and destroys himself.

"From the worship of dancer-gods, the worship of the dancer is a natural evolution. Rather than places of worship, the temples of Belur and Halebid were, in effect, scarcely more than dancing pavilions for the beautiful queen Santala-devi, one of history's greatest Bharata Natya dancers. Inside the sanctum before images of the central deity Vishnu, the queen danced on large circular slabs of black marble. Outside on the walls are carved layer upon layer of friezes depicting battle scenes from the great religious epics, Ramayana and Mahabharata, erotic scenes (*mithuna*, an indispensable adjunct of Indian temple architecture), and portraits of the gods in various incarnations. The best carving is reserved for the large bracket figures depicting the life and dances of the queen....

"**Devadasi.** Preservation of dance traditions in South India was not left entirely to lifeless temple statues and words in a dead language. Inevitably the close interrelation between religion, temple, and dance, produced a cult of temple dancers attached to temples. These dancers were called devadasis* or servants of the deity, and their part in history and culture is pertinent. Had it not been for them and their teachers, Bharata Natya, the pride of In-

dian dance, would certainly never have survived the vicissitudes and vagaries of history.

"The prototype of the devadasi in religious mythology is the Apsaras* or heavenly nymph, who dances for the entertainment of the gods. She is found wherever Hindu thought has penetrated, whether in the guise of 'flying angels' as in the Tunyuam Buddhist caves in northwest China, or as 'celestial dancers' in the sometimes Buddhist, sometimes Brahmanical temples of Angkor in Cambodia. Few cave paintings or temple sculptures of India ignored the Apsaras. Few temples were without at least one devadasi dancer.

"In actual practice in South India the private lives of these repositories of art, the devadasi, became a difficult question. The profession of prostitution they naturally followed brought odium upon them and their art. In the wake of the many social reform movements that arose in mdoern India, attempts were made both by legislation as well as by creation of public opinion, to abolish the cast and institution of devadasis....

"**Effect of Bharata Natya.** A Bharata Natya evening of dance begins with devotional songs by the musicians who set the mood for an ecstasy. With the appearance of the dancer, the program bursts into a swift, restless, joyous mood which does not abate or subside until the concluding item. The Western spectator is first dazzled by the extreme articulation of almost every part of the dancer's body and by the use of every member of the body in a seemingly endless series of varied postures, leaps, turns, and bends. After witnessing several performances, he begins to recognize repetitions of the fragmentary basic movements. These each time are differently chained together and seem to be completely new movements. Few dance techniques have the vitality, comprehensive and all-inclusive play of the body demanded by Bharata Natya. For the Westerner, its movements present a new concept of the human body. Nearly all of the basic gestures of Bharata Natya are scrupulously avoided in the classic ballet of the West. Bharata Natya proves them not only beautiful but essential to the universal pool of dance resources....

"Bharata Natya is a kind of mesmerism, overpowering in its insistent meter, astounding speed, and succession upon succession of body patterns....

"Bharata Natya is also a suggestive art, and here it offers an analogy with music. Music in dealing with sound is denied a concrete form for explicit realism. Bharata Natya by dealing with abstraction and conventions functions on a purely aesthetic and remote plane. Bharata the sage forbade realism so that godlike and unlimited ideals may be suggested by the artist and realized in the minds of the spectators. Even when Bharata Natya is being specific it presents its meaning through conventions and symbols, leaving the idea to become as great and as near-perfect as the combined imaginations of the dancer and audience can make it.

"Sastric texts propound high-flown rules for the dancer in saying that: hands must be like the movements of fishes swimming in pools; the walk must be like the gliding of the swan, or quick and animated like the movements of a fantail; the body must be held like a horse about to leap; all the body, the hands, and the arms must have the suppleness of silk; the feeling of the dance must be like the ecstasy of a peacock when he dances before his mate at sunset....

"**Accompanying music.** To watch the musicians [which include singer, drummer, and players of flutes and stringed instruments] as they perform is akin to watching a kind of self-induced hypnosis. There is an element of trance in the fact that despite their lengthy performances of continuous singing, musicians rarely tire. Within the rigid rules controlling fractional entries on 1/4 and 1/16 beats, and working within the minute, 22 purely tempered, tonal divisions (*srutis*) of the Indian octave, they abandon themselves to a mood of ecsasy. In joyous release the singer shouts his song and the drummer forces his rhythms out of his hide-and-wood instrument. Together, they bend their bodies, shake their heads in approbation (although the gesture looks to Westerners as if they are saying 'no, no'), and apparently remain seated with difficulty as they bring out their music. The singer is the core of the music; the drummer, music's life. The drummer and singer focus their attention on each other with a svengali-like intensity. Each seems to draw out of the other effort upon effort, precision upon precision, perfection upon perfection....

"**Manipuri dancing** [of the territory of Manipur, at India's most northeastern frontier, surrounded by nine converging mountain ranges]. Mythology connects Manipur's origin with dancing. According to the Meithi people (whose holy scriptures or *puranas* are often not in agreement with orthodox Hinduism), Manipur was created so that gods might have a place to dance. The story of Manipur's creation is that Krishna and the Gopis (milkmaids who always accompany him) had created a dance of ecstasy in heaven, the Ras Lila, with which they amused themselves in secret. Shiva (in Manipur, a lesser god than Krishna) asked to see this enchanting Ras Lila. Krishna declined in part, but allowed Shiva to stand porter at the gate providing he, on oath, kept his back to the Ras Lila, and did not peek at the dance itself. Shiva kept his promise. Afterwards he became intoxicated with the memory of the ravishing music, the clank of the bells around the feet, and the whirl of the turning skirts. He could think of nothing else. Parvati, Shiva's wife, grew irritated by his constant preoccupation. Together they decided to recreate a Ras Lila of their own. The problem was where to perform it.

"They walked down the Himalayas until they reached Manipur. Shiva stood on Mount Kobru and saw that the valley was submerged in water. He took his sacred trident to make a gash in the side of a mountain, and the waters immediately drained into the Irrawaddy River of Burma where they still flow. Shiva and his consort were elated at the sight of the prospective land for the much desired Ras Lila. They summoned nine celestial nymphs (*Apsaras*) and each stood on the nine ranges of hills surrounding the valley. The musical instruments of Manipur were created, the *ping* drum (something like the mridanga of Bharata Natya) and the *pena* (a small stringed instrument a little like a violin). Dressed in the Manipuri Ras Lila costume, the group danced their imitation of the heavenly dance. The serpent god, Pakhan-ba, who dwells at the core of the world, kept the area lit with the radiance of his jeweled, cobralike hood. At the conclusion of the dance, the serpent was in such ecstasy that the glitter of his jewels was released in a spray over the entire area. And so it is that the place was called *mani* (diamond) *pur* (place), and thus it is, that the Ras Lila costumes of Manipuri dancers are sprinkled with shiny mica to sparkle like the original diamonds....

"The religion of Manipur expresses itself in a synthesis of music, singing, dancing, and drama. Since Manipur is a deeply religious nation, the majority of its population is proficient in several of these arts. Dancing, widespread as it is, constitutes only one emotional outlet for the people. The dominant element of the Manipuri's religion and life is music, and it subtends all the rituals as well as the arts. Of music's many facets, kirtan singing [singing of hymns of praise, originally of Radha and Krishna] occupies the highest position of honor....

"Every night from every temple of Manipur (and their number is legion since every house has its own private temple and attached dance pavilion or *mandal*), sounds of devotional singing ensue. This performance is called Shanda Arathi or offering of the sacred fire to Lord Krishna.

Manipuris say the custom developed because each night as Krishna returned home from tending his cows, his mother, fearing that harm might have come to him, lit a fire in order to inspect his body and reassure herself of his safety. A more likely explanation, however, is that it is a carry-over of primitive fears that the setting sun might not rise again without propitiation and human inducements. Nightly singing is as important a part of the Manipuri's daily ritual as are his morning ablutions and affixing of the sandalwood-paste *tika* marks on his forehead....

"The guiding spirit [of Manipur] is religion, and the body and its movements are the highest dedication of the human being to his gods. Sports and dance are also inextricably connected in Manipur. God is worshiped through boat racing, Ras Lila, polo ('In case of epidemics, offer a stick and a ball to the gods,' it says in the Meithi holy books regarding hockey and polo), folk dances, mountain climbing (necessary to reach where the best Ras Lilas are often performed), and Lai Haraoba [dance imitation of the Ras Lila]. All are part of one devotion. Manipuris say that religion without physical culture is no religion. As for the dance; according to them it is physical culture made most 'ornamental' and all for the glory of the gods." — Bowers, pp.13-19, 22-24, 43-44, 109-110, 123-24, 147.

HORN. *(See also p.369.)*

§152.3 See **ORLANDO (Rinaldo)***.

§152.4 "As a musical instrument, [the horn] figures in emblems symbolizing the spiritual call to join the Holy War. This particular meaning is corroborated by the crosses, trefoils, circles and fleurs-de-lis associated with the horn.[254]" — Cirlot, p.151.

---

254 See Harold Bayley, *The Lost Language of Symbolism* (London, 1912; reprint 1951).

§152.5 "During the Middle Ages many legends emerged connected with the old families of Cumbria [in the Lake District of England] with the object of explaining the symbols on the coats of arms of the family to which they belonged. One of the most interesting of these is the story of the Horn of Egremont. Slightly differing versions are given by the local antiquaries Denton, Sandford and Machel. The main facts, however, relate that the heir to the barony of Egremont was captured in war and held to ransom. His brother at home refused to send the money necessary to obtain the prisoner's release but instead made himself lord of the barony. Meanwhile the captive had been strung up by his hair to a beam. The chieftain's daughter, however, who loved the young man, aided by her maid, cut him down one night, but severed the skin of his scalp while doing so. The lovers fled and arrived some time later at the closed gate of Egremont Castle, where the usurping baron was feasting in the Great Hall. Suddenly, the horn at the gate which could be rung only by the rightful heir was sounded. The guilty baron sprang up in alarm, but, we are told, a reconciliation was eventually effected between the brothers sealed by the grant of the lordship of Millom to the younger."[255] — Rowling, p.53.

HUNGARIAN FOLKTALES AND MYTHS.

§153A.1 "How People Got a Taste of Tobacco and How They Took to Dancing. In the beginning, after the world was finished and Adam and Eve had been settled in Paradise, it so happened that they had to move out and set to tilling the soil for their living.

"And in the course of time they had taken to procreation, and a hundred years later their offspring had multiplied. But not any of them had ever heard of such things as smoking a pipe or dancing. It is true that every now and then they used to come together, but the time was passed in conversation and the singing of songs by the women, while Adam was telling the people about the beauty of Paradise, of the wonderful life they had there, their expulsion from it, or about the murderous Cain and the death of his son Abel.

"And sometimes he would tell the people about the things he had heard from the archangels, Gabriel and Raphael, about the bliss of Heaven, the Fall of the defiant angels, of the torments of Hell, and about the advent of Jesus Christ. And he would always find something to tell the folks, and they liked to listen to him. It's no wonder that Adam and Eve had known such a lot about these matters, since they had been told about them by the Archangel Gabriel himself. So their leisure time was passed amidst such useful conversation, or in singing, but never was there anything wrong in their amusements.

"But Satan, the archenemy of all that is good and holy, would not indulge such seemly conduct on their part.

"He thought to himself, 'If they go on forever like this, then what is the use of Hell? If folks are going to behave in this manner, I shan't ever get a single soul into damnation. Surely I shan't gain anything by sitting tight and looking on idly. I've forfeited my right to go back to Heaven, and I can't go back to Hell unless I do something to my credit.'

"Satan has plenty of wits and he always finds the easiest way to entice people into folly. So he thought to himself, 'I will teach them to do something which will bring them right into my net.'

"Once when the people came together to pass the time, as they were wont to do, conversing, praying, and singing, Satan dressed up as a gentleman and, holding a

---

255 Thompson Folklore Motif D1222 (Magic horn [musical]). (Ed.)

walking stick in his hand and a *chibouque* [long pipe] in his mouth, walked up to the house where the gathering was held and knocked at the door. But the people inside the house had not been used to knocking and did not know what it meant. So nobody answered the first knock, and only after the second and third knock did one of them go to open the door. Then Satan entered and greeted the people, and they returned his greeting, wondering what sort of a man this stranger might be, as never before had they seen a man with a pipe in his mouth, breathing out smoke like a chimney. They offered a seat to him, and he sat down on a bench, beside one of the men. There he sat quietly pulling at his pipe. For a while the conversation went on as usual, but this did not suit the visitor. After all, he had not come here to sing with them. So he rose and said, 'I must be leaving now because I have a long way to go. I came here to see whether you did not know a better way to amuse yourselves than this. I think it is pretty dull.'

"The people said, 'We do not find it dull. For us singing hymns and praying is a good enough recreation, and besides it is an entertainment which joins us in a friendly community.'

" 'All right,' the stranger said, 'but I know something better, and why shouldn't I teach you how to get more fun. You could learn that sort of amusement which is the custom in my country. I could teach you to dance, and I am sure you'd like it very much. It's a poor sort of entertainment to go on praying and singing forever.'

"The women asked him, 'What is a dance? Will you please show us what it is, since never before did we hear of such a thing.'

"With an ugly grin the visitor answered, 'Well, as it is your wish I will teach you to dance, but you must listen to me attentively and keep your eyes open. But before I begin teaching you to dance you must try my pipe and take a draw at it in turn, till all of you have got a taste of it. You'll see how delightful you'll find its smoke, feel-

ing better after each pull at it.' And he handed the pipe to the man sitting next to him, adjusting the mouthpiece in the right way between his lips.

" 'Just hold on to it and you'll never regret it,' he said, and he thought to himself, 'Now I've got you, my man. Once you've had a taste for it, you'll never give up smoking, and you'll be willing to pinch the egg from under the hen to get yourself a pipeful of tobacco.'

"The man began pulling at the pipe and found it so much to his liking that soon he was loud in its praises. When he had enough of it, he gave it to his neighbor, and thus, from one man to the other the pipe was passed along, and they found it so much to their liking that it went around and around, and all of them had a pull at it. And while they were having their pleasure in the pipe, the stranger broke suddenly into a song and began dancing a *csárdás* in the fiery way of the Magyars, shaking his feet and clapping at his bootlegs and clicking his heels in a fury.

"The people stood around him and were staring in open-mouthed astonishment at this performance. Never before had they seen a dance, and now the strange gentleman was leaping to one and then to the other, taking a round with each of them in turn, until they got out of breath and the tears came into their eyes from the frantic whirl of the dance. Then he bade them sit down and have a short rest so that they would not dance themselves tired. He asked them if they didn't think it was greater fun than praying and singing for their amusement.

"The people cried out, 'Thank you very much indeed! We shall never forget what you've taught us.'

"And great was Satan's joy upon hearing them say this because he knew that many of them would now dance themselves into perdition.

" 'Fine!' he thought to himself. 'It seems that I will reap where I have not sown. Many a bird will I catch in my snare by this dance.' And he started anew with his frenzied dancing, but this time he was not dancing alone; all the others were shaking a leg.

"Satan looked at the dancers with no end of pleasure. 'Well, that did the trick,' he said to himself. 'I've got my birds in the snare.'

"And since that day people have taken such a fancy to dancing that they have never stopped going on with this folly. And they have grown so fond of smoking their pipes that even their children have taken to that habit.

"Satan enjoined them to stick to the pleasures of smoking and dancing. Again he started dancing, and with him were dancing all the others, and they went waltzing around and around the room, and Satan knew very well that they would not think of praying as long as they were dancing.

"And he gave them his pipe and plenty of tobacco for it, and also tobacco seeds so that they should never be in want of it. And he taught them to make brandy and enjoined them to make merry by smoking and drinking, as a wetted whistle will make for merrier songs.

"Now we know beyond doubt that it was Satan's doing that people have taken to brandy and fallen into the habit of smoking. Confound it all! Hasn't it worked toward the undoing of many a good man!

"If it had not been for the pipe and brandy there'd be less quarreling between people. Because if a man has to do without a pipeful he'll raise hell in his own house."[256] — Dégh, pp.177-181.

HYMN. *(See also p.371.)*

§156.4 "In Christian tradition, a song of praise to God, usually sung to music in public worship; the ancient Greeks composed hymns in honour of their gods and heroes, the most notable being the Homeric hymns; there are records of early hymns from ancient China, Egypt, Babylon and India, usually in praise of their gods, but sometimes also sung to enlist aid in averting sickness or disaster." — Cavendish [Man, Myth and Magic], p.1379.

INDIAN (ASIAN) PRACTICES AND BELIEFS. *(See also p.376.)*

§161.8 See **PAKISTANI FOLKTALES AND MYTHS*** *(p.1310).*

§161.9 "MAHAVIRA. The last Jaina saviour, he was a contemporary of the Buddha, and died about 500 BC. His childhood was distinguished by miracles. One day he overcame a serpent that threatened his friends, thus earning the title Mahavira, 'great hero'.... At the age of thirty-two he distributed his personal possessions to the needy and commenced his inner quest, a terrestrial event that brough an immediate response from the heavens; the firmament glowed like a lake covered in lotus flowers, the air was filled with the sounds of celestial music, and gods descended to pay their respects to Mahavira." — Cotterell, p.78.

---

256 In this story the age-old controversy between "music as elevating" (and therefore sacred) and "music as intoxicating" (and therefore profane or Satanic) is resolved by relegating *singing* to the former category, and *dancing* (along with smoking) to the latter. However is there not — also — a note of gentle enthusiasm for these awful ways of Satan — for the *csárdás,* danced "in the fiery way of the Magyars" — for the merry pleasures of "shaking a leg"? The narrator's "Confound it all!" seems scarcely genuine (it was uttered, perhaps, in the presence of a priest...). See also **DANCING TO DEATH (OR INSANITY)*** (Ed.)

§161.10 "**PARSVA**. The twenty-third Jaina tirthankara, Parsva, or Parsvanatha, is reputed to have lived in the eighth century BC, some 84,000 years after the death of his saintly predecessor, Neminatha. According to legend, he dwelt on earth for a century, having quit his family at the age of thirty to become an ascetic. Parsva was an incarnation of Indra [king of the gods in the *Rig Veda*, the early collection of Hindu hymns], a handsome and noble man whose relations accepted only as a last resort his determination to take the vow of world-renunciation known as sannyasa. His father, King Asvasena of Benares, had been informed through the pre-natal dreams of his queen that their son would be either a world monarch or a world-saviour.

"The encounter between the eight-year-old Parsva and his maternal grandfather Mahipala appears to have been something of a turning point in his development. Parsva was riding an elephant in the jungle when he chanced upon Mahipala, an ascetic since the death of Parsva's grandmother over a decade before. The old hermit was beside himself with anger: had he not once been a king, had he not been disturbed in the midst of the severest penances, and had he not received from the young prince an improper salutation! Seizing an axe, he was about to split a log into two pieces, when Parsva told him that he would kill two serpents within the wood. 'And who are you? Brahma [the Creator, first of the triad of Hindu gods]? Vishnu [the Preserver, second in the triad of Hindu gods]? Shiva* [the Destroyer, third member of the triad of Hindu gods]? I perceive that you can see everything, no matter where.' said Mahipala scornfully. Then he swung the axe, and did slice in half the serpents hidden inside. Grudgingly the recluse acknowledged his grandson's rank as a great sage, especially when the hymn-singing of Parsva was sufficient to ensure the reincarnation of the dying snakes as Ananta, the cosmic serpent, and Lakshmi, the spouse of Vishnu....

"[As a man Parsva fasted] without break, till he attained the supreme consciousness. Nothing could distract him, except the earnest prayers of the gods and his chief disciple, Svayambhu, who successfully requested that Parsva teach the way of escape from eternal rebirth." — Cotterell, p. 81-82.

§161.11 "**VISHNU**. As preserver and restorer, Vishnu is a very popular deity with Hindu worshippers. The root of his name, *vish*, means 'to pervade', and he is regarded as the all-pervading presence, whose power has been manifested to the world in a variety of forms called *avataras*, or 'descents', in which a part of his divine essence was incarnated in a human or supernatural form....

"Vishnu is generally represented pictorially as a handsome youth of a dark blue colour, and dressed like an ancient king. In his four hands he holds a conch shell, a discus, a club, and a lotus flower. His vehicle is Garuda, the sun bird, enemy of all serpents. This antagonism is dramatically portrayed in Krishna's defeat of the water serpent Kaliya. Reminded of his divine nature by Balarama, Vishnu, lying as Krishna [the eighth avatar of Vishnu and the most celebrated hero of Hindu mythology (Ed.)] at the bottom of a pool bestirs himself and dances upon the threatening Kaliya's mighty head. Sparing the exhausted serpent king, Krishna said: 'You shall no longer reside in the Yamuna River, but in the vastness of the ocean. Go! Moreover, I tell you that Garuda, the golden sun bird, deadly foe of all serpents and my vehicle through infinities of space, forever shall spare you, whom I have touched.' It has been suggested that this popular legend recounts the supplanting of the local nature divinity by an anthropomorphic god, Krishna, who in turn was merged with Vishnu." — Cotterell, pp.89-90.

§161.12 "**[MAGICAL POWER OF DRUM.** As part of an ancient Vedic ritual observed during a] festival of the winter solstice.... there is beaten an earthen drum, doubtless to scare away the demons who might attempt to overthrow the power of the sun; the Hotr sits on a swing and is swung to and fro, to represent the path of the sun in the sky.... Women celebrate to the sound of the lute in the south the patrons of the ceremony; maids dance round the fire with water pitchers, while the Stotra is being performed: they pour water on the fire, and their song shows that they desire richness in milk with water for the cows. The desire of heat and rain seems clearly united: the position of the sun nearest earth is indicated by the priest, who touches the board of the swing and the earth with one hand, and says, 'The God hath united with the goddess [clearly the wedding of sun and earth, a form of that of sky and earth].'...

"[DEIFICATION OF DRUM. In the Vedic world] there is no very essential distinction between the worship of natural objects conceived as living and the worship of objects made by human hands [although] it is obvious that the worship of such objects tends to be restricted in effect and importance.... We find [in the *Rigveda*] that two implements of the ploughman, Cuna and Sira, which may be the plough-share and the plough, are invoked, and that in the Catapatha Brahmana a cake is assigned to them in the sacrifice. The warrior invokes his arrow as divine, and begs it to protect him and assail his foes: his armour, his bow and quiver, are also celebrated, and the drum is invoked to drive away the demons and the danger; in the Atharvaveda a whole hymn is devoted to its praises.... The mortar and pestle were deified also, and the Atharvaveda adds to the category various ladles and invents a great deity in the remnant of the sacrifice, the Ucchista.

"It is possible to draw a distinction between the cases of the deities of the plougher and warrior, and those of the priest. In his case the presence of the deity at the sacrifice may be held to be the cause why the instruments of the sacrifice are treated with so much reverence, while in the former cases the reverence is not due to anything save the essentially valuable character of the objects, and the mystic powers which are deemed by man to lie within them. It is particularly easy to understand how the arrow or even the plough can be regarded as animate: the worship of the priestly implements would thus be rather more fetishistic in origin than real and direct worship of the implements for themselves....[257]

---

257 This passage invites a little sorting out. By the single act of "deifying" the drum, the warrior apparently seeks both to address a particular god or divinity *and* to assure that the drum in question has the magical power to drive away demons and the danger at hand. Normally — if I may put it that way — one might expect the warrior to, first, address a particular deity independently, and then, secondly, request of such a god that the implement (drum) be given the magical capacity of driving away the demons and the danger. In our case however the warrior (or farmer etc) has telescoped these activities, by simply identifying the implement (drum or ploughshare etc) *with* divinity, in the first place. But, what is it indeed that "deifying" itself signifies, to begin with? It is, after all, only a recognition that "divinity" (or more exactly the Cosmic or Life Force or Energy) does in fact "inhabit" all aspects of being, both "animate" and "inanimate"; thus to appeal to a particular god to work a certain magic through a particular object or implement would be — in a sense — somewhat redundant. The "appeal", if you will, can be made directly to the object itself, which (again) is already inhabited or possessed by the divine — i.e., is already "animated" in some sense by the Cosmic or Life Force or Energy. (Ed.)

"[MUSIC AND DANCE AS OFFERING TO – OR ENTERTAINMENT FOR THE BENEFIT OF – THE GOD(S); OR TO ATTRACT THE GOD(S) ATTENTION. At a given ritual] it was of course essential that the god invited should be received in a due place, and that any honours which were possible should be paid to him. Hence the hymns of praise, the sound of music, and the dance: even perhaps the theosophical riddles with which at the great horse sacrifice the priests delighted one another.... In addition to these features there was much more in the Vedic sacrifice, mimic combats, ribaldry, chariot racing, archery, dicing, and much else, which cannot be deemed save in quite a secondary way to have been thought to be a part of the entertainment provided for the god. In the vast majority of these cases [although not always] the nature of the ritual can be solved at once by the application of the concept sympathetic magic, and this is one of the most obvious and undeniable facts in the whole of the Vedic sacrifice: it is

from beginning to end full of magic elements....

"The nature of the ordinary offering to the god is expressly stated to be an offering made to the god for the purpose of attracting his attention and good-will, so that, delighted himself, the god may reward in the appropriate way his worshipper." – Keith, pp.188-89, 258-59, 351-52.

§161.13 "The Mimamsa darsana, [one of the six classifications or philosophies or 'points of view' which recognize the authority of the Vedas,] supports a theory of the infallibility of the Vedas and a theory of meaning as inherent in sound: Sanskrit, the holy language of the Vedas, that is to say, is not a historical tongue based on convention, but an emanation of Being*(sat)* in sound *(sabda)*; hence the power of the sacred mantras and of the Vedic hymns to touch the quick of truth and so to work magic. It is from this potency that the effects of the sacrifice are derived, not from divine intervention; for

though the offerings are addressed to deities, the deities are themselves supported by the power of the sacrifice." — Zimmer (Philosophies), pp.607-08.[258]

§161.14 "[DUMRU [DAMARU] DRUM.] The *dumru* is the hour-glass shaped, tiny drum with a leather thong attached to the narrow waist. This thong is flicked to hit each side of the parchment-skin heads.

"Shiva* in his Dance of Creation — the *Tandava Nrittya* — plays the *dumru* as symbol of sound and revelation of creation. Now [1972] it is to be seen most in use by the monkey wallahs beating out the simple beat for their monkey charges to dance to....

"[BANSARI FLUTE.] This is the poor man's musical instrument, be it only the simple *bansari* made of bamboo, a hollowed sugar cane or a metal tube. In North or South India it is universally played by the villagers, and in the spring one can hear all the little shepherd boys in the surrounding open plains of the Punjab fluting their simple, haunting melodies. It is associated with the Lord Krishna who claimed the gopis with it.[259]

"[VEENA (VINA).] To be able to play this doyen of all Indian instruments is to be able to play any instrument. This is the South Indian instrument *par excellence*....

"It has been said by Yajnavalkya, the ancient Indian writer and philosopher: 'He who knows the art of *veena*-playing and *sruti shastra*[260] can attain God easily.'...

[Additional note (1) about the *veena (vina)*: "Vedic *veenas* were of the harp, lyre, and dulcimer types. We hear of *vipanchi* (nine stringed) and *sata tantri* (hundred stringed) *veenas;* some of these, along with *venu* (flute) were used for the vedic chant.... These harps and dulcimers disappear completely by about the 15th century, giving place to finger-board instruments. Today we have *sitar, sarode* and *veena* (finger-board lutes) as the most popular and accepted ones. The stray survivors of the ancient *veenas* are *santoor* and *svaraman-*

---

258 Although music is not mentioned specifically here, of course music is an expression or manifestation of sound. Sound itself in turn is — is an "emanation" of — the Life or Cosmic Force or Energy referred to in our preceding footnote. Indeed, the gods themselves appear to be no more than "emanations" of this same force or energy; they do not create the cosmic energy, after all, but are, themselves, supported by it. Thus again music — as an expression or "emanation" of Being (of the life force or energy) — tends rather to *support* the gods than to be created *by* them. In Judeo-Christian philosophy it might be said that the divine (God) invents or creates music, or sound; in Vedic philosophy, certain gods may indeed contrive certain musical instruments, however they do not invent or create music (sound, the cosmic life force or energy) itself. Indeed, in Vedic philosophy the "divine" (i.e. life force or energy) is clearly *superior* to (in the sense of being still more fundamental than) even the gods. (Ed.)

259 "As a young man Krishna's interests turned to milkmaids. There are numerous tales of his dalliances with the *gopees*, maidens, in the glades of Vrindaban by the banks of the sacred river Yamuna. As Murli Manohar or Govinda (flute playing cowherd) he would steal their affections by the magic of his divine music." — Massey & Massey, *The Music of India*, p.41. (Ed.)

260 *Srutis (shrutis)*, microtonal intervals — from Sanskrit *sruti*, "to hear"; *shastra* (or *sastra*), book which covers a given subject in detail — also theory or doctrine (see e.g. discussions of the *Natya-sastra* of Bharata, below). "Indian music 'divides' a *saptaka* [roughly analogous to a Western octave] into 22 intervals known as *srutis*." — Deva, *An Introduction to Indian Music*, p.16. (Ed.)

dal." — Deva, *An Introduction to Indian Music,* p.76.]

[Additional note (2) about the *veena (vina):* The modern instrument has seven strings; it consists of a hollow fingerboard attached to two gourds, one of which is larger than the other. A North Indian version of the instrument — having two gourds of the same size — is called *Been* or *Bin.* "But the glory of all stick zithers is the Indian *vina,* or *bin* as it is called in the north. Already mentioned in the *Yahur Veda* (the word then probably designated the harp), the term is clearly related to *bint,* the harp of ancient Egypt. After the harp disappeared from India some thousand years ago, the word was apparently transferred to the stick zither. It is also possible that theretofore *vina / bin* was a generic term for chordophones; at any rate, the word is older than the form of instrument it designates today. *Vinas* are consecrated to Sarasvati, goddess of wisdom." — Sibyl Marcuse, *A Survey of Musical Instruments* (Harper & Row, 1975), p.184. (Ed.)]

"MARGA. 'The sought' in Sanskrit. In musical terms *Marga Sangeet* was one primary stage of development beyond the earliest Vedic music of chanting mantras or magical incantations of symbolic sound. Marga combined elements of the early folk-music and harvesting-songs into the ritual music....

"NAAD or NADA. Literally 'resonant sound', but like most Sanskrit words its overtone are more than the literal and precise English. It is much more complex, implying 'vital power'.

"Acording to Sir John Woodruffe who wrote *The Serpent Power,* 'the universe of immovable and movable things is linked together and pervaded by this shakti (female energy as seen in a universal and biological sense) which is called by such names as *naad, prana,* etc.' In another book, the *Sangeet Sar,* it is put this way: 'Without *naad* there is no *sangeet,* without *naad* there is no knowledge of the universe and without *naad* there is no existence of the Lord Shiva. In fact the whole universe is illumined by *naad,* the divine energy.'

"Lord Shiva symbolizes this energy, expressing it visually in the Cosmic Dance — the source of all classical dancing — hence the spiritual overtones to dance and music in even modern India....

"NADA BRAHMA. *Na = praña = * life breath; *da = agni = * fire; *Brahma = * omnipotent, absolute, male manifestation of Brahman, the neuter creative energy that motivates the whole entire cosmos.

"According to the *Yoga Shastra, nada* is the source of music inseparably connected

with the *kundalini* or vagus nerve. The *Sangeet Ratnakara* of Sarangadeva gives profound metaphysical connotations to these Hindu and musical concepts: vocal music is considered pure, primary sound, different from instrumental sound which is struck sound. Vocal music emanates from the internal spirit of man. It wells up from the soul and floats out through the vocal chords — which explains the particular Hindu attachment in supersensory or magical terms to the chanting of certain word patterns in Sanskrit mantras, for example the evocative sound OM.[261]

" 'The notion that the power of music, especially the intoned word, can influence the course of human destiny and even the order of the universe goes back to the very oldest surviving form of Indian music, namely the music of the Vedas. The intoned formula is the pivot of the whole elaborate structure of Vedic offerings and sacrifice. It is the power of words, enunciated with the correct intonation, that determines the efficacy of the rites; a mistake may destroy everything.' ...[262]

"TALA or TAAL. The root 'ta' stems from *tandava* = the Cosmic Dance of Shiva; and 'la' from *lassya* = the dance of Parvati, the female Principle of the Universe. It means a palm of the hand in Sanskirt, indicting the clapping of hands to keep the strict beat and time measure. *Tala* is the basic

connection between the three constitutents of *sangeet* [i.e. *sangita* (Ed.)]: vocal music, instrumental music and dance. It comprises the metric patterns, the actual beat of the music rather than the inherent pulse or laya. The origin of the word is connected with the Hindu metaphysical belief in the all-embracing, comrehensive rhythm of the universe as personified in Shiva. [Although] most authorities agree to the figure of 108 main *talas*... the basic [most often played] *talas* used in Hindustani [i.e. North Indian] music are these: *Dadra*, a rhythmic cycle of 6 beats divided 3-3, generally in fast tempo for light music; *Rupak, 7 beast divided 3-2-2, in slow tempo for serious music; Deepchandi,* 7 beats, divided as for Rupak tala; *Adi*, 8 beats divided 4-2-2, in fast tempo with a beat and three counts, a beat and throw, a beat and throw; *Kerrvaa*, 8 beats divided 4-4; *Chandrakada*, 9 beats divided 5-4, divided irregularly and subdivided, with emphasis on beats 1, 3 and 5; *Jhaptal*, 10 beats divided 2-3-2-3; *Mandari*, 11 beats divided 3-2-3-3, divided irregularly; *Ektal*, 12 beats divided 4-4-2-2, for slow tempo and serious music; *Jaital*, 13 beats divided 9-2-2, divided irregularly; *Adachautal*, 14 beats divided 2-4-4-4, for slow tempo and serious music; *Jhumra*, 14 beats divided 3-4-3-4, for slow tempo; *Gaja Jhampa*, 15 beats divided 4-4-4-3, divided irgularly; and *Teentaal*, 16 beats divided 4-4-4-4, a very common *tala* much used in fast

---

261 Concerning the *Sangeet Ratnakara* of Sarangadeva (Sarngadeva): "A monumental work came to be written in the 13th century AD. This was the *Sangeeta Ratnakara* (The Ocean of Music) penned by Sarangadeva, an emigrant from Kashmir, who became the Chief Accountant of Raja Sodhala, a Yadava king of Devgiri in South India. A work so stupendous in depth and extent is it that it is difficult to believe that it could have been scribed by the one man. The *Ratnakara* gives in great detail descriptions of scales, *ragas*, *talas*, musical forms, instruments, and many other subjects. Of greater significance is the fact that it is, perhaps, the first major work dealing with Northern and Southern musical systems. It is opined by many scholars... that it was during this period Indian music got bifurcated into the two systems of North [Hindustani] and South [Karnatak]." — Deva, *An Introduction to Indian Music*, p.74. See additional references in §161.17, below. (Ed.)

262 Dr. Arnold Bake, 'Music in India' in *The New Oxford History of Music*, Vol I, *Ancient and Oriental Music*.

tempo." — Holroyde, pp.258, 261-62, 265, 273-75, 281-82.

§161.15 "[THE VEDAS etc.] In India from the earliest times music has been closely associated with religion. In particular it was associated with the *Sama Veda,* one of the four ancient books of the Hindu religion which are written in Sanskrit. Scholars hold that parts of the Vedas were already in writing when the Aryan tribes began to invade India from the northwest between 2000 and 1000 BC. While the high priest conducted the solemn rite of the Soma drink-offering to God, using the *Atharva Veda,* another priest is said to have sung chants from the *Sama Veda.* In Hindu temples today one can still hear chants in praise of the deity which doubtless originated in very ancient times.

"Hindus believe that the art of music is especially patronized by the goddess Saraswati [Sarasvati*], the consort of Brahma. She is often pictured or represented in the form of an image seated upon a lotus flower and playing upon a stringed instrument. Rev. H. A. Popley has written [in *Music of India,* p.7]:

In Hindu mythology the various departments of life and learning are usually associated with different *rishis* [sage or hermit], and so to one of them is traced the first instructions that men have received in the art of music. *Bharata rishi* is said to have taught the art to the heavenly dancers (Apsarasas*) who afterward performed before the god Shiva*. The rishi Narada, who wandered about the earth and heaven singing and playing

his *vina** [or *veena*], taught music to men....

"Indian musicians have sometimes claimed that a deity resides in each of the seven main tones of the scale. There is an interesting story from the *Ramayana,* one of the two great epic poems composed in the early centuries of the Christian era. The story is told that Hanuman, king of the monkeys, boasted to Prince Rama, the hero of the *Ramayana,* about his skill in song. Rama determined that he should be humbled. There was a certain rishi living in a jungle who by his occult powers had caused seven lovely nymphs to live each in one of the seven main notes of the scale. One day Rama took Hanuman to a spot near the rishi's abode and induced him to play on the *vina* and to sing. While this went on, the seven nymphs happened to pass on their way to bring water from a spring. When Hanuman sang one of the notes incorrectly, the nymph connected with that particular note dropped dead. As soon as the rishi heard the bad singing, he came out of his house smiling, took up the *vina,* and played all seven notes correctly. As he did so, the dead nymph came to life again, and gaily joined her companions. So runs the legend....[263]

"Rabindranath Tagore, the famous Nobel prize-winning poet of Bengal, has written the following significant words:

For us, music has above all a transcendental significance. It disengages the spiritual from the happenings of life; it sings of the relationships of the human

---

263 For another version of the tale, featuring Vishnu and Narada in place of Rama and Hanuman, see §161.17 below. Note the mythologizing (personification) of the elements of music — seven lovely nymphs reside in the seven principal notes of the scale — recalling our themes **T1c** (Music as medium through which the spirit world [of divinities, supranatural beings] attempts to signal or contact man) and **T6a** (Music as herald of otherworldly or supernatural being), *Introductory Remarks,* Vol I above. In this way music provides a link between human beings and the divine or spirit world. (Ed.)

soul with the soul of things beyond. The world by day is like European music; a flowing concourse of vast harmony, composed of concord and discord and many disconnected fragments. And the night world is our Indian music; one pure, deep and tender *raga*. They both stir us, yet the two are contradictory in spirit. But that cannot be helped. At the very root nature is divided into two, day and night, unity and variety, finite and infinite. We men of India live in the realm of night; we are overpowered by the sense of the One and Infinite. Our music draws the listener away beyond the limits of everyday human joys and sorrows, and takes us to that lonely region of renunciation which lies at the root of the universe, while European music leads us a variegated dance through the endless rise and fall of human grief and joy.

"From this one can discern that *raga* is the very soul of India's music.... *Raga* has been roughly defined as a *melody-scale* or *melody-type*. [However] it must be borne in mind that the term 'scale' is not an accurate description of a *raga*. A *raga* is a combination of musical phrases, shapes and contours which give a characteristic melodic identity in a way that the term 'scale' cannot give. It is a succession of tones, or notes, which bear a relationship to the basal pitch (Sa) of the drone-chord. Each *raga* has its individual name and charac-

teristic ascending (Arohana) and descending (Avarohana) notes....

"*Ragas* are said to be able to cause not only emotions but certain physical effects. For example, the snake-charmer claims to attract or control the cobra by playing a certain *raga* on his pipe. Although a snake does not have ears, it is in some way affected by the music. The use of the raga *Bilahari* is believed by Indian musicians to be helpful in reducing body pains and promoting health.[264] There is also a *raga* which is said to cause fire, and another which will cause rain....

"There is an interesting story about the Fire Raga. A certain king had at his court a famous musician. One day the king heard about this *raga* and ordered the musician to demonstrate his powers with it. He commanded the musician to descend into the Jumna River, stand in the water up to his neck, and then to intone the Fire Raga. As he did so, flames burst from his neck and consumed him! Another legend adds that a musician friend then sang the Rain Raga, which quenched the flames and saved the court musician. Whatever historical facts underlie these legends, this certainly illustrates the popular belief in the power of music to work unusual effects....[265]

"At this point the reader is cautioned to keep in mind a very important fact about the *raga*. The ability to sing or to play the characteristic notes of a *raga* does not necessarily mean that [one] has mastered the *raga* itself. A *raga* is something more than its characteristic notes. What is that

---

264 See our themes **T1b** (Music gives magical power to musician [e.g. shaman, doctor, priest]), **T2b** (Music has magical effect upon orderly process of nature) and **T4b** (Music as magical restorative of mental or physical health), *Introductory Remarks*, Vol I above. (Ed.)

265 The story is told in many versions; see also e.g. story involving the singer Tansen, the emperor Akbar, and jealous courtiers in §161.17 (*Ragas*), below. (Ed.)

'something'? In Indian terms it is called the *raga-bhava*, or the life of the *raga*. It is not easy to explain this in a book. It has to be demonstrated by an expert singer or player. When the expert demonstrates a *raga* by voice or instrument, he brings it to life both to himself and to his hearers. The effect is usually produced by the use of *gamakas* (grace notes or embellishments)." — White, pp. 7-8, 21, 24-25.

§161.16 "[The earliest musicologists — NARADA and BHARATA.] It is a great pity that no one can place in time — with any degree of exactitude — the earliest musicologists of India. The first of these was Narada who undertook the task of finding a relationship between sacred and secular music. He also discovered the features common to folk and art music. Tradition has it that Narada was a sage, a *muni* who, after accomplishing his work on earth, left for the Elysian fields where he still plays his lute*.[266] To further complicate matters later theorists took the cognomen 'Narada', so that we now have four books by different Naradas. Research has, nevertheless, proved that the first Narada was the author of *Siksa* ('learning' or 'training'). This was the first work that examined music in a spirit of scientific enquiry.

"India's greatest writer on the arts, the sage Bharata, is also a misty figure of antiquity. His book the *Bharata Natya Shastra* was regarded as a sacred book and was called the Fifth Veda. It was, and still is, the most important work on Indian aesthetics and covers music, dance, drama and criticism....

"When Bharata was asked to explain the origins of his book, he replied that when the people of the world strayed from a righteous path 'their happiness was mixed with sorrow'. The gods then asked Brahma, the Great Father, to devise a new *Veda* which could be seen as well as heard and which would belong to all the people. Brahma, therefore, agreed to create the Fifth Veda which would induce 'duty, wealth, as well as fame, and contain good counsel,' which would be 'enriched by all the teaching of all the scriptures and give a review of all arts and crafts.' So Brahma took recitation from the *Rig-Veda*, song from the *Sam-Veda*, histrionic representation from the *Yajur-Veda* and the sentiments from the *Atharva-Veda*, and with a combination of these created the new *Veda*.

"Brahma then asked the god Indra to teach it to the other gods, but Indra said that the gods would neither understand nor interpret the *Veda* skillfully enough. He suggested instead that the sages were better fitted to receive the new scripture. Brahma, therefore, taught the *Veda* to Bharata who, in turn, instructed his hundred 'sons', by which is probably meant men who followed him in becoming authorities on music, dance and drama.

"These 'sons' of Bharata have been the cause of much confusion. Many musicologists after Bharata used his surname and so we have Adi-Bharata, Kohala-Bharata, Matanga-Barata [Matanga, fl. 5th century AD], and Nandikeshvara-Bharata.

"The date and authorship of the *Bharata Natya Shastra* are both in dispute. The book has been variously dated from the 2nd century BC to the 3rd [or, according to some

---

266 Perhaps members of the American or International Musicological Societies ought to reflect on this promise for a future which — by extension — Indian tradition holds out for all who testify to this profession! Indeed, let all degree candidates only contemplate that — some day perhaps — each may advance to the Elysian Fields plucking at his or her lute. (Ed.)

sources, the 4th (Ed.)] century AD, but there is even less certainty about the author [himself]." — Massey & Massey, pp.18-19.[267]

§161.17 "[DRUMS.] The musical uses of drums* start... with primitive dance-music rites and rituals. Even today the great variety of folk drums is *nrityanuga*, i.e., accompaniments to dance. Of course, in primitive and folk levels dance and music are inseparable and because of the ritualistic association in early human societies, *avanaddha vadyas* [the membraphone class of musical instruments, comprising covered instruments or drums (Ed.)] have had magical value. 'The drum is indispensable in primitive life; no instrument has so many ritual tasks, no instrument is held more sacred.' The sacred symbolism of *damaru* [or *dumru* (Ed.)] of Lord Shiva* is profound to the highest degree. Once the Lord was dancing in ecstasy on Mount Kailas. Great sages gathered round the Divine Dancer, entranced and spellbound. When the dance came to an end, they prostrated [themselves] at His feet and begged that the knowledge of the Sound be made available to humans. He then took up His *damaru* and played on it fourteen times, giving birth to the fourteen aphorisms of grammar which also are the base of all music.

"*Pushkara* is the ancient Sanskrit word for the drum. This is how the instrument came to be invented: Once the sage Svati went to fetch water from a lake (*pushkara* also means a lake or pond) near his abode. Just then Indra (Pakasasana) sent torrential rains onto the earth. Svati listened deeply to the patter — sweet and pleasing — of the rain drops on the lotus leaves (*Pushkara* again means blue lotus). With the sounds

still ringing in his ears, he returned to the hermitage. Then he made *mridanga* [one of the most ancient drums of India — in its present form, a barel-shaped wooden body, bulging in the middle and tapering towards the ends (Ed.)] and *pushkaras* such as *panava* and *dardura*, with the assistance of Visvakarma, the godly craftsman. On seeing *dundubhi* [kettledrum] he fashioned *muraja* and other drums....[268]

"[FLUTE.] Earlier and later vedic texts refer to flute* as *venu*. It was used as an accompaniment to vedic recitations along with *veena*. These sources also refer to a kind of flute called *tunava* employed during sacrifices. *Nadi* was another variety, probably made of reed, played to propitiate Yama, the Lord of Death. Not only was it an important instrument in religious ceremonies, but the flautist was one of the victims of human sacrifice in *Purushamedha yajna* ritual.

"The flute has thus been known from very ancient times in India, and is one of the most widely distributed instruments in this country, called by various names: *venu, vamsi, bansi, bansuri, murali* and so on in North India; in South India it usually goes under the names *pillankuzhal* (Tamil), *pillanagrovi* (Telugu), *kolalu* (Kannada), etc....

"Comparable only to *veena* of Sarasvati and *damaru* of Shiva, the flute has always held, for an Indian, a mystic significance. For it is the call of Lord Krishna to his beloved Radha. She is the human soul longing for union with the Lord. And Krishna is the Adored, for ever beckoning to the Soul of Man. His call is not merely the call of the lover to the *gopis* (milk maids), but the divine invitation to everyone. The soul of man responds:

---

267 The *Bharata Natya Shastra* [or *Natya-sastra*] is discussed again in section §161.18, below. (Ed.)

268 For another account of the sage Svati's invention or creation of the *puskara* [*push-kara*] drums, see §161.18 below. (Ed.)

Still must I like a homeless bird
Wander, foresaking all;
The earthly loves and worldly lures
That held my life in thrall,
And follow, follow, answering
The magical flute-call....[269]

"[CONCH. Wind instruments] form an important part in religious processions and the conch is even a sacred symbol of Lord Vishnu....

"[RAGAS.] Closely linked with the ethos of a *raga*[270] is its association with the seasons of the year and the time of the day, specially in Hindustani [i.e. North Indian (Ed.)] music. (South Indian [i.e. Karnatak] music, however, has no such traditions, except for a small number of melodic types.) For example, the North Indian *Basant* and *Bahar* are of spring time. *Malhar* is of the rainy season; indeed, this *raga* is famous for its magical powers. It is believed that rains can be made to come down by singing it [see our theme T2b (Music has magi-

cal effect upon orderly process of nature), *Introductory Remarks*, Vol I above (Ed.)]. Once the court musicians of Akbar became jealous of Tansen's eminence and friendship with the Emperor. [*Tansen* (1508-1589) is often regarded as the greatest singer ever to have lived in North India. *Akbar* (c.1556-1607) – a contemporary of Queen Elizabeth I – was a Moghul emperor who, having married a Hindu princess, achieved dominion over India. (Ed.)] To destroy him they played a ruse and suggested to Akbar that he command Tansen to sing *raga Deepak* (Melody of Lights), knowing fully well that it would burn him up. Not aware of such consequences, the Emperor requested the great singer to sing to him *Deepak*. The royal command could not be disobeyed; and so Tansen began the *raga*. One by one the lamps in the palace courtyard, where he was performing, began to light up by themselves. As the music proceeded, the heat started to consume his body. The stupefied king did not know of a way of

---

269 Sarojini Naidu, *The Sceptered Flute*, p.161. Kitabistan, 1946.
270 "*Raga:* a combination of notes, aesthetically pleasing, and capable of 'colouring the hearts of men'. Technically, a scale, a melody archetype." – Massey & Massey, *The Music of India*, p.173. "A melody is a flow of sound – up and down, with various rhythmic distributions. When we abstract these characteristics and make a 'type', it becomes a '*raga*' – a musical 'language'. Here again, out of a stream of sound, 'notes' are created and named, and a particular arrangement of these 'notes' becomes a *raga*. There is a general similarity between language and *raga*.... A *raga* may be defined broadly as a melodic scheme characterised by a definite scale or notes (alphabet), order of sequence of these notes (spelling and syntax), melodic phrases (words and sentences), pauses and stases (punctuation) and tonal graces (accent). Of course, there is always a rider attached to this: a *raga* must be pleasing; it must have emotional appeal. Therefore, an ancient definition runs, 'A *raga*, the sages say, is a particular form of sound which is adorned with notes and melodic phrases and enchants the hearts of men.' As a matter of fact, the word *raga* is derived from the root *ranj* (Sanskrit), to please." – Deva, pp.4-5. "*Ranj* = to colour or tinge with emotional colour.... *Ragas* developed as an arrangement of intervals so that seven notes are in a certain relationship with each other and thus define a melody.... *Raas* or *Rasa* = the emotional and aesthetic relish or flavour of the *raag*. The very sounding, for instance, of two or three tones in juxtaposition – such as ni[k] sa reh[k], or dh[k] pa ma[t] of *Kamavardhani Raag* and *Bhairavi Raag* – immediately sets up an electric response, and therefore a chemical one as well, in the adrenalin of the listener. The fluctuations of constant play through the *rasa* has a powerful effect on the practised Indian audience." – Holroyde, *The Music of India*, pp.277-78. (Ed.)

stopping this slow but sure death. Then someone thought of Tansen's lady who was herself a great musician. She was immediately informed of the tragic situation. On hearing of the danger to her lover, she began to sing *raga Malhar* and surely the rains came, drenching Tansen and saving his life.

"The seasonal associations of *raga* are grosser than diurnal relations. The immediate clues to this are the festivals of spring, rains, sowing and reaping. Of these, the most striking are the vernal and of monsoon with their sudden onset and deep biological symbols of procreation; they inspire music of the finest order, like the songs of *Vasant* (spring) and *Savan* (rains). *Raga Hindol* of the North is a good example. This is a *raga* invariably connected with the season of flowers and buds. *Hindola* 'is a lovely youth, surrounded by young ladies. He looks like an embodiment of love. The spring blossoms around him with all its beauty and lustre. He swings amongst maidens playing the *veena* and beating the drums. Lord Brahma created him out of his navel-lotus.' Now, the swing is one of the most ancient sexual auxiliary and symbol. It has always been recognized as an excitor of erotic desire[271] and so the music sung with the swings *(dol)* was quite naturally named *Hindol*. In *raga* iconography, therefore, it is always represented by the swing. There are also similar associations of *Vasant* with spring and *Malhar* with rain.....

"Indian art, whether it be painting, poetry, dance or music has a characteristically inward quality. This is a manifestation of the bias and world-view of this culture. The nature of creation and its forces are not felt and thought about commencing at the point of material phenomena. 'Indian thought at its deepest affirms, on the other hand, that mind and matter are rather different grades of the same energy, different organizations of one conscious Force of Existence.' Hence the external and its imitation have had little place in our art. The outside is only a projection of this 'Force of Existence', experienced within, and 'beauty does not arise from the subject of a work of art, but from the necessity that has been felt of representing that subject.' That is why programmatic music is not considered of really deep quality and it is a recent recurrence in the country, specially with the ballet and the films. Imitation of thunder and the ripple of water is not great music, just as realistic photographic painting is not great art. The langour of rains after an Indian summer is what *Malhar* expresses but not the patter of drops on a tin roof!

"A *raga* or a *tala*[272] is, therefore, the externalization of an inner consciousness. It is a concept or a mood unfolding itself. This 'concept' has also been iconized. For every *raga* is a man, a woman or a god in a particular state of mind. In effect, it is a personality — a *dhyanamoorty* — a form to be meditated upon — and the *dhyanamoorty* helps and intensifies the inward tendency of the artiste. 'Let the imager establish images in temples by meditation on the deities who are the objects of his devotion.... In no other way, not even by direct and immediate vision of an actual object, is it possible to be so absorbed in contemplation.'

---

271 As Keith also points out, however — §161.12 above — the swing may also represent the path of the sun in the sky. (Ed.)

272 *Tala* — approximately, a recurring arrangement of rhythmic patterns. "[The] rise and fall of tones has a certain accent in time or time division. This is the simplest meaning of the rhythm of a song. In a primitive stage this rhythm is a bodily activity of stamping and clapping which are developed and stylised into the complicated system of the 108 *talas* of classical music." — Deva, p.2.

"Narada, the divine singer [see also reference above, section §161.16 (Ed.)], was boastful of his musical genius; and Lord Vishnu wanted to teach him a lesson in humility. So the Lord invited the sage for a walk in the woods. As they were going along, they heard wails and moans, coming from a nearby cave. Their curiosity and pity aroused, the two entered the place and found men and women — all maimed — weeping and writhing in pain. Lord Vishnu solicitously enquired as to the cause of their sorrow. Amid their sobs they said, 'O Lord, how shall we describe our agony. We are the *dhyanamoortys* of *ragas* and *raginis*. There is a churl called Narada who thinks he is a great musician but he does not know a thing. See how he has sung everything wrongly and broken our arms and legs and disfigured our faces!' It was a sufficient lesson to Narada and to all musicians — it is not easy to grasp the esssential form of a *raga* and to project it without confusion....

"**[Personifications of music: *ragas* and *raginis*.** *Ed. note:* Throughout world mythology we often encounter music (or musical forms or instruments) as an invention or gift of the gods or divine beings; however, the following passage provides an instance in which music *itself* is personified (i.e. mythologized or deified). Further — or so I will conjecture here — insofar as it is to be hoped that a given performer and also the audience will achieve rapport with the mood or state which is being conveyed by the music, then in just that sense the performer and audience will also find themselves "in touch" if you will with the legendary personification (deifying or mythologizing) of the particular *raga* which is being performed. I would suggest that — however subtly — this is, after all, an illustration of our familiar theme **T1a** (Music as magical means of communication with god[s] or supreme being[s]) — for which see *Introductory Remarks* Vol I above.]

"A very interesting [development] became popular in North India. This was the *raga-ragini* tradition. Six major melodic genera were postulated and these were called as *ragas* (masculine). They were considered to be of prime importance and deemed as heads of six families. Each *raga* had wives, the *raginis* (feminine) who begot minor *ragas*, the sons. There were also the daughters-in-law of the family. Though the naming of such pedigree appears fanciful to us now, it seems to have had some musical significance.

"A beautiful extension of this idea resulted in the personification of *ragas* and *raginis*. Indian aesthetics has a well formulated theory of emotions (the *rasa* theory [discussed below. (Ed.)]) wherein different kinds of heroes *nayaka)* and heroines *(nayika)* have been classified. The details of their states of mind in union and separation have been described to the minutest detail. Originally related to drama and literature, this aesthetic tradition was taken over to music by imagining each *raga* or *ragini* to be a hero or heroine of a particular emotional character. A *raga* becomes a man with a definite feeling in a definite situation; similarly a *ragini* is woman in a dramatic context of her own. For instance, *Malkaus* [Hindustani nomenclature for a particular *raga* (Ed.)] 'wears a robe of blue; he holds a staff in his hand. He wears on his shoulders a string of pearls; he is accompanied by a number of lady attendants. Dressed in blue robe, his shining complexion puts to shame the prince of Kaushaka. With garlands on his shoulders and a white staff in hand, he is the very picture of the purity of the flavour of love. He overpowers the hearts of women and by his beauty attracts the gaze of all. At early dawn he is up and seated. Hero and lover, he is contemplating on his colourful exploits of love'. His *ragini, Todi,* beloved of *Malkaus,* 'has a complexion of yellow; with saffron and camphor on her body, and is dressed in white robe. Her developed breasts are firm, her waist is thin. Her navel is deep, she has the shine of gold. Her tresses are strings of clouds, her face is the full-moon, in which dance her eyes like those of a fawn and in which shine her teeth like a row of pearls. She wears bejewelled ornaments of incomparable beauty. Venus says to Cupid — 'Be sure, do not forget me, if you please'. Her patterned beauty lights up the four quarters; she plays on a *veena*, reposing in a meadow. The strings of the *veena* shine like the rays of effulgence, discoursing melodious music with the sweet *panchama*. She practices the form of the melody in her improvization; by hearing the melody, birds and animals are moved to tears. Absorbed in the songs the fawns dance before her without fear.'

"This ornate imagery caught the fancy of painters also. Inspired by the human qualities of *ragas* and *raginis,* excellent pictures in colour were created, visualizing the moods and feelings. Known as the *raga-mala* miniatures they are not only interesting as musically evoked paintings but also as some of the finest examples of Indian art *per se....*

"[Again,] this iconography of *raga* has produced for us the exquisite *raga-mala* miniatures of North India. The six major *ragas,* their wives, sons and daughters-in-law have all been given more or less definite situations of emotion and are depicted in such states. *Ragini Todi* is the beautiful maiden with a *veena* on her shoulders and enchanted deer as her com-

pany; the ascetic and the snakes always portray the mood of *ragini Asavari.*

"A *raga* or *ragini,* thus, is a hero or a heroine in a given emotional condition and a musician is expected to create this affective state and the audience to participate in this creation. That is why a listener, of really fine sensitivity, is a *rasika* and *sahridaya* — a person who can attain to a state of *rasa*[273] and one who attains the condition of empathy.

"Of course, not all music is 'contemplative' of the Force of Existence. The sensate value in human experience is not taboo in good art; and they find expresion in the lyrical songs of *thumri, tappa* and *javali.* These are certainly of an earthly quality like the sculpture of Konarak. It is how one creates music or responds to it that matters." — Deva, pp.22-23, 52-53, 55-56, 58, 68-69, 71-72.

§161.18 The following, highly abstracted and rather technical selections by R. Sathyanarayana first appeared in as the opening chapters of R. C. Mehta, ed., *Music and Mythology: A Collection of Essays [on Indian Music],* Bombay, 1989. The original articles include page and other references to the many sources cited, which have been omitted here. However, I have added approximate dates of these sources, where known, deriving most of these from Sathyanarayana's own indexes; and, I have inserted other notes of explanation. Readers may wish to consult Mehta's pub-

---

273 *Rasa:* very roughly, "an awareness of the totality of the emotional situation.... While finally *rasa* is a contemplative state of mind, there are said to be nine *rasas* corresponding to nine emotional conditions: *sringara* (erotic), *hasya* (humorous), *karuna* (pathetic), *raudra* (furious), *veera* (valorous), *bhayanaka* (fearful), *beebhatsa* (odious), *adbhuta* (wonderous) and *santa* (peaceful)." — Deva, p.67.

lication directly—a copy of which is owned by the Oriental Collection of the New York Public Library, Main (Fifth Avenue) Library. (The succeeding entry, §161.19, is also extracted from Mehta's volume.)

Note: an "(s)" at the end of certain words denotes plural alternative. (Ed.)

"INDIAN MUSIC: MYTH AND LEGEND. Some myths and legends occurring in treatises on Indian music and dancing may be listed here; the list is not comprehensive.

"Bharatamuni describes the mythical origin of *natya*[274] genesis of *apsara(s)**, origin of the Banner Festival of Indra and celestial presentation of the first play, origin of the flagstaff worship in *purvarangavidhi*, protection of the stage against evil spirits, presentation of *'Amrta-manthana'* (churning the milk-ocean by gods and demons for elixir of immortality), the first play of the *samavakara* type, presentation of the first *dima*-type of play viz. *Tripura-daha* (slaying of the demon Tripura), teaching of *angahara(s)* by Tandu to Bharata at the command of Shiva*, origin of *nirgita* or pure instrumental performance in a theatre, origin of *vrtstet* style, origin of *nyaya* representation of combat methods, origin of the percussive Puskara, curse of *bharata(s)*, i.e. actors, descent of *natya* on the earth and repentance of the cursed actors.[275]

"Nandikesvara [before 500 AD] extends Bharata's account of the origin of *natya* and gives a line of transmission of the art. This is followed by Haripala deva [c.1175; the word 'deva' generally means 'god'

---

274 *Natya* (dancing): "So close were the two arts of music and dance that both were included in the Sanskrit word *sangita*—the arts of singing, playing musical instruments, and dancing. For each of the three aspects of *sangita* there is a specific word—*gita* for singing, *vadya* for playing instruments, *natya* [also *nrtta* (Ed.)] for dancing—but the concept of *sangita* combines them all into one thought."—Wade, *Music in India: The Classical Traditions*, p.16. Bharata himself is, of course, traditionally the author of the celebrated *Natya-sastra*, discussed below. (Ed.)

275 *Puskara*—ancient Sanskrit word for drum—refers both to a type of percussion instrument and to a certain sage; however, the origins of the instrument (or family of instruments) are generally attributed to the sage Svati—described below and in §161.17 above. *Bharata*—the revered traditional author of the *Natya-sastra*—is also cited as a brother of Rama, the hero (and an incarnation of Vishnu, also called Ramachandra) whose exploits are depicted in the *Ramayana*. "A major landmark in musicology is the work, *Natya-sastra*, of Bharata (2nd century BC-4th century AD). This book on dramaturgy has a few chapters on music and all later writers invariably go back to it for reference."—Deva, *An Introduction to Indian Music*, p.20. Concerning the title, *Natya-sastra*: *natya* has been identified, already, with dancing—which together with *gita* (singing) and *vadya* (playing instruments) forms the concept of *sangita*. Sastra: "the Sanskrit term *sastra* means either a text containing an authoritative exposition of doctrine in a particular field, or the body of doctrine itself. A field of knowledge or an art must be embodied in a *sastra* to be fully legitimate, and *natya-sastra* is the theory of dramaturgy and its junior branch, *sangita-sastra*, is the theory of vocal music, instrumental music and dance. *Natya-sastra* now generally pertains only to representational performance, including dance, and *sangita-sastra*

covers only vocal and instrumental music.... The musical portions [of] the *Natya-sastra* probably belong to the Gupta period (4th and 5th centuries).... *Natya-sastra* (dramaturgy) is the origin not only of dramatic theory but also of musical theory, poetics, metrics and general aesthetics.... Although the *Natya-sastra* has now been published several times, in the 1970s a critical edition had not yet appeared. One of the major obstacles to such an edition is the music section, which is full of technical discussions and long lists of terms, most of which have not been understood or used for more than a milennium." — Harold S. Powers, in Sadie, ed., *The New Grove Dictionary of Music and Musicians*, 9:72, 77. See also footnote above. Arthur Berriedale Keith, in *The Religion and Philosophy of the Veda and Upanishads* (1925), also refers to the "Bharata people" and to the "Bharatan war" of c.950 or 850 BC; Emmons E. White, in *Appreciating India's Music* (1971), defines Bharata as a "name of ancient India". (Ed.)

CORREOS DE EL SALVADOR,C.A.

AEREO

25 c.   TAMBOR

(Ed.)], Sarngadeva [c.1230],[276] Srikantha [c.1575] etc.[277] The descent of dance on earth is differently mythified by Nandikesvara [before 500 AD] in the account of Natasekhara narrated in the form of a dialogue betwen Indra and Nandikesvara. In another version, claiming to be an abridgement of Bharatarnava, called the Bharatarnava Samgraha, Nandikevsara gives a slightly variant version of this legend which accounts for the transmission of the art of dancing from Indra to Sumati. Again a Nandikesvara gives a mythical account of the emanation of articulate, inarticulate and onomatopoeiac sounds from the shaking of Nataraja's hand drum, *dhakka*.

REPUBLIQUE RWANDAISE

---

276 Another major author of another major theoretical work with various legendary or sacred associations. "The 13th-century treatise *Sangita-ratnakara* by Sarngadeva [or Sarangadeva, a Brahmin of Kashmiri descent]... was the fount of *sangita-sastra* [traditionally the theory of vocal music, instrumental music, and dance — more recently, of vocal and instrumental music only; see above (Ed.)] until the 20th century.... In this work all the threads of ancient doctrine are woven into a complex but systematic pattern which, as a model, could hardly be improved upon. It is divided into seven large chapters. The first chapter discusses sound, including its generation, microtones and intervals, scales and scale degree patterns, and the *jati* (ancient modal patterns). The second chapter discusses *raga* (melody type), both doctrinal and current. The third chapter is miscellaneous, dealing largely with performing practice.... The fourth chapter is on composition.... The fifth deals with *tala* (time cycle), both doctrinal and current. The sixth discusses instruments (strings, winds, drums and idiophones) and includes lists of *ragas* with a few of their characteristics for the *kinnari-vina* and the flute*, plus playing techniques for strings and drums.... The seventh chapter is on dance." — Powers, *op. cit.*, 9:73. See also reference to Sarngadeva (Sarangadeva) in §161.14 above. (Ed.)

277 "Srikantha's *Rasa-kaumudi* was composed c.1575 in Gujarat and comprises two five-chapter divisions, of which the first is devoted to music. Most of the musical material is taken directly from *Sangita-ratnakara*, but two extensive passages in the chapter on *raga* are not. One of these passages is a description of the new forms of *vina* [or *veena*] and an outline of the general tonal system based on its tuning and fretting.... The other novel passage of *Rasa-kaumudi* is the description of the *ragas*, which are grouped according to a system of 11 *mela* (scale types) in the southern

"There is an interesting, but little known legend relating to Matangamuni, presumably the author of Brhaddesi.[278] According to it the sage had two sons, Dattila and Kohala (who are, however, mentioned as 'sons' of Bharatamuni himself in the Natyasastra, and who are known to history as authorities on music and dancing). They married Sukla (lit. 'white') and Krsna [Krishna] (lit. 'black'), daughters of the sage Jhilika. A local myth (Sthalapurana) from Srimusnam in South Arcot district says that these daughters-in-law of Matanga desired keenly to worship Lord Yajnavraha of Srimusnam and hence turned themselves into namesake rivers.

"Sarngadeva gives a myth relating to the origin of *kapala(s)* and *kambala(s)*. There are ancient, time honored songs comprehended in Marga Samgita.[279] Kallinatha [c.1430], his commentator,[280] expands the former myth with additional details. Sudhakalasa [1350] narrates a long myth which sets forth the origin of the percussive instrument *muraja*.[281] Astavadhana Somanarya narrates a humorous myth of the genesis of another membranophone, viz. *'dolu'*. Cikkabhupala [1960] invokes an unspecified source ('matantara', lit. 'different view') for a myth on the origin of *muraja*. An unpublished manuscript work called Mridangalaksana[282] deposited in the Government Oriental Manuscript Library, Madras contains the same myth with minor variations.

"*Literary References*. Besides the above legends and myths occuring in theoretical treatises, there are copious references in samskrta and vernacular works embodying music and dance legends and myths. Some instances will be given here.

"The earliest myth is renowned in Vedic literature as 'Somaherana'. It describes

fashion." — Powers, *op. cit.*, 9:83. (Ed.)

---

278 "[Another landmark is the treatise of] Matanga of about the seventh century AD... the *Brihadeshi* (a comprehensive account of deshi music) of late Buddhist times." — Holroyde, *The Music of India*, p.76. (Ed.)

279 "The Brahmins... divided music into two categories: *Marga Sangeet* — that which was 'pleasing to the gods' and which was sacred music — and *Desi Sangeet* — that which was 'pleasing to humans' and which was secular or profane music. Both used the seven *swaras* [also *svara*, a full tone or note (Ed.)]] but in *Marga Sangeet* the melodic patterns were clearly defined as falling into seven classes: *arcick* used one note, *gathik* two, *samik* three, *swarantar* four, *odava* five, *sadava* six, and *sampurna* seven." — Massey & Massey, *The Music of India*, p.14. (Ed.)

280 'Of the commentaries on *Sangita-ratnakara*, Kallinatha's *Kalanidhi* in particular is a tantalizing link between ancient and modern music. Kallinatha expanded considerably on the material in *Sangita-ratnakara*, in several places identifying 15th-century equivalents of its *ragas* by names still in use, and he clarified the important section on improvisation." — Powers, in Sadie, ed., *The New Grove Dictionary of Music and Musicians* 9:79. (Ed.)

281 Powers refers to "the unique mid-14th-century Tantric system of *ragas* and *bhasa* in the *Sangitopanisat-saroddhara* by Sudhakalasa", in Sadie, ed., *The New Grove Dictionary of Music and Musicians*, 9:82. (Ed.)

282 *Mridanga* — one of the most ancient drums of India. See entry §161.17 preceding. (Ed.)

how Gandharva* stole away the elixir of the gods, *Soma*. Deified prosodial structures attempted to rescue it but failed. The goddess of speech and music viz. Vak then assumed the form of the vedic prosody named *gayatri*, inviegled Gandharva with music and restored to the gods the *Soma*. This myth is given in Taittiriya Samhita [4000-3000 BC], Maitrayaniya Samhita [before 2000 BC], Aitareya Brahmana [before 1000 BC] etc.

"The samvada (dialogue) hymns of the Rigveda such as those between yamayami, Pururava-Urvasi, Visvamitra-Rivers, Sarama-Pani(s), Agni-gods, Vasistha-Vasistha(s) Indra and Agastya-Lopamudra are believed to be vedic prototypes of the later secular drama and histrionic representation.

"Soma Puranas contain a mythical or legendary account of the divine origin of music and dancing; a few contain even an exposition of their theory. An unequivocal association of gandharva(s) with music and aspara(s) with dancing emerges in India for the first time in *purana(s)* [i.e., stories concerning the gods (Ed.)] as discussed by me elsewhere (1967). These myths bear some correspondence with their analogues in other early cultures. For example, aspara(s) are conjectured to originate from the Nile valley in Egypt, the ancient Egyptian chordophone *baini* is equated with the vedic *vina* [or *veena* —

described above (Ed.)]. Tehuti, father of Egyptian musical instrumentarium, is surmised to correspond to the Indian sage Svati. Gandharva(s) of the purana(s) are comparable to the Greek centaurs. I have discussed such ancient myths and legends on music in other cultures elsewhere (1983).

"Several purana(s) contain frequent reference to the musical activity of gandharva(s) and dance activities of apsara(s); e.g. Matsya [300-600], Markandeya [300-600], Padma [c.1420] etc. Agni Purana [300-600] gives a brief account of the elements of the prosody and dramaturgical accessories; Markandeya Purana recounts in a myth how Sarasvati*, the presiding deity of learning and music, taught the elements of music to the serpent brothers Kambala and Asvatara, — as well as an account of the music and dancing of gandharva(s) and apsara(s). Vayupurana [300-600] devotes two entire chapters to the description of music theory. Visnudharmottara purana [before 6th century] also has two short chapters dealing with music theory. The entire Naradiya Siksa of Sama veda forms a chapter (5) of Naradiya purana. This Siksa [the 'learning' or 'training' of Narada—see also §161.16 above (Ed.)] is an ancient, golden bridge between sacred and secular music of India. Sivapurana has a myth according to which Shiva-Nataraja humbled and enlightened

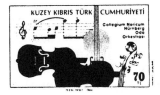

the sages of Daruka Forest who were arrogant of their power in black magic. Rudra slays the demon Tripura(s) (Taraksa, Kamalaksa and Vidyunmali) and performs victory dance (Mahabharata, Bhagavata purana [300-600], Matsya purana [300-600]). With Nataraja arises the myth of his subjugating the demon Apasmara or Muyyalaka (S. V. Chamu [1982]). An early dravidian legend[283] tells us of Sundara Pandyan king of Madurai. He witnessed Lord Nataraja's dance in Cidambaram. He became very distressed that the Lord danced unceasingly on the same, single foot, *sthirapada*. He repeatedly prayed, out of concern for the Lord, to rest or at least shift to the other foot. Since the Lord did not heed the prayers, the king immolated himself in despair. Then Nataraja was pleased that his devotee passed the final test and restored him to life and acceded to his prayer (J. Gonda [1970]). Sivapurana(s) in both samskrta [Sanskrit] and tamil[284] endow the concept of Nataraja's dancing with rich symbolism for the seven varieties of *tandava* performed in the Seven Halls in cosmic terms.

"Many local myths and legends (sthalapurana[s]) of Shiva-Nataraja are available in tamil literature, e.g. his dancing before Patanjali and Vyaghrapada, before his consort, Sivakamasundari, dancing in competition with Kali, etc. Some of these sources are Cidambara puranam, Cidambara mahatmyam, Tiruvalankkadu puranam, Koil puranam, Cidambaram Mummanikkovai, Unmaivilakkam etc. Myths relation to Nataraja's dances with his divine bride are discussed by D. D. Shulman [1980].

"Vira Saiva literature in Kannada, ranging from the 12th century to the 20th century, abound in ancient myths and legends; some even include historical figures of their own or slightly earlier times transformed from religious dogma into myth or legend. Some of these may be listed here from T. S. Shama Rao's Compilation [1967]. [As elsewhere throughout this article, chapter references are omitted. (Ed.)]

"Shiva slays the Andhaka demon and dances the *tandava* in victory;[285]

"Shiva slays the elephant demon Gaja and dances the *tandava* in victory;

"Allayya propitiates Shiva by singing *raga(s)*;

"Asphuti propitiates Shiva by singing *raga(s)*;

"Aditya bhupa please Shiva and devotees with music recitals;

---

283 *Dravidian:* "Since the second millenium BC, when a group of related tribes known as the *aryas* began to settle among the original Dravidian peoples and other indigenous tribes on the then sparsely settled land, the subcontinent [of India] has been populated by Aryan and Dravidian ethnic offshoots." — Wade, *Music in India,* p.14. (Ed.)

284 "[Tamil is] the main Dravidian language" — Sachs, *The History of Musical Instruments,* 153. "The oldest surviving poetry is in Tamil and dates from the 7th century to the 10th. The poems were assembled c.1000 into two great collections: the *Devarama* ('Garland of the gods'), which contains songs to Shiva, and the *Nal-ayira-prabandham* ('Four thousand compositions'), which is devoted to Vishnu. Hymns from these collections are still sung, in temples of the respective sects in the Tamil country. The Shaivite *Devaram* are sung only in temples, by a class of temple singer called *oduvar*." — Powers, in Sadie, ed., *The New Grove Dictionary of Music and Musicians,* 9:75. (Ed.)

285 "Shiva's dance was *tandav,* masculine, and Parvati's was *lasya,* feminine. The *ta* from *tandav* and *la* from *lasya* make up *tala* [i.e. cycle of rhythmic units, for which see e.g. §161.14 above]." — Massey & Massey, *The Music of India,* p.110. (Ed.)

"Anainaru delights Shiva by musicalising the five-syllable mantra on the flute;

"Kakkayyal makes Shiva dance to his own accompaniment on the percussive instrument viz. Kankari and excels Shiva in rhythm;

"Karikalamme witnesses Shiva's *tandava* dance and goes to Kailasa [region of Mount Kailas? (Ed.)];

"Kinnari Brahmayya is a professional performer of the Kinnari *(vina)*. He pleases Shiva with his music (in several legends);

"Gundayya plays rhythms on the earthen pot and is a potter; he attracts Shiva, Parvati and devotees with music;

"Gitakara was begotten by *ex voto* self immolation of Vira of Pandya country to the goddess. He excelled in singing jnanasambandha's devotional songs;

"Cerama was a singer-devotee. Shiva delights him with his dance and agrees to dance whenever Cerama sings;

"Caudayya is a quick change artist and musician *par excellence.* He pawns the *raga* Ramakriya to find resources in the propitiation of Shiva's devotees. Shiva redeems the *raga;*

"The demon Dhakka obtains the namesake percussive instrument as boon from Shiva and persecutes the world. Shiva slays him and plays on the *dhakka;*

"Marayya is a professional *dhakka* player. He makes a living by accompanying the dance of goddess Mari-amma. He defeats her in a contest through devotion to Shiva;

"Sages Durvasa and Sailada are born on Earth at Saunda and Vyagrapada respectively. They witness Lord Nataraja's dance at Cidambaram and are emancipated;

"Devasarman receives the percussive instrument *damaru*[286] as boon from god Bhairava of Kapalaksetra;

"Narada pleases Shiva with his performance on stringed instruments;

"Kambala and Asvatara are serpent brothers, sons of the serpent king Taksaka. They propitiate Shiva with music and become Shiva's ear-rings;

"Putavali, a devotee of Shiva, was directed to the Guha forest, witnesses Shiva's dance there and walks to Kailasa;

"Bacale worships Shiva with her drum music and obtains grace;

"Bhadra is a professional musician of Kozhikode, worships Shiva and his devotees with music. He trains an orphan boy in music but refuses to train the son of a proud rival singer viz. Gandharva bharati for money because he courts poverty. Shiva directs him to the king Cerama and in consequence makes him rich;

"Sankanna is renowned for singing *raga(s).* He collects firewood from a nearby forest and sells it for a living. Shiva is pleased with him and engages him to sing a *raga* before him every day in his forest temple on a small daily wage. Sankanna is content with this. King Vikramaditya gave him riches and the title ragada-Sankanna;

"Vatavarali of Cengaturu in Cola country sings a *raga* every morning to Shiva and competes with ragada-Sankanna at the royal court in Madurai. Shiva appears as his disciple and defeats all rivals. Then

---

286 Also *dumru,* Indian drum*. See also §93.12, **The Shamanic Drum**, above: "J. Przyluski had already drawn attention to the non-Aryan origin of the Indian name of the drum, *damaru;* cf. *Un Ancien Peuple du Punjab: les Udumbara,* pp.34 ff. On the drum in the Vedic cult, cf. J. W. Hauer, *Der Vratya,* pp.282 ff. Legend sometimes tells of the divine origin of the drum; one tradition records that a *naga,* (snake-spirit) teaches King Kaniska the efficacy of the *ghanta* (drum) in rain rites. Here we suspect the influence of the non-Aryan substratum — the more so since, in the magic of the aboriginal Indian peoples (a magic that, though not always shamanic in structure, is nevertheless on the border of shamanism) drums have a considerable place." — Eliade, *Shamanism.* (Ed.)

Vatavarali (which is also the name of a *raga* and is probably a titular name) came from Cengaturu and pleased the king with his music. Shiva is pleased and takes him to Kailasa.

"Siddhadevi is expert in singing and dancing. She worships Shiva every day with *raga* and *tala* and thus obtains his grace;

"The pair of gandharva(s) viz. Haha and Huhu dispute another gandharva pair, Tandana and Tana (which are also vocalise syllables in *raga* singing) in a musical contest. Hanuman umpires the contest and adjudges both pairs as equals;

"Hanuman propitiates Shiva with music in the hermitage of Gautama;

"Hanuman pleases Shiva with music;

"Haradatta, musician, acquires music disciple Nilakantha and witnesses Nataraja's dance at Cidambaram;

"In another legend, from Adbhuta Ramayana [1882], Narada is jealous of Tumbura for the esteem he received from Narayana, Laksmi and their attendants in vaikuntha for his musical excellence coupled with humble devotion.[287] Kusika is also similarly esteemed. In order to excel them and earn similar esteem, Narada learns the excellences of music from Ganabandhu, king of owls. Then he is drunk with arrogance at his musical powers. He is taken to the house of humble Tumburu where *svara(s)* [personification of *svara* — a full tone or note (Ed.)], *raga(s)*

and *ragini(s)* are found mutilated and miserable. They woefully explain their condition as due to Narada's very poor and inept singing. Narada is humbled. Narada tries to earn Narayana's esteem for his music repeatedly. Narayana promises Narada musical fulfilment during his own incarnation as Krsna [Krishna]. Then Narada receives musical instruction from Krsna's consort Satyabhama and assessment from Rukmini, another consort of Krsna. He is again pronounced as very inept even by Rukmini's servant maids. However, when Narada joins humility, faith and devotion to his technical excellence in music, Krsna pronounces him equal to Tumburu.[288]

"*Epics and folklore.* The epics Mahabharata and Ramayana also contain interesting legends on music and dancing. Mahabharata describes how Arjuna in his *ex voto* incognito wanderings learnt music and dancing from the gandharva chief Citraratha at the behest of Indra. At least five legends may be gathered from the Ramayana: When Bharata sojourned with his army, kith and kin into the jungle to persuade his brother Rama to return to Ayodhya and to be coronated, he and his train were [held] hostage by the sage Bharadwaja in his hermitage. By virtue of his supernatural powers, celestial gandharva(s) and apsara(s) entertained the guests with song and dance at the ban-

---

287 It might be added that a common theme in all of these accounts is that "musical excellence" or proficiency *is* identified with "humble devotion". On the other hand an excess of pride or arrogance in one's musical accomplishments is *ipso facto* no display of "humble devotion", at all, and must be corrected — see following lines of the present text. (Ed.)

288 To be arrogant or boastful in one's attitude of devotion or humility is, clearly, oxymoronic — a self-contradiction expressed in this case in musical terms as the initial "ineptness" of Narada's performance. When — instead — Narada's devotion is offered with true humility, then, correspondingly, his playing no longer gives offence and it too becomes truly pleasing. In sum: a musical performance is of itself held to signify devotion or humility — in short, is conceived as a means of approaching and therefore communicating with the gods or divine spirit beings; therefore, it must be rendered properly. (Ed.)

quet. Even trees and creepers of the hermitage performed music and dancing. When Anjaneya, Angada and other monkey chiefs were trying to locate Sita — Rama's wife kidnapped by Ravana — they came upon the Vindhya mountains. They entered a deep cave belonging to the celestial apsara, Hema originally; music and dancing were performed there incessantly. The gandharva Tumburu was once negligent of his duties and was cursed by Kubera to take birth on earth as the demon Viradha; the curse would be — and was — lifted when Rama slew him and buried him alive [sic]. The sage Dharmabhrt narrates the legend of the Lake of Five Apsara(s) to Rama. From this lake continuously emanated the sounds of celestial music and dancing. On another occasion Rama learns the legend of the Lake of Seven Jana — sages who from out of their supernatural powers created mansions below the lake and led a perennial life enjoying music and dancing in them.

"The primitive lore and folklore of every ancient culture have many meaningful myths and legends. India is no exception. I have discussed such folklore myths and classical myths on music and dancing of some ancient cultures elsewhere (1983). Verrier Elwin [1949] describes many interesting myths on the genesis of music and dance among the tribes of badu, binjwar, dhanwar dhobu, gond, pardhan, lanjengi pardhan bhuiya, mopka, etc. in Madhyapradesh.

"The intimate affiliation of music and dancing with gods and goddesses is recorded in myths and legend from the earliest times in India. Thus Visnu blows a conch; Krsna blows the conch named *pancajanya* and plays the flute. Rama is described as a musician *par excellence*. Shiva plays the *pinaka vina*. In the form of Nataraja, Rudra, Daksinamurti and Virabhadra, he is a dancer; in fact, he is the king of Dancers (Nataraja). He plays also the *dhakka* [hand-drum] and *damaru* [drum]. Krsna also performed the victory dance after defeating the demon Kalinga. Kali

and Durga dance in the terrrible *(raudra)* mood. The seven dances of Nataraja symbolise the fivefold cosmic processes of creation, sustenance, dissolution, withdrawal and recreation. Attendants of Shiva such as Nandi, Tandu, Bhringi, attendants of Visnu such as Narada, Tumburu, and Ramas's servant Hanumana are also musicians.

"Some authorities — e.g. Narada [300-600] in Samgitamakaranda, Sarngadeva [c.1230] in Saingitaratnakara, Vemabhupala [1400] in Samgita cintamani, Devendra [c.1375] in Samgita muktavali — associate gods and goddesses of the Hindu pantheon as well as sages with the genesis and promotion of music and dancing. The names of these may be eclectically gathered here: Shiva, Samkara, Sambhu, Mahadeva, Sasimauli, Sadasiva, Gauri, Parvati, Paramesthi, Prajapati, Brahma, Virinci, Sarasvati, Kamalesa, Srinatha, Hari, Laksmi, Sanmukha, Guha, Skanda, Vignesa, Indra, Brhaspati, Bhaskara, Sasamka, Santi, Visvakarman, Vallabha, Kinnaresa, Vikrama, Yajnavalkya, Bharadvaja, Narada, Agastya, Ayu, Aruvan, Usana, Ekadhanvin, Kanva, Kesa, Krtavarma, Kratu, Galava, Cyavanna, Durvasa, Dhruma, Dhaumya, Asvatara, Atri, Parvata, Pulastya, Pulaha, Pratimardani, Bhavana, Manu, Raibhya, Vatsa, Bhargava, Kapila, Bhrigu, Angada, Kusika, Guna, Yaksa, Daksa, Sumati, Vyali, Samudra, Citraratha, etc. The names of the one hundred and one 'sons' of Bharata, in Bharata, may be added to the list of sages. Alain Danielou [1949] has compiled many such names. Some of the foregoing names are probably synonymous [with each other].

"*Recent Legends*. Myth and legend indicate a process of continuous evolution of a living culture and are therefore by no means only ancient in origin. They only change their form and motivation from time to time in order to remain relevant to the space and time which generate them but retain their original structure, function and relationship to the parent culture. In view of the close affinity which Indian music and dance bear to religion, it is natural that the following miracle-legends are associated with saint-composers and saint-singers. It suffices to mention only a few of these.

"Lord Krsna disguised himself as Javadeva (12th century) to complete a stanza (16th century) from the Gitagovinda. Tansen lit the lamps of Akbar's court by singing the *raga* Dipak and brought rains by rendering the *raga* Megh Malhar.[289] Venkatamakhin (c.1650) was protected against robbers by Rama and Laksmana themselves. Once, when his royal patron Vijayaraghava enforced Vaisnava cult on unwilling subjects, Venkatamakhin became sad and agry; consequently, Vijayaraghava was afflicted with acute stomach pain. He became well again only when he removed the offending compulsion. Srinivasa was a devottee of goddess Minaksi of Madurai (17th century). The faculty of musical composition came to him when the goddess placed a betel leaf in his mouth. Margadarsi Sesayyangar migrated from Ayodhya to Srirangam in the South. He composed many songs on Sri Ranganatha.

"He wrote them down and left the MSS at the Lord's feet overnight. Next morning he found only sixty songs remaining in the MSS. The music composer Matribhutayya (17th-18th centuries) was directed by goddess Sugundhi Kuntatamba of Tirucirappalli in a dream to seek patronage of Pratapasimha, ruler of Tanjore. She also directed the king in a parallel dream to receive and patronise the composer.

"Ramasvami Diksita (18th century) cured the blindness of his son Cinnasvami through musical worship. His son Muddusvami Diksita brought rains to the parched Ettayapuram.[290] He received the faculty of musical composition from Lord Guha (Kumara Svamin) when the latter placed a piece of sugar candy in his mouth. He also calmed an enraged mad elephant, cured acute stomach ailment of his disciple, Suddhamrdangam Tambi (18th-19th

---

289 See our theme T2b (Music has magical effect upon orderly process of nature), *Introductory Remarks,* Vol I above. (Ed.)

290 I would hazard here that, in addition to making the common association of musical performance with magical performance — for which see again our themes T1b (Music gives magical power to musician) and T2b (Music has magical effect upon orderly process of nature), *Introductory Remarks,* Vol I above — one may continue to assume that musical proficiency is an indication and indeed expression of "humble devotion", as discussed in a previous footnote. But does not this attitude of "humble devotion" imply (then) union or harmony with the mood or spirit of the gods — in other words, with the underlying laws or "structures" of the world or being? In this context musical proficiency ultimately implies also our theme T2 (Music identifies individuals and a people collectively with the physical and spiritual universe, or cosmos. The laws [structure] of music parallel the laws [structure] of nature or the universe). (Ed.)

centuries). The life of the saint composer Tyagaraja[291] is surrounded with many legendary miracles (18th-19th centuries): He received the precious musical treatise, viz. Svararnavam, directly from the sage Narada. He had three visions of Rama in his lifetime. He restored to life a drowned boy. Devotees were directed in their dreams to meet him. He received materials and money needed for his daughter's wedding from God disguised as a merchant. The musical trinity (Tyagaraja, Muddusvami Diksita and Syamasashi, 18th-19th centuries) predicted their own last days correct to the exact date and time.

"Legend of Tripuskara: Preface. The legend on the origin of the group of percussive membranophones called *Tripuskara,* as narrated by Bharatamuni, will be analysed in this [section], prefaced with a few general observations.[292]

"Indian music theory offers one of the earliest classificatory schemes for musical instruments: *tata* (chordophones), *susira* (aerophones), *avanaddha* (membranophones) and *ghana* (idiophones)[293] Posterior to Bharata, it encompasses method, material, excitation, resonator, shape, size etc. and is still relevant today.... It has continuously evolved at the hands of eminent musicologists [such as] Bharata, Dattila, Narada, Kohala, Haripala (c.1175], Sarngadeva.[294]

"Membranophones [e.g. drums] fulfill a peculiar and important function in Indian music in both solo performance and in accompaniment. Inside a spiral temporal frame (viz. *tala* [rhythmic cycle]) made rigid, coherent and consistent through fixed, periodical recurrences they provide a foil for cross rhythm to the melody line besides emphasizing the rhythmic structure inherent in the latter. Indian music offers a wide range of percussive instruments—struck, rubbed, plucked, etc. The Vedic literature mentions *bakura, adambara, lambara, dundubhi* [kettledrum], *bhumidundubhi, diksu dundubhi, talava, muraja* (Sathyanarayana, 1968). Many

---

291 "The life and work of Tyagaraja [1767-1847], the bard of Tiruvayyaru, is a miracle of miracles. For no musician, with the exception of Purandara dasa, revolutionized and gave a new direction to Indian music as he did. So creative a musician and saint was he that he has come to be known as *Sri Tyaga Brahman,* which is a reference not only to his creativity but carries with it a part of his fathere's name, Ramabrahmam." — Deva, *An Introduction to Indian Music,* p.106. (Ed.)

292 Here it should be recalled that "Puskara" has been used to refer both to a type of percussion instrument (drum) and to a certain sage. (Ed.)

293 Chordophone — a member of the class of musical instruments having strings, including zithers, lutes, lyres and harps; aerophone — musical instrument (e.g. trumpet or flute) in which sound is generated by a vibrating column or eddy of air; membranophone — musical instrument (e.g. drum or kazoo) having a tightly stretched membrane as a vibrator or resonator and made to vibrate by percussion or friction; idiophone — musical instrument (e.g. bell, gong, rattle) the source of whose sound is the vibration of its elastic constituent material unmodified by any special tension (as in a drum). — Ed., after *Webster's Third New International Dictionary.* Since *vadya* = "instruments", the four classes are called *tata vadya* (chordophones/stringed instruments), *susira* (or *sushira*) *vadya* (aerophones/wind instruments), *avanaddha vadya* (membranophones/covered instruments or drums) and *ghana vadya* (idiophones/solid instruments). (Ed.)

294 Bharata, Narada and Sarngadeva have been mentioned a number of times above. Kohala-Bharata has been cited as one of the "sons" or disciples of Bharata. (Ed.)

membranophones are mentioned in the epics, e.g. *panava, dardura, gomukha, mridanga, mardala, bheri,* etc. Bharata himself mentions membranophonic percussives such as *dundubhi, mridanga, mardala, panava, jhallari, pataha, blemi, jhanjha, dindima,* etc. Later musicologists, notably the encyclopaedic Sarngadeva offer precise details of construction, expressive manual techniques, onomatopoeiac syllables etc. of these and many other instruments. Bharata also suggests a more detailed scheme of classifying them on the basis of primary component part or organ (*anga*) and secondary component part (*praty-anga*). This appears to have lost favour in later times....

"*Mridanga* is probably the best known, best developed and the most ancient among Indian membranophones.[295] It has not evolved into a technically and acoustically perfected state. Except perhaps in the composition of the damping paste called *karani* applied to the right membrane — which is of comparatively recent origin — the instrument has remained essentially the same for over two millennia. Its acoustical characteristics render the tone rich and complex. It offers a wide scope for the use of every part of the hand and wrist in generating both single, successive or simultaneous sounds on every part of each membrane. It also offers a wide range in tuning.

"*Reductionist Analsysis.* A study of the legendary origin of *puskara* as described in our early musicological texts provides

many points of interest. Such legends perform a dual function: They bestow upon the instrument a sacramental value by ascribing a divine or celestial origin thus helping [to] create an extra-musical attitude of devotion and dedication in the mind of the exponent.[296] This is well in consonance with *vedopavasali* — conceptual indwelling in the Veda — which music has received from the earliest times in India. For example, Bharata says that Brahma selected song from Sama veda in creating the composite theater art.

"Secondly, these legends are largely allegorical and often couch a phenomenological, ethnic or other symbolism. Some [of these] legends are considered here....

"Bharata's version of the origin of *mridanga* is largely phenomenological and only a little mythical. In the thirty-fourth chapter of his *Natya-sastra*, he describes membranophones and prefaces it with a legend of their origin deriving it on the traditional authority of the sages, Svati, Narada and Puskara. He seems to group the three percussive membraphones, viz. *mrindanga, Panva* and *dardara* together as *tripuskara,* i.e. three *puskara(s)*. This collective name is both appropriate and interesting. Abhinavagupta says that Narada's name is included in this list of authorities to emphasize that a vocalist should be familiar with these three (rhythm) instruments. He further holds that Svati is the most important of the three sages here because his name is associated with percus-

---

295 "*Mrdanga:* double-headed, externally barrel-shaped wooden drum (similar to Hindustani *pakhavaj*), the predominant percussion instrument of South India." — Wade, *Music in India,* p.239. (Ed.)

296 However, in a sense some divine origin or association of music or musical instruments has *already* been presupposed, which the naming of particular deities or episodes etc. therefore only supports or rationalises. Such a presupposition itself, presumably, is based on the assumption that music represents or allegorizes some universal principle or structure, has magico-sacred properties etc. If something along these lines had not been assumed, in the first place, then there would be no provocation *to* "create an extra-musical attitude of devotion and dedication in the mind of the exponent". (Ed.)

sive instruments even from the very first chapter of the *Natya-sastra*....

"[In the *Natya-sastra*, Bharata tells us that his] initial efforts at the presentation of [a certain] play lack the popular appeal of the Kaisiki style. Brahma recalls its use by Lord Shiva in his dance, suggests its inclusion and creates gandharvas and apsaras for music and dance in the play. Narada is among the gandharva(s) so created and is probably their leader. Brahma commissions Svati and his disciples to perform the percussives. Bharata then fully learns and assimilates the Kaisiki style into his play. Together with Svati and Narada, he goes to Brahma, announces his readiness and seeks an opportunity to present the play. Abhinavagupta [10th century commentator on Bharata's treatise] explains the passage [which recounts this in the *Natya-sastra*] thus: 'In order to show that *natya* should be practiced (and performed) with all four styles and qualities (*guna-nikaya*), the author combines singing and instrumental performance in the passage beginning with Svati, etc. — Svati who constructed the Puskara instruments in his own way according to his professional rules and requirements by imitative application of the peculiar (motely, wonderful, beautiful) syllables, which were formed when the continuous stream of raindrops struck lotus leaves (in a pond) in variegated ways in the rainy season. "Together with his (Svati's) disciples" (in the exemplar) means (the author) says that the auxiliary use of *panava*, *mridanga*, *jhallari* etc. which fulfil (the meaning and scope of) *tripuskara* instruments should be taken here as "side" instruments (cf the term *pakkavadya* in Karnataka music which means accompaniment).'

"Abhinavagupta thus anticipates and epitomises the legend which follows in the thirty-fourth chapter. It is clear from Bharata that Brahma created vocalists (and flautists etc according to Abhinavagupta) and dancing nymphs, but not percussionists. They were already there in the person of Svati and his disciples. So he

simply commissioned them with the job. This means that Svati had already invented the percussive membranophones (and idiophones), comprehended by the term *tripuskara*. Therefore, the prominence of Svati as the procreator of the instrument and in transmission of the story of the creation is fully justified. If Narada is the same as the gandharva created by Brahma for singing support in the Kaisiki style as Abhinavagupta sees fit to think, his role in the transmission of the legend accrues only from close association with Svati and is second hand in authority. Brahma's role in the transmission of the legend is thus even more remote, if [he plays any role] at all. It is suggested neither by collative consensus of Abhinavagupta's own exemplar, nor by the circumstances of the prior reference (in the first chapter) to Svati, nor by his own explanation of them. In fact, such [a] role is contradicted by these. This is one of many similar problems in constituting the text of the Natyasastra and of Abhinavabharati [Abhinavagupta's commentary on Bharata]....

"[Thus] the role of Svati as the inventor of Tripuskara is not in dispute. Bharata narrates the legend as follows:

"On a day of intermission from studies, the sage Svati went to a lotus pond to collect water, according to Abhinavagupta to quench his thirst. The sky was heavily overcast. Indra, god of clouds (and rain) was engaged in causing a heavy downpour in the region of the pond, as if the earth would be filled with water. Large rain drops descending in heavy streams were driven down by a fast wind and struck the lotus leaves making loud sounds.... The great sage perceived the sound (*nada*) of the streams of rain drops with wonder and intently observed the deep, sweet and appealing sound (*Svara*) produced on the large, middling and small lotus leaves. He then returned to his hermitage and contemplated the creation of *Puskara(s)* with an earthen body. With the assistance of the celestial engineer, Visvakarman, he created the *Tripuskara* con-

sisting of *mridanga, panava* and *dardara*....
Svati was inspired by *devadundubhi* (larger
celestial kettledrum; metaphor for thunder
clap) into constructing the *muraja* in three
performing postures: *alingya* (embraced),
ankya (played on the lap), and *urdhvaka*
(held vertically up). Expert in considering
pros and cons, possibilities and implications, he then created the *mridana* and *dan-
dara* by stretching leather membranes on
the faces of the earthen body and the
panava by using strings also in addition to
earthen clay and leather....[297]

"Nanyadeva's Version of Pushkara Legend.
Nanyadeva [1097-1133] offers a modified
version of the *puskara* legend at the beginning of the 14th chapter of his Saras-
vatihrdayalankarahara. Commencing
with a salutation to Shiva, he proceeds to
set forth the *puskara* chapter, 'not at length'
based on the words of (Bharata) muni.
Svati, the sage of musical notes
(Svaramuni) desired to bathe (according to
Bharata, to bring water; according to Abhinavagupta, to drink water) and went to
a lake. The lake was full of *kalhara* and lotus
flower, and vanquished in beauty all its
compeers in the heavens. It had garlands
of the jujube fruit; bees hummed musically, birds sang merrily; ospreys and swans
were melodious and loquacious. The sage
saw all this with wonder and pleasure. He
listened to the sonorous rhythms, which
were as if performed by the very king of
gandharva(s). At that time Indra made
rains so heavy that they appeared to support the skies. The streams of rain drops
fell on large, medium and small lotus
leaves and made such music as could not
be expressed by the mere streams. The sage

listened to this accompanied with the
rhythm of (the jumping) fish as if providing *tala* [rhythmic cycle]. Then he covered
a vessel with the leaves and beat the
membrane with left hand and right hand
strokes, singly and together. He perceived
the variegated and wonderful sounds, was
very pleased and went home quickly.

"Svati then remembered the *dundubhi*
[kettle-drum] of the gods and the celestial
engineer (who made it). He invited the latter and with his collaboration, made the
bhanda instruments, mounting wooden
resonators with skins, wrought into different shapes (and sizes) with hands
[handles? (Ed.)]. He performed on them,
heard the syllabic and nonyllabic sounds,
and was satisfied. In this manner he made
five instruments, viz. *mridanga, muraja,
panava, dardara* and *pataha* and gave them
the collective name of *puskara*.

"Brahma, together with the gods, heard
Svati's performance of [the] *mridanga* and
was very happy. Lord Samkara had, long
before, created all this on the *mridanga*
under the name of *nandi* in preface to the
performance of *lasya* and *tandava* forms of
dance [the dance of Parvati, signifying the
female Principle of the Universe, and the
Cosmic Dance of Shiva respectively (Ed.)].
Brahma had witnessed this performance.
The singing and instrumental performance [of] *nandi* was more sacred than a
thousand holy bathings. Whatever the
country in which the sounds of *nandi* were
heard, demons, evil spirits and obstruc-
tionist forces fled such [a] country.[298] If
they are performed at weddings, divine
worship, sacrifices and on auspicious royal
occasions, violent and evil forces are

---

297 Strictly speaking, this account of the origin of the drum or *puskara* family in India
refers to natural phenomena (the sounds of raindrops falling on lotus leaves) rather
than to merely supranatural occurrences. However, as in the case of the invention
or discovery of the lyre* by Hermes* — inspired perhaps by the sound of breezes
blowing across a hollowed tortoise shell — the "natural", itself, is depicted in a
supranatural setting or context. (Ed.)

298 See our theme T4a (Music as magical weapon against evil spirits, means for combat-
ing, routing, expelling evil spirits), *Introductory Remarks*, Vol I above. (Ed.)

driven away. Since Svati had brought it to earth and propagated it, it became known by his own name by Brahma's command. Then Brahma invited Bharata and his sons to learn the same and propagate it in the world because it is auspicious, removes sin and is like nectar to the ears. Thus Svati contemplated the *mridanga* and invented the *puskara*, then with Visvakarman's help constructed *panava* and *dardara*. He then saw the *dundubhi* of the gods and make *muraja* in its embraced, lapped and vertical postures....

"Myths on Muraja: (1) Sudhakalasa. Three myths are available on the genesis of *muraja* [drum] in Indian musical literature. These are from the Sangitopanisat sarodhara, Abhinava Bharata sarasangraha and Mridanga laksanam. They will be briefly examined here.

"The first [chronologically] is Sudhakalasa's Sangitopanisat sarodhara (1350). He is a *svetambara jaina* belonging to the *harsapuriya gaccha*. He gives two versions for the origin of *muraja*. The first conforms to his own religious dogma, according to which every cosmic emperor is vested with nine treasures (*nidhi[s]*): *kala, mahakala, naisarpa, panduka, padma, pingala, manavaka, sarvaratna* and *sankha* (Pampa, 941 AD). According to Sudhakalasa, musical instruments and dramaturgy belong to the ninth *nidhi* viz. *sankha*. In popular belief however, music is reputed to originate from Hara.

"The second is a popular, Hindu version. According to this, *muraja* orginated from the god Rudra himself. Once, Rudra [the ancient Vedic god of the dead and prince of demons — original form of Shiva] sat in meditation on the Kailasa mountain. A demon called Muraja wandered into the place by accident. Previously he had obtained from Brahma a boon that he would be slain by none but Rudra. He saw Rudra

deep in meditation and realised that if the meditation were allowed to continue undisturbed, it would end up in his own death. Therefore he created the spring season artificially to distract Rudra, and afraid to face the consequence ran away and hid himself. Rudra woke up from his meditation. He discovered the cause of his distraction and sought out Muraja. After a long battle he slew the demon, cutting off his head and limbs. He then returned to Kailasa. Eagles carried off the fleshy trunk for food, and ate a little. But the trunk proved too heavy for the birds and slipped from their beaks. It fell with trailing entrails on a tree. It gradually dried up in the hot sun; it was sealed off at both ends with the dry, stretched skin. The guts tightly entwined the boughs as if tautly [binding it] with thongs. The hollow ribcage and belly was then filled with air. This caused both skins at the ends to serve as drumheads and to make them resound and resonate.

"Shiva and Uma[299] were wandering in the forest at the time and heard the sounds. Impelled by curiosity, Shiva traced the sounds to the source and wondered at its strange form. Then he recalled his slaying Muraja and divined the sequence of events which led to the present situation. Then, out of curiosity, he gave the left membrane a gentle stroke with his left hand. This generated a pleasing sound which seemed like the syllable 'ta'. He repeated this on the right membrane with his right hand and generated the sound 'dhi'. He experimented again on the left and right membranes with harder strokes with his left and right hands and brought forth the sounds 'thom' and 'draim' respectively.

"Time passed and the rainy season came. Shiva commanded his attendants to build a hut with the leaves, twigs and boughs of the *patasa* (bastard teak, *butea frondosa*),

---

299 "*Uma*: Hindu corn goddess and mother goddess. Also known as Parvati, Durga, and Lakshmi." — Carlyon, *A Guide to the Gods*, pp.139-40. (Ed.)

sarja (vatica robsta), etc. in a lovely meadow at the request of Uma. Then the rains arrived. When raindrops fell on the dry leaves covering the hut, they produced sounds. Shiva and Uma both heard these. Then Uma said, 'Lord, please establish (by imitation) these sounds generated by the falling of raindrops on the leaves!' (Establish: make permanent, retain in memory.) Shiva then recalled and narrated to Uma his slaying of Muraja and the musical instrument which came into being because of it. He recalled his playing on it and then proceeded to establish 35 varieties of sound groups inclusive of both drumheads using single hand and double hand strokes on the *muraja* and the *mardala*.

"Thus Shiva created the musical instruments *(turya) mridanga, muraja* and *mardala*. In this way a veritable ocean of *pataksara(s)* was created on a percussive membranophone with two stretched membranes. Rudra created thus the *muraja* in the name of the demon for accompanying dance and drama; he also invented the above sounds in a mood of curiosity. Among mortals however the instrument came to be made of hollow wood, covered at both ends with stretched leather. It was made in the shape of the original *muraja*, substituting entrails with leather thongs, binding the two heads to the body in *nagapasa* ('snake noose') knots.

"Myths on Muraja: (2) Mridangalakshana. Mridangalaksanam is an unpublished treatise on *mridanga* of about the 16th century. Its author is not known. Its MS is deposited in the Government Oriental Manuscripts Library, Madras. It offers a slight variation on the above myth. The work is said to be revealed by Shiva to Nandi. But the creator of *muraja* is here Vishnu, not Shiva.[300] It is not unlikely that this myth arose in a spirit of sectarian rivalry. It says that once upon a time there was an invincible demon called Mura. He terrified gods and men with his violence and evil. Once, the sages gathered together to perform a *sattra* sacrifice in the Himalayan ranges. This demon blasphemed and sacrileged the same with his unholy acts. Then Vishnu, protector of the world, killed him and cut off his head and limbs. He covered the orifice of his neck with the skin of the Mura's own head and the anal orifice with the skin of the demon's legs. He attached both membranes to the trunk tautly with 24 thongs made from the demon's intestines. Thus Vishnu made the body into a percussive instrument and played on it with both hands. Various sounds like 'dhimi—dhima' emanated from both drumheads and from the demon's back. Nandikesvara [before 500 AD—possibly a legendary sage, musician, or theoritician (Ed.)] performed on this instrument in accompaniment to Shiva's dance.

"Myths on Muraja: (3) Cikkabhupala. Mummadi Cikkabhupala's account [1960] of the mythical origin of *muraja* is very similar to the above. He does not specify his source, but it is probably Astavadhana Somanarya. According to him, Lord Krishna slew the demon Mura and made a *mardala* (!) out of his body. He covered it with Mura's own skin and stretched it taut with the latter's nerves. Then he played on it; instrumental sounds emanated from the voice apparatus of the demon. Hence the instrument was

---

300 See our theme T1c (Music sent [to man, animals] as gift of the gods or heavenly beings; music as invention of the gods), *Introductory Remarks* Vol I above. (Ed.)

called *murajka*. Lord Hari gifted this *muraja* to Nandikesvara.[301] Hence the presiding deity is held to be Nandikesvara in popular usage. He should therefore be worshipped before commencing its performance. *Muraja* is of three varieties, played on the lap, played by hugging the instrument and played in a vertical position....

"*Comparison.* There are some minor variations in [the different versions of the myth.] In the Svati legend the rain drops fell on lotus leaves whereas they fell on [the] dry leaves of a leaf-hut in the Mura myth. This [suggests] different acoustic parallels: the lotus leaf is circular, stretched and is of different sizes. Since *puskara* means lotus and lotus pond, there is a nominal justification. The leaves are dry in the [Mura legend]: therefore the sound is somewhat magnified and the tone quality is different. Nominal justification is sought here also; but the name of the instrument is not that of the hero, but is of the vanquished villain; the instrument is the body of the killed enemy, a tangible token of victory. The celestial engineering skill of Visvakarman sought or invoked in the Svati legend lends it a degree of authenticity and realism. In the Mura myth such skill is displayed by God himself....

"In the Mura myth, the name of the instrument is derived by adding the genetive suffix '-ja' to the name of the mythical demon, Mura. The genesis of the instrument marks the celebration of triumph of good over evil, of divinity over demoniasm, of assurance-reassurance, of protecting the good and the meek by the good and the strong. Such myths are oblique expressions of a deep inner conflict between fear and hope, destruction and survival, good and bad....

"*[The Dolu.]* Astavadhana Somanarya [c.1550] records a myth on the origin of another percussive membranophone, the *dolu*. According to him it was invented by the demon king Ravana [a fallen angel, demon king of the Rakshasas, or Hindu evil spirits; they lived in an exquisite city specially built for them by Visvakarma, god of craftsmen (Ed., after Carlyon)] in order to wake up his younger brother Kumbhakarna from his proverbiablly profound slumber. 'Do' signifies presiding divinity of the demons and 'lu' the inventor, Ravana. It is performed with a mace (?drumstick). This is the abode of Brahma at its beginning, of Hari at the middle and Rudra at the end.

"This is a pure myth invented because of the loud and compelling sound of the instrument. It is based on a popular legend found in the Ramayana. It is narrated to Rama by Vibhasana about his own brother Kumbhakarna. No sooner was Kumbhakarna born than he felt so hungry that he went on devouring everything and everyone in sight in thousands. Unvanquished and undeterred, he did havoc with the heavens and the earth; he persecuted the sages and kidnapped women; earth soon came to be depleted of people, who then [sic] prayed to Indra for relief. Himself helpless, Indra led a delegation of men and gods to Brahma. Brahma listened to their tale of woe, commanded the presence of the raksasa(s) (demons) and cursed that Kumbhakarna should forewith fall asleep as if dead. Ravana pleaded for justice for his brother and requested the curse to be lifted periodically for Kumbhakarna who had reached after

---

301 *Hari:* "The early Vedic Vishnu was not personified; he was then the principle of light which pierces the entire universe. Epithets applied to this principle [include] Ananata, 'infinite'; Hari, 'stealer of souls; Mukunda, 'liberator; [and] Kesava, 'hairy' (because of the solar rays emanating from his head)." — Carlyon, *A Guide to the Gods*, p.141. (Ed.)

all the prime of life. Brahma relented and allowed one day of wakefulness (and appeasement and quenching) for every six months of sleep. It is therefore understandable that nothing less than *dolu* could have awakened this king of slumberers. The myth offers no natural physiological or musical correspondence or parallel. But it carries the seeds of magic: the syllables in the name *dolu* are construed to be seed mantra(s) to be incanted for attaining to proficiency in its performance since they are invocations and propitiations of the patron divinities of the instrument." — Sathyanarayana, in Mehta (Book I) pp.4-15, 19, 32-35, 38, 42-43.

§161.19 "[INDIAN AND OTHER MYTHOLOGIES COMPARED.] There are some broad parallels between certain mythical personages in India and the West, if one overloks the differentiating cultural details. The sage Narada is, perhaps, the closest Indian equivalent to Orpheus*, although the former's person is too enshrouded in reverence to be as well developed as our picture of Orpheus. And yet there are a number of legends which feature Narada's human attributes: stories in which he is confronted with the personified forms of the *svaras* [whole note or pitch] he had distorted and the *ragas* he had mutilated....

"Sarasvati* obviously occupied a prominent role in the Indian *mythos* of music, particularly because of her identifiction with *vac* (speech) and water imagery (one of the most vital of Indian musical metaphors), and because of her role as patroness of music and the liberal arts. She is the equivalent of all the Muses* in one person, as well as of St. Cecilia*, the most important patron saint of Western music. One may not hear Sarasvati's name invoked as frequently as that of others in the teeming pantheon of patron deities, but her role is secure.

"One extremely striking parallel between Indian and Western mythologies of music may be seen in the attending hosts of spirits who accompany visual representations of musical deities — the *gandharvas**, *apsaras**, *kinneras, naras,* and the like, presided over by their genial master Ganesha, whose name reveals his station as 'Lord of Hosts'.[302] These troops of celestial musicians are the precise counterparts to the hierarchies of musician angels depicted so colorfully and so lovingly in medieval European cathedral art. In contrast to the latter, however, the Indian hosts have undergone a much more intensive mythical development: many have individual names and stories, and some are virtually indistinguishable from such great figures as the seers Narada and Tumburu. The celestial musicians make their home in the sky and are connected with the dance, with battle songs, with amorous successes, with brilliant colors, with the purity and fertility of water and the mutability of vaporous cloud shapes, with animal forms and with pleasure and gaming. The message here is complex, but one may venture a partial interpretation: The practice and enjoyment of music is inexorably linked with *kama* in all its forms, manifesting the typically Indian blend of sensual ecstasy and religious devotion, yet authorized by the companion hosts of legendary and divine figures and associated with the images of fluid continuity that represent one of the highest values in the Indian musical tradition. The

---

302 "*Ganesa (Ganesh, Ganapati, Gajana— 'elephant-face')*: Elephant-headed Hindu god of wisdom, literature, and worldly success. Ganesa is thought to derive from an animistic deity. He is a propitious god, promising success, prosperity and peace and is invoked before any sort of enterprise. His pot-belly symbolizes a pitcher full of prosperity, a sort of abdominal cornucopia. Ganesa is said to have been the son of Parvati and Shiva*." — Carlyon, *A Guide to the Gods,* pp.122-23. (Ed.)

Indian musician is literally compassed about with a 'cloud of witnesses', a congregation of mythical forebears and celestial guides that form the resplendent yet unseen backdrop for the making of music.

"Two other important points need to be made here. First, the mythical placement of music and its 'parts' amidst a culturally authorized hierarchy of creatures of all kinds testifies to our need to explain music itself as a hierarchy (of tones, of scales, of rhythmic and formal configurations) that transcends limitations of time and space. And second, myth assigns to music symbolic meanings or 'resonances', by constructing complex tables of correspondences.... We shall explore these matters briefly and illustrate some cross-cultural comparisons.

"Figure 1 [below] summarizes an elaborate scheme of correspondences drawn from the first *adhyaya* of the 13th-century *Sangita-ratnakara* [the famed treatise of Sarangadeva, discussed in §161.18 above. The term *sangita* comprises the three arts of singing, playing musical instruments, and dancing (Ed.)]. Here no simple explanation will suffice. Such a network of cultural connections provides a wealth of material for analysis—more than our limited space allows. It is worth remarking that both the temporal (metres) and spatial *(svaras)* dimensions of music are represented, as well as their aesthetic consequences (*rasa*, emotional affect). One may easily infer the status of the various scale degrees by comparing the first and fourth vertical columns; music theorists will not be surprised to find scale degrees 1, 4, and 5 (Sa, Ma, Pa) established as the primary degrees by analogy to the Brahman or priestly class, 2 and 6 (Ri, Dha) as secondary by means of their analogy to the *kshatriya* or warrior class, and 3 and 7 (Ga, Ni) as tertiary and linked with the *vaishya* or merchant class. Not included in the table but explicit in Sharngadeva's text (verse 54) is the connection between the two altered scale degrees (*antara* Ga and *kakali* Ni) and the *shudra* or servant class. This may be mythology, but it is also music theory and extremely revealing. Readers who wish to explore these matters further

FIGURE 1

Figure 1. Table of Correspondences from the *Sangitaratnakara* of *Sarngadeva* 1.3.46–60

Svars	Dynasty	Color	Class	Continent	Rish	Deity	Metre	Rasa	Animal/bird sounds
SA	gods	lotus	brahman	*Jambu*	fire	Agni	*anushtubh*	vira, adbhuta, & raudra	peacock
RI	*rishis*	yellow	*kshatriya*	*Shaka*	creator	Brahma	*gayatri*	vira, adbhuta, & raudra	*cataka* bird
GA	gods	gold	*vaishya*	*Kusha*	moon	Sarasvati	*trishtubh*	karuna	goat
MA	gods	jasmine	brahman	*Kraunca*	Vishnu	Shiva	*brihati*	hasya & shringara	crane
PA	*pitris*	dark	brahman	*Shalmali*	Narada	Vishnu	*pankti*	hasya & shringara	cuckoo
DHA	*rishis*	saffron	*kshatriya*	*Shveta*	Tumburu	Ganesha	*ushnih*	bibhatsa & bhayanaka	frog
NI	asuras	spotted	*vaishya*	*Pushkara*	Tumburu	Sun	*jagati*	karuna	elephant

will find R. K. Shringy's analysis both thoughtful and penetrating.[303]

"Such lists of correspondences are seldom uniform from treatise to treatise, and authors frequently resort to repetition to fill out an otherwise incomplete scheme. A comparison of the correspondences mentioned in the *Naradiya-shiksha* and the *Sangit-ratnakara* reveals several discrepancies. The resonance is often phonetic: Narada's *shiksha* [*siksa*] develops an obvious phonetic analogy from the phonemes *(rish)* that links the *svara* Ri *(rishabha)* with the bellow of a bull *(rishabha)* and the class of sages *(rishis)* only the latter of which is preserved in the *Sangita-ratnakara*. Indeed I know of no other tradition of mythology in which the nature and structure of the mythical connections have been as profoundly shaped by the phonetic properties of the parent language, in this

case Sanskrit. It becomes all the more apparent when we observe early theories of music developing within the context of the literary genre of phonetic treatises. This connection demonstrates one of the most profound insights [into] the nature of myth: myth is an *oral* tradition—it is to be uttered, not read.

"Figure 2 [below] reproduces an equally informative set of correspondences from ancient Chinese tradition, in which the five degrees of the pentatonic scale (*kung* = Sa, *shang* = Ri, *chiao* = Ga, *chih* = Pa, *yii* = Dha) function as a single dimension amidst a hierarchy of relationships produced by the influence of the 'five agents'—wood, fire, earth, metal and water. Once again we find both temporal and spatial concepts drawn into the overall scheme.

FIGURE 2

Figure 2. Table of Correspondence for the traditional Chinese theory of the "Five Agents"

Correspondence	wood	fire	earth	metal	water
musical notes	chiao (E)	chih (G)	kung (C)	shang (D)	yu (A)
seasons	spring	summer		autumn	winter
sacrifices	inner door	hearth	inner court	outler court	well
animals	sheep	fowl	ox	dog	pig
grains	wheat	beans	panicled millet	hemp	millet
organs	spleen	lungs	heart	liver	kidneys
numbers	eight	seven	five	nine	six
colors	green	red	yellow	white	black
tastes	sour	bitter	sweet	acrid	salty
smells	goatish	burning	fragrant	rank	rotten
directions	east	south	centre	west	north
creatures	scaly	feathered	naked	hairy	shell-covered
beasts of the directions	Green Dragon	Scarlet Bird	Yellow Dragon	White Tiger	Black Tortoise
virtues	benevolence	wisdom	faith	righteousness	decorum
planets	Jupiter	Mars	Saturn	Venus	Mercury
Ministries	Agriculture	War	Works	Interior	Justice

303 Readers interested in correspondences of this type should also see the article on **HARMONY (HARMONIA) OF THE SPHERES*** by Joscelyn Godwin—§136.9 above. (Ed.)

"From early western tradition, I present one additional table of similarities from the treatise *Musica Practica* by the 15th-century author Bartolomeo Ramis [Figure 3, below].

"Some common strands run through these elaborate world-schemes. They represent not a tradition of linear, cause-and-effect thinking but a rich tapesstry of associations and cultural meanings. Such is the way myth communicates—side-ways, like poetry. The schemes also represent a concern for what the Germans refer to as *Ganzheit*—'totality'—a deep-seated human need to 'tell' the dimensions within which we are encompassed, in an attempt to get our minds 'around' the complex dimensions of human experience. These tables further reveal a culturally authorized connection between the basic components of music and vital, inner substance (of one kind or another), a notion which Indian readers will not fail to recognize and accept. There is an obvious parallel, if a limited one, between the Western doctrine of the four humors/temperaments and the Indian theory of the three *gunas* (*sattva, rajas,* and *tamas*), although the former is basically a theory of personality and the latter a more pervasive theory of qualities present in all phenomena. Each of the schemes I have outlined details also a set of *social* connnections—dynasties of beings, deities, social classes, government officials, patrons of the arts—as well as the more obvious cosmic connections (the planets and other heavily bodies, or their respective deities).

"*Musical Substance.* We have reached one of the most critical components of mythical thinking about music, and also the source of the greatest divergence between Indian and Western explanations. I submit that the ontological nature of music is and has been one of the central concerns of the philosophy of music. It is an immensely complex issue, and an intriguing one. Mythical explanations of the *being* of music are couched in a jumble of cultural imagery

FIGURE 3

Mode	Temperament	Humor	Element	Planet	Muse
1	phlegmatic	phlegm	water	Sun	Melpomene (tragedy)
2	phlegmatic	phlegm	water	Moon	Clio (history)
3	choleric	yellow bile	fire	Mars	Erato (elegiac poetry)
4	choleric	yellow bile	fire	Mercury	Calliope (epic poetry)
5	sanguine	blood	air	Jupiter	Euterpe (lyric poetry)
6	sanguine	blood	air	Venus	Terpsichore (dance)
7	melanchoic	black bile	earth	Saturn	Polyhymnia (sacred potery)
8	melancholic	black bile	earth	Earth	Erania (astronomy)

that resists one's efforts to sort it out: part naive acoustical science, part philosophy, part folklore, part superstition, and part clever speculation. Space does not allow me to do more than to clarify what I believe to be the two opposed fundamental conceptions—(1)the ancient Greek notion of harmony (based on the metaphor of the state of equilibrium maintained by a tensed string), and (2) the Indian theory of *nada* (continuous, emerging, causal sound, born of mind, impelled by heat energy, and discharged in the form of vital inner substance).[304]

"The philosopher Heraclitus (fl. 500 BC) boldly stated the primitive Greek concept in one of his typically enigmatic sayings: 'There is a harmony in the bending back, as in the case of the bow and the lyre.' In brief, the musical instrument was seen as the equivalent of the hunting bow, and the notion of musical sound was thereby developed by means of the metaphor of a tensed string, the impact thereon, and its return to a state of rest. It should be kept in mind that harmony was considered a property of, not a synonym for, music; the Greek definition of music required a compound of melody, rhythm, diction, and gesture. But the idea of harmony became the most potent concept of music, almost as a *pars pro toto*. Musical sound itself was described as a harmonization of opposites, the unification of disparate things, and the conciliation of warring elements. As Theon of Smyrrna put it: 'Music, as they say, is the basis of agreement among things in nature and of the best government in the universe. As a rule it assumes the guise of harmony in the universe, of lawful government in a state, and of a sensible way of life in the home. It brings together and unites.'

"Such a concept of music as an audible representation of the balance and agreement of opposing tension has had, I believe, enormous consequences for the development of music in the West. The embodied notions of tension and of the subsurface pull-and-tug between opposite poles of attraction eventually led musicians to seek audible forms for this underlying concept: with respect to rhythm, in the binary alternation of arsis and thesis[305] (metric 'lift' and 'descent'): and with respect to pitch, in the alternation of consonance/stability and dissonance/instability, applied first to musical intervals and subsequently to more complex simultaneities.

---

304 "*Nada*: sound. The word has peculiar philosophical connotations. *Nada* is cosmic energy; it is the First Cause. Chanted sounds such as '*Aum*' symbolize the creative power of *nada*." —Massey & Massey, *The Music of India*, p.172. "*Nada*: sound, conceived in metaphysical terms." —Wade, *Music in India*, p.239. "The importance of sound *(nada)* as a primeval organizing principle has its roots in the Vedic texts and the chanting of the *Samveda*. Music is a means of acquiring and expressing power; it is a method for achieving Supreme Bliss; it is also a means of devotion. This last idea has been popular since at least the eighth century AD, when the devotional movements sprang up in the South and spread through India. That music is a means of devotion is perhaps the most common idea expressed by musicians. For Sufis and the Muslim musicians today, music as a form of devotion to and worship of God is the rationale given to explain the performance of music in the light of its discouragement or prohibition in Islam." —Neuman, *The Life of Music in North India*, p.60. See also section §161.14 above. (Ed.)

305 *Arsis*: the upbeat, or unaccented part, of a measure; *thesis*: in music, the accented section of a measure (Ed.).

"The idea of music as harmony (or, equally valid, harmony as music) is also a notably abstract principle. While the harmony of the human body and the harmony heard in music were ruled by the same principle, the actual music is extrinsic to the self; music may have been viewed as a symbol of harmony in all things, but the connections between *musica instrumentalis* (performed music) and *musica humana* (the inner harmony of body and mind) were metaphorical. One might stimulate the other by means of the tendency for passive matter to assume the form of some homologous thing (this, in brief, was Aristotle's position), but this explanation stops short of asserting a causal connection between inner substance and musical sound.[306]

"How different is the Indian concept of *nada*. The production of musical sound is assigned cosmic power, and the progression of sound along the channels of the human body traces a continuous spiral pathway from subtle, inner, unmanifested sound to gross, outer, articulate sound — acquiring definition and divisions as it emerges. If the symbol of the tensed string of the hunting bow best symbolizes the ancient Western idea of harmony, nothing but the outpouring of vital substance throughout the bodily canals can represent the Indian concept. At the risk of overstating the contrasts, the following diagram illustrates something of the range of the two ideas; these should be read as relative tendencies and preferences, not absolute values [see Figure 4, below].

"The Indian concept of sound as emergence represents a cluster of cherished cultural ideas: the divine origin of sound, utterance as worship, the 'inner' and the 'center', breath as vital substance, activating power of heat energy, the fertility and purity of fluid, 'pouring forth' as an image of creation, undivided continuity as value, the mythical identification of music and speech, the metaphor of a creative spiral, the potential valued above the actual, 'unstruck' sounds valued about 'struck' sounds, and the nonmanifest valued above the manifest. Because of the long cultural development of India, it is impossible to chart the confluence of these ideas with any precision, but there are numerous and audible traces of these values in Indian music: in the focus upon vocal music and its *quintessential* humanity, in its unique dynamic vitality, in the preference for 'chainlike' forms, in the expansive organic development of melodic structure, in the atavistic role of

FIGURE 4

Greek : harmony	Indian : nada
Static	dynamic
objective	subjective
extrinsic	intrinsic
articulation as value	continuity as value
sound as impact	sound as emergence
abstract principle	concrete/human
tensed string as metaphor	emerging vital breath (*prana*)
equilibrium	outpouripg
material	immaterial
syntactical forms	organic, serial forms

306 Interested readers may wish to compare these sentiments with various entries for **HARMONY OF THE SPHERES***. (Ed.)

respiration and gesture as recreations of sacrificial ritual, and perhaps in the kinship that links the individual musical performance with its larger 'family' of formal archetypes and *ragas*.

"In Conclusion. We have sketched a structural basis for comparing the Indian and early Western traditions of mythical thinking about music. Certain of the themes and patterns of explanation were seen to be natural, perhaps even 'universal', and may represent a stratum so deeply imbedded in mankind's mythical consciousness that cultural modifications have been confined to details and shades of meaning. In other components of musical ideology, most notably in the concept of musical substance, the sharply contrasting ontologies have been profoundly reflected in the development of musical style in the two traditions. But the consequences of how a culture conceptualizes its music go far beyond technical facts — they are manifest in how the music is perceived, with what affect the listener responds, and how the music is valued.

"The distinctive propositions of the Indian and Western ideas of music have been thoroughly programmed in each culture's listeners: an Indian listener, for example, may or may not have studied philosophy; he may not have read the *shastras* [*sastra* — formal text or treatise; also a body of doctrine, itself (Ed.)], and his experience of music may have been conditioned more by the cinema than by the concert hall or by formal instruction in music. But myth has done its job. He is 'at home' with the ornamental patterns of Indian music; they are as much a part of his familiar aural environment as are the decorative patterns and contours he perceives in sculpture and the dance a part of his visual environment.

And he senses, no less deeply, the cultural meanings inherent in the smooth outwelling of vocal sound at the start of an *alapana*.[307] In what has been called the 'mythically instructed community', of which India is a superb (but surely not the only) example, a listener *knows* his relationship to musical sound — not by means of his technical command of acoustical facts pertaining to how sound waves impact upon the organs of hearing and are transmitted to the brain, but rather in the form of deep-seated cultural beliefs. He may not know the sophisticated particulars of Abhinavagupta's elegant analysis of the theory of *rasa* ['emotional and aesthetic relish or flavor of the *raga*' — Holyrode], but he senses that a good performance communicates something of its vital substance to the receptive listener, and he finds nothing mysterious in the notion that musical sound taps a deep-running inner stream, a stream in which performer and listener alike can become absorbed.

"But it is not for a Westerner [such as me] to describe how an Indian *feels* music, and the picture is far more complex than the foregoing remarks may have suggested. And as for what a Western listener feels about music, that too is no simple matter. Our concern here has been [with] the influence of myth, and our assumption has been that myth works at a geologically slow rate, with its roots quite beyond the horizons of human history. But myths, like rocks, do change, and newer myths appear on the scene. In the West the seventeenth century witnessed the crumbling of the ancient-medieval worldview which had held together for so long a time. Musical ideology evolved rapidly between 1600 and 1800, and the wave of romanticism in the nineteenth century brought with it a

---

307 *"Alaap, alapa* or *alapana*: introductory slow movement of a *raga*, in which attention is given to particular notes, their order, usage and emphasis.... The *alaap* is the invocation to the *raga*, calling forth its mood or *rasa*." — Holroyde, *The Music of India*, p.266. (Ed.)

virtual overhaul of musical values—
towards, interestingly enough, many of
the highest values which inform the arts of
India (the irrational, the subjective, the
primaeval, the continuous, the dynamic,
the organic, the inner, the ambiguous,
direct communication by means of emotion, *et al.*). But the Indian listener may not
hear these values in nineteenth-century
Western music, any more than his counterpart is able to identify them in an Indian
performance. Too much stands in the
way....

"Certain of the themes in the Western
mythology of music still seem foreign to
Indian musical ideology: the preoccupation with numbers and ratios, the concern
for music's transience, the link with
astronomy, the 'lore' associated with a
wide range of musical instruments. The
belief in the therapeutic power of music,
while not unknown in Indian literature, is
not as widely celebrated as it is in the West.
And one of the most familiar tropes in
Western literature—that music is, in a
sense, a conquest of nature, that it can
overcome natural law, even 'untune the
sky'[308]—is utterly incomprehensible
within the traditional Indian worldview.
To the Indian music is a manifestation of
natural law, more immediate than other
sensory perceptions and more real than
what he experiences of the visible tangible
world. To him music is pure natural *process*
and process is what he values. In the West,
we may say, music represents—or represented—a treasured cultural memory: a
memory of a natural *state*, the state of nature as we thought (and hoped) it was until
scientific investigations tore gaping holes
in the coherent fabric of ideas that held the
ancient and medieval worlds together." —
Rowell, in Mehta (Book II) pp. 20-28.[309]

INDIAN (NORTH AMERICAN) MYTHS — PRACTICES AND BELIEFS. *(See also pp.387, 874.)*

§162.15 See **BAGPIPES***.
           HIAWATHA*.

§162.16 **DANCE.** "*Dancing* is one of the most
valued amusements of the Indians, and
much more frequently practiced by them
than by any civilized society. It enters into
the forms of worship, and is often their
mode of appealing to the Great Spirit, or
paying their usual devotions to their

---

308 The famous concluding phrase from John Dryden's *A Song for St. Cecilia's Day, 1687.*
309 It seems to me that *some* of these statements can be challenged on specific points, in
    addition to which contrast with so-called "primitive" views (for which see e.g.
    Australian aboriginal, North and South American, and shamanistic etc practices and
    beliefs) has been omitted entirely. Certainly, for example, there is considerable In-
    dian "lore" concerning musical instruments; and while certain powers of music over
    "natural" phenomena *are* indeed supposed sometimes in Indian myth, it is also the
    case that in Western philosophy music is *not* merely set in opposition to "nature",
    so-called—but is construed as a medium of dealing *with* it, if you will. Moreover,
    the basic principle of "harmony" for the West (and also for the Chinese etc) is—
    precisely—that music is an expression of, and is not in opposition to, fundamental
    "cosmic" structure. Nevertheless, Rowell's essay remains interesting and provoca-
    tive. I would only stress—as a final note—that themes such as those which are out-
    lined in our *Introductory Remarks* at the head of Vol I do, in fact, appear to be
    "universal", and—on the whole—are only expressed differently at different times
    and in different places according to some local emphasis or nuance. (Ed.)

medicine, and of honoring and entertaining strangers of distinction.

"Instead of the 'giddy maze' of the quadrille or the country dance, the cheering smiles and graces of silkened beauty, the Indian performs with jumps and starts and yells, much to the satisfaction of his own exclusive self, and the infinite amusement of the gentler sex, who are always lookers-on but are seldom allowed so great a pleasure, or so signal an honor, as that of joining with their lords in this or any other entertainment.

"I saw so many different varieties of dances among the Sioux that I should almost be disposed to denominate them the 'dancing Indians'. They had dances for everything. There was scarcely an hour, day or night, but that the beat of the drum could not be heard. The dances are almost as various and different in their character as they are numerous. Some of them are exceedingly grotesque and laughable. They can keep bystanders in an irresistible roar of laughter. Others are calculated to excite pity and forcible appeal to sympathies. Others disgust. Still others terrify and alarm with frightful threats and contortions.[310]

"As is often done in the enlightened world, dancing is also done here to get favors — to buy the world's goods. In both instances it is danced with about equal merit, except that the Indian has surpassed us in honesty by christening it the 'beggar's dance'. This spirited dance was given not by a set of *beggars* but by the first and most independent young men in the tribe, beautifully dressed, with their lances and pipes and rattles in their hands, and a medicine-man beating the drum and joining the song at the highest key of his voice. In this dance everyone sings as loud as he can halloo, uniting his voice in an appeal to the Great Spirit to open the hearts of the bystanders to give to the poor, and not to themselves, assuring them that the Great Spirit will be kind to those who are kind to the helpless and poor.

"[Even the victory-dances of the Sioux have a religious element — in this case, regarding (at the very least) a "superstitious dread of the spirits of their slain enemies" — as the now author tells us. (Ed.)] The scalp-dance is given as a celebration of a victory. Among the Sioux it is danced at night, by the light of their torches, and just before retiring to bed. When a war-party returns from a war excursion, bringing home with them the scalps of their enemies, they generally 'dance them' for fifteen nights in succession. They make the most extravagant boasts of their prowess in war, while they brandish their war weapons. A number of young women are selected to aid (though they do not actually join in the dance), by stepping into the center of the ring and holding up the scalps that have been recently taken. The warriors dance around in a circle, brandishing their weapons and barking and yelping in the most frightful manner, all jumping on both feet at a time, with a simultaneous stamp and blow and thrust of their weapons. It would seem as if they were actually cutting and carving each other to pieces. During these frantic leaps and yelps and thrusts, every man distorts his face to the utmost, darting about his glaring eye-balls and snapping his teeth as if he were in the heat (and actually breathing through his inflated nostrils the very hissing death) of battle!

"There is no doubt that one great object in these exhibitions is public exultation. Yet there are other essential motives for formally displaying the scalp. Among some tribes it is the custom to bury the scalps after they have gone through this series of public exhibitions, which may be

---

310 For all the author's (George Catlin, 1841) view of the Indian as an "uncivilized" society, it is plain from this description that he regards Sioux and other dancing is a sophisticated art, capable of varied and forceful effects. (Ed.)

to give them notoriety, or award public credit to the persons who obtained them and now are obliged to part with them. The great respect which seems to be paid to them while they use them, as well as the pitying and mournful song which they howl to the *manes* of their unfortunate victims, and the precise solemnity with which they afterwards bury the scalps, sufficiently convince me they have a superstitious dread of the spirits of their slain enemies, and by performing many conciliatory offices, one of which is the dance, ensure their own peace." – Catlin, pp.250-52.

§162.17 ZUÑI TALES AND BELIEFS.

Although it appears to be the case that Native American "song" is probably closer to chant or rhythmic declamation than it is to the lyrical poetry of "art" song, still it *is* song and not speech; and – again – while Native American dance may seem closer to a sort of "prose" rhythmical gesturing than to ballet and other "artistic" musical forms, still this too is still dance. A point that deserves to be stressed, meanwhile, is that both song and dance are – at least in part – *magical* gestures, or instruments intended to accomplish certain tasks through magic. This is made especially clear in the following excerpts from the introduction (by John Wesley Powell) to Cushing's *Zuñi Folk Tales:*

"The gods of Zuñi, like those of all primitive people, are the ancients of animals, but we must understand and heartily appreciate their simple thought if we would do them justice. All entities are animals – men, brutes, plants, stars, lands, waters, and rocks – and all have souls. The souls are tenuous existences – mist entities, gaseous creatures inhabiting firmer bodies of matter. They are ghosts that own bodies. They can leave their bodies, or if they discover bodies that have been vacated they can take possession of them. Force and mind belong to souls; fixed form, firm existence belong to matter, while bodies and souls constitute the world. The world is a universe of animals. The stars are animals compelled to travel around the world by magic. The plants are animals under a spell of enchantment, so that usually they cannot travel. The waters are animals sometimes under the spell of enchantment. Lakes writhe in waves, the sea travels in circles about the earth, and the streams run over the lands. Mountains and hills tremble in pain, but cannot wander about; but rocks and hills and mountains sometimes travel about by night.

"These animals of the world come in a flood of generations, and the first-born are gods and are usually called the ancients, or the first ones; the later-born generations are descendants of the gods, but alas, they are degenerate ones.

"The theatre of the world is the theatre of necromancy,[311] and the gods are the primeval wonder-workers; the gods still live, but their descendants often die. Death itself is the result of necromancy practiced by bad men or angry gods.

"In every Amerindian language there is a term to express this magical power. Among the Iroquoian tribes it is called *orenda;* among the Siouan tribes some manifestations of it are called *wakan* or *wakanda,* but the generic term in this language is *hube.* Among the Shoshonean tribes it is called *pokunt.* Let us borrow one of these terms and called it 'orenda'. All unexplained phenomena are attributed to orenda. Thus the venom of the serpent is orenda, and this orenda can pass from a serpent to an arrow by another exercise of orenda, and hence the arrow is charmed. The rattlesnake may be stretched beside the arrow, and an invocation may be performed that will convey the orenda from the snake to

---

311 "The art that professes to conjure up the spirits of the dead and commune with them in order to predict the future; black magic, sorcery; magical qualities." – *American Heritage Dictionary of the English Language* (1969). (Ed.)

the arrow, or the serpent may be made into a witch's stew and the arrow dipped into the brew.

"No man has contributed more to our understanding of the doctrine of orenda as believed and practised by the Amerindian tribes than [Frank Hamilton Cushing, the collector and translator of the present volume of Zuñi folk tales]. In other publications he has elaborately discussed this doctrine, and in his lectures he was wont to show how forms and decorations of implements and utensils have orenda for their motive.

"When one of the ancients – that is, one of the gods – of the Iroquois was planning the streams of earth by his orenda or magical power, he determined to have them run up one side and down the other; if he had done this men could float up or down at will, by passing from one side to the other of the river, but his wicked brother interfered and made them run down on both sides; so orenda may thwart orenda.

"The bird that sings is universally held by tribal men to be exercising its orenda. And when human beings sing they also exercise orenda; hence song is a universal accompaniment of Amerindian worship. All their worship is thus fundamentally terpsichorean, for it is supposed that they can be induced to grant favors by pleasing them....

"The primitive religion of every Amerindian tribe is an organized system of inducing the ancients to take part in the affairs of men, and the worship of the gods is a system designed to please the gods, that they may be induced to act for men, particularly the tribe of men who are the worshipers. Time would fail me to tell of the multitude of activities in tribal life designed for this purpose, but a few of them may be mentioned. The first and most important of all are terpsichorean

ceremonies and festivals. Singing and dancing are universal, and festivals are given at appointed times and places by every tribe. The long nights of winter are devoted largely to worship, and a succession of festival days are established, to be held at appropriate seasons for the worship of the gods. Thus there are festival days for thanksgiving – for harvest homes. In lands where the grasshopper is an important food there are grasshopper festivals. In lands where corn is an important food there are green-corn festivals; where the buffalo constituted an important part of their aliment there were buffalo dances. So there is a bear dance or festival, and elk dance or festival, and a multitude of other festivals as we go from tribe to tribe, all of which are fixed at times indicated by signs of the zodiac. In the higher tribes elaborate calendars are devised from which we unravel their picture-writings.

"The practice of medicine by the shamans is an invocation to the gods to drive out evil spirits from the sick and to frighten them that they may leave. By music and dancing they obtain the help of the ancients, and by a great variety of methods they drive out the evil beings.[312] Resort is often had to scarifying and searing, especially when the sick man has great local pains. All American tribes entertain a profound belief in the doctrine of signatures, – *similia, similibus curantur,* – and they use this belief in procuring charms as medicine to drive out the ghostly diseases that plague their sick folk.

"Next in importance to terpsichorean worship is altar worship. The altar is a space cleared upon the ground, or a platform raised from the ground or floor of the kiva or assembly-house of the people. Around the altar are gathered the priests and their acolytes, and here they make prayers and perform ceremonies with the

---

312 However, as one commentator observes, if the shaman fails to drive out the evil beings and cure the patient, he may simply chalk it up to failure. If at first you don't succeed... (Ed.)

aid of altar-pieces of various kinds, especially tablets of picture-writings on wood, bone, or the skins of animals. The altar-pieces consist of representatives of the thing for which supplication is made: ears of corn or vases of meal, ewers of water, parts of animals designed for food, cakes of grasshoppers, basins of honey, in fine any kind of food; then crystals or fragments of rock to signify that they desire the corn to be hard, or of honeydew that they desire the corn to be sweet, or of corn of different colors. That which is of great interest to students of ethnology is the system of picture-writing exhibited on the altars. In this a great variety of things which they desire and a great variety of the characteristics of these things are represented in pictographs, or modeled in clay, or carved from wood and bone. The graphic art, as painting and sculpture, has its origin with tribal men in the development of altar-pieces. So also the drama is derived from primeval worship, as the modern practice of medicine has been evolved from necromancy.

"There is another method of worship found in savagery, but more highly developed in barbarism, — the worship of sacrifice. The altar-pieces and the dramatic supplications of the lower stage gradually develop into a sacrificial stage in the higher culture. Then the objects are supposed to supply the ancients themselves with food and drink and the pleasures of life. This stage was most highly developed in Mexico, especially by the Nahua or Aztec, where human beings were sacrificed. In general, among the Amerinds, not only are sacrifices made on the altar, but they are also made whenever food or drink is used. Thus the first portions of objects designed for consumption are dedicated to the gods. There are in America many examples of these pagan religions, to a greater or less extent affiliated in doctrine and in worship with the religion of Christian origin." — Major J. W. Powell (1901), in Cushing, pp.ix-xi, xiii-xvi.

* * *

In the preceding introduction, Powell describes the habit of seeking to address the gods or spirit world (in other words of seeking to address the *animals* — the original world beings) through song and dance. Appropriately, the *Zuñi Folk Tales* retold by Cushing in the book proper show various of these animal characters themselves naturally slipping into song or dance as a means of communicating with each other — of, indeed, bringing about some special (to us magical) effect or other. Thus the two reinforce each other: human beings who sing and dance in their religious observances tell stories featuring animals that communicate (and bring about magical occurrences) through song and dance.

Excerpts from *Zuñi Folk Tales:*
"[A young man eager to rejoin his beloved — whom, by a tragic turn of events, he has killed — has been following an elusive red prayer-plume which floats before him, just out of reach, and in his haste he had come to be suspended above a canyon, where he now hangs in risk of losing his life...] Whereupon the little chit [squirrel] ran chattering away and called his mate out of their house in a rock-nook: 'Wife! Wife! Come quickly; run to our corn room and bring me a hemlock, and hurry! hurry! Ask me no questions; for a lax fool of a man over here will break himself to pieces [fall to his death below] if we don't quickly make him a ladder.'

"So the little wife flirted her brush in his face and skipped over the rocks to their store-house, where she chose a fat hemlock and hurried to her husband who was digging a hole in the sand underneath where the young man was hanging. Then they spat on the seed, and buried it in the hole, and began to dance round it and sing, —

Kiathla tsilu,
Silokwe, silokwe, silokwe;

Ki'ai silu silu,
      Tsithl! Tsithl!

Which meant, as far as any one can tell now
(for it was a long time ago, and partly
squirrel talk),

Hemlock of the
      Tall kind, tall kind, tall kind,
Sprout up hemlock, hemlock,
Chit! Chit!

And every time they danced around and
sang the song through, the ground moved,
until the fourth time they said *'Tsithl!
Tsithl!'* the tree sprouted forth and kept
growing until the little Squirrel could
jump into it, and by grabbing the topmost
bough and bracing himnself against the
branches below, could stretch and pull it,
so that in a short time he made it grow as
high as the young man's feet [were, and so
saved his life]....
[The plume continues to float away, with
the young man in pursuit of it.] Toward
the middle of the night he heard strange,
happy voices. The doorway to the Land of
Spirits opened, and the light shot up
through the dark green waters from many
windows, like sparks from a chimney on a
dark, windless night. Then [a ladder of
flags came up out of the middle of a lake],
and he saw the forms of the dead pass out
and in, and heard the sounds of the
Kâkâ,[313] as it danced for the gods. The com-
ers and goers were bright and beautiful,
but their garments were snow-white cotton, stitched with many-colored threads,
and their necklaces and bracelets were of
dazzling white shells and turquoises un-
numbered. Once he ventured to gain the
bright entrance, but the water grew deep
and chilled him till he trembled with fear

and cold. Yet he looked in at the entrances,
and lo! as he gazed he caught sight of his
beautiful bride all covered with garments
and bright things. And there in the midst
of the *Kâkâ* she sat at the head of the dancers. She seemed happy and smiled as she
watched, and youths as bright and as
happy came around her, and she seemed
to forget her lone lover.

"[Very much as in the myth of Orpheus*
and Eurydice, the young man almost
claims his love from the Land of the Spirits
and — at the very last minute — fails to
bring her back to life.]

"Alas! alas! Thus it was in the days of the
ancients. Maybe had the young man not
[done what he had done yonder by] the
Lake of the Dead, we would never have
journeyed nor ever have mourned for
others lost. But then it is well! If men and
women had never died, then the world
long ago had overflown with children,
starvation, and warring.

"[*The Youth and the Place of the Dead.* Once
upon a time] when night came [another
youth] went with the Eagle people to the
city [of the damned]. A beautiful place it
was, large and fine, with high walls of
stone and many a little window out of
which the red firelight was shining. The
smoke was going up from its chimneys, the
sparks winding up through it, and, with
beacon fires burning on the roofs, it was a
happy, bustling scene that met the gaze of
the youth as he approached the town.
There were sounds and cries of life
everywhere. Lights shone and merriment
echoed from every street and room, and
they were ushered into a great dance hall,
or *kiwitsin,* where the audience was already assembled.

---

313 "The kâkâ, or Sacred Drama Dance, is represented by a great variety of masks and
      costumes worn by Zuñi dancers during the performance of this remarkable
      dramatic ceremony. Undoubtedly many of the traditional characters of the Sacred
      Drama thus represented are conventionalizations of the mythic conceptions or per-
      sonifications of animal attributes." — p.229.

"By-and-by the sounds of the coming dance were heard, and all was expectation. The fires blazed up and the lights shone all round the room, making it as bright as day. In came the dancers, maidens mostly, beautiful, and clad in the richest of ancient garments; their eyes were bright, their hair black and soft, their faces gleaming with merriment and pleasure. And they came joking down the ladders into the room before the place where the youth sat, and as they danced down the middle of the floor they cried out in shrill, yet not unpleasant voices, as they jostled each other, playing grotesque pranks and assuming the most laughter-stirring attitudes:

" 'Hapa! hapa! is! is! is! (Dead! dead! this! this! this!)' — pointing at one another, and repeating this baleful expression, although so beautiful, and full of life and joy and merriment.

"Now, the youth looked at them all through this long dance, and though he thought it strange that they should exclaim thus one to another, so lively and pretty and jolly they were, he was nevertheless filled with amusement at their strange antics and wordless jokes. Still [as he had been warned not to,] he never smiled.

"Then they filed in again and there were more dancers, merrier than before, and among them were two or three girls of surpassing beauty even in that throng of lovely women, and one of them looked in a coquettish manner constantly toward the youth, directing all her smiles and merriment to him as she pointed round to her companions, exclaiming: 'Hapa! hapa! is! is! is!'

"The youth grew forgetful of everything else as he leaned forward, absorbed in watching this girl with her bright eyes and merry smiles. When, finally, in a more amusing manner than before, she jostled some merry dancer, he laughed outright and the girl ran forward toward him, with two others following, and reached out, grasped his hands and dragged him into the dance. The Eagle-maiden lifted her wings and with a cry of woe flew away with her people. But ah, ah! the youth minded nothing, he was so wild with merriment, like the beautiful maidens by his side, and up and down the great lighted hall he danced with them, joining in their uncouth postures and their exclamations, of which he did not yet understand the true meaning — 'Hapa! hapa! is! is! is!'

"[When morning comes, the youth found the scene much changed...] The rafters, dried and warped with age, were bending and breaking, and pieces of the roof fell now and then when the wind blew more strongly. He raised himself, and clammy bones fell from around him; and when he cast his eyes about him, there on the floor were strewn bones and skulls. Here and there a face half buried in the sand, with eyes sunken and dried and patches of skin clinging to it, seemed to glare at him. Fingers and feet, as of mummies, were strewn about, and it was as if the youth had entered a great cemetary, where the remains of the dead of all ages where littered about.[314]

"The Poor Turkey Girl. Long, long ago, our ancients had neither sheep nor horses nor cattle; yet they had domestic animals of various kinds — amongst them Turkeys.

"In Mátsaki, or the Salt City,[315] there dwelt at this time many very wealthy families, who possessed large flocks of these birds, which it was their custom to have their slaves or the poor people of the town herd in the plains round about

---

314 This episode, featuring a dance of the dead (in the form of eagles), puts one in mind of British folktales about elves and fairies who — similarly not of this world — dance the whole night to the fiddler's never-resting tune! (Ed.)

315 Presumably Salt Lake City, Utah. (Ed.)

Thunder Mountain, below which their town stood, and on the mesas beyond.

'[Now near the border of the town] there lived alone a very poor girl,—so poor that her clothes were patched and tattered and dirty, and her person, on account of long neglect and ill-fare, shameful to look upon, though she herself was not ugly, but had a winning face and bright eyes; that is, if the face had been more oval and the eyes less oppressed with care. So poor was she that she herded Turkeys for a living; and little was given to her except the food she subsisted on from day to day, and perhaps now and then a piece of old, worn-out clothing....

"[As for the Turkeys] they loved their mistress so much that at her call they would unhesitatingly come, or at her behest go whithersoever and whensoever she wished.

"One day this poor girl, driving her Turkeys down into the plains, passed near Old Zuñi,—the Middle Ant Hill of the World, as our ancients have taught us to call our home,—and as she went along, she heard the herald-priest proclaiming from the house-top that the Dance of the Sacred Bird (which is a very blessed and welcome festival to our people, especially to the youths and maidens who are permitted to join in the dance) would take place in four days.

"[The poor girl would so love to go. Then one of the turkeys—a fine big Gobbler—addressed her thus:] 'Maiden mother, we know what your thoughts are, and truly we pity you, and wish that, like the other people of Mátsaki, you might enjoy this holiday in the town below.... Now, listen well, for I speak the speech of all the elders of my people: If you will drive us in early this afternoon, when the dance is most gay and the people are most happy, we will help you to make yourself so handsome and so prettily dressed that never a man, woman, or child amongst all those who are assembled at the dance will know you; but rather, especially the young men, will wonder whence you came, and long to lay hold of your hand in the circle that forms round the altar to dance. Maiden mother, would you like to go to see this dance, and even to join in it, and be merry with the best of your people?'

"[The girl promises not to forget her friends, the Turkeys, and they prepare beautiful clothes for her.] Before the maiden donned all these garments, the Turkeys circled about her, singing and singing, and clucking and clucking, and brushing her with their wings, until her person was as clean and her skin as smooth and bright as that of the fairest maiden of the wealthiest home in Mátsaki....

"[They produce gems for her, and—promising once again not to forget her dear friends, and to return home before the hour has grown too late—the beautifully transformed Cinderella of the plains makes her way into the town to the dance court. Now the finest youths among the dancers vie with one another for her hand. In her joy at dancing and dancing, she fails to notice the hour, or think at all of her friends. When at last she does remember, and returns to them—they have gone. Why should they remain in captivity, if the mistress whom they trusted has forgotten them? They have trooped out of their cages, and run up toward the Cañon of the Cottonwoods, and then round behind Thunder Mountain, through the Gateway of Zunñi, and so on up the valley.]

"Behold, not a Turkey was there! Trailing them, she ran and she ran up the valley to overtake them; but they were far ahead, and it was only after a long time that she came within the sound of their voices, and then, redoubling her speed, well-nigh overtook them, when she heard them singing this song:

K'yaanaa, to! to!
K'yaanaa, to! to!
Ye ye!
K'yaanaa, to! to!
K'yaanaa, to! to!
Yee huli huli!

Hon awen Tsita
Itiwanakwin
  Otakyaan aaa kyaa;
Lesna akyaaa
Shoya-k'oskwi
teyathltokwin
  Hon aawani!D

  Ye yee huli huli
    Tot-tot, tot-tot, tot-tot,
      Huli huli!
    Tot-tot, tot-tot, tot-tot,
      Huli huli!

Up the river, *to! to!*
Up the river, *to! to!*
  Sing *ye ye!*
Up the river, *to! to!*
Up the river, *to! to!*
  Sing *yee huli huli!*

Oh, our maiden mother
To the Middle Place
  To dance went away;
Therefore as she lingers,
To the Cañon Mesa
And the plains above it
  We all run away!

  Sing ye yee huli huli,
    Tot-tot, tot-tot, tot-tot,
      Huli huli!
    Tot-tot, tot-tot, tot-tot,
      Huli huli!

"Hearing this, the maiden called to her Turkeys; called and called in vain. They only quickened their steps, spreading their wings to help them along, singing the song over and over until, indeed, they came to the base of the Cañon Mesa, at the borders of the Zuñi Mountains. Then singing once more their song in full chorus, they spread wide their wings, and *thlakwa-a-a, thlakwa-a-a,* they fluttered away over the plains above.

"The poor Turkey girl threw her hands up and looked down at her dress. With dust and sweat, behold! it was changed to what it had been, and she was the same poor Turkey girl that she was before.

Weary, grieving, and despairing, she returned to Mátsaki.

"Thus it was in the days of the ancients. Therefore, where you see the rocks leading up to the top of Cañon Mesa (Shoya-k'oskwi), there are the tracks of turkeys and other figures to be seen. The latter are the song that the Turkeys sang, graven in the rocks; and all over the plains along the borders of Zuñi Mountains since that day turkeys have been more abundant than in any other place.

"After all, the gods dispose of men according as men are fitted; and if the poor be poor in heart and spirit as well as in appearance, how will they be aught but poor to the end of their days?

"How the Coyote Joined the Dance of the Burrowing Owls. [A long time ago, in a valley beyond the foot-hills of the great mesa called Middle Mountain,] there lived a village of Prairie-dogs, on fairly peaceable terms with Rattlesnakes, Adders, Chameleons, Horned-toads, and Burrowing-owls. With the Owls they were especially friendly, looking at them as creatures of great gravity and sanctity. For this reason these Prairie-dogs and their companions never disturbed the councils or ceremonies of the Burrowing-owls, but treated them most respectfully, keeping at a distance from them when their dances were going on.

"It chanced one day that the Burrowing-owls were having a great dance all to themselves, rather early in the morning. The dance they were engaged in was one peculiarly prized by them, requiring no little dexterity in its execution. Each dancer, young man or maiden, carried upon his or her head a bowl of foam, and though their legs were crooked and their motions disjointed, they danced to the whistling of some and the clapping beaks of others, in perfect unison, and with such dexterity that they never spilled a speck of the foam on their sleek mantles of dun-black feather-work.

"It chanced this morning of the Foam-dance that a Coyote was nosing about for Grasshoppers and Prairie-dogs. So quite naturally he was prowling around the by-streets in the borders of the Prairie-dog town. His house where he lived with his old grandmother stood back to the westward, just over the elevations that bounded Sunken Country, among the rocks. He heard the click-clack of the musicians and their shrill, funny little song:

I yami hota utchu tchapikya,
        Tokos! tokos! tokos! tokos!

So he pricked up his ears, and lifting his tail, trotted forward toward the level place between the hillocks and doorways of the village, where the Owls were dancing in a row. He looked at them with great curiosity, squatting on his haunches, the more composedly to observe them. Indeed, he became so much interested and amused by their shambling motions and clever evolutions, that he could no longer contain his curiosity. So he stepped forward, with a smirk and a nod toward the old master of ceremonies, and said: 'My father, how are you and your children these many days?'

" 'Contented and happy,' replied the old Owl, turning his attention to the dancing again.

" 'Yes, but I observe you are dancing,' said the Coyote. 'A very fine dance, upon my word! Charming! Charming! And why should you be dancing if you were not contented and happy, to be sure?'

" 'We are dancing,' responded the Owl, 'both for our pleasure and for the good of the town.'[316]

" 'True, true,' replied the Coyote; 'but what's that which looks like foam these dancers are carrying on their heads, and why do they dance in so limping a fashion?'

" 'You see, my friend,' said the Owl, turning toward the Coyote, 'we hold this to be a very sacred performance—very sacred indeed. Being such, these my children are initiated and so trained in the mysteries of the sacred society of which this is a custom that they can do very strange things in the observance of our ceremonies. You ask what it is that looks like foam they are balancing on their heads. Look more closely, friend. Do you not observe that it is their own grandmothers' heads they have on, the feathers turned white with age?'

" 'By my eyes!' exclaimed Coyote, blinking and twitching his whiskers; 'it seems so.'

" 'And you ask also why they limp as they dance,' said the Owl. 'Now, this limp is essential to the proper performance of our dance—so essential, in fact, that in order to attain to it these my children go through the pain of having their legs broken. Instead of losing by this, they gain in a great many ways. Good luck always follows them. They are quite as spry as they were before, and enjoy, moreover, the distinction of performing a dance which no other people or creatures in the world are capable of!'

" 'Dust and devils!' ejaculated the Coyote. 'This is passing strange. A most admirable dance, upon my word! Why, every bristle on my body keeps time to the music and their steps! Look here, my friend, don't you think that I could learn that dance?'

" 'Well,' replied the old Owl; 'it is rather hard to learn, and you haven't been initiated, you know; but, still, if you are determined that you would like to join the dance—by the way, have you a grandmother?'

" 'Yes, and a fine old woman she is,' said he, twitching his mouth in the direction of his house. 'She lives there with me. I dare say she is looking after my breakfast now.'

---

316 See **DANCE AND RELIGION***, above. (Ed.)

" 'Very well,' continued the Owl, 'if you care to join in our dance, fulfill the conditions, and I think we can receive you in our order.' And he added, aside: 'The silly fool; the sneaking, impertinent wretch! I will teach him to be sticking that sharp nose of his into other people's affairs!'

"[The Coyote's grandmother] was singing to herself when he dashed up to the roof where she was sitting, and, catching up a convenient leg-bone, whacked her over the pate and sawed her head off with the teeth of a deer. All bloody and soft as it was, he clapped it on his own head and raised himself on his hind-legs, bracing his tail against the ground, and letting his paws drop with the toes outspread, to imitate as nearly as possible the drooping wings of the dancing Owls. He found that it worked very well; so, descending with the head in one paw and a stone in the other, he found a convenient sharp-edged rock, and, laying his legs across it, hit them a tremendous crack with the stone, which broke them, to be sure, into splinters.

" 'Beloved Powers! Oh!' howled the Coyote. 'Oh-o-o-o! the dance may be a fine thing, but the initiation is anything else!'

"[In great pain he returned] to the Prairie-dog town, his poor old grandmother's head slung over his shoulders.

"When he approached the dancers, — for they were still dancing, — they pretended to be greatly delighted with their proselyte, and greeted him, notwithstanding his rueful countance, with many congratulatory epithets, mingled with very proper expressions of welcome. The Coyote looked sick and groaned occasionally and kept looking around at his feet, as though he would like to lick them. But the old Owl extended his wing and cautioned him not to interfere with the working power of faith in this essential observance, and invited him (with a *hem* that very much resembled a suppressed giggle), to join in their dance. The Coyote smirked and bowed and tried to stand up gracefully on his stumps, but fell over, his

grandmother's head rolling around in the dirt.

"[At last Coyote understood that he had been duped, and vowed to smoke out the Burrowing-owls from their holes, with yucca, and grease-weed, and yellow-top weeds, and pitch-pine. Then Coyote returned home and washed the blood and dirt from his grandmother's head, and sewed it back to her body with sinew as carefully as he could. Then he opened her mouth, and, putting his muzzle to it, blew into her throat, in the hope of resuscitating her; but the wind only leaked out from the holes in her neck, and she gave no signs of animation. Then he expressed his regret over what he had done, and implored her to revive. At last, weakened by his injuries, and filled with grief and shame and mortification, he wandered off a little ways, and lay down.]

"He was so engrossed in howling and thinking of his woes and pains that a Horned-toad, who saw him, and who hated him because of the insults he had frequently suffered from him and his kind, crawled into the throat of the beast without his noticing it. Presently the little creature struck up a song:

Tsakina muuu-ki
Iyami Kushina tsoiyakya
Aisiwaiki muki, muki,
Muuu ka!

" 'Ah-a-a-a-a-a,' the Coyote was groaning. But when he heard this song, apparently far off, and yet so near, he felt very strangely inside, so he thought and no doubt wondered if it were the song of some musician.

"[Then the Horned-toad sang again, and still again. At last the Coyote discovered where he was. Meanwhile the Horned-toad explored him from inside, touching his liver, and feeling the sides of the Coyote's food-bag. 'Mercy! mercy! Be very careful — that is the very source of my being — my stomach itself' the Coyote exlaimed. Then the Horned-toad locked one of his horns into the Coyote's heart. The Coyote gave one gasp, straightened out his limbs, and expired.]

" 'Ha, ha! you villain! Thus would you have done to me, had you found the chance; thus unto you' — saying which [the Horned-toad] found his way out and sought the nearest water-pocket he could find.

"So you see from this, which took place in the days of the ancients, it may be inferred that the instinct of meddling with everything that did not concern him, and making a universal nuisance of himself, and desiring to imitate everything that he sees, ready to jump into any trap that is laid for him, is a confirmed instinct with the Coyote, for those are precisely his characteristics today.

"Furthermore, Coyotes never insult Horned-toads nowadays, and they keep clear of Burrowing-owls. And ever since then the Burrowing-owls have been speckled with gray and white all over their backs and bosoms, because their ancestors spilled foam over themselves in laughing at the silliness of the Coyote.

"*How the Coyotes Tried to Steal the Children of the Sacred Dance.* In the times of the ancients, when our people lived in various places about the valley of Zuñi where ruins now stand, it is said that an old Coyote lived in Cedar Cañon with his family, which included a fine litter of pups. It is also said that at this time there lived on the crest of Thunder Mountain, back of the broad rock column or pinnacle which guards its western portion, one of the gods of the Sacred Drama Dance (*Kâkâ*), named K'yámakwe, with his children, many in number, and altogether like himself.

"One day the old Coyote of Cedar Cañon went out hunting, and as he was prowling among the sage-bushes below Thunder Mountain, he heard the clang and rattle and the shrill cries of the K'yámakwe. He pricked up his ears, stuck his nose into the air, and presently discovered the K'yámakwe children running rapidly back

and forth on the very edge of the mountain.

" 'Delight of my senses, what pretty creatures they are! Good for me!' he piped, in a jovial voice. 'I am the finder of children. I must capture the little fellows tomorrow, and bring them up as Coyotes ought to be brought up. Aren't they handsome, though?'

"[Coyote summons his brother Coyotes — with whom he plans to share the beautiful children of the god — and with himself at its head the crowd of Coyotes advances on Thunder Mountain, bent on mischief. In order to climb up the mountain they form a chain — each holding on to the tail of the Coyote before him. Then — just when they are in sight of their goal — the chief of the Coyotes has the bad fortune of sneezing, and loses his hold on the rocks, and so down the whole string, hundreds of Coyotes, fell, and were completely flattened out among the rocks.]

"The warrior of the *Kâkâ* — he of the Long Horn, with frightful, staring eyes, and visage blue with rage, — bow and war-club in hand, was hastening from the sacred lake in the west to rescue the children of the K'yámakwe. When he arrived they had been rescued already, so, after storming around a little and mauling such of the Coyotes as were not quite dead, he set to skin them all.

"And ever since then you will observe that the dancers of the Long Horn have blue faces, and whenever they arrive in our pueblo wear collars of coyote-skin about their necks. That is the way they got them. Before that they had no collars. It is presumable that that is the reason why they bellow so and have such hoarse voices, having previously taken cold, every one of them, for the want of fur collars." — Cushing, pp.27-30, 33, 46-49, 54-64, 203-14, 229-34.

Nearly every creature of the animal world expresses itself under certain circumstances by singing and dancing. In one story about an ugly old Tarantula who has stolen the beautiful garments of the son of the priest-chief of the town of K'iákime, several attempts are made to reclaim them. First the Great Kingfisher swoops by—in vain. Tarantula sings from inside his hole,

> *Ohatchik'ya ti Tákwà,*
> > *Ai yaa Tákwà!*
> *Ohatchik'ya lii Tákwà,*
> *Ohatchik'ya lii Tákwà!,*
> *Ai yaa Tákwà!*
> *Ai yaa Tákwà!*
> > *Tákwà, Tákwà!*

"Thus singing, he danced,—surely a song that nobody but he could dance to, if it be a song, but he danced to it. And when he had finished jigging about, he looked at his fluttering garments, and said: 'Ha, ha! Just look at my fine dress! Now am I not handsome? I tell you I am handsome! Now, let's have another dance!' And again he sang at the top of his wheezing voice, and pranced round on his crooked hind legs, with his fine garments fluttering.

"[Great Eagle tries next.] But his wings hissed and buzzed past the hole harmlessly, and his crooked talons reached down into the dark, clutching nothing save one of the plumes in Old Tarantula's head-dress. Even this he failed to bring away.

"The Old Tarantula tumbled headlong into his lower room, and exclaimed: 'Ha, ha! Goodness save us! What a startling he gave me! But he didn't get me! No, he didn't get me! Let's have a dance! Jig it down! What a fine fellow I am!' And he began to prance about, and jig and sing as he had sung before:

> *Ohatchik'ya ti Tákwà,*
> > *Ai yaa Tákwà!*
> *Ohatchik'ya lii Tákwà,*
> *Ohatchik'ya lii Tákwà!,*
> *Ai yaa Tákwà!*
> *Ai yaa Tákwà!*
> > *Tákwà, Tákwà!*

"As soon as he paused for breath, he glanced askance at his fluttering bright garments and cried out: 'Ho! what a handsome fellow I am! How finely dressed I am! Let's have another dance!' And again he danced and sang, all by himself, admiring himself, answering his own questions, and watching his own movements.

"[Hatchutsanona, the Lesser Falcon, tries next to reclaim the beautiful garments of the son of the priest-chief of the town of K'iákime.] With a sweep of his wings like the swirl of a snowdrift, [the Lesser Falcon] shot into the mouth of Old Tarantula's den, grasped at his head, and brought away with him the macaw plumes of the youth's head-dress.

"Down into his den tumbled Old Tarantula, and he sat down and bent himself double with fright and chagrin. He wagged his head to and fro, and sighed: 'Alas! alas! my beautiful head-dress; the skulking wretch! My beautiful head-dress; he has taken it from me. What is the use of bothering about a miserable bunch of macaw feathers, anyway? They get dirty, they get bent and broken, moths eat them, they change their color; what is the use of troubling myself about a worthless thing like that? Haven't I still the finest costume in the valley?—handsome leggings and embroidered skirt and mantle, sleeves as pretty as flowers in summer, necklaces worth fifty head-plumes, and earrings worth a handful of such necklaces? Ha, ha! let him away with the old head-plumes! Let's have a dance, and dance her down, old fellow!' said he, talking to himself. And again he skipped about, and sang his tuneless song:

> *Ohatchik'ya ti Tákwà,*
> > *Ai yaa Tákwà!*
> *Ohatchik'ya lii Tákwà,*
> *Ohatchik'ya lii Tákwà!,*
> *Ai yaa Tákwà!*
> *Ai yaa Tákwà!*
> > *Tákwà, Tákwà!*

"He admired himself as much as before. 'Forsooth,' said he; 'I could not have seen the head-plume for I would have worn it in the back of my head.'

"[Then the people called Swift-runner himself, from whom the clothes had been stolen. Aided by the Gods, Swift-runner succeeded at last in conquering that huge beast, the Old Tarantula. And then] the people assembled and heaped up great quantities of dry firewood; and they drilled fire from a stick, and lighted the mass. Then they cast the struggling Tarantula amid the flames, and he squeaked and sizzled and hissed, and swelled and swelled and swelled, until, with a terrific noise, he burst, and the fragments of his carcass were cast to the uttermost parts of the earth. These parts again took shape as [smaller] beings not unlike Old Tarantula himself.

"Thus it was in the days of the ancients. And therefore today, though crooked are the legs of the tarantula, and his habit of progress backward, still he is distributed throughout the great world. Only he is very, very much smaller than was the Great Tarantula who lived below the two rocky columns of Thunder Mountain." — Cushing, pp.352-64.

§162.18 "ELVES AND FAIRIES [Northeast Algonquin]. It was well known unto all Indians who still keep the true faith of the olden times that there are wondrous dwellers in the lonely woods, such as elves and fairies, called by the Micmacs [of New Brunswick] *Mikumwessos*, and by the Passamaquoddies [of Maine] *Oonahgawessos*. [They were created by the great, benevolent divinity Glooskap—a giant whose head touches the stars, who also created man and all the beasts.] And these can work great wonders, and also sing so as to charm the wildest beasts. From them alone come the magic pipes or flutes, which sometimes pass into possession of noted sorcerers and great warriors; and when these are played upon, the woman who hears the melody is bewitched with love, and the moose and caribou follow the sound even to their death. And when the *Megumawessos* are pleased with a mortal they make him a fairy, even like themselves.

"In old times there was an Indian village, and in it were two young men, who had heard that Glooskap, ere he left the world, would bestow on those who came to him whatever they wanted. So they went their way, an exceeding long pilgrimage, until they came to a great island, where he dwelt. And there they first met with Dame Bear and Marten, and next with the Master himself. Then they all, sitting down to supper, had placed before them only one extremely small dish, and on this there was a tiny bit of meat, and nothing more. But being a bold and jolly fellow, the first of the pilgrims, thinking himself mocked for sport, cut off a great part of the meat, and ate it, when that which was in the dish grew in a twinkling to its former size; and so this went on all through the supper,

every one eating his fill, the dish at the end being as full as ever.

"Of these two, one wished to become a *Mikumwess*, and the other to win a very beautiful girl, the daughter of a great chief, who imposed such cruel tasks on all who came for her, that they died in attempting them. [However, the latter gains her hand in marriage, and the pair share many adventures.]

"And the first was taken by Glooskap; and after he had by a merry trick covered him with filth and put him to great shame, he took him to the river, and after washing him clean and combing his hair gave him a change of rainment and a hair string of exceeding great magic virtue, since when he had bound it on he became a *Mikumwess*, having all the power of the elfin world. And also because he desired to excel in singing and music, the Master gave him a small pipe, and it was that which charmed all living beings;[317] and then singing a song bade him join in with him. And doing this he found that he could sing, and ever after had a wondrous voice.

"[Later — at the wedding of his friend to the chief's daughter, mentioned above — the *Mikumwess*,] at the great dance which was held that evening at the wedding, astonished all who beheld him. As he danced around the circle, upon the very hard beaten floor, they saw his feet sink deeper at every step, and ever deeper as the dance went on; ploughing the ground up into high, uneven rides, forming a trench as he went, until at length only his head was to be seen.[318] And this ended the dancing for that night, since the ground was no longer to be danced upon by anybody except wizards and witches." — Leland, pp.81-83, 88-89.

§162.19 IROQUOIS MYTHS AND LEGENDS. "*A 'Medicine' Legend.* A...

legend is told by the Senecas to account for the origin of their 'medicine'. Nearly two hundred years ago — in the savage estimation that is a very great period of time — an Indian went into the woods on a hunting expedition. One night while asleep in his solitary camp he was awakened by a great noise of singing and drum-beating, such as is heard at festivals. Starting up, he made his way to the place whence the sounds came, and although he could not see any one there he observed a heap of corn and a large squash vine with three squashes on it, and three ears of corn which lay apart

---

317 The identity of these incidents with those of 'classic' times is worth noting. There is a lustration and the clothing the neophyte in a new garment, and he receives the magic fillet, as in the Mysteries of the old world. Nor is the resemblance of the pipe to that of Orpheus less striking. In many respects this is the most remarkable old Indian myth I have ever met with. [*Ed. note:* Elsewhere the author observes that Eskimos once ranged as far south as Massachusetts, and that for three centuries they had had intimate relations with Scandinavians; thus, points of contact between local Indian legends and incidents of e.g. the Eddas, the Sagas, and the popular tales of Scandinavia are not suprising. Here I think one should note the resemblance of the powers of the *Mikumwess* who charms all living beings with his pipe-playing to those of the aged Väinämönen (in the Finnish *Kalevala**), who similarly holds sway over the very winds and the beasts with the magic of his song.]

318 This is very characteristic of the true magician, both in the Algonquin and Eskimo folk-lore. 'The *angakok*,' or sorcerer of Greenland, 'after meeting with *tomarsuk*, or guardian spirits, sometimes manifested it by his feet sinking into the rocky ground *just as if into snow*' (Rink).

from the rest.[319] Feeling very uneasy, he once more pursued his hunting operations, and when night came again laid himself down to rest. But his sleep was destined to be broken yet a second time, and awaking he perceived a man bending over him, who said in menacing tones:

" 'Beware: what you saw was sacred. You deserve to die.'

"A rustling among the branches denoted the presence of a number of people, who, after some hesitation, gathered round the hunter, and informed him that they would pardon his curiosity and would tell him their secret. 'The great medicine for wounds,' said the man who had first awakened him, 'is squash and corn. Come with me and I will teach you how to make and apply it.'

"With these words he led the hunter to the spot at which he had surprised the 'medicine'-making operations on the previous night, where he beheld a great fire and a strange-looking laurel-bush, which seemed as if made of iron. Chanting a weird song, the people circled slowly round the bush to the accompaniment of a rattling of gourd-shells. On the hunter's asking them to explain this procedure, one of them heated a stick and thrust it right through his cheek. He immediately applied some of the 'medicine' to the wound, so that it healed instantly. Having thus demonstrated the power of the drug, they sang a tune which they called the 'medicine-song', which their pupil learnt by heart.

"The hunter than turned to depart, and all at once he saw that the beings who surrounded him were not human, as he had thought, but animals—foxes, bears, and beavers—who fled as he looked at them. Surprised and even terrified at the turn matters had taken, he made his way homeward with all speed, conning over the prescription which the strange beings

had given him the while. They had told him to take one stalk of corn, to dry the cob and pound it very fine, then to take one squash, cut it up and pound it, and to mix the whole with water from a running stream, near its source. This prescription he used with very great success among his people, and it proved the origin of the great 'medicine' of the Senecas. Once a year at the season when the deer changes his coat they prepare it as the forest folk did, singing the weird song and dancing round it to the rhythmic accompaniment of the gourd-shell rattles, while they burn tobacco to the gods."—Spence [North American], pp.230-32.

§162.20 "TALIGVAK [Story of the shaman's magic singing and dancing— Eskimo folklore]. A long time ago, in a village on the shore of the Arctic Ocean, the seal hunters had a bad winter. Snowstorms blew constantly, making it impossible to hunt; the people went hungry.

"The hunters invited well-known shamans* to call upon their spirits in the big dance igloo which they called the *qalgie*. However the shamans were unable to make the seals come and famine threatened the settlement.

"A young man named Taligvak lived with these people. No one liked him and he lived alone at the edge of the settlement apart from the other people. He was very poor, lacking nearly all necessities. No one wanted to give him a daughter for a wife and so Taligvak had no one to sew warm clothing for him. He did own a knife and with that was able to build a snow house. But it was so small that he could not lie down inside it and instead had to remain in a sitting position even when trying to sleep. Moreover, as there was no stone lamp in his igloo, Taligvak suffered from the cold. When his mittens became frozen with frost he had to put them under his

---

319 The Iroquois 'Three Sisters'—as in some accounts they are called—include corn, squash, and beans. (Ed.)

clothes, next to his skin, and as he slept the heat from his body would dry them.

"It is possible that everyone avoided Taligvak because they were afraid of him. As young as he was, he was reputed to be a powerful shaman. It was said that he commanded strange magic forces. It was believed that there was nothing that Taligvak could not do: his aides were the spirits in the air and the darkness who, taking pity on him, would come at his call and do wonders for him. All of the people spoke in awe of the young man's strange powers but, not liking him, they had kept him at a distance. However now that they were threatened with starvation the people wondered if they should ask his help.

"The people met in the *qalgie*, the big dance igloo, to discuss what they should do. They agreed that the only one who could help them in this period of ill fortune was Taligvak. Quickly, they sent three young men to bring him to the *qalgie*.

"When the three men arrived at Taligvak's igloo, two of them were so afraid that they did not dare to look inside. The third man, having more courage, looked in and said, 'Taligvak, the people want you to come to the *qalgie*. Come see them.'

"Taligvak remained silent for awhile. Finally he answered. 'The wind is blowing up a storm. It is cold out and I have nothing warm to wear, not even mittens or boots. I shall not go to them.'

"Hearing his refusal, the messengers returned to the *qalgie*. A woman was then sent to Taligvak with a present of mittens and boots. She took him by the arm and led him back to the big igloo.

"Taligvak entered the igloo by crawling through the low passageway. When he reached the entrance of the large room he refused to go inside, preferring to stand by the door, motionless, without saying a word. The people had their eyes fixed on him. One of them spoke out: 'You want a warm igloo; you want to stay with us, to have good clothes, mittens and warm skins to sleep under. We shall give you all this if you will cut a hole in the ice right here at the edge of the iglo and if you will make the seals come. We are going to starve to death for certain. Catch some seals for us!'

"Taligvak stayed where he was for some time. Then he went over to the wall of the *qalgie* and knelt down on the ice. 'Do not watch what I do,' he commanded the people. 'You must begin to dance.'

"The people started to sing and dance while he worked at making a hole in the ice. He blew on the ice again and again and each time the magic force of his breath hollowed the surface. Eventually the ice was broken and water bubbled up into the hole.

"The young man then invited the dancers to come and look. Each saw the water at the bottom of the hole with his own eyes and let out a cry of joy.

" 'Now,' Talgivak said, 'begin dancing again and do not watch what I shall do.' He was holding a small magic weapon in his hand. It was a harpoon which was as small as a child's toy. He brandished it over his head and sang an invocation to the spirits that would help him:

What joy to hear climbing from the
    bottom of the water
A very fat animal
Who will give to all
As much to eat as they will want!
What joy to see it stretched out
On the floor of the igloo,
When they have pulled it from
The bottom of the water!

"While singing he had harpooned a seal which had come to answer his call and he had pulled it onto the floor of the igloo. On his orders the people dragged the beast to the far side of the *qalgie* to a snow lean-to which formed a secondary room. He told them to remove the head of the harpoon from the seal's body.

"When the harpoon head was brought to him he replaced it on the shaft of his weapon. He then ordered that the animal be cut up and the meat distributed. While some ate and others sang, he again took up his vigil near the hole. He forbade the people to watch what he was doing and began to sing once more:

> What joy for the men
> When on the ice
> A big seal is hauled
> From the hole where he came to
>   breathe.
> My harpoon line is for him
> Like a snare which squeezes him!

"And again, thanks to the magic of his song, Taligvak pulled a big, fat seal onto the ice. The people cried with joy; they no longer feared that they would starve to death.

"Winter passed and the darkness lifted from the sky and the earth. Spring returned and with its return the people left their camp on the ice to go inland, to hunt caribou and fish in the lakes.

"By this time, Taligvak was receiving help from the others, but he was always left somewhat alone. He also went inland, but he walked behind the others, carrying his sleeping skins, his knife and sewing implements on his back. (It was said that his sewing needles were cut from the bones of a rabbit's foot.)

"[The snow gradually disappeared, the rivers opened up. Caribou descended toward the river. Encouraged by these signs of spring Taligvak built a kayak. He snared rabbits, and cleaned their skins. As the sun warmed he caught fish, and snared a loon. Later he killed a caribou with his knife. After he had eaten, he made a spear from its hammered and split shin-bone, mounted on a piece of wood. With this he hunted for caribou, with great success — wasting nothing from each kill. The meat and skins were put out to dry; he also preserved the marrow and tongues in bags made from the stomachs of the first animals. Then, when his famished people came by, he set out a small amount of the food on a plate.]

"The plate, which he placed on the ground, was an old scrap of seal skin which they had thrown away because they did not find it good enough for them. On this piece of skin Taligvak placed a little bit of meat, a small helping of marrow and a few tongues; not much of anything for a large, hungry crowd. He made the people sit on the opposite side of the plate from him, told them not to watch what he was going to do, and began to sing:

> They have arrived at Taligvak's
> And it is lucky that I have some
>   tongues to offer them
> And that I killed a very fat caribou
> That, you know all about!
> No need to tell you.
> But look at this plate,
> This poor plate of nothing.
> It is full to overflowing...
> It is overflowing!

"And the people saw the plate in which Taligvak had put so very little fill itself more and more. Taligvak continued his magic chant:

> From the banks of the Padleq River,
> They came to my place
> And I killed a very fat caribou
> With my kayak sewn with thin straps
> That, you know all about!
> No need to tell you.
> But look at this plate,
> This poor plate of nothing,
> It is full to overflowing...
> It is overflowing!

"The meat continued to grow on the plate made from skin. Many people were there and they were very hungry. They had not eaten meat for a long time. They ate until they were gorged, but they were not able to finish the contents of poor Talgivak's magic plate."[320] —Metayer, pp.61-69.

§162.21 HUICHOL INDIANS (MEXICO).

As a part of the reliqious ceremonies of the Huichol Indians of the Sierra Madre Occidental of North-Central Mexico, a complicated mythical account is narrated which concerns the origins of the annual pilgrimage to gather peyote, undertaken "so that we may have life." The hunt itself is an event which is rich in complex symbolism; the story includes details about a great flight through the sky.

"The myth is related as the central part of the Drum* and Calabash ceremony, which is a kind of 'first fruits' festival, held before the peyote hunt so that the children 'will understand all'. It takes place during the dry season, usually late fall when the maize is still green but the squash is ripe. At this time, the mara'akame plays the drum, beating the deerskin head with his palms while he and his assistants chant. During the chant, he 'transforms' the children into a flock of little birds and leads them in magical flight from the Sierra to the land of peyote. The row of bird-children is symbolized by a fiber cord to which bunches of cotton have been tied, one for each child. One end of the string is attached to the drum, the other to the sacred chair of Kauyumari on which the mara'akame is seated." —Myerhoff, pp.115-16.

§162.22 PAÍYATUMA AND THE MAIDENS OF THE CORN—Origin of the "Dance of the Corn Maidens" (Zuñi folklore). *Ed.note:* In this story, music is a talisman which guides life into being—is a conveyor of the spirit of life itself.[321]

"Whence came they, the Maidens who are told of in the stories and sung of in the songs of our Fathers, the seven Maidens with their magic wands and plumes who were lovelier than the seven bright stars that are above us now? Paíyatuma the Flute-player, the God of Dew and of the Dawn, brought them to our Fathers; they were his foster-children. And when he had brought them to where our Fathers were, he sang a song that warned all who were there that these were virgins and must be forever held as sacred beings. Paíyatuma sang:

> The corn that ye see growing upward
> Is the gift of my seven bright maidens:
> Look well that ye nourish their
>   persons,
> Nor change ye the gift of their being
> As fertile of flesh for all men
> To the bearing of children for men,
> Lest ye lose them, and seek them in
>   vain.

The mists of the morning were clearing away. Even as his voice had already gone into them, Paíyatuma the Flute-playing God went into the mists. Seven plants of corn he had left before our Fathers; seven Maidens he had left who would cause the

---

320 This simple tale perhaps disguises an event of truly major local importance — namely, the appearance of the deliverer "once upon a time", at a critical moment in the history of the people. Taligvak is, as well, teacher, moralist ("waste not, want not") and outsider — the misunderstood savant, perhaps. Given his overall importance, the powers of music and dancing enjoy a corresponding significance. (Ed.)

321 For another version of the legend, see p.399 above. See also theme T2 (Music and/or dance invokes or induces the world or cosmos itself *into being*) — *Introductory Remarks,* Vol I above.

corn to grow. 'Thanks, thanks to thee, O Paíyatuma ,' our Fathers cried into the mists that closed round him. 'Verily we will cherish the Maidens and the substance of their flesh.'

"Thereafter, as the season came round, our Fathers would build for the Maidens a bower of cedar-wood that was roofed with timbers brought from beyond the mountains. They would light a fire before the bower. All night, backwards and forwards, the Corn Maidens would dance to the music of drum* and rattle* and the songs sung by the elders. They would dance by the side of the seven growing plants of the corn, motioning them upward with their magic wands and plumes.

"Then the first Maiden would embrace the first growing plant. As she did this the fire would leap up, throwing out a yellow light. The second Maiden would embrace the second growing plant, and the fire would burn smokily with a fuller grasping of the brands; blue would be the light the fire would throw out. The third Maiden would embrace the third of the growing plants, and at this the fire would reach to the fulness of its mastery, and the light it would throw out would be red. Then the fourth Maiden would embrace the fourth growing plant, and the fire, flameless now, would throw out a white light. As the fifth Maiden embraced the fifth growing plant the fire would give up its breath in clouds of sparks and its light would be streaked with many colours. The sixth Maiden would embrace the sixth growing plant; the fire would be sleeping then, giving out less light than heat. And as the seventh Maiden embraced the seventh growing plant the fire would awaken afresh in the wind of the morning, and, as the fire of the wanderer stays glowing with many colours, it would stay glowing. Beautiful the dance of the seven Maidens, delightful the music they would dance to. And when the mists of the morning came they would go within the bower and lay down their magic wands and plumes, and their soft and shining dresses, and thereafter they would mingle with the people.

"All rejoiced in the dance of the white-robed Corn Maidens. But a time came when certain of the young men of the village began to speak of a music they heard sounding from Thunder Mountain. This music was more wonderful than the music we had for the dance of the Maidens. And the young men declared that the dance that went to it, the dance they had not seen, must be more wonderful than the dance that our Maidens were praised for. They spoke of these things so often that they made our dance seem a thing that was of little worth. Then the Fathers summoned two messengers and bade them take the trail that went up the mountain. They were to find out about the music and the dance. Perchance they might be joined with ours, and a music and a dance that would seem wonderful to all might be given between the bower and the fire.

"The messengers took the trail that went up Thunder Mountain. As they climbed they heard the sound of flutes. They went within the cavern that the music was being played in—the Cavern of the Rainbow. Mists surrounded them as they went within; but they knew what being was there, and they made reverence to him. Here was Paíyatuma the Flute-Player, the God of Dew and the Dawn.

"They heard the music and they saw the dance that was being given in the Cavern of the Rainbow. The music was not as our music, for the musicians were flute-players. The Maidens who danced were as beautiful as our Corn Maidens; seven were they also. They carried in their hands wands of cottonwood: from the branchlets and buds of these wands streamlets flowed. 'They are like your Maidens as the House of the Seven Stars seen in water is like the House of the Seven Stars as it is in the sky. They are fertile, not of seed, but of the Water of Life wherein the seed is quickened.' So said Paíyatuma, the God of Dew and of the Dawn. And when the messengers looked upon them they saw that the Maidens were taller than ours were, and that their colour was fainter.

"Then did Paíyatuma lift up his flute and play upon it. A drum sounded also, and the cavern shook as with thunder. And as the music was played a white mist came from the flutes of the players. 'Athirst are men ever for that which they have not,' said Paíyatuma the Flute-player through the mist. 'It is well that ye have come, and it shall be as ye wish,' said he to the messengers. They knew then that he was aware of what errand they had been sent upon.

"They went back and told the elders of the village that Paíyatuma's flute-players would come amongst them and make music for the dance of the Corn Maidens. The flute-players came down to the dancing-ground. Out of their bower came our white-clad, beautiful Corn Maidens. The flute-players lifted up their flutes and made music for the dance. And as the Maidens danced in the light of the fire they who played their flutes looked on them in such wise that they were fain to let their hair fall down and cast down their eyes. Seeing the players of the flutes look on the Maidens amorously, our own youths looked on them amorously also. They plucked at their garments as they, in their dancing, came near them. Then the players of the flutes and our own youths sprang up and followed them, shouting and laying unseemly hands upon the beautiful, white-clad maidens.

"Yet they finished their dance, and the seventh Maiden embraced the seventh growing plant. The mists came down, and unseen, the Maidens went into their bower. They laid their magic wands and their plumes upon the ground; they laid their white robes down also. Then they stole away. They were gone when Paíyatuma appeared. He came forth from the mists and stood amongst the assembled people. The flute-players, waving their flutes over the people who were there, followed Paíyatuma as he strode, wordless, through

the mists that were rolling up the mountain.

"The drum was beaten, the rattles were shaken, but still the Maidens did not come forth from their bower. The Elders went within and they found nought there but the wands and plumes and the garments that had been laid away. Then it was known that the Corn Maidens had gone. Grief and dismay filled the hearts of the people. 'We must seek for and find our Maidens,' they all cried, 'for lacking them the corn-seed, which is the life of the flesh, cannot flourish.' But where could one go seeking? The Maidens had left no trail behind them. 'Who can find them but our great Elder Brother, the Eagle,' the people said. 'He is enduring of will and surpassing of sight. Let us send messengers to the Eagle and ask him to make search for our Maidens white and beautiful.'

"[The messengers were sent to the cave where the Eagle had his nest, where they beseeched the Eagle to help them. Over the heights he circled and sailed, to the north and the south, the east and the west. But he did not see them. Then the messengers were sent to the Falcon, on the same errand. But he could not find the Corn Maidens either. Then the people went to Heavy Nose the Raven, and gave him the best of tobacco to smoke, and brought him the best of corn. But Heavy Nose told them that only Paíyatuma himself could find the Corn Maidens, and bring them back.

"[Then the Fathers went to Paíyatuma. And] in his presence they purified themselves, putting away from them all that disgraced them in his eyes. From the youths in the village they chose four who had not sinned in their flesh. These four youths they brought to Paíyatuma.

"And with the four youths he set out for Summerland. Where he paused he played upon his flute, and butterflies and birds came around him and fed upon the dew that was breathed forth from his flute. In a little while he came to Summerland. The seven Maidens of the Corn were there.

They heard his flute-playing, and when they saw his tall form coming through the fields of corn that was already quickened they went to meet him. The butterflies and the birds came and fluttered over them — over the seven Maidens of the Corn, over the four youths from the village, over Paíyatuma, as he played upon his flute.

"Back to the village they went, the Maidens, the four youths, and Paíyatuma. O greatly did the people rejoice at having their Maidens back once more amongst them. The bower was built and the fire was lighted as before. All night, backwards and forwards, the Corn Maidens danced to music and to songs sung by the elders. They danced by the side of the seven growing plants, motioning them upwards. And as each Maiden embraced the plant that was hers, the fire threw out its yellow light, its blue light, its red light, its white light, its streaked light, its dim light, its light of many colours.

"Ah, but as each Maiden embraced her growing plant, she put into the corn and, by a mystery, the substance of her flesh. Then, as that light of many colours was thrown from the fire, the Maidens went forth as shadows. Into the deep night they went, and they were seen no more of men. The dawn came and the Fathers saw Paíyatuma standing with folded arms before the fire. Solemnly he spoke to them all; well have the solemn words he uttered been remembered. The corn would grow because of the substance of their flesh that the Corn Maidens had put in it; in future seasons maidens chosen from amongst our own daughters would dance backwards and forwards to the music of the flute as well as the drum, and would embrace the seven growing plants in the light of the fire. And all would be well for the growth of the corn. But as for the Maidens white and beautiful whom he had twice brought to us, they were gone from us forever. They have departed since the children of men would seek to change the sustaining blessedness of their flesh into humanity which sustains not, but is sustained. In the loving of men and the cherishing of men's children, they—even they—would forget the cherishing of their beautiful seed-growing. The Mother-maidens have gone, but their subtance is in the plants of corn.'

"For that reason the corn that is for seed is held by us as a thing sacred. Through the nights and days of the Moon Nameless, of the Moon of Sacred Fire and Earth, of the Moon of Earth Whitening, of the Moon of Snow-broken Boughs, of the Moon of Snowless Pathways, of the Moon of Lesser Sand-driving Storms, the seed of the corn is held. Then it is put in the earth reverently; it is buried as a tribe might bury its beloved dead. The seed which has in it the substance of our Maiden-mothers becomes quick beneath the earth. Paíyatuma, the God of Dew and of the Dawn, freshens the growth with his breath; then Ténatsali, the God of Time and the Seasons, brings the plants to maturity; then Kwéwele, the God of Heat, ripens them with the touch of his Fire-brother's torch, giving them their full vitality. And our own maidens dance beside the corn-plants in the light of the fire, motioning them upwards—upwards."—Colum, pp.311-18.

§162.23 "**THE DEAD WIFE (Alabama).** *The dead are lamented, but they are also feared. Their power is to be avoided, yet it must be utilized. The various possibilities are explored [in a variety of North American Indian] tales.*

"A man and his wife were going along a trail, when the man picked some berries of the button snakeroot and threw them gently at his wife, who was ahead of them. They passed through her body[322] and she died. Then the woman's relatives took her

---

322 A husband is similarly killed [by his wife's poking her sinew threader through him, making tiny holes,] in an Eskimo myth [called 'The Origin of Nunivak Island'].

and buried her, and her husband with her, although he was alive.

"When night came, she went to a dance.[323] The next night night she was gone again. She came back covered with sweat. Then she said to her husband, 'You have nothing to do here but lie still and be sad. Get on my back.' So he got on her back; she jumped up and put him down outside, going through the earth with him. And when he reached his house and the people saw him, they said, 'He has broken through the earth.' They set out for the place and, when they got there, looked all about, but nothing was disturbed." — Bierhorst (Red Swan), p.235.[324]

INDIAN (SOUTH AMERICAN) MYTHS — PRACTICES AND BELIEFS. *(See also p.407.)*

§163.7 MAKIRATARE (Indians of the upper Orinoco River in Venezuela) — practices and beliefs.

"AICHUDI: One of the two types of sacred song (the other being *ademi*) found amongst the Makiratare, the *aichudi* are most often associated with the shorter, more private 'blowing' songs used to exorcise evil spirits, expel storms, purify food, and cure the ill.

"ATTA ADEMI HIDI: Literally 'To sing house', this is the festival held at the completion of a new *atta* [communal roundhouse]. Lasting several days, the *Watunna* [compendium of religious and social models of the 'true people', or So'to] recounting the construction of the first house by Wanadi [god and culture hero — the unknowable, unseen force in Heaven] is sung, and all evil spirits are exorcised.

"KAICHAMA: Mominaru's [Makiratare deity] reincarnated form with which he returns to Earth to avenge himself of Sahatuma [from whose blood the first jaguar, Mado, was born]. The name Kaichama is no doubt a variant of 'Kachimana', the plant spirit who 'makes fruits ripen' and is called by the use of ritual flutes or *momi*.

"MARACA: The shaman's gourd rattle whose great magical powers are attributed to the *wiriki* crystals inside it. The maraca, the first of which was created by Wanadi, is used in virtually all shamanic activities.

"SIWO: A horn made from the bark of the *nikua* tree which is used to begin the *Adahe ademi hidi* [most important annual Makiritare festival, for the new *conuco* — gardens yielding yuca, bananas, pineapple, sugar cane, chili peppers, squash, sweet potato, tobacco and gourd — held between the time of its clearing and its planting]. It is said that Semenia's [redbilled scythebill, chief of Wanadi's Bird People] voice is hidden inside this horn and that he made the original *siwo* to call the animals to the first *adahe ademi hidi*.

"TEKOYE: Classified as clarinets because of their inner, adjustable reeds, these fivefoot-long instruments are always played in pairs, male and female. Often referred to as *wanna*, which is the name of the bamboo they are made from, the *tekoye* are not subject to any of the strict taboos to be found among other Amazonian tribes concerning similar instruments." — Civrieux, pp.175-177, 183, 186, 191.

§163.8 SIONA (Indians of the Northwest Amazon basin, Southern Colombia) — SPIRIT SONGS. "The shaman* has the knowledge and experience to contact and influence the spirits and to lead others in the visions. This 'knowledge' is gained

---

323 Dancing is widely regarded as the typical activity of the dead.

324 Source: John R. Swanton, *Myths and Tales of the Southeastern Indians*, Bureau of American Ethnology, Bulletin 88, 1929, pp.144-45. Obtained by Swanton between 2908 and 1914 'from the Alabama Indians living in Polk County, Tex.' "

through prolonged training with an experienced or 'master' shaman. When a young man decides to undergo apprenticeship, he first spends a month or more in isolation, purging his body of the substances that would otherwise obstruct his learning and cause bad visions. Then he begins prolonged periods of ingesting *yagé* [a hallucinogen], such as drinking for three nights in a row, resting one, and resuming again. This continues for periods ranging from two weeks to two months at a time. Throughout these sessions, the apprentice attempts to pass through a set of 'culturally influenced' visions. It is recognized that all men must pass through the same experiences and visions if they are to accumulate knowledge.

"The knowledge gained by *yagé* is not a limited concept, nor is it conceived as a single stage of enlightenment. If the comparison can be made, it is more like our educational system with a series of subjects in which one may master and specialize. All the spirits have their 'design' as well as their songs which the novice learns when he 'arrives' at their place. He first must pass through the visions necessary for all who wish to leave their bodies and travel. Then he is shown the visions that his teacher shaman has acquired. As the novice increases his repertoire of visions and songs, he increases his power with the spirits he knows and can deal with. Once well established in his knowledge, he may visit other shamans and learn their specialities. He may find that he has a facility for certain specialties, i.e. drinking to see specific spirits, for hunting, or for curing. Once he is sufficiently trained to lead his own *yagé* sessions, he may show others what he knows, but the road to knowledge never ends, for a shaman constantly strives to contact more and more spirits and see their visions....

"[Here is an excerpt from one informant's early visionary experiences with *yagé*, which includes an 'out-of-body' experience:]

First a big screaming fire came burning the whole world.... Then a big machine burning with fire came to me. As it came toward me, it was grinding up everything in sight....

The Jaguar Mother appeared and gave me her breast to suck. 'Suck this, child, the breast of the Jaguar Mother,' she said to me. So I sucked her breast. 'Now, good, grandson, you have sucked my breasts,' she said.

Then seeing, I turned and when leaving [my body] I saw the *yagé* people all pretty and gold. They are like people, like us.

They came to me singing. The youths came down singing their songs, 'To you little parrot the visions have been ugly, and you have suffered and cried. But now you have left and now you will cry no more, for when you drink *yagé*, you will see us here. When you arrive to us, you will no longer think of crying. Here we are, the living *yagé* people. We are coming to you. And you personally have come to know us; thus there will be no bad visions.'

They spoke, and I saw them. Then the reed flutes* came down hanging in the air. It was not yet the time for me to play them, so I just looked at them.

'If you have arrived, you would have played these flutes,' they said to me. 'But you still have not arrived to play them. Drinking another house of *yagé*, you will play them,' they said to me. I watched as they spoke.

Thus I saw what my father gave me to see. When I saw, 'Good,' I thought, and I was very happy. Later I woke up on this side. I came back to this side and the visions were over. 'Now it is good; I saw the visions,' I thought.

The informant said that he was about twelve years old when he had this experience....

"After passing through the [initial] stage of drunkenness, the narrator [has seen] his first set of visions, which are marked by an intense fear of death, and his first acqaintance with the Jaguar Mother. Facing the idea of death is a very important aspect of drinking *yagé*. It is said by all Siona that a man must be very strong to drink *yagé* and become a shaman. Thus, facing an intense fear of death is a test he must pass through to prove he has the strength. Throughout his entire career in *yagé* he is constantly threatened by death from spirits and other shamans. Only the strongest are able to continue living and drinking; the weak must give it up or perhaps even die....

"The Jaguar Mother, also known as the *Yagé* Mother, is a principal figure in the *yagé* system, for she is also the mother of the shamans, who are jaguars in their transformed state. Before she accepts the novice as her son, she also tests him as to his strength and fearlessness by reinforcing the fear of death. She cries and tells him that he will die. As his 'grandmother' she sings the Siona mourning chants as she points to his coffin and personal effects. According to Siona myth, the mourning chants practiced by the Siona were originally learned from her.[325]

"When the novice sucks her breasts, we can see another aspect that is necessary to gain knowledge. Not only does the novice have to be strong, but the mystical death also symbolizes a return to a state of innocence and dependence upon the Jaguar Mother. Shamans transform into jaguars when they drink *yagé*, and the Jaguar Mother becomes their mother when they become shamans. Thus, this vision is a symbol of mystical death in which the apprentice leaves this world through death and is reborn as a child of the Jaguar Mother. His dependency and infant status are symbolized by drinking from her breasts....

"The term 'parrotlet' (*kihi*) refers to a small parrot that is regarded as a representation of the novice's soul. Very often in dreams and *yagé* visions, the soul of the Siona appears in the form of a bird. The shaman's soul appears as a scarlet macaw; an adult's soul as a species of oriole; and that of children and youths as the parrotlet.

"As mentioned, the spirits all have their songs, and the learning of their songs and other music is an important aspect of acquiring knowledge. All shamans play small reed flutes bound in red or white thread. The Siona say that these flutes fall from the sky where the *yagé* people live. In this case, the informant sees the flutes, but cannot reach them yet in order to play them. The *yagé* people inform him that he must drink another night (house) of *yagé* to do so. This demonstrates the cumulative nature of the visions. Each night of drink-

---

325 See our theme **T1c** (Music sent [to man, animals] as gift of the gods or heavenly beings. Music as medium through which the spirit world [divinities, supranatural beings] attempts to signal or contact man), *Introductory Remarks*, Vol I, above. Also pertinent to this selection are **T1a** (Music as magical means of communication with god[s] or supreme being[s]) and **T1b** (Music gives magical power to musician [e.g. shaman, doctor, priest]). (Ed.)

ing the novice sees and learns a little more of what he is desiring and expecting to see.

"The informant tells us that he is happy to have seen what his father intended for him to see. His father conveyed this when he 'arranged' the *yagé,* singing about the visions that would occur, and when he sang during the time that they were both under the effects of *yagé.*...

"The informant continued to drink *yagé.* He 'arrived' to play the flutes and continued to build up his knowledge.[326]" — Langdon, in Browman & Schwarz, pp.68-72.

§163.9 DESANA (Tukano Indians of the Northwest Amazon basin, Colombia) — .

"The Desana are a small subgroup of some thousand Tukano Indians who live in the equatorial rain forests of the Vaupés territory in the Colombian Northwest Amazon. Their principal habitat is the basin of the Papurí River, but their territory extends southward to the Tiquié River and onto Brazilian soil where other representatives of the aboriginal group are located....

"[*Portion of the Desana creation myth:*] When the first Desana cohabited with the Daughter of Aracú, there were several animals who were witness to the fact. The water turtle saw it, and from that time on it has had the color of the vagina; when one eats the meat of this turtle, welts break out on the skin. The curassow saw the penis of the man, and since that time it has had a red neck and always lives on the riverbank. The sloth was also watching,

but the Daughter of Aracú saw it and changed it into a slow animal; before this it had been a very nimble climber....

"The centipede and a large, black poisonous spider came to lick the blood of the childbirth, and from that time on the centipede looks like an umbilical cord and the spider like a vagina. Also the scorpion and a large black ant licked the blood, and from that time on the bite of these two makes one vomit and produces great pains similar to those of childbirth. The stingray is the placenta of the Daughter of Aracú, and its poisonous sting produces the same pains....

"Thus, mankind was born and the tribe was formed. The second Desana also married a woman from the river, and when she became pregnant for the first time she asked her husband to bring her some fish because she was tired of the other food. The man went to the forest and cut a heart of palmito (*mihí*); he took it to the landing place where the woman was and put small pieces of palmito into the water, reciting at the same time incantations to the fish. Then bubbles began to rise, and suddenly a large wooden drum* came out of the water. It had the same shape as the Snake-Canoe, *pamurí-gahsíru,* and in its gills the fish were held fast. The man took hold of the fish and gave them to his wife, but he put the drum again in the river where it submerged. Since then, the large drums are kept at times under the water so that they may have a new life....

"[In one portion of the creation myth,] horseflies sting people, thus causing great

---

326 It can probably be assumed that flutes have an allegorical significance as surrogates for both male and female reproductive organs—concerning which see **FLUTES***, **§112.16, Rituals of Manhood: Male Initiation in Papua New Guinea** in particular. The identification of song and music with "knowledge" suggests that kind of non-representational, non-particularizable knowledge or intuition which is typically identified with *mythos,* in contrast to the sort of representational or *definable* knowledge which is typically identified with *logos,* and with a given spoken or written language in particular. On this topic see Victor Zuckerkandl on **MUSIC, MAGIC AND *MYTHOS**,** below. (Ed.)

disturbance. With the help of [an] inform-ant, we were able to clarify the obscure symbolism of this [portion of the myth] that, at first sight, lacks all meaning. Let us analyze for a moment the purely zoologi-cal aspect. The horsefly in question (*Der-matobia hominis*) is a large insect that, when flying in circles around a person or an animal, produces a loud buzz that is bothersome and threatening. This fly, however, does not oviposit directly but seeks a small mosquito as an intermediary host upon whose abdomen it deposits its eggs. When the host mosquito bites a per-son, the eggs are transferred, maggots develop, and, when full grown, produce a painful inflammation. What does this process symbolize?

"According to the Desana, the horsefly (as do other stinging insects) represents a masculine principle, and the act of biting or stinging is accompanied by a fertilizing insertion. As a matter of fact, the horsefly is called *nura-mëe*, a word derived from *nurirí*/to bite or to insert the penis, and the suffix *m137e*, which means the power to produce something, as we have seen in the case of the name of the supreme deity. The sting is then the penis, and the maggot that develops is the result of sexual impregna-tion; it is an embryo whose growth causes a swelling accompanied by pain. The in-sect that stings indiscriminately represents the man who, also indiscriminately, cohabits with any woman [in other words, a lewd person].

"Let us return to the myth. When the horseflies were biting the people, the men suddenly decided to kill them, to get rid of this loathsome pest. [Our] informant says: 'When the men killed the horseflies, the norms began to rule. They killed them; that is to say, they began to fulfill them.' In other words, the law of exogamy and the

rest of the prohibitions that regulate sexual relations were established; chaos was ended, and order was reestablished. But let us turn back once more. The [licen-tious] beings disturbing the social order [in another part of the creation myth] 'had a language like the buzz of an insect,' the myth says. This is another aspect of the horsefly theme that is left for us to explain. We said above that this insect flies in circles around people in a threatening manner. Considering this fact it is not surprising to find that among the Desana the bull-roarer* exists and that it is called precisely *nurá-mëe*/horsefly. This wooden slat, suspended from a string, is swung rapidly in a circle to make a distinctive noise. It has religious significance as 'the voice of the power of the Sun' through which the Creator exhorts society to ob-serve the rules of exogamy....[327]

"*Symbols and Associations.* Many objects of Desana material culture, and not only those that form part of their ceremonial paraphernalia, contain a profound sym-bolic meaning....

"Musical instruments have a very com-plex symbolism because in this instance the fundamental criterion of interpreta-tion is not only the specific form of the in-strument but the type of sound that the in-strument produces. We can classify these objects into wind instruments, vibration instruments, and percussion instruments.

"On many occasions, youths as well as adult men play panpipes [see entries for both Pan* and pipes* (Ed.)] (*veó-páme:* from *veó*/cane, *páme*/composed of parallel objects). The number of tubes and the size of these panpipes vary according to the age of those who are playing them and ac-cording to the occasion on which these in-struments are played. If the player is be-

---

327 "Exogamy: the custom of marrying outside the tribe, family, clan, or other social unit. Compare *endogamy:* marriage within a particular group, caste, class, or tribe in accordance with set custom or law; inbreeding." —*American Heritage Dictionary of the English Language* (1969). (Ed.)

tween five and nine years of age, the pan-pipe will have only three tubes; the boys who have attained puberty have flutes that are somewhat larger, having from four to five tubes, and adult men play even larger instruments composed of eight or nine tubes. Again, we find in these instruments a sexual symbolism explained by the informant in the following terms: the development of the sexual organs is compared with the number and size of the tubes. The instrument and the sounds it produces—sustained whistles—symbolize male sexuality, first latent, then fully developed. The act of playing the instrument is compared directly with the sex act. It is usual for the youths to play their pan-pipes on the trail to the forest or on the riverbanks because this music is sexually exciting to *Vaí-mahsë* and thus contribute to the fertility of the game animals.

"The large flutes played on the occasion of the *yuruparí* ceremony [described below] are painted yellow, but the upper part, the mouthpiece, is red. On the upper and lower edges of the rectangular aper-ture two thin, movable blades are fastened that must be gauged with precision before the instrument can be played. We mentioned that there are two flutes, one male and the other female. The male flute produces a sustained sound that excites, while the sound produced by the female flute is interpreted as a threatening vibration. In these two instruments we then have a combination of two principles, one that invites incitingly and the other that rebuffs threatingly.[328] The symbolism of these two actions was explained by the informant as the promulgation of exogamic norms.

"We find the vibrant sound in other large flutes in which the tone is also gauged by a thin, movable vibrating blade. This flute is called *mëhte palo*, a name derived from *mëhte*/fly, and *páli*/to touch slightly, to pet. The vibrating reed is compared to a large fly, a horsefly, which is licking or 'petting', and the act of playing these flutes is interpreted again as the sexual act insinuated but not consummated. This instrument is also characteristic of youths and adoles-

---

328 The "threatening" aspect of female sexuality—from the point of view of males—is also associated with the fear of being consumed (and therefore destroyed) by the female "mouth". (Ed.)

cents, and involved when it is played is an erotic game well known to all. Especially when a group of girls goes to bathe in the river, the playing of these instruments causes great hilarity among both men and women.[329]

"Another instrument that produces a vibrant sound is made from a turtle shell. The upper end of the plastron is covered with a thick lump of black beeswax; when the shell is kept tightly under the left arm and the wax is rubbed with the palm of the hand, the instrument produces a rapid croaking sound. The object is called *peyú vári*/turtle-to scratch, and symbolizes the vagina and clitoris of the Daughter of the Sun, clearly indicating its threatening character.

"In some gatherings and rituals the men use long, thin stick-rattles [see also rattles* entry (Ed.)]. These lance-shaped objects are adorned at their lower end with yellow feathers and have an oblong, sonorous chamber containing fruit kernels that produce a strong rattling hum when the stick is shaken. This stick is called *ye'e-gë* (from *yeru*/penis, *ye'éri*/to cohabit, *-gë*/male suffix). Being a phallic symbol, the stick is essentially a cosmic axis. When it is struck vertically in the ground, it is imagined that its lower part, called 'yellow', penetrates to *Ahpikondiá*, while the sonorous 'blue' part represents the communication with the Milky Way. The central 'red' part where the payé or another man grasps it is symbolic of our world. Moreover, the small, dry kernels in its resonating chamber are called 'embryos' (*se'erí*) and are precisely the elements that communicate the warning. The rattle-sticks are an important symbol of power of the payé and, theoretically, each sib possesses one of these ritual objects.[330] The sound is 'the voice of the sib' or 'the voice of the payé' because [the latter] is the representative of his group.

"We have already mentioned the bull-roarer, another musical instrument of vibrating sound....

"Passing on now to the percussion instruments, we shall first mention the

---

329 It may be asked why the sexual associations of musical instruments have therefore a *mythical* or *mythological* dimension, as well. The answer I believe lies in at least these two directions: the realization that "life" itself is precarious, a tenuous event, and that in consequence procreation *itself* is dependent upon the "favor" of the gods etc; and the looking upon sexuality as, indeed, a vastly "mysterious" sort of thing. Indeed is there anyone among our more "sophisticated" societies who *truly* believe that he or she has mastered *all* of the intricacies and politics and "symbolisms" and consequences if you will of love, of love-making, of sexual conquest, or of that very special "community" which is brought into being (and, so often, so precariously!) — which is *launched* so to speak by love? Then, I think that he or she has not read his great French novels closely enough, such as *Rouge et noir* and *Dangerous Acquaintances, Manon Lescaut, Vie de bohème, Nana, La dame aux camelias,* and *Madame Bovary...* *Chéri,* and *Blé en herbe...* (Ed.)

330 Two terms used throughout this account are "phratry" and "sib". A phratry is "an exogamous subdivision of the tribe, comprising two or more related clans", while a sib is "a blood relation; kinsman; or, relatives collectively — kinfolk" (*American Heritage Dictionary* — see for example our English word "sibling", a brother or sister); in other words, here, the word "sib" would appear to mean "clan" generally. In Desana society a phratry usually consists of up to 20 or 30 ranked sibs. Each sib of 4-8 nuclear families occupies a single *maloca,* or large communal house. (Ed.)

drum*. In times past, the Desana used large drums that consisted of a thick, hollow cylinder carved from a single tree trunk. The wood was the same as that used for the manufacture of canoes. These drums had a longitudinal opening in the form of two circular preforations joined by a straight slit. The instrument was suspended horizontally from ropes held up by a frame or four thick stakes and placed outside the maloca, near the main door. When the drum was not in use, it was generally kept in the center of the maloca. The drum was called *toá-toré* (from *toá*/onomatopoetic, *toré*/cavity, hollow trunk) and represents the uterus of the sib or phratry. The drumstick (*toá-toré padígë*) was called the 'penis of the Sun', and the slit represented a vagina.[331] The drum was painted yellow on the lower outside and red on the upper part; it was also decorated with the diamonds and stripes of *pamurí-gahsíru*, the Snake-Canoe. The drum was thus considered to be a replica of the Snake-Canoe in which humanity arrived. Generally, the drum was played at dawn on the day of a gathering, and in the past it was also played on occasions of intertribal war. When the drum was played to convoke the neighbors, it was 'the voice of the uterus' that called the members of the group.

"Another instrument, the gourd rattle (*nyahsánu*/to shake), is divided into three parts: the handle, painted red and symbolizing the penis and the terrestrial world; a decoration of yellow feathers where the handle joins the resonating chamber, representing the fertility of the Sun; and the gourd body, a uterine element. Its exterior is covered with incised motifs that, in part, imitate those that adorned *mamurí-gahsíru*. The noise the rattle produces when it is shaken by a payé is

believe to be the 'echo' of the sound made by the thorns and splinters that the payé carried hidden in his forearm.

"Small rattles are made from the dry seeds of a tree (*uatúgë*; from *uatí*/bell) and, tied to the ankles, are used by the dancers, especially by prominent 'counselors'. The word *uaitú* is derived from *uai*/name, and *tu'úri*/to name, to designate, to point out; the explication given by the informant is that these rattles call attention to the name or status of the person who uses them.

"In many dances the rhythm is marked by the beat of thick hollow sticks made of light *guarumo* (Cecropia) wood. With the lower end the dancers stomp the ground rhythmically, keeping the stick vertical. These instruments are called *borépu deariyuhkë* (from *boréri*/white, *deári*/to strike the ground, *yuhkë*/stick, branch). The white wood is decorated with the black and red designs of the Snake-Canoe. Although, by their decoration, these stomping tubes are identified with a uterine concept, they are also interpreted as phallic objects. According to our informant, these objects are a cultural borrowing from the Cubeo and are not a traditional Desana element.

"Some instruments of lesser importance may be mentioned here. The young men sometimes make small flutes of tubular deer bone (*nyamá go'á*) that they carry on their belts and play on the trails to the forest or to the riverbanks. It is said that those boys who during their puberty do not show much interest in myths and tradition become very pale due to the harmful influence of these bone flutes. 'The bone is harmful for those who do not comply with the norms,' the informant says, alluding to the phallic symbolism of the 'bone' and making it understood that this refers to the prohibition of masturba-

---

331 As in the case of the flute and other instruments, one and the same instrument represents sexual characteristics of *both* male and female genders. For a detailed discussion of the sexual aspects of primitive musical instruments, see e.g. Marius Schneider essay, **PRIMITIVE PRACTICES AND BELIEFS***, pp.667*ff*. (Ed.)

tion. Similar ideas are connected with a musical instrument made of the cranium of a deer.

"An instrument that, until some two or three generations ago, was very characteristic of the Desana but today is found only in a few isolated regions is a kind of flute or ocarina made of pottery. The object is shaped like two cones joined at their bases and open at one end. As this opening is touched rhythmically with the palm of the hand, one blows over the circular orifice located on the upper surface. This instrument is called *gahpí soró* and symbolizes the vagina of the Daughter of the Sun.

"We have said above that the musical instruments of the Desana could be roughly grouped into three categories, wind, vibration, and percussion instruments. Our informant elaborated on this classification in the following manner: the wind instruments, the flutes, produce a sustained whistling sound that always has the connotation of sexual invitation. It is a sound that incites others to commit a prohibited or, at least, a dangerous act. The deer and certain rodents 'whistle', inciting the hunter, just as do certain birds of prey that symbolize female sexuality. The opposite sound is that of vibration, a buzzing or humming noise. It is the aggressive male principle associated with the hummingbird, bees, ants, and the horsefly, those animals that 'buzz' when they fly, that 'bite' and 'sting', that 'suck honey'. The buzzing is a warning, a threat: it is the voice that warns and thus establishes a dialogue with the whistling sound. The model of the symbolic interpretation of the buzzing is, essentially, the sound of the kettle on the fire; water as it begins to boil; the combustion of firewood and tobacco; the creaking of elastic reeds when a basket

is being filled; the distant roar and murmur of the rapids. When he said: 'The buzzing is the result of accumulation,' the informant expressed the concept of retained energy, ready to explode, to overflow. Associated with the buzzing and humming instruments are the yuruparí flutes, the bull-roarer, and the stick-rattle, when they are swung in a wide, circular movement. They are 'the voices' that warn of the dangers of incest, promulgate the law, and, finally, conserve sexual energy.

"In between these two categories of sounds, the sustained whistle and the humming buzz, is percussion, the dry clap, the staccato of realization. These instruments are the drum, the gourd rattle, and the seed rattles of the dancers; they represent the pecking of the woodpecker against a hollow tree trunk, or the dry, smacking sound (*'tái-tái-tái'*) produced by the lizard, symbolic of *Vaí-mahsë* when he sees a woman. When the drum or the rattle is played, or when the dancers stomp the ground to make their seed anklets ring, the act is being fulfilled, they have arrived at a synthesis of opposites. It is an act of creation in which male and female energy have united....

"*Invocations and Spells.* Invocations play an important role in collective and individual rites. To invoke is *bayíri*, a word related to *bayári*/to dance, that indicates that the dances should essentially be interpreted as imploring attitudes. In all invocations tobacco smoke is the principle medium because the request (or threat, as the case may be) is directly transmitted through the smoke....

"The occasions on which these invocations are made fall into the following categories: curing of illnesses, success in hunting and fishing, the attainment of food in general, fecundity of women, social cohesion, and harmonic relations on the phratric, sib, and family level....[332]

"[*Other Religious Symbolisms.* A ritual or ceremonial song may consist] essentially of two phases. In the first (*bayári*/to sing) the song only describes [a particular] animal, its form, its movements and colors, its fleetness, and other characteristics. In the second phase (*bayíri*/to invoke; *bayíri uri*/to invoke and to call) the song changes rhythm, and the words now compare these characteristics with desirable qualities, especially those referring to the Sun. The color red is invoked to ask for help from *Diroá-mahsë*, and allusions are made to the procreation and fertility of the animal, speaking of the 'power of the Sun' in fostering the abundance of the species.

"A group dance is generally initiated with *mahkaá piru bayári* (village-snake-dance), a name that is derived from that of a large snake (boa constrictor?) whose markings are said to represent a 'village', and *pamurí-gahsíru*, because it has many greenish, yellow, and black spots. It is said that this snake twists a great deal, 'like a brook', and the dance repeats these undulating movements. The dancers move in zigzag, turning and returning rapidly to the place of starting, all with quick steps and in a joyful mood. This dance is connected, in part, with the idea that the snakes are the procreators of fish and that, by imitating them, 'the children of the dancers will be great fishermen'. On the other hand, fishing symbolizes, for the Desana, coitus and 'to catch fish' expresses exogamy....

"The Desana say that those members of their phratry who, after their death, have had to return to the dominions of *Vaímahsë* exist there as animals but, during feasts, wear masks of painted bark-cloth. By dressing up in these masks, which are the symbol of terrestrial though not of human existence, the ancestors sometimes appear to the living. This belief in the transformation of masked beings is very probably derived from the Cubeo who, according to what the Desana say, believe that all their dead, without any distinction between the sinners and the virtuous, go back to a particular hill located some distance upriver from Mitú. This hill, which is called *suriró-gë*/garment hill, is a sacred spot for the Cubeo, and at the foot of it they say there is a small clearing where the dead sometimes gather to hold celebrations. On the eve of the death of a Cubeo, music is heard there along with voices, and they say that the dead, disguised in their masks, dance in order to celebrate the immediate arrival of a kinsman....

"*The Yurupari.* The name yuruparí is a term borrowed from the Lengua Geral, and its etymology has not yet been satisfactorily clarified. It refers to a ceremonial complex that, for the past century, has caught the attention of ethnologists, missionaries, and travellers. An abundant literature exists concerning it, although much of this literature deals with speculations that only seldom seem to approach reality, that is, the ideas formed by the natives themselves about this ceremony. Thus, yuruparí has been interpreted by various authors as the commemoration of a culture hero, as a fertility rite, as a diabolic orgy, and even as a romantic

---

332 These *desiderata* — here associated with the magical (invocative) function and capacities of dance alone — can be generalized to include musical performances of any kind. The purpose of any such (musical) communication with the divine or spirit world *is*, that is to say, to promote e.g. the curing of an illness, fertility, social cohesion etc. (Ed.)

legend, full of poetry. As to general features, the 'yuruparí' can be described as an exclusive ceremony of initiated men during which large flutes are played. The women are not allowed to see or hear these on pain of severe punishment. At the same time, the men bring large quantities of wild fruit for the event, a procession or dance is organized, the participants sometimes wear masks, and occasionally the ceremony is combined with the initiation of a group of youth who in this manner are incorporated into a secret society....[333]

"The ceremony is held about once a year, generally at a time when there is an abundance of small fish, fruits of *vahsú, sëmé, toá,* and hearts of *palmito mihí* or of other palms such as *nyumú* or *më'ë.* A group of men gather in the forest to collect these fruit, to smoke meat and fish, and to prepare other foods. They then carry them back to the maloca that has been chosen as the center of the celebration. Days or weeks beforehand the members of the other phratries such as Pira-Tapuya, Tukano, and Uanano have been invited and large quantities of chicha have been prepared. The choice of the place of the gathering is determined by the number of pubescent girls in the maloca — that is to say, when a Desana maloca is disposed to enter into the reciprocal relationship of interchange of women with a sib of another phratry. Once the food is prepared, the men, now gathered at the landing, march off. On the path to the maloca they play various large, tubular flutes and conical trumpets* that are made from a piece of bark wrapped into a spiral shape and provided with wooden mouthpieces.

"We must first look at some of the details of these musical instruments that, obviously, fulfill a central function. The flutes or trumpets are manufactured in the same place in the forest where the men gather fruit, and consist of long pieces of wrapped bark about one meter long. In order to give this conical tube stability it is reinforced by tying two or three thin sticks secured by fibers around it. While the tube can be made out of any available bark, the mouthpiece (*dihsiró*/mouth) must be made from the wood of a macana palm (*Guilielma speciosa Mart.*) The flute consists of a short, heavy tube some fifteen or twenty centimeters in length that is inserted in the narrower end of the bark tube. The flutes are always played in pairs, a 'male' one called *poré* and a 'female' one called *ponenó.*

"Now, when the dull sounds of these flutes are heard approaching, all the women, except those who have passed menopause, leave the maloca and hide in the underbrush while the men arrive. Playing their instruments, they enter the maloca and there deposit the fruit and the rest of the food on a large basket tray near the main door. Each man, however, keeps for himself a small bunch of fruit, some fish, or a bit of smoked meat. Playing another set of flutes that are not taboo, they now walk in line through the maloca toward the rear door; before arriving at the other end, they suddenly disperse and pretend to look for the young women while they touch the old women with the food they carry in their hands. After leaving through the back door and contnuing to play their flutes, the men then leave and return to the landing where they hide their instruments under water.

"While the men are busy at the landing, the old women call the young girls to return to the maloca. Simultaneously, the men return, now without their flutes but carrying handfuls of nettles in their hands as well as the fruit or smoked meats. They enter the maloca with laughter, joking and shoving, attacking the women and the girls. Striking them on the back or the breasts with the meat and the fruits or scratching them with the nettles, they

---

333 For a related essay see FLUTE* —§112.16, **Rituals of Manhood: Male Initiation in Papua New Guinea (Sambia)**, above. (Ed.)

stage a sham battle. The women pretend to flee but, with laughter and shouts, they allow themselves to be touched by the men who pursue them inside and outside the maloca. After a while, and in the same atmosphere of joy and excitement, the various foods are distributed. What follows then is a gathering like any other, during which chicha is served, food is eaten, and there is dancing. We can observe clearly two phases: the first is solemn, and threatening, producing a separation of the sexes, the second is joyful and seeks union.

"In order to understand these ritual attitudes, we must first consider the mythical background of this ceremony. The Sun Father, as we know, committed incest by violating his own daughter who had not yet reached puberty; this is the highest sin among the Desana, and thus is a mythical event of extraordinary importance for them. The scene occurred at the Wainambí Rapids, at the foot of a *vahsúpë* tree, and on the large boulders of the river bank marks can still be seen in the stone, reminders of this violation: the impression of the buttocks of the girl, the red spots of blood, and a series of small holes where she urinated. The only witness of the violation was a small insect, the praying mantis, which is called *bári bugë* or *bári uáhti*, after the name of a fruit that is said to smell like onion (*Anacardium excelsum?*). The insect heard the laughter of the Daughter of the Sun and went closer to see what had happened. Being a witness of the act, the insect changed into a person (the myth does not give more details) and manufactured a trumpet, the first trumpet of yuruparí, and used it to denounce publicly the crime that he had observed. On the rocks of Wainambí a circle (or spiral) marking the spot where he put the mouthpiece of the flute can still be seen. The sound that this instrument produced was sad and menacing because it proclaimed the existence of a great sin, and the instrument itself smelled like the *bári* fruit, having the odor of the genitals of the Daughter of the Sun.

"But the myth continues, relating a new stage. Some time after the introduction of the flutes and of the ceremonial playing of them, still during the time of Creation, some women followed the men when they went to the landing to hide the instruments. When the men had gone, the women took out the flutes to look at them; they took them into their hands and touched them with their fingers. But when they touched their own bodies with the hand that had been touching the flutes, suddenly hair grew on their pubis and under their armpits, places that previously had no hair. When the men returned to the landing, the women seduced them and, although they belonged to the same phratry, they cohabited with them. Only after supernatural punishments, which the myth does not describe, were the men able to establish order again. Since then the rules that are observed at present have been enforced.

"This fragmentary myth shows us again the passage from Creation to chaos because of forbidden sexual acts, followed by the reestablishment of the social order in terms of exogamic law. Since then the flutes are played periodically as a reminder of this great sin. But while the commemorative ceremony has as its objective the prohibition of incest, it also indicates what sexual relations are to be permitted. After the commemorative and threatening phase, a phase of sexual excitation comes during which the permitted relationships are expressed symbolically.

"We can now complete this interpretation by analyzing some details of the story. We have said that there are two flutes, a male and a female one. The sound which the male one produces is said to be *poré-e-e-e-e*, which is interpreted as *koré*/vulva. When one blows into the mouthpiece, the sound of *k* is necessarily changed into a *p*, but all know the erotic meaning of the sound in question. It may be said here that the term *koré* is considered to be rather obscene and that in conversation the word *sibiá* (from *sibí*/quail, a euphemism for clitoris) is generally substituted. The conical form of the instrument is compared to the clitoris. When the flutes approach the maloca, the women and girls who are hidden nearby shout together *'bi-bí, bi-bí'*, an expression of scorn and rejection, but they also laugh loudly, imitating the laughter of the Daughter of the Sun before coitus. This cry imitates the *sibí*, a bird whose song is of evil augury for the hunter (who, not only symbolically, is a man who is excited sexually). When they cry *bi-bí*, the women want to express their wish that 'bad luck will stay away from them', i.e., they will not commit the sin of incest. The sound of the female flute, on the other hand, is harsh, monotonous, and threatening. It is transcribed as a long-drawn *li-li-li-li-li*. While the male flute incites and insinuates, the female one rejects and threatens.

"It is interesting to observe here that the Pira-Tapuya, who also have yuruparí ceremonies, call the flutes *minia-poári* and the people who play them are designated as *miniá-poári mahsá*. This name is derived from *miníye*/to be drowned, to sink, and from *paári*/hair, pubic hair. We have already mentioned that the sexual act is compared with the act of 'submerging oneself in water', to cast oneself into the water, and thus this alludes to the sexual character of the flutes. The men who play them represent those who are 'drowned', those who committed the sin.

"We now pass on to the second phase of the ceremony. The distribution of food is called *po'ori*, a word that has several meanings. It is derived from *po'o píri*/to scatter something, to broadcast, to sow a very fine seed like tobacco, to make a present. When it is related to the verb *puri*, it means to cohabit. In any case, we are now concerned with a markedly erotic aspect of the ceremony. The impetuous entrance of the men into the maloca carrying fruits and meats is interpreted as sexual aggression, but within permissible limits, and the very

symbolism of the different fruits and of smoked meat, with which they try to touch the bodies of the women, makes this celebration an event with an orgiastic connotation. The act of rubbing the bodies of the women with nettles, a 'male' plant, is called *nya-suári* (from *nya*/nettle, *suá)ri*/to make penetrate, to penetrate with force), and is interpreted as an act that is symbolic of permitted sexual contact. It remains for us to add here a phrase from our informant: 'Yuruparí is not a person; it is a state— it is a warning not to commit incest and to marry only the women from another group.'

"According to our data, this interpretation of yurupari is the one that all the Tukano tribes give to this ceremony, principally the Desana, Tukano, and Uanano, but probably their neighbors, too. Among the Desana, masked dancers do not participate in this celebration, but among some other groups they may do so." — Reichel-Dolmatoff, pp.3, 30-32, 58-59, 111-16, 153-54, 164-71.

§163.10 "'DEVIL' WORSHIP.[334] When applied to the ceremonies of barbarous races, devil-worship is a misnomer, as the 'devils' adored by them are deities in their eyes, and only partake of the diabolic nature in the view of missionaries and others. But inasmuch as the gods possess a demoniac form they may be classed as diabolic. Among these may be enumerated many South American and African tribes. The Uapès of Brazil worship Jurupari, a fiend-like deity, to whom they consecrate their young men. His cult is invested with the utmost secrecy. The myth of his birth states that he was born of a virgin who ceonceved after drinking a draught of *chahiri*, or native beer. She possessed no sexual parts, and could not give birth to the god until bitten by a fish whilst bathing. When arrived at man's estate Jurupari invited the men of the tribe to a drinking-bout, but the

---

334 This entry from an account first published in 1920. (Ed.)

women refused to provide the liquor, and thus gained his illwill. He devoured the children of the tribe because they had eaten of the *uacu* tree which was sacred to him. The men, enraged at the loss of their offspring, fell upon him, and cast him into a fire, from the ashes of which grew the *paxiuba* tree, which the Uapès say is the bones of Jurupari. Whilst it was night the men cut down the tree and fashioned it into sacred instruments which must never be seen by the women, on account of the dislike Jurupari conceived for them. Should a woman chance to see the sacred symbols pertaining to the worship of Jurupari, she is at once poisoned. On hearing the 'Jurupari music' of the priests on the occasion of one of his festivals the women of the tribe wildly rush for concealment, nor dare to emerge from it until all chance of danger is past. In all probability this custom proceeds from the ancient usage common to most American tribes that the rites of initiation of the men of the tribe must not be witnessed by the women thereof, probably on account of some more or less obscure totemic reason or sex-jealousy analagous to the exclusion of women from the rites of freemasonry, to which, strange to say, the worship of Jurupari bears a strong resemblance."— Spence [Occultism], pp.123-24.

§163.11 "TURTLE AND FOX (Anambé people—Brazil). One day as Turtle was playing his flute*, Fox came close to listen.
" 'Lend me your flute,' he said.
" 'No,' said Turtle, 'you'd keep it.'
" 'Well, then let me hear you play.'
"Turtle began to play: [narrator sings in a mocking voice] 'fah-fah-coulo-faw-fah.'

" 'Turtle, you play beautifully! Now can't I try?'
" 'Here,' said Turtle, 'but don't run off with it. If you do, you'll be sorry.'
"Fox took the flute, tried it, and began to dance. Delighted, he ran off with it.
"Turtle started after him but stumbled and flipped over on his back. 'Just wait!' he said. 'I'll catch up with you by and by!'
"Then Turtle went off through the forest and came to the edge of a river. He cut some wood, built a bridge, and on the opposite bank felled a tree that had a nest of bees in it. He took out the honey and went back and positioned himself along Fox's path. He hid his face in the leaves and daubed his anus with the honey. Soon Fox came along.
" 'Uh-oh! What's this?' he said, seeing the honey shining there. He stuck his finger in and tasted it. 'It's honey!'
"Just then another fox, who happened to be passing by, cried, 'Come now! That's turtle's anus!'
" 'No, no. It's honey. It really is.' Then he greedily stuck in his tongue—and Turtle squeezed his anus shut.
" 'Turtle! Let go of my tongue!' cried Fox.
" 'So!' retorted the other fox. 'Wasn't I right? I told you what it was, but you kept saying "No, no. It's honey." '
" 'Aha!' said Turtle. 'What did I tell you? I've got you now, haven't I! And you so clever? Now, where is my flute?'
" 'Turtle, I haven't got it!'
" 'You lie. Give me my flute, now! Or I'll squeeze harder.'
"Then Fox gave Turtle his flute."—Bierhorst (Red Swan), pp.222-23.[335]

§163.12 **CUSTOMS AND BELIEFS OF THE XINGU REGION.** "The Xingu Na-

---

335 Source: J. Viera Couoto de Magalhaes, *O Selvagem,* Rio de Janeiro, 1876. The English translation is mine [John Bierhorst], after the Portuguese of Malgalhaes (who also gives the text in lingua geral). Collected by Magalhaes. Émile Allain's French version is in Magalhaes *Contes Indien du Brésil,* Rio de Janeiro, 1882 [Bierhorst]. The flute typically has phallic significance among primitive peoples of the Brazilian Amazon and similar regions; see entries following. (Ed.)

tional Park is a federal reservation created by the Brazilian government in 1961 and enlarged in 1968 to its present [1970] area of approximately thirty thousand square kilometers, or about eleven thousand five hundred square miles. The park is situated in the north of the state of Mato Grosso, in a zone of floral transition between the Planalto Central and the Amazon. [In this region — which, geographically, also extends into Colombia — a number of native tribes continue to live according to old and traditional ways.]

"[SELECTED GLOSSARY OF TERMS:] "**Curatá.** A small Pan flute* or pipe which is both the voice of the spirit and the spirit itself; higher pitched than the *jakuí* flute but frequently played at the same time and particularly during rituals held around the men's house, or *tapaim*....

"**Horí-Horií.** A bull-roarer* carved from wood in the shape of a particular species of fish and swung above the head by a rope attached to a tall pole. The loud whining noise made by the spinning bull-roarer is the voice of the spirit that the bull-roarer itself represents....

"**Jakuí.** Perhaps the most important spirit for the tribes of the Alto-Xingu; it lives at the bottom of rivers and lagoons and has a village at the Morená. The four-foot-long flutes played by the tribesmen are both the manifestation of *Jakuí* and the spirit itself. The tribeswomen are forbidden to see these flutes, as they are a symbol of the malevolent supernatural and the human male sexuality. When the flutes are played and danced to in the village, always in groups of three, the women remain sealed inside their family houses; if they should see the flutes, they would be raped by the tribesmen, who are felt to become spirits themselves while playing the flutes....

"**Maracá-Êps.** Singers; song specialists who inherit or 'purchase' the privilege and right to sing over the posts which represent the dead individuals at an Alto-Xingu funeral *(kuarup)*. The singers are said to become the voices of the dead and the songs serve both to narrate the ritual taking place and to remind the mourners of the possibility of the dead returning....

"**Mavurauá.** A festival song performed in exchange for food (usually *mingau* [a liquid made with manioc or pequi paste] and boiled or grilled fish); a dance of spirit origin.[336]

"**Mearatsim.** A spirit associated with the flute spirit *Jakuí* whose village is found at the river bottom; a mask of the spirit....

"**Nhumiatotó.** A flute made of bamboo in Kamaiurá. The Alto-Xingu tribesmen are also accomplished musicians and play flutes that look like Panpipes and are associated with the spirits. The longest flute made is between eight and ten feet long and is played at the funeral, or *kuarup*, ceremony. Adolescent girls, recently emerged from house seclusion, dance behind the pairs of flutists, who move around the village circle, briefly entering each house to dance in front of the central hearth....

"**Tapaim.** The men's house or flute house (the home of the spirit *Jakuí*), located in the center of Alto-Xingu villages. Women are forbidden to enter because the flutes which they must never see are hung from the rafters inside. The tribesmen use the *tapaim* during the day as a gathering place where they may sit talking while making new arrows or fish traps or spirit masks and costumes. Much of the daily body painting and ornamentation is done inside the men's house....

"**Tauarauana.** Both a Kamaiurá festival song and a dance performed by the Trumái are known by this name. The dance, frequently seen in the Xingu, involves a number of men dressed in buriti-fiber skirts, feather headdresses, and leafy branches

---

336 See our theme T6 (Song as "energy exchange", e.g. song given in exchange for food, offspring, protection, etc.), *Introductory Remarks* Vol I above. (Ed.)

which are tied to arms and shoulders. The leaves are from a highly aromatic bush that is of great importance in the curing rituals of the tribal shamans. The center of the village plaza is the usual area for tribal dancing, and the music is provided by two men who sing while keeping the rhythm with a rattle* and a percussive instrument made from a hollow bamboo tube beaten on the ground.

"**Tavarí.** The mask of a water spirit; the spirit itself, which is associated with the *jakuí* flute.....

"[SELECTED LEGENDS AND TALES.] *Mavutsinim: The First Kuarup, the Feast of the Dead (Kamaiurá tribe).* [Magical singing restores the dead to life.] Mavutsinim wanted his dead people to come back to life. He went into the forest, cut three logs of *kuarup* wood, carried them back to the village, and painted them. After painting them, he adorned the logs with feathers, necklaces, cotton threads, and armlets of macaw feathers. Then Mavutsinim ordered poles to be fixed in the ground at the center of the village. He called for *cururu* toads and agoutis (two of each) to sing near the kuarups. On the same occasion, he brought fish and *beijus* [flat roasted bread] to the center of the village to be given out to his people. The *maracá-êps* [singers], shaking gourd rattles in their right hands, began to sing without pause to the kuarups, pleading with them to come to life. The village men kept asking Mavutsinim if the logs were actually going to turn into people or whether they would always be wood as they were. Mavutsinim answered that no, the kuarup logs were going to transform themselves into people, walk like people, and live as people do. After eating the fish, the people began to paint themselves and to shout as they did so. Everybody was shouting. The only people singing were the maracá-êps. Around midday the singing ended. The people wanted to weep for the kuarups, who represented their dead, but Mavutsinim would not let them, saying that the

kuarups were going to turn into people and for that reason there was nothing to weep about.

"On the morning of the second day, Mavutsinim would not let his people look at the kuarups. 'No one can look,' he said. Mavutsinim had to keep repeating it from moment to moment. His people must wait. In the middle of the night on the second day, the logs began to move a little. The cotton thread belts and the feather armlets were trembling, the feathers moving as if shaken by the wind. The logs wanted to turn themselves into people. Mavutsinim kept telling his people not to look. They had to wait. As soon as the kuarups began to show signs of life, the singers—the cururu toads, and the agoutis—sang to make them go and wash themselves as soon as they came to life. The posts moved, trying to get out of the holes where they had been planted. At daybreak, from the waist up, the kuarups were already taking human form, with arms, breasts, and heads. The lower half was still wood. Mavutsinim kept telling his people to wait, to keep themselves from looking. 'Wait... wait... wait,' he said over and over. The sun began to rise. The singers never stopped singing. The kuarups' arms kept growing. One leg was already covered with flesh. But the other was still wood. Around midday, the logs were nearly real people. They were all moving around in their holes, more human than wood. Mavutsinim ordered all house entrances to be covered. Only he stayed out at the side of the kuarups. Only he could look at them, no one else. When the transformation from wood into people was nearly finished, Mavutsinim ordered the villagers to come outside and shout, make a commotion, spread joy, and laugh out loud near the kuarups. Then the people came out of their houses. Mavutsinim suggested that those who had had sexual relations with their women during the night ought to stay inside. Only one of them had had relations, and he stayed inside. But he was unable to contain his curiosity, and after a while he came out too. In that very instant, the kuarups stopped moving and turned back into wood.

"Mavutsinim was furious at the young man who had failed to follow his orders. He ranted and raved, saying, 'What I wanted to do was to make the dead live again. If the man who lay with his wife had not come out, the kuarups would have turned into people, the dead would have come back to life every time a kuarup was made.'

"After his tirade, Mavutsinim passed sentence: 'All right. From now on, it will always be this way. The dead will never come back to life again when kuarups are made. From now on, it will only be a festival.'

"Mavutsinim then ordered that the kuarup logs be taken out of their holes. The people wanted to take off their ornaments, but Mavutsinim would not let them. 'They should remain this way,' he said. And right afterward, he ordered them to be thrown into the water or into the forest. No one knows where they were thrown, but they are at the Morená today....[337]

"*The Iamuricumá Women and the Jakuí: Women and Men Fight for Possession of the Jakuí (Kamairuá tribe).* The Iamuricumá women played a flute called the jakuí. They played, danced, and sang every day. At night, the dance took place inside the tapaim [flute house], so that the men could not see. The flutes were forbidden to the men. When the ceremony was performed during the day, outside the tapaim, the men had to shut themselves indoors. Only the women were allowed outside, playing, singing, and dancing, decking themselves out with necklaces, feather headdresses, armbands, and other ornaments today worn only by the men. If a man by accident

saw the jakuí, the women immediately grabbed him and raped him. The Sun and the Moon knew nothing of this, but in their village they were always hearing the chants and shouts of the Iamuricumá women.

"One day the Moon said they had to go see what the Iamuricumá were up to. They decided to go, and they went. They came close to the village but stayed a way off, watching. The Moon did not like to watch the women's movements: the old one's playing the *curatá* [small Pan flute or pipe] and dancing, others playing the jakuí, still others shouting and laughing out loud. To get a better view, the Sun and Moon went into the village. The women were having a festival.

"As the Sun and Moon came closer, the chief of the women said to her people, 'Don't say anything, or they'll do something to us.'

"As soon as they got there, the Sun said to the Moon, 'I can't stand to hear women playing the jakuí. This can't go on.'

"Then they discussed how to solve the problem, and the Sun said to the Moon, 'Let's make a *horí-horí* [bull-roarer] to frighten the women away.'

" 'Let's do, and stop this thing. This is a dreadful state of affairs.'

"Having said that, they left to make the horí-horí. It took them an entire day. When the bull-roarer was ready, the Moon asked who would attack the women with it, to frighten them.

" 'Let me take it,' said the Sun.

"And he began to adorn himself with feather armbands, headdresses, and other things. After covering himself completely, he went off in the direction of the Iamuricumá women. The Moon waited in the village. As he got close, the Sun started to whirl his giant bull-roarer over his head. The women went on dancing, but they

---

337 See our theme **T4b** (Music as magical restorative, of mental or physical health, from regions of evil, from regions of the dead [music as agency for restoration to life], etc.), *Introductory Remarks*, Vol I above. (Ed.)

were starting to get frightened by the approaching roar. When they turned around and saw the Sun making his frightful horí-horí roar, they were terrified. The Moon shouted to the women to get inside their houses. They abandoned everything on the spot and ran inside. The men, in turn, came out of their houses shouting with joy and grabbed the jakuí. Seeing what was happening, the Moon said, 'Now everything is all right. The men will play the jakuí, not the women.'

"At that very moment the men began to play and dance instead of the women. One of the women, who had left something in the middle of the village, asked them from inside her house to bring it to her. When the Moon saw this he said, 'From now on it will always be like this. This is the right way. Women should stay inside, not men. They will be shut away when the men dance the jakuí. They may not go out, they may not look. Women may not see the bull-roarer either, because it is the companion of the jakuí.'

"The men learned everything that the Iamuricumá women had known: the music of the jakuí, its songs and dances. At first only the women knew these things...."

"Uuatsim: The Ear-Piercing Ceremony in the Village of the Birds (Kamaiurá tribe). Uuatsim invited his brothers to go fishing. Four people went out, seated inside a single canoe. When the sun was sinking, they passed a village called Tsariuaparrét. Uuatsim stopped there and asked the owner of the house for manioc drink, but he only had cauim [manioc bread dissolved in water]. Uuatsim and his brothers did not want any. They really wanted *morrét* [manioc flour mixed with water]. They refused it and went on their way.

"[Uuatsim and his brothers pass through other villages on their way to the fishing, drinking the manioc drink. At night they reach the fishing area, light torches, and

begin to kill all kinds of fish. They encounter a *pintado*, which Uuatsim shoots with an arrow. The brothers pursue the pintado fish upstream, in their canoe. At the top the wounded fish enters a lake. The fishermen abandon their canoe and continue the pursuit on land.]

"They went laughing and shouting after the fish. The jakuí, who were playing their flutes underwater, heard the shouts and laughter.[338] They looked up and saw the fishermen walking along the *ivacacapé* [the Milky Way]. The jakuí put their flutes away in the tapaim and came out of the water to call the fishermen back. They yelled, but the men did not hear. But when the jakuí blew on their flutes, the fishermen heard and realized they had lost their way. They put out their torches of fire and turned to go back, but a giant snake appeared in the path and blocked their retreat. So Uuatsim and his brothers began to accuse each other.

" 'Who told you to shoot an arrow?' said one.

" 'You told me to,' answered another.

"And there they stood, putting the blame on each other for a long time. When the argument subsided, one of the brothers asked Uuatsim, 'Wasn't it you in our house who raised parrots, ibises, and parakeets?'

" 'Yes, it was I.'

" 'Well then, let us go find the birds.'

[The brothers look for the village of the birds. They discover that an ear-piercing festival is being held for the parakeets. Uuatsim says that he has come to take part in the festival, which is for his son: it was the spirit of the little parakeet that he had brought up. At last the brothers reach the village of the birds.]

"When the travelers came into the village, the parakeet took Uuatsim by the hand and led him to his house. He hung up a hammock for him and asked his father to stretch out, saying, 'How about that,

---

338 See also **WATER SPIRITS***. (Ed.)

Father? They're making this feast to pierce my ears.'

" 'I know, my son, I came to take part.'

"In the afternoon the birds all emerged from their houses to sing the namim, the festival song. They sang in the center of the village. The main singer was the *ueravapirum* [stork]. The parakeet told Uuatsim it was the song of the ueravapirum. 'Listen carefully to the way he is singing, so that you can learn. When the people sing, you have to give the singers some fish.'

"The next day the birds sang the same song again. They sang for several days in a row, day and night, without stopping. Two days before the ear-piercing, the people began to prepare the manioc, pulling it up, carrying it to the village, making the dough.

"[Uuatsim and the birds go fishing. They catch many fish by various means. They return to the village bringing the fish — piles of them.]

"In the village the birds decked themselves out, and started up their songs and dances again. They sang the rest of the day and all night long. The parakeet again begged his father Uuatsim to listen to the songs to learn everything.

"When the day began to break, the singers, who were singing inside the houses, going from one to another, came out to the center of the village where this first phase of the festival of the namim ended. Then the preparations for the ear-piercing ceremony. First, the hair-cutting ceremony, to the accompaniment of new songs. Then, the piercing of the ears, together with other songs, took place.

"[At last Uuatsim and his brothers wish to leave. The vulture transports Uuatsim's brothers one by one back to where they live, in his canoe, but each one jumps to the land earth quickly and is killed. The parakeet instructs his father Uuatsim how to avoid the same fate.]

"The parakeet had not taught the others, because they had been mean to him when he was growing up. They would not feed him, they kicked him, they threw him out of the house, and they made all kinds of trouble for him. That is why the parakeet let them die and did not show them how to get out of the vulture's canoe [properly]. Uuatsim got off near the village of the Kuikúru. After teaching the villagers the songs of the namim, *mavurauá, pequeiatsin, tauarauana,* and jakuí, Uuatsim went to the Kalapalo village and then to Arapatsiuatáp, and there too he taught everyone the songs. He stayed a long time in these places. From these villages, Uuatsim went to the village of the Auetí, and all the people there learned to sing with him. From the Auetí, he went to the village of the Iaualapití. As in the other places, he taught everybody all the songs: tauarauana, mavurauá, the song to ask for food, and still others. He left the village of the Iaualapití and went over to the Kamaiurí village, where he spent less time, only ten moons. When Uuatsim's brother, who was from the village of the Waurá, found out that he was staying with the Kamaiurá, he went to find him. Uuatsim asked his brother to wait, saying, 'Let's stay here awhile longer, I want to teach these people something.'

" 'I'll wait.'

"Uuatsim then started to sing day and night, so that the people of the village could learn. Before leaving, he told his whole story to the Kamaiurá. The people all listened to him.....

"The Kamaiurá listened attentively to the story that was being told. And Uuatsim went on telling it all: the arrival at the village of the birds, the festival of the namim, the songs that he had heard, the return to earth in the vulture's canoe. After finishing the story, which the Kamaiurá listened to crowded around him, Uuatsim said he was going to stay only two more days in the village.

" 'I would like to stay longer,' said Uuatsim , 'but I must go, because my brother came to get me.'

"Early the next day he departed.

"Ever since this happened, the Kamaiurá have said, 'If Uuatsim had come to our village first, today we would know all the songs better than anybody else. But since he first came down about the Kiukúru, the Kalapalo, and others, they know more than we do. We also don't know much because Uuatsim did not stay long in our village.' " — Villas Boas & Villas Boas, pp.55-56, 119-21, 147-52, 254-55, 257, 269-62, 266-67.

§163.13 "OI. According to the tribes living along the Xingu River in Brazil, the remote past belonged to such legendary nations as the Oi, who were very tall and had a curious habit of singing in chorus as they walked. Since the Oi have disappeared only in recent times, the Indian people have remembered their chant and can still intone it today. Another mythical nation was the Minata-Karaia, whose men had a hole in the top of their heads that produced a high, loud whistle. They also had bunches of coconuts growing from under their armpits; these fruits they snatched, broke against their heads, and ate." — Cotterell, p.221. (For other peoples of the Xingu River region, see following entry regarding Kalapolo myth and ritual.)

§163.14 **A MUSICAL VIEW OF THE UNIVERSE: KALAPALO MYTH AND RITUAL.** *Ed. note:* I have included the following anthropological account because it amplifies and explains some of the materials given above, and because in its own way it addresses the familiar question of how non-verbal modes of expression (such as musical — but also e.g. visual and kinesthetic) can be said to have or convey "meaning".... in particular, how musical performances *as music* can be said to express or convey e.g. "knowledge" or "truths" concerning spiritual and historical aspects of a given community. Speaking for myself, I would propose that the answer has to do with how the concept of "meaning" itself is construed. If the "meaning" of a thing is exclusively that to which

some verbal construction (e.g. word, phrase or sentence) which is associated with it refers, then of course by definition we have excluded non-verbal communications from having or conveying "meaning" at all. If, on the other hand, we propose that meaning has to do with revealing or disclosing the nature or character of a given class, group, society or culture etc., itself — whose languages or communications systems (verbal, but also non-verbal) the languages or "systems" under review happen to be — then at least it becomes a legitimate or authentic question to ask, in what sense *do* they possess or convey "meanings" with respect to such a class or group or society etc?

However — having established that non-verbal expressions can indeed be said to have "meanings" of some kind (namely, insofar as some aspect of the general character of the group or culture itself is revealed or disclosed by non-verbal modes of expression) — the equally vexing question, of determining what *sort* of meanings e.g. music specifically might be said to have, now presents itself.

I have already suggested — throughout the present work as a whole, beginning with my *Introductory Remarks* — that music can be said to have some meaning or intent on a purely local or parochial level insofar as a given musical performance is designed to perform or accomplish a given utilitarian purpose or function. The "meaning" of a march, for example, may be precisely to set the beat or rhythm for marching crowds; that of a battle signal *to* commence some military manoever; that of a dance, to establish a basic rhythmic pulse for communal dancing; that of a lullaby, to put a child to sleep; that of "program" music, to depict a scene or impression of a natural or emotional kind (such as love or anger, agitation, or the depicting of a storm at sea, or matinal appearance of the sun over mountaintops). With respect to religion and mythology in particular, I have suggested that the meanings of music (including song, dance, and purely instrumental performance) typically have to do with mediating (establishing some communication and, subsequently, negotiation) between man and gods, or between representatives of a given culture and a "nature" which is conceived as that to which such a culture, itself, is held to be in some opposition.

But what does e.g. music mean or signify as an expression *of* a given group, or culture, itself? It is difficult to say since (again) we cannot resort to words themselves in order to render such a "meaning". However, let me propose the following:

Musical performance as a collective enterprise *expresses* one's sense of "community", in itself.

Musical performance as a *ritual act* expresses or indicates continuity between past, present and (perhaps) the future of a given community.

Music as harmonic structure expresses (echoes, resonates with) some sense of communal (i.e. "world") structuring.

Music as itself a phenomenon or "force" of nature expresses the community's own sense of identity or unity with "nature" itself.

Music as (precisely) a *nonverbal* form of communication reminds us if you will that "meaning" or "signification" itself is not

fixed or determinable, but is ultimately only symbolic — i.e. that in truth *verbal meanings or significations are — of themselves — incomplete and misleading.*

These are some possible "meanings" which "being a community" may have — or which may be sensed by individuals within such a community — which are (precisely) nonverbal, and which musical expression in particular may be able in part to "disclose" or "reveal".[339]

Indeed there is also I think a linkage of aspects of musical expression such as these and a *mythical* (mythological) dimension of music. For we have not been speaking of literal, precise meanings of music, but of "sensed" or "intuited" meanings having to do with one's sense of community, nature, overall "being" etc. One cannot in fact *point to* or literally *define* community, nature etc of the kinds we are speaking of, the "nature" or "character" of which music and musical performances might be said to be a revealing, or disclosing. Rather, we are speaking in an intuitive, provisional, hypothetical or indeed *mythical* idiom, to begin with: of a kind of "higher" truth regarding the supposed nature of things, which is not the same thing at all as their merely practical or utilitarian nature, or dimensions. In speaking of "community",

---

339 For example, in support of the hypothesis that "musical performances in part reveal or disclose what it 'means' to enjoy membership in a given community or culture", consider the following instances in modern "sophisticated" societies such as our own: congregational singing and other music-making in a church, temple or synagogue, at which a particular spiritual bonding — elevation — is felt, which is the "essence" therefore *of* there being such a community; concerts of non-religious art and popular music at which, once again, performers and audiences form some spiritual bond — with each other and indeed with perceived aspects of "nature" generally; other music-making occasions, especially ceremonial, at which (again) some sense of community is *being expressed*. With respect to the latter, for example, doesn't Mel Tormé's Christmas song "Chestnuts on an open fire" invoke feelings of tradition, community, "being human", "being alive", one's family, loved ones, spirituality etc — not in a specific (verbal) but nevertheless in a powerfully "felt" manner?

for example, we refer less to the political boundaries and constitution of a given state or other unit, than to a sense of our "belonging" to or having some emotional identification with something which cannot, itself, precisely be defined. In that sense, our reflections have indeed taken a "mythical" or philosophical turn.[340]

So much by way of preface to the following selections. In these excerpts, the author treats of the myths and rituals of a fairly circumscribed, "primitive" community — which, precisely as a more or less clearly observable "case history" if you will, do I believe have a more general relevance along lines such as those I have just proposed.

"The Kalapalo are a community of about two hundred Carib-speaking people who live in their settlement called Aifa in a region of central Brazil that is protected as a national reserve, the Parque Nacional do Xingu. Within the southerly region of the park, the Kalapalo together with seven other Indian groups live artificially segregated from national Brazilian society and economy, cultivating fields of manioc, corn and rice, and orchards of piqui fruit, and fishing in the many lakes and streams that cross the region. Although they are considerably less isolated than in the recent past, their protected habitation has made possible their continued survival in the face of increasingly disastrous demographic, social, and economic pressures which on several occasions have threatened the integrity of the reserve....

"[It may be observed that] culture constitutes and contains within itself explanations of human life and thought and of so-cial, psychological, environmental, and cosmological events and processes. By 'explanation' I mean the ways knowledge is organized and used — in persuasion, debate, reflection, and especially narrative — to clarify that which is considered problematic or puzzling, thereby effecting a particular orientation towards something in the world. Explanation (an aspect of concretization of epistemological principles) is a process that is embedded in the very general cultural function of interpretation, of making experience intelligible through symbolic codes that are ever subtly shifting to accommodate new insights, new applications, newly available forms, and new contexts of use. Hence the explanatory aspects of culture seems most critical for understanding the efficacy of creative play — a process of experimenting with symbols and concocting new ones that involves extending meaning beyond what is commonly accepted and understood.[341] The relation of explanation and symbolic play is suggested by the fact that what we hold to be true about the world and the meanings given to our experience of it are most often developed and expanded in situations of action — found in all cultures — that are marked or foregrounded by virtue of their performed, artistic, and fantastic attributes. These cultural modes of action give scope and meaning to daily experience through images that reveal both the most deep speculation and concern with the fascinating and mysterious aspects of human life and the role of human beings in a sensory universe of polymorphic entities and problematic events.

---

340 Some of these matters are given further consideration in the "language" portion of the present editor's *Essay on Myth and Reality*, which follows as Part II of the present work.

341 Another way of putting this might be to say, simply, that we devise, comprehend and communicate "meanings" through idioms other than verbal or linguistic alone, for example, through the various "symbolisms" of play, games, music and dance — or, indeed, through some type of "action" generally. (Ed.)

"Anthropologists see [musical and other] performances as especially heightened forms of cultural expression wherein creative experimentation is appropriate, even often expected, where the performer is responsible to a critical audience and therefore needs to adjust the action to satisfy that audience. Hence the success of symbolic play in performed events is judged by the participants according to criteria specifically suited to the genre and context; in performance, responses to play strongly influence and are thus an integral part of the process, for it is in such situations that the performer becomes an affecting presence (to use Robert Plant Armstrong's expression) eliciting anticipated responses from an audience for whom the performance is both meaningful and interesting.

"Not all performance involves the transmission of traditional knowledge, but when it does conditions for consecration of that tradition arise. If judged successful the playful use of symbols to transmit knowledge and to communicate explanatory messages in turn has a strong affirmative, even venerating effect. The essential comprehensibility of the world is assured in the minds of people involved, and the suitability of the models is reconfirmed. Not surprisingly, the suggestion has been made that oral tradition and performance may be inseparable components of the same cultural phenomenon....[342]

"The forms of Kalapalo culture that are the most directly associated by them with performance are storytelling and collective ritual, processes participated in by virtually everyone so often as to be considered familiar but hardly commonplace or trivial in their lives. The relations between Kalapalo myth and ritual are in part a matter of homologies resulting from references to similar themes and personages, but more fundamental is the complementarity between the two symbolic media resulting from the special performance processes typifying them. These processes distinguish myth and ritual as unique expressive events in Kalapalo life that construct and clarify fundamental cosmological ordering principles, the enhanced awareness and understanding of which constitute a special experience of the performers. The heightened form of expression in Kalapalo myth is verbal; in ritual it is musical.

"Unlike our own attitude toward art as a professed speciality, the Kalapalo do not

342 In the present editor's own terminology — see "language" portions of the *Essay on Myth and Reality*, Part II of the present work — a given cultural or social order may be regarded as a "coherence" which is being formed provisionally, which both defines and is defined by the language, thinking and behaviors generally of individual members of such a group or coherence. To express oneself verbally, musically or otherwise is at the same time a "being disclosed" or revealed — tentatively or hypothetically — of what it is to be such a group or culture. (Ed.)

restrict artistic activity to specialists or to people exhibiting virtuosity. The Kalapalo understand that everyone has the capacity for creativity and expressiveness. Indeed, the importance of participation in verbal and ritual art indicates that they virtually insist upon people actively developing such capacities from childhood. This is not to say that performative events are not evaluated or that virtuosity is not occasionally significant for identifying some people of unusual accomplishment and for creating distinctive roles and relations for them. The point is that the processes through which various performed events are constructed are integral to social life and are a significant aspect of the ordinary person's means of comprehending reality. Hence both creative performance and non-performative creativity are of vital significance for understanding the general experiences of Kalapalo life....[343]

"Kalapalo Narrative Art

"The Kalapalo refer to narrative art by the form *akina,* a transitive verbalization of the noun *akisi,* '(someone's) speech'. Although the Kalapalo word subsumes any form of narrative speech (including personal accounts and oral tradition or 'ancestral stories'), topic is not as important to their idea of narrative performance as are two elements critical to the narrative process: the speaker's adherence to a set of conventional discourse structuring elements and the participation of a listener-responder, who is responsible for creating the conditions under which a speaker's story can unfold... As verbal art, the Kalapalo use of grammatical categories and discourse features is as crucial to understanding their mythology as are the characters, events, and themes. For a storyteller creates an interpretive and explanatory matrix through poetic and rhetorical organization of these resources of the Kalapalo language, and this matrix mentally engulfs the listeners

---

343 In sum, the author seems anxious to establish the following points: (1) nonverbal modes of expression and communication (e.g. ritual involving music and dance) are of no less importance than verbal modes of expression and communication as preservers and transmitters of "knowledge" and of "meanings" generally pertaining to the group's supposed history, organization, constitution or character and beliefs etc; (2) the myths and rituals of this particular group or culture generally tend to express the views of *all* (or most) of its members individually—that is, they are not the inventions of a special artist/performer class merely, but truly do reveal or disclose what it is (what it signifies or implies) to belong to (to be a member of) the group or culture. Thus, the myths and rituals of this particular group apparently do reflect its overall philosophy or belief system. It remains now to describe the nature and content of some of these myths and rituals. (Ed.)

until they understand, or 'see', the point of what is being said....[344]

"Kalapalo storytelling is an imaginative activity, high entertainment that involves great attention to form through the creative manipulation of language and the use of tropic imagery, repetition, purposive structuring, and other poetic [i.e. musical-poetic? (Ed.)] devices. Kalapalo storytelling should be approached as an extremely efficient means of communication, compressing a great amount of information, interpretation, speculation, and imaginative play. In Kalapalo myths, we meet a fascinating blend of poetry and science, fascinating not only because it forces the mind to focus on esoteric matters, but, more important, upon otherwise hidden, secretive matters that are prohibited expression elsewhere, and upon those things that have been too often taken for granted.[345]

"Although the worlds of mythic narrative are in the imaginative sense illusory, the Kalapalo understands the characters in their myths to be real and the events described therein to be true. Kalapalo describe their narrative speech as a way of teaching or imparting knowledge (*ikanigi*) and of explanation (*ifanigi*). It has been said that myth is true in the sense that our own poetry is true. We can think of Kalapalo mythology more prosaically as a kind of science fiction constructed out of the people's most advanced and learned scientific understanding of their world to convey narratives of very unusual lives. But whereas the writer of science fiction speculates about an imaginary future, the tellers of Kalapalo myths evoke an illusory past. In so doing, they clarify the conditions of the present world.

"Kalapalo Ritual Art

"Collective music-making (MIan) is also directly associated with performance. As with Kalapalo myth, the particular conditions under which collective ritual performances occur permit the expression of meanings that have at best a limited field in nonritual life....

"Kalapalo rituals are shaped by the use of sound as symbol. The manner in which the performance of sound (especially music) emerges from and is related to other ritual conditions (altering their subsequent forms) indicates that it is an enacted symbol that is expressive of the literal physical and mental processes that produce it; it is the bearer of visions of fundamental cosmological, environmental, social, and personal truths.

---

344 This suggests that no less importance is given to the *formulaic* aspect of the narratives that are being recited and performed than to the literal (verbal) content of the utterances themselves. In a sense such narratives already have a "musical" (ritualistic) significance, then, insofar as — by virtue of tradition — these formulas themselves invoke certain "meanings" or significations among the participants in the myth-telling event in addition to (or even apart from) the literal references of the spoken texts. (Ed.)

345 Here the body of Kalapalo myth as a whole brings to mind such more sophisticated bodies of myth as Biblical, ancient Greek (embodied e.g. in the Homeric poems and in Hesiod), and Virgilian — each of which similarly includes elements of literature/drama/poetry, historical narrative, epic or heroic narrative, cosmology, philosophy or religion, and natural history or speculative science.... all of them rolled into a single package. (Ed.)

"Because Kalapalo ritual life is essentially musical, Lévi-Strauss's much repeated proposal that an understanding of music might be the key to an understanding of myth seems a particularly useful guide to examining Kalapalo ritual experience.[346] Lévi-Strauss's primary concern was with the profound homologies of transformative semiotic structure between music and myth and with the assymmetric relation between them resulting from their different connections to natural language, but he also writes of the analogies between the unconscious structure of Western music and 'primitive' myth. Moreover, until the end of the final volume of *Mythologiques*, when he rejects its pertinence for mythological studies, he is virtually unconcerned with ritual. Lévi-Strauss's rejection of ritual's pertinence for myth is especially misleading because through the New World musical performance is crucial to ritual action. Musical ritual therefore represents a third cultural mode that might have assisted understanding the phenomena of thought to which his life's work has been dedicated. For ritual that is musical is meaningful music, not only (or necessarily) in a programmatic sense or through conventional reference (which is the position Lévi-Strauss understandably rejects) but in its significance as a performed event, from which both its structural and semantic links to cosmology and cosmogony arise. As Lévi-Strauss himself points out in a passage equating mythical and musical experience: 'Mythology and music have in common the fact that they summon the listener to a concrete form of union, with the difference, however, that myth offers him a pattern coded in images instead of sounds. In both cases, however, it is the listener who puts one or several potential meanings into the pattern, with the result that the real unity of the myth or the musical work is achieved by two participants, in and through a kind of celebration.'

"For the Kalapalo, mythological narrative, musical ritual, and the 'sound rituals' of a person's life crises (especially mourning, which uses all possible human sounds, and puberty, which is soundless) are all symbolic action aimed toward comprehension of the world and of the self through active imagining and performative experience, and sound is the primary symbolic form uniting these processes.[347] The Kalapalo mythological perspective is therefore close to what the philosopher Victor Zuckerkandl calls a 'musical view of the universe', which he suggests is attained not through faith and revelation as in Western culture but through sense perception and observation or, in the words of that most musical of anthropologists, through the 'science of the concrete'. In Kalapalo myth, this 'science' organizes

---

346 For excerpts from the writings of Claude Lévi-Strauss, see **MUSIC AND MYTHOLOGY***, pp.555-70 above. The word "semiotic" — used below — generally means "of or relating to semantics" — in logic, the study of relationships between signs and symbols and what they represent. (Ed.)

347 The present author seems to have become involved in the familiar difficulty of attempting to describe or depict the *meanings* of non-verbal activities or processes (death, puberty, making music, performing some physical action) *in*, precisely, non-verbal terms. For how, indeed — one may ask — *are* e.g. the "sound rituals of a person's life crises" aimed toward a "comprehension of the world and self"? That is to say: in what sense can we speak of "comprehension" which is (also) non-verbal? In fact, I should think that we too must attempt a creative leap of some kind as we, too, endeavor to understand what it is to e.g. "think musically" (i.e. rather than to think verbally, using language) or to "think kinesthetically" (i.e. by means of some physical action or process in place of words). (Ed.)

signs into implicit ordering modes. In life-crisis rituals, these models take the form of explicit propositional statements effective through sound symbols and *techniques du corps* that serve to orient personal identity and justify and explain the efficacy of the performative process and the general value and understanding of the performed self. Yet Kalapalo myth is the speech genre that most deemphasizes by a compression of categories the boundaries of such cosmological structures. It is performative action striving for a merging of the speaker with the listeners and of both speaker and listeners with what is spoken about. Kalapalo storytelling resembles the experience of performing music, the hearing of tones produced by the self, the experience of something that is at once external and internal, and the merging of the self with what is produced. Musical ritual goes beyond myth, of course, by putting into collective practice what is normally shared verbally and occasionally among only a few persons, thus creating the conditions for total communication, for experiencing power of community that is a consequence of collective understanding. To use Lévi-Strauss's experession, musical ritual moves doubt 'right outside language', first because it is a performed process and second because it is musical. Kalapalo myth and ritual are connected not only by thematic homologies but more particularly by their respective ability to create—through a performative frame that is conditioned by a unifying social aesthetic—a distinctive consciousness and to construct complementary visions of a comprehensive reality....

"Saturated with Music, Submerged in Sense
"Although Dawn People and powerful beings [conceptions of Kalapalo myth (Ed.)] are distinguished by their use of speaking and musicality, these symbolic channels of Kalapalo narrative art are also complementary communicative codes that establish a world to which both types of entities belong and in which they reciprocally attend to each other. This world is reproduced during ritual performances, in which Kalapalo collectively adopt the powerful mode of communication through which they engender the experience of a unity of cosmic forces, developed through the unity of sound formed by creative motion. In rituals, too, they most vividly realize their powers of presence. For by collectively performing music, they not only model themselves upon their images of powerful beings, but they feel the worth of those models by experiencing the transformative powers inherent in human musicality. Unlike trance states or those of alternative, illusionary states of consciousness, these transcendant powers unite within a heightened state of sensual consciousness bodily feelings of great intensity, transforming for a time the meanings given to the personal self and to the collectivity as well as the environmental setting.

"Many Kalapalo rituals are associated with a mythological idea of the origin of some musical phenomenon (a song or a musical instrument) which is an integral part of the ritual. Rarely, though, is a ritual in its entirety as it might be observed today described in myth, and certainly never in connection with an instrumental goal.

(Sometimes we learn the appropriate context for some rituals: the story of Kanasini describes the first memorial ritual held by Taugi after his mother's death, while elsewhere we hear about Kumagisa, the man who learned the *Auugufi* from Snake People, of Jagifunu, who learned the Fishes' *undufe* from the Fish People, or of the origins of the women's *Yamurikumalu*.)[348] The most obvious way, then, that Kalapalo myth and ritual are connected is that myths describe something which we can observe in the present as the most fundamental aspect of ritual performance, namely music, and it informs us as well of some aspects of the context of music's origins.

"Aside from the songs used in connection with shamanistic curing, the most important ritual use of music occurs in public, collective events which take place for weeks and sometimes months at a time during the six-month dry season (roughly between May and September). During that season, and especially at the period of its onset, the Kalapalo are intensely occupied with these complex collective efforts that involve both a musical, performed component and one that is economic and not performed. The Kalapalo at this time of year are constantly involved in musical performances that are associated with the most basic and unquestioned or sacred values and cosmological principles, and which thus seem to be among the most fundamental religious events in their lives....

"[Meanwhile] the phenomenon of musical ritual forces us to ask several fundamental questions. First, if we cannot understand musical ritual chiefly from meanings given to the musical content, must we consider it in the main a nondiscursive physical and emotional experience? Second, what are the connections and differences at the formal and logical levels on the one hand and of performance and experience on the other between linguistic modes of constructing meaning and musical modes? The answers to these questions will have implications for contemporary theories of religion and for our anthropological understanding of musicality, which is (as Zuckerkandl reminds us) as crucial to our understanding of ourselves as spiritual beings as is language. [In the remarks that follow] I address these issues by examining several Kalapalo performances, showing what is distinctive in general about Kalapalo musical rituals and how different musical performances create a variety of transmundane experiences for them.

"Talking About Music
"[Music understood as a process of living.] For the Kalapalo, music is, like speech, a process of living, but, because it encompasses all other types of utterances, especially speech (thereby yielding song), it is the

---

348 *Taugi* and *Aulukuma:* Sun and Moon, trickster twins. *Yamurikumalu:* the myth of the Monstrous Women, which "focuses upon the nature of gender, identity and sex role and plays with various transformations of these ideas: how people of one gender might acquire the physical and characterological attributes of the other; how the merging of these characteristics within a single person is associated with the transformation of the individual into a powerful being [etc.]" (p. 26). The Yamurikumalu ritual includes collective performances by the women of a variety of songs. (Ed.)

clearest manifestation of the highest degree or level of animacy: that of powerful beings. The transitive verb *an-* is used in reference to collective instrumental or song performances during which people 'dance', or more correctly, make rhythmic motions with their feet (*tetsuiti*, 'shuffling'). By 'collective' I refer (as do the Kalapalo) to performances of the same music by members of a community; from one instance of performance to another the relations between participants and observers change, resulting in virtually full group participation. 'Collective', in other words, does not imply that everyone is participating all at once but that all eventually do participate and also actively observe at some time during the ritual process.[349]

"In contrast to the performance of music, which is a collective process, a noun (*igi-*) is used in reference ot a musical piece — a song or a line of instrumental music — and the verbalization of this noun (*iginu-*) refers to an act of singing; playing on an instrument is *on-*. These acts may or may not be performed; the terms do not imply collective participation as does *an-*. 'Collective musical performance' is thus constructed from 'musical pieces'; the latter may be played or sung independently of performance and are frequently quoted in nonritual contexts (such as storytelling) so that listeners may learn them. Finally, the word *itolotepe* ('birding') refers to the performance of songs that have concrete referential meaning and that, unlike music that occurs during *an-*, have been 'pieced together' by human beings (*fes-*; the same verb means 'articulate a skeleton' and 'sew together pieces of a garment').

"*[Music identified with the life force itself; music a talisman by which to gain power over natural beings and forces.]* By naming an aspect of life, the verb *an-* implies animacy of a supreme degree, the hyperanimacy of powerful beings that involves dangerous creativity and lack of personal restraint, especially that control of aggressive urges with which the Kalapalo seem so occupied. The hyperanimacy of powerful beings, the source of music, is life in its most complete, unrestrained, and infinitely varied expression, the creative source but also one of dangerous transformative power, of violence, witchcraft, and destruction. Human beings can use music to charm and soothe powerful beings by engaging them in a performance that temporarily controls their ferocity, enticing them into forgetting for the moment their antipathy toward the performer. It is important,

---

349 I would suggest that this implies that each member of the group both *is defined by* — and, *himself defines* — the group or culture, the nature or character of which is being revealed or disclosed through (and is also being represented by?) the ritual process. Therefore, it is essential that each member of the group participate in this process. (Ed.)

Kalapalo say, to be able to perform music when in the presence of powerful beings, for music disarms dangerous monsters so as to make them forget themselves.[350] This is also an important theme in many stories about personages who outwit the most dangerous monsters. Music 'soothes a savage breast' in ways that language cannot.

"Similarly, the *kefege* or song spells that contemporary Kalapalo shamans* own and the songs they use in curing rituals can be called to help cure seriously ill people.[351] In addition, the music associated with particular powerful beings that is performed during collective ritual performance can be used in serious cases to attract those *itseke* to the settlement so that they may be persuaded to help a victim whose *akua* has been temporarily lost.[352]

"In these several contexts of people's relations with powerful beings, then, music (or more exactly, musical performance) is identified by the Kalapalo as having controlling force over aggressive, transformative, and wandering power; it is also a manifestation of that power. The ability of music to control and channel aggression, to limit hyperanimacy in ways that are helpful to people, has further consequences for understanding its importance within ritual contexts. This is because in such contexts of use, political life — the relations of control that some people effect over others — achieves its most concrete and elaborate expression.

"Musical Rituals

"Musical performance as such does not have fixed or assigned meanings, but in ritual contexts music is always an important symbol. Musical performance is associated with the imagined characteristics of certain primordial inventors or composers, namely, the transformative and dangerous hyperanimate power of specific powerful beings (though not, it seems, specific kinds of transformative power). This meaning is further extended in the experience of 'affecting presence' generated by music; music's power over a listener (and even more so, over the performer) is defined as the power embodied in the mythological creator. This meaning, hwoever, refers to the phenomenon 'musical performance', not to the particular characteristics of particular pieces....

"The association made between music and hyperanimacy appears at a number of levels of meaning and experience within the ritual performative frame, for it is expressed not only in the general ideas concerning sound symbolism... but in the contexts of costuming, the aesthetic of musical performance, and the complex semantic connections the Kalapalo makes between musicality and sexuality....

---

350 In my *Introductory Remarks* (Vol 1) I have identified this as theme **T4a** (Music as magical weapon against evil spirits, means for combatting, routing evil spirits etc). (Ed.)

351 Themes **T1b** (Music gives magical power to musician [e.g. shaman, doctor, priest] partly as a result of being in communication with gods or members of spirit world); **T4a** (Release or exorcism of the spirit or soul, incl. expulsion of devils, evil spirits etc); **T4b** (Music as magical restorative, of mental or physical health); and **T5b** (Calming effect on persons suffering or undergoing spiritual turmoil, madness etc). See *Introductory Remarks*, Vol 1, above. (Ed.)

352 *Akua*: interactive self. The author refers to "the Kalapalo idea that sleeping may be accompanied by the wandering of the sleeper's *akua* or 'interactive self', during which future goals are fixed upon" (p. 30). (Ed.)

"Egitsu and Undufe Rituals

"The Kalapalo classify their public rituals into two general categories. The word *egitsu*, meaning 'visited' or 'attended upon', refers to events that culminate in a climactic performance in which formally invited communities within the Upper Xingu social realm participate. Included in this category are the Egitsu proper, a ritual that commemorates dead *anetau* or 'leaders'; the Ipone or boys' ear-piercing ritual (an event that is a classic rite of passage); the women's Yamurikumalu and men's Kagutu rituals; the Katugakugu ('mangabeira sap object'), a rubber ball game ritual; Takwaga, in which flutes* of the same name are played; and Ifagaka, the spear-throwing ceremony. All of these rituals involve repeated performances of music in the host community over a considerable period of time before the climactic performance that includes the visitors. In addition, because *egitsu* rituals involve athletic competition between guests and hosts, for several months before the appearance of the guests, the hosts practice their skills (as the guests are doing in their own settlements).

"The rituals called *undufe* are performances that include only the members of a particular settlement.[353] Among these are the Kana undufegï, 'Fishes Undufe'; Eke undufegï, 'Snakes' Undufe'; Fugey Oto, or 'Arrow Master' ritual; Agë, the manioc ritual; Afugagï; and several in which masks associated with the *itseke* 'owners' of the music are manufactured and used; Kafugukuegï (howler monkey ritual), Afasa (the forest cannibal monster), Zak-witkatu, Kwambï, and Pidyë (powerful beings who were placed in the water by Taugi), and the Whirlwind undufe, Atugua.

"The Structure and Experience of a Musical Performance

"The climactic performance of a Kalapalo ritual always follows a series of preliminary events that sometimes occur over an entire year. For this reason, we have to be concerned with a long series of repetitive incidents and a process that extends over a long period of time rather than with single events. People often learn music and dances during these preliminary performances, so they are used by the performers to practice their skills and to try out the effect of their costumes, but these are not events designed solely for practice. Especially significant is the constant redefinition of space in the community as ritual space and of certain times of year as ritual time, or more precisely, as liminal space and time ['liminal' = having to do with the threshold of a physiological or psychological response (Ed.)], 'time out of time' and space that is literally siteless. These attributes result from the way musical performances are structured.[354]

"Most Kalapalo music is measured in that it is accompanied by rattles and dances in which the body is used as an instrument for measuring time, for establishing a common pace. A beat group is the dominating feature of a piece of music, repeated small groups of beats constituting the structure of the piece. Musical pieces are almost invariably structured in rhythmic and text

---

353 When visitors come to trade (*uluki*) they are asked to perform whatever *undufe* music their hosts are engaged in and are joined by the host women.

354 It would appear that music by its very nature is thus identified with a kind of "timeless" and "spaceless" realm or order of "being" itself, if you will, though to be sure these are essentially "European" concepts and may not accurately reflect what is intended by the Kalapalo themselves. But is that not also partly the point, that music (or musical performance) is used as a kind of language or communications system (communication with the divine or supra-natural) in *other than* a literal, verbal sense? (Ed.)

patterns of four or eight; first, a softly sung or played tone center is rapidly repeated four times within a rhythmic beat that is measured by a performer's step or by a flute being raised and lowered (the tone center occurs within a four- or eight-beat measure); second, an initial part or 'portion' (akwalu) of the piece proper in which the first melodic line is structured in four- or eight-beat measures that vary in rhythm; third, a second 'portion' with a second melodic line (similarly structured as to meter but also rhymically varied); fourth, a third portion (less common); and fifth, the tone center repeated to mark the end of a section before a new verse or repetition of the whole. In full performance each of the constituent portions is repeated. When a single person or a group is performing, the repetition of each piece occurs either two or four times in each house or in the plaza, but some performances feature pairs of singers, in which case each singer takes a portion in turn, singing it twice before a new song is started.[355] Pairs of singers or players are usually mis-

matched, in that an older or more knowledgeable person who teaches is coupled with a younger or less experienced one or one who is learning. Finally, when men and women sing in unison (during the *ipone* or ear-piercing songs and the Agï, a manioc-planting ritual) each gender-based group deliberately sings a whole pitch apart from the other, so that a sense of two distinct but united voices is evident.

"The nature of Kalapalo musical motion seems designed to emphasize the hypnotic rhythm of the music.[356] This rhythmic experience involves a structure of continuously repetitive motion: repetition of the steps of the performers, repetition of the tones, repetition of the performance by each participant in a single event, repetition of the entire event from day to day, repetition of the ritual through time, from the original performance that a Dawn Person saw (described in a myth, perhaps) until the present event. But this repetition is patterned; it is not simply the occurrence of precisely homogeneous forms over and

---

355 Thus a linkage is established between repetition of certain musical materials as a part of the purely *musical* structure, and repetition which is intended to accommodate participation by various members of a given community. This makes me think at once of Britten's *Young Person's Guide*, in which repetitions of Purcell's melody not only create the musical form of the piece but also permit each of the instruments and instrument-families to "participate" — as members of the (in this case) musical community — in the performance or *doing* of the work. If we should only move the concert hall to the center of a Kalapalo village, then it might be said that the strings, winds, brass and timpani etc are each to be given their own special opportunity to address and speak of the gods and "hyperanimate" beings and forces of nature. (Ed.)

356 See theme T5 (Music as a hypnotic force), *Introductory Remarks* (Vol 1). (Ed.)

over. For the aesthetic of ritual repetition incorporates the use of structured variation, which is as much a matter of individual differences among the performers as it is a consequence of the melodic, rhythmic, and textual changes in the music.

"The continuously repetitive movements of groups of Kalapalo dancing in unison seem to bring out what Zuckerkandl calls the 'ceaseless repeated beating of the metric wave'. A tune cannot be easily sung without the movement of the body, especially the legs (in nonperformative contexts, a person might swing in his or her hammock or merely tap a hand on a nearby house post to represent this bodily motion), nor is the song complete without the rhythmic accompaniment of the dancers' feet. The movements of Kalapalo dance also help to mark changes in the direction of the melody. As I discussed above, Kalapalo musical pieces typically consist of a pair of melodic lines of complex rhythm that are repeatedly exchanged, and with each change the dancers reverse their movements; sometimes this exchange is between a pair of singers. Dance motions also emphasize changes from one of these repeated pairs to the start of a new verse, a return to the beginning of the old melody, or the start of an entirely new melody and set of rhythms. Finally, Kalapalo dance brings out the spatial side of the musical symbol by uniting discrete places, dissolving the differences between autonomous houses, and uniting the residents into an undifferentiated whole.[357] From a musical point of view, space is used as an important compositional resource, as important as are the tones themselves, for Kalapalo melodies are constructed from at most four tones (entire vocal pieces have no more than six tones and many flute pieces have but three), and those of a single ritual convey a somewhat stereotyped impression as a consequence, an impression that is compounded by the incessant repetition of the performance. Hence the salience of rhythm and space as devices for structur-

---

357 Once again demonstrating the particular interest of this account of "primitive" musical/dance performance ritual, since the element of *community* participation is so clearly pronounced. The point I have made before, and would stress again, is that by "revealing" or "disclosing" what it is to "be" the community or culture itself, individual members who participate in this ceremony or ritual of disclosure are themselves equally *defined by* and *defining of* that same community or culture. The musical experience — so often emphasized throughout the present work as constituting a "mediating" between man and nature, or between civilized (acculturated) being and "being" or nature itself — here suggests a kind of bonding or identification between individual, community, and some "essential" or "true" aspect (which e.g. "unifies" or comprehends all time and space) of "being" itself. (Ed.)

CORREOS DE EL SALVADOR, C.A.

50 c.   AEREO

SONAJAS

ing a ritual event would seem especially important for developing the aesthetic of patterned repetition.[358]

"Although everyone strives for correct performance, it is recognized that each person has a slightly different interpretation, an impression formed by the performer's physical appearance, the care taken in selecting the elements for a costume (and how well these conform to the generalized ideal to which everyone subscribes), and of course a person's musical abilities, the care with which an *itseke* is represented, and how the performer's own character influences what is actually done.[359] Some people are said to know much more about a particular powerful being and thuse represent that being more clearly than do others. (I have heard, for example, some people speak admiringly of how well their Arawak neighbors the Waura represent the difficult *auugufi* polyrhythmic motions — body, voice, and rattles — of the Snake People.)

"The patterning that involves this subtle variation in each act of repetition also occurs in collective performances, in which people group themselves into lines. When such a line of dancers moves from one place to another, it is led by the 'beautiful ones' of the community, the young secluded boys or girls who are also *anetau* (in the case of the *egitsu* rituals, which are always sponsored by *anetau*), or, during an *undufe,* by the most experienced song leaders. In the middle of the line dancer the 'ordinary' (*talokito*) people, and at the very end, perfunctorily decorated and barely able to keep up with their elders, are the young children. When a line of performers remains relatively stationary, they face in a single direction with the song leaders in the center, flanked by the less experienced singers and finally the youngest of the group. As with the patterned repetition that occurs as dancers move from one house to another, uniting different houses into a spatial whole, this linear formation emphasizes personal differences among

---

358 According to Robert P. Morgan, in tonal music the tonal system — the octave — constitutes the basic structure for musical space. But the less emphasis placed upon tonality to structure space, the more a composer uses performance space (and even visual space as represented by the score) to do so. In this connection, 'A weakening of one kind of musical space was countered by a strengthening of another, more literal one. Indeed, the more removed a composition is from the older conventions the more likely it is that the performance space will be incorporated into its overall conception' (1980).

359 In more "advanced" social settings, we are not usually concerned with the performer's *character* in considering his or her performance of a given work. But is not such a "character" implied, after all — do we not indeed hear "Heifetz" or "Perlman" as well as the composer's own voice, and the sound of the instrument? In this account of more primitive music-making, the importance of the individual community-member's own "character" is acknowledged from the very beginning, as an essential part of a "fabric" which includes individual, community, and nature (or "being") — all of which are fused (magically?) by the sounds of the music itself. (Ed.)

the participants while paradoxically uniting all those individuals into a collective whole. This unity creates a tension within patterned repetition that involves simultaneous collective homogeneity and individual difference.

"The musical performances of both *egitsu* and *undufe* rituals typically involve a simple, recurrent patterning in which virtually everyone of the appropriate sex and age participates, either at once or sequentially. The first performance, marking the opening of ritual time, occurs in the central plaza (*fugombo*), the central communal space beneath which are the graves and in which is located the ceremonial house (*kuakutu*), where costumes are made and stored during the ritual period. The dancers move from this area to the house of the sponsor, performing either inside by encircling a central storage platform or dancing in a line facing the front entrance (there may also be a performance outside in front of the house), then emerge and continue the same performance in every other house in the village circle.[360] The events end with a final performance in the plaza. Normally this first enactment occurs during a liminal time of day: at the very beginning of dawn (*mitote*) or at the end of the day just before sunset (*kohotsi*). I stress this timing because during such times of day people normally are at their most idle, reflecting upon their dreams of the previous night, seeking out their lovers, or sitting in the plaza or before the entrances to their houses, gossiping about what has happened during the day. All these activities emphasize personal relationships,

introspection, and thinking about the effectiveness of one's relationships with others, in marked contrast with those ocurrences during the ritual events. The timing of Kalapalo ritual performances thus seems to restrict people in their thoughts about matters that are potentially destructive of group harmony.

"Just as the communally performed *an*- established in a performative manner the time of year as that of ritual, so the interior movement of the event unites the two halves of each house (separated by the storage platform), and the house-to-house movement links each autonomous social space into a ritual whole that is communal and egalitarian. Similarly, because the performance is communal, people from different households and of different families are expected to work collectively for the ritual. In other ways there is a purposive homogenization of the factional divisions resulting from kinship and marriage ties. Men who are brothers do not dance next to each other, nor do they play flutes together, and women must not dance with their husbands but with men from other households. Furthermore, as the movement of th performers within the space of the settlement creates a spatial unity, so the dance and music together unify the bodies of the participants physically, thereby creating or at least enhancing an experience of unity of persons, of space, and of time that differs from that of nonritual life.

"As the series of preparations continues (they may be year-long in the case of the *egitsu* or only a few weeks long in the case

---

360 What could involve each individual community member more intimately than this having the dancing/music-making group *enter one's own house!* In our modern societies we are less accustomed to regarding music performance as a collective or *community* enterprise in this fashion — specifically linking each individual to the group, and the group in turn to "nature" itself — but a hint of this type of experience is given during congregational music-making in a church or synogogue, and at a "mass" e.g. rock concert at which an audience may indeed swoon and shout and become somewhat frenzied by the piercing cries and beats of the music which unites them all. (Ed.)

of the *undufe*), each performance intensifies—indeed, visually compresses or condenses—these temporal, spatial, and social images by means of the spatial movements and ritual components that occur. As the date of the climactic event draws nearer and the level of economic activity accompanying it increases, along with greater public work by the ritual officers, so (in the case of the *egitsu*) do the ritual performances occur more and more within the central plaza, and the participants in both *egitsu* and *undufe* are more numerous. Sometimes there is obvious movement from house circle to plaza, as in the case of the Egitsu performances. Similarly, the ritual becomes more complex. Earlier performances, led by a few undecorated and poorly rehearsed song leaders (*iginoto*), are followed by larger, more spontaneously formed, and more elaborately decorated groups; in the final performances masks are sometimes used, portraying the faces of the *itseke* inventors of the music. This intensification and compression of ritual time and space and of the unity of the community seems to be felt by the performers through the cumulative effects of their dance movements, repeated costuming of their bodies, and increasing satisfaction resulting from greater performative success. In other words, an intensification of feeling occurs, not about a ritual object but about the ritual experience. In particular, it is the experience of a wonderful power of community emerging from a group performance, with a concomitant deemphasis on the inner self and the problems of in-

dividuals that is the Kalapalo sense of their ritual musicality.

"Let us consider first the 'tone' aspect of the performance. A curious aspect of most Kalapalo ritual music is that with the exception of the *itolotepe* and songs associated with the Kwambï, it is rarely accompanied by intelligible words; it consists either of the playing of flutes unaccompanied by songs or of virtually meaningless song texts. Songs are sometimes said to be in another of the local Upper Xingu language or in a language identified as Kalapalo but unintelligible to current speakers (the Yamurikumalu songs, for example, some of which are in Arawak—a fact the Kalapalo singers deny). Some are in effect tone syllables (similar to our 'do re mi') that repeatedly assert a tone center (in Kalapalo, *igitomi*, 'in order to sing it'). When songs are sung in Kalapalo the text consists of seemingly banal descriptions of mythological events, such as 'Anteater, the long-nosed one', 'Look, look, I'm wearing *itali* paint, I'm wearing red paint', or of repetitive metaphorically constructed lines, such as 'the other Parrot's mouth is opened'. To interpret the latter, one must know the story behind the song, that is, the situation in which the song was invented. Few people (mainly older song leaders) know these stories, and those who do not know them claim to be unable to interpret the songs though they know the words. For these people, the words have no signification.

"How, then, are we to interpret these 'meaningless' songs? My answer is that the specifically musical nature of the performance is the symbolic medium out of which ritual communication is fashioned. With several important exceptions... all Kalapalo songs approach 'pure' singing and focus the efforts of the singer on the experience of musicality. Thus the peformers are afforded a privileged relationship with the special temporal-spatial frame of myth, 'the Beginning', the time when human beings could 'approach' *itseke* and gain firsthand an experience of their musicality.[361]

"Musical performance is associated with powerful beings and is a means of communicating with them although it is not directly addressed to them."[362] The apparently banal and repetitive nature of the lexically meaningful songs emphasizes the crucial objects and attributes that make them distinctive, which the singers need to focus on during the performance — the powerful beings such as Anteater or Ulejalu. Communication may be said to occur not by singing *to* a powerful being but by singing it *into being*.[363] Highly focused mental images of the powerful being are created in the minds of the performers by means of the performance, an act of magic. There is a consequent merging of the self with what is sung about; just as in myth powerful beings participate in human speech, so in ritual humans participate in *itseke* musicality and thereby temporarily achieve some of their transformative power.[364] In public ritual, this is power of community. Rather than implying danger and ambivalence, however, it is collective solidarity emerging out of a performative experience of social restructuring and communal labor, representing a transformative power with markedly creative effects, including the ability to create its own social organization and to help cure the most seriously ill.[365]

"In a masterful exposition of the meaning of musical experience, Victor Zuckerkandl writes of the function of singing to create 'an enlargement, and enhancement of the self, a breaking down of the barriers separating the self from things, subject from object, agent from action, contemplator from what is contemplated: it is a transcending of this separation, its transformation into a togetherness'. In situations without singing 'self and object are sharply distinguished'. Zuckerkandl continues, 'Thus music is appropriate, even helpful, where self-abandon is intended or required — where the self goes beyond itself, where subject and object come together' (1976). In choral singing, as often

---

361 All mythologies of any substance have a "beginning" or are set, in Eliade's famous phrase, *in illo tempore*; rarely however have these "origins" of the world, being, humanity etc been so explicitly presented in a musical idiom, or identified as a kind of "musical" event. However, such a view is compatible with (Chinese, ancient Greek or Egyptian etc) notions of the "universe" itself being constructed along musical (i.e harmonic) lines or principles; while the very "amorphousness" of music if you will seems suited to the "mistiness" (non-specificity) which most of us even today would tend perhaps to associate with the first beginnings of time. (Ed.)

362 See theme **T1a** (Music as a magical means of communication with god[s] or supreme being[s]), *Introductory Remarks* (Vol 1). (Ed.)

363 See theme **T2** (Music (and/or dance) invokes or induces the world or cosmos itself *into being*) — *Introductory Remarks* (Vol 1) — for an example of which see also **SHIVA***, dancer of the cosmos into and out of being. (Ed.)

364 See theme **T1b** (Music gives magical power to musician) — *Introductory Remarks* (Vol 1). (Ed.)

365 Theme **T4b** (Music as magical restorative, of mental or physical health) — *Introductory Remarks* (Vol 1). (Ed.)

occurs among the Kalapalo during their rituals, the roles of singer and listener are combined, resulting in a person's feeling at one with the group through what (s)he/they are producing and which (s)he/they listen to. In such situations, a person feels, first, at one with the group, and second, an awareness as a musical performer of the concreteness of objects, their exteriority, while experiencing their essential unity with the self, and finally, there is a sense of 'space without distinction of places' and 'time in which past and future coexist within the present', that is, of the movement of tones which is music itself.

"We can now begin to think of the musical aspect of Kalapalo rituals as liminal in many of the senses of the term that Turner developed for it because, through the unification of space and time on the one hand and of persons on the other, Kalapalo musicality enhances among both performers and observers an awareness of the possibility of communitas. This result is achieved by concretely effecting that experience. The economic, instrumental events in Kalapalo ritual which parallel these musical performances also exhibit qualities of communitas in that ordinary relations between the residents of a settlement which tend to divide households, promote jealousies, and prevent group unity are transcended, overcome temporarily by means of the enactment of ritual office and communal labor. Although liminality is usually treated as an antistructural vision that is at once opposed to but a commentary upon the structure of social life, Kalapalo rituals of the sort I have been desribing are, like Turner's 'normative communitas', liminal events that peridocially emerge from the experience of one kind of social structure — of hierarchically defined obligations and ways of speaking, a temporary experience of the communal whole, of equality of person and feeling.

"The Kalapalo speak of their experience of communal performance, especially in a ritual context, by means of the verb *-ail-*.

This verb is most often used to speak of rituals in which several types of musical performances occur simultaneously, as during the Egitsu or the Kana Undufegï, when flute playing and several types of communal singing occur at once. The word is also used to refer to a sense of satisfaction resulting from the resolution of a group problem or the accomplishment of a difficult task by a group. Fnally, the word is often used to describe a group of people cheering as a sign of that collective feeling of satisfaction. In each usage, the term refers to a collective feeling or its manifestation resulting from a group effort; for this reason I have translated it 'feeling harmony', in the sense of 'agreement in feeling', or 'appropriate combination of elements in a whole' (following *Webster's*). I do not think it would be going too far to call this a South American version of the experience of communitas. Turner's use of this term emphasizes a process of homogenization or equalization of personal qualities and of structurally pertinent differences that characterize social life, whereas the Kalapalo are inclined to use differences among individuals within their aesthetic of repetition that is both experiential and performative. For the Kalapalo (and perhaps other central Brazilian peoples who devote much of their lives to collectively performing musical ritual) it is music as an enacted symbol that communicates and at the same time creates an experience of communitas. Applied to musical ritual, *-ail-* expresses the joy of experiencing communal action....

"[Kagutu ritual — Music and gender, sexuality]
"The language used by the Kalapalo to talk about the *kagutu* [flute-like musical instruments] is characterized by metaphors of female sexuality. The shape and appearance of these large, tubular instruments, rather than seeming phallic to them, are likened to the female sexual organ: the mouth of this flute is called its 'vagina' (*igïgï*), and when the set of *kagutu*

is stored high in the rafters of the sponsors' house during periods when it is not played, the instruments are said to be 'menstruating'.[366] During this time the sponsor, like a husband avoiding his menstruating wife, is not supposed to fish for the players, nor are the flute players supposed to eat fish given them by the sponsor. Yet when the flutes are played, women must avoid seeing them lest they be gang-raped, and they are also supposed to avoid seeing the men prepare the flute-sponsor's manioc field (from which food will be made to pay the players and feed guests at the *kagutu egitsu*). Sometimes... the manner of playing the flutes suggests they are used to express this potentially violent potency, as when the players beat them against the closed doors of the houses, allegedly so as to frighten the women inside. I never saw adult women reacting in fright, but younger girls were markedly affected, and in calming them, the older women did not laugh as they would on other occasions when children became frightened; there is no doubt that they view the threat as serious. Some men, however, seemed unsure of their capacity for such violence when I questioned them about the threat of rape.

"The *kagutu* songs are of several types, and some seem to parallel those of the Yamurikumalu. Others, however, are distinctive to the *kagutu*. One aspect of the *kagutu* ritual music I did not observe in the Yamurikumalu are what I call oratorical songs. After the flutes have been played for several hours, a song-master will sing out in a falsetto voice combining oratorical

and musical styles, asking the sponsor (*oto*) for food and drink to be given to the players. Two of these oratorical songs follow. Unmeasured, they are sung in falsetto, which indicates that the singer has taken on the role of a powerful being:

a. *Ohsi tuikefa kagifagu fomisu baba baba*
   [You should go pick Bull Frog's chili pepper, baba baba]

b. *Ande wokino timbukugu wokino*
   [Here's my future meal of manioc starch, my future meal]

The *kagutu* sponsor is identified with *kagutu oto*, who are powerful beings that live in the water, such as Bull Frog and Shrimp. Some *kagutu* music is identical to songs performed by women during their ritual.... But in addition to these forms of music, the men play other songs which women sing in contexts other than the Yamurikumalu process. These are called *itolotepe*, 'birding'. These songs are said to have been composed by women, and they clearly reflect a woman's point of view for they refer to food taboos women should follow when their children are sick, the relations between women and their lovers and husbands, and female rivalries. The songs are commentary upon past incidents involving known and frequently named ancestors, but most people were not able to describe these incidents to me, and none could provide any detail.

"Women are interested in music played on the *kagutu* flutes, particularly the women's songs, some of which they may

---

366 In connection with the present discussion as a whole, see *Introductory Remarks* theme **T2d** (Identification of musical instruments with male and female sex characteristics, i.e. insofar as the life cycle is affected); see also e.g. **PRIMITIVE PRACTICES AND BELIEFS***. Speaking for myself, I would guess that aside from the obvious associations of some instruments with male and female genitalia — e.g. flute with penis (for which see especially flute article §112.16) — the larger association *is* of music, or music-producing, with "fundamental" and indeed *mysterious* aspects or "forces" of nature. Is not sexuality, itself, inherently fascinating and "mysterious" — no less so perhaps than *nature* (so to speak) itself? (Ed.)

not know as well as the Kagutu ritual performers. During a Kagutu ritual in 1979, Ambo, a young leader and song authority always ready to learn new music, called Kudyu, who was visiting in her house, to sit by her hammock so he could sing for her some of the songs that were being played outside. She also asked him who was playing. Indeed, many women are aware of which men are playing the *kagutu*, perhaps because they remember having heard certain individuals practising on their *kuluta* flutes.

"In the Kagutu and Yamurikumalu rituals people play songs that refer to members of the gender opposite to that of the performers. Some of this music is said to have been originally 'pieced together' by persons of the opposite sex. Other songs, composed by persons of the same sex as the performers, explicitly refer to commonly held images of the typical sociosexual behavior of members of the opposite sex. Furthermore, the symbols — forms of performance, costumes, instruments — used in each ritual carry sexual meanings that concern the opposite gender. In the Yamurikumalu, the women perform and behave aggressively like men. As the story describes so well, they adopt this role because the original female inventors of the Yamurikumalu acquired masculine characteristics by applying substances used only by men: *itali* resin, whose 'pungency' is dangerous to women and which is worn by men during wrestling because it is supposed to impart physical strength; chili peppers (that originally swelled the women's genitalia into those of men) that are associated with a man's potential ability to control and use hyperanimate (*itseke*) power, *kugitse* or love medicine that is supposed to attract

women fatally to men and thus represents the sexual desire that men can generate in women. I have already shown that the men are handling a powerful symbol of female sexuality when they play the *kagutu*.

"The men literally handle a representation of female sexuality when, at the time the sponsor receives payment from the *taiyopke*, they flourish before the women large gourds upon which beeswax vaginas are modeled. During this phase of the Kagutu ritual women and men engage in dances that end in debris-throwing brawls between *ifandau*.

"But the particular sexual attributes that are referred to in these rituals are precisely those that are considered repellent and pose the most danger to persons of the opposite sex. For the men, these are the insatiable female vaginal mouth and its mysterious and fearful menstrual process. For the women, masculine dangers are ever-present in the form of potentially dangerous seminal substance (an excessive quantity from a number of men can rot inside a women and make her seriously ill, for it cannot agglutinate to form a child), and even worse, the aggressive sexual passion of men that constantly threatens to turn into rape.

"Yet despite these references to what persons of each gender understand to be the most difficult and threatening aspects of sexuality, during their rituals they enact those very qualities of sexual being. When people of one sex are performing, they are associating themselves with and even adopting qualities of feeling that are part of the imagined model of the opposite sex. These feelings include those that are directly linked to gender identity (uncontrollable sexual feelings, dangerous sexual substances) and others that emerge in the course of social life (jealousy, excessive modesty, fear of the opposite sex, absurd passions[367]). Music is the enacted metaphor in each case.

"Let us look more closely at that exceptionally violent (for the Kalapalo) and therefore strange injunction: women must not watch the flutes being played lest they be gang-raped, being taken, some men told me, to a place where a hornets' nest had been found so that the insects would later sting the victim to death. This might appear to be a punishment, and women are not afraid of the flutes but of the men raping them. The rape is described as if it were a reaction men have if they see women watching them play the flutes, and the Kalapalo suggest that this reaction is a consequence of the flutes' temporary association with female sexual parts and qualities of sexual passion. The men are, in fact, combining their own sexual feelings (aggression, initiating relations before women) with a particularly intense form of female sexual feeling that comes from their contact with the powerful beings that most clearly manifest those feelings, the *kagutu.* In combination with that of men, this female sexuality becomes violent and aggressive, marked by antipathy toward the victim. So rape may not be so much a punishment, something that men do to 'get back' at women who have violated a serious injunction, as it is considered a compulsive effect of performance observed....[368]

"During the time of year when the Yamurikumalu ritual is held, women attack and beat up any man other than the sponsor who dares to enter the plaza. A visitor from the nearby settlement of Anafutu was so upset by the violence of

their attack on a relative that he likened them to men clubbing to death an accused witch. As the women pound on the man's body with their fists and pull his hair, they smear him with *ondo,* the variety of red paint that only women use and that, when mixed with the resin called *tifa,* some men liken to menstrual blood. This symbolizes the dangers to men of sexual contact with women. Yet, a man who suffers this ordeal has the right to ask his female cousins for sexual relations, as if in defiance of the women's counterpart to the men's threat of rape that is ever present during the Kagutu. In the Yamurikumalu, the women violently repel men by means of a symbol of what seems to provoke the greatest overt anxiety in men concerning their relations with women. In both Kagutu and Yamurikumalu, neither male sexuality nor female sexuality alone is inherently violent or merely aggressive, but in conjunction they become seriously threatening. As the myths propose and the Kalapalo enact during their musical rituals, this combination is socially lethal, and it can be extremely dangerous – even fatal – to a member of the opposite sex.

"What of the other musical instruments [used in ritual performances]? The *meneuga* was described to me as an instrument resembling the *kuluta* but no longer made. The *kuluta,* on the other hand, is still important, and its manner of use seems to represent an aspect of male sexuality that markedly contrasts with what is expressed through the *kagutu* playing. Whereas the *kagutu* flute performances suggest the aggressive and violent aspects of male sexuality, the older *kuluta* sister suggests what is charming and seductive in Kapalalo masculine behavior. This flute,

---

367 I find it terribly intriguing that this entirely casual ennumeration of "jealousy, excessive modesty, fear of the opposite sex, [and] *absurd* passions" – for I cannot resist italicising to underline the somewhat comic aspect – would form the basis for a novelist's catalog of themes regarding the progress (or lack of progress) of love... (Ed.)

368 The position of the musical instrument itself in all of this remains central... (Ed.)

being older, is less powerful, less beautiful, and hence not forbidden to women. On the contrary, men play the *itolotepe* songs on their *kuluta* to charm and seduce women, to let their lovers know they are approaching as they walk along the paths that wind among the manioc fields. And there are other flutes—the *atana* and the *takwaga*—which are not associated with Kafunetiga and played by men who are dancing with women in highly positive erotic contexts....

"Although I—and the Kalapalo—emphasize the dangers and difficulties [of sexuality] through a focus on certain rituals and myths, there is always also the pleasurable, erotic feelings (described in the same, as well as other myths) that draw men and women to each other and that are the very basis for continued human existence.

"Conclusion
"In the Yamurikumalu and Kagutu ritual processes, the performance of music effects a paradoxical relationship between the two categories of gender. First, the symbols it calls to mind emphasize the differences and antagonisms between the sexes through their reference to the dangerous powers inherent in human sexuality. Yet at the same time the music effects communication between the performers (of one sex) and the listeners (who are of the opposite sex), a situation of communicative control over those dangerous powers. Just as music is defined within narrative art as both a manifestation of transformative and aggressive attributes of powerful beings and a means available to people for controlling these forces, so

Kalapalo use music ritually as a means of communicating between what they define as insurmountably separated or grossly unequal categories of beings.

"This communication is effected not so much by establishing a mood of sympathy as by entrancing the listeners through explicit reference to their own power, using the powers of the listeners to disarm them temporarily. Such control cannot be effected through language, which obliquely deceives by creating mental illusions. It is true that Kalapalo music—like their speech—can emphasize boundaries and create antagonisms, as we see during the Kwambiï, Kagutu, and Yamurikumalu rituals. But music has as well the paradoxical effect of simultaneously transcending boundaries, allowing people to communicate across the formidable divisions they create among and between themselves and the rest of their concerned existence. What is most successfully expressed in the environment of music paradoxically emphasizes formally opposed categories of being by bridging the chasms that separate them....

"When people perform music, they have the ability to move powerful beings because the latter can most clearly recognize something of themselves in humanity.[369] Human beings, on the other hand, discover their pedigree through music.

"The formal parallels between the myths of the New World and Western music that Lévi-Strauss understood so clearly may indeed be a consequence of how experience is created, organized, and interpreted by the indigenous inhabitants of the Americas, where not only are mythologi-

---

369 Other American instances of music that moves powerful beings come to mind: the Inuit shaman who by singing to the life-controlling water demoness Sedna revives the dead; the Navajo Night Chant hero myth, in which figure the maimed twins, who—by song—finally move the gods into curing them, after speech, prayers, payment, and weeping each fails in turn. Only when their weeping turns to song are the gods moved by the yearnings of human beings for the beauty that comes with health, strength, and order.

cal genres complex poetic performed processes, but ritual is essentially a series of musical events. For the Kalapalo, the two are linked, first, by a sound symbolism that gives meaning to language and to music as signifying forms implying feelings and relations between entities, and second, by a performative frame that dissolves social and personal differences so as to create an experience of unity that is simultaneously physical and mental and therefore has deep moral significance. In Kalapalo verbal art, the performance of sound creates a sense of multiple presences through shifts in rhythm, tempo, tonality, contouring, and timbre – a musical process, though it need not always incorporate music per se. In Kalapalo mythic discourse, unity of participants occurs by means of mental imagining; hearing leads to 'seeing' and understanding, and the meanings of words are taken to be shaped by illusionary images. In ritual performance, the unity of persons is effected through musical expression, wherein the body is an important musical instrument that helps to create a feeling about the motion of sounds in space, an understanding of a particular sense of time and of the most intense expression of life itself, which is the experience – however transient – that one is indeed a powerful being.

"The mingling of different sounds in various situations of performed Kalapalo art is therefore a truly ecological representation of the universe. Through sound symbols, ideas about relations, activities, causalities, processes, goals, consequences, and states of mind are conceived, represented, and rendered apparent to the world. It is through sound that cosmic entities are rendered into being and represented by the Kalapalo – not as object-types but as beings causing and experiencing action in a veritable musical ecology of spirit." – Basso, pp.xi, 1-2, 6-10, 243-46, 248-55, 304-11.

IRISH MYTHS AND FOLK-TALES. *(See also p.417.)*

§170.3 See **BAGPIPES*** – The Piper and the Pooka, §34.6.
HARP*.

§170.4 **ANGUS MAC OG [Aengus, Oengus]**. "God of youth. Son of Dagda [see **HARP***, above] and Boann. He was called Mac Og (or the Young Son) after his mother's words, 'Young is the son who was begotten at break of day and born betwixt it and evening', referring to his magical conception and gestation.... An eighth-century text, *Aislinge Oenguso* (The Dream of Angus), tells how he was visited by an otherworldly maiden, Caer Ibormeith, in his sleep and conceived such a love for her that he fell ill until he found her, with the help of Bodb [King of the Sidi of Munster]. She was in the form of a swan one year and assumed human shape the next. He found her at Loch Bel Dracon at Samhain [the Celtic festival which marked the New Year – held on 1 November], together with 149 other girls all in swan-form, with silver chains between each pair. Angus also assumed the form of a swan, and together they circled the lake three times, singing sleep-music so profoundly moving, that everyone in the vicinity fell asleep for three days and nights. They returned to his other-worldly palace, Bruig na Boinne (New Grange, Meath). W. B. Yeats' poem 'The Song of Wandering Aengus' is a retelling of this event." – Matthews and Matthews, p.23.

§170.5 **CORMAC MAC AIRT**. "The Irish Solomon. His famous reign could have been 226-66, when Tara enjoyed a period of unprecedented prosperity. A contemporary was Finn MacCool, who led his band of warriors in great deeds. The wisdom of Cormac derived from a wonderful golden cup. If three lies were spoken over it, into three pieces it would break; whereas three truths made it whole again.

The King also possessed a musical branch, made of silver with three golden apples on it. When Cormac shook the branch, the sick, the wounded, and women in childbed would fall asleep until the next day.[370] Both the magic cup and branch were gifts from Mananna mac Lir, 'a renowned trader who dwelt in the Isle of Man'. Art Cormac'd death, they vanished." — Cotterell, p.150.

§170.6 **LEANAN SIDHE.** "The Fairy Mistress who encounters poets and musicians inspiring them with her muse-like power. She appears frequently in Irish poetic tradition as the central figure of the Aisling or vision, in which the poet meets her on a hillside. The music and poetry which she inspires is usually indicative of otherworldly sadness and regret for the past glories of Ireland." — Matthews, p.104.

§170.7 **MAG MOR.** "The great plain: the heartland of the gods where men and maidens lived together without shame, where music always sounded, where possessions were unknown and where the ale was more intoxicating than the best produced in Ireland." — Matthews, p.113.

§170.8 **LEGENDS OF MUNSTER — PROVINCE OF MUSIC.** "After they had gained possession of the island [of Ireland], a contention arose between [the brothers] Éremón and Éber concerning the kingship. Amairgen, as arbitrator, said 'The heritage of the chief, Donn, to the second Éremón; and his heritage to Éber after him', but Éber insisted upon a division. Here we have the inception of a territorial dichotomy which is fundamental to the cosmographic structure of Ireland. Éremón took the kingship in the North and Éber in the South, or according to some texts, Éber took the South and Éremón took the North *with the kingship*....

"Before parting, the two brothers cast lots upon their artists, a poet and a harper. The poet, 'learned man of mighty power', went with Éremón northward, 'so that henceforth in the North he secured dignity and learning'; the harper went to Éber southward: 'string-sweetness of music... in the South part of Ireland; thus shall it be till the mighty Judgment'.

"Throughout Irish literature the Northern Half of Ireland is known as *Leth Cuinn*, 'The Half of Conn', and the Southern Half as *Leth Moga*, 'The Half of Mug'. As a common noun *conn* means 'head', 'chief', 'sense', 'reason', while *mug* means 'servant'. The traditional boundary-line between the two halves runs along Eiscir Riada, a broken ridge of low mounds running between Dublin and Galway Bay, and the names of the two halves are explained by the story of a struggle between Conn, the eponymous ancestor of the Dál Cuinn dynasties of the Northern Half, and Mug Nuadat ('Servant of Nuadu'), also known as Eogan, the eponymous ancestor of the Eoga-natchta, the rulers of Munster. Mug Nuadat, by storing up provisions for a coming famine, gains the Southern kingdom for himself....

"Modern Ireland comprises four great provinces, Connacht, Ulster, Leinster, and Munster, whose origin lies beyond the beginning of recorded history. Yet, the Irish word for 'province' is *cóiced*, which means a 'fifth', not a 'fourth', and the expression 'five fifths of Ireland' is familiar to all who speak the Gaelic tongue. The antiquity of this five-fold conception cannot be doubted, but tradition is divided as to the [precise] identity of the fifth fifth....

---

370 Theme of healing or consoling properties of music — see also **DAVID (Jewish)***, **JAPANESE MYTHS — PRACTICES AND BELIEFS (Jizo-Bosatsu)***, **SHAMAN(S), SHAMANISM*** etc. (Ed.)

"The four great provinces and the centre constitute a hierarchic system which corresponds to that of the invasions from Partholón to the Sons of Míl. When the representatives of the four quarters and of the Manor of Tara had been assembled together... the supernatural Trefulngid asked: 'O Fintan, and Ireland, how has it been partitioned, where have things been therein?' 'Easy to say,' said Fintan, 'knowledge in the west, battle in the north, prosperity in the east, music in the south, kingship in the center.' Then Trefuilngid proceeded to indicate in detail the attributes of each quarter and the middle. [And these are as follows: CONNACHT (West) is identified with the attributes of Learning (*Fis*, foundations, *teaching*, alliance, *judgement, chronicles, counsels, stories, histories, science*, comeliness, *eloquence*, beauty, modesty (lit. blushing), bounty, abundance, wealth. ULSTER (North) is identified with Battle (Cath), *contentions, hardihood, rough places, strifes, haughtiness, unprofitableness, pride, captures, assaults, hardness, wars, conflicts*. LEINSTER (East) is identified with Prosperity (Bláth), *supplies, bee-hives* (? = ceasa), contests, feats of arms, *householders*, nobles, wonders, *good custom, good manners, splendour, abundance, dignity*, strength, *wealth, house-holding, many arts*, accoutrements (?), *many treasures, satin, serge, silks, cloths* (?), *green spotted cloth* (?), *hospitality*. MUNSTER (South) is identified with Music (Séis), waterfalls (esa), *fairs* (oenaigi), nobles, *reavers*, knowledge, subtlety, *musicianship, melody, minstrelsy*, wisdom, honour, *music*, learning, teaching, warriorship (fiansa), *fidchell-playing*, vehemence, fierceness, poetical art, advocacy, modesty, code, *retinue*, fertility. In addition MEATH (Centre) is identified with Kingship, stewards, dignity, primacy, stability, establishments, supports, destructions, warriorship, charioteership, soldiery, principality, high-kingship, ollaveship, mead, bounty, ale, renown, fame, prosperity.]

"It will be remembered that Mug Nuadat gained possession of the Southern Half [of Ireland], the Half of Mug, by feeding the people, and that when Éremón and Éber originally divided the country into two, the harper went to the South and endowed the Southern Half with music in perpetuity. In the fivefold division which we are now discussing, these two attributes, 'Prosperity' and 'Music' are [additionally] separated and allocated respectively to Leinster and Munster, the two provinces of the Southern Half, here identified with 'East' and 'South'...."

"The attributes of Munster are almost as all-embracing as those of the Central Province—they include knowledge, wisdom, learning, teaching, and poetic art, warriorship, and fertility, as well as attributes which connect it with the fourth 'function'. It is a world in itself.

"This separateness and self-sufficiency of Munster is... a concomitant of its peculiar role in the wider cosmology—a role which has many facets. Firstly, Munster is associated with the dead. The House of Donn and the world of the dead lie off the coast of West Munster....

"Secondly, Munster is pre-eminently the province of female supernatural personages. 'The Síd of Munster' is known as 'The Síd of the White Women'. Ireland is sometimes called 'the land of Anann', and Anann, described in Cormac's Glossary as 'the mother of the gods of Ireland', is commemorated in the name of two hills, 'The Paps of Anann', near Killarney in Munster....

"Munster is the primeval world, the place of origin. On its west coast are the landing places of several of the mythical invaders, including Dún na mBarc in Corco Duibne where Cessair came to land. Under the name of Banba, this first woman lived to meet the Sons of Míl on Sliab Mis, again in Corco Duibne. Tul Tuinde where Fintan, or alternatively Banba, survived the Flood, is likewise in West Munster, according to the Fir Bolg division of Ireland. On Valentia Island off the west coast of Munster dwelt the wizard Mug Ruith who lived through nineteen reigns. *Sen* means 'old', and Sen, Sengann, Ro-shen, Senach, Sengarman, Senláech, Senan, Senfiacail — who appear in diverse stories — are all Munster characters....

"To describe Munster as the province of the dead, and as the province of female and ancient personages, is to stress only some of the more obvious peculiarities of its character. It is a land of surprises....

"The paradoxical nature of Munster manifests itself in many ways. If the kingship of Munster is 'like a fly', the people are 'like bees', and in Celtic tradition, bees have a secret wisdom and hail from Paradise. The supernatural beings of Munster have a dual nature. Cessair, the outcast, is also Banba the queen, Fintan the idolator is the sage of the ages. Mug Nuadat, the 'Servant' king is also known as Eogan the Great (*Eogan Mór*). Mugan, the Munster queen, seems to be the same person as Mór of Munster. The story goes that the kings of Ireland were seeking Mór. Her 'House' is pointed out at the western extremity of Corco Duibne, and when the sun is shining it is said that 'Mór is on her throne'. Fintan changes his form, and the Old Woman of Beare renews her youth,

time and time again. A similar metamorphosis appears in a Fenian story in which Finn's destiny is revealed by a visitant from the Other World. This stranger was Crónánach — his name is suggestive — from Síd ar Femuin, the Síd of Munster, and he appeared, an enormous, black, misshapen churl, upon Finn's hunting-ground. He brought out two pipes* and played 'so that wounded men and women in travail would have fallen asleep at the exquisite music which he made'.[371] Later, 'As the light of day came there came upon the churl a beautiful form and shapeliness and radiance, so that there was a delightful beauty upon him... and he had the demeanour of a high-king, and there was the charm of a youth in his figure.'

"We have connected the Music of the South with low-class entertainers, but this gives only one side of the picture. Time and again, both in the early literature and in folktales, sweet music is revealed to be one of the essential attributes of the Other World. Its sound often heralds the approach of the supernatural, and by means of it the *síd*-folk place men and women under enchantment.[372] Just as, in the story of the Sons of Míl, the learning of the North is set over against the music of the South, so the *Rig Veda* bears witness to the

---

371 See themes **T4b** (Music as magical restorative, of mental or physical health, from regions of evil, from regions of the dead), **T5** (Music as hypnotic force), **T5b** (Calming effect on persons suffering or undergoing spiritual turmoil, madness etc), *Introductory Remarks* (Vol I, above). See also Thompson motifs D1224 (Magic pipe) and D1364.25.3 (Pipe causes magic sleep), **FOLKLORE AND FOLKTALES — TYPOLOGY***, pp.282, 284 above. (Ed.)

372 See themes **T1a** (Music as magical means of communication with god[s] or supreme being[s]), **T3** (Making and enjoyment of music as characteristic or identifying feature of earthly or heavenly paradise, place of ultimate safety or security, eternal rest or peace, eternal life, fulfillment of all one's desires), **T4** (Music as magical means by which spirits or other supernatural beings or forces take possession of human or other victim), **T4b** (Music as instrument of enchantment), **T6a** (Music as herald of otherworldly or supernatural being), *Introductory Remarks*, Vol I above. (Ed.)

fundamental opposition of the brahmans and the *Gandharvas**—beings who dwell in a world apart and whose name is also used with reference to human musicians. In the *Satapatha Brahmana*, Words and Chant (*Rik* and *Saman*) are equated with Earth and Heaven, respectively, and in China* 'right behavior' (*Li*) and music are similarly contrasted: 'Music... is of the order of heaven, *Li*... is of the order of earth.... Music was made manifest in the genesis of all things, and *Li* has its abode in their completion.' It is a universal belief that words have a creative power; they symbolize the manifest world. Music, on the other hand, brings us into harmony with the non-manifest,[373] and 'to understand music is to be at the secret source of *Li*.' " — Rees and Rees, pp.100-101, 118, 122-25, 134-37.

§170.9 SOME BACKGROUND ON THE CELTIC GODS IN IRELAND; MENTION OF DAGDA AND THE HARP.[374] "Irish mythology is a great contrast to Greek mythology because the gods were not organized in early times by the poets into a great heavenly community like the gods of Olympus. They never live in the sky or on the mountain tops. They live individually either underground or on the earth, often across the seas or on distant islands.

"The ancient mythological stories of Ireland may be divided into four chief groups. We do not include here stories of local cults of springs and rivers and lakes, such as are prominent in Gaulish religion. These are not prominent as independent cults in Ireland, and occur chiefly — and not even very commonly — in connexion with important gods, such as the *Dagda* [Irish earth and father god (Ed.)] whose

home was Bruig na Bóinne, close to the Boyne.

"*Group 1* is of the older Celtic gods, who are known from early times in Gaul, and also, perhaps later, from Britain.

"*Group 2*, a much larger group, the native Irish gods of underground, whose homes are in the *síd*-mounds, the great barrows of the dead. This is the group of whom the majority of our most picturesque stories are told. They are by far the best known to modern scholars.

"*Group 3*, the gods of re-birth, also known from sources outside Ireland, and not originally, or at least obviously, associated with the *síd*-mounds, but with the sea.

"*Group 4*. Stories of the supernatural world — *Tír Tairngiri*, 'the land of Promise'; *Tír na nÓc*, 'the land of the Young'; *Mag Mell*; and stories of mortals who visit it. These are commonly referred to as *echtrai*, 'adventures' and *baili*, 'visions, ecstasies'.

"It is natural to suppose that the earliest gods are those who belonged originally to the ancient Celts of Gaul. Perhaps the chief was the god Lug* [Celtic hero god].... His name has survived in many place-names in Gaul and possibly Britain. Various stories have survived as to how he came to Ireland; but his foreign origin is recognized by early allusions, for he is said in one story to come from overseas, and he is referred to as a *scál balb*, a 'stammering spirit', doubtless with reference to his foreign tongue. In Wales his name is cognate with that of *Lleu Llaw Gyffes* who is a prominent hero in the *Mabinogi* of *Math fab Mathonwy*. But he has been integrated with the Irish pantheon, being claimed as the originator of the Fair of Teltown, held a fortnight before the Festival of Lugnasad on the first of August and a fortnight after it, resembling the Olympic games. He was fostered and trained by the wife of one of

---

373 See theme **T2** (The laws [structure] of music parallel the laws [structure] of nature or the universe), *Introductory Remarks*; also discussion of **MUSIC, MAGIC and MYTHOS**, §263C.1, below. (Ed.)

374 See also **HARP***, §137.12 above. (Ed.)

the *Tuatha Dé Danann* [tribes of the goddess Danann] till he was fit to bear arms....

"[LUG (Welsh *Llew*).] *Lugus* must have been a great Celtic god, but we do not know what his special character was. In Ireland he was the god of *Lugnasad*, 1 August, which was evidently a harvest festival, and Lug may have been the god of fertility....

"[The invading gods of Ireland, collectively called *Tuatha dé Danann*, made an alliance with the Fomoiri — beings that were half-human, half-monster, with one hand, one leg, and three rows of teeth, 'undersea phantoms'. The latter, in turn, staged a second great invasion and were defeated by their former allies, the *Tuatha Dé Danann*, in the second Battle of Moytura. Meanwhile Lug has arrived from overseas, to help the *Tuatha Dé Danann*. He is called 'Lug of all the arts' — *Samildánach* — and it is he who leads the *Tuatha* — it would seem to be identified now with the native peoples of Ireland — to victory.]

"During the battle Lug was heartening the men of Ireland, 'that they should fight the battle fervently so that they should not be any longer in bondage [to the Fomoiri]. For it was better for them to find death in protecting their fatherland than to bide under bondage and tribute as they had been'. The words of Lug still ring down through the ages. They might have been spoken yesterday. Then the Mórrígan[375] came and was heartening the *Tuatha Dé* to fight the battle fiercely and fervently, and the Fomoiri were beaten to the sea.

"Now Lug and the Dagda and Ogma [god of eloquence, inspiration and language] pursued the Fomoiri for they had carried off the Dagda's harper. When they reached the banqueting-hall of the Fomorian king Bres, there hung the harp on the wall. That is the harp on which the Dagda had sounded the melodies, so that they would only sing out by his command; and the harp left the wall and came to him. And he played to them three melodies — the wailing-strain, so that women wept; and the smile-strain, so that their women and children laughed; and the sleep-strain, so that the host fell asleep. And through that strain the three gods escaped unhurt from the murderous host of the Fomoiri. And after the battle was won the Mórrígan and Bodb [Irish goddess of battle] proclaimed the battle and the mighty victory which had taken place, to the royal heights of Ireland and to its *síd*-hosts, and its chief waters and its river mouths; and Bobd described the high deeds which had been done, and prophesied the degeneration of future years." — Dillon & Chadwick, pp.13, 142-43, 149.

§170.10 Arthur Cotterell (1989) retells the familiar story in the following way, laying particular stress on the figure of (the) Dagda: "**Dagda**, in Irish mythology the father of the gods. A kindly figure, his name means 'the good god'. He was portrayed as a fat man dressed in simple attire, dragging a gigantic club on wheels.

"Dagda was Ruad Ro-fhessa (lord of perfect knowledge), and was therefore patron of the druids. As Ollathair (all-father), he ruled over an already created world. The source of fertility, he sustained mankind but also apportioned death. He could kill nine men at a time with his club, but with the other end he restored them to life.

"Dagda had several typically Celtic* magical possessions, including a powerful harp*, two marvelous pigs, ever-laden fruit trees and an inexhausible cauldron which represented material abundance and the restoration of life. A parallel

---

375 Goddess of battle, 'Great Queen' — forerunner of the Arthurian Morgan le Fay, "an extremely unpleasant lady, hag-like and with a demonic laugh" — Carlyon, *A Guide to the Gods*. (Ed.)

cauldron was that of Annwyn, lord of the Welsh underworld.

"Dagda, the son of Dana, was the chief of the Tuatha De Danaan, 'the peoples of the goddess Dana', who were continually at war against the Fomorii, a race of evil beings. The Formorii once stole Dagda's harp and the god, together with his son Ogma, the god of eloquence, and Lugh, the sun god, set off in search of it. He found it in the dwelling-place of the Fomorii and, entering their great hall, demanded its return. Before the Fomorii could reply, the harp leapt from the wall, killed those who had put it there and then sang a tune so sad that it put all the Fomorii to sleep.

"Accounts of Dagda's actions on the battlefield are contradictory. At the first battle of Magh Tuireadh, 'the plain of towers', he slew countless numbers of the enemy, helped by the crowlike form of the war goddess Morrigan, who delighted in the terror of the fray.

"At the second battle of Magh Tuireadh, Dagda degenerated into an old man, burdened with excessive weight. Ignoring the battle, he busied himself with the contents of his cauldron which held 80 gallons of milk as well as goats, sheep and pigs. His ladle was so large that a man and woman could easily have slept in it."—Cotterell (Macmillan Myths and Legends), p.81.

JAPANESE MYTHS—PRACTICES AND BELIEFS. *(See p.426.)*

§177.11 "**AMIDA-NYORAI.** Of all the deities in the Japanese Buddhist pantheon 'the Buddha of Infinite Light' approaches closest to the West Asian and European idea of an exalted yet personal god. Amida-nyorai, the Japanese Amitabha [Indian Buddhist boddhisattva of 'infinite light', who represents the primordial, self-exis-

tent Buddha], is the great refuge that the devotte thinks of at the moment of death.

"Strictly speaking, Buddhism denies a permanent resting-place to the soul and teaches a perpetual process of change in an individual's moral character. But this continuity, the endless round of rebirth cause by *karma*, sin, has come to encompass in Mahayana tradition nuemrous realms of existence, from highest heavens to nethermost hells. Japanese mythology is full of details about the pilgrimage of the soul to and from these realms, and the spirits of those who hover between them, perhaps as Tengus [demonic spirits]. Most popular are the legends clustered round the Paradise of the Pure Land, Gokuraku Jodo, the realm of Amida-nyorai. This celestial abode has a lotus pond brimming with ambrosia groves of jewel-studded trees, on the branches of which perch marvellous birds and hang melodious bells, and above the Buddha and his saints circle angels, scattering petals on the gentle breeze."—Cotterell, pp.104-105.

§177.12 "**BENTEN.**[376] In Japanese folklore Saraswati, the Hindu river goddess, was transformed as Benten into the genius of music, the guardian of eloquence, and the giver of wealth. As a deity of good fortune she has been popular since the twelfth century, many local legends collecting about her and her shrines."—Cotterell, p.105.

§177.13 "**JIZO-BOSATSU.** Ti-tsang of China, Jizo of Japan—the bodhisattva Ksitigarbha—wanders eternally through the realms of hell, comforting tortured souls and rescuing them from darkness by his very presence.... He is usually depicted as a gentle-faced monk with a shaven head, dressed in a long robe and holding a staff with clattering rings on one end. The staff—originally called a khakkhara in India, on account of the khak sound it made—announces the otherwise silent

---

376 See also entry, p. 101 above. (Ed.)

mendicant as he walks along the street or comes with his begging-bowl for his daily meal. The Buddhist monk never asks for alms, nor does he acknowledge them. The only sound comes from the staff, which in the hands of Jizo-bosatsu is potent enough to disperse the powers of evil."[377] — Cotterell, pp.116-117.

§177.14 "KIYOHIME. The legendary murderess of a Japanese monk named Anchin, and a character in a No play. Overwhelmed with desire for the monk, Kiyohime [Kiohimé] chased Anchin into a Buddhist* temple, where he hid under a great bell. As she approached his hiding place, the wooden supports holding up the bell collapsed, trapping Anchin inside its wide body. At once Kiyohime turned from a young girl into a scaly monster, breathing fire. Her breath was so hot that the bell melted, burning Anchin and herself to death." — Cotterell (Macmillan Myths and Legends), p.213.[378]

§177.15 SHINTO SHRINES. Joseph Campbell has described impressions of a Shinto shrine in the following manner: "Such a place of worship is without images, simple in form, wonderfully roofed, and often painted a nice clear red. The priests, immaculate in white vesture, black headdress, and large black wooden shoes, move about in files with stately mien. An eerie music rises, reedy, curiously spirit-like, punctuated by controlled heavy and light drumbeats and great gongs; threaded with the plucked, harplike sounds of a spirit-summoning koto. And then noble, imposing, heavily garbed dancers silently appear, either masked or unmasked, male or female. These move in slow, somewhat dreamlike trancelike, shamanizing measure; stay for a time before the eyes,

and retire, while utterances are intoned. One is thrown back two thousand years. The pines, rocks, forests, mountains, air, and sea of Japan awake and send out spirits on those sounds. They can be heard and felt all about. And when the dancers have retired and the music has stopped, the ritual is done. One turns and looks again at the rocks, the pines, the air and sea, and they are as silent as before. Only now they are inhabited, and one is aware anew of the wonder of the universe." — Campbell [Masks/Oriental], p.475.

JEWISH FOLKTALES / FOLKLORE. *(See also p.449.)*

§182.2 "THE WONDROUS GIFTS AND THE WICKED OLD WOMAN [Moroccan Jewish Folktale]. [Once upon a time a spirit gave a poor old unmarried man a magic pot, which would fill up with whatever kind of food the old man wished of it. The old man entertained his friends and neighbors with many marvelous dishes. One day a poor old woman secretly robbed him however, replacing the magic pot with an ordinary one of her own. Then, when the old man knocked on the pot, nothing would happen. Enraged, he complained bitterly to the spirit, which gave him another. On command, this second pot would fill up — not only with food — but also with gold and silver. Once again, the old woman stole the wondrous pot. Once again, the old man lost his temper, and complained to the spirit.]

"The spirit began to plead with him. 'Twice I have given you a pot to enable you to live in comfort. But what can I do if it is stolen from you? Now listen to me: For the last time I am giving something to you. This time I shall not give you food or money, but an instrument that reveals

---

377 While a staff with clattering rings on one end is not precisely a musical instrument, this story has obvious affinities with the lore of bells and is consistent with the function of music as a dispeller (or summoner?) of evil. (Ed.)

378 For an alternate telling of this story, see BELLS* §40.10, pp.83-86 above. (Ed.)

thieves and restores what is stolen. But you must conduct yourself in keeping with my instructions. Invite your friends to your house for a party. Sit in a large circle. Then you will take this instrument out and place it in the centre of the circle. It will begin to dance, to jump up and down, until it will come down on the head of the man who stole the pots from you. That will be your sign. Then a negro will come out of the instrument and will strike the thief until he confesses and says: I am the thief! When the thief restores what he has stolen, your command can put an end to the blows.'

"The man went home and invited all his friends to a big party. He did not invite the old woman because he did not know her at all. They all sat in a large circle, while the old woman stood at a distance, outside the house. She was waiting for the party to end so that she could steal the new thing, too.

"The man put the instrument in the middle of the circle and addressed it: 'Do what you have to do!'

"The instrument began to dance and to sing. Suddenly it rose to the roof and made straight for the old woman, though she was far away. When the old man saw this he said to her: 'Grandmother, I should like you to sit here with us. Enjoy yourself together with us.'

"The old woman entered the room. The host seated her and said to the instrument: 'Do what you have to do!'

"Once again the instrument began to sing and to dance, until it leaped onto the head of the old woman again and again. The old man understood that it was the old woman who had stolen the pots from him, and that the spirit had spoken the truth. Immediately a negro armed with a stick came out of the instrument, forced her into the middle of the circle and began to beat her until she cried out: 'Enough! Enough! I will tell you everything!'

" 'Don't tell us anything but return what you have stolen from me,' said the old man. 'Only then will I put an end to the blows.'

"The old woman ran to her home. The negro was behind her all the time striking her, until she had brought the pots back to the old man. It was only then that the old man commanded the negro to stop.

"What did the old woman do next? She went to the king and told him: 'My lord the king! You are no longer king!'

"The king was astonished: 'What do you mean I am no longer king?'

" 'I will tell you what comes to pass in your country,' the old woman explained. 'You know nothing about it.'

" 'Tell me, grandmother.'

" 'In such and such a street there is such and such a house, in which an old man lives. He has things which belong to kings. I do not know where he has got them from. Perhaps he has stolen them. Perhaps they are the property of your family?'

"The king sent police to the house of the old man to bring him before the king. 'Bring me the two pots and the dancing instrument,' commanded the king. 'Also tell me where you got them.'

"The poor old man, escorted by two policemen, went to his home, took the three articles and gave them to the king. He himself was cast into prison.

"The king made use of the wondrous pots, and he had everything his heart desired. One day the king wished also to make use of the instrument, which began to dance until it came down on the head of the king. The king cried out for help and all the courtiers and all the men of his palace came to help but the negro kept on beating him, crying out all the time: 'You are not my master! You are not my master!' And the blows continued. The king sent a messenger to the prison to bring the old man to him. When the man came he asked him to stop the beating.

"When the beating stopped the old man told the king all about himself. How he had been poor and had not had anything to eat.... [and how he] had received precious gifts from the spirit, how they had been stolen from him by the wicked old woman, in short the whole story of his life.

"The king let the old man go and in his stead put the wicked old woman in prison."[379] — Noy, pp.37-39.

LAPP PRACTICES AND BELIEFS. *(See also p.498.)*

§214.5 "The Laplanders have a reputation for magical practice which is almost proverbial throughout Europe, and certainly so among the peoples of the Scandinavian peninsula. Indeed the Finns still [1920 (Ed.)] credit them with extraordinary power in sorcery and divination. Many Scandinavian scions of nobility were in ancient times sent to Lapland to obtain a magical reputation, and Eric the son of Harold Haarfager found Gunhild, daughter of Asur Tote, sojourning among the Lapps in AD 922 for that purpose. English literature abounds with reference to Lapland witches. But Sorcery in Lapland was a preserve of the male shamans or magicians. Like the Celtic witches the Lapps were addicted to the selling of wind or tempests in knotted ropes.

"Scheffer in his *Lapponia* (1674) writing of Lapp magic says: — 'The melancholic constitution of the Laplanders, renders them subject to frightful apparitions and dreams, which they look upon as infallible presages made to them by the Genius [apparently a sort of personal spirit guide — possibly related to Moslem *jinni* (pl. *jinn*), *jdinni* (pl. *djinn*), or *genie?* (Ed.)] of what is to befall them. Thus they are frequently seen lying upon the ground asleep, some singing with a full voice, others howling and making a hideous noise not unlike wolves....

" 'Lundius observes that some of the Laplanders are seized upon by a demon, when they are arrived to a middle age, in the following manner: — Whilst they are busie in the woods, the spirit appears to them, where they discourse concerning the conditions upon which the demon offers them his assistance, which done, he teaches them a certain song, which they are obliged to keep in constant remembrance. They must return the next day to the same place, where the same spirit appears to them again, and repeats the former song, in case he takes a fancy to the person; if not, he does not appear at all. These spirits make their appearances under different shapes, some like fishes, some like birds, others like a serpent or dragon, others in the shape of a pigmee, about a yard high; being attended by three, four, or five other pigmees of the same bigness, sometimes by more, but never exceeding nine. No sooner are they seized by the Genius, but they appear in the most surprising posture, like madmen, before bereaved of the use of reason. This continues for six months; during which time they don't suffer any of their kindred to come near them, not so much as their own wives and children. They spend most of this time in the woods and other solitary places, being very melancholy and thoughtful scarce taking any food, which makes them extremely weak. If you ask their children, where and how their parents sustain themselves, they will tell

---

379 This tale of life in a sorry land — which discriminates against women, and merely accepts (out of necessity, from the point of view of his subjects) the lordship of a greedy king — represents Aarne-Thompson Folktale Type 839*C and includes Thompson Folktale Motifs Q581.0.1, *Loss of life as a result of one's own treachery*, and R325.2, *Idol cracks open to grant refuge to fugitive in answer to prayer, then closes again*. See also **SINGING BONE***, p.719. (Ed.)

you, that they received their sustenance from the Genii....

" 'Whenever a Laplander has occasion for his familiar spirit, he calls to him, and makes him come by only singing the song he taught him at their first interview; by which means he has him at his service as often as he pleases.[380] And because they know them obsequious and serviceable, they call them *Sveie*, which signifies as much in their tongue, as the companions of their labour, or their helplates. Lundius has made another observation, very well worth taking notice of, viz.: — That those spirits or demons never appear to the women, or enter into their service, of which I don't pretend to allege the true cause, unless one might say, that perhaps they do it out of pride, or a natural aversion they have to the female sex, subject to so many infirmities.'[381]

"For the purpose of augury or divination the Lapps employed a magic drum*, which, indeed, was in use among several Arctic peoples. Writing in 1872, De Capell Brooke states that the ceremonies connected with this instrument had almost quite disappeared at that date. The encroachments of Lutheranism had been long threatening the existence of the native shamanism. In 1671 the Lapp drum was formally banned by Swedish law, and several magicians were apprehended and their instruments burnt. But before that date the religion which the drum represented was in full vigor. The Lapps called their drum *Kannus* (Regnard, 1681), also *Kaunus, Kabdas, Kabdes Gabdas,* and *Keure*

(Von Düben, 1873), its Scandinavian designations being *troll-trumma*, or *Rune-bomme*, 'magic or runic drum', otherwise *Spa-trumma*, 'fortune-telling drum'. J. A. Friis has shown that the *sampo* of the Finnish *Kalevala* * is the same instrument. According to Von Düben, the best pictures and explanations of the drum are to be found in Friis's *Lappish Mythologi* (Christiana, 1871), pp.30-47, but there are good descriptions in Von Düben's own work (*On Lapland och Lapparne*, Stockhold, 1873), as also in the books of Scheffer, Leem, Jessen, and others. The appearance of the Lapp drum is thus described by Regnard in 1681: — 'This instrument is made of a single piece of wood, hollowed in its thickest part in an oval form, the under part of which is convex, in which they make two apertures long enough to suffer the fingers to pass through, for the purpose of holding it more firmly. The upper part is covered with the skin of the reindeer, on which they paint in red a number of figures, and from whence several brass rings are seen hanging, and some pieces of the bone of the reindeer.' A wooden hammer, or, as among the Samoyeds (1614), a hare's foot was used as a drum-stick in the course of the incantation. An *arpa* or divining-rod was placed on a definite spot showing from its position after sounding the drum what magic inference might be drawn. By means of the drum, the priest could be placed *en rapport* with the spirit world, and was thus enabled to divine the future; to ascertain synchronous events occurring at remote distances; to forecast the measure

---

380 See our theme **T1a** (Music as magical means of communication with god[s] or supreme being[s]), *Introductory Remarks* Vol I above. (Ed.)

381 Or simply to buttress up their own power over women by fostering superstitions of this type; see also in this connection various Australian aboriginal* and African* customs and beliefs, and also e.g. those revolving around the Jurupari (see **INDIANS (SOUTH AMERICAN) MYTHS — PRACTICES AND BELIEFS***, §163.9-10 above — wherein freemasonry is also mentioned in this context). (Ed.)

of success attending the day's hunting; to heal the sick; or to inflict people with disease and cause death.[382] Although obsolete in Lapland these rites are still [1920] performed among the Samoyeds and other races of Arctic Asia and America.... The same practices can be traced eastward through Arctic America, and the drum is used in the same fashion by the Eskimo shaman priests in Greenland (Henry Rink's *Tales*, etc., 1875, 60-61). The shape of the drum varies a little according to locality. The shape of the Eskimo drum is that of a tambourine*.

" 'Their most valuable instrument of enchantment,' says Tornaeus, 'is this sorcerer's kettle-drum, which they call Kannas or Quobdas. They cut it in one entire piece out of a thick tree stem, the fibres of which run upwards in the same direction as the course of the sun. The drum is covered with the skin of an animal; and in the bottom holes are cut by which it may be held. Upon the skins are many figures painted, often Christ and the Apostles, with the heathen gods, Thor, Noorjunkar, and others jumbled together; the picture of the sun, shapes of animals, lands and waters, cities and roads, in short, all kinds of drawings according to their various uses. Upon the drum there is placed an indicator, which they call *Arpa*, which consists of a bundle of metallic rings. The drumstick is, generally, a reindeer's horn. This drum they preserve with the most vigilant care, and guard it especially from the touch of a woman. When they will make known what is taking place at a distance, — as to how the chase shall succeed, how business will answer, what result a sickness will have, what is necessary for the cure of it, and the like, they kneel down, and the sorcerer beats the drum; at first with light strokes, but as he proceeds, with ever louder stronger ones, round the index, either till this has moved in a direction or to a figure which he regards as the answer which he has sought, or till he himself falls into ecstasy, when he generally lays the kettle-drum on his head. Then he sings with a loud voice a song which they call *Joghe*, and the men and women who stand round sing songs, which they call *Daura*, in which the name of the place whence they desire information frequently occurs. The sorcerer lies in the ecstatic state for some time — frequently for many hours, apparently dead, with rigid features; sometimes with perspiration bursting out upon him. In the meantime the bystanders continue their incantations, which have for their object that the sleeper shall not lose any part of his vision from memory; at the same time they guard him carefully that nothing lilving may touch him — not even a fly. When he again awakes to consciousness, he relates his vision, answers the questions put to him, and gives unmistakable evidence of having seen distant and unknown things. The inquiry of the oracle does not always take place so solemnly and completely. In everyday matters as regards the chase, etc., the Lapp consults his drum without falling into the somnambulic crisis....

" 'The use which they make of their power of clairvoyance, and their magic arts, is, for the most part, good and innocent; that of curing sick men and animals; inquiring into far-off and future things, which in the confined spheres of their existence is important to them. There are instances, however, in which the magic art is turned to the injury of others.' " — Spence [Occultism], pp.246-48.

---

382 See our themes **T1b** (Music gives magical powers to musician [e.g. shaman, doctor, priest]) and **T2b** (Music has magical effect upon orderly process of nature), *Introductory Remarks* Vol I above. (Ed.)

LYRE. *(See also p.519.)*

§227.4 "A symbol of the harmonious union of the cosmic forces, a union which, in its chaotic aspect, is represented by a flock of sheep.[383] The seven strings of the lyre correspond to the seven planets. Timotheus of Miletus raised the number of strings to twelve (corresponding to the signs of the Zodiac). A serial development of a similar kind is that effected by Arnold Schoenberg in our day by giving the same value to chromatic notes as to the notes of the diatonic scale, creating in place of the old scale of seven notes, a new one of twelve. Schneider draws a parallel between the lyre and the fire, recalling that in the temple of Jerusalem (according to Exodus 38:2) there was an altar with horns 'overlaid with brass' on either side, and the smoke of sacrifice rose up between them. The lyre, similarly, produces its sounds through the horns forming the sides of its structure, and representing the relationship between earth and heaven.[384]" — Cirlot, p.195.

MAYAN MYTHS—PRACTICES AND BELIEFS. *(See also p.531.)*

§237.3 "AH PUCH. The Maya god of death. He was portrayed as a skeleton or a bloated corpse, adorned with bells. As Hunhau the chief of demons, he presided over the ninth and lowest of the underworlds, the horrible *mitnal*. In modern folklore he survives as Yum Cimil, 'lord of death', prowling the houses of the sick in his endless search for prey." — Cotterell, p.201.

MELANESIAN PRACTICES AND BELIEFS.

§240A.1 See **FLUTE*** (§112.16, Rituals of Manhood: Male Initiation in Papua New Guinea).

§240A.2 Among the **Melanesian Karavar people** of the Bismark Archipelago, songs and dances are performed by two classes of male masked figures, the "female" tubuan and "male" dukduk, at certain religious ceremonies.

"Some [of the dukduk-tubuan songs] are the gifts of spirits encountered by men of the Duke of York Islands during vigils in the deep bush. At that time they may be visited by bush spirits or ancestors who sometimes give them songs, patterns for new tubuans or dukduks [i.e. masks], and magic. The songs often refer to images from the fantasy experience itself. One, for instance, desribed a man becoming very small and hiding with a tiny bush spirit inside a vine." — Errington, pp.177-78.

MENNONITE PRACTICES AND BELIEFS.

§241A.1 "Among Pennsylvania Mennonites the belief was held that any musical aid (instrument) was known to cause a schism in a congregation. Scripture forbade the use of organs*." — Ferm, p.157.

MEXICAN FOLKTALES AND MYTHS.

§248A.1 See **AZTEC PRACTICES AND BELIEFS***.

---

383 See M. Mertens Stienon, *L'Occultisme du zodiaque* (Paris, 1939).

384 See Marius Schneider, *El origen musical de los animales-simbolos en la mitologia y la escultura antiguas* (Barcelona, 1946).

INDIAN (NORTH AMERI-CAN) MYTHS — PRAC-TICES AND BELIEFS* (§162.21 Huichol Indians).

§248A.2 "LITTLE SAINT MICHAEL. A man was going along a road toward Bochil. Suddenly he saw a *morral* [woven bag] lying on the ground. He went and picked up the bag to see what was in it and found three bottles of liquor inside. He uncorked one of the bottles and took a drink. Then he left the bag where it was and went on his way.

"He hadn't traveled far when he felt like drinking some more, so he came back to the *morral*. He took another drink, but then he decided to take the *morral* with him so he wouldn't have to come back again.

"When he got home he hung up the bag with the bottles on a hook. He was pretty drunk by then, so he lay down to sleep. About midnight he began to hear music and singing. He woke his wife up and asked her if she heard music and singing.

" 'You're crazy and drunk,' she told him, and she didn't stir out of bed.

"He kept hearing the music, and since it seemed to come from the *morral*, he took it down and hung it in another part of the room. Then he saw that it was from the *morral* that the singing and music came. He lighted the light and searched the *morral*, and found little Saint Michael inside. It was the saint who was singing and from whom the music came.

"This man died some time ago, and he left the image of the saint to his son, who lives in Soyaló. The owner of the image allows people to consult the saint; they take the little box out and take it wherever they wish, and it speaks to them." — Paredes, p.31.

Ed. note: Music is often used by man in order to communicate with the spirit world, to summon (good spirits) or expel (bad spirits), etc. See theme T1a (Music as magical means of communication with god[s] or supreme being[s]), *Introductory Remarks*, Vol I, above. Here, however, is a case where the reverse seems to be true — where the spirit world attempts to reach *us*, through music — for which see theme T1c (Music as medium through which spirit world [divinities, supranatural beings] attempts to signal or contact man).

§248A.3 **THE GREENISH BIRD.** A prince takes the form of a Greenish bird and, in that form, makes love to and falls in love with Luisa, a poor orphan girl. Mistreated by her sisters, he goes away. Distraught, Luisa searches for him, taking along her guitar. She visits the Sun and his mother, the Moon and hers, and the Wind and his. At last she finds her way to the prince's palace, where she finds him ill and leprous. He is soon to marry a princess who loves him, but, he still loves Luisa. Luisa sings to him, and plays on her guitar. This helps him to get well. The prince announces that he will marry whosever's cup of chocolate he drinks — and drinks the chocolate that Luisa has made.[385] — See Paredes, pp.95-102.

MINSTREL (THE).

§249A.1 "The first enigma of the Tarot pack, this figure of a minstrel is a symbol of the original activity and the creative power of Man. He is depicted on the Tarot card wearing a hat in the form of a horizontal eight (the mathematical sign for infinity); he holds up a magic wand ('clubs') in one hand, and the other three symbols of the card-pack are on the table facing him; these are the equivalent of diamonds, spades

---

385 See Thompson Folktale Motifs D1234 (Magic guitar), D1500.1.24 (Magic healing song), and E55.5 (Resuscitation by playing guitar). (Ed.)

and hearts, which, together with the wand ('clubs'), correspond to the four Elements (as well as the points of the compass). These attributes symbolize mastery over a given situation. The minstrel's garb is multi-coloured, but the predominant colour is red—denoting activity. In its transcendental implications, the enigma is related to Mercury.[386]." — Cirlot, pp.210.

MITHRAIC PRACTICES AND BELIEFS.

§250A.1 *The Mysteries of Mithra—Mithraic Liturgy.*[387] "The role of the clergy was certainly more extensive than in the ancient Greek and Roman religions. The priest was the intermediary between God and man. His functions evidently included the administration of the sacraments and the celebration of the services. The inscriptions tell us that in addition he presided at the formal dedications, or at least represented the faithful one on such an occasion along with the Fathers; but this was the least portion only of the duties he had to perform; the religious service which fell to his lot appears to have been very exacting. He doubtless was compelled to see that a perpetual fire burned upon the altars. Three times a day, at dawn, at noon, and at dusk, he addressed a prayer to the Sun, turning in the morning toward the East, at noon toward the South, at evening toward the West. The daily liturgy frequently embraced special sacrifices. The celebrant, garbed in sacerdotal robes resembling those of the Magi, sacrificed to the higher and lower gods divers victims, the blood of which was collected in a trench; or offered them libations, holding in his hands the bundle of sacred twigs which we know from the Avesta. Long psalmodies and chants accompanied with music were interspersed among the ritual acts. A solemn moment in the service, — one very probably marked by the sounding of a bell*, — was that in which the image of the tauroctonous [word having to do with 'bull'? (Ed.)] Mithra, hitherto kept veiled, was uncovered before the eyes of the initiates. In some temples, the sculptured slab, like our tabernacles, revolved on a pivot, and alternately concealed and exposed the figures that adorned its two faces. Each day in the week, the Planet to which the day was sacred was invoked in a fixed spot in the crypt; and Sunday, over which the Sun presided, was especially holy.[388]" — Cumont, pp. 165-67.

---

386 See Oswald Wirth, *Le Tarot des imagiers du Moyen Age* (Paris, 1927).

387 "Mithraism: an oriental mystery cult incorporating elements from Zoroastrianism*, the primitive religions of Asia Minor, and Hellenism, having as its deity Mithras [or Mithra], the saviour hero of Persian myth, admitting only men to its seven degrees of initiation, and constituting a serious rival of Christianity in the Roman Empire between the second and fourth centuries AD." — *Webster's Third New International Dictionary.*

388 I will conjecture that the employment of music (including bell) may have served the purpose not only of intending to establish communication with divine, sacred or spiritual beings, but also of empowering the communicants in some fashion; see our themes T1a (Music as magical means of communication with god[s] or supreme being[s]) and T1b (Music gives magical power to musician [e.g. shaman, doctor, priest] partly as a result of being in communication with gods or members of spirit world), *Introductory Remarks* (Vol I, above). (Ed.)

MUSIC—SYMBOLISM.

§260A.1 See **HARMONY (HARMONIA) OF THE SPHERES***.

§260A. 2 "The symbolism of music is of the greatest complexity and we cannot here do more than sketch out some general ideas. It pervades all the component elements of created sound: instruments, rhythm, tone or timbre, the notes of the natural scale, serial patterns, expressive devices, melodies, harmonies and forms. The symbolism of music may be approached from two basic standpoints: either by regarding it as part of the ordered pattern of the cosmos as understood by ancient, megalithic and astrobiological cultures, or else by accepting it as a phenomenon of 'correspondence' linked with the business of expression and communication. Another of the fundamental aspects of music-symbolism is its connexion with metre and with number*, arising out of the Pythagorean theory.[389] The cosmic significance of musical instruments—their allegiance to one particular Element—was first studied by Curt Sachs in *Geist und Werden der Musikinstrumente* (Berlin, 1929). In this symbolism, the characteristic shape of an instrument must be distinguished from the timbre, and there are some common 'contradictions' between these two aspects which might possibly be of significance as an expression of the mediating role of musical instruments and of music as a whole (for an instrument is a form of relationship or communication, substantially dynamic, as in the case of the voice or the spoken word), For example, the flute* is phallic and masculine in shape and feminine in its shrill pitch and light, silvery (and therefore lunar) tone, while the drum* is feminine by virtue of its receptacle-like shape, yet masculine in its deep tones.[390] The connexion of music-symbolism with self-expression (and even with graphic art) is well in evidence in primitive music-making, which often amounted to almost literal imitations of the rhythms and movements, the features and even the shapes of animals. Schneider describes how, hearing some Senegalese singing the 'Song of the Stork', he began to 'see as he was listening', for the rhythm corresponded exactly to the movements of the bird. When he asked the singers about this, their reply confirmed his observation. Given the laws of analogy, we can also find cases of the expressive transferred to the symbolic: that is, a melodic progression as a whole expresses certain coherent emotions, and this progression corresponds to certain coherent, symbolic forms. On the other hand, alternating deep and high-pitched tones express a 'leap', anguish and the need for Inversion; Schneider concludes that this is an expression of the idea of conquering the space between the valley and the mountain (corresponding to the earth and the sky). He observes that in Europe the mystic designation of 'high music' (that is, high-pitched) and 'low music' (low-pitched) persisted right up to the Renaissance. The question of relating musical notes to colours or to planets is far from being as certain as other symbolic correspondencs of music. Nevertheless, we cannot pass on without giving some idea of the profound, serial relationship which exists in phenomena: for instance, corresponding to the pentatonic scale we usually find patterns grouped in fives; the diatonic and model scale, since it has seven notes, is related to most of the asstrobiological systems, and is unquestionably the most important of all the series; the present-day tendency towards

---

389 See René Guénon, *L'Esotérisme de Dante* (Paris, 1949).
390 See Marius Schneider, *El origen musical de los animales-simbolos en la mitologia y la escultura antiguas* (Barcelona, 1946).

the twelve-note series could be compared to the signs of the Zodiac. But, so far, we have not found sufficient evidence for this particular facet of music-symbolism. All the same, here are the correspondences as set down by Fabre d'Olivet, the French occultist: Mi—the Sun, fa- Mercury, sol—Venus, la—the Moon, ti—Saturn, do—Jupiter, re—Mars.[391] A more valid series of relationships, at least in the expresssive aspect, is that which links the Greek modes with the planets and with particular aspects of the *ethos,* as follows: the mi-mode (the Dorian)—Mars (who is severe or pathetic); the re-mode (the Phrygian)—Jupiter (ecstatic); the do-mode (the Lydian)—Saturn (pained and sad); the ti-mode (the Hypodorian)—the Sun (enthusiastic); the la-mode (the Hypophrygian)—Mercury (active); the sol-mode (the Hypolydian)—Venus (erotic); the fa-mode (the Mixolydian)—the Moon (melancholy).[392] Schneider's profound investigations into the symbolism of music seem to us well-founded. The tetrachord formed by the notes do, re, mi, fa, he considers, for instance, to be a mediator between heaven and earth, the four notes corresponding respectively to the lion (signifying valour and strength), the ox (sacrifice and duty), man (faith and incarnation) and the eagle (elevation and prayer).[393] Conversely, the tetrachord formed by sol, la, ti, do, could represent a kind of divine duplicate of the previous tetrachord. Fa, do, sol, re are regarded as

masculine elements corresponding to the Elements of fire and air and to the instruments of stone and metal, whereas la, mi, ti, are feminine, and pertain to the Elements of water and earth. The intervals fa-ti, known to musicologists as a tritone (or augmented fourth), expresses with its dissonance the 'painful' clash between the Elements of fire and water—a clash occurring in death itself.[394] We have been able to suggest here only a few outlines of the music-symbolism developed by Schneider in his work *The Musical Origin of Animal-Symbols,* the scope of which is so wide that, as he has privately intimated to us, he believes all symbolic meanings are at root musical or at least have to do with sounds. This becomes easier to understand when we recall that singing, as the harmonization of successive, melodic elements, is an image of the natural connexion between all things, and, at the same time, the communication, the spreading and the exaltation of the inner relationship linking all things together. Hence Plato's remark that the character of a nation's music cannot be altered without changing the customs and institutions of the State.[395]"—Cirlot, pp.223-225.

MUSIC AND MYTHOLOGY.
(See also p.555.)

§261.2 "Italy is the motherlode of ancient pre-historical myths and the living source of new myths, born and taking shape in

---

391 See René Guénon, *Man and His Becoming according to the Vedanta* (London, 1945).

392 See Schneider, *El origen musical de los animales-simbolos.*

393 At this point, two principal themes of the present work may be mentioned: that the *meanings* of music lie in the functions it performs in a given context or situation (for which see *Introductory Remarks,* above); and that in a religious or mythological context, music typically functions as a mediation between man and the divine, or between aspects of a culture (civilization) and of pre-cultural "nature". "Symbolism", itself, is perhaps essentially a rendering of one term or concept by some other, without (therefore) any essential change in the *meanings* or the *functions,* at least, of the original which is thus being symbolized. (Ed.)

394 Schneider, *op. cit.*

395 See Guénon, *Man and His Becoming according to the Vedanta.*

our historical age of reason. The ancient legends of gods and heroes, of Diana and Aeneas who arrived mysteriously from ancient lands to sanction the sacredness of Rome, are still alive among the precious archaeological finds of ancient Tusculum. Now as then humans celebrate their rituals. Cristopher Columbus, the fabled navigator from Genoa and a mythical figure for our time, is honored from the Mediterranean to the Atlantic and Pacific Oceans.

"The esoteric and mysterious archetype of the Voyage emerges again, as it always does, in the Man of Destiny, whether he is ancient or modern, Aeneas or Columbus. It is an eternal odyssey that constantly renews itself, from Homer's Ulysses who disappeared beyond the Pillars of Hercules, to the burning flame that roves in Dante's hell, and to Joyce's Dublin wanderer. The voyager expresses a primordial human need, a faustian desire to know. It is the need to discover the mystery of new realities outside of ourselves, as well as the meaning of ancient and precious values secretly guarded in our souls....

"The end of the ancient world marked the birth of 'historical time'. *Myth*, reduced to naive fable, was substituted [for] by *logos*, the sacrilegious analytical thought. However, the historical world, through the *logos*, cyclically recreates *myth* and gives birth to new archetypes.

"There are two different aspects to our discourse. In the cycles of time myth always wins — albeit with different contents and forms — and the fascination for the primordial mystery renews itself. Our ability to know is enriched by the process through which certain and objective realities are brought back into the realm of the spirit and sublimated into new archetypes. From the deep and mysterious levels of the spirit will emerge the archetypal world created by the accumulation of human experience. Through the connections linking new myths to old ones we will find the universal archetypes that are at the core of Frazer's theory.[396]

"Creation — death — rebith. Music is the eliciting factor of this constantly self-reproducing process that involves both the macrocosm and the microcosm. The 'cry' and the 'sound', in their meaning of primary musical substances as suggested by oriental cosmogonies, are the counterparts of the Biblical saying 'In the beginning was the word.' Music is at the origin of the world, and sounds, according to the leading music historian Franco Abbiati, are the synthesis of concepts and of spiritual operations. They are the connecting elements between the limits of life and the unlimited world of the divine.

---

396 [In *The Golden Bough,* Sir James] Frazer demonstrates fascinating similarities among many distant and disparate cultures. These similarities give rise to the concept of 'archetypes' and have continued to play a major interpretive role throughout history.]

"Elmire Zolla says that the world was created by Death singing the song of death. Music has therefore an initiation role. Each musical tone corresponds to a star, a moment of the year, a sector of nature, a part of the human body. In the story of the king-priest of Nemi [perpetually slain by his successor as recounted in *The Golden Bough*], the wandering at night and the deadly challenge are accompanied by music. The dying king, a mortal as an individual but eternal as the incarnation of the Word of the Spirit of Life, must go back to the origins and pass through the initiation rituals. The first phase corresponds to the labyrinth of the forest in the darkness of night, the second to the violence of the fight, and the third to the transferral — through death — of the spirit of the tree, of fertility and life, to the new king-priest."[397] — Siniscalchi, pp.64-67.

MUSIC AND RELIGION.

§263A.1 See **CHRISTIAN PRACTICES AND BELIEFS***.
DANCE AND RELIGION*.
HINDU PRACTICES AND BELIEFS*.
ISLAMIC PRACTICES AND BELIEFS*.
JEWISH PRACTICES AND BELIEFS*.
MUSIC AND MYTHOLOGY*.
MUSIC AS AN APPROACH TO GOD (Christian)*.

ORIGINS OF MUSIC*.

§263A.2 "There are few religions in which music has played no part at all. On the surface there is all the difference in the world between the music of an African tribal ritual, for instance, and Bach's *St. Matthew Passion*, but beneath the differences there is the fundamental resemblance that music is being used to help express and heighten the content of ritual action of some kind. Music is part of the universal language of ritual, and without it ritual must always be impoverished. Remove the musical content from the average Christian act of worship and most members of the congregation would feel deprived of something essential.

"Even in those cases where music has no immediate connection with the ritual act, it is common to find people claiming to derive 'spiritual sustenance' from music of all kinds — from pop to Pergolesi, from Bach to beat. Music, then, can become an emotional substitute for ritual....

"Music is one of several elements in cult or ritual, for it is in the context of ritual that 'religious music' has found, and still finds, it main areas of expression. First there is purely physical movement and action, with the dance* as its most important aspect. Probably imitative in its earliest forms, the dance came to include a vast range of symbolic actions, no doubt partly magical in intention. For instance, by dancing in such a way as to imitate the movements of an animal which was to be hunted, the dancer 'became' for magical

397 [Whatever slave] was able to take a branch of mistletoe [from the oak tree in the Sacred Grove by Lake Nemi] — called *Golden Bough* because the leaves of the plant, during a certain season of the year, turned a golden yellow — became the *Rex Nemorensis*. However, in order to become the new *Rex*, he had to kill his predecssor. In turn, the new *Rex* would be killed by another stronger and younger slave holding a branch of mistletoe. The oak-tree appears in the great Judeo-Christian and Moslem traditions. It is present in Medieval science as the life-giving tree out of whose roots spring the waters of the alchemical fountain. It exists in the Scandinavian mythology as the 'Tree of the World' — the Yggdrasill oak-tree that has come down to us through the custom of the Christmas tree.

purposes the animal in question; the symbolical hunt culminated in the 'killing' of the individual. The action itself was such as to remove the partcipants from the limitations of the everyday world, and to establish them temporarily on the 'other side' among the powerful supernaturals.

"The second element begins with the rhymical movement of the dance. The rhythm of the dance, which in primitive societies often has directly sexual connotations, particularly where fertility rites are involved, is 'accompanied' at first by means of hand-clapping, stamping and the beating of improvised percussion instruments. Improvisation passes into more deliberate acocmpaniment, usually by the drum*, probably the most widespread of all ritual instruments. Examples of 'sacred' drums are found all over the primitive world. Among the best-known are those of the shamans of northern Europe, Asia and North America, indispensable items of equipment, for by them the spirits were called, and in them they were gathered.

"A further stage is reached when the voice is brought into play. The participant may strain his or her voice to imitate animal noises, or to pass outside the normal range of vocal expression. This, too, could be thought of as a potentially or actually sacred act, forming a link with the all-powerful spirit world. A particularly gifted performer would assume the role of leader, and the remainder would respond, usually by simply repeating the short phrases first announced by him. The dance, then, leads naturally into a simple form of music, with heavily accentuated rhythms but little or no harmony, and very simple and short melodies. Both together combine to provide a setting for a magically effective ritual which breaks the bounds of the everyday and normal....

"Dance and rhythmical melody are two aspects of religious music. The third is verbal and conceptual: to dance and music is added the holy word. As man began to live in more permanent settlements, music tended to become less spontaneous and

more elaborate. This was largely because of its use in connection with sacred texts such as hymns and prayers which were used in temples and other holy places. The development of writing rendered these more permanent. It is a curious fact, incidentally, that many of the holy scriptures of the ancient world were composed in verse forms rather than in prose, and it is known that these were originally chanted in order to heighten their sacred quality. In ancient Mesopotamia, Egypt, India and elsewhere, holy places were commonly provided with a complement of musicians and dancers, whose task was to praise and give pleasure to the gods, and to enrich the various daily and seasonal cycles of worship." — Sharpe, in Cavendish [Man, Myth and Magic], pp.1910-11.

§263A.3 From Ter Ellingson essay in Mircea Eliade (Editor in Chief), *The Encyclopedia of Religion* (1987).

"Music and religion are closely linked in relationships as complex, diverse, and difficult to define as either term in itself. Religious believers have heard music as the voices of gods and the cacophony of devils, praised it as the purest form of spirituality, and condemned it as the ultimate in sensual depravity; with equal enthusiasm they have promoted its use in worship and sought to eradicate it from both religious and secular life. Seldom a neutral phenomenon, music has a high positive or negative value that reflects its near-universal importance in the religious sphere. This importance — perhaps difficult to appreciate for post-industrial-revolution Westerners accustomed to reducing music to the secondary realms of 'art', 'entertainment', and occasionally 'religious' music isolated behind sanctuary walls — has nonetheless been pervasive.

"Religious 'texts' have been sung, not written, throughout most of human history; and religious behavior has found musical articulation in almost every religious tradition. Navajo priests are 'singers'; the primary carriers of Sinhala traditional religion are drummers and dancers; and the shamans of northern Eurasia and Inner Asia use music as their principal medium of contact with the spirit world. Through the centuries, priests, monks, and other specialists have sung the Christian masses, Buddhist *pujas*, Islamic calls to prayer, Hindu sacrifices, and other ceremonies that form the basis of organized religious observances in the world's major religions.

"The values, uses, and forms of religious music are as diverse and culture-specific as the religious traditions in which they are found. Christian liturgical music is generally as characteristically 'European' as Hindu devotional music is 'Indian'; both use sounds, forms, and instruments from the respective cultures and have contributed greatly to the overall musical life of their own regions. Yet music, like religion, can transcend cultural limits; the religious musical systems of Ethiopia and Tibet, for example, differ almost as greatly from the secular musics of their own respective cultures as the musics of foreign countries.

"Religious musical systems may also extend across cultural boundaries. Islam, for example, has forged musical links across vast regions of Asia and Africa; and North American traditions such as the Ghost Dance and the peyote cult have created musical bridges between very diverse ethnic groups. Other well-known intercultural religious musical traditions include Jewish, Christian, Hindu, Buddhist, and West African/Latin American possession music. Additional cases may include (1) the drumming and singing of Asian shamans, perhaps constituting a related tradition stretching from Scandinavia to the Himalayas, and possibly even extending into the Americas; (2) the epic songs, based on improvisatory recombinations of traditional song segments, of Central Asia and eastern Europe; (3) the bronze gong ensembles, associated with cosmological and calendrical symbolism and functions, of Southeast Asia; (4) perhaps the ancient sacrificial chants, linked to modal systems built on tetrachrods, of Indo-European poeples extending from India to Greece; and (5) conceivably an even wider connection between Chinese, Indian, and Greek conceptions of music as an embodiment of universal cosmological and mathematical laws.

"Yet, second only to its universal occurrence, diversity is the most characteristic feature of religious music, even in the great intercultural traditions. Christian music, for example, includes not only Gregorian plainsong, Palestrina masses, Protestant hymns, and Bach oratorios but also the resonant basses of the Russian orthodox choir, the ornate melodies of Greek orthodox chant, and the percussion-accompanied dances of Ethiopian Coptic worship; in the postcolonial era, it encompasses West African rhythms, and metallic sonorities of the Javanese *gamelan* orchestra, and the driving beat and electronic tones of the rock band as well. Hindu music aimed at helping to achieve the meditative state of *samadhi* can employ the very non-Indian sounds of Indonesian bronze instruments....

"**Definitions and concepts.** Given the close links between musical and religious concepts, a nonsectarian definition of music may be impossible. For example, one common definition of music as 'humanly patterned sound' conflicts with widely held religious beliefs that music is not humanly, but rather, divinely patterned. To members of traditions holding that music or, at least, religious music originates with the gods or with devils, the assertion of the human origin of music must seem the ultimate in Western materialistic dogmatism, however scientifically neutral it may seem to the outsider.

"Even definitions as simple as the dictionary staple 'art of sounds' carry ethnocentric and sectarian implications. In many religious contexts, music is less an expressive 'art' than a technology applied to produce practical results, from the storage and retrieval of information contained in religious narratives and teachings memorized in song to the attraction of animals in hunting, increase of harvests, curing of diseases, communication with the divine, supplication, and control of the various levels of psychocosmic experience. While aesthetic beauty may or may not be integral to such technologies, individual self-expression plays little part in them and may be detrimental to their intended results.

"The concept of music as an 'art' carries overtones of a late European ideology based on the sanctity of self-expression and individualism, ultimately rooted in Greek and Judeo-Christian notions of ego, self, and soul. For some traditions, music is antithetical to the very notion of an individual self or soul. One group of Buddhist texts takes music as the archetypal embodiment of impermanence and conditioned causality, dependent on external sources and conditions, in order to show that there can be no such thing as an individual self. By contrast, modern Western scholars tend to view music, at least in its ideally purest forms, as fundamentally independent of external causes and conditions; they draw a sharp line between 'extramusical' elements such as symbolism, function, purpose, and so forth, and 'the music itself', which is supposed to consist of pure arrangements of tones. This concept of music seems to reflect European post-Renaissance religious concepts of an autonomous and inviolable soul wholly contained in the body of the individual. Perhaps it also reflects postfeudal economic concepts of individual entrepreneurial freedom, just as the Buddhist concept of an impermanent music resulting from temporary combinations of causes and conditions reflects basic Buddhist religious beliefs.

"Even sound may not play a decisive role in religious concepts of music, at least not in any technical sense. When fundamentalist Muslims ban recordings of Western popular music and fundamentalist Christians burn them, they are not necessarily reacting to the melodic or chordal structures that constitute the essence of music for the technically oriented outsider. The 'music of the spheres' extolled by early Christian writers was not sound in the sense of physical waves propagated in a gaseous medium; and, in Tibetan Buddhist thought, music consists of both the 'actually present music' produced by sound-making voices and instruments and the 'mentally produced music' perceived and imagined by each listener, with different results according to individual differences in experience, skill, and imagination. Religious traditions have by and large no more conceived music to consist of sounds and the 'extramusical' than they have considered persons to be made up of the physical body and the 'extrapersonal'. Hence, even the most basic technical definition of music will ignore or deny essential aspects of music as conceived by many religions, while labels such as 'symbolism' applied to nonacoustic aspects may appear misguided or even hostile from a believer's perspective.

"The very attempt to define music neutrally and openmindedly might be objectionable from some religious viewpoints. For certain Christians, some kinds of secular music and the musics of other religions are the works of the devil and should not be mentioned without condemnation; on the other hand, for the Mahayana Buddhist author Sa-skya Pandita, all music deserves praise because it relieves human suffering. Some Muslims would object to a discussion of Qur'anic vocalizations and other songs under the same heading and would assign negative connotations to music in general; but some Sufi writers discuss music only in terms of highest praise for its capacity to lead to spiritual fulfillment, and they would consider a neutral approach as evidence of a lack of real understanding or appreciation of music's most important meanings and values.

"Many religions and cultures do not have a concept corresponding to 'music' or 'religious music'. For Islam, *al-musiqi* ('music') is, in principle, what the West might consider secular music, controversial for its potential to mislead believers into sensual distractions; melodic vocalizations of the Qur'an and certain religious poetry are not 'music', however musical they may seem on technical and aesthetic grounds. To avoid violating the integrity of a tradition by imposing a dissonant external viewpoint, it might help to consider all such cases of performances that sound musical to the outsider, but are not music to the insider, as 'paramusical'.

"Cultures as diverse as those of Ethiopia and modern Tibet have distinct terms and concepts for religious and secular music, with no common category of 'music' to unite them. The music of the Chinese *ch'in* (a type of zither), on the other hand, is clearly conceived as music and has strong roots in Confucian and Taoist concepts and practices; but it certainly is not 'religious' in the same sense as the singing of monks in Buddhist or Taoist temples. And, although the point lends itself all too easily to distortion and romanticism, it is a well-known fact that in many small-scale kinship-based societies of hunters, nomads, and subsistence farmers, where formal role distinctions are much less prominent than in bureaucratized state civilizations, it is often as difficult to draw a clear line between 'sacred' and 'secular' musics as it is between religion and everyday life. Are Pgymy honey-gathering songs part of a traditional ritual, a comic entertainment, a social regulatory system designed to ensure and enhance egalitarian universal participation in community life, or an aesthetically exquisite polyphonic art? The question, if not meaningless, is at least inelegant.

"Musics, like religions, are most meaningfully defined in their own terms. Along with aspects of musical sounds and their structural relationships, religious definitions frequently take into consideration such factors as cosmological and mathematical laws, divine origin or inspiration, psychological and emotional effects, social and ethical implications, relations or contrasts between religious and secular musics, and a wide range of other elements....

"**Origins, Myths, and Symbolism.** The close relationship of music and religion may imply, as some myths and legends claim, a common or related origin. From the eighteenth to the early twentieth century, evolution-oriented scholars debated theories of musical origins in the sounds of birds and animals, emotional cries of grief at funerals, language intonations, stylized recitations of religious texts, and animistic awe of 'voices' heard in natural objects such as shells and bamboo tubes, and so forth. All such theories proving no less speculative and resistant to objective investigation than the traditional myths they were meant to replace, the issue gradually lost scientific interest, and it is now all but ignored in musical research. But, as if in discouragement at having failed to construct their own myth of musical origins, scholars also made little effort to explore the origin question in its traditional context of religious mythology; and today we still find ourselves in the 'surprising' position of finding, as did Alan P. Merriam (1964), 'that there seem to be almost no available accounts of beliefs concerning the ultimate origin of music'.

"Accessible information, while insufficient to allow for generalization or systematic analysis, is abundant enough to show that music is as diverse in myths of origin as in any other of its aspects. Music may be thought to originate in a primordial divine power, as in the *nada-brahman* 'God-as-sound' of Hinduism, or in the efforts and discoveries of such human originators as Jubal* and his father Lamech, briefly mentioned in Jewish and Islamic traditions (see Genesis 4:21), or Fu-Hsi and Huang-ti, in Chinese legend the discoverers of music and its mathematical-cosmological basis. Music may also play a cosmogonic role in the origin or maintenance of the world, as in the drum-playing and cosmic dance of the Hindu god Siva Nataraja [Shiva* (Ed.)] or in widespread stories of gods who 'sing' their creations and creatures into existence.

"The creation of individual pieces of music and musical instruments may involve contact with the divine. In the vision quest of the Plains Indians,[398] individuals would go out alone into the wilderness to fast and seek divine messages revealed in songs, which they would then bring back to enhance the religious and musical life of the community. The Asian shaman's[399] quest for a drum may take him to the center of the world and the beginning of time, just as the Australian Aborigine's* dreaming of songs may provide a link to the primordial Dreaming. Musical creation may even move in the opposite direction, from the human world to the divine, as in the case of the Tibetan composer Mi-la-ras-pa (1040-1123), whose songs are said to have been 'imported' to heaven by the Mikha'-'gro-ma goddesses who, like their counterparts in other religions, fill the Tibetan Buddhist heavens with their music.

"The idea that music originally belonged to 'other' places, times, persons, or beings is found in many myths, sometimes with connotations of conflict and conquest, as in the South American and Melanesian legends of male theft of sacred flutes from the women who originally possessed them. However, the discovery or creation of music is more often a joyful or ecstatic experience, as in the many vocal and instrumental pieces and religious dances of Tantric Buddhism experienced in dreams and meditations as celestial performances and then recomposed by the meditator for performance in the human world. Handel's often-quoted account of seeing God and the angels while composing the 'Hallelujah' chorus—to say nothing of the religious experiences the chorus continues to evoke for many of its performers—may indicate the viability of such concepts even in cultures that favor ideas of human composition of music over divine creation and that tend to conceptualize musical 'inspiration' in more secular terms.

"Specific beliefs in music coming to us from other realms and beings may be a special case of a more general belief in the otherness, the special or extraordinary nature, of music in human experience. Such beliefs are seldom rooted in simple perceptions of music as strange and alien but rather seem based on recognition of the beauty and power of music. Thus, even when some traditions condemn music, they are condemning aspects of it that other traditions find worthy of praise: music exerts a strong appeal on humans, spirits, or gods; it stimulates sensual, bodily, and mental involvement, and so on. Does the power of music come from physical sensations of breath, motion, and vibration, from cognitions of proportion and symmetry as unexpected and serendipitous in the auditory realm as geometric arrays in nature, from socially and culturally conditioned associations? Is there one explanation, or are there separate causes for different kinds of musics and experiences? Whatever the answer, music enhances, intensifies, and—in ways that may elude precise analysis and control but which are nevertheless apparent both to participants and observers—transforms almost any experience into something felt not only as

---

398 See INDIAN (NORTH AMERICAN) MYTHS—PRACTICES AND BELIEFS*. (Ed.)

399 See SHAMAN(S), SHAMANISM* for cross-references. (Ed.)

different but also as somehow better. In this transformative power, music resembles religion itself; and when the energies of music and religion are focused on the same object in an isofunctional adaptation of both toward a common meaning and goal,[400] intensification reaches a peak greater perhaps than either might achieve by itself. Thus, the 'otherness' of music and the 'other' levels of reality and beings encountered in religion merge into a heightened synthesis of religious-musical experience. The possibility of such a synthesis may help to explain the aspect of music in religion that we usually call symbolism.

"Symbolism is a problematic concept for both religion and music. Like the gods and spirits who remain invisible to an outside observer or to a camera, music's religious meanings and functional effects that elude capture by microphones and tape recorders may strike the uninitiated outsider as pure symbolism and yet be at least as real as its physical sounds to the aware and sensitive insider. For the Aztec, songs were flowers, birds, pictures, and the spirits of dead warriors called back to earth (Bierhorst, 1985); we ourselves would probably find it easier to agree that a song 'is' a picture than that a song *is*, rather than *symbolizes*, a spirit. And if we adopt the kind of viewpoint that reduces the symbolic relationship between symbol and meaning to questions of physical-intangible and real-unreal, thus disposing of the spirits,

we still have not decided whether songs are symbols of flowers or vice versa. One senses that either choice is equally arbitrary; but if both are admissible as the real basis of the symbol, then why not the spirits as well?[401]

"Even if we take musical symbolism as a comparative and technical question of meanings attributed to sounds and forms, there are further questions of how so abstract and nondiscursive a medium can symbolize effectively, other than by purely arbitrary association, in the absence of explicit content that would lend itself to unambiguous communication. Some hear the diabolical in sounds that others find sacred; cross-cultural searches for even the most general aggreement on music's cognitive or emotional significance have been unrewarding. There even seems to be a contradiction in the attempt to encode or decipher symbolic meanings in music: its aesthetic power seems to rely on the manipulation of abstract forms, however defined by a given culture and style, to the extent that subjecting form to an externally imposed system of meanings and functions might imply conflicts of purpose and musically inferior results.

"Yet, if a symbol is that which stands for and reveals something other than itself, then music throughout the world has been accepted as successfully symbolizing the 'other' of religion. Part of its success must derive from its generally perceived qualities of otherness and extraordinari-

---

400 "Isofunctional" = "having the same function"? This particular word does not appear in either of my dictionaries! (Ed.)

401 In my own, very simple efforts to grapple with issues of the possible "meanings" and the "language" of music (see *Introductory Remarks*, above), I have settled tentatively on the notion that musical meaning or significance relates essentially to function — i.e. to some purpose served, or intended to be served, by the composition or performance of a given musical composition or effect. In my view this avoids the problem of "extra-musical" meanings of a musical work or segment (e.g. as such meanings or significations might be expressed in a verbal language such as English or French) and, equally, it avoids the problem of which ought to be thought of as *symbolizing* which — the music something which is not itself (such as a spirit, flower, emotion etc), or the something else music. (Ed.)

ness, and perhaps even from the very abstractness that frees it from associations too narrow to be associated with religious goals and meanings. But symbolic effectiveness must also rely on more specific associations than arbitrary applications to meanings or goals, which, even though they may be isofunctionally linked to the goals of religious practice, may still appear extrinsic to the music. If such associations do not arise from explicit musical content, then they must result from specific forms that accord with other meaningful forms in the religious sphere. Isoformalism of shared musical and religious forms, then, may combine with isofunctional applications to produce music that effectively symbolizes a religious object, and moreover without compromising the aesthetic integrity or viability of music as a medium of structured forms. Taking religious inspiration as the primary element in the process, this synthesis would occur when the form of a religious experience, action, image, or statement stimulated the creation of a corresponding musical form appropriate to and effective in the context of the musical system of its particular culture or religious tradition.

"When religious and musical forms and purposes thus coincide, we have the kind of congruence that allows religious mean-

ing to pervade every aspect of music from its assumed origin to the forms of individual instruments, songs, and pieces, and at every level of meaning from the most central to the most peripheral, from the most general to the most specific. The synthesis may be so complete as to leave no certainty whether either component, religion or music, takes precedence over the other; and it certainly allows for influence in both directions. There are, for example, not only myths of music, but also musics of myths; and the influence of music on mythology is almost certainly more pervasive and more important than the influence of mythology on music.[402]

"Contrary to a famous assertion by Lévi-Strauss, Wagner was far from the first, even in the Judeo-Christian tradition, to structurally 'analyze' myths through music, for there are European precedents for the musical structuring of mythic narratives and themes going back to the Middle Ages, and far older examples from other parts of the world. These range in complexity from dramatizations as musically elaborate as Bach's or Wagner's (for example, the many performance genres of the Hindu epics *Ramayana* and *Mahabharata* in South and Southeast Asia), to the almost universal forms of mythic vocalization that utilize a simple binary contrast of sung

---

402 This, of course, points to the *raison d'être* of the present work—to indicate "influences" of each (music and mythology) upon the other, by recalling a number of typical references which have been made throughout human history to music in a mythological context. However, this seems to me not to be quite the same thing as suggesting that musical elements have *shaped* this or that myth. Personally, I should think it is enough to say that mythical accounts which happen to involve musical elements simply express certain views which people do have concerning the nature of music, musicians, and musical instruments; or, express views which people do have concerning the *place* of music in the general scheme of "nature" or the "cosmos". So much, then, for the question of whether or not music "influences" mythology. Does mythology influence music? Obviously it does—insofar as composers and performers (dancers, for example) have so often set mythological themes and subjects to music and dance; however—again—speaking personally, the question itself seems slightly beside the point. In saying this I do not mean to detract from the present author's discussion, which I think is a most appealing summary of "music and religion". I mean only to add this comment by way of a parenthesis. (Ed.)

myth/unsung ordinary discourse, or melodic and rhythmic highlighting of important words and passages to create a musically enhanced structure for a mythic narrative. For most religions throughout history, myths have been embodied not in written literature but in musical performance; and such performances provide one of the most characteristic bridges between religious belief and action, between myth and ritual.

"Time, Space, and Ritual. Music is widely used as a demarcator of ritual time and space. In traditional settings all over the world, one may enter a community just before or during a ritual performance and be drawn toward the center of religious activity by musical sounds that grow progressively stronger as one moves toward the center. At the ceremonial site, music may emanate from the exact center of action; or musicians may be placed at the borders of the ritual site, creating a boundary zone of maximum sensual stimulation through which one passes to enter the ritual area itself. In either case, the ceremonial space is pervaded by musical sounds that, more than any other element, fill the entire sacred area with a tangible

energy and evidence that a special situation has been created.

"Sometimes architectural or geographic isolation is used to confine the sound to the ritual space, and the music beocmes an intimate or secret experience restricted to ritual participants and unheard by the general public. In other contexts, musical contrasts may mark the boundaries of sacred spaces by reserving different styles or sounds for sacred centers and profane peripheries: for example, Christian churches with bells that ring on the outside and organ music on the inside, or Theravada Buddhist monastic ordinations with royal processional instruments outside the temple and choral chanting inside.

"Unlike works of visual art, which exist in their entirety and all their details at any given moment, music unfolds through time. Thus, it creates a temporal framework that may be synchronized with ritual time in various ways. At the simplest level, the beginning and ending of a musical performance may coincide with the beginning and ending of a ritual performance. Music may begin before a ritual and end after it, enclosing the performance in a temporal bracket or frame; or music may be performed selectively at temporal high

REPUBLIQUE RWANDAISE

REPUBLIQUE RWANDAISE

points in ritual activity, highlighting significant periods of religious action.

"But music also structures the experience of time in more complex ways. The tempo of the sounds that constitute the 'events' of a musical performance may be considerably faster or slower than the pace of everyday experience, and they may combine in unusual temporal patterns. Music uses formal devices such as cyclicity, repetition, contrast, variation, and development of one pattern of organization into another. Any or all of these devices may be used to create perceptual impressions of the extension or compression of a moment of experience to a longer or shorter time than normal, the return of a previous moment, or the building of intensity toward a climax and emergence of a new structural and experiential framework.[403]

"For both time and space, the structuring effect of music and other performance media may thus function in quite distinct ways. The most obvious way is by contrastive marking of boundaries between music-filled sacred space/time and profane space/time without music. The musical preludes and postludes performed before and after Christian services, or the conch-shell trumpet notes sounded before and after many South Asian rituals, often from a temple door or gateway, exemplify the boundary-marking aspect of music used to highlight ritual activity by creating a sonic frame around it in time and space.[404]

"A different mode of organization is used when the spatial and temporal centers, rather than the boundaries, of ritual activity are brought into concentrated focus by music. This phenomenon occurs at a conceptual or 'symbolic' level when music is perceived as a spatio-temporal *axis mundi*, a channel of communication with spiritual realms and primordial eras. For example, singing the 'drum lineage' songs of the Tibetan Bon religion evokes a link with the beginning of time and the center of the world.

"More concretely, the spatiotemporal foci of ritual actions in the physical world may be highlighted by musical intensification, while movement toward or away from the center is marked by gradually changing intensity rather than a sharp boundary. For example, the religious and musical focus of a Sinhala Kohomba Kankariya ritual is in the drumming, singing, and dancing of the priests themselves; their sound is heard with decreasing in-

---

403 Perhaps it could be said that music establishes not only its own rhythmic pulse etc but also its own time-scale generally, which is not necessarily that of human (worldly) time — nor exactly that of an other-wordly timelessness or "eternity", either — but, is something in between, or serves indeed as a kind of temporal median (mediation) between one and the other. For example, in folktales about magically-possessed fiddlers, or the dancing of elves and fairies, what in earth time is the passing of a hundred years is only, for the participants in the story — which is to say with respect to musical duration — the passing of a night, or of a few hours or minutes! The musical time in question seems like a meeting point between e.g the eternity of elves and the everyday clock of our own world. (Ed.)

404 Similarly, perhaps, with respect to the musical overture to a play or drama, even if the drama itself also be musical — and to films, which typically begin with some music played against the titles, even if little music is written for the action that follows: in dramatic terms, merely, a hint of things to come, or mood-setting; in spiritual terms, however, a temporary farewell to the profane world of everyday work and cares, and invitation or crossing-over to some more elevated, sacred plane of being and contemplation. This, too, is consistent with a principal theme of the present book — of music as mediator (go-between) between the natural and supernatural worlds, or between the profane and sacred etc. (Ed.)

tensity as one moves outward through the concentric rows of the audience in the open-walled ritual enclosure, through the streets of the village, and on out through the fields of the surrounding district, which may be the ultimate space concecrated by their performance.

"In such cases, the consecrated space is defined by its relation to the ritual action at its center, rather than by a boundary at its edge; and the gradually diminishing intensities of musical sounds emanating from the center serve well to embody this central-focal mode of spatial demarcation. A similar mode of temporal demarcation seems to occur in, for example, the Shona Bira ritual described by Berliner (1978), in which the *mbira* musicians begin their performance with unobtrusive, unelaborate playing and gradually build to a peak of musical and religious interaction with the audience. Both musical intensity of creative improvisaton and religious experiences of spirit possession occur within this focal period, and both gradually fade away to more ordinary levels as the ritual draws to an end. In such modes of application, music ceases to be a simple boundary marker, enhancer, or accompaniment to ritual action and religious experience: musical and ritual structure and content begin to take on more vital and significant relationships.

"The most basic and widespread musical and ritual time-structuring device is repetition, often carried to such lengths as to perplex or bore the outside observer. It may be that repetition and redundancy serve to impart sensations of continuity, stability, and security, that they aid concentration and provide safeguards against distraction, or that they simply allow con-

tinuation of a 'state of music' to enhance a ritual performance. Whatever the cause, the use of reptition is surely wide enough to show the importance of this little-understood formal device. However, except in unusual cases such as South Asian *mantra*, Japanese Nembutsu chanting, and some kinds of instrumental accompaniments to rituals, which may involve very prolonged repetitions, musical repetition is almost always found in conjunction with variation, and each depends on the other.

"For example, we might consider three possible musical settings for the beginning of the Christian Mass, *'Kyrie eleison / Christe eleison / Kyrie eleison'*. (1) The same melody, musical form, and so forth, is repeated in all three phases. This would appear to minimize the effect of the textual variation *'Kyrie... / Christe... / Kyrie'* and create a musical analogue of the textual continuity provided by the triple repetition of *'eleison'*, reinforcing the conceptual unity of the plea for mercy expressed in all three phrases. (2) Each phrase is set to a different melody or form. Here, the formal analogue is with the variation of initial words, rather than continuity and repetition, and the cognitive effect might be a heightened awareness that each phrase represents a new act of asking mercy, even though there is textual repetition in the first and third phrases. (3) The beginning and ending *'Kyrie...'* phrases are set to the same or a similar melody or form, with the intervening *'Christe...'* set to a different one.

"Here, the use of musical variation and repetition corresponds exactly with the variation and repetition of *'Kyrie... / Christe... / Kyrie...'*; continuity and conceptual unity are given cyclic expression in the identity of the beginning and ending phrases, while the middle phrase receives the special treatment of being given its own individual musical setting.[405] Both repetition and variation in this context acquire a different significance than in (1), with its triple repetition, or (2), with its ongoing changes. The individualized setting in the second phrase is likely to be experienced by performers and observers alike as a special or climactic moment between the pattern established in the first phrase and repeated at the end; and a participant might experience it as a special enhancement of asking mercy in the name of Christ, without special attention to the role played by musical forms. But the formal differences remain: (1) with its repetition and sense of continuity and prolongation of a moment and action already begun, (2) with its emphasis on change and newness, and (3) with its variation-repetition structure and sense of return to a previous moment when the text and music of the first phrase are repeated at the end.

"Similar cases can be found in many religious traditions; for example, in the various settings of the Buddhist Triple Refuge, with its three-phrase invocation of Buddha, Dharma (teaching), and Samgha (religious community). The actual use of musical structuring through repetition and variation is frequently much more complex, and each tradition tends to develop its own characteristic styles. For example, many Christian Mass settings use extensive repetitions of text phrases such as 'Kyrie eleison' with increasingly different variations of the melody, developing it into new forms, and building to climaxes of musical intensity. Buddhist settings of the Triple Refuge, on the other hand, tend

to use melodic variation in more restrained ways, and concentrate instead on text/music repetitions that build to mathematical or exponential permutations such as triple repetitions of a three-phrase structure, resulting in a 32 formal structure, and perhaps a sense of transcending cyclic repetition to reach a more abstractly perfect state. However such structures may be felt or interpreted in their own traditions, it is clear that they make equally sophisticated but formally quite different use of such features as continuity, change, and development of basic elements into more complex forms. And since each in its own context is only a small part of a much longer ritual performance, opportunities for complex structuring of musical time are obviously great.

"Yet, however natural the concept 'musical time' may appear to us, we must treat the issue with caution. Westerners may not be the only ones to conceive of music and its structures in temporal terms. For example, the Javanese prince Mangkunegara VII (1957) and others see the *wayang kulit* (shadow play) in such terms. For them, this all-night performance, with its chronological ordering of musical modes and its complex alterations of repeating sections and new developments, encapsulates the experience of progress through a prolonged state of *samadhi* meditation and through life from bith to spiritual fulfillment. And Judith Becker (1979, 1981), in a series of provocative articles, suggests that Javanese music embodies local and Hindu-Buddhist time concepts from cyclicity to the coincidence of differently ordered calendars.

"Alan P. Merriam (1981) has warned that we may be imposing our own prejudices

---

405 Somewhat fancifully, it might also be suggested that an ABA musical form proposes "A" as unity—the truth—fundamental identity, to which a return is always made after the departures and divergences of "B". Again in symbolic terms, in music in which the "A" also provides some tonal center or resolution, the "spiritual truth" of "A" would also provide a foundation on which the (musical) structure as a whole is built etc. (Ed.)

on African music by discussing it in terms of a 'musical time' for which African languages have no corresponding terms. Nevertheless, we find areas in Africa with both musical coincidence of different-length beat cycles and calendrical coincidence of different-length week cycles, and the parallel seems too exact and complex to be unrelated. Perhaps one solution would be, in studying a culture, to adopt a comparative perspective that takes musical time as one of the fundamental modes of human time perception and organization, whether or not the culture calls it by a term that also applies to calendrical or experiential time, just as we continue to identify and study 'music' and 'religion' in cultures that have no equivalent terms. Since each culture and religion has its own concept of time, some such artificially neutral viewpoint may be necessary to think clearly about questions of musical and ritual durations and structures, questions that transcend both cultural and religious boundaries." — Ellingson, in Eliade (vol. 10), pp.163-71.

§263A.4 "Emotive music. Sacred to early man were man-made sounds in imitation of animals or of birds deemed messengers, spirit vessels, totem representatives, and the like. Another type of sacred sound would be the 'abnormal' noises made by adapting natural objects to produce sounds (bull-roarer*, drum*, ram's horn*) and by employing the human voice outside its familiar gamut of speaking. Hence singing, chanting, intoning have always been associated with religion; it is often deflating to observe the banality of the words accompanying celebrated oratorios and other sacred music. Oracles and shamans* regularly project a rhythmic voice that is disturbingly unusual. Ghosts and spirits are frequently characterized by high-pitched squeekings or deep sepulchral tones. Each Amerindian of the Great Plains was supposed to receive a unique 'spirit song' from his guardian spirit. Musical instruments with the mar-velous facility of providing more than one note, even if no more than a didgerydoo, are obviously of divine origin, as Hermes* invented the lyre* and Pan* invented the syrinx*. Most especially, highly rhythmic music is peculiarly emotive. Intensive and repetitive cadences help achieve trance and spirit possession as in modern 'Holy Rollers'. Shamans have long used drum-beating to contact the spirit world. Some shamans report that specific musical patterns evoke specific visions or types of visions. Temple musicians have been commonplace from Japan through the Near East and ancient Egypt. The Olympian worship made meager use of music, but the Greek mystery cults emphasized ecstatic music; conservative critics especially objected to the inflammatory effect of the *aulos** (a reed instrument) in such cults as the Dionysian. In general the emphasis in classic times seems not upon the aesthetic qualities of music but upon the ability of music to stir the listener to action, as the Dorian mode supposedly induced martial valor and the Lydian mode lured to the pursuit of love.

"In the passive forms of physical stimulus the recipient of religious impulses does not employ his own muscularity, but has his senses powerfully assailed to arouse feelings of altered awareness." — Day, pp.78-79.

MUSIC AND TRANCE.

§263B.1 The following extended exerpts from *Music and Trance: A Theory of the Relations Between Music and Possession* by Gilbert Rouget (1980) illustrate, I believe, our contention that, in a religious, mythological, or magico-sacred setting, music commonly serves (or is meant to serve) as a medium of communication or exchange between man and god(s) or supreme being(s) — e.g. summoning or invoking the presence of such gods *to* or, indeed, *in* the musician, or subject upon whose behalf the musician acts, etc. (Ed.)

"Trance is to be defined as an altered, transitory state of consciousness, conforming to a cultural model....

"[Trance may be identified with 'possession' which, in turn, is widely associated with music and dance.]

"We are able to distinguish three broad types of mystic trance.

"The first is characterized by the fact that, during trance, the subject is thought to have acquired a different personality: that of a god, spirit, genius, or ancestor—for which we may use the general term 'deity'—who has taken possession of the subject, substituted itself for him, and is now acting in that subject's place. [This particular] representation of things is often founded on the idea that an individual possesses several souls, so that, using the *bori* of the Niger Hausa as an example, there is one soul that 'the gods send away during possession in order to take its place' (Monfouga-Nicholas 1972). For a longer or shorter period the subject then becomes the god. He *is* the god. We can call this possession in the strict sense of the word.

"In the second category, rather than having switched personalities, the subject is thought to have been invested by the deity, or by a force emanating from it, which then coexists in some way with the subject but nevertheless controls him and causes him to act and speak in its name. The most frequent example of this relationship is that found in trances attributed to the Holy Ghost. I shall refer to this category of trances not as possession, but as inspiration.

"In the third category the relationship between divinity and subject is seen as an encounter which, depending upon the individual, is experienced as a communion, a revelation, or an illumination. Unlike the previous two relationships, this one does not involve embodiment of any kind. I shall therefore refer to the trance state

brought about by *wajd,* and achieved by the practice of *dhikr,* which [is described later on in our discussion of the relations between music and trance among the Arabs], as communion or 'communial' trance. For a Sufi, or for any Muslim, there can obviously be no question of embodying Allah, or identifying oneself with him.

"Having defined these three categories—not as abstract models but on the basis of concrete examples—let me hasten to add that, in reality, things are not always as simple as this division might suggeset, and that it is often difficult to know with which of the three categories one is dealing. To return to the case of the Sufi, it can happen, contrary to all principles of the Muslim faith, that it does take the form of an indisputable embodiment. Among other examples, there is this description of a *dhikr* séance by a Fez derqwa votary in which, speaking of God (Allah), the trance subject cries out: 'He is in me! He is in me! *Huwa! Huwa!* [meaning He! He!]' Many people would say that this, whether one wishes to accept it or not, is purely and simply a case of possession. For my part, I shall say that it is inspiration, but that in any event more than mere communion is clearly involved, contrary to what the logic of Sufism might lead us to expect.... The Shakers of Saint Vincent in the Antilles regard their trances as resulting from the presence of the Holy Ghost. They say they are 'shaken' by him (Henney 1973), but they do not identify themselves with him in any way. Jeannette Henney nevertheless explains these trances as resulting from possession by the Holy Ghost....

"[By 'music' we shall mean here] any sonic event that... cannot be reduced to language, and that displays a certain degree of rhythmic or melodic organization. Music will therefore be taken in its most empirical and broadest sense. In other words, it will not be treated here as an art but as a practice displaying the greatest possible variety of aspects, extending from the most discreet rustling sounds produced by the shaking of a basketry rattle to the deafening unleashing of a large group of drums*, from the solitary tinkling of a tiny iron bell* to the orchestral splendors of a Balinese gamelan, from the most elementary monody, chanted *recto tono*, to the most complex vocal polyphonies (such as those of the Bushmen), from the linearity of a simple motif produced by clapping hands to the extremely complex interplay of a large percussion ensemble, from the refinement of a violin tune skillfully varied by a professional virtuoso to the rustic sound of a summons bellowed through an animal horn or tapped out with a nail on the side of an empty beer bottle....

"What does possession music signify? What is its meaning? What are the words of the songs saying? What do the dance rhythms express? Or, rather, to what dances do those rhythms correspond and what do those dances signify? We can say in a general sense that the vast majority of [the songs which accompany or are otherwise involved with the trance state] concern divinities that have come to be embodied, or that are expected to do so. They can concern these divinities in several different ways. Sometimes they are addressed directly to them, summoning them or, on the contrary, asking them to go away; sometimes they describe them, usually in a flattering way, and often by referring to their genealogies or their mottoes, which comes to the same thing.

"Jane Belo, in her book on Bali, does not provide very much information about the texts sung during trances caused by the gods. But the songs for the popular trances brought about by *sanghyang* spirits (the *sanghyang* who inhabit the dolls and the little girl dancers on the one hand, and the *sanghyang* of animals on the other [Belo 1960]) fit in well with what I have just said. Judging from Simon and Simon-Barough's chapter on the subject, the same is true of the 'hymns of invocation to the genii' sung in Vietnam during *hâu bóng* cermonies. In

Tibet*, the chant used to trigger the oracle's trance is formed of two parts (Nebesky-Wojkowitz 1956). The first is an 'invocation to the *dharmapâla* and also of the abode in which he is supposed to reside.' Then follows 'a litany... praising the *dharmapâla* — who by now should have occupied the body of the oracle — enumerating and eulogizing his various capabilities'.

"In Madagascar, the songs (*ântsa*) sung to summon the divinities (*tsumba*, a dialectical variation of *trômba*) are 'fairly slow'. The words 'aim to describe and flatter the god' (Koechlin). 'These solemn chants' alternate with other songs accompanied by a board-zither, an instrument 'also used on a schooner, to summon the winds when the boat is becalmed'. Once the trance is well established and the dances take on a purely playful character, it is dynamism of movement that is mainly required. The importance of the words decreases, and they are often reduced to simple exclamations. But for slower dances, the words may acquire importance again, and the singing consists of 'success songs', occasionally humorous in content but no longer connected with possession as such. Among the Thonga of Mozambique, the importance of the rhythm and sound level provided by the drums in possession séances have been strong emphasized by H. A. Junod, but 'that which is the most essentially necessary,' he also writes, 'is the *singing* (1913). This is provided by experienced possessed persons: 'They address the spirit in laudatory terms, trying to cajole it by flattery, to get the right side of it, and thus to induce it to grant the signal favor of a surrender'. Such phrases as 'Rhinoceros, thou attackest man!' show that these songs obviously fall into the category of mottoes.

"In Ethiopia, 'apart from the songs used to evoke the *zar*, which are called *wadaga* like the gatherings during which they are performed,' and apart from 'songs with prophetic intentions... often contributed by professional possessees' and consisting more often of 'a very general lament about vicissitudes of the times,' Leiris (1958) also describes a great many songs 'performed for the purpose of entertainment.' Elsewhere, however, he makes reference to a 'song intended to make the *zar* descend onto a novice' and also mentions — though without expressly linking it to the singing — the use of mottoes *(fukkara)* which he defines as a 'fairly free accumulation of stereotypes recalling Homeric epithets.'

"In Niger, in the *bori,* the songs used to trigger trance (and on occasion to calm it too, when the possession is a false one) are essentially mottoes. At least this is what emerges from the work of Jacqueline Monfouga-Nicolas (1972). Still in Niger, among the Songhay the 'musical mottoes' (that is to say, the ritual texts) which are sung 'usually with instrumental accompaniment' (Rouch 1960), but which are also frequently played on the fiddle without being sung, provide the very substance of their possession music. 'Each divinity has one or several musical themes specific to him,' writes Rouch, who then assigns those themes and texts, the dance steps associated with them, and even such objects as altars, ritual furniture, and costumes, to one and the same general category of 'more or less materialized signs of the divinities.'

"In Senegal, the *bak,* a 'theme-song or motto-song is one of the *rab's* attributes... It is with the aid of the *bak,* a short and more or less explicit phrase, that the spirits are summoned one by one during the *ndöp* and the *samp'* (Zempleni 1966). In the warming-up phase, chanting of the *bak* plays a decisive role. At the start of the session, after the drummers have played the summons, the *ndöpkat* form a procession, enter, stop in front of the drums, and 'consult over the choice of the first *bak.*' Then, when everything is ready, the women officiants, in order to achieve 'a suitable degree of excitation', 'summon those possessees who are particularly easy to excite, by manipulating the appropriate *baks.* In the course of the extremely impor-

tant session known as the 'naming of the *rab',* various *bak* are intoned in succession. At the end, 'it is when a new *bak* is called out by the assistants that A. G.... suddenly utters a long cry, then announces: "*Wali Ndiaye Sene!*" This is the name they had been waiting for.' We shall return later to the role of chanted mottoes in the process of identifying a deity.

"Among the Dogon, in the course of the ceremonial enthronement of one of the priests of the *binu* (mythical ancestors), when the priests hear the drum theme of their own *binu,* 'they move into the center of the circle and dance more quickly, or give themselves up to a ritual crisis that a colleague then calms with an application of sacred bastard-mahogany bark' (de Ganay 1942). What is happening here is that 'when the *binu's* rhythm is played that *binu's* *nyama* [life force] possesses the priest, who then performs the movements specific to the theme being drummed out.' 'For each *binu* there is a specific drum rhythm *(binu boy),*' G. Dieterlen writes. When he hears the rhythm specific to his *binu,* the priest goes into trance, because 'at the mere beating of the drum, the *binu's* soul is thought to rise onto [his] head... and provoke the crisis.' Here again, then, among the Dogon we are dealing with musical mottoes (which must not be confused with verbal mottoes, *tige*) that trigger possession. But possession can equally well be induced, not by rhythms played on a drum, but by song. At least this is implied in a remark made by S. de Ganay (1942), who relates the trance of a *binu* priest 'crawling on his belly to imitate the *Nommo* [water spirits] who move in to deep holes in the earth' to a song about the god *Nommo.* But at the level of myth, the onset of the trance is attributed neither to the singing, nor to the musical instruments, nor to the dance, but to the sound of speech. It was when he heard *Nommo* utter the first word intended for the first men that Binu Seru, the first totemic priest, 'underwent the first fit, analogous to those that still make all priests seized by inspiration "tremble" today' (Calame-Griaule 1965). Here again, then, in every case a sound bearing a meaning is seen as being at the origin of the trance.

"In Nigeria and Dahomey, among the Yoruba and also among the Fon or the Gun, the *oriki* of the *orishi* and the *mimlan* of the *vodun* respectively occupy an important place in the invocations chanted to summon the divinities to manifest themselves, or to make them dance once they have been embodied (Verger 1957, Rouget 1965). These *oriki* and *mimlan* are nothing other than mottoes, which may be spoken, sung, or drummed depending on the circumstances. In Brazil, in the *candomblé*, each deity has his or her specific 'canticles', which 'constitute, together with the sonorous drum rhythms that accompany them, so many leitmotifs, to borrow a Wagnerian term, intended to attract the orixa' (Bastide 1958). 'As these canticles unfold,' Gisèle Cossard writes, 'so the initiates go into trance' (1970). The texts she quotes elsewhere (1967) demonstrate that we are once again dealing primarily with mottoes.

"The sun invocations requesting the divinity to come and take possession of the adept combine mottoes, exhortations, prayers, and, on occasion, insults — a sign of the familiarity that reigns between men and gods. Thus among the Vandau: 'They are not afraid to insult the possessing spirit, like the chief's daughter who is mocked for being a prostitute, or like the almost untranslatable song of the *Mandiki*' (Junod 1934). In nearby Zimbabwe, among the Tonga, A. Tracey (1970) reports that when people grow tired of waiting for the medium to become possessed, a certain *mbira* player specializes in singing a song so insulting to the *mhondoro* (spirit), who is usually addressed in flattering terms, that shame forces him to 'come out' immediately. Whether they are prayers, praises, or insults, these songs are addressed to the deity, and this is the important thing to remember. They constitute communication with him.

"When they are specific to a particular deity, melodies played on an instrument have the same function as sung mottoes: they are call-signs. Indeed, these melodies often are mere instrumental versions of the sung mottoes which are deprived of their text; but, when they hear them, 'men and gods also hear the words that relate to them' (Rouch 1960). Whether linked to a text or not, these tunes are used for dancing, and the resulting dance constitutes the motto's choreographic aspect; it expresses the deity's personality just the same, but in movement rather than words. Whether it is a rhythmic theme played on a drum or a melodic theme played on, say, a fiddle, this theme, when linked to a particular deity, has a 'signified' referring to that deity, either because it is related to him or her by some expressive correspondenc (it depicts the deity) or because it simply has been arbitrarily attached to him or her. Thus the rhythmic themes specific to the various *orisha* in the *candomblé* are described by Gisèle Cossard (1967) as 'dramatic', 'full of vivacity', 'aggressive', 'tempestuous' — each of these adjectives corresponding to the nature of the divinity in question. On the other hand, I am unable to say whether or not the 'tunes of the genii', which constitute the repertoire of the *holey* (genii) cult among the Songhay, also have an expressive content. In tarantism, each variety of tarantula has its own particular tune. But is the correspondence in this case expressive or is it purely arbitrary? We do not know. We do know, however, that in order to cure tarantulees 'the piper or zither player plays for them various motifs related to the quallty of the venom, so that they are ravished by the harmony and fascinated by what they are hearing, and the venom either dissolves away within the body, or is slowly eliminated through the veins' (early sixteenth-century text quoted by De Martino 1946). Since each tarantula 'likes its own tune,' there is 'a traditionalized series of tunes and songs from which one must choose the one (or ones) best suited to each particular case.' It is the 'right' music, in other words, the one that best fits the case, that 'will make the tarantula *scazzicare* (leap about),' just like the appropriate canticle in the *candomblé* or *bak* in the *ndöp* will attract the corresponding *orisha* or *rab*. But although there are different varieties of tarantella, each differing from the other in tune, key, and rhythm, it seems that the dance—or rather the sequence of the dance's various movements—always remains the same, no matter which tarantula is involved. One of these movements consists in imitating the spider. It is thus a figurative dance, as are so many other possession dances in Bali, in Vietnam, and in Africa. Depending on whether it involves a warrior (sword dance), a loving woman, a wild animal symbolizing power (tiger or panther) or fertility (snake), the dance will naturally differ in character, and with it the music that sustains it. And in this case one is also dealing with more or less directly figurative music.

"The situation offered by tarantism, in which the same dance is performed to different tunes, corresponds among the Mundang to an inverted situation where, on the contrary, different dances are performed to the same music. The film and recordings made by Adler, Pineau, and Zempléni... show that different possessed women all dance at the same time, one the panther dance, one the sun dance, one the rain dance, and still another the milling dance. In a small group, they all dance to the same music. This music varies only in its details and... nothing shows it is linked to one or the other choreographic figure. We are thus dealing here with music that, in contrast with the figurative music in tarantism, one might describe as abstract. Another example of nonfigurative music is the *adarum* rhythm.... The saint's daughters, who ordinarily respond only to the summons of the rhythm specific to their own particular *orisha*, all go into trance when the *adarum* is played. In the *ndöp*, while the *rab's bak* (the genius's tune) is what most distinguishes one genius

from another (Zempléni 1966), and while each class of *rab* has its own mimicry (its 'identificatory behavior'), contrariwise certain dance movements, particularly those of the 'labor of crisis', together with the drum music directing them, of course, are the same for all *rab*. This is true among the Songhay as well: 'Although each *Holey* has one or several specific mottoes, one or two special musical themes, the dances that lead to his incarnation are not particular to him' (Rouch 1960). These dances comprise several distinct phases, characterized by different figures and following one another at a steadily increasing pace until they finally lead to the crisis, but here again, as with the 'labor of crisis' in the *ndöp*, the drumbeats, and not the played or sung melodies, control the dancing. And since the same drum music works for all the *holey* or for all the *rab* and is thus impersonal in a way, it does not function as a musical motto, which is also the case with the *adarum* rhythm. The list of such examples could be extended considerably. It is consequently necessary, with respect to music accompanying possession dances, to distinguish between sung or played themes on the one hand, which are usually musical mottoes, and on the other drum music which may or may not function as a motto. This does not, however, alter the fact that in practice the music may be an intimate mixture of melodic music and of rhythmic music, the two being associated in combinations that vary from cult to cult, and in which one of the other sometimes predominates.

"Let us now return to the musical motto, which, as we have seen, plays a central role in possession. It can be defined as a sign whose 'signified' is the god to which it refers, and whose 'signifier' has three facets: linguistic, musical, and choreographic. The signifying power of the sign is peculiarly extensive, since it involves spirit and body, intelligence and sensibility, and the faculties of ideation and movement, all at the same time. This is evidently what makes it, for the adept, the most powerful means available for identifying himself with the divinity possessing him. In certain cases when the deity's unknown identity must still be established, it will also be the principle means of identifying him or her.

"Tarantism provides a particularly striking example of the use of music or, more precisely, of the musical motto, as a means of identifying the divinity (here, the spider) responsible for the possession. In the late nineteenth century, one could still find 'in Naples twelve different tarantella themes used to diagnose tarantulees in order to establish which one corresponded with which particular case, and consequently triggered the dance,' writes E. De Martino (1966), who elsewhere quotes a passage from G. Baglivi, the celebrated iatromechanist of the late seventeenth century, describing 'musical exploration' (or diagnosis) as follows: 'The musicians who were summoned asked the patient the color and size of her tarantula so they could adapt their music accordingly; but the patient replied she did not know if she had been bitten by a tarantula or by a scorpion. They began trying out their themes: at the fourth, the tarantulee immediately began to sigh, and at last, no longer able to resist the call of the dance, she leapt half naked from her bed, without a thought for conventions, and for three days kept up a sprightly dance, after which she was cured.' We find the very same process at work in the case of the Sardinian *argia*, a variant of tarantism that departs considerably from the Apulian model. Like the tarantula in Italy or Spain, or the scorpion, in Sardinia a mythical creature, the *argia*, is responsible for the patient's poisoning. This creature 'is categorized under three distinct species, the nubile, the wife, and the widow, and the treatment of the poisoned person differs according to the type of *argia* that bit him or her. In particular, the widow *argia*, symbolically associated with the color black, always requires dirges... the musical exploration [is] intended to determine the type involved

in the given case [and] it unfolds through the successive use of musico-choreographic themes and songs traditionally associated with each type.' The success of this musical 'exploration' depended on the skill of the musicians, as did the efficacy of the cure, once the 'right music' had been found, De Martino also tells us.

"This 'right music' is, in fact, to give another example, what Plato speaks of when he describes the Corybantes* 'falling into a trance when they hear the melody specific to the divinity by whom they are possessed' (Jeanmaire 1951). And again, it is the 'right song', played for the medium among the Tonga, that proves irresistible: as soon as the deity hears it 'he is unable to refuse to incorporate him' (Tracey 1970).

"Among the Thonga, 'as among the Wolof, it does not suffice for the possessed woman to declare the name of the divinity possessing her—a crucial episode in her initiation: she must also sing the deity's theme. In the *ndöp*, after they have extracted the name of her *rab* from her, the officiants continue to press the sick woman: 'They begin shaking her again in order to get the *rab*'s song-motto out of her. It was some time before the young woman began to sing in a staccato voice, the *bak* required of her, and which all those present then repeated in chorus' (Zempléni 1966). Among the Thonga (or Tsonga), things unfold slightly differently. The patient sings his song, but he has to invent it himself: 'Every possessed person invents a song which will be henceforth *his*, and by means of which crises, or trances will be provoked or cured' (Junod 1913). If the spirit responsible for the trance is a Zulu one, as is most frequently the case among the Thonga, the words will be in Zulu, even if the man involved does not know this language. This is an extreme case of personalization of the sung theme, which, among the Tonga, corresponds to the inverted case of 'songs, which while identified with *mbondoro* spirits in general, are not tied to any one' (Tracey 1970). This recalls what I said above about the *adarum* rhythm in the *candomblé*, at the sound of which all the *orisha*, without distinction, go into trance.

"*Who Makes the Music and in What State Is He?* Who makes this music played at various points in the ritual, which triggers adepts' trances and which makes them dance when they are possessed? Who plays these instruments, who beats these drums, who sings these songs? [There are usually two categories of individuals who provide such music:] those whose activity is expressively and exclusively to make music, in other words, those appointed to make it... and those whose activity is to make music only episodically, or accessorily, or secondarily....

"*Music and Trance Among the Greeks*. In ancient Greece, trance, although this is too often forgotten today, constituted a very important aspect of religious life. Dionysiac practices, with their wild behavior and violence, do of course form an integral part of the picture we tend to have nowadays of Greek religion. Rohde, and many others after him, have given accounts of these practices. Nietzsche celebrated them at length. Even though Jeanmaire and Dodds (respectively in *Dionysos* and in *The Greeks and the Irrational*, both published in 1951) made it quite plain more than thirty years ago, we still too often ignore the fact that possession trance was the mainspring of the cult of Dionysis-Bacchus. That Bacchus was the god of the vine and wine is obviously no mere chance; to get drunk is ultimately no more than a particular way of no longer being oneself. But Dionysiac frenzy can no more be reduced to drunkenness than Dionysus can be reduced to Bacchus, contrary to what current usage of his latinized name would lead us to believe. From the standpoint of the history of religions, the feeling of elatedness due to wine is no more than an anecdotal and fairly recent

aspect of the much more ancient, and much more universal elatedness due to trance. Moreover, religious frenzy was not limited among the Greeks to the worship of Dionysus. Everyone knows that the actual functioning of the Delphic oracle, another essential aspect of Greek religion—this time linked with Apollo*, god of music—relied in part at least upon the practice of mediumistic trance. In addition, like so many other peoples, the Greeks regarded the inspiration of the poet (and of the musician, since the two were for a long while inseparable) as being nothing other than a trance. Finally, Plato, as we shall see, held that there was no true love other than mad love, and that this madness, also stemming from the gods, was a trance....

" *'Mania' and Its Terminology*. That the word *mania* among the ancient Greeks meant what I have been calling a 'trance'... is something that will become apparent [in the remarks that follow]. For the moment let us take this for granted and begin by asking ourselves what Plato's concept of *mania* was. Even so, one point should be clarified. Although from our perspective, the word *mania* can be considered as the exact equivalent of 'trance', depending on the context, I shall translate it sometimes by 'madness' and sometimes by 'frenzy'. The reader should see no inconsistency in this. 'Madness' and 'frenzy' are in fact more accurate translations of *mania* as the Greeks understood it, and it is their viewpoint that is important to us at the moment. We should note, however, that although 'madness' (or the French *folie*) is, along with 'frenzy', the most frequently used translation of the Greek *mania*, this has not always been the case. During the Renaissance, to mention only one period, it was rendered in French as *fureur* and in Italian as *furore* (Cicero said 'furor'), both of which were just as legitimate as *folie*, albeit signifying another aspect of things. Today, *Orlando furioso* ought to be translated 'Mad Orlando' rather than 'Furious Orlando'. In the seventeenth and eighteenth centuries, Michel Foucault points out in his *Histoire de la folie a l'âge classique,* that *fureur* was a 'technical term in jurisprudence and medicine' designating 'a very precise form of madness.'

"This said, what did the word *mania* mean for Plato? The answer is to be found partly in the *Timaeus* and partly in the *Phaedrus.* In the *Timaeus* (86b), having given a general account of the diseases of the body *(soma nosemata),* he turns to those of the soul *(psyche),* whose specific disease, he says, is dementia *(anoia),* which is of two kinds: either madness *(mania)* or ignorance *(amathia).* And he adds: 'Whatever affection a man suffers from, if it involves either of these conditions, it must be termed "disease"; and we must maintain that pleasures and pains in excess are the greatest of the soul's diseases.' Oddly enough, but significant no doubt, Plato's reflections in the *Timaeus* on the classification of *mania* stop there. It contains no allusion whatsoever to something found in the *Phaedrus,* a much earlier work, in which he makes what is for us a crucial distinction (265a-b) between two different kinds of *mania,* one arising from human diseases *(nosematon anthropinon)* and the other from a divine state *(theias exallages)* 'which releases us from the customary habits.' He then divides this state into four sorts of mania, four different kinds of madness each inspired *(epipnoian)* by a God: 'mantic' (by Apollo), 'telestic' (by Dionysus), 'poetic' (by the Muses), and 'erotic' (by Eros and Aphrodite). This is how in a celebrated and often quoted passage, Socrates summarizes and characterizes in one word the four forms of madness he had just described in his discourse to Phaedrus on love.

"This manner of characterizing the four forms of madness merits closer attention. Three of the four are defined by means of

epithets concerning their function: the one leading to divination is called 'mantic', the one stirring the poet to creation is 'poetic', and the one inspiring the lover to transports of frenzied love is 'erotic'. The fourth, however, is defined from a quite different standpoint, a formal rather than a functional one. It is called 'telestic', meaning it entails *teletai,* or rites. In other words it is 'ritual' madness. [And] this telestic frenzy is nothing other than what we have been calling possession trance. For Plato, then, that which characterizes the possession trance first and foremost and distinguishes it from other forms of trance, is the fact that it is ritual. About these rites themselves he provides few details, no doubt considering it pointless to elaborate on facts with which the reader of his day would be familiar, and presuming that the latter would know them well enough. Fortunately, he nevertheless writes enough about them *(Laws* 791a-b) for us to know they essentially consisted of sacrifices, dances, and music. We can also be sure, moreover, whatever the arguments aroused by the interpretation of the word *teletai...,* that these rites also comprised an initiatory aspect, of varying importance, and that they must have been secret, to some extent at least....

"On the basis of the data given by the three... dialogues *Phaedrus, Laws,* and *Ion,* Plato's theory of the relations between trance and music can be formulated as follows: 'People who are psychologically somewhat fragile, and who as the result of god's anger suffer from divine madness, cure themselves by practising ritual trance, which is triggered by a musical motto and takes the form of a dance; music and dance, by the effect of their movement,[406] reintegrate the sick person into the general

---

406 Reference is also made to the effect of a mother's rocking her troubled infant to sleep, in consequence of which she appears to "drive off" the troubling spirits. Quiet or stillness without movement at all seems not to accomplish this: it requires singing (lullaby fashion) and rocking. (Ed.)

movement of the cosmos, and this healing is brought about thanks to the benevolence of gods who have been rendered propitious by sacrifice.'...

"What exactly was the place of the *aulos** [reed instrument] among the ancient Greeks? Both textual and pictorial evidence clearly show that it was closely associated with trance, [though by no means] exclusively....

"[Let us consider] the relation of *aulos* to *mania*. Apollo was seen among the Greeks as the inventor of the lyre and Marsyas* the Silenus as the inventor of the *aulos*. And about the melodies of Marsyas, Plato categorically says: 'whether played by a fine *aulos* player or a paltry *aulos* girl, they are the only ones capable of inducing possession, because of their divine origin, and to indicate those who are recipients of the deities and their [proper] rites' (*Symposium* 215c). Why is this? Because they 'are themselves divine.' An explanation as unexpected as it is peremtory! But who provides it? Alcibiades, who is drunk and delivering his celebrated and highly ironic speech in praise of Socrates. In other words, it should not be taken seriously. In short, Plato tells us that tunes on the *aulos* entrance people, and this is corroborated by too many other sources for us to doubt it; but he abstains from explaining this particular effect of *aulos* music. This fact is important and deserves to be stressed. Although Plato has a theory of the effects of music and dance on the curing of madness, as we have seen, he lacks one to explain the effects of music on the triggering of trance.... Aristotle, on the other hand, had very precise ideas on the subject, so we will now turn to him.

"*Aristotle, the Ethos* of Modes, and the Phrygian Mode.* Plato tells us that if the 'productions' of Marsyas have the strange power of causing trance, this is 'because

they are themselves divine.' His explanation is a bit brief. Aristotle proposes a different view of the matter. In the *Politics* (1340a), having talked about the tunes composed by Olympus, 'which make our souls enthusiastic,' and having given a long account of the imitative virtues of music and the nature of 'harmonies' — or musical modes — he makes the general statement that 'the Phrygian mode makes men enthusiastic [*enthusiastikous*]' (1340b). Marsyas the Silenus and his pupil, Olympus, are both, as we know, Phrygians. The *aulos* is Phrygian in origin. If the tunes of Marsyas and Olympus induce trance, they must do so because they are in the Phrygian mode — a more interesting explanation, it will be conceded, than Plato's. And all the more so because it is part of a general theory of music's effects based on the idea that music is able to 'represent' and 'imitate' states of the soul.[407] Melodies (*Mele*) 'do actually contain in themselves imitations of character' (*mimemata ton ethon*), Aristotle tells us, and in 'melodies there are differences, so that people when hearing them are affected differently and do not have the same feelings with respect to each of them' (1340ab). The same is also true of rhythms, he adds. Returning a little later on to the Phrygian mode, he writes (1342b): 'the Phrygian mode has the same effect [*dynamin*] among harmonies [*harmonion*] as the *aulos* among instruments, both are orgiastic and passional [*orgiastika kai pathetica*]... all Bacchic transport [*baccheia*] and all movement of this sort belongs to the *aulos* more than any other instrument, and find their suitable accompaniment in tunes in the Phrygian mode among the harmonies.'

"Being 'passional' or 'pathetic', the Phrygian mode is thus opposed to the Dorian mode, which is 'ethical'. Properly speaking, then, the Phrygian mode is not endowed with *ethos* or moral character, but with *pathos* or passion. For this reason, un-

---

407 See also entries on **ETHOS*** (Greek) and **HARMONY OF THE SPHERES***. (Ed.)

like melodies in the Dorian mode, which the man or youth of high birth may learn because they are 'ethical' (ethikotatai) and therefore suitable for educational purposes, those in the Phrygian mode must only be listened to, and their performance must be left to musicians of servile or low condition. It is worth noting, in passing, that here we return, though by an unexpected path, to a fact we established in an earlier [place], namely that possession music is music one listens to and that is played by others.

"Aulos music is Phrygian, then, and it excites 'enthusiasm' among those persons in whom the effect of the 'sacred melodies' (hieron melon) incite that kind of emotion. Those persons are then thrown into a state comparable to that produced by administering a remedy or purge (katharsos), and the result of these 'purgative' or 'cathartic' melodies is to produce a feeling of liberation in those to whom they are administered. Briefly summarized, this is the well-known theory of the relations between music and trance that Aristotle advances in book 8.7 of the Politics. CLearly it is very different from Plato's. Not a word here of either dance or movement: everything centers upon a theory of the effect (dynamis) of music, which is ethical when the mode is Dorian, orgiastic when the mode is Phrygian. In Plato, this aspect of the matter is not even mentioned, the reason being that he does not hold the same views as Aristotle on the ethos of modes. Aristotle is at the same time clearer and more liberal. For him, the Dorian alone is 'ethical', which is to say moral and worthy of figuring in the educational program of well-born youths. The Phrygian, being 'orgiastic' and 'passionate', must be excluded from such a program, and should only be listened to when played by employees of low estate or slaves. This said, however, all modes are good provided they are used in the correct way at the right time....

"Plato's and Aristotle's interpretations of the relations between music and trance are thus quite different. Plato's theory of movement in harmony with the cosmos carries on the Pythagorean tradition.[408] By systematizing the ideas inherited from the past concerning the ethos of modes, and at the same time relativizing them, which is to say giving them a much more psychological than moral content, Aristotle branches off in a quite different direction. We are not concerned here with deciding which theory is the better. What is interesting is to observe the extent to which the views of the two philosophers differ on the subject of music's relation to trance, even though they are separated by only about fifty years, and they both interpret what must have been currently observable facts presenting much the same aspect to each of them....

"The Phrygian [mode] undoubtedly was—and here we concur with Jacques Chailley—as much a style as a mode [italics mine (Ed.)]. To use Isobel Henderson's terms (1957), the word harmonia did not only designate a certain scale but also an 'idiom'. Should we conclude from this that Phrygian melodies were so charged with expressivity and emotional content that they were capable of inducing trance by virtue of this quality alone? This would mean accepting the idea that music has a power sui generis, an idea refuted at length in earlier chapters [of the present work]. But this, one may say, is nevertheless Aristotle's theory! Not quite, I would reply. True, he writes (Politics 1340a) that the tunes of Olympus make men's souls 'enthusiastic' and enthusiasm is an affliction (pathos) of the soul. True, he repeats

---

408 "Harmony" not in a polyphonic or "chordal" sense, however, but with respect to the ratios of different intervals to each other. See discussion by John Hollander, **HARMONY OF THE SPHERES*** §136.10 above. (Ed.)

elsewhere (1342a) that under the influence of these 'sacred melodies' certain persons are 'possessed' by a form of agitation known as enthusiasm. But he presents this effect of the Phrygian only as a particular — and, without doubt, extreme — case of a more general action tending to produce emotion in those inclined to 'pity or terror'.

"The well-known passage in the *Politics* (1342a) in which Aristotle's views on the relation of music to trance are expressed is quite significant. The *katharsis* that occurs in possession rituals, as a result of 'enthusiastic' harmonies and 'sacred melodies', is presented as being of the same order as that which is at work in the theater. (In passing, let me point out that this is probably the earliest text associating possession and theater in this way.) More generally still, these 'purgative melodies', which arouse 'a pleasurable feeling of relief' in emotional people, provide men with 'harmless delight'. The Phrygian mode thus covers a very broad musical field, one that includes trance music, theater music, the equivalent of variety show music (I mean those songs that move souls subject to 'pity and terror,' just cited), and last, dance music, when the latter is agitated or unbridled in character. Moreover, as it emerges from book 8 of the *Politics*, this Dorian/Phrygian opposition subsumes a whole series of other oppositions: calm vs. agitated, virile vs. effeminate, worthy vs. unworthy, aristocratic vs. plebian, beauty vs. banality, educational vs. entertaining. The Phrygian side of this opposition could be summed up in one word: release. For Aristotle, then, Phrygian does not mean only 'enthusiastic' in the religous sense of the term, but rather 'orgiastic' in its general and rather late sense. When Aristotle writes (1341a) that the *aulos* — and therefore the Phrygian mode — is not 'a moralizing but rather an orgiastic influence,' so that it should only be used for purposes of 'purification rather than instruction,' he is certainly not thinking only of Dionysiac

ceremonies. He is also thinking of theatrical performances or banquets; in short, all situations in which people seek release. On the contrary, when he specifcally targets possession (*Politics* 1339b) and the music that induces it, he does not merely talk about the Phrygian, but is much more specific: the tunes of Olympus are the ones that make our souls 'enthusiastic'. Naturally, this must be set alongside the passage I have often quoted from the *Symposium* (215c) in which we are told that only the tunes of Marsyas are capable of 'inducing possession.' Why this insistence on the two names? Obviously because, by using them, Aristotle and Plato are indicating *ipso facto* that it is not just any Phrygian melody or just any *aulos* tune that triggers trance.

"By thus specifying that only the tunes of Olympus and Marsyas are capable of inducing trance, both writers obviously have a particular repertoire in mind. What might its characteristics have been? The text tells us nothing. But the reference to two legendary if not mythical characters implies that the repertoire in quesiton was ancient and traditional. This is not all, however. Marsyas and Olympus, and particularly the first, are strongly branded, if one may say so, as Phrygians. To mention Marsyas is almost to name Phrygia. And what was Phrygia if not precisely the homeland of Dionysus? 'From the fields of Lydia and Phrygia, fertile in gold, I traveled first to the sun-smitten Persian plains,' he tells us himself in the *Bacchae* (14-15). And a little later: 'O my sisterhood of worshipers, whom I lead with me from barbaric countries, from Tmolus, bastion of Lydia, who live and travel at my side. Raise the music of your own country, the Phrygian drums* invented by Rhea the Great Mother, and by me.' And lastly, in a later passage the chorus describes the Corybantes as 'wedding their frenzies to the gentle breath of the Phrygian pipes.' In the time of Plato and Aristotle, 'Phrygian melody' clearly meant 'melodies in the Phrygian mode', but not necessarily 'melodies originating in Phrygia'. Evidently this is what was meant by 'melodies of Marsyas' or 'of Olympus'. As we have seen, the Phrygian mode was probably very recognizable as music, but it was less by virtue of being in the Phrygian mode than by virtue of originating in Phrygia that these melodies were endowed with the power of 'inducing possession'. In other words, their effect was due less to their musical characteristics than to the fact they they were signs: signs of Phrygia, the land from which Dionysus himself had come; in short, from the cradle of Dionysus worship. This process conforms with the general logic of possession which frequently makes a point of revealing the foreign origin of the god responsible for trance through all sorts of external signs. Possession is essentially identification with another. To assign that other a precise homeland is to assert his identity and thus his reality. As [may be seen in another context], in Benin, when people belonging to Gun tribes are possessed by Yoruba divines, they speak Yoruba and sing Yoruba songs. In South Africa, when the Thonga are possessed by spirits of Zulu or Ndau origin, then they sing Zulu or Ndau tunes. In Greece, in order to become possessed by Dionysus, one needed tunes originating in Phrygia....

"*The Renaissance.* There has never been a period when musicians, peots, and 'humanists' — all united at this time by one and the same desire, that of reviving Greek art — have been so deeply concerned about the power of music as the Renaissance. In Italy, as in France, the main concern was to rediscover the secret power than music was believed to have had in antiquity. People referred, with utmost seriousness, to the story of Orpheus* taming the wild beasts with the spell of his songs and to that of Amphion* displacing stones with

the sound of his lyre* to build the walls of Thebes. Even the kings put their word in. Like the emperors of ancient China, they held music responsible for public morality.[409] In his *Lettres patentes*, which created the Académie de Poesie et de Musique in 1570 in Paris, Charles IX declared: 'It is of great importance for the morals of the citizens of a town that the music current in the country should be kept under certain laws, all the more so because men conform themselves to music and regulate their behavior accordingly; so that whenever music is disordered, morals are also depraved, and whenever it is well ordered, men are well tutored.' Created to 'restore the usage of music in its perfection,' that is to say, in the style of antiquity, this Académie was intended to makes its 'listeners... capable of higher knowledge, after they have been purged of whatever may remain in them of barbarity.' One might think one is reading the *Li Ki* (Memorial of the Rites) of the ancient Chinese*. In fact, via Florence and the work of Ficino, adapted to French taste by Pontus de Tyard, what is being revived here is Plato's *Laws* and *The Republic*. And in the 'purged' we just read, we may also recognize Aristotle's catharsis from the *Politics*. With these *Lettres patentes*, which merely repeat the terms of the letter in which Baïf requested the creation of the Académie by the king, the whole program of the Pléiade poets was given official recognition. Through them, Ronsard's very theory of the union of poetry and music was made state policy; hence their importance.

"Immediately associated with poetry, music was seen in the Renaissance as a decisive factor of civilization. It raises the soul and refines manners. By what means? Essentially by its capacity to arouse emotions. Among the ancients, Pontus de Tyard writes in his *Solitaire second ou dis-*

---

409 The discussion in this particular section complements others given under the headings of **ETHOS* (Greek)** and **HARMONY OF THE SPHERES***, above. (Ed.)

cours de la musique, 'music served as an exercise to temper the soul into a perfect condition of goodness and virtue, arousing and calming, by its native power and its secret energy, the passions and affections, while its sounds were borne from the ears to the spiritual parts.' Such is the model to be followed. Thanks to the intimate union of words and melody, of 'measured verses' and music, also 'measured', it is possible to obtain the three desired 'effects', which are, Baïf writes in his letter to Charles IX, to 'tighten, untighten, and calm men's minds.' The supreme aim of music is thus clearly defined: it should move us. And the result of these 'effects' is described for us by Ronsard in his hymn to the cardinal of Lorraine, a poem in which, in praising the cardinal's musician, called Ferabosco, the poet also praises what he sees as the ideal in the field of music:

Oh heavens, what sweetness, what
    ease and what pleasure
The soul receives when it feels itself
    seized
By the movement, the sound, and the
    voice combined
That your Ferabosco on three lyres
    conjoins
When the three Apollos*, singing
    divinely
And gently wedding the lyre to the
    voice
Suddenly, with agile throat and hand
Make Dido die again through Virgil's
    verse
Almost dying themselves; or with
    louder trill
Rethunder the sieges of Calais or
    Guienne
Your brother's victories. Thus there is
    no soul
That does not leave its body and
    swoon away
At their sweet song, just as, up there in
    the skies
At the god Apollo's song, the gods all
    swoon
As he plays his lyre....

"The ideal, as we see, is that music should make one swoon. And what is swooning if not falling into ecstasy or trance, in short to be beside oneself? 'There is no soul that does not leave its body.' Again we are reminded of that great coming and going of the souls [which one encounters] in Haiti and Africa.

"Exagerration, one may say. A mere figure of speech that should not be taken seriously. Not at all! The literature of the time is replete with references to *fureur* and *furore*, words that translate the Greek *mania*, and that alternate with 'enthusiasm'. In his *Histoire et chronique de Provence* (1614), Nostradamus (not the astrologer but his son) writes that the troubadours derived their poetic invention from 'a certain inspiration and divine frenzy called enthusiasm by the Greeks.' A century later, in his *Le Parnasse ou l'Apothéose de Corelli*, François Couperin was to express in music 'the enthusiasm of Corelli caused by the waters of Hippocrene'. How are we to explain this rather unexpected resurgence of 'enthusiasm'? Largely by the influence of two 'humanists' somewhat forgotten today, but who in their time played a decisive role in this return to antiquity that so profoundly marked artistic life in the Renaissance: Ficino, the great translator of Plato, and then Pontus de Tyard, the masterthinker, so to speak, of the Pléiade. Tyard's book *Solitaire premier, ou Discours de Muses et de la fureur poétique* was published in 1552 and reprinted in 1575, and its title evidently echoes that of Ficino's commentaries on the *Ion* published earlier under the subtitle *'vel furore poetico'*.

"This 'poetic furor' is nothing other than Plato's poetic *mania*, which was attributable, as we saw, to the Muses. Both Ficino and Tyard resuscitated the Platonic theory of the four aspects of *mania*, which, via Latin, became *furore* or *fureur*. In resuscitating it, however, they also transformed it somewhat. Times had changed since Plato. Of the four aspects of *mania*, three had become rather difficult to celebrate: First, erotic *mania*, totally identified with pederasty by Socrates; second, prophetic *mania*, which had acquired a whiff of fire and brimstone; last, telestic *mania*, that of possession, which of course was no longer overtly practiced, under the penalty of being brought before the Inquisition. Of these three, however, the last was to survive the best, owing to a certain amount of clever juggling that enabled Bacchus, with the help of communion wine, to become identified with Jesus, and Dionysianism with religious fervor. But the only one that had remained at all easily defensible was poetic *mania*, with the result that it eclipsed the other three, and 'poetic furor' came to be the only state representative of 'enthusiasm'. Let there be no mistake, however: this poetic 'furor' was still very close to the religious frenzy, and was regarded as an inspiration, in the religious sense of the term, as a visit from the spirit; in other words, as a trance state, if not as possession.

"Let us now return to the 'effects' of music.[410] If in the Dorian mode, music will incite men to moderation and virtue, thus exerting the moral influence referred to in the *Lettres patentes*. If Phrygian, it will unleash the passions, enthusiasm, and ultimately violence. Here, in a much simplified form, we recognize the theory of the ethos* of modes as set forth by Aristotle. The poets and musicians of the Pléiade took it very seriously indeed. 'If it please God to be able by the Dorian mode to extinguish the furor that the Phrygian may have aroused,' Claude Le Jeune writes in the dedication of his *Dodécacorde* to Turenne. Forty years later, Marin Mersenne himself, having first expressed the opinion, in his *Harmonie universelle*, that 'bad music [meaning Phrygian] should be banned from society,' wishes that 'magistrates would institute prizes and rewards for those who practice none but

Dorian music.' In that time of religious wars it was apparently the secret hope of Baïf that the psalms in 'measured verses' would disarm the rebellious Huguenots and that the pacifying effect of the Dorian mode would restore harmony between Catholics and Protestants. The least we can say is that Renaissance man took music seriously!

"[Overall, a number of anecdotes demonstrate a characteristic Renaissance interest in,] first, music that renders you beside yourself; [and,] second, music that restores you to yourself.... [With respect to the first, for example,] Pontus de Tyard (1555)... passes on a story told to him at first hand by a contemporary, the count of Vintimiglia. The count tells how, in Milan, where he had been invited to 'a sumptuous and magnificent feast, held in honor of that city's most illustrious company,' he heard a lute* player who had 'so divine a fashion of touching' and making 'the strings die beneath his fingers,' that all those who heard him 'remained deprived of all feeling, apart from that of hearing, as if the soul, having deserted all the seats of sensibility, had withdrawn to the edge of the ears, so as to take its pleasure more easily in so ravishing a symphony'....

"*Music and Trance Among the Arabs.* Of all the peoples in the world, the Arabs are undoubtedly those who have associated music and trance the most closely: first, in their religious life, with Sufism*, in which trance (*wajd*), which for many adepts occupies a very large place in the search for God, is achieved very often through music; and second, in profane life, in which musical emotion (*tarab*) traditionally leads, very frequently, to trance behavior. These two aspects of the relations between music and trance among the Arabs are what we must now examine.

"*Religious Trance. Kith adab al-sama°y wa al-wajd*, 'Book of the Right Uses of Audition

---

410 Again, see also our entry for **ETHOS* (Greek)**, Vol I above. (Ed.)

and Trance'—such is the title given by Ghazzali (al-Ghazzali, known as Algazel during the Middle Ages) to the eighth section of his renowed *Ihya^c ulum al-din*, 'Book of the Revivifying of the Sciences of the Faith', which dates from the early years of our twelfth century and constitutes one of the most immportant writings on Sufism. 'Audition', let it be clear from the start, means audition of what we have here decided to call 'music'. To be sure, one could not have found a book more closely connected with the problem of the relations between music and trance. But before coming to it, let us first examine the words *sama^c* and *wadj*, which I have translated as 'audition' and 'trance', whereas Duncan B. MacDonald, to whom we owe the English translation of this work, most often renders them by the terms 'listening' and 'ecstasy'.

"The word 'Sama^c'. Given the context in which Ghazzali uses it, the word *sama^c* is in fact untranslatable, for two reasons. The first is that it denotes a very particular thing, peculiar to Sufism, which is the ceremony made up of prayer, music, and dance that brings dervishes together for the purpose of adoring God and practicing trance. This ceremony is called the *sama^c* and, taken in this sense, it is similar to the word *islam* in that it has no equivalent in French or English. The second reason is that Ghazzali's book is above all an attempt to justify *sama* and his justification rests upon the ambiguity of the word, or rather upon the fact that the word has two meanings, a very particular one, which I have just given, and a general one, which is 'listening' or 'audition'. If 'audition' *(sama^c)*—'of poetry and music' is understood—is lawful in the eyes of the faith because it can cite illustrious precedents in its support, then the same *sama^c* (ceremony) is also lawful. This, in extremely simplified forms, is his argument. Now we must look at the meaning, or rather the meanings, of *sama^c* even more closely.

"The relation between *sama^c* as ceremony and trance *(wajd)* is so close that the word *sama^c*, in this sense, also signifies the trance state. One can in fact say 'to go into *sama^c*' or 'to be seized by *sama^c*,' or again, 'to be in that state.' Molé writes (1963) that the term is practically equivalent to 'ecstatic dance'. At the beginning of the first chapter of his book (MacDonald 1901), Ghazzali says, 'knowest that the *sama^c*... bears as fruit a state in the heart that is called trance [*wajd*].' Taken to its limits, *sama^c* can also mean 'music', or something very like it, since one can say 'hear *sama^c*'—which is surprising since it runs counter to the very logic of the word, for such a usage amounts to the same thing as saying 'hearing the audition'. But, once again, *sama^c*, which derives from the root *s.m.^c.* (hear, listen) denotes, in its first and general sense, the act of hearing or listening, without reference to any particular acoustic phenomenon, or, let us say, 'audition'. Granting this, in the Sufi texts that interest us here, the verb 'hear' *(s.m.^c)* in its various forms always includes an implicit object, which is either poetry, the Koran, or music, though a particular kind of music only. But which one? In order to answer this, I must first digress on the word 'music'.

"The Arabic word *musiqi*—which comes directly from the Greek, need I say?—does not appear even once in Ghazzali's book. This is clearly not because he does not know the word; at the time he was writing his book, the translation of Greek authors into Arabic had already been going on for a hundred and fifty years. It is because he is avoiding it. For several reasons. First, because in his time the word *musiqi* denoted the rules or the art of music but not music itself as a product of that art, or, if one may say so, as a concrete thing. In order to refer to what we would call music in the concrete sense, Ghazzali talks either of song *(ghina)* or or instruments used for entertainment *(malahi)*, depending on whether he has vocal music or instrumental music in mind. And so of course, he had many other words at his disposal, such as 'entertainment' *(lahw)*, in the sense of 'entertainment music', 'melody' *(lahn)*, or 'sound' *(sawt)*, for example, without mentioning the names of the various musical instruments. But he does not have a word that covers a very general concept comparable to that we convey by the use of our word 'music'. (Although, as we all know, this word can have different, and even opposing meanings on occasions, according to who is using it.)

"If Ghazzali does not use the word *musiqi* it is also because this word, referring as it does to the rules for composing music, relates much more to the music maker than to the listener. And it is precisely the listener he is interested in, not the musician — for a very good reason, indeed, since in the eyes of the faith the musician is always a suspect, if not blameworthy person. His third and last reason for not using *musiqi* is that it does not connote any moral value. The rules of music apply to all kinds of music; not only to that played for spiritual purposes but also to that played at 'gatherings where wine is drunk' (Mole 1963) in which the songs are mere 'amusement and futility.' From Ghazzali's point of view, which is essentially that of finding a moral justification for *sama^c*, it is indispensible to make a distinction between what we might term 'light' music and 'serious' music. Only the latter is lawful. To confuse the two by using the same term to cover both would thus be aberrant. That which is lawful consisted of: first, the cantilation *(taghbir)* of the Koran, of course; second, sung poetry, on the condition that its sentiments and thoughts were sufficiently elevated; and third, accompanied song, provided that the musical instruments utilized were permitted, which is to say instruments that were never associated with blameworthy musical practices. But this is not all. Another restriction must be added to these. It is permissible to hear only that which one hears when one is oneself in a certain state of inner purity. It is not only what is sung or played that counts; it is also the disposition of the listener. Heard with a pure heart, music can be lawful even though it would not be if

one listened to it in a lascivious state of mind. This delimitation of the repertoire (Koran, poetry, accompanied song), made all the stricter by the proviso applying to the listener's own intention, is precisely what is conveyed by the word. This conceptual patterning of reality to which it corresponds is comparable to no other, and certainly not to that of the word 'music'.

"Thus, in a Sufi text, the range of things possible for 'audition' *(sama^c)* is restricted to poetry, the Koran, and, let us say, serious music, and these three things combine, for this very reason, to constitute a particular category of sound. This category, which is covered by no particular Arabic word (unless it is *sama^c*), may thus be defined, in the context of Sufism, as the category of the objects of audition *(sama^c)*. This category of sounds, as we have seen, is not only constituted by the different intrinsic qualities of its three components; the fact that it is heard also plays a role. It exists only insofar as it is perceived by the ear and insofar as it affects the hearing. Twice, on the first page of his book, Ghazzali stresses the importance of the ear: 'There is no way of extracting their hidden things save by the flint and steel of listening to music and singing, and there is no entry into the heart save by the antechamber of the ears' (MacDonald 1901). The category is, therefore, not constituted at the level of the message itself, nor at that of its sender, but at the level of its receiver, or, if one prefers, at the level of perception.

"Why is this? Apparently because the three components of this category of sound are all capable, from the listener's standpoint, of the same effects. This is what emerges form a reading of the 'Book of the Right Usages of Music and Trance', which clearly shows that the Koran, poetry, and serious music are all three equally capable of inducing *wajd*, which is to say trance, and of doing so in any context, not only during *sama^c* (the ceremony) but also outside it. However, let us observe that the manifestations of this trance will be very different depending on whether the 'audition' takes place during *sama*^c or outside it. This is a point of great importance for our purposes, and we shall return to it.

"The Word 'Wajd'. This word, which is more often translated as *extase* or ecstasy, but which I shall render as 'trance'..., is only used in the Sufi vocabulary and is derived from the root *w.j.d.*, 'to find, to meet with'. Speaking about the 'reality of trance' *(wajd)* for Sufis and the relation of 'audition' to the soul, Ghazzali writes: 'Wajd is an expression of what is found [*yujadu*] through audition [*sama*^c]'. This discovery, this encounter, involves something that is in close connection with the deepest part of one's being, or that is in intimate harmony with the situation being experienced. It manifests itself suddenly, like an illumination (I imagine that Saint Paul on his way to Damascus was experiencing *wajd*). It is revelation or inspiration. Its relation to 'audition', Ghazzali says, derives from the fact that it 'produces purity of heart and the purity is a cause of revealing'. Trance *(wajd)* consists of 'Revelation proceeding from the Truth,' he says elsewhere, and the man who experiences trance achieves it 'because he has found [*wajada*] what was lacking with him.'

"How does this trance manifest itself? Let us begin with the case in which it is induced by audition of the Koran. 'The stories indicating that trance [*wajd*] has shown itself in the possessors of heart at hearing the Koran are many,' Ghazzali tells us, and then cites several of them, beginning with three anecdotes concerning the Prophet himself. The latter is depicted as follows: 'his eyes were flowing with tears...; then he fell, fainting,' and weeping, while listening to three different passages from the Koran. 'And much is transmitted from the Companions and the Follower concerning ecstasy through the Qur'an. Of them were some who fell swooning, and some who wept, and some who fainted, and some who died in their

fainting.' He then recounts: 'And 'Umar heard a man reciting, *Verily the punishment of thy Lord surely descends; there is none to keep it back!* [Qur., 52:8]. Then he cried with a great cry and fell fainting, and was carried into his house and ceased not to be sick in his house for a month. And Salih al-Marri recited to Abu Jarir, and he sobbed and died. And ash-Shai^ci heard one reciting, *This shall be a day when they shall not speak and shall not be permitted to excuse themselves* [Qur., 83:6] and he fell fainting....' 'And similar stories are transmitted from a number of them,' Ghazzali adds.

" 'So, too, is the case with the Sufis,' Ghazzali tells us: 'One night of Ramadan ash-Shibli was in his mosque, and he was praying behind an Imam of his, and the Imam recited, *And, verily, if We willed We would bring to thee him whom We inspired* [Qur., 17:88], and ash-Shibli shrieked a great shriek, the people thought that his soul had fled; his face grew red, and his shoulder muscles quivered, and kept saying, "With such words He addresses the beloved," repeating that over and over.'

" 'Audition' of the Koran does not have the power of inducing trance solely among devotees. The following story concerns a slave girl, a *tar* player, who were numerous among the Arabs of that time. This story does not come from Ghazzali, of course, but from a quite different source. As she passed close to a Koran reader who was chanting the verse, 'Truly hell surrounds the impious,' the girl threw away her *tar*, uttered a cry, and fainted. When she came to, she broke her instrument into pieces and embraced religious life.

"Trance induced by the 'audition' of poetry manifests itself in the same way: by cries and fainting; occasionally, too, by madness and self-destruction. For instance, Ghazzali recounts a story of how the famous Abu-l-Husayn an-Nuri, hearing at a gathering a certain line from a poem on the subject of religious love, 'arose and constrained himself to an ecstasy, and ran wildly on, and happened upon a cane-break which had been cut, but the stems in which remained like swords. Then he kept running in it and repeating the verse until the morning, and the blood flowed from his legs so that his feet and shanks swelled. And he lived after that a few days and died.'

"Now we come to an example of trance brought on by singing.[411] The scene is set in the vicinity of Baghdad, beside the Tigris. On the verandah of a fine residence there is a man; before him a slave girl is singing. Beneath the verandah a very handsome young man is listening. He asks the slave girl to repeat the line she has just sung: ' "Every day thou changes!" Then she repeated it, and the youth kept saying "This, by Allah, is my changing in my state with Truth!" and he sobbed a sob and died.'

"One last example is also very representative of the situation in which trance results from the shock of hearing sung words that unexpectedly correspond precisely to the dramatic situation in which the hearer finds himself. The coincidence triggers an inner upheaval so intense it can be fatal. This story, taken from Isfahani's *Book of Songs* and wholly profane in character, is that of a woman whose husband is taking her away against her wishes, to the country where he lives. The wife, 'having heard a singer reciting some lines by Abu-Katifah, sighs convulsively and drops dead.' The lines of poetry were: 'I spend the night in grief and moan... thinking of my fellow countrymen, who live so far away from me.'

"All our examples thus far are of unexpected trances linked with situations in which the Koran, poetry, or a song was heard accidentally, as it were. The audition (*sama*[c]) was fortuitous. It did not occur during a *sama*[c] in the sense of a 'ceremony'. When, on the contrary, trance does occur during such a ceremony, it may still manifest itself by cries, tears, and fainting (and eventually even death), but Ghazzali tells us that according to the 'right usages' (*adab*) one should not abandon oneself to trance unless it is really too strong; one should always try to dominate it. 'Then think not that he who throws himself upon the ground in agitation is more perfect as to trance than he who is still and does not agitate himself; yet, often he who is still is more perfect as to trance than he who is in agitation,' he writes.

"The second part of his book is devoted, first, to the 'effects' (*athar*) of *sama*[c], then to the 'right usages' that should govern it. The latter are five in number and relate to (1) the time, place, and participants in the *sama*[c]; (2) the precautions to be taken regarding the presence of neophytes (*murid*) to whom the *sama*[c] could be injurious; (3) attention and inner concentration; self-control, consisting in not-yielding to the trance unless it is impossible not to (absence of external manifestations may be a sign of the trance's weakness, but it may also be a sign of the subject's strength of will); (4) control of tears and dancing, neither of which should be indulged in unless it is impossible to restrain them; similarly with the tearing of garments, which should not be practiced except within certain limits; (5) courtesy toward other participants and the behavior one should observe while dancing.

---

411 I would suggest that recitation from the Koran or of poetry and singing or other musical performance in a suitable context are, alike, an announcement or heralding of the fact of one's being or existing — i.e. of the divine spirit itself, then — through *sound*, which only happens to be directed upon a particular spiritual being through the particular formulas of the reciting or singing in question. Thus as alike renderings of sound, music *is* a kind of poetry (words presented in a formulaic way), and recitation *is* a kind of music (pitches presented in a formulaic way): *both are equally ritual performances of (certain modes of) sound.* (Ed.)

"Let us look for a moment at that curious manifestation of trance called *tamziq*, which consists in tearing one's clothes. The same behavior, which the evidence suggests is a stereotype, can also be observed outside the *sama*^c ceremony. One famous example is that of a certain Umayyad caliph (living in our eighth century) who, so the story goes, was so affected by the music of a great singer of the day that he tore his clothing. The singer was given a thousand pieces of gold as a reward, Farmer tells us (1929), but at the same time the caliph warned him: 'When you return to Al-Medina you may be inclined to say, "I have sung before the Commander of the Faithful and so entranced him that he tore his garments," but, by Allah, if a word escapes your lips of what you have seen, you will lose your head for it.' We see how much this form of trance behavior, however conventional and stereotyped it may be, is regarded as irresistible. It is also interesting to note that it is both and at the same time highly valued — even a caliph may be subject to it — and somehow shameful — it must not be disclosed. During a *sama*^c, one can tear one's garments ony if the need is irresistible, and only on the condition that the remaining pieces of clothing are still usable afterwards (MacDonald 1902).

"We have seen that outside the *sama*^c, trance manifests itself quite often not only by fainting but also by sudden death. Ghazzali also reports on a case of death during a *sama*^c caused by struggling too hard to overcome trance. 'It is related,' he tells us, 'that a youth used to accompany al-Junayd, and whenever he heard aught of the mention *(dhikr)* of God he would cry out. Then al-Junayd said to him, "If you do that another time, you shall not accompany me." And thereafter he kept putting pressure upon himself until from every hair of him there would drip a drop of water, and he did not cry out. And it is related that he choked one day through the force of the pressure upon him and sighed

a single sob, and his heart broke and he died.'

"Whether trance takes place during or outside the *sama*^c, we see it can produce the same manifestations: sudden death, fainting, cries, tears, tearing of garments. The only difference is that 'right usages' of the *sama*^c consist in not succumbing to trance but precisely in controlling these agitations and manifestations: 'Think not that he who throws himself upon the ground in agitation is more perfect as to trance than he who is still and does not agitate himself; yet, often he who is still is more perfect as to trance than he who is in agitation.' But after having stated in the first lines of his first chapter that the fruit of the *sama*^c is trance, Ghazzali adds: 'and trance bears as fruit a moving of the extremities of the body, either with a motion that is not measured and is called agitation or with a measured motion which is called clapping of the hands and swaying of the members.' In other words, he establishes an opposition between 'agitation' *(idtirab)* — or 'nonmeasured' motion — and 'measured' motions — or dance — to which trance leads when it is controlled. 'Agitation', with its ensuing cries, tears, fainting, and madness, is observed above all, as we have seen, when trance occurs outside the *sama*^c or, in other words, when there is no ritual. Let us say that, from our perspective, this is a nonritualized crisis or trance. Dancing, on the contrary, is observed only during the *sama*^c, which is to say during a ritual. Let us say that this is a ritual trance. So once again we find the opposition between ritual and nonritual trance, which is familiar by now and which we have encountered so often in matters of possession. Nonritualized trance is frequently lethal (as Zempléni tells us), even within the *sama*^c ritual, when it is so violent that it cannot conform to the ritual (as with the young follower of Al-Junayd). Ritual trance, on the contrary, consists in a state of plenitude and exaltation.

"The kind of trance, Ghazzali tells us, that is 'found with Hearing *(sama*^c*)*,' and which is a 'Revelation proceeding from the truth,' is at the same time 'Witnessing of the Watcher' (i.e., knowledge of God), presence of understanding, beholding of the unseen, communion with the secret, and relation to what is lacking. It is pleasure and purity of heart — love, or rather passion, for God. It is not, of course, a possession trance, and Ghazzali who clearly has Halladj in mind, denounces the heresy of the man who claims to be 'inhabited' (hulul) by God and to become 'one' with him. It is a trance, however, in the sense in which we defined our terms at the beginning of this [essay], and not an ecstasy, since it manifests itself by movement ('it bears an excitation of the bodily extremities like a fruit'), is produced by sensorial stimuli (sounds), and is achieved not in solitude but in the company of other particpants (the sama^c has three essential ingredients according to Al-Junayd: time, place, and company).

"Perhaps, in order to distinguish it from possession trance, we may call it a trance of communion or a 'communial' trance. It is not conceived as the effect of God occupying a person — which would be totally impious — but as the result of a more or less immediate relation to God, one that can have the shattering nature of a revelation, the calm nature of contemplation, or even, at the very limit, the nature of a union. The word 'communial' seems to me capable of covering all three.

"Although it is a trance, then, and not an ecstasy, one might say that when wajd is completely controlled, mastered, sublimated, it is nevertheless at the very frontier of ecstasy. This frontier is crossed when wajd becomes fana, which lies somewhere beyond and is a state of annihila-

tion (Molé 1963), or 'disappearance' of human qualities in God. This state of ecstasy is frequently the result of another practice known as dhikr, which is often closely associated with sama^c.

"The Word 'Dhikrh'. In a very general way dhikr — a word often translated as 'recollection' — may be defined as an exercise of piety consisting in repeating the divine name in order to recollect God and at the same time to make him recollect one's existence, in the hopes of attracting his blessing. The word dhikr in fact derives from dhakara, 'to recollect, remember'. The practice of dhikr, like that of sama^c, has been the subject of many works by Arab authors, particularly by the Sufis. To be sure, our interest in this practice is limited to its use as a means of attaining the trance state.

"If we broadly schematize this very complex question, we can say that dhikr has two principal aspects: solitary dhikr and collective dhikr (Gardet 1952). The first is also called the dhikr of the privileged and the second the dhikr of the commoners. The first, the solitary, that of the privileged, displays three different degrees of ascetic discipline and ultimately leads to what we have agreed to call ecstasy. The second, the collective, that of the commoners, is on the contrary an attempt to reach the trance state and contains only one degree of ascetic discipline. Solitary dhikr, which uses a very elaborate technique of breath control and which involves the silent and inner repetition of the divine name, leads to a state of annhilation, fana, which consists in a total absorption of the self into God. Attained in solitude, silence, and immobility, this ecstasy — or as some say, following Mircea Eliade (1948), this 'enstasy'—is accompanied by hallucinations that are mainly auditory when the *dhikr* is of the second degree, and visual when it reaches the third, the one called 'inner' or 'secret' *dhikr*. Clearly this form of *dhikr* is of no interest to us here, since it is practised in silence.

"The 'collective' *dhikr* or *dhikr* 'of the commoners' *dhikr al-'awamm*) (Garet 1952), on the contrary, is of the utmost interest to us since it is closely associated with music and dance.[412] This is the *dhikr* (or *zikr*) often called 'public' (in opposition to the other, which is 'secret'), since it is practiced by a number of dervish brotherhoods from India to Morocco. Its very spectacular aspects, with its violent trances during which the dervishes pierce their flesh, walk on burning coals, grasp red-hot pieces of iron without burning themselves, swallow broken glass—in short give visible proof of their invulnerability— have been described innumerable times. These practices were introduced into *dhikr* at a relatively late date, sometime around our twelfth century, it seems. The style and repertoire of the singing, the use of musical instruments, the dance techniques, the demonstrations of, let us say, fakirism, vary from brotherhood to brotherhood, each having developed its own particular form of *dhikr* over time. But among those that practice collective *dhikr* aloud, the manner of intoning the divine name by shouting, if not howling, it out remains more or less the same everywhere. Hence the name of 'howling dervishes' that has sometimes been applied (very improperly, I might add) to the members of these brotherhoods.

"Nothing could be more different from the *sama*ᶜ described by Ghazzali very early

in the twelfth century, or from the *sama*ᶜ of the Mawlawiyya (the 'whirling dervishes') as it was instituted some hundred and fifty years later by Jalal al-Din Rumi, then the *zikr* of the Rifaᶜiyya or the *hadra* of the ᶜIsawiyya, as they can be observed in our day. We will now turn to the relationship between music and the diverse manifestations of trance that characterize these two broad types of ritual, *sama*ᶜ and *dhikr*. But before we do so, we must first explain in greater depth the opposition we posit between *sama*ᶜ and *dhikr*.

"According to Massignon, in the course of time the practice of *dhikr* gradually replaced the *sama*ᶜ among the Sufis. 'The masters of mysticism,' he writes (1934), 'gradually abandoned free musical séances [*sama*ᶜ]... for fixed recitations of litanies based on the Koran [*dhikr*].' We shall return to this point before long, but let us specify first of all that *ama*ᶜ and *dhikr* are as different from one another as the words used to designate them, and second, that they have coexisted in the past and still coexist today. As Molé states (1963), *dhikr* and *sama*ᶜ 'must be carefully distinguished, even though a certain correlation does exist between them, and despite the fact that anti-Sufi polemicists frequently confound *sama*ᶜ and public *dhikr*.' Ghazzali, in his treatise of *sama*ᶜ, refers on several occasions to *dhikr*. His brother Ahmad also mentions *dhikr* in his short description of a *sama*ᶜ séance (Robson 1938). In both of these cases *dhikr* seems to be an episode within the general framework of the *sama*ᶜ. This was some nine centuries ago. More recently, Brunel (1926) found that in Morocco the *dhikr*, accompanied by very violent trances, was practiced by the ᶜIsawiyya, whereas the

---

412 The fact that, in the present author's account, trance-states can so often be achieved *without* music suggests to me at least that the role of music, song and dance—or of rhythmic or ritualized sound or utterance generally—is or can be nevertheless a *facilitator* to achieving such a state. Thus in this context it is not a case of the latter being "unnecessary" to achieving a trance state, but of understanding those (additional?) paths which music, song and dance make available to one. (Ed.)

sama^c, with very calm trances, was practiced by the Tijaniyya. In our day [1980], in Iraq, the word *dhikr* is the one used to denote the trance rituals practiced by the Qadiriyya and the Rifa^{c}iyya, while sama^c is used for those of the Yezidi (Hassan 1975), about which we admittedly have little information, but enough to presume that they are very different from the first.

"It is clearly by the extension of its original meaning that the word *dhikr* has come to denote not merely the 'mention of the divine name', as Gardet puts it, but also the entire ritual during which this recitation occurs, when it is collective and performed aloud. In the West, and also in some Muslim regions of the East and Africa, *dhikr* has become known as a ritual that is more or less open to the public and that gives rise to spectacular manifestation, and it is in this sense, consequently, that the word is most often understood outside the narrow circle of Sufism.

"This being so, there nevertheless has been, and still is, a great deal of uncertainty in the use of the two words. For example, *dhikr* is often used nowadays when referring to the sama^c of the Mevlevi. Judging from the extracts quoted by Molé (1963), the ancient writers spoke only of sama^c, so that the house where the dervishes met was called sama^{c}khana and the principal dancer sama^{c}zan (he who makes the sama^c). Inversely, in the fourteenth century, Ibn Batutah, in the story of his encounter with the Rifa^{c}iyya in India, gives the name sama^c to the displays of fakirism customary among this sect, whereas today we would speak of *dhikr*, or, better yet, *hadra*. This last word, which means 'presence' (not that of God, as one might think, but that of the Prophet), and which in many brotherhoods designates the weekly *dhikr* séance, has, according to Trimingham, 'taken the place of the term sama^c of older usage' (1971).

"It is not only with respect to terminology, however, that things have changed over the centuries. As Massignon says, there have been even greater changes in the ritual practices themselves. The practice of sama^c, as described by Ahmad (brother of the great Ghazzali), which took the form of a 'spiritual concert' that gave rise to highly controlled mystical emotions closer to ecstasy than to trance, progressively lost ground to collective *dhikr*, which became an extremely violent affair that generated rather frenzied trances. This change, which began in the twelfth century, consisted, Trimingham says, in 'the mechanization (if one can put it that way) of mystical experience' (1971), which from then on became accessible to 'the ordinary man in a relatively short space of time, by rhythmical exercises involving postures, control of breath, coordinated movements, and oral repetitions.' It is worth observing, in passing, that this evolution paralleled a similar trend in the domain of possession, in which, it has often been said, violent trances are signs of a relatively late stage in the cult's development.

"*'Sama^c Music According to Ghazzali.* We... have enough data to be able to say that at the end of the eleventh century a sama^c was a kind of 'spiritual concert', as Mokri (1961) terms it, in which the music was mainly sung, sometimes by a soloist, sometimes by a chorus, but which also included an instrumental element of varying importance. The concert took place under the direction of a master (*shaikh*) who led the ceremony and was at the same time the spiritual director of the faithful who attended. The solo singing was provided by a cantor, the *gawwal*, chosen for his musical talent and beautiful voice. The concert consisted of several successive phases, some vocal, some instrumental, some a combination of the two. The faithful listened to the music seated, in a state of great inner contemplation, and allowed themselves to be gradually overcome by trance (*wajd*), which they did their best to control. When the trance became too intense, they rose (MacDonald 1902) and began to dance. Return to calm and normality was brought about by the sound of music suitable for that purpose (Robson 1938), after which everyone went home filled with a memory of 'the revelation of what appeared to them in the state of their absorption in trance'.[413]

"Pleasure *(ladhdha),* divine love, and beauty are the three words that recur constantly in Ghazzali's account of how 'audition' produces trance, after he has first described how, in other contexts, it can arouse profound love, joy, grief, courage, warlike feelings, and how, in other circumstances, it can also be a summons to pilgrimage. The cause of these states *(ahwal)* that invade the heart when one is hearing music is the secret of God Most High, Ghazzali tells us and 'consists in a relationship of measured tones to souls' *(al naghamat al mauzuna).* And 'knowledge of the cause why souls receive impressions through sounds,' he adds, 'belongs to the most subtle of the sciences of the Revelations to which Sufis are granted.' The pleasure *(ladhdha)* given by music is something that only madmen, the insensitive, and the hard of heart do not experience. Such people are amazed that it is possible to feel pleasure and go into trance as a result of listening to music, and their amazement is like that of the impotent man who marvels at 'the pleasure of sexual intercourse, and the youth [who] marvels at the pleasure of governing.' Because 'in the case of him whose power of perception is imperfect, that he should have pleasure through it cannot be imagined.' We clearly see just how sensual Ghazzali's theory on the relations between music and trance is. Elsewhere, when he explains what the onset of trance owes to understanding of the words as opposed to the pure sound of the melody, Ghazzali

still talks about pleasure: one faints 'from the force of joy, pleasure, and gladness,' he says. But this joy, this pleasure, this gladness, are associated with love of, or rather passion for, God. Pleasure, understanding, love of God—these, then, are the three components of trance *(wajd),* which is a revelation of God when it is the result of the 'audition' of music, poetry, or the Koran.

"If singing *(ghina^c),* writes Ghazzali, has greater power than the Koran to cause trance, this is due to seven reasons: (1) because the verses of the Koran do not always match the state of the person hearing them, so that he may not understand them; (2) because the Koran is so well known that there is no surprise effect when one hears it; (3) because the sound *(sawt;* i.e., of the voice) is more pleasurable when it is measured (has a regular meter) than when it is not measured, and such 'measure' is what distinguishes poetry from the Koran; (4) because the variety of 'measured poetry' has great expressive power, even if the melody is purely instrumental and consequently has no meaning; (5) because 'measured melodies are helped and strengthened by the rhythms' of the drum, whereas the Koran never is; (6) because song can be used more freely than the Koran; (7) because 'the Koran is the word of God' and because 'it is uncreated'; because its composition does not lie in the realm of language since it is a miracle, whereas poetry, which is composed by men, is in harmony with their natural qualities.

"If both the Koran and sung poetry can induce trance *(wajd),* this is because both are capable, through the medium of a pleasant voice, of making us meet *(w.j.d.),* of revealing to us, that which is in

---

413 What I find so compelling about this particular account is that, fundamentally, it describes any normal experience of "live" music—in the concert hall where one becomes "entranced" by the swelling grandeur of a Brahms, Bruckner, or Tchaikovsky (*sans* dancing perhaps)—or swept up by the enthusiasms of a hymn-singing, Lord-praising Baptist congregation of a Sunday morning. (Ed.)

profound harmony with ourselves; but if sung poetry is more capable of doing this than the Koran, this is especially because poetry is measured and has rhythm. With respect to the arousal of trance, rhythm and measure are thus regarded as an important dimension of music. But it is not more important than the quality of the sound, the beauty of the voice, and the meaning of the words. It is the combination of several causes that gives birth to trance, as we have just seen. The drum, whose rhythm helps the melody and strengthens the measure, is mrely one among many others, an interesting point we need to remember. Although for Ghazzali the drum is the only instrument, except for the small flute*, that could be played in the $sama^c$, it nevertheless only occupies a somewhat secondary place in his list of the effects of music and, ultimately, in his theory of the relations between music and trance. This is a further example of the inanity of the theory... that the drum is always and everywhere the principal, if not the only, cause of the arousal of trance....

"*Conclusion.* Among all the types of trance we have discussed, emotional trance—profane or religious—as we observed it among the Arabs is undoubtedly the one that has the most direct and evident relation to music. Upon hearing music that has a strong emotional power over him, the subject, overwhelmed by emotion, goes into trance. From what source does the music draw this power? From the meaning of the words and from the perfection of their relation to the music. The emotion is not only affective; it is to an equal extent aesthetic, and calls upon either the subject's sense of the beautiful, or his sense of the divine, or upon both simultaneously. In this case music is pure message, and it in fact produces trance by virtue of a *sui generis* power. It must nevertheless be emphasized that this power is indissociable from that of the words—it is the 'union of poetry and music,' as they said in the

Renaissance, that is at work. The relations between music and trance are thus, in this instance, as simple as they can be. The only problem they present is that of knowing why musical emotion so commonly leads to such conduct among the Arabs and does so less frequently than elsewhere. The answer is clearly that this behavior among the Arabs is a cultural phenomenon, an expression of emotions that have been learned, stereotyped, and assigned a certain value. And although the phenomenon is less usual elsewhere, we do have some examples of it. In Europe, I [may cite] the '*Ranz des vaches*' and its effect on the Swiss. We have also recently learned that in Melanesia, among certain New Guinea Papuans and also among the 'Are'are of the Solomon Islands, musical emotion frequently gives rise to certain forms of trance. In the West, the emotional impact of military bugle calls, which can reduce the bravest men to tears, is another example. There is also justification for thinking that the more or less hysterical behavior of pop music fans can be categorized as musical emotion that has become an accepted and valued stereotyped form of behavior.

"Of all the arts, music is undoubtedly the one that has the greatest capacity to move us, and the emotion it arouses can reach overwhelming proportions. Since trance is clearly an emotional form of behavior, it is not surprising that musical emotions should prove to be destined to some extent, under the pressure of cultural factors, to become institutionalized in this form. This would mean that we are dealing here with a relation between music and trance that, although strongly influenced by culture, is nevertheless based on a natural—and thus universal—property of music, or at least of a certain kind of music. Moreover, in emotional trance it is music alone that produces the trance. This trance, which frequently is nearer to nervous crisis than to true trance, is of short duration, since it does not result, or only to a very small extent, in dance. Contrary to what happens in the case of other sorts of trance, music does not function to maintain it.

"Communial trance, as I have said, occurs in two forms, induced and conducted. When induced... it is always emotional, but can be either ritualized or not. When it is ritualized and blossoms into dance, it is the classical Arab *sama*^c. Music brings about the trance as a result of the emotional power—entirely steeped in religious feeling in this case, to be sure—of the sung poetry; it then prolongs it—maintains it, we could say—during the dancing by means of its rhythm. It therefore has two effects: first, triggering the trance; second, maintaining it—the two resulting from two very distinct actions, first that of the words, then that of the rhythm.

"When communical trance is conducted... we have the Muslim *dhikr* or, among Christians, the trance practices of the Shlustes, the Shakers, and various other sects. Here, the role of the music in producing trance is of a quite different kind. Being indissociable from dance—for it can only be made whilst dancing—it is above all a corporeal technique. The dancer and the musician, or more precisely the dancer and singer, are merged into one and the same person. It is both the subject's own singing and dancing that lead him to trance. The *dhikr* is a certain way of singing. But this singing, which calls for a particular technique of breath control, is at the same time a recitation of the name of God (among Christians it refers to the Holy Ghost or Christ). The words also play a role (and many would say that it is the essen-

tial one) and are, here again, bearers of emotion—religious emotion, naturally, but at the service of a religion of love and fervor conducive to many ambiguities. In content and in form this music is above all invocatory. If one dissociates it from the meaning of the words, the music—singing and dancing combined—seems to have the function of creating excitation. What we are dealing with then is a very particular form of autoexcitation, since it makes use of breathing, a certain overstimulation of the vocal cords, a very accentuated rotary movement of the neck and head, and a whole variety of physical movements that must certainly consume (or liberate?) a great deal of energy. There are two musical characteristics specific to *dhikr:* a particular sort of vocal delivery (the 'saw' *dhikr*)—which raises the question of whether or not it has neurophysiological repercussions—and a systematic use of *accelerando* and *crescendo,* the object of which is to increase the emotional tension. Although it is not as monotonous as people tend to claim—even if only because the increasing agitation just mentioned contributes to a renewal of the musical interest—repetition (and above all the repetition of words) also plays a role. Let us say, to sum up, that music, words, and dance create at the same time a great physical effervescence and a state of 'monoideism' that, in combination, create psychophysiological conditions apparently very favorable to the occurrence of trance. In this case trance is quite deliberately sought for, and if it occurs—which is not always the case, for the 'mechanism' is not automatic, even though it is certainly very efficacious—it is only very rarely that it does so in an unexpected manner, unlike emotional trance, which very often does occur unexpectedly....

"The role of music [in triggering possesion] is multiple. At the level of the ceremony—or if one prefers, of the theater—it creates a certain emotional climate for the adepts. Second, it leads the adepts toward that great mutation, occurring at the level of imagination, that consists in becoming identified with the spirit possessing him.[414] In this operation which is so aleatory and which is subject to so many variables, the relation between music and trance often appears quite strained. Third and last, it provides the adept with the means of manifesting this identification and thus of exteriorizing his trance [e.g. through dance or other bodily movement]. Why? Because it is the only language that speaks simultaneously, if I may so put it, to the head and the legs; because it is through music that the group provides the entranced person with a mirror in which he can read the image of his borrowed identity, and because it is the music that enables him to reflect this identity back again to the group in the form of dance [or other physical expression]." — Rouget, pp.26-27, 56, 63, 97-103, 187-89, 205, 214-15, 219-22, 224-26, 230-33, 255-266, 268-69, 315-17, 325.

MUSIC, MAGIC AND *MYTHOS*.

§263C.1 *Ed. note:* In the extended excerpt from Volume 2 of *Sound and Symbol* (1973) reproduced below, Victor Zuckerkandl writes "Nonsense plus feeling does not make music". That is to say, music has a dimension of "meaning" in its own right, and it does not imply an *absence* of thinking but only a mode of thinking which is distinctly its own (which is not the same as that type of thinking which is expressed e.g. in or by means of a verbal language).

Zuckerkandl's presentation is sufficient in itself, but I should like to add an element from my own *Essay on Myth and Mythology* which appears as Vol III of the present work. I will argue that any "expression" of something—not only through language or a "communications systems" of one type or another, but through the very appearing or occuring of a given phenomenon at all (i.e., in the very *existing* of a given being)—is, therefore, in a sense, a projecting or putting forward *of* "meaning" of some kind. However, such a meaning (in my view) is (a), only provisional or hypothetical—it is subject to "confirmation" of some kind or other; and (b) it is also "mythical", insofar as it represents an attempt, if you will, by some being to take its own measure; to disclose what it is or may be to *be* the being in question.

I will not attempt to develop these ideas in detail here (for which see the *Essay* itself), however, I do feel that they link with Zuckerkandl's argument in the following way:

---

414 One must stress again—as throughout the present essay—that this recalls our own basic themes **T1** (Music identifies one with the god[s] or supreme being[s]), **T1a** (Music as magical means of communication with such god[s] or supreme being[s]), **T1c** (Music as medium through which the spirit world [of divinities, supranatural beings] attempts to signal or contact man; music announces the presence of a god or spirit), **T5** (Music as magical means of promoting or inducing state or condition of ecstasy, frenzy, madness, losing oneself, etc.), **T5c** (Negatively or positively, identification of music with love, sex, lust, physical release or abandon etc, e.g. Dionysian attributes), for which see *Introductory Remarks*, Vol I above. (Ed.)

How can a thing adequately or correctly describe itself? In fact it cannot, and in that sense the apparent preciseness of our written/spoken languages (with which we *do* attempt to judge our own character and dimension, and our own "status" as existents) is entirely misleading.

Music, on the other hand, is "non-representational", in a strict sense, to begin with. It makes the inescapable point that "representational" thinking itself is misleading — or *wrong*.

Musical expression is a kind of parable on the peculiar position of e.g. human beings who come to appreciate that they do *not* in fact "know" that which they presume to know.

Music (to employ a Heideggerian sort of phrase) is a "calling" to us who presume to "know" nevertheless, not from the self-defined "objectivity" of the "logos" of (artificially) organized thought, but (it would seem) from the *opening out* of "language" itself, to embrace all possibility...

A written/spoken language points to itself, to the "object-ness" of its own symbols. A musical language on the other hand prides itself if you will on its own failure to objectify objects in the manner of a written/spoken language, and to *intimate*, instead, that which cannot be specified.

Music (in a fable- or parable-like manner) points to the *mythical* (undefined) aspect of our own being.

Musical performance is in part a response to (or acknowledgement of) our own *not knowing*, i.e. in a "rational" or "logical" sense. ("Logic" or "knowing" ought not to be contrasted with *feeling* — but only with *not-knowing*.)

Zuckerkandl proposes that "the same gulf separates prelinguistic utterance from the first melody *and* from the first [written or spoken] sentence." Ernst Cassirer has made a similar point in his *Language and Myth*, in which he argues (if I may paraphrase it so) that myth-making and the inventions of a language are similarly responsive to the mere *fact* of the existential situation in which a given being finds

itself. I have only stressed this same "mythical" element with respect to musical expression and meaning in particular: in a sense whereas a verbal language is — in the face of one's "not-knowing" — a protestation that in a sense one *does* "know", nevertheless (e.g. insofar as one is able to name, categorize or "define" [as we call it — though all we mean by this is a kind of pointing to] this and that object in the natural inventory), a musical performance — in the face of this same "not-knowing" — is a kind of tacit admission or acknowledgement *that, truly, one does not...* is a kind of refusal, if you will, *to* give things any particular names or definitions, or to insist on relegating them to this or that category...

Zuckerkandl writes: "We believe that man's early relation to the world is most comprehensively characterized by what has been termed his 'magic mentality'." Is not such a "mentality" of itself an admission that one does not know — an attitude of wonder... of acceptance of one's own lack of knowing? I would suggest that musical performance — insofar as it may be identified with the "magic mentality" of which the author speaks — is a carrying-over of this same acknowledgement *that* one does not know, onto a "rational" (thinking) plane. (Roughly: musical and verbal idioms are, alike, "rational", but whereas one in a way is an assertion *of* one's ability to "know", the other remains an admission that — even in this "knowing" — one *fails* after all to know...) Indeed, to *know* is also to separate, or divide (to distinguish or break up into categories); to know that one *does not* know is, in a sense, to regain the wholeness and indivisibility of "nature" or "being" which exists unquestioned and unchallenged before the "artificialities" if you will of knowledge, itself, have intruded... (The author writes that in both magic and music, together, "man's sense of being at one with the world outweighs his sense of being distinct from it". I am proposing that it is precisely *knowledge* — which we are impelled to cultivate in ourselves, and with respect to our own situations — which forces a "distinction" between ourselves and "world", and that magic and music alike imply a certain *failure* to know: magic, in the case of beings who genuinely do not; music, in the case of beings who — *in* their very "knowing", itself — acknowledge something of the degree to which they remain ignorant.)

I also find Zuckerkandl's careful distinction *between* magic and myth — for all their affinities — particularly instructive. If "magic" implies, on the whole, a lacking in a certain sense of self-consciousness, or self-awareness, "myth" most decidedly does *not* — indeed, in my own, personal view, it suggests a very special sophistication with respect to appreciating various fundamental limitations concerning our own "knowledge" (of "ourselves" — or, indeed, of anything else), itself.

"*Phaedo*, the great dialogue on the immortality of the soul held on the eve of Socrates' death, opens with a remarkable admission on the philosopher's part concerning music. Socrates' friends are questioning him about a rumor current in Athens that in the last days of his imprisonment he has turned to the practice of music, of all things. In reply, Socrates tells them that repeatedly, throughout his life, he has had a dream in which a voice has told him to 'make music and work at it'. Until recently, he tells them, he had not felt obliged to take the admonition literally. Rather, he had taken it the way a runner takes the urgings of the crowd: isn't he already doing his utmost? After all, had he not devoted his life to philosophy, the true art of the Muses? (To the Greeks, the art of sounds and that of words were intimately related: there was no music without words, and poetry was not spoken, but sung or chanted.) Since his trial, however, Socrates had begun to wonder whether he might not have taken the admonition too lightly, and so had occupied himself in the last days before his execution by compos-

ing a hymn to Apollo and by turning into verse some of Aesop's fables.

"The story is too ancient and too well known not to be taken seriously. Though it is told self-deprecatingly, its sense is perfectly clear. Like Socrates' last words, 'We owe a cock to Aesculapius', it refers to payment of a debt. The philosopher is being scrupulous to the last. His whole life has been devoted to the service of a single power, that of the spoken word. Now, before it is too late, he must make amends for not having served the only power that shapes man's spiritual essence. He will make one last gesture of reverence and gratitude to the power of music: he will raise his voice in song at least once before dying.

"Nietzsche was the first to grasp the sense of Socrates as 'music maker', no doubt out of some underlying kinship. To him that last gesture in the *Phaedo* is an acknowledgement of the limitations of logical-scientific thinking. Nietzsche views Socrates as the archetypal 'abstract thinker', as the 'mystagogue of science'. 'These words heard by Socrates in his dream,' he writes in *The Birth of Tragedy*, 'are the only indication that he ever experienced any uneasiness about the limits of his logical universe. He may have asked himself, "Have I been too ready to view what was unintelligible to me as being devoid of meaning? Perhaps there is a realm of wisdom, after all, from which the logician is excluded? Perhaps art must be seen as the necessary complement of rational discourse?" ' Yet surely Socrates was already well aware of this. For time and again, in the course of dialgoue after dialogue — and at the moment some especially important point is reached — the strict dialectician suddenly starts to tell a story; the logician turns into the purveyor of myth; the Logos is bolstered up and made more vivid with recourse to Mythos. And the voice in the dream is a warning voice: even when Logos and Mythos work hand in hand, words are not enough. To give utterance to the whole of things, to be whole oneself, tones are needed, and song. Nietzsche must have experienced something like it himself when he said of his work, shortly before he went mad, 'It ought to have sung, this "new soul", not spoken!' No doubt music, song, underwent the most extraordinary developments between Socrates and Nietzsche, but one thing has not changed. Music still is, just as it has always been, the *other* power which, along with language, fully defines man as a spiritual being. No one who has not recognized and honored music as such can be said to have paid his full debt to the world, to himself, to mankind.

"The notion to which the *Phaedo* gives expression is that of *homo musicus,* of man as musician, the being that requires music to realize itself fully. This dimension of our humanity has largely been in shadow over the course of Western thought. It is time to bring it into the light....

"Music pure and simple is part of the general human endowment. It is not confined to the masterworks of art music, but inherent in people everywhere. There is no people or tribe without music, however primitive. Wherever there is speech, there is also song. The harps* from the graves of Ur and the sounding stone disks from the Malayan jungle bear witness to the fact that music is older than recorded history. Nor is there any real argument against the assumption that music is coeval with language and that the appearance of the human race in time announced itself both in word and sound. From this music of the beginning we who witnessed the culminating phase are the farthest removed, so far indeed that we have lost sight of it. How, then, can we hope to understand the innermost essence of music, including that of the culminating phase, unless we consider its entire trajectory and take into account both the beginning and the culmination? The beginning of music is not a historical event — man had music long before he had a history — nor is it a prehistoric event, something that occurred at an indefinitely remote time of the human past. If we cannot separate man, time, and music in our thinking, then it is impossible to think of a beginning of music; in other words, the beginning of music lies in the realm of myth. As legend has it, music was the gift of a god to mankind. What this means is quite clear. It could not have been that a god intoned a song for people to sing after him. Gods do not give in this way, from the outside. A god's gift comes from the inside; he opens men's hearts and unseals their lips. Another legend is even clearer on this point: men first raised their voices in song when they witnessed the death of a divinely beautiful young hero. At the beginning, music comes from men, not to them — or, rather, also to them but on the rebound. The singer or player cannot help hearing what he sings or plays: the circle must be closed. Here the notion of a confrontation between listener and work makes no sense. Music is both the gift and the giving, the musician both giver and recipient....

"Wittgenstein was wrong to write, 'What we cannot speak of we must consign to silence.' Not at all: what we cannot speak of we can sing about.

"Just what we mean here should be clear. Singing man does not raise himself above speaking man; musical man does not supersede rational man. The otherness of tones is not of another world. It does not derive from some transcendental beyond or from some 'purely interior' self or thought or feeling. It is singing man's different attitude toward his world. That from which speaking man sets himself apart and which he holds in front of himself, singing man brings as close as he can to himself, becomes one with. The two acts are like breathing in and breathing out, in one process, or the Chinese sage's complementarity of love and respect.

"MUSIC AND MAGIC. We have still to consider a not infrequently expressed opinion... that singing man, far from marking any sort of advance over speaking man, actually marks a reversion to earlier, prelinguistic, prerational stages of development. If it is true that speech creates objects, objective reality, sharp boundaries, and a radical opposition between subject and object, then—it is argued—music, which tends to abolish this opposition and to blur these boundaries, can aim at nothing other than annulling the achievements of speech and reviving the superseded prerational stage. This leads to two contradictory evaluations of music. Briefly stated: where 'spirit' is looked upon as the 'adversary of life', music is praised as the healing power that keeps open our lines of communication to the wellsprings of life; by contrast, where salvation is sought in a spiritual order, it is felt that music tempts us to relapse into animal darkness, and therefore that we should shun it. Common to both evaluations is the mistaken opinion that music originated at some prelinguistic stage of evolution, and that the radical opposition between subjectivity and objectivity can only be transcended 'from below', by going back to some prerational stage. That the same result can also be achieved by going forward to a broadened rationalism is overlooked.

"This mistaken opinion finds its strongest support in the widespread belief that song is first and foremost an expression of emotion. The assertion that music is to speech as feeling is to thought is rarely contradicted. Furthermore, because the child's development is generally viewed as an abridged version of the development of the human race, and because the child passes through a period of predominantly emotive utterance before learning to speak, we conclude without further ado that singing man existed prior to speaking man. 'Man sang out his feelings long before he was capable of uttering his thoughts.'

"This sentence and the passages quoted below are taken from Otto Jespersen's *Language, Its Nature, Development, and Origin*. It is astonishing that even in a discipline as exact as modern linguistics the popular correlation between musicality and emotionality should be uncritically accepted and serve as foundation of a theory according to which speech marks an advance over a primitive 'feeling' stage. 'It is a consequence of advancing civilization that passion, or at least the expression of passion, is moderated; and we must therefore conclude that the speech of uncivilized and primitive men was more passionately agitated than ours, more like music or song.... There was once a time when all speech was song, or rather when these two actions were not yet differentiated.... Our comparatively monotonous spoken language and our highly developed vocal music are differentiations of primitive utterances, which had more in them of the latter than of the former. These utterances were at first, like the singing of birds and the roaring of many animals and the crying and crooning of babies, exclamative, not communicative.... Our remote ancestors had not the slightest notion that such a thing as communicating ideas and feelings to someone else was possible.... How did the association of sound and sense come about? How did that which originally was a jingle of meaningless sounds come to be an instrument of thought?... We may perhaps form an idea of the most primitive process of associating sound and sense.... In the songs of a particular individual there would be a constant recurrence of a particular series of sounds with a particular cadence.... Suppose... a lover was in the habit of addressing his lass "with a hey, and a ho, and a hey nonino". His comrades and rivals would not fail to remark this, and... banter him by imitating and repeating his "hey-and-a-ho-and-a-hey-nonino". But when once this had been recognized as what Wagner would term a "person's leitmotiv", it would be no far cry from mimicking it to using [it]... as a sort of nickname.... It might be employed, for instance, to signal his arrival. And when once proper names had been bestowed, common names (or nouns) would not be slow in following.' Thus, according to Jespersen, speech developed from song.

"We may leave aside the question of whether it is legitimate to call a living being still incapable of speech 'human': actually we know no human community, however primitive, whose language consists only of calls, does not include names, words. That prelinguistic utterance, however, should unhesitatingly be designated as a kind of song will certainly not pass unchallenged. Utterances such as meaningless noises, animal growls, and infant gurgles have just as much and just as little in common with speaking as with singing. The 'hey-and-a-ho' is certainly just as (perhaps even farther) removed from the primitive musical phrase as it is from the primitive sentence. However primitive, a musical phrase is a structure no less meaningful than a verbal phrase. Nonsense plus feeling does not make music. Such notions are based on a totally mistaken conception of what music and song really are. A sound of more or less defined pitch, no matter how expressive, is not a musical tone; a sequence of tones of varying pitch, by which feeling is expressed, is not yet song, nor can it become song merely by repetition. Song begins precisely where successive sounds rise above their ties to feeling and form new ties—ties with one another. A tone is a sound of definite pitch, referring primarily not to a feeling expressed by it—or, more generally, to a thing—but to other sounds of definite pitch, to other tones. A sequence of tones is a musical structure, a melody, when its unity results primarily from the audible relations of sounds to one another, not from their relations to something else—for example, feeling. Tones can be audibly interrelated only because they form a system, an order. The step from the prelinguistic call to the primitive melody is in no way less fundamental than the step to the primitive sentence. In either case, the step

leads to order, signifies the discovery of structure; it is a spiritual act that creates meaning. The meaning of the sound is constitutive of the tone just as it is constitutive of the word; and even though tones are not meaningful in the same sense as words, the problem of how sounds became associated with meaning is a musical as well as a linguistic one. The same gulf separates prelinguistic utterance from the first melody *and* from the first sentence. As measured by this gulf, the most primitive song is not a bit closer to prelinguistic stages of culture than a Bach fugue is. Similarly, the most primitive sentence and the most fully developed speech are, as word language, just as different in kind from prelinguistic utterance. There is no evidence against the hypothesis that the step which led to the word was the same which led to the tone, that man began to sing and to speak at the same moment, and that later differentiations of musical and verbal modes of utterance hark back to a stage when speech and song had not yet been clearly separated. But such a stage would in any case lie on this side of the gulf: in respect of origin, singing man and speaking man stand together. Singing man did not precede speaking man; he misunderstands himself when he seems himself as the representative of an evolutionary stage closer to the animal stage. It would be more just to ascribe a higher spiritual rank to song than speech, for speaking man finds a kind of material support in the fact that words refer to tangible things, but where can the musician find such tangible support? This may be the reason why Greek and Chinese myths associate mankind's emergence from the stage of barbarism with the appearance of a *musician*, half man, half god.

"To view musicality as falling within the domain of the rational, however, is merely to shift the problem to another plane. Human rationality did not come into the world at one stroke, ready-made. Beginning at a primitive stage, it ran through a long evolution before fully unfolding in the advanced civilizations. And it is precisely at the early stages of this evolution that music, as a cultural phenomenon, played a dominant part. The domain in which its importance is most strikingly manifested is defined by the notion of magic.

"We believe that man's early relation to the world is most comprehensively characterized by what has been termed his 'magic mentality'. As can be inferred from anthopological studies of today's primitive tribes, the basic traits of this mentality are as follows: The distinctions between animate and inanimate nature, between persons and things, also between one person and another, lack the sharpness and exclusiveness that today are taken for granted; the world is not yet split into subject and object, matter and mind. Thinking remains at a concrete level, does not yet tend to generalization and abstraction; life manifests itself most intensely in the group, is not yet concentrated in the emancipated individual, remains in an intermediary state before falling asunder into extremes. The negative features of the magic mentality include inability to make clear distinctions and decisions; the vagueness is an obstacle that must be overcome before rationality can develop. The positive features—which are largely lost on the way to the next stage—are the original closeness of man to man, man to thing, and thing to thing; the oneness of man's being with nature was once actually experienced, not merely conceived. This is not the same thing as the 'unconscious' oneness with nature of prehuman living beings. Man at the magical stage might well see nature, but he sees it from the inside, so to speak. (It was to express this that Edgar Dacqué coined the term *Natursichtigkeit*.) He was probably able to influence nature 'from within' in ways incomprehensible to us. At this stage man already faced nature, conceived of it as something distinct from him, but his sense of being at one with it was still much stronger.

"That music is closely related to magic is obvious at first glance. No primitive magic ritual can do without music, and even in modern civilized societies scattered islets of ritual have survived. The church no less than the circus, the ceremonial of public as well as of private life, cannot do without music. Conversely, certain principles of magic ritual—repetition, structures based on the numbers three, four, and seven, to name only the most important—play a crucial role, not just in primitive music but in the culminating stages of art music. To how surprising an extent even today musicians practise magic in the literal (not the metaphorical) sense, Jules Combarieu's voluminous *La musique et la magie* demonstrates with a great many documented examples. The affinity between music and magic does not just come down to superficial similarities; it is rooted in their very nature. The same terms serve to characterize the essence of musicality and of the magical mentality; in both, man's sense of being at one with the world outweighs his sense of being distinct from it: what links man to man, man to thing, and thing to thing outweighs what separates them. If it is true that tones build a bridge over the boundaries which words spell out between subjectivity and objectivity, the correspondence between music and magic seems complete. Thus it is natural to recognize in music the form in which magic survives down to our day.

"In his book *Ursprung und Gegenwart*, Jean Gebser does not content himself with noting a close correspondence, as well as affinities, between music and magic: according to him, music actually determines the very structure of magic. 'If the links between music and magic disclose that they are closely related,' he writes, 'and thereby that music is eminently magical, it will not be surprising if we believe we are justified in singling out the ear as the inner organ that plays the predominant role at the magical stage. The magical world, and with it an essential part of what constitutes our own world, originated in magical sound, operating through the ear, giving rise to an audible world.' In this book's broad perspective, expounding the overall development of mankind in terms of a few decisive evolutionary steps, the mythical stage supersedes the magical stage at the same time as the word supersedes the tone in the latter's fateful function. Music and speech would stand for two stages of development. The magical stage: the world experienced as one; existence as egoless, timeless, spaceless; the opposition between man and world not yet present to waking consciousness but as though in a dream, buried under the awareness that man and nature are originally at one; the individual dissolved in the group, not yet opposed to it. The mythical stage: awakening of the individual spirit, opposition between man and the world felt as a polarity; awareness of self as existing in time; the individual in process of emerging from the group.[415] At the magical stage the crucial organ was the ear, the crucial sense the sense of hearing. At the mythical stage it was the mouth, the organ of speech. There is no mouth in the earliest representations of human figures; only later is the mouth fully delineated.

"In this view of mankind's development, words and musical sounds are sharply contrasted and assigned radically different origins. Their relationship is reduced to one of temporal succession, a crucial evolutionary leap in the history of the human race. The two are diametrically opposed, musical sounds treated as something due to be superseded by words, and it is claimed that the supersession has ac-

tually occurred. Even though Gebser lays special emphasis on the fact that in every living development the earlier stages remain operative in the later ones, his interpretation helps us understand why fanatics of the word look upon the presence of music among us as a dangerous atavism, while those who have lost hope in the word believe they hear in music the glad tidings of ultimate return to a lost paradise. Such overstatements dictated by partisan passion are frequent enough; relegating music to the status of magic makes it all possible.

"I am listening to people singing; they are rehearsing one of the miracles of art music, a double canon by Purcell. Two melodies closely intertwined are being sung by different voices at different times. To what stage does such a microcosm of the highest quality belong? Is this the mode of utterance of a still slumbering soul, without awareness of self or time, a spirit still imprisoned within nature? What is so splendidly unfolded here is nothing other than an order of tonal space and tonal time, the same order already contained in germ in the musical tone as such. If with the creation of the word man emerges as a principle of order, if the word marks the rise of a spiritual order above nature, then tones and words must have a common origin. Where could a spiritual order, where could man conceiving of himself as a spiritual power distinct from nature be more purely revealed than in tone structures? Where could the soul be more awake than where it represents itself in tonal movement? Where could it be more deeply aware of

---

415 In my own view, any mythical "stage" also acknowledges that the "self" etc which comes to be differentiated through logical or rational thought is of a *provisional* or *hypothetical* — i.e. mythical — nature, our own being differentiated as a separate and distinct "being" or "entity" being, itself, in the way of being a sort of fable or parable which we tell *upon* (or with respect to) ourselves, in order to suppose or guess what we imagine we might be. It essential to "mythical" thinking that one does not regard the being of the myth in question — including one's own being, that is to say — as something which is or can be "defined" or determined absolutely. (Ed.)

time as one of the roots of its existence than in music? Verily, the mouth that opens to sing, no less than the mouth that opens to speak, is the human organ par excellence. As long as the mouth opens only to cry, to call, to utter merely expressive sounds, it is not yet human, and can be omitted in representations of the human figure confined to the essential. Only when pictorial representations disclose that the mouth has been discovered as the organ of human expression in the pregnant sense — i.e., at the mythical stage, not earlier — must we look for the origin of the tone as well as of the word.

"It is easy to see how this conclusion can be reconciled with the undeniable fact that music is closely related to magic. We must only keep clearly in mind that the same word, 'tone', denotes something different at each of the two stages in question. The tone of the still dream-imprisoned soul, unware of self and time, is a biological phenomenon, an expressive sound or sign (warning, calling, direction-showing) or both: an element in a chain of actual events. The tone of awakened consciousness, the musical tone proper, is a semantic phenomenon: part of a system of audible relationships, a structural element, a member of a symbolic whole. The special significance of the musical tone rests upon this, that here the crucial achievement of the mythical stage, the discovery of the symbol, becomes fruitful in the audible world itself, i.e., in the element that was the essential one of the superseded magical stage, the element that embodies that interpenetration of man and world. Music's content is magical, its form mythical. Music takes over and resettles the old in the new; it does not conjure up the past, does not glance backward, is not a reconstruction but, first and foremost, a construction: the past becomes symbol and in this form continues to be a living force in the present and in what is to come. Music achieves the appropriation of the magical by the spiritual: the essential core of magical existence is integration into a spiritual order. To infer from the affinity between music and magic that music originated in the world of magic is fallacious. Music did not originate in magic; it originated precisely because of the loss of the world of magic, following the law of all living development that each successive stage must incorporate the modes of existence of the preceding one. Speech and music are not antagonists representing two developmental stages, one of which superseded the other. Our discussion of the word-tone relationship in song [in a previous portion of the author's 2-volume work *Sound and Symbol* (Ed.)] has shown that the two work together, not one against the other; that they are not at cross-purposes, but enhance each other. Words divide, tones unite. The unity of existence that the word constantly breaks up, dividing thing from thing, subject from object, is constantly restored in the tone. Music prevents the world from being entirely transformed into language, from becoming nothing but object, and prevents man from becoming nothing but subject. Nor can the word aim at this; the objectifying word *needs* the tone, *demands* it: the stronger the tones, the freer the words are to perform their task of objectification. It is certainly no accident that the highest unfolding of the power of objectifying words in modern science coincide historically with the sharpest divisions ever drawn between subjectivity and objectivity. Not because the tone expresses the subject as adequately as the word expresses the object, not because the tone feeds the irrational element as the word feeds the rational element. Such either/ors are false and superficial. What the tone expresses is not the subject but the interpenetration of subject and object. Music does not thrive at the expense of rationality. Music originates, grows, and reaches its culmination within human rationality, together with it, not outside it or against it." — Zuckerkandl (Sound/Symbol 2), pp.1-3, 11-12, 66-76.

MUSICIAN.

§268A.1 "The musician is a common symbol of the fascination of death (personified by the Greeks as a youth). The Pied Piper of Hamelin in the well-known tale,[416] the harpist and the citharist in legends and folktales, all allude to this one symbol. Music represents an intermediate zone between the differentiated or material world, and the undifferentiated realm of the 'pure will' of Schopenhauer. Hence its use in rites and liturgies (together with fire and smoke)." — Cirlot, p.225.

NORSE MYTHS AND LEGENDS.

§277A.1 See **EDDIC MYTHS AND LEGENDS*.**
HEIMDALL, HEIMDALLR*
(Teutonic).
ODIN*.

§277A.2 **BRAGI, THE GOD OF MUSIC.**
"Men worshipped [Odin] as patron of eloquence, poetry, and song, and of all scalds. [However,] although Odin had... won the gift of poety, he seldom made use of it himself. It was reserved for his son Bragi, the child of Gunlod, to become the god of poetry and music, and to charm the world with his songs.

White-bearded bard, ag'd
Bragi, his gold harp
Sweeps—and yet softer
Stealeth the day.
— *Viking Tales of the North*
(R. B. Anderson)

As soon as Bragi was born in the stalactite-hung cave where Odin had won Gunlod's affections, the dwarfs presented him with a magical golden harp*, and, setting him on one of their own vessels, they sent him

out into the wide world. As the boat gently passed out of subterranean darkness, and floated over the threshold of Nain, the realm of the dwarf of death, Bragi, the fair and immaculate young god, who until then had shown no signs of life, suddenly sat up, and, seizing the golden harp beside him, he began to sing the wondrous song of life, which rose at times to heaven, and then sank down to the dread realm of Hel, goddess of death.

Yggdrasil's ash is
Of all trees most excellent,
And of the Æsir, Odin,
And of horses, Sleipnir;
Bifröst of bridges,
And of scalds, Bragi.
— *Lay of Grimnir*
(Thorpe's transl.)

"While he played the vessel was wafted gently over sunlit waters, and soon touched the shore. Bragi then proceeded on foot, threading his way through the bare and silent forest, playing as he walked. At the sound of his tender music the trees began to bud and bloom, and the grass underfoot was gemmed with countless flowers.

"Here he met Idun, daughter of Ivald, the fair goddess of immortal youth, whom the dwarfs allowed to visit the earth from time to time, when, at her approach, nature invariably assumed its loveliest and gentlest aspect.

"It was only to be expected that two such beings should feel attracted to each other, and Bragi soon won this fair goddess for his wife. Together they hastened to Asgard, where both were warmly welcomed and where Odin, after tracing runes on Bragi's tongue, decreed that he should be the heavenly minstrel and composer of songs in honour of the gods and of the heroes whom he received in Valhalla.

---

416 See **PIPE(S) AND PIPERS***, p.650 (Ed.)

* * *

"As Bragi was god of poetry, eloquence, and song, the Northern races also called poetry by his name, and scalds of either sex were frequently designated as Braga-men or Braga-women. Bragi was greatly honoured by all the Northern races, and hence his health was always drunk on solemn or festive occasions, but especially at funeral feasts and at Yuletide celebrations.

"When it was time to drink this toast, which was served in cups like a ship, and was called the Bragaful, the sacred sign of the hammer was first made over it. Then the new ruler or head of the family solemnly pledged himself to some great deed of valour, which he was bound to execute within the year, unless he wished to be considered destitute of honour. Following his example, all the guests were then wont to make similar vows and declare what they would do; and as some of them, owing to previous potations, talked rather too freely of their intentions on these occasions, this custom seems to connect the god's name with the vulgar but very expressive English verb 'to brag'.

"In art, Bragi is generally represented as an elderly man, with long white hair and beard, and holding the golden harp from which his fingers could draw such magic strains." — Guerber [Norsemen], pp.100-102.

NUMBERS.

§277B.1 See **CORRESPONDENCES***.

§277B.2 *Ed. note:* Number symbolism generally — with which the following article deals — may be applied more specifically or narrowly to the musical symbolisms of e.g. intervals, harmonics, chordal relationships and the number of notes in a scale. Much numerical symbolism has to do with relations of heavenly bodies, of heaven and earth, of directions or dimensions in physical space — thus, much numerical symbolism relates to the placement of physical bodies relative to each other, leading to (or expressing) ideas of an overall harmony or coherence.

"In symbolism, numbers are not merely the expressions of quantities, but idea-forces, each with a particular character of its own. The actual digits are, as it were, only the outer garments. All numbers are derived from the number one (which is equivalent to the mystic, non-manifest point of no magnitude). The father a number is from unity, the more deeply it is involved in matter, in the involutive process, in the 'world'. The first ten numbers in the Greek system (or twelve in the oriental tradition) pertain to the spirit: they are entities, archetypes and symbols, The rest are the product of combinations of these basic numbers. The Greeks were much preoccupied with the symbolism of numbers. Pythagoras, for example, observed that 'Everything is disposed according to the numbers'. Plato regarded number as the essence of harmony, and harmony as the basis of cosmos and of man, asserting that the movements of harmony 'are of the same kind as the regular revolutions of our soul'. The philosophy of numbers was further developed by the Hebrews, the Gnostics and the Cabbalists, spreading to the alchemists as well. The same basic, universal notions are found in oriental thought — Lao-tse, for example: 'One becomes two; two becomes three; and from the ternary comes one' — the new unity or new order — 'as four' (Maria Prophetissa). Modern symbolic logic and the theory of groupings go back to the idea of the quantitative as the basis for the qualitative. Pierce suggests that the laws of nature and of the human spirit are based on these same principles, and that they can be ordered along these same lines. Apart from the basic symbols of unity and multiplicity, there is another general symbolism attached to the even numbers (expressing the negative and passive principle) and the uneven numbers (the positive and active). Furthermore, the numerical series possesses a symbolic dynamism which it is essential not to overlook. The idea that one engenders two and two creates three is founded upon the premiss that every entity tends to surpass its limits, or to confront itself with its opposite. Where there are two elements, the third appears as the union of the first two and then as three, in turn giving rise to the fourth number as the link between the first three, and so on. Next to unity and duality (expressing conflict, echo and primordial duplication), the ternary and the quaternary are the principal groupings; from their sum comes the septenary; and from their multiplication the dodecanary. Three is the more direct derivation of seven (since both are uneven) and four more closely related to twelve (both being even numbers). The usual symbolisms are as follows: The ternary represents the intellectual or spiritual order; the quaternary the terrestrial order; the septenary the planetary and moral order; the dodecanary the universal order. Here now are [some of] the most generally accepted symbolic meanings of each number:

"*Zero.* Non-being, mysteriously connected with unity as its opposite and reflection; it is symbolic of the latent and potential and is the 'Orphic Egg'. From the viewpoint of man in existence, it symbolizes death as the state in which the life-forces are transformed. Because of its circular form it signifies eternity.

"*One.* Symbolic of being and of the revelation to men of the spiritual essence. It is the active principle which, broken into fragments, gives rise to multiplicity, and is to be equated with the mystic Center, the Irradiating Point and the Supreme Power. It also stands for spiritual unity — the common basis between all beings. Guénon draws a distinction between unity and one, after the Islamic mystic thinkers: unity differs from one in that it is absolute and complete in itself, admitting neither

two nor dualism. Hence, unity is the symbol of dvinity. One is also equated with light.

"*Two.* Two stands for echo, reflection, conflict and counterpoise or contraposition; or the momentary stillness of forces in equilibrium; it also corresponds to the passage of time — the line which goes from behind forward; it is expressed geometrically by two points, two lines or an angle. It is also symbolic of the first nucleus of matter, of nature in opposition to the creator, of the moon as opposed to the sun. In all esoteric thought, two is regarded as ominous: it connotes shadow and the bisexuality of all things, or dualism (represented by the basic myth of the Gemini) in the sense of the connecting-link between the immortal and the mortal, or of the unvarying and the varying. Within the mystic symbolism of landscape in megalithic culture, two is associated with the madorla-shaped mountain, the focal point of symbolic Inversion, forming the crucible of life and comprising the two opposite poles of good and evil, life and death. Two, then, is the number associated with the *Magna Mater.*

"*Three.* Three symbolizes spiritual synthesis, and is the formula for the creation of each of the worlds. It represents the solution of the conflict posed by dualism. It forms a half-circle comprising birth, zenith and descent. Geometrically it is expressed by three points and by the triangle. It is the harmonic product of the action of unity upon duality. It is the number concerned with basic principles, and expresses sufficiency, or the growth of unity within itselff. Finally, it is associated with the concept of heaven and the Trinity.

"*Four.* Symbolic of the earth, of terrestrial space, of the human situation, of the external, natural limits of the 'minimum' awareness of totality, and, finally, of rational organization. It is equated with the square and cube, and the cross representing the four seasons and the points of the compass. A great many material and spiritual forms are modelled after the quaternary. It is the number associated with tangible achievements and with the Elements. In mystic thought, it represents the tetramorphs.

"*Five*. Symbolic of Man, health and love, and of the quintessence acting upon matter. it comprises the four limbs of the body plus the head which controls them, and likewise the four fingers plus the thumb and the four cardinal points together with the centre. The *hieros gamos* is signified by the number five, since it represents the union of the principle of heaven (three) with that of the *Magna Mater* (two). Geometrically, it is the pentagram, or the five-pointed star. It corresponds to pentagonal symmetry, a common characteristic of organic nature, to the golden section (as noted by the Pythagoreans), and to the five senses representing the five 'forms' of matter.

"*Six*. Symbolic of ambivalence and equilibrium, six comprises the union of the two triangles (of fire and water) and hence signifies the human soul. The Greeks regarded it as a symbol of the hermaphrodite. It corresponds to the six Directions of Space (two for each dimension), and to the cessation of movement (since the Creation took six days). Hence it is associated with trial and effort. It has also been shown to be related to virginity, and to the scales.

"*Seven*. Symbolic of perfect order, a complete period or cycle. It comprises the union of the ternary and the quaternary, and hence it is endowed with exceptional value. It corresponds to the seven Directions of Space (that is, the six existential dimensions plus the centre), to the seven-pointed star, to the reconciliation of the square with the triangle by superimposing the latter upon the former (as the sky over the earth) or by inscribing it within. It is the number forming the basic series of musical notes, of colours and of the planetary spheres, as well as of the gods corresponding to them; and also of the capital sins and their opposing virtues. It

also corresponds to the three-dimensional cross, and, finally, it is the symbol of pain.

"*Eight*. The octonary, related to two squares or the octagon, is the intermediate form between the square (or terrestrial order) and the circle (the eternal order) and is, in consequence, a symbol of regeneration. By virtue of its shape, the number is associated with the two interlacing serpents of the caduceus, signifying the balancing out of opposing forces or the equivalence of the spiritual power to the natural. It also symbolizes—again because of its shape—the eternally spiralling movement of the heavens (shown also by the double sigmoid line—the sign of the infinite). Because of its implications of regeneration, eight was in the Middle Ages an emblem of the waters of baptism. Furthermore, it corresponds in medieval mystic cosmogony to the fixed stars of the firmament, denoting that the planetary influences have been overcome.

"*Nine*. The triangle of the ternary, and the triplication of the triple. It is therefore a complete image of the three worlds. It is the end-limit of the numerical series before its return to unity. For the Hebrews, it was the symbol of truth, being characterized by the fact that when multiplied it reproduces itself (in mystic addition). In medicinal rites, it is the symbolic number *par excellence*, for it represents triple synthesis, that is, the disposition on each plane of the corporal, the intellectual and the spiritual.

"*Ten*. Symbolic, in decimal systems, of the return to unity. In the *Tetractys* (whose triangle of points—four, three, two, one—adds up to ten) it is related to four. Symbolic also of spiritual achievement, as well as of unity in its function as an even (or ambivalent) number or as the beginning of a new, multiple series. According to some theories, ten symbolizes the totality of the universe—both metaphysical and material—since it raises all things to unity. From ancient oriental thought through the Pythagorean school and right up to St. Jerome, it was known as the number of perfection.

"*Eleven*. Symbolic of transition, excess and peril and of conflict and martyrdom. According to Schneider, there is an infernal character about it: since it is in excess of the number of perfection — ten — it therefore stands for incontinence; but at the same time it corresponds, like two, to the mandorla-shaped mountain, to the focal point of symbolic inversion and antithesis, because it is made up of one plus one (comparable in a way with two).

"*Twelve*. Symbolic of cosmic order and salvation. It corresponds to the number of the signs of the Zodiac, and is the basis of all dodecanary groups. Linked to it are the notions of space and time, and the wheel or circle.

"*Thirteen*. Symbolic of death and birth, of beginning afresh. Hence it has unfavourable implications.

"*Fourteen*. Stands for fusion and organization and also for justice and temperance." — Cirlot, pp.230-34.

OCEANIA (MYTHS OF) — PRACTICES AND BELIEFS. *(See p.906.)*

§278A.3 "BUE. In Gilbertese mythology, son of a woman magically impregnated by the sun [i.e. sun god]. Bue travelled to the east by canoe, seeking his father and his inheritance of cleverness, *te rabakau,* and knowledge, *te ataibai.* Like the Polynesian hero Maui, the determined Bue assaulted the sun god and obtained his desire. Although the father tried to hamper the later exploits of the son, Bue was the cultural founder hero. He taught men how to build canoes and houses, how to raise winds by magic, how to ensure health and prosperity, and how to compose dance chants."[417] — Cotterell, p.272.

§278A.4 "KADAKLAN. The thunder god in the mythology of the Tinguian people, who live in the mountainous interior of Luzon, the northernmost island of the Philippines. He lives in the sky and produces thunder by beating his drum*. His faithful dog, Kimat, is the lightning that 'bites' trees, houses and anything else that Kadaklan chooses. However, the thunder god receives less reverence than the ancestral spirits, whose goodwill the Tinguians are very concerned to retain....

"MESEDE. In Melanesian mythology,[418] a champion marksman whose bow burst into flames when it was drawn. Mesede saved Abele's son from the jaws of a crocodile and claimed as his reward Abele's daughters, who were then killed by Mesede's wife in a jealous rage. A magic drum* was made from a daughter's head. It is used in the rites of several Melanesian peoples." — Cotterell (Macmillan Myths and Legends), pp.211, 221.

ODIN. *(See also p.613.)*

§279.2 "According to [one] myth, it was in his search for knowledge that Odin lost an eye. He gave this, according to one of the poems, as payment for a drink from the spring of Mimir [a god about whom little is known, who was said to be exceedingly wise], the spring beneath the root of the World Tree, whose water gave inspiration

---

417 In *The Macmillan Illustrated Encyclopedia of Myths and Legends* Cotterell writes that "Bue taught people how to build houses and canoes, how to cast spells, and how to dance" (p.190). Presumably dancing and "dance chants" were a principal form of music making in the Gilbert Islands, with magical-sacred significance. In some respects Bue recalls certain origins and functions of APOLLO*. (Ed.)

418 Melanesia — "an island group in the southwestern Pacific Ocean, extending southeastward from the Admiralty Islands to the Fiji Islands." — *American Heritage Dictionary of the English Language* (1969). (Ed.)

and knowledge of things to come. Another account of how Odin gained wisdom is that he kept the head of Mimir after it was cut off by the Vanir [fertility gods—gods and goddesses of plenty; rivals of the Aesir], preserved it with herbs and sang spells over it until it could speak with him and answer questions. He consulted it when he wished to learn the future."— Davidson, p.48.

ORCHESTRA.

§283A.1 "Symbolic of the activity of a corporate whole. This is the idea behind Schneider's remark that when the high and the low orchestras (that is, heaven and earth) perform the counterpoint of the cosmos, these two antithetical voices are 'descanting'. But when one of the voices imposes its own rhythm upon the other, then that voice is 'enchanting' its opponent.[419]"—Cirlot, p.244.

ORIGINS OF MUSIC. (See p.615.)

§286.2 Readers of the present work will be familiar with the "primitive" belief that music originates with or is the gift of certain gods or celestial beings—for which see our themes T1a (Music as magical means of communication with god[s] or supreme being[s]), T1c (Music sent [to man, animals] as gift of the gods or heavenly beings. Music as medium through which the spirit world [of divinities, supranatural beings] attempts to signal or contact man), T6 (Music a mediator between world of nature and world of man [culture])—and perhaps others—which are given in the *Introductory Remarks*, Vol I above.

In fact, such beliefs are characteristic not only of "primitive" societies, but of the early history of many so-called "modern" or "sophisticated" societies of Europe, Asia, and the Americas as well. The lesson would appear to be that such a belief in the divine or heavenly origins of music is to a degree *universal...* not subscribed to by everyone at any given time, to be sure, but nevertheless popular at some stage at least in the evolution of nearly every society or culture, regardless of type, historical period, or geographical location. This fact alone suggests certain characteristics which many people tend to associate with music itself, such as its overall magic or sacred, spiritual, elevating, transporting, transcending etc qualities.

The following excerpts from *Philosophies of Music History: A Study of General Histories of Music, 1600-1960* by Warren Dwight Allen conveniently summarize representative early "Western" (i.e. European and Near Eastern, or West Asian) views of the origins and nature of music.

"*CALVISIUS.* In 1600, Seth Kallwitz, Cantor of the Thomasschule and Musikdirector of the Stadtkirche in Leipzig, having Latinized his name as Sethus Calvisius, published one of several important works on musical theory. The first of these had been printed in the year of his double appointment (1594), a *Compendium musicae practicae pro incipientibus,* which reached a third edition in 1612, under the title *Musicae artis praecepta nova et facillima.* His original and compilatory work in hymnology is also known to all students of the Lutheran chorale and its history. There is evidence, therefore, for his active interest in music education, and in the general Lutheran tendency to *simplify* and *popularize* the music of the church.

"But the work published in 1600 is a distinct novelty in the field of theoretical

---

419 See Marius Schneider, *El origen musical de los animales-símbolos en la mitología y la escultura antiguas* (Barcelona, 1946).

treatises, because the book contained an Historical Supplement, entitled *De origine et progressu musices [Of the Origin and Progress of Music]*....

"Before Calvisius, many a book had been written on the origins of music. There [appears to have been a general agreement among them as to] the divine origins of the art....

"Calvisius [himself], like all his contemporaries, believed that the music of the voice was God-given, at Creation; that instrumental music, beginning with Jubal*, 'the father of all such as handle the harp and the organ', came afterward;[420] but that the sounds of Nature's instruments 'invented' and perfected by man are worthy to rank with vocal music in the praise of God.

"This [last] came to be contrary to Roman and Puritan theory, so that later histories argue interminably over the 'priority' of vocal over instrumental music, for all sorts of reasons—theological, mythological, esthetic, and anthropological.

"Calvisius goes on to name, in chronological order, the various 'inventors', theorists, and innovators through whose *labor* and *industry* the art of music was developed. He quotes Horace's *Art of Poetry*, which is probably one of the earliest applications to music history of the theory of progress from simple to complex.[421]

"It has already been noted that Calvisius followed Martin Luther's desire to '*simplify* and *popularize* the music of the church'. But this did not prevent him from writing eight-part motets and advanced treatises on the scientific aspects of music. And just as Luther had admired that master of polyphony, Josquin des Près, so did Calvisius. Josquin, Clemens non Papa, and Orlandus Lassus are mentioned by Calvisius with great admiration. He mentions these dominating figures of the century previous, in fact, as proof of his belief that Pope John XXII had been entirely wrong in condemning figured music (polyphony) in 1324-1325.

"In short, Calvisius was interested not merely in the ancient beginnings (*initio*) of music, but in its meaning for him as a practical musician, composer, and teacher. He was willing to accept the theory of music's divine origin in the first vocal utterance of man, at Creation, but was able to see progress in a continuous series of men who had inherited accumulating musical traditions, and who had passed them on with worthy contributions of their own....

"In his genealogical résumé of the subject, Apollo", inventor of the cithara, or lyre*, is, as always, the first and foremost of the 'inventors', followed by Mercury*,

---

420 "Jubal" is the name given to the putative first musician or inventor of musical instruments, in Genesis 4:20-22. (Ed.)

421 For a modern translation of the passage from Horace, see T. A. Moxon's, in Everyman's Library, No. 901, pp.67-68. In this passage Horace shows the development of the simple flute* with a few holes to the new instrument, 'bound with brass', which rivals the trumpet. This development correlates with the change in the audience, beginning with simple rustics and ending with sophisticated crowds in larger cities, for whom strings were added to the lyre, and 'dancing and wanton gesture to the simple art of old'. But this did not mean 'decadence', because 'daring eloquence rivaled the pronouncements of Delphi'.

Terpander with his added strings, Pythagoras, John of Damascus of the Eastern Church, and Guido d'Arezzo, 'inventor of modern music' according to some, and of notation and counterpoint according to others.[422] The disagreements between Aristoxenus and the Pythagoreans as to whether music is for the ear or for the reason as a science of numbers is dealt with (pp.91, 92) and citations appear from Boethius' *De Musica*, as in every treatise of the day.

"But Calvisius condenses these conventional items with admirable brevity to get down to an explanation of the different methods of metrical music and of solmisation. He gives not only Guido's hexachord system with the syllables *ut, re, mi, fa, sol, la* at the beginning of each line of the famous hymn to *Sanctus Johannes* (repeated in nearly every history of music to this day), but also a system for singing syllables for the major scale, for treble voices in the G clef, our most common clef today (then just coming into favor). These predecessors of the 'movable *do*' system were *Bo, ce, di, ga, lo, ma, ni, Bo,* and are used in transposition (pp.121-122).

"At the end of this little treatise, which covers much ground in a few pages, Calvisius says that these matters discussed show that 'from the beginning of the world to our own times,' *Musica* has progressed from very small beginnings, little by little, thanks to the labors of men who have added so much to it to make the art that we enjoy today.

"Then follows the usual benediction, in which the heavenly choirs are anticipated, in the perfection of music beyond this life:

perfectissimae illius musicae in vita coelesti, ab universo
triumphantis Ecclesiae & beatorum Angelorum choro,
propediam inchoendae, et per omnem aeternitatem
continuandae
FINIS

"*PRAETORIUS.* Calvisius was born in Thuringia and died in Leipzig. Another native of Thuringia, fifteen years younger than Calvisius, was Michael Praetorius (1571-1621). Praetorius began publication of his great *Syntagma musicum* in 1615, the year of Calvisius' death....[423]

"As for the origins of music, the divine origin of psalmody is probably taken for granted, but little is said about it, even in Part I. But the scientific interests of the day are apparent in Part II, at the beginning of which he finds the origins of music in Nature, 'the mother of all things and the mistress of all the arts' (*rerum omnium mater et omnium artium Magistra,* p.167). This part goes on to explain the functions music serves in society, its usefulness in peace and war, in triumphal celebrations, in physical education, and so on.

"Place is found for genealogy, the great-man theory, in Section II of Part II, devoted, as the register promises, to *Anfängern und Vorstehern aller zusammen stimmenden Harmoney und Gesangen,* and is dedicated to Apollo and the muses....

"*CERONE.* [Two] priests should [now] be mentioned, Dom Pietro Cerone, the Italian who wrote in Spanish (1566-c.1613), [and] Père Mersenne (Marinus Mersennus), the French Minorite (1588-1648).... These men

---

422 Such eclecticism! Here Calvisius records the supposed contributions of Biblical, Greek mythological, Greek historical, Roman mythological, Greek theological (Saint John of Damascus, AD700?-754?, a Doctor of the Eastern Church) and Christian historical personages (Arezzo, on the Arno in central Italy, having been the birthplace also of Petrarch and Vasari) *in one and the same breath...* (Ed.)

423 *Praetorius* is also a Latinization (of Schultheiss, according to Moser; of Schulz, according to Riemann). The *Syntagma* was originally planned to comprise four volumes, of which three were completed.

did not write histories, but provided a great mass of materials for future historians.

"Cerone spent years in Spain, and published *El Melopeo y Maestro* in Naples in 1613. After that date very little is known concerning his career....

"For Cerone there is no connection whatever between the ancient music and modern music since Guido. There is no persistence of Hebrew tradition as for Praetorius, and no genealogical chain *ab initio mundi ad praesens tempus* as for Calvisius. Ancient music had its inventors (Vol. II, Ch. XVII) but they had nothing to do with *la nuestra musica* (II, Ch. XVIII). Ancient music was simple, with no instruments, and had no *variedad de bozes — come agora se haze* (I, p.239). Nature may have inspired their music, but not our modern art (I, p.227). Cerone accepts the old legends of the music of the spheres [see **HARMONIA OF THE SPHERES*** (Ed.)], carefully repeats the old reasons why we cannot hear it (II, Chs. XII, XIII), and finds the three great 'divisions' of music accepted by medieval theory [for which see below] His training in hierarchized thinking leads him to set up comparisons, scales of value.... The ancients held music in better respect than the moderns (I, Ch. LIII); the Italians are better *professores* of music than the Spanish (I, Ch. LIII), and the heresies within the church of God *impede* the development of the art (I, Ch. LXVII). In other words, music is divided into fixed categories that can only be compared, not connected.

"However, with all his conservatism in these fields, Cerone ranks as one of the great theorists of his day, especially in the field of vocal counterpoint....

"*MERSENNE*. The outstanding contributions of the other great Catholic theoriest, Père Mersenne, date from the decade 1627-1637. In 1627 the first complete statement of his musical philosophies and researches appeared in a small volume entitled *Traité de l'Harmonie universelle où est contenu la Musique Thérique et pratique des Anciens et des Modernes, avec les causes de ses effets, enrichi de raisons prises de la Philosophie, et des Mathematiques par le Sieur de Sermes (nom de plume)*, Paris, 1627.[424] Mersenne belongs, properly speaking, to the history of musical theory, and the musical world is indebted to him for researches in the realm of acoustics, musical intervals, and tuning....

"Theology had its place for the Lutheran pioneers, so long as sacred music was under discussion; but for Cerone and Mersenne [who were both Catholic priests] it was still the queen of the sciences, never to be left out of the picture for a moment. For Mersenne, *Harmonie universelle* was completely dominated by the *first* 'cause of its effects', God himself. Cerone and Mersenne were not interested in Protestant research into Old Testament chronology [as Lutheran pioneers such as Calvisius and Praetorius had been]; for them all the phenomena of musical science was contained in a great Triunity, timeless as all creation. For example, in Mersenne, the three great *genera* of music — the diatonic, the chromatic, and the enharmonic — constituted a Trinity comparable to the Holy Trinity.

"The Father is represented by the diatonic, because this mode with its whole steps and half steps includes the two other modes, just as God contains within himself the Son and Holy Ghost principles. The Son parallels the chromatic mode (which

---

424 Not to be confused with Mersenne's greatest work, *Harmonie universelle, contenant la théorie et la pratique de la Musique*, 2 large folio volumes, Paris, 1635, 1636.

takes its name from the Greek word *chroma*); both represent beauty, equality, and wisdom. Thus the Son and the chromatic mode proceed from the Father and the diatonic, respectively; the enharmonic proceeds from the chromatic and the diatonic, just as the Holy Ghost proceeds from the Father and the Son. Beyond the Holy Ghost and the enharmonic no further development is possible.[425]

"Similar uses of analogy are found in Mersenne's second book of the *Traité*. This is entitled *Des Paralleles de la musique*. Here he proposes to show the relationships which *intervals* bear with 'rhythm, meter, and verse; also with colors, tastes, figures, geometrical forms, virtues, vices, sciences, the elements, the heavens, the planets, and several other things.'

"In the parallels with poetry, the hexameter is comparable to the octave, because one has six feet and the other six whole steps, or twelve half feet to the octave's twelve half steps. 'The smallest meter, which has one and a half feet, corresponds to the smallest consonance, which has a tone and a half tone [the minor 3rd].' (Bk. II, *Theorème II*, p.311.)...

"Similarly, consonances and dissonances are comparable to taste and colors. Black and white are dissonance and consonance, and chromatic intervals give 'color'. This analogy is still current and useful, but Mersenne finds that in taste, the 5th has a *saveur grasse*, the 4th a *saveur salé*, the major 3rd a *saveur astringente*, and the minor 3rd a taste that is 'insipid'. (Bk. II, *Theorème II*.)

"In astronomy, Mersenne follows Kepler, who found parallels between the interval ratios and the distances between the planets.[426] Mersenne concludes that a 'concert of the planets' would involve a spacing of distances between the planetary voices that go to make up the 'music of the spheres', or 'world music', as it was called during the Baroque era. Thus the bass would be assigned to Saturn and Jupiter; the *taille* (tenor) to Mars; the *haute-contre* (the alto) to the Earth and Venus; the *dessus* (soprano) to Mercury.

"Mersenne also found hierarchical analogies between the numerical ratios of intervals and the hierarchical stages of Being in scholastic philosophy. The lowest audible fundamental corresponded to the earth itself, the ground-tone, as the bass is still called. Living beings are 'higher' forms of life in the same sense that 'higher' notes are represented by higher numbers. Inaudible high notes beyond the reach of computation are comparable to the nine orders of invisible angels that surround the Holy Trinity. The twelve modes, as he says, on his last page, are comparable to the twelve pearly gates of the Celestial City. In other words, all of the esthetic beauty of medieval scholastic theory is bound up with the musical theory of Père Mersenne....

"*PRINTZ.* Third and last of the Luthern historians of the seventeenth century [was] Wolfgang Printz von Waldthurm, whose work *Historische Beschreibung der edlen Sing- und Klingkunst*, in 1690, is usually hailed as 'the first history of music'....

---

425 The passage summarized here is in Part I of the *Traité*, pp.60-61. In modern parlance, the enharmonic scale would be a scale having divisions or intervals smaller than half steps, the chromatic one consisting entirely of half steps.

426 Kepler had published his *Harmonices Mundi Libri V* in Linz, Austria, only seven years before, in 1619.

"Printz was a well-trained church and court musician. His book is the first historical treatise on music written in German....

"He also accepts the theory of divine origins [of music], without allowing it to conflict with other theories. In his first chapter, the following origins are all deemed possible: (a) man's powers of reason; (b) irrisistible natural impulse; (c) the accents and inflections of the voice under emotion; (d) the wind in the trees, and other sounds of nature; (e) the ambition to outdo others,[427] and many other psychological origins. For Printz *all* these theories had validity. His genial sense of humor might have made him very appreciative of the quest for origins conducted in nineteenth-century histories of music....

"Printz is probably regarded as the 'first' music historian because he is the first one of these scholars to attempt systematic biographies in chronological order, beginning with Jubal. According to *der seelige Herr Luther*, Jubal was father of all such as handle *all* instruments, not merely the harp and organ. In direct line of genealogical descent, Apollo was the inventor, not merely of the cithara, but of the flute as well.

"After Luther, one of the most frequently quoted authorities is [the Jesuit] Father [Athanasius] Kircher. Whole pages are quoted, occasionally, but in all cases Printz cites his authority for the statements that the Egyptians were the first to 'restore' music after the Flood, and that the Greek inventors Linus*, Orpheus*, and Am-

phion* inherited all they knew from David* and Solomon.

"A large proportion of Printz's work is devoted to contemporary musicians and those of a previous generation, and evidently Lutheran taste of his day could still look back with admiration upon the complicated polyphony of earlier centuries, as Luther's encomium of Josquin des Près is repeated....

"MEDIEVAL AND RENAISSANCE CLASSIFICATIONS. Today we speak of theoretical and practical, or applied, *branches* of music study. But medieval and Renaissance classifications gave independent reality to 'inspective' or 'speculative' music as something quite apart from 'active' music. And these were fixed and independent divisions of a larger division. Roughly, there were three great kinds of music: first, the mystic 'world music', the music of the spheres, which was so important to the Catholic scholars Cerone and Mersenne; second, human music; and third, instrumental music. The second had to do with the ethical phases stressed by Cerone. All Baroque research was interested in the third, which was divided into 'harmonical' and 'organical' music. Theory and practice were both parts of 'harmonical' music. There were various and different schemes of classification,[428] and the order of superiority or inferiority was apt to vary with the interests of the writer on the subject. This is the scheme proposed by Ornithoparcus, whose *Micrologus* was translated by John

---

427 Here Printz shows that his origin theories are not mere speculation. He points to actual Nature music then in vogue, for voice and instruments, and to the new developments in wind instruments themselves, as much as to say, 'Lucretius is right today'. And certainly the ambition of music-patrons 'to outdo each other' was the actual origin of much music.

428 Grassineau [transl. English 1740] mentions 45 different kinds of *Musica*.

Dowland, the famous song writer and singer of the Elizabethan era:[429]

> The world's Musicke is an Harmonie, caused by the motion of the starres, and violence of the Spheares.... Now the cause wee cannot heare this Sound, according to Pliny is, because the greatnesse of the sound doth exceed the sense of our eares.
>
> Humane music is the concordance of divers elements in one compound, by which the spirituall nature is joyned with the body, and the reasonable part is coupled in concord with the unreasonable, which proceedes from the uniting of the body and the soule.... Every like is preferred by his like, and by his dislike is disturbed. Hence it is, that we loath and abhor discords, and are delighted when we heare harmonicall concords, because we know there is in ourselves that concord.
>
> Instrumentall Musicke is an Harmony which is made by helpe of Instruments. And because Instruments are either artificiall, or naturall, there is one sort of Musicke — the Philosophers call Harmonicall; the other Organicall.... Organicall Musicke is that which belongeth to artificall instruments; or it is a skill of making an Harmony with beating, with fingering, with blowing.... Yet such Instruments as are too voluptuous, are by Coelius Rodiginus rejected.
>
> 'Harmonical Musick' is divided into Inspective Musicke, a knowledge censuring and pondering the Sounds formed with naturall instruments, not by the ears, whose judgment is dull, but by wit and reason: and Active Musicke, which also they call Practick (as St. Augustine in the first Booke of his *De Musica* writeth), the knowledge of singing well.

"From the above it is evident that Ornithoparcus and his translator were both interested in 'Active Musicke... the knowledge of singing well', and that they looked down upon instrumentalists with undisguised scorn. They, however, were looked upon with equal contempt by pure theorists who argued for the supremacy of 'inspective', or 'speculative Musicke'....

"*FROM ANCIENT TIMES TO THE PRESENT*. Two analogies based on harmony have been of great service to philosophers seeking to explain the fundamentals of political science; first, that of a leader holding and guiding his singers, with their different parts, in a harmonious ensemble; second, the notion of the power of the fundamental tone, to which all the partials are subordinate. The first concept was stated by Aristotle thus:

> The single harmony produced by all the heavenly bodies singing and dancing together springs from one source and ends by achieving one purpose, and has rightly bestowed the name not of 'disordered' but of 'ordered universe' upon the whole. And just as in a chorus, when the leader gives the signal to begin, the whole chorus of men, or it may be of women, joins in the song, mingling a single studied harmony among different voices, some high and some low; so too it is with the God that rules the whole world....
>
> As is the steersman in the ship,... the law in the city, the general in the army, so is God in the Universe;... he

---

429 Andreas Vogelmaier (Ornithoparcus), *Musice active micrologus*, Leipzig, 1517. The English version is entitled: Andreas Ornithoparcus, his *Micrologus, or Introduction, Containing the Art of Singing*, digested into foure Bookes, not only profitable, but also necessary for all that are studious of Musicke. London, 1609.

moves and revolves all things, where and how he will, in different forms and natures; just as the law of a city, fixed and immutable in the minds of those who are under it, orders all the life of a state. — *De Mundo,* ch. 6, 399a, 400b, in *Works,* Vol. III, ed. by W. D. Ross, Oxford, 1931.

"The second analogy is illustrated by a remarkable passage written in the late sixteenth century. Jean Bodin concluded his *Six Books of a Commonweale*[430] with a statement of 'Harmonicall Principles', in which the traditional preferment for perfect intervals is referred to as a means of unification of differences. Bodin proposes that Harmonicall Justice will be preferable to Geometrical Justice, as the latter would merely reward the leaders in each particular field:

We must also, to make an harmonie of one of them with another, mingle them that have wherewith in some sort to supply that which wanteth in the other. For otherwise there shall be no more harmonie than if one should separate the concords of musique which are in themselves good, but yet would make no good content if they were not bound together; For that the default of one is supplied by the other. In which doing the wise Prince shall set his subjects in a most sweet quiet, bound together with an indissoluble bond one of them unto another together with himself and the Commonweale. As in the first foure numbers to be seene; which God hath in harmonicall proportion disposed to show unto us, that the Royal estate is harmonicall, and also to be harmonically governed. For two to three maketh a fift; three to four, a fourth; two to foure, an eight; and againe afterwards, one to two maketh an eight; one to three a twelfth, holding the fift and the eight; and one to foure a double eight or Diapason; which containeth the whole ground and compasse of all tunes and concords of musicke beyond which he which will pass into five, shall in so doing marre the harmonie, and make an *intolerable discord.*

"Every harmonic innovation, in the past, has been met by theorists and historians

---

430 Tr. by Richard Knolles, London, 1606, pp.790-794.

REPUBLIQUE TUNISIENNE

REPUBLIQUE TOGOLAISE

Cor Bassar

Musique d'aisselle

Castagnettes

100F

POSTE AERIENNE   INSTRUMENTS DE MUSIQUE

with statements similar to the last phrase above....[431]

"RELIGIOUS, NATURALIST, AND ETHICAL TRADITIONS. I. Biblical Periodization and Ethical Classifications. The purpose of this chapter is to show that churchmen and moralists dictated the fundamental bases of early music histories, that certain secular concepts were debated by them from the first, and that in spite of the preponderance of secular theory today, occasional texts still appear which show the persistence of old traditions.

"For the early schemes of periodization in music history, evidence is first brought from Bonnet's *Histoire*....[432] His periods were as follows:

I. From the Divine Origins at Creation to the Flood.

II. From the Flood to King David and Solomon.

III. From King Solomon to Pythagoras.

IV. From Socrates (3600 years after Creation) to the Birth of Christ.

V. From the Birth of Christ to Gregory the Great.

VI. From Pope Gregory to St. Dunstan.

VII. From the Eleventh to the Sixteenth Centuries (Chap. X and XI).

VIII. to musicians of the author's own day.

"Supporting the theory of Aristides Quintilianus, Bonnet divides music into *Musica Mondana* (music of the spheres), *Musica Humana* (a harmony of the one and the other in man, made by the body, and controlled by the mind), *Musica Rhithmica* (the consonant harmony one feels in prose), *Musica Metrica* (music of verse), *Musica Politica* (the harmonious organization of the State), and *Musica Harmonica* (musical science and theory).

"Bonnet, although a priest, shows less concern with Christian tradition than the laymen, stressing rather the Greek *ethos** of music so important in didactic music history....

"In [1757] Padre G. B. Martini, Italy's most learned scholar, began publication of his *Storia della musica.* Beginning with a presentation of evidence from the Holy Scriptures, and deductions therefrom, no attempt is made to go beyond the music of the Greeks. The epochs of Biblical history are as follows:

---

431 The paradigmatic "harmony" is indeed musical harmony; musical harmony has ever been held as the model for "harmony" itself—according to many in all parts of the globe, and through all recorded history, the supposed fundamental being of the "cosmos" itself (for which read also "being" itself). In a sense this is only the *complement* to the view that such harmony (i.e. music itself) is the gift or invention of the gods, or supreme beings or spirits—of the Creator, however this last may be conceived. See also our theme T2 (Music identifies individuals and a people collectively with the physical and spiritual universe, or cosmos. Music [and/or dance] invokes or induces the world or cosmos itself *into being.* The laws [structure] of music parallel the laws [structure] of nature or the universe, e.g. those having to do with the relation of heavenly bodies or other natural components to each other, or with the conduct of such bodies or components with respect to each other. Such laws may also regulate or serve as model for the politics of heaven [privileges and responsibilities of divine beings] and earth [privileges and responsibilities of each member of a given state, from king or emperor to common citizen])—in addition to other themes mentioned at the head of this section—given in the *Introductory Remarks,* Vol I above. (Ed.)

432 Bourdelot-Bonnet, *Histoire de la musique, et de ses effets depuis son origine, les progrès successifs de cet art jusqu'à preésent.* Cochart, Paris, 1715.

I. Music from the Creation of Adam to the Flood.

II. Music from the Flood to the Birth of Moses.

III. Music from the Birth of Moses to his Death.

IV. Music from the Death of Moses to the Reign of King David.

V. Music from the Reign of David to that of King Solomon.

VI. From the Reign of King Solomon to the Destruction and Rebuilding of the Temple.

"Vol. II begins with a chapter on the origins of music according to the ancients, particularly in Greece.

"In 1744 Martin Gerbert published *Di cantu et musica sacra a prima ecclesiae aetate usque ad praesens tempus*. This work, by a learned and active Benedictine monk, although a history of sacred music only, is perhaps the most important German music history of the eighteenth century. Gerbert, as shown by his correspondence with Martini, expected to collaborate with the latter; Martini was to write the introduction and general summary, with a discussion of secular music, while Gerbert reviewed sacred music.

"Gerbert had a zealous purpose in writing his history of sacred music. The abbot saw the dangers to theology from the En-lightenment and tried to stem the tide with an appeal to history. Theology, for him, was divided into three categories: first, dogmatic theology, in its historical development; second, moral theology, concerning the Christian life; third, liturgical theology, including music. Gerbert strenuously opposed the mixing of secular elements in sacred music, and demanded a return to simple, severe plainsong and chorales. Instruments were recommended only for support of the voices, and instrumental music independent of the service was condemned. No *coloratura* singing was to be permitted.[433]

"Music itself must be *sacra* (in contrast to the Protestant view that music is sacred or profane, depending on the spirit with which it is performed). As a basis for this in history, the divine-origin theory is inevitable. Gerbert's history begins with the creation of Adam and Eve, therefore, not because of mere concession to convention, but as a basis for theoretical 'proof'. Music, for Gerbert, began with origins in special creation, then showed steady progress, slowly, but surely, through the ages, up to Palestrina. Since that great master's period, the art has steadily declined. The three periods are given the terms now used so frequently: Ancient, Medieval, and Modern. In this case the periodization is

---

433 On account of the association of florid singing with operatic arias, Gerbert chose to disregard the florid elements in medieval Alleluias.

CORREOS DE EL SALVADOR, C.A.

AEREO

25c.   TAMBOR

used, however, to denote growth, maturity, and decay....

"II. Was Music Revealed, Imitated, or Invented? In 1754, J. A. Scheibe, a German *capellmeister* in the service of the Danish king, wrote his *Abhandlung vom Ursprung und Alter der Musik,* in which he expressed the notions that had long been current. Adam and Eve must have lifted their voices in grateful song on the day of their creation, so vocal music was *erfunden* by the first human beings, in Paradise. As in all early histories, Jubal is mentioned as the inventor of instrumental music, 'the father of all such as handle the harp and organ' (Genesis 4:21), but Scheibe explains that instrumental music, man's invention, became separated from vocal music before the Flood, on account of the godless race of Cain. After the long abuse of instrumental music, due to the Fall of Man, the two branches of the art remained separated, until united in the service of God by Moses. The question still raging as to the priority of vocal or instrumental music was thus settled very simply.[434]

"There has always been a conservative element in the Christian tradition which has looked with disfavor on 'invented', 'artificial' instrumental music.[435] Although much of this may have been due to the association of instruments with the pagan rites of Greece and Rome, it is possible that this prejudice is rooted in this theory of music's twofold origin and separation.

"At any rate, the evidence of music histories shows conclusively that whenever the historian recognizes a long, proud tradition of religious music, the divine-origin theory survives, even today, in modified forms. Following the ecclesiastical tradition down to modern times, we find it thinning out into esthetic, linguistic, and psychological theories in England and Germany and among philologists of France and Italy. But with some writers, the church traditions persist in all their vigor, especially in France, Italy, and Ireland....

"[In his *A History of Music,* Edinburgh, 1830, the English Protestant William Cooke Stafford,] like many of his contemporaries, accepted Bishop Ussher's date for Creation (4004 BC), and followed the usual Biblical chronology:

> Though the records of the state of music in the antediluvian period are so scanty, *we shall not be wrong in supposing that in the 1600 years and upwards which elapsed between the Creation and the Deluge, considerable progress was made in the science....* though the Deluge swept away all the glory and grandeur of the antediluvian world, yet we can-

---

434 Those who would congratulate "modern man" on his tremendous wisdom and sophistication, and dismiss "primitive" beings on account of the stupidity and naïvté of their inventions concerning e.g. the origins and nature of music (of the drum, rattle, flute or bullroarer for instance), might ponder that both the present author *and those "first" subjects he means to describe* walked this earth in the not-too-terribly-distant past. Allowing two or three generations per century, the four hundred years counting backwards to the year 1600 encompass the entire life stories of fewer than a dozen of us. Our "unenlightened" (from today's point of view) forebearers are — in the grand scheme of things — nearly our contemporaries. Indeed there are many today who would hold — in faith, and by conviction — that some of these views are in fact correct, either literally or metaphorically. (Ed.)

435 Medieval musical theorists were all churchmen, who believed that music's sole purpose was that of enhancing and emphasizing the sacred text. Certain papal edicts condemn all other music.

not suppose that Noah and his family were ignorant of the arts and sciences taught before that event....

"Jean Baptiste Labat, a cathedral organist interested in church-music reform, and also a royalist who is pleased with the 'regeneration' of France after the restoration of the monarchy, says, in 1852, that

Music, since the beginning of time, since the foundation of religions, has been wholly identified with them, with an essence wholly divine.[436]

"Father L. F. Renehan [observes], in the only Irish *History of Music* [Dublin, 1858]:

It does not appear that Music can justly be reckoned among the results either of chance or industry: for, it seems to be *coeval with man himself* and *the bountiful gift of his Creator*.... That music made considerable progress before the deluge, is manifest from the earliest invention of musical instruments, and from its being then of sufficient importance to be made a profession.

"In other words, it must be admitted that man invented instruments, but not that he invented music.

"In 1846, an anonymous *Manual of Music* [London] 'containing a Sketch of its Progress in all Countries', began as follows:

Music *did* originate with that great Being who endowed the man he had created with speech and thought — and gave him, in the sense of hearing, and

the love of the agreeable and the beautiful, the faculty of perceiving and appreciating the concord of sweet sounds. This faculty is universal....

"In 1869, an Inaugural Dissertation at the University of Rostock, *On the History of Music down to the End of the Seventeenth Century*, was delivered by the Rev. Charles Booker.

"Booker begins with divine origins, and closes thus:

I have now accomplished the task which I proposed to myself... tracing most imperfectly, yet with some degree of precision, the rise, spread, progress and perhaps perfection of music as a science... hoping that even so imperfect a sketch of this noble science may cause us to feel thankful that we live in an age when it has probably reached its highest pitch, and may each of us in our several stations and callings endeavor to praise our Creator on earth as the archangels do in heaven....

"Félix Clément was an organist and director of church music, historian of the fine arts, and author of *Histoire générale de la musique religieuse* (1861). He asserts that *musique humaine* had the same origins as those of language, that the principal sounds (intervals), those of the tetrachord and the octave, were revealed to man by the Creator, at the same time that an articulate language was vouchsafed to him. The idea of origins in the imitation of Nature is repugnant to Clément: 'One would not be able to reproduce Nature in servile fashion without degrading this human art from the high rank it occupies in Creation.'[437]

---

436 *Études philosophiques et morales sur l'histoire de la musique...*, Paris, 1852.
437 Lucretius on the origin of music, *De rerum natura*, Book V, 1379-1412: 'Through all the woods they hear the charming noise / Of chirping birds, and tried to frame their voice / To imitate. Thus birds instructed man, / And taught them songs before their art began. / And whilst soft evening gales blew o'er the plains / And shook the sounding reeds, they taught the swains: / And thus the pipe was framed, and tuneful reed.'

"III. Theories Concerning the Ethos of Music.
The Greeks recognized the value of music
(which for them included all phases of
mental culture) in the education of youth;
thus we find Plato greatly concerned with
music's origin in the soul and its effect on
the individual....

"Later, when the church became responsible for the morals of her children it was
inevitable that ecclesiastical recorders of
medieval music should ignore the raucous,
immoral *modus lascivus* of the common
folk, to leave for posterity only the music
approved by authority. (Hence the one-
sided nature of earlier music histories,
especially those works written in ages of
piety by men who accepted both the
theories of musical origins in the soul of
man, and the theories of divine creation.)
Thus the church has remained for many,
even until recently, the final arbiter of taste
concerning music, the 'handmaid of
religion'. In 1887 Louis S. Davis could say,
'Music is but one effect of the great cause,
the Christian Church, and upon its rituals
and institutions depended the fate of the
whole tone-system'.[438]

"IV. A Modern Reversal of Causal Theory.
Cyril Scott has presented the point of view
of theosopy in *The Influence of Music on History and Morals, a Vindication of Plato* [Lon-
don, 1928]:

"For Scott, music is the first cause, not a
mere result of natural causes or of human
effort:

Throughout the ages, philosophers,
religionists and savants have realized
the supreme importance of sound. In
their most ancient scriptures, the
Vedas, it is stated that the world was
brought into manifestation though the
agency of sound.... The writer of the
Book of Joshua must have possessed
some knowledge of the power of
sound, otherwise it is unlikely that he

would have written the story of the
Fall of Jericho.....

"Reversing the old hypothesis, in a sense,
Scott believes that music is the Great Cause
in history:

It may seem extravagant to say that
*through music the first conception of God
was aroused in the human mind,* yet
when primitive Man came, deemed his
prayers (sung) were heard, he naturally came to conceive of a Being higher
than himself.... Hitherto his conceptions had been entirely phallic... but
after he had discovered song, he conceived the idea of the great Mother....
*The next stage in the evolution of
religion* is common knowledge; when
once the idea of the Great Mother had
been formulated, Man fashioned her
image in wood and stone.... *Finally,*
having fashioned his idols, he appointed someone to guard them; and
in this manner the office of priest
originated. It was the priests who discovered that if certain notes were
reiterated, definite emotional results
could be obtained and definite
powers brought into action. Thus
music became associated with
ceremonial magic in the very earliest
ages of Mankind....
One of the effects was to increase
religious fervour, with the result that
men began to sway with their bodies,
and to clap their hands. In the course
of time the most elementary form of
drum was invented to accentuate the
rhythm; this led to the invention of
other instruments and so to the actual
birth of music as an art....
So far, with our earthly music we
have only been able to imitate the
faintest echo of the music of the
Spheres, but, in the future, it will be
given us to swell the great Cosmic
Symphony....

---

438 *Studies in Musical History,* N.Y., 1887, p.iv.

"In our own day a calculating musician of the highest intellectual gifts waxes romantic over the mystic Greek notion of the music of the spheres:

Music is a part of the vibrating universe.... It may be that we must leave earth to find that music. But only to the pilgrim who has succeeded on the way in freeing himself from earthly shackles, shall the bars open....[439]

"*[A Brief Summation.]* Summarizing... various psychological theories, [which at the same time is to put theories concerning the divine origins of music into perspective,] we find the origins of music located [by various writers and theorists] as follows:

"(1) *In divine creation,* coeval with the first attempts at vocal expression or language by the first human beings, endowed, as Adam was, with necessary knowledge.

"(2) *In numbers,* as illustrated by the music of the spheres, made by the planets in their orderly movements, and as demonstrated in the laws of sound-relations in Nature.

"(3) In the *imitation of Nature,* as illustrated by childish and primitive practices, and in the empirical invention of instruments.

"(4) In the *moods* (emotions) of the individual, in the 'soul'. As music could directly imitate these moods, the *ethos of music,* in its various modes, was an important problem in education. The laws for 'good' music, then, are not of 'Nature', but of the cult, church, academy, or tribunal that decides what music is good for its adherents. This function was performed by the church in the Middle Ages, and today [1939] is performed for Germany by the *Kultusministerium.*[440]

"(5) In the *genius* or *talent* of the individual. This theory is always popular in an age that glorifies the virtuoso.

"(6) In *national consciousness,* group solidarity, in folk music 'instinctively' expressive of the characteristics and aspirations of one nation in one area. These theories are especially popular in countries where the militaristic ideal is fostered.

"(7) In *class consciousness,* in the group solidarity engendered by common enterprise, work, and play. Rhythm is the prime factor in this theory.

"(8) In the *religious* impulse, in the communal feeling of awe leading to rites of worship, beginning with music in *magic.*

"(9) In the *dramatic* instinct—impassioned speech, sexual selection, the emotion of fear, heroic narration, desire for social approval.

"(10) In the *dance* instinct—the desire for exercise, the play impulse....

"It is essential to note that all of [these] recognize certain truths. Together they illustrate the many-sided nature of music." —Allen, pp.5-9, 10-17, 23-25, 29-30, 32-33, 48-53, 55-61, 191-92, 215-16.

ORLANDO (ROLAND).

§286A.1 "**Roland.** The Frankish hero of Roncesvalles, where his men slew 100,000 Saracens. When his forces were reduced to fifty, a fresh phalanx of Saracens suddenly appeared from over the mountains. Only

---

439 Ferrucio Busoni, *A New Musical Aesthetic,* New York, 1913.

440 Another factor which perhaps is overlooked here stems from the notion that "Music [is] a magical means of communication with god(s) or supreme being(s). Music as magical conveyance to territory of gods or spirit beings"—our theme **T1a,** *Introductory Remarks,* Vol I above. For someone who is convinced that music does indeed possess this power, it could be essential that the *right* sort of music is employed, which is performed in the *right* sort of way—or else the intended result may fail of achievement. (Ed.)

then did honour permit Roland to blow on his ivory horn, Oliphant, in order to summon Charlemagne to his assistance.

"The sound of the horn was so shrill that it killed birds in the sky, split the horn itself in two, and caused the Saracens to retreat in alarm. But by the time Charlemagne arrived, Roland had died of his battle wounds.

"The actual encounter that gave rise to this legend occurred in AD 778 when the Basques annihilated the rearguard of Charlemagne's army, which was withdrawing after a campaign in Spain. The eleventh-century *Chanson de Roland* tells the story in epic fashion." — Cotterell (Macmillan Myths and Legends), p.235.

§286A.2 "**Orlando or Roland.** Nephew of Charlemagne, and one of the most celebrated knights in medieval romance. His exploits are described in the *Chanson de Roland* and *Orlando Furioso*, and he appears in Bishop Turpin's *Chronicles*. He perished in the battle of Roncesvalles (AD 778)....

"[Among his many adventures, Orlando promised his beloved Angelica to destroy the garden of the enchantress Falerina, in which many valiant knights had been entrapped, and were imprisoned. Along the way the knight rescues another maiden, and the two make their way together.]

"While they rode another damsel approached on a white palfrey, who warned Orlando of impending danger, and informed him that he was near the garden of the enchantress. Orlando was delighted with the intelligence, and entreated her to inform him how he was to gain admittance. She replied that the garden could only be entered at sunrise and gave him such instructions as would enable him to gain admittance. She gave him also a book

in which was painted the garden and all that it contained, together with the palace of the false enchantress, where she had secluded herself for the purpose of executing a magic work in which she was engaged. This was the manufacture of a sword capable of cutting even through enchanted substances. The object of this labor, the damsel told him, was the destruction of a knight of the west, by name Orlando, who she had read in the book of Fate was coming to demolish her garden. Having thus instructed him, the damsel departed.

"Orlando, finding he must delay his enterprise till the next morning, now lay down and was soon asleep. Seeing this, the base woman whom he had rescued, and who was intent on making her escape to rejoin her paramour, mounted Brigliadoro, and rode off, carrying away Durindana.[441]

"When Orlando awoke, his indignation, as may be supposed, was great on the discovery of the theft; but, like a good knight and true, he was not to be diverted from his enterpise. He tore off a huge branch of an elm to supply the place of his sword; and, as the sun rose, took his way towards the gate of the garden, where a dragon was on his watch. This he slew by repeated blows, and entered the garden, the gate of which closed behind him, barring retreat. Looking round him, he saw a fair fountain, which overflowed into a river, and in the centre of the fountain a figure, on whose forehead was written:

The stream which waters violet and
    rose,
From hence to the enchanted palace
    goes.

---

441 Brigliadoro: in Bioardo's *Orlando Innamorato*, the name of Orlando's horse. It means literally 'golden bridle'. Durandana or Durindana: Orlando's sword, given him by his cousin Malaggi. It once belonged to Hector, was made by the fairies, and could cleave the Pyrenees at a blow.

Following the banks of this flowing stream, and rapt in the delights of the charming garden, Orlando arrived at the palace, and entering it, found the mistress, clad in white, with a crown of gold upon her head, in the act of viewing herself in the surface of the magic sword. Orlando surprised her before she could escape, deprived her of the weapon, and holding her fast by her long hair, which floated behind, threatened her with immediate death if she did not yield up her prisoners, and afford him the means of egress. She, however, was firm of purpose, making no reply, and Orlando, unable to move her either by threats or entreaties, was under the necessity of binding her to a beech, and pursuing his quest as he best might.

"He then bethought him of his book, and, consulting it, found that there was an outlet to the south, but that to reach it a lake was to be passed, inhabited by a siren, whose song was so entrancing as to be quite irresistible to whoever heard it; but his book instructed him how to protect himself against this danger. According to its directions, while pursuing his path, he gathered abundance of flowers, which sprung all around, and filled his helmet and his ears with them: then listened if he heard the birds sing. Finding that, though he saw the gaping beak, the swelling throat, and ruffled plumes, he could not catch a note, he felt satisfied with his defence, and advanced toward the lake. It was small but deep, and so clear and tranquil that the eye could penetrate to the bottom.

"He had no sooner arrived upon the banks than the waters were seen to gurgle, and the siren, rising midway out of the pool, sung so sweetly that birds and beasts came trooping to the water-side to listen. Of this Orlando heard nothing, but, feigning to yield to the charm, sank down upon

the bank. The siren issued from the water with the intent to accomplish his destruction. Orlando seized her by the hair, and while she sang yet louder (song being her only defence) cut off her head. Then, following the directions of the book, he stained himself all over with her blood.

"Guarded by this talisman, he met successively all the monsters set for defence of the enchantress and her garden, and at length found himself again at the spot where he had made captive the enchantress, who still continued fastened to the beech. But the scene was changed. The garden had disappeared, and Falerina, before so haughty, now begged for mercy, assuring him that many lives depended upon the preservation of hers. Orlando promised her life upon her pledging herself for the deliverance of her captives."[442]....

"[Other episodes also mention the horn of Astolpho—an English duke who had joined the Emperor in his struggle against the Saracens, and who thus became (like Orlando and Rinaldo) one of the twelve paladins of Charlemagne. A blast upon this horn was sufficient to dispel the most terrible of enemies. For example, Astolpho visits Senapus, king of Abyssinia, who is beset by Harpies (winged monsters—half women, half birds—armed with sharp claws—who defiled everything they touched).]

"King Senapus received [the hero Astolpho] graciously, and ordered a splendid repeast to be prepared in honor of his arrival. While the guests were seated at table, Astolpho filling the place of dignity at the king's right hand, the horrid scream of the Harpies was heard in the air, and soon they approached, hovering over the tables, seizing the food from the dishes, and overturning everything with the flapping of

---

442 See Thompson Folklore Motifs B53 (Siren: Bird with woman's head), D1275 (Magic song), J672.1 (Ears stopped with wax to avoid enchanting song); see also **WATER SPIRITS***. (Ed.)

their broad wings. In vain the guests struck at them with knives and any weapons which they had, and Astolpho drew his sword and gave them repeated blows, which seemed to have no more effect upon them than if their bodies had been made of tow.

"At last Astolpho thought of his horn. He first gave warning to the king and his guests to stop their ears; then blew a blast. The Harpies, terrified at the sound, flew away as fast as their wings could carry them. The paladin mounted his Hippogriff [winged horse, with an eagle's head and claws, whose father was a griffin and mother a filly], and pursued them, blowing his horn as often as he came near them. They stretched their flight towards the great mountain, at the foot of which there is a cavern, which is thought to be the mouth of the infernal abodes. Hither those horrid birds flew, asif to their home. Having seen them all disappear in the recess, Astolpho cared not to pursue them farther, but alighting, rolled huge stones into the mouth of the cave, and piled branches of trees therein, so that he effectually barred their passage out, and we have no evidence of their ever having been

seen since in the outer air."[443]—Bulfinch, pp.687-89, 770-71, 914, 923, 956.

§286A.3 "[Astolfo attempts to rescue his friends from the land of the killer-women.] The horn, to which he always resorted in desperate situations, he now set to his lips; the earth, indeed the whole world, seemed to quake when the dreadful noise was unpent. So terrified was the populace that in their haste to flee they tumbled out of the arena aghast and stupefied; nor were any guards left on the gates. Just as a startled family will risk death and throw itself out of windows and off great heights if they see the whole place ablaze with a fire which has spread little by little while drowsy slumber sat in their eyelids; thus, little prizing their safety, everyone fled from the appalling noise. Hither and thither, up and down the dazed mob surged, seeking to escape. More than a thousand were piled up at each gate, blocking each other's way. Some lost their lives in the mêlée, others were smashed to pieces in their fall from terraces and windows. Many an arm was fractured, and many a skull—leaving their owners maimed or dead. A confusion of eries and shrieks, chaos, and cataclysm assailed the

---

443 See Thompson Folklore Motif D1222, *Magic horn (musical)*. This incident is described in *Orlando Furioso*, Canto 33. (Ed.)

sky. Wherever the sound of the horn penetrated, the panicking mob fled headlong....

"The horn's magic power had the same dire effect on Astolfo's friends as on all the rest. Samsonet, Guidone, and the twins [Grifon and Aquilant] bolted away after terrified Marfisa [the Saracen warrior-damsel, who sides with Charlemagne]. However far they ran, they could not put enough distance between themselves and the ear-splitting racket. Astolfo scoured the entire neighbourhood, blowing on his horn with ever-increasing vigour. Some fled down to the sea, some up to the hills, others vanished into the woods. A few simply kept running, without a backward glance, and never stopped running for ten days. Some were in such a state as they sped out across the drawbridge that they never in all their life returned within the walls. The squares, houses, and temples were so cleared of people that the city remained almost deserted."[444] — Ariosto, pp.239-40.

ORNAMENTATION.

§286B.1 *Ed. note:* The following entry applies to the symbolism of visual/pictorial ornamentation, but suggests some intriguing possibilities with respect to musical ornamentation, as well. "This is a symbol of cosmic activity, of development in space and of the 'way out of chaos' (chaos being denoted by blind matter). Ornamentation by virtue of graduated motifs — its progressive reconciliation with order — signifies the gradual stages in this evolutive development of the universe.... For Moslems, art is a kind of aid to meditation, or a sort of mandala — indefinite and interminable and opening out onto the infinite, or a form of language composed of spiritual signs, or handwriting; but it can never be a mere reflection of the world of existence. In Islamic ornamentation — which we may regard as one of the basic prototypes — the essential constituents are as follows: plaits, foliage, polygons, arabesques, inscriptions, the twenty-eight letters of the alphabet, five or six stylized flowers (such as the hyacinth, the tulip, the eglantine, the peach-blossom), certain of the fabulous animals and the seven smalts in heraldry. Patterns such as these are

---

444 Here the horn's magic power is in the way of being an extension of its customary nature and function, which is to make a loud sound, call assembly, stir others to action, confuse or terrify an opposing enemy, etc. The question is raised, then, as to whether or not many (or even all) of the magical powers and properties of music and musical instruments are not also extensions (or heightenings) of what music, and musical instruments, normally are and do? And if this should be the case, might it not be said that music — precisely in its normal or customary aspect — itself is magical, then, to begin with? Thus it might be argued that music generally is seductive (magical, enchanting) — not only in some particular tale or situation, but according to its nature; is elevating or transporting not only in virtue of some spell which is put upon a player, but on account of what it normally is and does; that music can summon (or drive away) spirits, not only in the hands of a magician or shaman or sorcerer but in virtue of what music itself (apparently) is. A charmed fiddle may have the power to cause its hearers to dance themselves to death; however — is this not an extension or heightening of the (perhaps equally magical?) power of fiddles to make their listeners want to dance — and dance — and dance, in the first place? (Ed.)

blended into a vast symbolic network reminiscent of polyphonic music and the aspiration towards the harmony of infinity.[445]" — Cirlot, pp.245-46.

ORPHEUS (Greek). *(See p.627.)*

§287.11 ORPHEUS: Music as an Instrument of Civilization (as Civilizing Agency). "The influence of Orpheus [who was regarded not as a god but as a hero in the sense of one who could claim close kinship with the gods—who though he had certain superhuman powers, had to live the ordinary span of life and die like any other mortal,] was always on the side of civilisation and the arts of peace. In personal character he is never a hero in the modern sense. His outstanding quality is a gentleness amounting at times to softness. From warlike attributes he is entirely free, differing in this from the archer-god whom in some other ways he so closely resembles. The atmosphere of calm which surrounds him differs strangely too from the normal habits of the wild mountain-god whose religion he adopted. Music may excite as well as soothe, but the cymbals and tympana of a Thracian or Phrygian orgy seem at first to have little to do with the sweet tones of Orpheus' lyre. The power of the lyre was to soften the hearts of warriors and turn their thoughts to peace, just as it could tame the wildest of the beasts. Not only animals but men gathered round to listen to the song. In the vase-paintings which show this scene, the expressions of the faces of the listeners leave no doubt of the effect which the music is having. This is reflected in the statement of a later author that Orpheus 'by his playing and singing won over the Greeks, changed the hearts of barbarians and tamed wild beasts'. He made men give up cannibalistic feasts, an achievement which in Graeco-Roman times was attributed to many gods without much discrimination; but, for Orpheus it can be traced back to the fifth century. He taught men also the arts of agriculture and in this way inclined their natures towards peace and gentleness. Themistios, who lived in the first century of the Byzantine Empire, but was a zealous reader of Plato and Aristotle, writes: 'Even the initiations and rites of Orpheus were not unconnected with the art of husbandry. That is in fact the explanation of the myth when it describes him as charming and softening the hearts of all. The cultivated fruits which husbandry offers us have a civilising effect on human nature in general and on the habits of beasts; and the animal passions in our hearts it excises and renders harmless.' " — Guthrie [Orpheus], pp.40-41.

§287.12 "THE SONGS OF ORPHEUS AND THE NEW SONG OF CHRIST.[446] Orpheus, the singer whose music moved animate and inanimate creatures, is a figure by which Christ and his power may be understood. Such was the impression of Clement of Alexandria, a Christian

---

445 See Luc Benoist, *Art du monde* (Paris, 1941).
446 My thanks to the Canada Council, who granted me a Leave Fellowship for 1974-5 when the first version of this paper was written, and to Scarborough College for research leave; also to Peter Toon, Oak Hill College, London, for a fresh look at psalms and songs in the Old Testament. For a general discussion of music and the figure of Orpheus in early Christian writings, see Robert A. Skeris *On the Origins and Theological Interpretation of the Musical Imagery Used by the Ecclesiastical Writers of the First Three Centuries, with Special Reference to the Image of Orpheus* (1976).

apologist and a student of Greek philosophy. Other writers from the New Testament period on had used Old Testament figures as types of Christ: Melchizedek as a type of Christ's high priestly function and Isaac as a type of Christ's sacrifice, to name only two. But Clement took the daring step of typifying Christ through a figure of Greek mythology.

"Clement was writing near the end of the second century of the Christian era, when Christians were at times severely persecuted and at times merely despised by the world in which they lived.[447] Many Christian writers of this period defended their community against the attacks and insinuations of their pagan neighbours. This defence usually took the form of showing that Christians were doing no harm to anyone and that, because the sources of their faith were older than in other cultures, their beliefs were superior to those of their opponents. Some of these writers attempted to demonstrate a dependence of Greek ideas on Jewish thought.[448]

Clement wrote his *Protrepticus* or *Exhortation to the Greeks* to explain to his readers in terms which were familiar to them the meaning of his faith and its superiority to their religious beliefs and practices.[449] In this work he shows himself conversant with Greek literature and Jewish Scriptures, with Greek cults and Christian tradition. Quotations and verbal reminiscences are woven into his text with missionary zeal; for however much he may have admired Greek culture, he was quite certain that the Greeks had so far missed the 'greatest of good things' — salvation through Christ the Word (*Protrepticus* 12, 162; 1.86.25-6). Odysseus had his men bind him to the mast of his ship so that he might be restrained from responding to the Sirens who lured sailors to their doom as his ship sailed past their shore. Instead of emulating Odysseus Clement's readers ought to depend on the power of the cross to protect them from evil. 'Bound to the wood [of the cross],' he tells them, 'you will be freed from all corruption' (12, 252; 1.83.25-6). In a later section he compares

---

447 Christians might be brought into the arena as at Vienne and Lyon in AD 177 (Eusebius *Historia Ecclesiastica* 5.1.3-2.8) or might be regarded with suspicion as baby-eaters and committers of incest (cf. Tertullian *Apology* 7.1.

448 Eg Moses was supposed to have influenced the Greeks. The *Testament* of Orpheus, quoted only by Christian writers, shows Orpheus repenting of polytheism and embracing monotheism through the influence of Moses. O. Kern *Orphicorum fragmenta* (Berlin 1922) 255-63 distinguishes three versions (his fr 245-47) preserved by Justin, Clement, and Eusebius. Undoubtedly this poem smoothed the way for Christians to compare Christ and Orpheus.

449 *Protrepticus* 12, 254; 1.84.7. First part of the reference is to the section of the work, followed by the page number in Clement of Alexandria, ed and tr G. W. Butterworth (Loeb edn; London and New York 1919); second part of the reference is to volume, page, and line number of the standard edition of *Clemens Alexandrinus* ed O. Stählin (4 vols; Leipzig 1905-36). References to *Protrepticus* will be given in this manner throughout.

the experience of becoming a Christian to initiation into a mystery religion — but one which was far superior to the rites of Dionysus (12, 254-6; 1.84). Clement manages to convey a genuine appreciation of Greek literature and culture, yet he refuses to be seduced by it.

"Clement began his *Exhortation* by references to famous singers of antiquity: Amphion* who was said to have used music to move stones into position to build the walls of Thebes; Arion* of Methymna who attracted a dolphin by his singing and with its help was rescued from wicked sailors; and Orpheus, more ancient and renowned than these, who tamed wild beasts and moved mighty oak trees by the power of his music. We learn of another singer, Eunomus, who was competing at Delphi when one of the strings of his lyre broke. Thereupon a grasshopper which had been chirping in the shade of the leaves jumped up on Eunomus' lyre and twittered there. Eunomus, so the story goes, adapted his music to the grasshopper's song, and thus compensated for the loss of the string. The Greeks thought that the insect was charmed by Eonomus' song, but Clement disputes that. Instead, he would have it that the grasshopper was singing praises to God spontaneously.[450]

"Eunomus and the grasshopper makes an odd fourth with the others: stones, fish, animals, and trees are surely not to be compared with one small insect. Eunomus himself is a dwarf beside the great musicians. By suggesting a different interpretation of the story of the grasshopper, Clement implies without stating that the supposed influence of music in the other accounts may be susceptible to other interpretations.

"Clement's next section deals with the contrast between myth and truth. The Greeks believed myths such as these about the power of song, but they did not recognize the 'shining face of truth' (1, 4; 1.3.24). They held that certain mountains were sacred and they enjoyed watching the stories of past misfortunes made into tragedy. But Helicon, Cithaeron, and the mountains of the Odrysians and Thracians[451] have been replaced by the holy mount Sion and a drama greater than any tragedy has been enacted, with the chief actor, the Word of God, 'crowned in the theatre of the whole world' (1, 16; 1.4.15-16). The Word, the title which Clement gives to the second person of the Trinity, is the true *agonistes*, a word which often means 'champion', although it occasionally means 'actor', a meaning attested to by the Aristotelian *Problemata*. In

---

450 Frequently, in mythology (and also in modern composition — e.g. Beethoven's *"Pastorale" Symphony*), a musician attempts to imitate sounds of nature: the song of birds, a peaceful breeze, a storm, a flowing brook, ocean swells — even the roaring of a lion (Saint-Saëns). One greater or lesser purpose of such an imitation could be an attempted mediation between our human, civilized world and the pre-civilized, non-human world of natural and supernatural gods and forces; indeed, the very animals which are so represented — or appealed to in some fashion — sometimes *represent* these same gods or natural phenomena. (Ed.)

451 J. B. Friedman *Orpheus in the Middle Ages* (Cambridge Mass 1970) 55 attempts to link all these mountain references to Orpheus; he is the son of Calliope, a Muse with her home on Helicon; he sang hymns and codified the theology of Dionysus of Cithaeron; and he tamed savage beasts and men in the mountains of Thrace and Odrysi. But a careful examination of Clement shows that he is not thinking solely of Orpheus.

this passage the appearance of the Word is contrasted with the dramas of the Greeks; the whole world—not just the tragic stage—is the theatre in which he acts; and the chorus is the company of the holy prophets who have interpreted his coming as the chorus in a tragedy comment on the action of the play (1, 16; 1.4.9). The crowning mentioned by Clement is a symbol of the reward which, in Christian writings from the New Testament on, comes from God to the faithful.[452] Clement seems to abandon the theatre in this detail and to think rather of the crowning of the victor. By this change he emphasizes the difference between re-enactments of past (untrue) stories in tragedy and the actual, historical unfolding of truth through the activity of the Word. Herein lies the suitability of the term *agonistes*. The Word is more than an actor who represents someone else's action; he is himself both actor and champion.

"As the Word is the true champion, not merely an actor, so for Clement he is the (true) singer: 'my Eunomus' in Clement's words (1, 6; 1.4.17). The song of the Word is not an old Greek one, nor is the mode Greek; it is the eternal song, with new harmony, bearing the name of God. It is the new song, the Levitical song, which in the words of Homer is the 'banisher of pain and anger, causing all evils to be forgotten'.[453] It is typical of Clement that he should introduce a Greek verse just at the moment when he is most insistent on the uniqueness of the Christian message. But his argument is that as Old Testament prophets wrote without complete understanding about Christ, so Greek poets may without comprehending have seen the truth. The words of Homer are truer of the song of the Word than of the poet's original application of them to Helen and the drugs she learned about in Egypt.

"The other singers, Orpheus, Amphion, and Arion, deceived mankind by relating stories of violence and sorrow, and let them into idolatry by the enchantment of their music. But 'far different is my singer,' Clement continues. Unlike those musicians honoured by the Greeks, the Word frees those who listen to his music. He tames not wild beasts but human beings who resemble them: birds who represent the 'unstable', reptiles the 'cheaters', lions the 'passionate', pigs the 'pleasure-lovers', wolves the 'plunderers'. People without sense are wood and stones; just as it was recounted that those famous singers moved trees and stones, so God the Word transforms senseless people. Clement introduces into his presentation quotations from the Gospels to justify his interpretation. Jesus said that God could raise up from stones children to Abraham (Matthew 3:9, Luke 3:8). These stones which could be transformed into

---

452 Lampe *Patristic Lexicon*.
453 *Odyssey* 4.221.

Abraham's children are interpreted by Clement as Gentiles who trusted in stones or idols, and who are spoken of as Abraham's children by faith elsewhere (for instance, in Galatians 3:7-9). Pharisees and Sadducees were called a 'generation of vipers' (Matthew 3:7, Luke 3:8) and false prophets were 'wolves in sheep's clothing' (Matthew 7:15). Clement declares that even these can repent and be transformed.

"Non-Christian writers previously had made Orpheus a bringer of civilization,[454] but Clement claims that the taming of beasts is an allegroy, not of Orpheus, but of the activity of the Word in dealing with mankind. Clement's treatment of this interpretation suggests that he feels that he is breaking ground. He is explicit about identifying animals and birds with kinds of human beings, he relies on quotations from Scripture to back him up, and his claim that the Word is the only one to tame human beings suggests that he is unaware of attempts to allegorize Orpheus.

"The new song does more than tame the savage and revive the insensible; it gives order to the universe.[455] Clement reminds his readers of the tempering of the extremes of heat and cold, the stability of the land, and the limits fixed to the encroachment of the sea. The word here used for world or universe is [Greek term], which basically means 'order' and in a derivative sense 'universe', because of its order.[456] The harmony in the universe extends from the centre to the edges and from the limits to the centre. One is reminded of the Pythagoreans' concept of harmony in the universe, and in particular of their theory of the music of the spheres,[457] music produced by the revolution of the heavens.[458]

"The Pythagoreans were speaking of literal music, though the ear did not hear it, being accustomed to it from birth. Clement, however, makes it clear that the music he means is not produced on instruments like the lyre and cithara, but that the Word uses the macrocosm and the human

---

454 See §287.11, above. (Ed.)

455 Whether music gives harmony (order) to the universe — or merely reflects such harmony (order) — is an interesting question which recalls to my mind a somewhat parallel distinction mentioned by Sybille Bedford in her Aldous Huxley biography — between supposing, on the one hand, that the human brain *produces* consciousness, and supposing, on the other, that the brain only *transmits* it somehow (see *Aldous Huxley: A Biography*, Alfred A. Knopf/Harper & Row, 1975, 539). I should think it all hinges on what one intends by the various terms: if a working of the brain in a certain way *is* what we call "consciousness", then, where there is that kind of working of a brain, there must also be what it is that we call "consciousness". Similarly, if music *is* order (harmony), then, where there is music, there must also be that which we call harmony (order). (Ed.)

456 Most Greek philosophers were convinced of this order: D. R. Dicks *Early Greek Astronomy* (London and New York 1970) 63; G. E. R. Lloyd *Early Greek Science* (London 1970) 27; W. K. C. Guthrie *The Greeks and Their Gods* (London 1950) 198.

457 See **HARMONY (HARMONIA) OF THE SPHERES***. (Ed.)

458 Lloyd *Early Greek Science*; Dicks *Early Greek Astronomy* 71; Aristotle *De caelo* 190b12f.

microcosm to make music to God. He quotes from an unidentified source, 'You are my cithara, my flute, and my temple,' and interprets this to mean '[you are my] cithara because of the harmony, flute because of the breath/Spirit, and temple because of the Word—God's purpose being that the music should resound, the Spirit inspire, and the temple receive its Lord.' The line quoted by Clement must be addressed by God to a human worshipper. The metaphor of the believer as a temple is found in the New Testament (cf. 1 Corinthians 6:19). Prophets were used by God 'as a flautist might blow into a pipe' according to a contemporary of Clement, Athenagoras.[459] A worshipper touched by God was compared by the heretic Montanus to a lyre awakened by the plectrum. What is true of the individual is also true of groups of believers and of the whole of creation.[460]

"Having established that the Word does not use a musical instrument like Orpheus or Jubal* 'father of those who play the lyre and pipe' (Genesis 4:21), but that he uses his creation as an instrument, Clement focuses briefly on David* 'the sweet psalmist of Israel' (2 Samuel 23:1), who is both like and unlike Orpheus. Like him, David played a stringed instrument, and composed and sang actual songs, but unlike him he did not sing false songs to enslave men to idols. Rather he drove away daemons by the power of his music, as his healing of Saul illustrated (1 Samuel 16:23). It is important to establish that David differed from Orpheus, because the Word incarnate was considered to be 'of the house and lineage of David' (Luke 2:4, 3:23, 3:31) and was to sit on 'the throne of his father David' (Luke 1:32).

"As the created order is the instrument of the Word, so the Word is the instrument of God.[461] By this figure Clement means that God revealed himself or 'spoke' through the Word (cf. Hebrews 1:2). The Word is the Singer in that he brings order to the world and to people by his music; he is the Song, in that he sings of himself and of God; and he is the Instrument in that he is being used to reveal God. Using the figures of Orpheus and other musicians and the idea of the power of music, Clement has drawn forth a number of pictures by which Christ may be understood. I have made explicit in my discussion what is only implicit in Clement, in order to show how he has explained Christian theology through ideas familiar to his Greek readers.

"Clement turns to expound the activity of the Word, both incarnate and pre-incarnate. He does not entirely forget the figure of the singer though he combines it with other figures, such as the doctor (1, 20; 1.8.25) and the teacher (1, 18; 1.7.30). But the imagery of music continues to appear

---

459 *Legatio* 9.1. Not much is known of Athenagoras: Philip of Side, a fifth-century Christian historian, says he was the head of the school in Alexandria and teacher of Clement, author of *Stromateis*, but this is not confirmed by, and is hard to reconcile with, other sources. He was active in the time of M. Aurelius and was therefore Clement's contemporary. Cf W. R. Schoedel *Athenagoras* (Oxford 1972) ix. Cf also the 'pipe of my lips' in G. Vermès *Dead Sea Scrolls in English* (London 1962) 89.

460 Epiphanius *Heresies* 48.4.1-3.

461 On the word as God's instrument, a favourite theme of Athanasius (eg *De incarnatione* 42.22) and Eusebius (*Praise of Constantine* chapters 11 and 12). Cf also Athenagoras *Legatio* 16.3 and Clement *Stromateis* 6.11.1-5.

as the Word 'sings to some'; is 'many-toned'; and 'encourages [people] by singing to his instrument' (1, 20; 1.8.25-30). At the end of the first chapter of his *Exhortation*, Clement returns to Greek religious imagery. He urges each of his readers to be purified 'not with laurel leaves and fillets adorned with wool and purple, but bind righteousness [round your head] and wreath yourself with the leaves of self-control.'

"Laurel leaves and fillets, if they are meant to have a specific association, may speak of Apollo to whom the laurel was sacred and who presided over purifications.[462] Since Orphics, who claimed Orpheus as their founder, were forbidden to use wool,[463] this cannot be a reference to the singer and is best taken as general imagery.

"Through this first chapter of the *Exhortation*, wherever the singer appears or Orpheus is mentioned, the power of music to influence is the point of comparison. Later Christian writers compared the story of Orpheus descending into the lower world to rescue his dead wife, Eurydice, to the action of Christ rescuing souls from the power of death. So Eurydice is analogous to the human soul, the snake which caused her death to 'that old serpent,' the devil, and Orpheus to Christ.[464] At times this becomes a general statement of the salvation of the soul, but more frequently it is applied to the rescue of the souls of those who died before Christ's coming and who were released by him when he 'descended into Hell'.[465] In most, but not all, versions of the myth, Orpheus failed to bring his wife back to the upper world; this failure is contrasted with Christ's success, as in a fourth-century hymn by Ephraim of Syria. In it Death scornfully denies the power of music to charm him: 'as for the wise that are able to charm wild beats, their charms enter not into my ears.' Later in the hymn, 'the voice of our Lord sounded in Hell and he cried aloud and burst the graves one by one.'[466] Death, according to Ephraim, had not given up his prey to one who was able to charm wild beasts, that is Orpheus, but he was defeated by Christ, in the harrowing of Hell. Clement makes no use of this part of the Orpheus story, even in the one place in the *Exhortation* (1, 18; 1.8.3-14) where we might have expected it. There he describes the serpent who 'buries people alive' through worship of idols, who also 'carried off Eve to death'. 'Our rescuer and

---

462 W. K. C. Guthrie *The Greeks and Their Gods* (London 1950) 192-3.
463 W. K. C. Guthrie *Orpheus and Greek Religion* (London 1935) 198.
464 P. Bersuire *Metamorphosis Ovidiana moraliter explanata*, quoted by Friedman, *Orpheus in the Middle Ages* 127.
465 As in the Apostle's Creed; cf also Ephesians 4:8 and 1 Peter 3:19.
466 In *Post-Nicene Fathers* vol 13 tr J. Gwynn (Oxford and New York 1898) 196-7, Nisibene Hymns 36 stanzas 5 and 11; Ephraim wrote AD 350-78.

helper is the Lord' he adds, but he makes no use of the figure of the singer.[467]

"For Clement, then, Orpheus is the singer, not the psychopomp he became for later Christian writers. The emphasis which later ages placed upon his great love for Eurydice and his attempted rescue of her from death, though not unknown in the ancient world, is overshadowed by the tradition of the power of Orpheus' music over animals.

"Clement is not alone in comparing Christ to Orpheus and his activities to that of the singer's. Eusebius in the fourth century in his speech 'In Praise of Constantine', the first emperor to identify himself as a Christian, includes in that speech an extended comparison of Christ to Orpheus. He says that Christ used an instrument, man, 'as a musician displays his skill by his lyre'.[468] Thus the human body assumed by the Word at his incarnation is treated as an instrument by which he acted. He refers then to Orpheus 'who tamed all kinds of wild beats by his song and softened the anger of fierce creatures by striking chords on an instrument with

a plectrum'. The Word, however, who is 'all-wise and all-harmonious' strikes up 'odes and epodes' which 'soften the fierce, angry passions of the souls of Greeks and barbarians'. Wild animals are, as in Clement, compared to human beings, but not in the same detail. One feels that it has become a more common and accepted comparison by this time.[469]

"Elsewhere in this speech, Eusebius refers to creation as the 'system of perfect harmony which is the workmanship of the one world-creating Word' and compares the harmony of a properly-tuned stringed instrument to the harmony of the world in God's hands. Those who honour what is created and fail to honour the creator are like children who admire the lyre and pay no attention to the musician who produces the music.[470] These are themes which have been used by other writers.[471] They show us the power of music in the minds of these early writers as well as the use of a pagan figure to interpret and symbolize Christ.

"Beside these two explicit comparisons of Christ to Orpheus, there are references to Christ as a musician, maintaining harmony

---

467 We might note in contrast *Ovide moralisé* 8.264: 'by Orpheus... we must understand the person of Our Lord Jesus Christ... who played his harp so melodiously that he drew from Hell the sainted souls of the holy fathers who had descended there through the sin of Adam and Eve' (see Friedman *Orpheus in the Middle Ages* 125-6) and the sequence 'Morte Christe celebrata' in A. Mai *Nova patrum bibliotheca* (Rome 1852) vol 1 part 2, 208 (a thirteenth-century hymn: 'Sponsam suam ab inferno / Regno locans in superno / Noster traxit Orpheus.'

468 The frequency with which people of all historical periods have identified music, and the making of music, as a force or instrument of truly supra-natural (sometimes "cosmic") capacities becomes quite overwhelming! (Ed.)

469 For the figure of Christ-Orpheus in art, cf F. Cabrol and H. Leclerq *Dictionnaire d'archéologie chrétienne et de liturgie* (Paris 1936) vol 12 part 2 sv 'Orphée'.

470 Eusebius, *In Praise of Constantine*, chapters 11 and 12.

471 See Footnote 458 above [Lloyd/Dicks/Aristotle] and Athenagoras *Legatio* 16; Tertullian *Ad nationes* 2.5.9.

in the universe or revealing himself by joining 'various tongues in one song'.[472] There are also references to the untamed nature of human beings without Christ, but these are not explicitly connected to the figure of the singer or Orpheus.[473]

"The usual figures for Christ—Teacher, Physician, and Shepherd—can all be traced back to scripture. There are many examples of teaching and healing in the Gospels; and the title 'The Good Shepherd' is familiar from John 10. But none of the Gospel writers describes him as singer or musician. Where then does the Singer come from?

"First of all we should consider singing and playing of instruments in the worship of God in the Old Testament. One whole book, the book of Psalms, is a collection of songs addressed to God. There are a few secular songs: David's lament for Saul and Jonathan (2 Samuel 1:17-27) or the popular song comparing the military prowess of Saul and David (1 Samuel 18:7). Most songs, whether in Psalms or elsewhere, praised God, and it is evident, therefore, that God was pleased with music and singing.[474]

"Many psalms were attributed to David; to succeeding generations he was the shepherd boy anointed to be shepherd over Jacob, or Israel (Psalms 78:70-1), and skilled in playing the lyre (1 Samuel 16:18).

As son of David, Christ inherited his kingship and was also, like him, known as a shepherd. It would not be a great step to attribute David's musical skill allegorically to Christ, especially when one recalls the way David soothed Saul's savage spirit with his music (1 Samuel 16:23).

"This blending of the figures of Orpheus, David, and Christ can be seen in early Christian art.[475] The singer is usually clothed in the style of Orpheus: short tunic, Phrygian cap, lyre held to one side. But although sometimes he is accompanied by the kind of animals which in myth he is said to have charmed, at other times his audience is reduced to sheep or increased to include centaurs and satyrs. Many 'Orpheus-Christ' figures are found in the catacombs, and some are set among otherwise biblical scenes. In the Jewish synagogue at Dura-Europos there is a figure with a lyre in a wall-painting which is interpreted variously as Orpheus or David.[476] Goodenough in his *Jewish Symbols in the Greco-Roman Period* has shown that Jews borrowed a vocabulary of pagan symbols during this period and used them on official Jewish structures because, as he argues, they represented the same mystic and eschatological hope for Jews, pagans, and Christians, too. He suggests that the lyre player in the synagogue at Dura-Europos symbolizes the power of the

---

472 *Damasi Epigrammata* ed. M. Ihm (Leipzig 1895) 66.

473 A. Heussner *Die altchristlichen Orpheusdarstellungen* (Leipzig 1893) 8-9; c.f Irenaeus *Adversus haereses* 5.8 and Cassiodorus on Psalm 49.10 (Migne *Patrologia Latina* 70.352).

474 By no means a self-evident phenomenon: curiously, perhaps, Islamic theology— which, after all, derives in part from Judaeo-Christian traditions—seems not to reflect this view, and it appears that music plays little or no part in the *formal* or *official* customs and practices of this faith. (Ed.)

475 On the use of Old Testament and pagan symbolism in early Christian art, see M. Gough *The Origins of Christian Art* (London 1973) and Fiedman *Orpheus in the Middle Ages* 38-85.

476 For discussions see H. Stern 'The Orpheus in the Synagogue of Dura-Europos' *Journal of the Warburg and Courtauld Institutes* 21 (1958) 1-6; A. Graber, *Christian Iconography: A Study of Its Origins* (London 1969) 24; E. R. Goodenough *Jewish Symbols in the Greco-Roman Period* 5 (New York 1956) 103-11 and 9 (New York 1964) 89-104.

spiritual to calm the turbulence of our material nature.[477] He compares the use of the lyre on nine coins of the second Revolt period (AD 132).

"Finding the lyre and lyre player outside the Christian community confirms its significance as a symbol rather than as a representative of a particular figure. One might conclude, then, that 'David' in the synagogue painting is not the historical king, but an idealized musician who symbolizes the coming 'peaceful kingdom' when natural enemies will become friends (cf. Isaiah 11:1-9 and 65:25). Similarly when the figure of the Singer appears in Christian art or writing, it symbolizes the harmony of God which is at work now through the activity of Christ the Word but will be better seen in the future.

"Music and the lyre in particular represent harmony; the Musician or Singer also represents this harmony. But according to Clement, the Word is not only Singer, he is also the New Song (1, 14; 1.6.26-7.28). In the Old Testament many times the Lord and his mighty works are the subject of song and he is the one who inspires the singers. Three times we read: 'The Lord is my strength and song, and he has become my salvation' (Exodus 15:2, Isaiah 12:2, Psalms 118:14). Clement surely had in mind these and other verses when he called the Word the New Song. Six times in Psalms a new song is mentioned: 'sing to him a new song' (33:3); 'he put a new song in my mouth' (40:3); 'O sing to the Lord a new song' (96:1, 98:1); 'I will sing a new song to thee, O God' (144:9); and 'Praise the Lord! Sing to the Lord a new song' (149:1).[478] The phrase recurs in Isaiah (42:10) and in the New Testament in the Revelation (5:9, 14:3). Judith in the Apocrypha (16:2) sings a new song of praise for her deliverance. The new song may be called forth by a recent act of deliverance (as at Psalms 40:3 and 98:1) or by a change in circumstances (Revelation 5:9). These are implicitly contrasted with the 'old song' (not so called), which sang of God's deliverance from Egypt.

"When Clement calls the Word the New Song, he means that he recently took human form and brought salvation to all. He reminds his readers specifically that the Word is not new 'in the same sense as a tool or a house' is new (1.14; 1.7.4); the Word is eternal, existing in the beginning.

"The redeemed in heaven 'sing the song of Moses, the servant of God, and the song of the Lamb' (Revelation 15:3-4). The song of Moses here must surely be a song of praise from the deliverance from Egypt, the great deliverance of the Old Testament;[479] the song of the Lamb is a song of

---

477 Goodenough *Jewish Symbols* 5, vii-x and 105.

478 The effect is especially lovely, and moving, when texts such as these *are* — themselves — put to music, as in the various psalmodies (psalters) and individual settings by Josquin, Monteverdi, Andrea Gabrieli, Schütz, Handel, Bach, Gluck, Schubert, Mendelssohn, Brahms, Reger, etc. See e.g. Heinrich Schütz' Psalm 98, *Singet dem Herrn ein neues Lied [Sing unto the Lord a new song]*, SWV 35 (also set by Mendelssohn — also in German) in the collection *Psalmen Davids samt etlichen Moteten und Concerten [Psalms of David]*, Op. 2, of 1619. (Ed.)

479 See e.g. Part II of Handel's oratorio *Israel in Egypt*, titled "The Song of Moses". The concluding numbers proclaim triumphantly that "The Lord shall reign", enjoining us all to "Sing ye to the Lord". (Ed.)

praise for the deliverance which is its spiritual parallel, salvation wrought by Christ. Similarly Clement speaks of the 'Levitical song' together with the new song (1, 6; 1.4.17ff). The Levites supplied the singers and musicians in the temple worship (1 Chronicles 15:16, 2 Chronicles 5:12). 'Levitical song' as a category includes praise for all God's acts in the Old Testament period; in this connection it is essential to remember that for Clement God acting in the Old Testament was always God the Word. The Levitical song praises the pre-incarnate Word; the new song, the Word incarnate.

"Christ the Singer and Song in Clement is a complex figure. First, he is compared to musicians of mythical powers, especially over the world of nature. The debt to Orpheus here is obvious and openly acknowledged; I have suggested that David as a musician who soothed Saul acts as a kind of intermediary in the comparison between Orpheus and Christ. Secondly, the instrument itself in the hands of the musician represents harmony and the subjugation of evil, as we see it in the stories of David and Orpheus. The lyre is also used as a type of the harmony found in creation. Thirdly, the song praises God and his deliverance, and because the Word brought deliverance, he is the Song. He can sing of himself because he is God the Word. The Song is the Word set to music.[480]

"There are prophecies of an age of peace when a descendant of David would come as a righteous judge, and when natural enemies in the animal world would become friends and be so tame that a little child could lead them (Isaiah 11:1-9). Reconciliation of the animals also occurs in the promise of new heavens and a new earth (Isaiah 65:25). Mosaics with animals and inscriptions from these passages have been preserved: a lion, a leopard, and a goat with Isaiah 11:6; a lion and an ox with Isaiah 11:7.[481] Since these prophecies looked forward to the coming of the Christ, it was natural that Christ should be placed in the midst of the animals he had tamed. Orpheus in the midst of wild animals was accepted as a prototype of Christ in the peaceful kingdom.

"Clement's figure of the Singer is more complex than would appear from his choice of Orpheus and the others as his starting-point. Instead of narrowing the discussion to a strict comparison, he widens it to cover more adequately the activity of the Word. Eusebius, whose comparison is reminiscent of his, is not so successful; nowhere else in this period does Orpheus foreshadow so majestically the divine Singer." — Irwin, in Warden, pp.51-62.

§287.13 ORPHEUS, HERMES, PAN, AMPHION ETC. IDENTIFICATION WITH NATURAL PHENOMENA: THE WINDS. In his book *Mythology of the Aryan Nations* (1887), George W. Cox treats of various figures in Greek mythology who, in his view, represent/relate to a number of important natural phenomena — among which he includes the winds (so vital to sailors and thus to commerce).

"HERMES. If Hermes* be the son of the twilight, or the first breeze of the morning,

---

480 Cf. Tertullian *De carne Christi* 20.3 where the author says that through David's Psalms, Christ sings of himself. On the 'new' song, cf F. A. Brigham 'The concept of "New Song" in Clement of Alexandria's exhortation to the Greeks' in *Classical Folia* 16 (1962) 9-13 and R.A. Harrisville *The Concept of Newness in the New Testament* (Minneapolis 1960) 18-20 and 96-9.

481 Stern 'The Orpheus in the Synagogue' 4, also compares a secular picture of 'friendship' — five pairs of wild and domestic animals — found at Daphni near Antioch. See also M. Gough *The Origin of Christian Art* 73-7.

his worship would as certain begin in Arkadia (the glistening land), or at Athens (the home of the Dawn), and his first temple be built by Lykâôn (the gleaming), as the worship of Phoibos would spring up in the brilliant Dêlos, or by the banks of the golden Xanthos in the far-off Lykia or land of light, whence Sarpêdon came to the help of Hektor....

"The staff or rod which Hermes received from Phoibos, and which connects this myth with the special emblem of Vishnu, was regarded as denoting his heraldic office. It was, however, always endowed with magic properties, and had the power even of raising the dead. The fillets of this staff sometimes gave place to serpents; and the golden sandals, which in the Iliad and Odyssey bear him through the air more swiftly than the wind, were at length, probably from the needs of the sculptor and the painter, fitted with wings, and the Orphic hymn-writer salutes him accordingly as the god of the winged sandals.[482] In the legend of Medousa these sandals bear Perseus away from the pursuit of the angry Gorgons into the Hyperborean gardens and thence to the shores of Libya.

"ORPHEUS. Of the myth of Orpheus it may also be said that it brings before us a being, in whom some attributes which belong to the light or the sun are blended with others which point as clearly to the wind. The charm of the harping of Hermes is fully admitted in the Homeric hymn,[483] but its effect is simply the effect of exquisite music on those who have ears to hear and hearts to feel it. In the story of Orpheus the action becomes almost wholly mechanical. If his lyre has power over living beings, it has power also over stones, rocks, and trees. What then is Orpheus? Is he, like Hermes, the child of the dawn, or is he the sun-god himself

[Phoebus Apollo] joined for a little while with a beautiful bride whom he is to recover only to lose her again? There can be no doubt that this solar myth has been bodily imported into the legend of Orpheus, even if it does not constitute its essence. The name of his wife, Eurydikê, is one of the many names which denote the wide-spreading flush of the dawn; and this fair being is bitten by the serpent of night as she wanders close by the water which is fatal alike to Melusina and Undine, to the Lady of Geierstein and to the more ancient Bhekî or frog-sun. But if his Helen is thus stolen away by the dark power, Orpheus must seek her as pertinaciously as the Achaians strive for the recovery of Helen or the Argonauts for that of the Golden Fleece. All night long he will wander through the regions of night, fearing no danger and daunted by no obstacles, if only his eyes may rest once more on her who was the delight of his life. At last he comes to the grim abode of the king of the dead, and at length obtains the boon that his wife may follow him to the land of the living, on the one condition that he is not to look back until she has fairly reached the earth. The promise is not kept; and when Orpheus, overcome by an irresistible yearning, turns round to gaze on the beautiful face of his bride, he sees her form vanish away like mist at the rising of the sun. This, it is obvious, is but another form of the myth which is seen in the stories of Phoibos and Daphnê, of Indra and Dahanâ, of Arethousa and Alpheois; and as such, it would be purely solar. But the legend as thus related is shorn of other features not less essential than these solar attributes. Orpheus is never without his harp. It is with this that he charms all things conscious or unconscious. With this he gathers together the bright herds of Helios and all the beasts of the field. As he

---

482 *Hymn XXVIII.*

483 For Hermes' alleged creation of the lyre, and his subsequent conflict with Apollo*, see **HERMES***, p.359. (Ed.)

draws forth its sweet sounds, the trees, the rocks, the streams, all hasten to hear him, or to follow him as he moves onwards on his journey. Only when Eurydikê is dead, are its delicious sounds silenced; but when at the gates of the palace of Hades the three-headed hound Kerberos growls savagely at him, its soft tones charm away his fury, and the same spell subdues the heart of the rugged king himself. It is thus only that he wins the desire of his heart; and when Eurydikê is torn from him the second time, the heavenly music is heard again no more. It is impossible to regard this part of the story as a solar myth, except on the supposition that Orpheus is but another form of Phoibus after he has become possessed of the lyre of Hermes. But the truth is that the myth of the Hellenic Hermes is not more essentially connected with the idea of sound that is that of Orpheus together with the long series of myths based on the same notion which are found scattered over almost all the world. In the opinion of Professor Max Müller 'Orpheus is the same word as the Sanskrit Ribhu or Arbhu, which though it is best known as the name of the three Ribhus, was used in the Veda as an epithet of Indra, and a name for the Sun'.[484] Mr. Kelly, following Dr. Kuhn, sees in the Ribhus the storm-winds which sweep trees and rocks in wild dance before them by the force of their magic song.[485] But even if the Sanskrit name can be applied only to the sun, this would only show that the name of Orpheus underwent in its journey to the west a modification similar to that of the name Hermes. It must, however, be noted that Orpheus acts only by means of his harp, which always rouses to motion. The action of Hermes is twofold, and when

he is going forth on his plundering expedition he lays aside his lyre, which he resumes only when he comes back to lie down like a child in his cradle. Hence the lyre of Hermes only charms and soothes. Its sweet tones conquer the angry sun-god, and lull to sleep the all-seeing Argos of the hundred eyes, when Hermes seeks to deliver Iô from his ceaseless scrutiny. But among the Greek poets the idea which would connect Orpheus with the sun was wholly lost. In Pindar he is sent indeed by Apollôn to the gathering of the Argonauts, but this would point simply to a phase which spoke of the sun as sending or bringing the morning breeze; and with the poet he is simply the harper and the father of songs. In Æschylos he leads everything after him by the gladness with which his strain inspires them. In Euripedes he is the harper who compels the rocks to follow him, while in speaking of him as the originator of sacred mysteries the poet transfers to him the idea which represents Hermes as obtaining mysterious wisdom in the hidden caves of the Thriai. In the so-called Orphic Argonautika the harper is the son of Oiagros and Kalliopê, the latter name denoting simply the beauty of sound.... No sooner does he call on the divine ship which the heroes had vainly tried to move, than the Argo, charmed by the tones, glides gently into the sea. The same tones wake the voyagers in Lemnos from the sensuous spell which makes Odysseus dread the land of the Lotos-eaters. At the magic sound the Kyanean rocks parted asunder to make room for the speaking ship, and the Symplegades which had been dashed together in the fury of ages remained steadfast for ever-more. But it is singular that when it be-

---

484 *Chips, &c.*, ii.127. The converse of the story of Orpheus is found in the legend of Savitri as recounted in the Mahâbhârata. Here Savitri marries Satyavan, knowing that he must die within the year. When Yama comes for Satyavan, she insists on following him, and at last succeeds in winning back the life of her husband, with whom she reaches her home at the break of day.

485 *Curiosities of Indo-European Folklore*, 17.

comes needful to stupify the dragon which guards the golden fleece, the work is done not by the harp of Orpheus, but by the sleep-god Hypnos himself, whom Orpheus summons to lull the Vritra to slumber.

"The same irresistible spell belongs to the music of the Seirens [Sirens — see WATER SPIRITS* (Ed)], who are represented as meeting their doom, in one legend, by means of Orpheus, in another, through Odysseus. Whether these beings represent the Seirai, or belts of calm, which are so treacherous and fatal to mariners, or whether the name itself is found again in the Syrinx* or pipe of the god Pan*, and in the Latin susurrus,[486] the whisper of the breeze, is a point of no great importance, so long as we note the fact that none who listened to their song could be withheld from rushing under its influence to their own destruction. In the story of the Odyssey, Odysseus breaks the spell by filling his sailors' ears with wax, while he has himself stoutly tied to the mast of his ship. In the Orphic myth the divine harper counteracts their witchery by his own

strain, and the Seirens throw themselves into the sea and are changed into rocks according to the doom which granted them life only until some one should sing more sweetly and powerfully than they.

"This mysterious spell belongs also to the Piper of Hameln [see PIPE(S) AND PIPERS* — p.649 (Ed.)], who, wroth at being cheated of his promised recompense for piping away into the Weser the rats which had plagued the city,[487] returns to take an unlooked-for vengeance. No sooner is a note of his music heard than there is throughout the town a sound of pattering feet, all the children of the town hurrying to listen to the strange melody. The musician goes before them to a hill rising about the Weser, and as they follow him into a cavern, the door in the mountain-side shuts fast, and their happy voices are heard no more. According to one version none were saved but a lame boy, who remained sad and cheerless because he could not see the beautiful land to which the piper had said that he was leading them. At Brandenburg the plague from which the piper delivers the people is a

---

486 The name is more probably connected with the Latin Silanus.

487 This tale at once carries us to the Sminthian worship of Apollôn. Sminthos, it is said, was a Cretan word for a mouse, and certain it is that a mouse was placed at the foot of the statues of the sun-god in the temples where he was worshipped under this name. But the story accounted for this by saying that the mouse was endowed with the gift of prophecy, and was therefore put by the side of the deity who was possessed of the profound wisdom of Zeus himself. This in the opinion of Welcker is a mere inversion, which assigned to the mouse an attribute which had belonged exclusively to the god near whom it was placed; accordingly he refers the myth without hesitation to Apollôn as the deliverer from those plagues of mice which have been dreaded or hated as a terrible scourge, and which even now draw German peasants in crowds to the churches to fall on their knees and pray God to destroy the mice. — *Griechische Götterlehre*, i.482. But the Hindu Ganesa, as well as the Hellenic Apollôn, is represented as crushing the mouse. — Gubernatis, *Zoological Mythology*, ii.68.

host of ants, whom he charms into the water. The promised payment is not made, and when he came again, all the pigs followed him into the lake — a touch borrowed probably from the narrative of the miracle at Gadara. In this myth there is a triple series of incidents. Failing to receive his recompense the second year for sweeping away a cloud of crickets, the piper takes away all their ships. In the third year all the children vanish as from Hameln, the unpaid toil of the piper having been this time expended in driving away a legion of rats.

"The idea of music as charming away souls from earth is common to all these legends, and this notion is brought out more fully not only in Göthe's ballad of the Erlking, who charms the child to death in his father's arms, but also in superstitions still prevalent among certain classes of people in this country, who believe that the dying hear the sound of sweet music discoursing to them of the happy land far away.[488]

"The idea of the shrubs and trees as moved by the harping of Orpheus has run out into strange forms. In some myths, the musician who compels all to dance at his will is endowed with the thievish ways of Hermes,[489] although these again are attributed to an honest servant who at the end of three years receives three farthings as his recompense. In the German story of the Jew among the Thorns the servant gives these farthings to a dwarf who grants him three wishes in return. The first two wishes are, of course, for a weapon that shall strike down all it aims at, and a fiddle that shall make every one dance, while by the third he obtains the power of forcing every one to comply with any request that he may make. From this point the story turns more on the Homeric than on the Orphic myth. Strangely enough, Phoibos is here metamorphosed into the Jew, who is robbed not of cows[490] but of a bird, and made to dance until his clothes are all torn to shreds. The appeal to a judge and the trial, with the shifty excuses, the dismissal of the plea, and the sentence, follow in their due order. But just as Hermes delivers himself by waking the sweet music of his lyre when Phoibos on discovering the skins of the slaughtered cattle is about to slay him, so the servant at the gallows makes his request to be allowed to play one more tune, when judge, hangman, accuser, and spectators all join in the magic dance. Another modern turn is given to the legend when the Jew is made to confess that he had stolen the money which he gave the honest servant, and is himself hanged in the servant's stead.[491]

"In a less developed form this story is the same as the legend of Arîon, who, though supposed to be the friend of the Corinthian tyrant Periandros, is still represented as a son of Poseidôn. In this case the musician's harp fails to win his life at the hands of the men who grudge him his wealth; but his wish seems to carry with it a power which they are not able to resist, while his playing brings to the side of the ship a dolphin who bears Arîon on his back

---

488 Gould, *Curious Myths*, second series, 160.

489 A rather fascinating linkage between the (benign) effects of the playing of an Orpheus or Väinämöinen (see **KALEVALA***) and the more frightening aspect of music as an instrument of sorcery or witchcraft, for which see e.g. **DANCING TO DEATH (OR INSANITY)***, **FAIRIES***, **FIDDLERS*** (fiddle as devil's instrument). (Ed.)

490 A reference to Hermes' trickery — see **HERMES***. (Ed.)

491 This marvellous piper reappears in Grimm's stories of the Wonderful Musician, of Roland who makes the witch dance against her will to a bewitched tune, and of the Valiant Tailor who thus conquers the bear as Orpheus masters Kerberos.

to Corinth. In the trial which follows, the tables are turned on the sailors much as they are on the Jew in the German story, and Arîon recovers his harp which was to play an important part in many another Aryan myth.

"The German form of the myth has been traced into Iceland, where Sigurd's harp in the hands of Bosi makes chairs and tables, kings and courtiers, leap and reel, until all fall down from sheer weariness and Bosi makes off with his bride who was about to be given to some one else. The horn of Oberon in the romance of Huon of Bordeaux has the same powers, while it further becomes, like the Sangreal, a test of good and evil, for only those of blameless character dance when its strains are heard. Still more marvellous are the properties of the lyre of Glenkundie:

> He'd harpit a fish
> out o' saut water,
> Or water out o' a
> stane,
> Or milk out o' a
> maiden's breast
> That bairn had
> never nane.[492]

The instrument reappears in the pipe of the Irish Maurice Connor, who could waken the dead as well as stir the living; but Maurice is himself enticed by a mermaid, and vanishes with her beneath the waters. It is seen again in the magic lyre which the ghost of Zorayhayda gives to the Rose of the Alhambra in the charming legend related by Washington Irving, and which rouses the mad Philip V. from his would-be coffin to a sudden outburst of martial vehemence. In Slavonic stories the harp exhibits only the lulling qualities of the lyre of Hermes. It comes before us again in the story of Jack the Giant-Killer, in which the Giant, who in the unchristianised myth was Wuotan himself, possessed an inchanting harp, bags of gold and diamonds, and a hen which daily laid a golden egg. 'The harp,' says Mr. Gould, 'is the wind, the bags are the clouds dropping the sparkling rain, and the golden egg, laid every morning by the red hen, is the dawn-produced Sun.'[493] This magic lyre is further found where perhaps we should little look for it, in the grotesque myths of the Quiches of Guatemala. It is seen in its full might in the song of the Finnish Wäinämöinen, and in the wonderful effects produced by the chanting of the sons of Kalew on the woods, which burst instantly into flowers and fruit, before the song is ended. The close parallelism between the myth of Wäinämöinen and the legends of Hermes and Orpheus cannot be better given than in the words of Mr. Gould.

" 'Wäinämöinen went to a waterfall and killed a pike which swam below it. Of the bones of this fish he constructed a harp, just as Hermes made his lyre of the tortoiseshell. But he dropped this instrument into the sea, and thus it fell into the power of the sea-gods, which accounts for the music of the ocean on the beach.[494] The hero then made another from the forest wood, and with it descended to Pohjola, the realm of darkness, in quest of the mystic Sampo, just as in the classic myth Orpheus went down to Hades to bring thence Eurydice. When in the realm of gloom perpetual, the Finn demigod struck his kantele and sent all the inhabitants of Pohjola to sleep, as Hermes when about to

---

492 Jamieson's *Scottish Ballads*, i.98; Price, *Introduction to Warton's History of English Poetry*, lxiv.

493 *Curious Myths*, ii.160.

494 Another marvelous touch — the *music* of those sounds which are made by the ocean rolling on the shore! (Ed.)

steal Iô made the eyes of Argos Panoptes close at the sound of his lyre. Then he ran off with the Sampo, and had nearly got it to the land of light when the dwellers in Pohjola awoke, and pursued and fought him for the ravished treasure, which, in the struggle, fell into the sea and was lost; again reminding us of the classic tale of Orpheus."[495]

"Wuotan again in the Teutonic mythology is Galdner the singer: and in the Gudrunlied the time which it would take one to ride a thousand miles passed in a moment while any one listened to the singing of Hjarrandi. The christianised form of this myth, as the Legend of the Monk and the Bird, is well known to the readers of Longfellow and Archbishop Trench, and is noteworthy chiefly as inverting the parts, and making the bird charm the wearied and doubting man.

"Still more remarkable is the connexion of this mystic harp in the legend of Gunâdhya with a myth which reproduces that of the Sibylline books offered in diminished quantities, but always at the same price, to the Roman king Tarquin. In the Eastern tale the part of Tarquin is played by King Sâtavâhana to whom Gunâdhya sends a poem of seven hundred thousand slokas written in his own blood. This poem the king rejects as being written in the Pisâcha dialect. Gunâdhya then burns a portion of the poem on the top of a mountain; but while it is being consumed, his song brings together all the beasts of the forest who weep for joy at the beauty of his tale. The king falls ill, and is told that he must eat game; but none is to be had, for all the beasts are listening to Gunâdhya. On hearing this news, the king hastens to the spot and buys the poem, or rather the seventh portion which now alone remained of the whole.[496] It is scarcely necessary to add that in this tale, as in that of Wäinämöinen, we have two stories

which must be traced to a common source with the myths of Hermes, Orpheus, and the Sibyl, — in other words, to a story the framework of which had been put together before the separation of the Aryan tribes.

"PAN. The harp of Orpheus and the lyre of Hermes are but other forms of the reed pipe of Pan*. Of the real meaning of this name the Western poets were utterly unconscious. In the Homeric Hymn he is said to be so called because all the gods were cheered by his music. Still through all the grotesque and uncouth details of the myth, which tells us of his goat's feet and horns, his noisy laughter and capricious action, the idea of wind is pre-eminent. It is the notion not so much of the soft and lulling strains of Hermes in his gentler mood, or of the irresistible power of the harp of Orpheus, as of the purifying breezes which blow gently or strong, for a long or a little while, waking the echoes now here now there, in defiance of all plan or system, and with a wantonness which baffles all human powers of calculation. To this idea the Homeric Hymn adheres with a singular fidelity, as it tells us how he wanders sometimes on the mountain summits, sometimes plunging into the thickets of the glen, sometimes by the stream side or up the towering crags, or singing among the reeds at eventide. So swift is his pace that the birds of the air cannot pass him by. With him play the water-maidens, and the patter of the nymphs' feet is heard as they join in his song by the side of the dark fountain. Like Hermes again and Sarameya, he is the child of the dawn and the morning, and it is his wont to lie down at noontide in a slumber from which he takes it ill if he be rudely roused. Of his parentage we have many stories, but the same notion underlies them all. Sometimes, as in the Homeric Hymn, he is the

---

495 *Curious Myths*, ii.177.
496 *Katha Sarit Sagara*, i.8; Gould, *Curious Myths*, ii.172.

son of Hermes and of the nymph Dryops, sometimes of Hermes and Penelopê, sometimes of Penelopê and Odysseus' but Penelopê is the bride of the toiling sun, who is parted from her whether at morning or at eventide, and to be her son is to be the child of Saramâ. Nor is the idea changed if he be spoken of as the son of heaven and earth (Ouranos and Gaia), or of air and water (Aithêr and a Nereid).

"Pan then is strictly the purifying breeze, the Sanskrit pavana,[497] a name which reappears in the Latin Favonius, and perhaps also in Faunus; and his real character, as the god of the gentler winds, is brought out most prominently in the story of his love for Pitys, and of the jealousy of the blustering Boreas, who hurled the maiden from a rock and changed her into a pine-tree. The myth explains itself. In Professor Max Müller's words, 'We need but walk with our eyes open along the cliffs of Bournemouth to see the meaning of that legend,'—the tale of Pitys, the 'pine-tree wooed by Pan, the gentle wind, and struck down by jealous Boreas, the north wind.' Of Boreas himself we need say but little. His true character was as little forgotten as that of Selênê, and thus the name remained comparatively barren. The Athenian was scarcely speaking in mythical language when he said that Boreas had aided his forefathers by scattering the fleets of Xerxes. The phrases were almost as transparent which spoke of him as a song of Astraios and Eôs, the star-god and the dawn, or as carrying off Oreithyia, the daughter of Erechtheus, the king of the dawn-city.

"Another myth made Pan the lover of the nymph Syrinx; but this is but a slight veil thrown over the phrase which spken of the wind playing on its pipe of reeds by the river's bank; and the tale which related how Syrinx, flying from Pan, like Daphnê from Phoibos, was changed into a reed, is but another form of the story which made Pan the lover of the nymph Echo, just as the unrequited love of Echo for Narkissos is but the complement of the unrequited love of Selênê for Endymiôn.

"AMPHÎON AND ZETHOS. The same power of the wind which is signified by the harp of Orpheus is seen in the story of Amphîon*, a being localised in the traditions of Thebes. But Amphîon is a twin-brother of Zethos, and the two are, in the words of Euripedes, simply the Dioskouroi, riding on white horses, and thus fall into the ranks of the correlative deities of Hindu and Greek mythology. But the myth runs into many other legends, the fortunes of their mother Antiopê differing but little from those of Augê, Tyrô, Evadnê, or Korônis. The tale is told in many versions. One of these calls her a daughter of Nykteus, the brother of Lykos, another speaks of Lykos, as her husband; but this is only saying that Artemis Hekatê may be regarded as either the child of the darkness or the bride of the light. A third version makes her a daughter of the river Asôpos, a parentage which shows her affinity with Athênê, Aphroditê, and all other deities of the light and the dawn. Her children, like Oidipous, Têlephos, and many others, are exposed on their birth,[498] and like them found and brought up by shepherds, among whom Antiopê herself is said to have long remained a captive, like Danaê in the house of Polydektes. We have now the same distinction of office or employment which marks the other twin-brothers of Greek myths. Zethos tends the flocks, while Amphîon receives from Hermes a harp which makes the stones not merely move but fix themselves in their proper places as he builds the walls of Thebes. The sequel of the history of

---

497 Max Müller, *Chips*, ii.159.

498 A more or less standard event in the life of the hero—see e.g. Otto Rank's comparative study in *The Birth of the Hero*. (Ed.)

Amphîon exhibits, like the myths of Tyrô, Inô, and other legends, the jealous second wife or step-mother, who is slain by Amphîon and Zethos, as Sidêrô is killed by Pelias and Neleus. Amphîon himself becomes the husband of Niobê, the mother who presumes to compare her children with the offspring of Zeus and Iô....

"The mournful or dirge-like sound of the wind is signified by [a] Boiotian tradition, which related how the matrons and maidens mourned for Linos* at the feast which was called Arnis because Linos had grown up among the lambs,—in other words, the dirge-like breeze had sprung up while the heaven was flecked with the fleecy clouds which, in the German popular stories, lured the rivals of Dummling to their destruction in the waters. The myth that Linos was torn to pieces by dogs points to the raging storm which may follow the morning breeze. Between these two in force would come Zephyros, the strong wind from the evening-land, the son of Astraios the starry heaven, and of Eôs who closes, as she had begun, the day. The wife of Zephyros is the Harpyia Podargê, the white-footed wind, Notos Argêstês, who drives before her the snowy vapours, and who is the mother of Xanthos and Balios, the immortal horses of Achilleus. But as the clouds seem to fly before Podargê or Zephyros, so the phenomenon of clouds coming up seemingly against the wind is indicated in the myth of the wind Kaikias, a name which seems to throw light on the story of Hercules and Cacus.

"AILOS AND ARÊS. In the Odyssey all the winds are placed by Zeus under the charge of Aiolos, who has the power of rousing or stilling them at his will. But beyond this fact the poem has nothing more to say of him than that he was the father of six sons and six daughters, and that he dwelt in an island which bore his name.... [The Iliad and Odyssey] simply speak of Aiolos as a son of Hippotês and the steward of the winds of heaven.

"But Hermes, Orpheus, Amphîon, and Pan, are not the only conceptions of the effects of air in motion to be found in Greek mythology. The Vedic Maruts are the winds, not as alternately soothing and furious, like the capricious action of Hermes, not as constraining everything to do their magic bidding, like the harping of Orpheus and Amphîon, nor yet as discoursing their plaintive music among the reeds, like the pipe of Pan; but simply in their force as the grinders or crushers of everything that comes in their way. These crushers are found in more than one set of mythical beings in Greek legends. They are the Moliones, or mill-men, or the Aktoridai, the pounders of grain, who have one body but two heads, four hands, and four feet,—who first undertake to aid Heraklês in his struggle with Augeias, and then turning against the hero are slain by him near Kleônai. These representatives of Thor Miölnir we see also in the Aloadai, the sons of Iphimedousa, whose love for Poseidôn led her to roam along the sea-shore, pouring the salt water over her body. The myth is transparent enough. They are as mighty in their infancy as Hermes. When they are nine years old, their bodies are nine cubits in breadth and twenty-seven in height—a rude yet not inapt image of the stormy wind heaping up in a few hours its vast masses of angry vapour. It was inevitable that the phenomena of storm should suggest their warfare with the gods, and that one version should represent them as successful, the other as vanquished. The storm-clouds scattered by the sun in his might are the Aloadai when defeated by Phoibos before their beards begin to be seen, in other words, before the expanding vapours have time to spread themselves over the sky. The same clouds in their triumph are the Aloadai when they bind Arês and keep him for months in chains, as the gigantic ranges of vapours may be seen, sometimes keeping an almost motionless guard around the heaven, while the wind seems to chafe beneath, as in a prison from which it cannot get forth. The piling of the cumuli clouds in the skies is the heaping up of Ossa on Olympos and of Pelion on Ossa to scale the heavens, while their threat to make the sea dry land and the dry land sea is the savage fury of the storm when the earth and the air seem mingled in inextricable confusion. The daring of the giants goes even further. Ephialtes, like Ixîon, seeks to win Hêrê while Otos follows Artemis, who, in the form of a stag, so runs between the brothers that they, aiming at her at the same time, kill each other, as the thunderclouds perish from their own discharges.

"Arês, the god imprisoned by the Aloadai, whose name he shares, represents like them the storm-wind raging through the sky. As the idea of calm yet keen intellect is inseparable from Athênê, so the character of Arês exhibits simply a blind force without foresight or judgment, and not unfrequently illustrates the poet's phrase that strength without counsel insures only its own destruction. Hence Arês and Athênê are open enemies. The pure dawn can have nothing in common with the cloud-laden and wind-oppressed atmosphere. He is then in no sense a god of war, unless war is taken as mere quarrelling and slaughtering for its own sake.[499] Of the merits of contending parties he has neither knowledge nor care. Where the carcases are likely to lie thickest, thither like a vulture will he go; and thus he be-comes pre-eminently fickle and treacherous, the object of hatred and disgust to all the gods, except when, as in the lay of Demodokos, he is loved by Aphroditê. But this legend implies that the god has laid aside his fury, and so is entrapped in the coils cast round him by Hephaistos, an episode which merely repeats his imprisonment by the Aloadai. Like these, his body is of enormous size, and his roar, like the roar of a hurricane, is louder than the shouting of ten thousand men. But in spite of his strength, his life is little more than a series of disasters, for the storm-wind must soon be conquered by the powers of the bright heaven. Hence he is defeated by Heraklês when he seeks to defend his son Kyknos against that hero, and wounded by Diomêdês, who fights under the protection of Athênê. In the myth of Adonis he is the boar who smites the darling of Aphroditê, of whom he is jealous, as the storm-winds of autumn grudge to the dawn the light of the beautiful summer."[500] — Cox, pp.459-72.

PAKISTANI FOLKTALES AND MYTHS.

§293A.1 "**THE SONG OF BHELUA.** [Long ago there lived a wealthy merchant named Manik in the town of Safiapur, a small port on one of those numerous islands which lie off the coast of East Pakistan. He had a

---

499 In this context the Roman version—Mars—perhaps better suits the epithet "god of war". (Ed.)

500 I have included in this section much material not relating directly to music, such as non-musical events in the careers of Orpheus, Pan, Hermes and Amphion, and accounts of the entirely non-musical Aeolus and Ares. However the narrative weaves a spell of its own—of the elements (here mighty winds and gentle breezes—daily transversal of the light-giving sun and, at end of day, the spreading again of darkness) through which now and then one discerns the human-like faces of mighty beings: all the several gods and heroes. *Some* of these beings having musical talents and abilities—some have musical (magical) powers. Is this only accidental, or does it play some important, perhaps essential role in the drama of nature? The author does not give a defensible argument, one way or another. He merely records. The reader is left to sense, if he will, what "nature" is all about, then. (Ed.)

handsome, intelligent and generous son called Amir, and an ugly, ignorant and spiteful daughted named Bivala. Amir was seized with a great desire to sail abroad in search of adventure. At sea the waters became rough and strong winds blew the ship off its course. For two days and two nights it was all whirl and confusion, but on the third day the tempest subsided. Amir and his companions sighted land and steered their ship towards it and disembarked.

Before them lay a beautiful garden where birds were singing sweetly. Alas, Amir took up his bow and arrow and shot a *maina* bird perched on the branch of a tree, that was chanting verses from the holy Quran. Now this *maina* was a pet of Bhelua, the enchantingly beautiful only sister of seven brothers who were wealthy merchants on this island. When she discovered that her *maina* was dead she was stricken with grief.

Her brothers found out the culprit and threw Amir and his friends into prison. A heavy stone was placed on his chest. But the widowed mother of Bhelua and her brothers heard the groans of the young merchant and went to see him. When she saw so fine a youth helpless and enduring such agonies, she felt sorry for him. He told her the story of his life, whereupon she called her seven sons and had the prisoners released.

'This is the son of my very own sister,' she said. 'My sister and I are bound by a vow that should either of us bear a son and the other a daughter, these two should be married.' Her wish was fulfilled. Amir and Bhelua were married — fell deeply in love — and returned to Amir's home at Safiapur.

On seeing Amir's bride the people were filled with wonder at her beauty. The couple lived happily. Then Amir left again in search of further adventure. However, on his first night out, a thick fog prevented him from making any headway. Unseen, he returned to shore and to his own bed-

chamber, and remained there with his wife. In the morning he departed again.

However, Amir's sister Bivala had noticed the door of Bhelua's room which had been left open by Amir in his haste. Deep suspicions were roused in her mind which she confided to her mother. Together the two women saw that Bhelua was also sleeping much later than usual. Bivala shook her till she awoke.

'Oh wicked woman,' said Amir's jealous sister. 'You have disgraced our house.'

'My husband came here last night,' Bhelua protested, with tears in her eyes. 'I swear by the holy Quran that no one but he was with me last night.' But no one believed her as none had witnessed the coming and going of his ship.

What was to be done with this wretched girl? Rather than having her drowned, or setting the dogs upon her, her mother-in-law, taking pity, decided she would henceforth serve as a menial in the house. Bhelua worked night and day. She was ill-fed and insulted. All her jewels and ornaments were taken away from her.

A year of grief and torment passed for Bhelua, but still there was no sign of her husband.

One day a merchant named Bhola was passing by in his ship, when he saw a young woman of dazzling beauty bathing close to the shore. It was Bhelua. He had her seized and taken off with him. Her cries for help went unanswered.

Bhelua refused to eat or drink. 'I am already married,' she said. 'My husband's name is Amir.'

'Believe me, oh damsel, Amir died only the other day at the port of Maslibandar. I was present at his funeral,' the crafty Bhola said.

Bhelua was numb with grief, but would not surrender to Bhola's advances. She begged to be left alone for six months of mourning, which as a Muslim girl was her right and her duty. Meanwhile fortune had favored Amir, and he returned to his home at Safiapur exceedingly rich.

'Where is Bhelua?' he demanded. 'What have you done with her?'

'She died three days ago,' his sister Bivala lied.

'Take me to her grave,' Amir demanded. Maddened with grief he tore at the earth with his fingers, and to his great surprise uncovered the body of a black dog. He realized at once that his wife had been the victim of some villainy.]

"For a long time [Amir] travelled over the countryside crossing rivers and canals, passing through forests and over hill-tracts. He traversed with great difficulty the whirlpools of the Karanaphuli and reached the mouth of the river Issamuti. In despair he wandered from place to place until he reached the valley of Syed Nagar, where lived a musician of great talent called Tona Barui. It was rumoured that he had supernatural powers, and that by his music he could make the wild tiger tame, and cause the river to change its course.

"Amir went to him, and told him his tale of woe, and begged to be allowed to become his pupil.

" 'You could not have done better than to come to see me my son,' said the old sage gently.

"Tona Barui made a small *sarangi* for his love-sick pupil.[501] He applied all the skill of his art in the making of this instrument, the body of which was made of *Bailan* wood, its pegs were made of fine *Manpaban* wood, the strings were made of the veins of the *Daras* snake and the bow was made with the wood of *Narsha*.

"The *sarangi* thus fashioned had a wonderful quality of tone. Such was the skill of the master that when the bow was drawn over the strings it gave out a sweet bewailing sound as if someone were calling 'Bhelua! Bhelua!'

"Amir left the musician and taking the *sarangi* with him went from door to door, and from city to city playing the same tune again and again with tears streaming from his eyes. After some time he reached the city of Kattani where Bhola had confined Bhelua in his house.

"Chance had brought Amir to the very door of the merchant's house just when he was saying to Bhelua:

" 'Now the time of mourning is over. Six months have passed, and you must fulfil your promise and marry me.'

"Bhelua hung her head and said nothing. Bhola took her silence for consent and was overjoyed.

"Just then her name in sweet notes reached her. Bhelua, startled, came out on to the balcony and looking over the edge saw a poor beggar playing on his *sarangi*. Their eyes met and it did not take them long to recognize each other. She then requested Bhola that the beggar be fed and given shelter in their house as he was looking so miserable.

"In the dead of the night Bhelua quietly got up and went to the corner of the courtyard where her husband was lying awake. In whispers they told each other the circumstances which had led them to their present state.

---

501 A variety of North Indian short fiddle, which may be hooked over the player's shoulder, resting on his arm, and played horizontally with a bow. "It is a clumsy instrument, hollowed out of a single block of heavy wood, with a waisted front which is entirely covered with skin. The short, broad neck has no frets, and the button-headed pegs are laterally inserted in a cubic block of wood which forms the pegbox. Three gut strings in c' g c are the regular equipment; but usually a fourth wire string in d is added.... Behind the three or four *bowed* strings, a quantity of thin wire strings, eleven to fifteen, are attached to smaller pegs in the neck. These wires resound sympathetically, as in the European *viola d'amore*. The bowing hand is held with the palm upwards." — Curt Sachs, *The History of Musical Instruments*, 226-27.

" 'The night will soon be over,' Bhelua said. 'Let us fly from this place at once.'

" 'No I can't,' Amir replied. 'I am the son of an honest man, and cannot steal you as Bhola did.'

"The next day Amir filed a petition in the court of the Kazi of the town whose name was Munaf. Whereupon a warrant for Bhola's arrest was issued, and he was brought to the court.

" 'This beggar is a wicked creature,' Bhola told Kazi Munaf. 'He visits people's houses and by playing on his *sarangi* seduces their wives.'

"Hearing this the Kazi ordered that the woman be brought to the court.

"When Bhelua appeared before the Kazi, he was dazzled by her beauty, for though he was ninety years old and toothless he still had a passion for a beautiful women such as Bhelua was.

" 'Tell me dear lady,' he asked Bhelua gently, 'which of the two men who claim you is your husband?'

" 'Sir,' Bhelua replied, 'This beggar is the Lord of my heart.'

"The Kazi was furious with Bhola, and drove him from the court. Then turning to Amir he said:

" 'You are not a fit person, my man, for this lady. If I give her to you now somebody else will soon take her away from you and you will again come pestering me to get her back for you. Leave me and proper care will be taken of her.'

"Before Amir could say a word in protest he was forcibly turned out of the court.

"Amir was dismayed. There was only one thing for him to do. He must go back to his own country and bring help.

"When Amir's parents came to know the truth about Bhelua they felt ashamed and were only too eager to redress the wrong they had done her. An army was raised in no time, and fourteen ships were made ready. Thirteen of these carried the troops, the ammunition, the provisions and other equipment necessary to wage war for six months. The fourteenth ship called *Furqan*

carried copies of the Holy Quran and library of other religious books.

"Meanwhile the Kazi came to know that the beggar whom he had turned out of his court was Amir, the young merchant of Safia and that he was coming with a large army to claim his wife. He was so frightened by this news that he hurriedly called at the house of Bhola.

" 'I have been put to great trouble on account of Bhelua,' he told him. 'She has rejected me because I am old and is really in love with you so I should like to send her to you, but unfortunately she is unwell at the moment.'

"Just then a great roar was heard coming from the direction of the coast; whereupon the Kazi told Bhola of the intended invasion of the town by Amir. Bhola was taken aback, but realized that he had no alternative but to join forces with the Kazi in the defence of their town.

"For seven days the battle raged with great fury. Hundreds of people were killed. Finally the combined armies of the Kazi and the merchant Bhola were completely defeated.

"A search was made for Bhola. He was arrested and taken before Amir who ordered him to be put to death instantly. The Kazi was also brought before him but was pardoned on account of his old age.

"Amir learned from the Kazi that Bhelua was confined in his house. When he went there he was horrified to find her very ill and weak. So great had been her grief that she had refused to eat or drink and had finally lost her reason.

"She was brought to the ship. Amir took her hands in deep affection, but she only stared at him blankly.

"There was a general rejoicing in the town of Safiapur over Amir's victory. The fourteen ships had all returned; but the citizens were unaware that one of them carried the dead body of Bhelua who had breathed her last while they were still at some distance from Safiapur. She was buried near the sea-shore with all the reverence due to the wife of Amir, the young merchant of Safiapur.

"Such was the intensity of Amir's grief that he lost all interest in life. During the day he was always to be seen at the grave of his beloved and at night the echoes of his *sarangi* rent the air calling Bhelua! Bhelua!

"And even today when the sea waves strike against the coast of Safiapur in the stillness of the night are heard the bemoaning notes as though someone was calling softly: Bhelua! Bhelua!" — Abbas, pp.11-23.

RADIN (Folklore of Borneo).

§330A.1 "An eighteenth-century leader of the Ibans, the Sea Dayaks of Borneo. A legend about him concerns a hungry ghost, which visited his people with smallpox. After winning a battle near Betong and taking many heads, Radin decided to hold a bird festival, *gawai burong*, and to this feast he invited all the other war leaders and persons of rank. As they wer feasting, some of the older guests told him that the image of the rhinoceros hornbill, sacred to the bird god Sengalang Burong, the patron of head-hunters, must be removed from the village three days after the celebration was over, and that the site must be vacated too. Radin adhered to custom in respect of the sacred image, but he did not quit the longhouse, the village under one roof. Some days later his people started to die of smallpox. Then, three nights in succession, as he was lying sleepless, worried by the increasing number of deaths, Radin heard the music of a lovely song, which took apparent pleasure at their plight. On the fourth night Radin took his machete and hid himself inside a roll of matting. When the hungry ghost came near to his place of concealment, singing about the sweetness of human flesh, Radin jumped out and cut down the invisible spirit. He heard something fall, but he could see nothing. Next morning, on going to look at the hornbill carving, he found it had been slashed as if by a powerful knife, and thrown to the ground. Baffled, Radin sought advice from his peers, who told him that the sacred image was too powerful and recommended immediate removal. This he and his people did thereafter using the old longhouse as a burial ground." — Cotterell, p.123.[502]

RAGNAROK (Norse myth).

§331A.1 See also **HEIMDALL***.

§331A.2 "Norse *doomsday*, the end of the present universe. Heimdall would announce the last battle of the gods by blowing the Last Trump on his horn; there would follow the destruction of the earth, the disapperance of the sun, the death of all the gods, and the return of the world to its original state of chaos."[503] — Walker, p.839.

---

502 Since in this story music (singing) is a kind of language through which the hungry ghost announces its presence, it may be regarded then as a kind of *mediating device* between the world of nature (or the supernatural) and that of man. In this respect the story has possibile affinities with e.g. the practice of shamans, wherein music is used to "mediate" the other way round — from man to nature (or the supernatural). (Ed.)

503 See also **TRUMPET — SWAHILI CREATION MYTH (the archangel Serafili)***, following. (Ed.)

RITES.

§338A.1 *Ed. note:* This topic has general application, and as such is included here. "In
essence, every rite symbolizes and
reproduces creation.[504] The slow-moving
ritual, characteristic of all ceremonies, is
closely bound up with the rhythm of the
astral movements.[505] At the same time,
every rite is a meeting, that is, a confluence
of forces and patterns; the significance of
rites stems from the accumulated power of
these forces when blended harmoniously
one with the other." — Cirlot, p.274.

ROLAND (Orlando).

§.1 See ORLANDO*.

RUSSIAN FOLKTALES — PRAC-
TICES AND BELIEFS. *(See p.690.)*

§342.2 "THE BRAVE AZMUN — Amur folktale (Russian Far East). To the bold, misfortune never bars the way. The bold will go
through fire and flood and only become
stronger. People long remember the bold
and the brave. Fathers tell tales of the bold
and the brave to their sons.

"This story took place long ago. Then the
Nivkhs still made their arrowheads of
stone. Then the Nivkhs still fished with
wooden hooks. Then the Amur estuary
was called the Little Sea.

"In those days there was a village on the
very edge of the Amur River. The Nivkhs
lived there neither too well nor too badly.
When the fish ran heavily, the Nivkhs
were merry, sang their songs, ate their fill.
When the fish ran lightly, the Nivkhs were
quiet, smoked moss in their pipes, and
pulled their belts in tighter. One spring
this is what happened.

[One day something came floating down
the Amur — a whole island of trees jammed
together so firmly you couldn't pull them
apart. On it the Nivkhs saw a whittled pole
with a red cloth tied to it, flapping in the
breeze. They heard a child's cry coming
from the moving island. How could the
Nivkhs not help? They pulled the island to
shore, and discovered a child there, all
white, round, his black eyes shining like
little stars, his face round like a full moon.
He held an arrow and an oar.

[An old Nivkh — Pletum — said 'I will call
him my son. I will give him a new name.
Let him be called Azmun.'

[The child began to grow at once! By the
time they had reached the old man's
house, he was all grown up!

[The lad was very kind — always thinking
of others. He caught fish for his adopted
father. When Azmun went to fish, his boat
would leap into the water by itself! He
caught many fish with his net, which he
shared with everyone in the village.

[Time passed. Soon there were fewer fish
to be caught. The village folk became
dejected. Azmun began to think. He
lighted his adopted father's pipe. He
puffed enough smoke to fill three
storehouses. Then he said, 'I will go to
Tayrnadz — the Old Man of the Sea. The
reason there are no fish in the Amur is that
the Master has forgotten all about the
Nivkhs.']

"Pletun became frightened. No Nivkh
had ever gone to the Master of the Sea.
That had never happened before. How
could a mere person go down to the sea
bottom to Tayrnadz?

" 'Are you strong enough for this journey?' asked the father.

"Azmun stamped his foot on the earth —
he sank into the earth up to his waist from
the force of his stamping....

" I am strong enough!' said Azmun.

---

504 See Mircea Eliade, *Tratado de historia de las religiones* (Madrid, 1954).
505 See Gaston Bachelard, *L'Air et les Songes* (Paris, 1943).

"Azmun got ready for the journey. He put a little bag of Amur earth in his bosom, took a knife, a bow and some arrows, a rope with a hook at the end, and a bone musical instrument — a *kungakhkei* — to play, in case he felt lonely on the way.

"He promised his father that he would send a message about himself soon. [Then he went off. He traveled far. The sea stretched before him — you could not see the end of it. Where to look for the Master? How to get to him? He asked the seagulls, and the whales.

[He sat on the sand among the dunes, leaned his head on his arms, and started to think. He thought, and he thought, and he fell asleep. In his sleep he heard people making a lot of noise on the shore. Azmun half opened his eyes, and saw young men playing on the shore. Then seals came up on shore. The men began to strike the seals with their swords. 'Oh,' thought Azmun, 'if only I had a sword like that! He managed to throw out his rope with a hook, and caught one of the swords, and pulled it slowly toward him. 'Oy-ya-kha!' said the man whose sword he had taken. 'The Master will give it to me now! What will I say to the Old Man? How will I get back to him?']

" Oh-ho,' thought Azmun, 'they know the Old Man. They must be from the Sea Village!'

[He followed the men onto the sea. But what was happening? Suddenly there were no boats or men ahead. Only whales were swimming in the sea, cutting through the waves; they raised their back fins up like swords, and pieces of seal meat were impaled on the fins. Now Azmun's boat came to life and began to move strangely. He was sitting not in a boat, but on a whale's back!]

"Whether he sailed this way for a long time I don't know — he didn't say. But he did sail long enough to grow a mustache.

"At last Azmun saw an island ahead; it looked like the roof of a yurt [circular domed portable tent used by the nomadic Mongols of Siberia and Gobi Desert (Ed.)].

On the highest point of the island was a hole, and from the hole smoke was curling up. 'The Old Man must live there!' Azmun said to himself. So Azmun put an arrow to his bow and sent the arrow back to his father.

"The whales swam up to the island, threw themselves on the shore, rolled over, and became men — men holding seal meat in their hands. [They saw Azmun, frowned, and said, 'Who are you? How did you get here?']

" 'What's the matter with you — don't you recognize one of your own? I fell behind while I was looking for my sword. Here it is, my sword,' Azmun said.

[He went to the highest point of the hill, and threw his rope through a hole at the top. He climbed down the rope and, when he got to the bottom, he found himself in the home of the Old Man of the Sea. Everything in the house was like a Nivkh's house: a bunk, a hearth, walls, posts — only here everything was covered with fish scales. And outside the window was water instead of sky.]

"The Old Man was lying on the bunk, asleep. His gray hair was spread across the pillow. A pipe sticking out of his mouth was scarcely lit, the smoke barely coming out of it, drifting up the chimney. Tayrnadz snored away, hearing nothing. Azmun touched him with his hand — no, the Old Man wouldn't wake up, and that's all there was to it.

"Azmun remembered the musical instrument, the *kungakhkei*. He took it out of his bosom, gripped it between his teeth, and plucked at its tongue. The *kungakhkei* began to vibrate, to hum, to buzz — now chirping like a bird, now babbling like a brook, now buzzing like a bee.

"Tayrnadz had never heard anything like it. What was it? He stirred, he awoke, he rubbed his eyes, he sat up, putting his legs under him. He was big, like a reef; his face was kind, and his mustache hung down like a catfish's. The scales on his skin were iridescent, like mother-of-pearl. His clothing was made of seaweed. He saw a little fellow standing before him, like a smelt before a sturgeon, holding something in his mouth and playing it so well that Tayrnadz's heart began to jump. Instantly Tayrnadz was awake. He turned his kind face to Azmun, squinted at him, and asked, 'Of what people are you?'

" 'I'm Azmun, of the Nivkh people.'

[Azmun explained that his people were dying of hunger. Tayrnadz became embarrassed. He blushed and said 'A bad thing happened – I lay down only to rest, and I fell asleep! Thank you for waking me!' At once he reached into a tank where giant kaluga, sturgeon, trout, and all kinds of salmon were swimming. More fish than you've ever seen. He threw them into the sea. He said to the fish, 'Swim to the Nivkhs on Sakhalin and on the Amur. Swim fast! Be a good catch in the spring.']

"Azmun bowed to him. 'Father! I am poor – I don't have anything to repay you for your kindness. Take my *kungakhkei* as a present.'

"He gave Tayrnadz his musical instrument, first showing him how to play it.

"And the Old Man had been itching to have it; he couldn't take his eyes off it! He liked the toy so much.

"Tayrnadz was happy. He took the *kungakhkei* into his mouth, gripped it between his teeth, plucked at its tongue.

"The *kungakhkei* began to hum and to buzz, now like the sea wind, now like the surf, now like the rustle of the trees, now like a bird at dawn, now like a gopher whistling. Tayrnadz was playing and making merry. He started to walk about the house, then to dance. The house began to shake, outside the windows the waves raged, seaweed was being torn to pieces – a storm was rising in the sea.

"Azmun saw that Tayrnadz was too busy for him now. He went to the chimney, took hold of his rope, and began to climb up. [It was difficult to find his way home. He saw

a rainbow hanging in the sky. One end was resting on the island, the other on the Big Land.]

"And in the sea, waves were raging – Tayrnadz was dancing in his yurt. White crests were breaking on the sea.

"Azmun climbed onto the rainbow. He barely made it. He got all smudged – his face was green, he hands yellow, his belly red, his feet blue. [At last he found his way home. He came to his own village. The Nivkhs were sitting on the bank, barely alive.]

"Pletun came out to the threshold of his house to meet his son and kissed him on both cheeks.

" 'Did you visit the Old Man, my son?' he asked.

" 'Father, don't look at me, look at the Amur!' answered Azmun.

"And on the Amur the water was seething – so many fish had come....

"The Nivkhs began to live well. Fish were running in the spring and in the fall! Since that time the Nivkhs have forgotten many people. But to this day they remember Azmun and his *kungakhkei*.

"When the sea becomes stormy, waves surge onto the rocky shore, white crests break on the waves – and in the whistle of the sea wind you can hear now the cry of a bird, now the whistle of a gopher, or now the rustle of the trees. That's the Old Man of the Sea; in order not to fall asleep, he is playing on the *kungakhkei* and dancing in his yurt under the sea.[506] – Nagishkin, pp.13-26.

SINGING BONE. *(See also p.719.)*

§365.4 "THE MIRACULOUS PIPE [Sample Version 4 of "Singing Bone" story – Russian]. Once there lived a priest and his wife; they had a son, Ivanushka, and a daughter, Alionushka. Once Alionushka

---

506 See our theme T6 (Song as 'energy exchange', e.g. song given in exchange for food, offspring, protection , etc.), *Introductory Remarks* (Vol I, above). (Ed.)

said to her mother: 'Mother, mother, I want to go to the woods and get berries; all my little friends have gone there.' 'Go, and take your brother along.' "Why? He is so lazy, he won't pick any berries.' 'Never mind, take him! And whichever of you gathers the most berries will receive a pair of red slippers as a present.' And so the brother and sister went to pick berries, and they came to the wood. Ivanushka picked and picked and put the berries in a pitcher, but Alionushka ate and ate the berries she picked; she put only two berries in her box. She still had almost nothing when Ivanushka's pitcher was full. Alionushka became envious. 'Brother,' she said, 'let me pick the lice out of your hair.' He lay on her knees and fell asleep. Alionushka took out a sharp knife and slew her brother; she dug a ditch and buried him, and took the pitcher with the berries.

"She came home and gave her mother the berries. 'Where is your brother, Ivanushka?' the priest's wife asked. 'He straggled behind me in the woods and must have lost his way; I called and called him, sought and sought him, but could not find him anywhere.' The father and mother waited for Ivanushka for a very long time, but he never came back.

"Meanwhile, there grew on Ivanushka's grave a clump of tall and very straight reeds. Shepherds went by with their herds, saw the reeds, and said: 'What excellent reeds have grown here!' One shepherd cut off a reed and made himself a pipe. 'Let me try to play it,' he said. He put it to his lips, and the pipe began to play a song:

Gently, gently, shepherd, blow,
Else my heart's blood you will shed.
My treacherous sister murdered me
For juicy berries, slippers red.

" 'Ah, what a miraculous pipe!' said the shepherd. 'How clearly it speaks! This pipe is very precious.' 'Let me try it,' said another shepherd. He took the pipe and put it to his lips, and it played the same

song; a third one tried, and again it played the same song.

"The shepherds came to the village and stopped near the priest's house. 'Little father,' they said, 'give us shelter for the night.' 'My house is crowded,' said the priest. 'Let us in, we will show you a marvel.' The priest let them in and asked them: 'Have you not seen anywhere a boy called Ivanushka? He went to pick berries and all trace of him has been lost.' 'No, we have not seen him; but we cut a reed on our way, and what a marvelous pipe we made of it! It plays by itself.' The shepherd took out the pipe and played, and it sang:

Gently, gently, shepherd, blow,
Else my heart's blood you will shed.
My treacherous sister murdered me
For juicy berries, slippers red.

" 'Let me try to play on it,' said the priest. He took the pipe and it played its song:

Gently, gently, father, blow,
Else my heart's blood you will shed.
My treacherous sister murdered me
For juicy berries, slippers red.

" 'Was it not my Ivanushka who was murdered?' said the priest. And he called his wife: 'Now you try to play on it.' The priest's wife took the pipe and it played its song:

Gently, gently, mother, blow,
Else my heart's blood you will shed.
My treacherous sister murdered me
For juicy berries, slippers red.

" 'Where is my daughter?' asked the priest. But Alionushka had hidden herself in a dark corner. They found her. 'Now, play the pipe!' said her father. 'I don't know how.' 'Never mind, play!' She tried to refuse, but her father spoke sternly to her and made her take the pipe. She had no sooner put it to her lips than the pipe began to play by itself:

Gently, gently, sister, blow,
Else my heart's blood you will shed.
You treacherously murdered me
For juicy berries, slippers red.

"Then Alionushka confessed everything,
and her father in his rage drove her out of
the house." — Afanas'ev, pp.425-427.

§365.5 ZIRILI AND KUFOGO (Sample version 5 — from African folklore).

Excerpt: "Na Gbewa was now very old
and blind; but as the Kussasi and the
Busansi very often raided his settlement
near the capital, and were not entirely
crushed, he sent his eldest son [Zirili] and
Kufogo against them, and they remained a
long time away at the war. Now Na Gbewa
considered Zirili a wicked man in his manner
of life and quite unfit to reign. He
therefore proposed to leave the kingdom
to Kufogo. Having arranged this with his
elders he sent his 'hazo', i.e. one who sits
in front, to call Kufogo's mother [to come
to him, so that he could tell her of his
mind]....

"For some reason, which no one knows,
the messenger went and called Zirili's
mother (it is stated that Zirili's mother was
good and Kufogo's mother wicked, and
that that was the reason that the front sitter
had done this).

"Na Gbewa, not knowing the mistake, for
he was, as stated, blind, began to tell the
woman [who came before him] all he had
arranged with the elders. Zirili's mother
said never a word; but leaving the
presence of her husband the king, she
went directly to the camp and informed
her son Zirili what his father had said.

"During the night Zirili ordered a big
hole to be dug and covered with grass
reeds. Before dawn he ordered skins and
embroidered leather cushions to be placed
over the hole. Then he sent for all the
elders in the camp.

"When they had come Zirili seated himself
near the trap and ordered his younger
brother Kufogo to sit on the pillows over
the hole by his side. Nobody knew that a
trap had been set for Kufogo, and no
sooner had he sat on the pillows than he
dropped into the hole and was there
buried alive by Zirili's orders. Great terror
reigned in the camp and none dared leave
it. Men remained in the camp until
Gushiag Na, i.e. Chief of Gushiago, broke
off, and with his party repaired to Pussiga
to inform Na Gbewa of what had occurred.

"As they drew near the town, the Chief
of Gushiago ordered a halt, to consider
how Na Gbewa could best be informed of
the murder of Kufogo; for according to the
customs of those days he could not inform
him verbally. At last it occurred to him to
fashion a pipe, a drum, and a horn of an
elephant tusk. On entering the town he ordered
men to play upon these instruments
which are preserved to this day, and
whenever a chief of Gushiago visits Yendi,
are carried and played as he enters that
town.

"The pipe says:

> Gbewa! Gbewa!
> Zirili ku Fogo!
> Zirili ku Fogo!

"The drum answers:

> M-ba ye! M-ba ye!

"The horn then wails:

> U-uhu! U-uhu!

Meaning:

> Gweba! Gweba!
> Zirili has killed Fogo
> Zirili has killed Fogo
> Oh! Father, Oh! Father
> U-uhu! U-uhu!

"At the time Na Gbewa was sitting outside his compound, and when he understood what the music said he began to throw himself about in such grief that the ground opened and he disappeared from sight."[507] — Cardinall, pp.246-47.

SOUND.

§371A.1 "In India, the sound of Krishna's flute* is the magical cause of the birth of the world. The pre-Hellenic maternal goddesses are depicted holding lyres*, and with the same significance.[508] There are other traditional doctrines which hold that sound was the first of all things to be created, and that which gave rise to all others, commencing with light, or, alternatively, with air and fire. An instance of this is the lament quoted in the *Poimandres* of Hermes Trismegistos.[509]" — Cirlot, p.300.

SUFI PRACTICES AND BELIEFS. *(See also p.731.)*

§375.3 "The Sufi tradition within Islam... stands out for its distinctive practices. While orthodox Islam frowns upon any use of music in religious rituals, Sufi orders throughout the Islamic world, particularly in Turkey, Iran and the Indo-Pakistani reigion, have developed a wide variety of ritual observances involving singing, drums* and other musical instruments, and dance*. Music is used in ritual processions, often commemorating the birthday *(mawlud)* of the founder of the order. Each order also developed its own distinctive ritual observance called a *dhikr*, a Qur'anic term meaning 'remembrance (of God)'. These rituals often include some form of dance, the best known in the West being that of the Turkish Mevlevi order, often called the 'whirling dervishes', whose cos-

---

507 Aarne/Thompson Folktale Type 780 (The singing bone); Thompson Folklore Motifs D1211 (Magic drum), D1222 (Magic horn [musical]), D1224 (Magic pipe [musical]), D1300 (Magic object gives supernatural wisdom), D1610.34 (Speaking musical instruments), D1615 (Magic singing object). As can be seen from the present category (above and pp. 719-23) variations on the "Singing Bone" motif are extremely widespread, both culturally and geographically. We have noted that music and musical instruments are frequently resorted to as devices through which shamans, sorcerers etc attempt to reach the "other world" of spirits etc; here is an instance of "other wordly" beings attempting to communicate with this world through music (song). Common to both is the view that music mediates between the natural and supernatural orders, or between culture (the world of man) and pre-culture (the forces of nature — including life and death). (Ed.)

508 See Ania Teillard, *Il Simbolismo dei Sogni* (Milan, 1951).

509 See C. G. Jung, *Symbols of Transformation* (London, 1956).

mic dance around their master *(shaykh)* simulates the rotation of the planets around the sun." — Welch, in Hinnells, pp.152-53.

TAMBOURINE. *(See also p.742.)*

§381.3 "MIRIAM'S TAMBOURINE [Jewish folklore — Eastern Europe c.19th century]. Long ago, in the land of Babylon, there lived a rabbi and his son who made their home in a small hut deep in the forest, where they spent their days in the study of the mysteries of the Torah. During the day they read from the sacred texts, and at night they peered into the stars and read in them as clearly as in any book. And they were the purest souls to be found in that land.

"In those days the Jews of Babylon led lives of peace, for since the days of Daniel there had always been a Jewish adviser to the king, who had protected the interests of his people. There was a remarkable tradition connected to the appointment of this minister. For since the time of Daniel each king had kept a golden chest beside the throne, and in that chest was a precious Book. And that Book could be opened only by the one man in each generation who was destined to serve as the king's minister. In the past, this one man had always been found among the Jews of Babylon, and now, it was time once again to seek out the one who would advise the King.

"[However, this time none of the Jews who applied was able to open the Book. Searching everywhere, messengers heard at last of the rabbi and his son living in the woods, who agreed to try. As they walked to the palace they spoke of the Book.] It had been delivered (so the legend went) to Daniel by an angel while he sat inside the lion's den. He had read it while he waited there, in the presence of the lions. And from it he had learned that he was the first mortal to open that Book, and that only one man in every generation after him

would be able to do so. It was said that the secrets in that Book were so deep that they had not been revealed even to the angels. Both the rabbi and his son longed to read that Book and share in those mysteries.

"[On their way to the palace the rabbi and his son became lost.] Yet they did not become frightened; they had complete faith that God would not lead them astray. [Soon they came upon a splendid palace, inside of which they found an old woman with beautiful wise eyes.]

"She was taking leaves out of a silver basket and crushing them between her fingers, into fine powder which she let fall into a golden basket at her side. When the rabbi and his son entered [the palace], she looked up; she did not seem surprised to see them. They approached her and the rabbi said, 'Peace be with you.' 'Peace be with you,' she said. Then the rabbi asked her what she was doing. 'I have children everywhere who suffer from one Sabbath to the next,' she said. 'But on the eve of the Sabbath, I take the powder made from these leaves and cast it into the wind. And the wind carries it to the four corners of the earth, so that all those who breathe in even the smallest speck have a taste of Paradise, and the Sabbath is filled with joy for them.'

"[The old woman's name was Sarah, and she was the bride of Abraham. She had fetched the freshly fallen leaves from the Garden of Eden. It was then that the rabbi's son saw the hand of fate in their coming to that place. He told Sarah of their journey, and their wish to open the Book that once belonged to Daniel.] She nodded as the young boy spoke, and then she said, 'That Book can be opened only by one who has the purest soul. And while both of your souls are very pure, still they are not pure enough to open the Book.' The rabbi and his son were very sorry to hear that. The rabbi said, 'But tell us, Sarah, is there any way that we can purify our souls enough so that we may open the Book?' And Sarah replied, 'Yes, there is one way. You must descend into Miriam's Well, and purify yourself in those sacred waters.'

"Now both the rabbi and his son had heard of Miriam's Well. That was the Well that had followed the children of Israel in their desert wanderings, the well God had given them in honor of the righteousness of Miriam, sister of Moses and Aaron. But that well had not been seen since the days of the wandering in the wilderness.... The rabbi asked Sarah where the well could be found, and she told them that they would come to it if they followed the path outside the palace. But she also told them that it would be futile to go there, for the Evil One had placed serpents all around the entrance to the Well. No one could enter there and purify themselves.... With a sad voice the boy asked Sarah if there were any way to get past the serpents. Sarah smiled and said, 'Yes, but only with the help of Miriam's tambourine.'

"Once again, hope burned in their hearts, and they wondered where they might find Miriam's tambourine, and if it were the same one that she had played after the Israelites had crossed the Red Sea. So they asked Sarah about this, and she told them that it was indeed the very same tambourine which the maidens of Israel had played as they danced at the Red Sea. And when they asked her where they might find it, she said simply, 'Why, with Miriam.' And when they asked where Miriam could be found, Sarah told them that if they went through that palace, into the garden, and passed through a hollow tree, they would find the entrance to a cave. And if they traveled through that cave, they would reach the shore of the Red Sea. And there, at the shore of the Red Sea, they would find Miriam, for that is where she made her home.

"[Thanking Sarah with all their hearts the pair set off and, at last, they reached the shore of the sea.] There they found a beautiful young woman, sitting on a rock beside the shore and playing a tambourine, with schools of fish crowded around her, and dolphins doing turns in the air. And as soon as they heard the wonderful rhythm of that tambourine, both the rabbi and his son were spellbound, and began to dance. They danced with the greatest joy they had ever known, for they were feeling the same joy the Israelites had felt after they had escaped the clutches of the Egyptians by passing through the parted waters of the Red Sea.[510]

"Now they might have danced there forever had the young woman not put down the tambourine. When she did, their feet came to rest, and they knew they had indeed found Miriam the Prophetess, and that the tambourine she played must be the very one they were seeking. The rabbi and his son introduced themselves to Miriam, and told her of their quest. She hesitated not a moment but handed them the tambourine, and said, 'Go, and, God willing, you wil! expel the serpents nesting there. For know that none of us who inhabit this place can accomplish that, only mortals such as yourselves, who have found your way here. Meanwhile I will wait here for you to return, for this is my home, beside the sea. Know that the sound of this tambourine has great power; it causes those with pure souls to be filled with joy, and evil creatures to cringe and flee as fast as they can. Now please hurry, for if I go as long as a day without hearing the music of my tambourine, my eternal life will come to an end.'

"[The rabbi gratefully accepted the tambourine, and the two hurried back to the cave, and the palace, where at last they dis-

---

510 On being made to dance by the sounds of a magical instrument — here in a joyful context — compare with the more familiar (and ominous) effects of e.g. fiddle playing under **DANCING TO DEATH (OR INSANITY)*** (Thompson Motif D1415.2, *Magic musical instrument causes person to dance*). See also Thompson Motif D1440, *Magic object [musical instrument etc] gives power over animals*, p. 286 above. — Ed.

covered the miraculous well which, with its living waters, had followed the Israelites as they wandered from place to place. And there the rabbi and his son saw a multitude of serpents nesting at its entrance, depriving the world of its wonderful powers.]

"They had reached the most solemn moment of their lives. When they stood there all the serpents raised their heads, as if to strike, but they paid them no heed. The rabbi handed the tambourine to his son and told him to start to play. Then the boy struck the tambourine for the first time, and as soon as he did, a wonderful, spell-binding music emerged from it, with a strong, insistent rhythm. This time the rabbi and his son were not compelled to dance, for Miriam was not playing; instead the sounds made all of the serpents writhe in agony, and they began at once to slither and crawl away from there as fast as they could go. They headed directly for the garden gate, and slipped beneath it, never to return, and the purity of the Well and the garden were restored at last.

"Then, while his son continued to play that tambourine, the rabbi found that the wonderful music gave him the strength to climb down the stones on the inside of the well. When he reached the water and immersed himself, he felt his soul purified to its very kernel. So it was that when the rabbi climbed out of the well, he took the tambourine from his son, and played its wonderful music once again as his son descended into those life-giving waters, and likewise purified his soul. And when they departed from that place, they found that their eyes had been opened, and that all manner of angels and spirits that had flocked around that garden now became apparent to them. Then they hurried back to the hollow tree and passed through the cave, for they wanted to take the tambourine back to Miriam as soon as possible. It was not long before they stood before her shining beauty, and when they returned the tambourine she blessed them

both and told them that their wonderful deed would always be remembered.

'[By morning the rabbi and his son reached the palace of the king, and were given an audience.] The rabbi had only to touch the cover of the Book lightly, and it opened to him, and all who surrounded him cheered, for the new minister of the king had finally been found.

"Thus it came to pass that the rabbi became the king's trusted adviser and served him for many years, referring to the Book for every important decision, and making certain that his fellow Jews were spared any persecution. And when the rabbi took his leave of this world, they did not have to look far to find the one who would take his place. For his son, who had also immersed himself in Miriam's Well and had been cleansed as fully as his father, had no difficulty in opening the Book and understanding its wisdom. He too served as the king's minister for many years, and that was a time of abundance for the Jews of that land." — Schwartz [Miriam], pp.1-7.

TIBETAN PRACTICES AND BELIEFS.

§393A.1 "The indigenous religion of Tibet is Bon, which evolved from northern and Inner Asian shamanism. During the periods of the first kings (seventh-tenth centuries CE), North Indian Mahayana Tantric Buddhism was introduced to Tibet. Subsequently Bon and Tantric Buddhism merged and resulted in a highly syncretic form of Tibetan Buddhism.

"**Music in Bon ritual.** Monastic forms of Bon have been largely assimilated by Tantric Buddhism. Many ritual practices of Bon have also been influenced by Buddhism. Bon ritual music employs chanting and instrumental music; the chief instruments are the indigenous *phyed-rna* (single-headed drum) and the *gshan* ('flute bell'). Flutes and trumpets made of animal bones are also used. In the instrumental part of the ritual the drum occupies a central place. According to legend when a Bon priest plays a drum he is thought of as mounting a flying steed to heaven to communicate with the gods. Bon chants are organized in strophic form, and in performance a large variety of vocal techniques are used, such as gliding before and after a given note, whistling, shouting, or masking the voice. Some of these sounds are said to represent the voices of spirits heard through the singer as medium. As the ritual progresses, the tempo of chanting and instrumental music accelerate, and the volume also increases; great intensity is generated as a result.

"**Buddhist liturgy.** Tibetan Buddhists hold that music prepares the mind for spiritual enlightenment. Accordingly, music (vocal as well as instrumental) is employed in the monastic routines that focus on five daily assemblies held in the monastery shrine hall between sunrise and sunset. The daily services consist predominantly of choral chants, with or without instrumental accompaniment, and antiphony between choral chant and instrumental interludes. All music is notated. Important liturgical items include the monks' 'invitation' to the deities to visit the place of worship, the ritual of offering, thanksgiving hymns, and hymns of praise to the Buddha and the *bodhisattvas*....

"**Liturgical drama.** The *'cham* is a quasi-liturgical ritual drama performed to exorcise evil spirits. The ritual is performed outdoors and involves the use of music (both vocal and instrumental), mime, and dance, as well as elaborate costumes and masks. The music ensemble consists of groups of chanters and an instrumental ensemble similar to that used in monastic liturgical services, with the addition of special sound effects not found in those services." — Wong, in Eliade (v10), pp.201-202.

§393A.2 *Musical Instruments in Tibetan Legend and Folklore*, from a monograph by Peter Crossley-Holland.

"The instruments referred to in the legends we are about to present are the following:

lute* (*sgra-snyan; vina**)
conch-shell trumpet* (*dung-dkar*)
thigh-bone trumpet (*rkang-gling*)
long trumpet (*dung-chen*)
frame-drum* of the *Bön-po* (*phyed-rnga*)
hand-drum (*damaru*)

"Apart from the lute, now essentially a secular instrument, these instruments are all used in Buddhist rituals today [1982]....

"**1. sGra-snyan (The Lute).** The instrument most frequently found in our sources is the lute (*sgra-snyan*). Although the lute is a secular instrument in Tibet today, there is much to suggest that a form of lute, referred to by its Indian name *vina*, was important in Buddhist symbolism at an early time. Some relevant material is to be found in *The Forty-Two Points of Instruction*, a Tibetan religious work whose essential content has been attributed to the Buddha himself. A passage from the eighth section, as translated by Huc and Gabet (1928), tells us, it would seem anachronistically, about a meeting between the Buddha and a *charmana* or monk of the Tibetan Buddhist hierarchy.

"*The Properly Tuned Lute.* A monk, who had passed the whole night in chanting prayers, manifested one morning, by his sad and suppressed voice, great depression and the desire to withdraw from his calling. The Buddha sent for this monk and said to him, 'When you were with your family, what used you to do?' The monk replied, 'I was always playing on the lute.' The Buddha then said to him, 'If the strings of the lute became slack, what happened?'
" 'I obtained no sound from them.'
" 'If the strings were too tight, what happened then?'
" 'The sounds were broken.'

" 'And when the strings obtained the exact equilibrium between tension and flexibility, what happened then?'

" 'All the sounds accorded in perfect harmony.'

"Whereupon the Buddha pronounced these words: 'It is the same with the study of the doctrine; after you shall have achieved dominion over your heart, and regulated its movements to harmony, it will attain the acquisition of truth.' (Huc and Gabet 1928).

"In this episode the Buddha is represented as using the properly tuned lute as a symbol for the harmony of being, and he likens the tuning of it to the study of the doctrine. Just what kind of lute the story is referring to we are not told, although the Indo-Tibetan texts usually refer to the *vina*, and most of the iconography shows an instrument which is pear-shaped but unlike the lute (*sgra-snyan*) found in Tibet today. Tibetan paintings sometimes actually depict a Buddha holding the lute. The Buddha of the Deva Loka, for instance, is shown holding such an instrument. The picture has been reproduced by Evans-Wentz (1949), who believes it to symbolize 'excellence in art and science and in the harmony of existence'. In Tibetan paintings depicting the 'offerings of the five senses' the conch-shell trumpet, which normally represents the sense of hearing, is sometimes replaced by the lute or may even be found in company with it (Waddell 1934)....

"[There is some mystery concerning likely or unlikely Buddhist origins of the lute as this instrument finally appears in Tibet. In fact we may be witnessing something like a *Graeco-Buddhist* contribution which found its way into the country through northern India.] This probably occurred not so long after the seventh century when, at lastest, Buddhism was beginning to reach Tibet and India was again becoming Hindu. This possibility is strengthened by the fact that the musically gifted angelic beings known as *Gandharvas** (Tibetan *Dri-za*) found their way into

the Tibetan 'Heaven of the Four Great Kings'. Of these, indeed, the King of the Gandharvas, who is also the Guardian King of the East *Yul-k'or-bsrun* (Sanskrit *Dhritarashtra*), is shown holding a pear-shaped lute (Waddell 1934). The lute is his special attribute, and in this character he appears on a fresco in the Potala, the Dalai Lama's palace in Lhasa (Sis, Vanis and Jisl n.d.); on another is the monastery at Litang (Duncan 1952); and in numerous illustrations elsewhere (Bryner 1956, Gordon 1959, Grünwedel 1900, Pott 1964, Riverside 1963, Roerich 1925). Further, a goddess from Gandhara sits across a lion as she plays a pear-shaped lute (Grünwedel 1900), while *gLu-ma* (Sanskrit *Gita*), one of a group of eight mother goddesses, holds a lute symbolizing music (Waddell 1934). Another painting in the possession of a former ruler of Sikkim, probably also of a Gandharva, shows this being playing a lute more closely resembling those still in use in Tibet (Pallis 1940). By extending our search, we find the lute at most levels of the Buddhist heavens. For instance, the Indian goddess *Saraswati*, adopted into the Tibetan pantheon as *dbYangs-can-ma*, 'Melody-Holder', goddess of euphony or of music and poetry (Jäschke 1881) frequently holds a pear-shaped lute in her hands (Gordon 1959, Meurs 1953). We find a similar instrument in the original two of the four arms of the Tantric goddess called *Aryajangulitara*, commonly known as the White Tara (Gordon 1959). This goddess is an aspect of *Tara*, the goddess of mercy of the Hindus who, under the name of *sGrol-ma*, has become the most popular female deity in Tibet....

"We have, then, so far found some lutes in Tibetan legend and iconography which are linked with ancient India, [as well as] some actual lutes and fiddles suggesting distant origins in Mongolia. A further legend raises the possibility of a connexion with China, and in this we find the lute for the first time mentioned in its more characteristic Tibetan context — the secular one. Before recounting this tale, we may note in passing that the Tibetan name of ther instrument *sgra-snyan* appears to be related to the Chinese word for lute *san-hsien* (compare Japanese *shamisen*), whereas the Sanskrit word for lute found in the Tibetan sacred texts, *vina*, relates to the name of the Chinese lute *p'i-p'a* (compare Japanese *wa*) and to the Tibetan word for fiddle *pi-wang*. To come to the tale: as is well known, *Srong-brtsan-sgam-po*, the first king of a united Tibet, who lived in the seventh century of our era, married two Buddhist princesses, one from China and the other from Nepal. Important statues and regalia are reported to have come with these royal and Buddhist brides, and the legend referred to, which was current in Lhasa around the turn of the century, connects the Chinese princess with a lute.

"The Princess's Lute Breaks a Spell. At the roadside on the northern border of Lhasa, there is a crystal spring which tradition connects with King *Srong-brtsan-gam-po*'s Chinese bride. Born out of a tear shed by the Compassionate Spirit for the poor Tibetans, the princess was sent as a bride to the great King Srong-brtsan, but she was prevented from seeing him through the spell of a wicked rival. She built a bower by the side of the spring, and languished there for two years. In her sadness she made a lute, on which she played so sweetly that the King, hearing her play as he was passing by one day, was at once freed from the jealousy of the wicked rival.[511] He married the princess and they lived happily ever after (Waddell 1906). The body of the princess is said to be enshrined in the temple of *Ra-mo-che*, some fifty yards to the west of the spring and quite near to the spot where a *chorten* [religious shrine—usually a small column or tower of piled-up stones (Ed.)] was erected by the Chinese in 1891 (*ibid.*).

"In this tale the princess's lute has unusual powers since, by playing it, its owner was able to break a spell. A definitely magical element is found in another lute, mentioned in two different Tibetan tales. The first of these, a folk tale collected early in the present century, is called 'The Story of Room Bacha and Bachi'; it concerns Bachi, the son of King Bacha of Room, who showed miraculous powers from his youth, and tells how he overcame an ogre.

"The Ogre's Magical Lute. One time Bachi is pursuing a deer, and he follows her at length into a cave where she turns into a beautiful woman. She explains that she is in the power of a terrible and bloodthirsty Ogre whose abode he has now reached. Just as she is telling him that she cannot escape without human assistance the Ogre's footsteps are heard approaching, whereupon the maiden goes over to the central glass pillar of the chamber, unscrews a portion of it, and bids the youth conceal himself within.

"Scarcely is the youth securely hidden within the pillar than the door of the cave flies open and a huge Ogre enters the central chamber. Calling the young woman to him, the Ogre commands her to bring his dinner and, after making a sumptuous repast, he seats himself on some cushions and begins playing on the lute. At the first sound of the music all the pillars in the room, save the one in which Bachi is concealed, begin a slow and stately dance; his pillar alone remains firm and

---

511 Although a "secular tale"—i.e. folk- or fairy-tale—with respect to mythological aspects see our theme **T4a** (Music as magical weapon against evil spirits. Release or exorcism of the spirit or soul, incl. expulsion of devils, evil spirits), *Introductory Remarks*, Vol I above. (Ed.)

unshaken. When the Ogre sees that one of the pillars is not dancing as usual he grows very angry, and seizing a huge hammer he advances upon it and threatens to shatter it into a thousand fragments; but the young woman, seizing him by the arm, begs him to spare it.

" 'Look,' says she, 'at the position of the pillar. It is the most central and the largest of them all. No doubt it feels some sense of dignity and wishes to be distinguished from the others. Spare it at any rate tonight, and it will probably dance as usual tomorrow.'[512]

"The remainder of the tale tells how the young man overcomes the Ogre and restores harmony to his own family (O'-Connor 1906). A three-headed Ogre playing the lute has been delightfully if somewhat primitively portrayed by a Tibetan artist from Gyantse (*ibid.*).

"The magical lute is found again in the story of *Susonri*, a tale originally said to have been related by the Buddha (Schiefner and Ralston 1926). This is contained in the collection known as *bKa'-gyur* — versions of the Sanskrit religious writings imported into Tibet and translated there, mostly in the ninth century. The episode concerning the lute is self-contained and runs substantially as follows:

"*The Top String of the Lute*. Asuga (Swiftfoot), son of a Brahmin and a *Kinnari* — that is, a celestial or fairy musician — has been sent by his father to a Brahmin as a pupil. He is missed by his mother, so she beseeches his friends in these terms.

" 'So soon as you shall set eyes upon him, give him a lute, so that he may support himself by means of it. Only he must be careful not to touch its uppermost string, for doing so would surely entail on him great misfortune.'

"One day, when Asuga had gone into the forest with the other young Brahmins to collect firewood, he wanders far away, and he is seen by his mother's friends who ask him what news he has to give. When the young man complains of hunger and thirst, they ask him, will he not go to his mother, for she is weeping and wailing. He cannot speak with his mother, he says, because of her hot temper. Then they give him the lute with which he may keep himself alive. But they tell him that, lest any misfortune may befall, he is not to touch its uppermost string. Asuga takes the lute to where the Brahmin youths are and, when he has played and sung to them awhile, without ever touching the top string, they ask him, why does he not touch it? He tells them the reason and then in spite of it, he touches the top string. Then they all begin to skip and dance, and this dancing makes them late, so that it is only in the evening that they return to their *Pandit* who asks them why they have stayed out so late. When the youths have told the whole story, the *Pandit* asks the young Asuga if he really understands how to play the lute and sing. When he says that he does, he is thereupon obliged to play. And when, at the *Pandit*'s instigation, he touches the top string, the Brahmin and his wife begin to dance; moreover, the whole house skips with a crash, and every pot and crock in it is broken to pieces. In a rage the Brahmin seizes the youth by the neck and turns him out of the house.[513]

"After that, Asuga made his living by lute-playing and singing. A company of

---

512 For other examples of the power of music over inanimate objects — such as walls — see AMPHION* (p.52) and JERICHO* (p.449). See also theme T2b (Music has magical effect upon orderly process of nature), *Introductory Remarks*, Vol I above. (Ed.)

513 See also DANCING TO DEATH (OR INSANITY)* and our (related?) themes T4c (Music as means for tempting subject to indulge in evil or carnal ways) and T5 (Music as magical means of promoting or inducing state or condition of ecstasy, frenzy, madness, losing oneself etc), *Introductory Remarks*, Vol I above. (Ed.)

merchants, some five hundred of them, who were putting to sea, took him on board with them as a musician. But one day when he was playing on board ship, at the request of the merchants he touched the top string, whereupon the ship began to bound in the air and at length capsized, and the merchants, all five hundred of them, lost their lives. Asuga, who held on to a plank, was driven by a storm to Kaserudvipa (Schiefner and Ralston 1926).

"For our presesnt study, the principal interest of these tales lies in the dance-compelling power of the lute, especially of its top string. The motif of the dance-compelling instrument is of widespread occurrence in the world's folklore (Thompson D1415.2). A dance-compelling lute is often found (D1415.2.6, compare D1232, D1234), and we even meet again with the motif of the pillars dancing to the sound of a magical instrument (D1599.1).[514] The references centre chiefly about the Indo-European world. We cannot, however, rule out the possibility of a link with Arab culture also.

"Whereas the secular music of Tibet favours stringed instruments, to which we may add the flute, these instruments find no place in religious music, which makes exclusive use of wind and percussion instruments.[515] The remaining instruments featured in our legends belong, one and all, in the religious domain.

"**2. Dung-dKar (The Conch-Shell Trumpet).** The conch-shell trumpet is familiar both as a signalling instrument and in the ritual ensembles of Lamaistic Buddhism. Some mysterious tales are told about this instrument. One account links the conch with the King of the *Nagas* (Tibetan *kLu*), serpent demi-gods or water-sprites who, like the *Gandharvas*, dwell in the Tibetan 'Heaven of the Four Great Kingdoms'. Their King, *Ja-mi-zan* (Sanskrit *Virupaksha*), Guardian of the West, is mentioned along with the conch in the life of the great Tibetan hermit and poet-saint of the eleventh and twelfth centuries, *Mi-la Ras-pa* (Milarepa).

"*The Magical Conch of the Naga King.* Milarepa had received a visit from Tserinma, the auspicious Lady-of-Long-Life, and her four sisters, and each of them had brought him a gift: incense, food and drink, musical instruments, fine apparel, and beautiful flowers. After bowing to him and going round him in a circle, they sing to him in chorus, and it is in one section of their song that the reference to the magical conch occurs:

> To the left of the mountain, Lhaman
>   Jalmo,
> Stands your hut by the bank of the
>   Lodahan River.
> The King of the *Nagas* sounded
> His magic conch trumpet,
> And into a wish-fulfilling Palace
> Was his hut transformed.
>   (Chang 1962)

"This passage makes the conch trumpet an attribute of the *Naga* King and credits it with magical power—a power capable of transforming a hut into a palace. Just as the *Nagas* are spirits of the water,[516] so also is

---

514 See **FOLKLORE AND FOLKTALES—TYPOLOGY***: D1415.2 (Magic musical instrument causes person to dance), D1415.2.6 (Magic lute causes dancing), D1232 (Magic lute), D1234 (Magic guitar), D1599.1 (Pillars dance when ogre plays guitar). (Ed.)

515 It is of interest that nevertheless, as we have seen, certain *secular* associations and traditions share features in common with certain religious or sacred traditions and customs. It might be said that the idea of an instrument causing a ship to capsize, for example—a folkloristic tradition—and of causing a wall to collapse—a Biblical/sacred tradition—unite nevertheless on the common ground of *mythology*. (Ed.)

516 See also **WATER SPIRITS***. (Ed.)

the conch (as a mollusc) connected with that element — we shall later see its connexion with weather control — and its magical transforming power has to be interpreted in relation to the spiritual context of Milarepa's life. It is very possibly a reference to the life-giving principle in the transformation of the saint's own body....

"Among several Tibetan deities, all having ancient Hindu connexions, the conch is also found as an attribute: sGrolma (the Blue Tara), who holds it in one of her four right hands; Vajratara (the Yellow Tara); and Jambhala, a non-Tantric tutelary god, who is sometimes shown seated upon a conch (Gordon 1959, Gordon 1963).

"3. rKang-gLing (The Thigh-Bone Trumpet). The trumpet made out of a human thigh-bone (rKang-gLing) is also the object of much traditional lore. The apertures at the end of the instrument are sometimes called 'the nostrils of the horse' and the belief is that the sound of the instrument reminds people of the neighing of the mystical horse that is believed to carry the faithful into paradise after death (Laufer 1923). The connexions of this belief with Eastern Central Asian shamanism are self-evident. A similar tradition is found in Mongolia, where the neighing of the horse is linked with a different instrument, the buré, a metal trumpet several feet in length (Deniker and Deshayes 1904). In any study of the playing styles of these instruments, these traditions should be taken into account, for they may provide significant clues.

"In Tibet the thigh-bone trumpet is thought to be possessed of special powers. Its blast can avert a hail-storm, and the Austrian ethnologist the late Nebesky-Woykowitz describes (1956) a ceremony for averting hail as probably practised in a certain sect to this day. It is also used in ceremonies for the promotion of fertility. In order to acquire their magic power, however, the instruments have to be prepared in a special way. The bones should come from persons of a very high

or a very low caste, or from one who has died violently (Combe 1926), Waddell 1934, Nebesky-Woykowitz 1956). According to the old Bön-po belief, the thigh-bone is the seat of the vital principle (Roerich 1953), and its use as an instrument gains significance in this regard.

"One legend explains how the instrument gave its name to a locality. The scene is set in Lhasa, where, immediately below the Potala, lies a spot named Pargo-rKang-gLing, or the 'Place of the Thigh-Bone Trumpet'. Colonel Waddell unearthed some information about this spot from work of local history in connexion with the life of Lha-tsün, the patron saint of Sikkim who was born in the year 1595. The description in the tale refers to a year probably corresponding to AD 1648 in the Western calendar.

"The Place of the Thigh-Bone Trumpet. While at his palace at Potala, the Grand Lama, through his powers of inspiration, told his attendants that a sage would visit him that day, and that the sage should be admitted into his presence. Lha-tsün, arriving immediately below the Potala at the site now named Pargo-rKang-gLing, blew loudly upon his rKang-gLing, or trumpet of human thigh-bone. But the castle guard, ignorant of who the man really was, seized him and tied him the the Do-ring monolith, as a punishment for daring to trumpet so close to the castle. The saint, thus bound, shook the whole hill of Potala, and so his arrival was brought to the notice of the Grand Lama, who ordered his instant release and admission into his presence. And the spot where the sage blew the trumpet is caled Pargo-rKang-gLing to this day (Waddell 1934)....

"As an attribute of deities, the rKang-gLing is found in the right hand of the guardian deity and Lord of Death Mahakala (Sanskrit), the Tibetan mGon-po Bran-zei grugs-pa (Grünwedel 1900), who also holds a skull-bowl in his left hand. The rKang-gLing is also found in the left hand of the 'Mistress of the Cemetary' (Nebesky-Woykowitz 1956); and, with a drum, in the hands of the tutelary deities of the White Lama Sect at Youngning (Rock 1931).

"4. Dung-chen (The Long Trumpet). The instrument by which Tibet is probably best known to the outside world is the long trumpet called *dung*, whose majestic sounds have never failed to impress those who have heard them....

"The episode which invites our attention is that in which *sGam-po-pa* (1079-1153)(who is later to be recognized as Milarepa's most gifted disciple) is seeking his master. In this account we meet not only the great trumpet but also a drum.

"The Trumpet's Mighty Voice and the Drum's Overwhelming Boom. One evening *sGam-po-pa* made offerings and said prayers to the Three Precious Ones. That night he blew a huge brass trumpet, whose mighty voice resounded in every corner of the earth. Even today there is no trumpet anywhere in all Tibet with a greater or more far-reaching sound. Then *sGam-po-pa* hung a drum in the air and beat on it a rhythm, producing a solemn, pleasant, and overwhelming boom heard by numerous men and animals. And on the same night he had a dream in which a girl, looking like a native of Mon, came to him and said, 'You

beat a drum for human beings, but many animals have also been blessed by the sound.'[517] Afterwards, sGam-po-pa explained, 'The human beings who heard the sound of the drum that night are those men of lesser capacity who must go through successive stages of the Path in gradual manner.... The animals who hear my drum are my great yogi disciples who practice meditation in caves.' Then sGam-po-pa set out to find Milarepa (Chang 1962). A shorter reference to this episode appears in *The Blue Annals* (Roerich 1953).

"The mighty voice of the trumpet is described as reaching 'every corner of the earth', just as, in Scandinavian mythology, the blast of the horn of Heimdal sounded through all the worlds. The drum is mentioned as being heard 'by numerous men and animals', sGam-po-pa explaining that the animals are his 'great yogi disciples'. Here we may have some affinity with classical Greek thought, whose Orphic lyre attracted and tamed the animals — that is, it subdued the animal nature in man.[518]

"The type of drum intended in the tale is not stated in the available translations, though it would almost certainly have been a form of the large religious drum *rNga*.

"5. Phyed-rNga (The Bön Frame-Drum. A drum of another kind figures in a number of Tibetan legendary tales. The best

---

517 On the blessing of animate and other living creatures by musical instruments, see also e.g. BELL*. One might guess that a reason *why* such instruments have this happy effect is, that through them contact is being made with beings of the divine or spirit world. See our themes T1a (Music as magical means of communication with god[s] or supreme being[s]), T1b (Musician as medium through which magical power is conveyed to a community or congregation), T2b (Music has magical effect upon orderly process of nature or life cycle), T2c (It can effect specifically crops, animals, the weather, etc. Music [or musician] blesses one's fields, household, family etc as a result of communication with gods or spirit beings), *Introductory Remarks*, Vol I above. (Ed.)

518 For another appearance of this theme — in which music not only subdues man's "animal nature", but *does* indeed demonstrate a magical mastery over the animal kingdom — see references to Vainamoinen (pp.476ff — also 255-257) in KALEVALA* entry, Vol I. (Ed.)

known of these describes a contest between Milarepa and *Na-ro-bo-c'un*, a sorcerer-priest of the pre-Buddhist Tibetan religion known as Bön. The scene is usually set in the vicinity of Kailas, the holy mountain, and a version is to be found in the twenty-second chaptr of the *Mgur 'bum*.

"*The Sorcerer who Flew on a Drum.* The Bön priest Na-ro-bo-c'un has challenged Milarepa to engage in a trial of magic designed to prove which of the two faiths might be the more powerful, Buddhism or *Bön*. It is agreed that whoever reaches the summit of Mount Kailas at the given hour should be deemed the winner of the prize, namely, dominion over the Holy Mountain itself. THe Bön-po sought to gain victory, while beating the tambourine and sitting on a drum (*nga*) which he was moving through the air (Hoffmann 1950).

"A shorter version appearing in *The Blue Annals* tells us that,

there was a Bön-po adept who had mounted a drum, and was about to proceed to the snowy summit. The Venerable One reached the snowy summit within a single moment, and then having spread his linen garment, he sent the Bön-po adept down with his drum, and showed many other similar miracles. (Roerich 1953)

"*Why the Sorcerer Hides his Face in the Drum.* The 'tambourine' referred to in the above legend is the drum held by a short wooden handle and beaten with a curved stick; the instrument is tuned with the skin facing downward and is then brought close to the face of the *Bön nag* sorcerer, who has to bring the stick upward, towards his face, in order to hit the skin of the drum. The Tibetan Buddhists seek to explain this by reference to the legend about the defeat of the 'Black Bön' sorcerer by Milarepa. The present day adherents of the *Bön nag* are ashamed of this defeat and they try — or so the Buddhists say — to hide

their face in the 'tambourine' (Nebesky-Woykowitz 1952).

"These traditions clearly represent a confrontation of the two religions and a Buddhist claim to have gained supremacy over the pre-Buddhist religion of Bön. The reason given for the strange method of playing seems almost certain to be an explanation euphemistically foisted by the new official religion onto some practice of the older faith whose meaning or connexions were inherently quite different. In any case, the striking of the drum from below is not unknown in other cultures, and it is worth noting here that into the present time the Eskimos* still bring the stick upward to strike the frame of the drum.

"*The Spirits Beating the Drum.* In a version of the confrontation of the two faiths given by the British mountaineer J. B. Noel, the contestants are somewhat different; they are Padmasambhava and the Bön priest of the Rongbuk monastery, and the mountain is Everest! Now Rongbuck is the shrine dedicated to Everest and it seems likely that Noel would have heard his version there. His conclusion of the tale adds some interesting information:

"When the sun appeared, Padmasambhava was conveyed by a beam, sitting in his chair, to the very top of the mountain. He sat there awhile, enthroned on the steeple of the world. When he descended he left his chair behind. The Bön-po lama perished, but the spirits of the mountain kept his drum. So now, when the rumble of rock avalanches is heard, the Tibetans say, 'the spirits are beating the drum' (Noel 1927).

"The account given in these tales is not the only instance of a Bön devotee flying on a drum. One of the priests summoned 'from the west' to participate in the funeral rites at the interment of King *Gri-gum* is praised for having been known 'to move through the air sitting on his drum' (Ohlmarks 1939, Hoffmann 1950, Hoffmann 1961).

"The rise to the realm of spirits by sitting and flying on a drum finds many parallels in shaman religions outside Tibet, and a number of these have been cited from Altaian, Buryiat, and Yakut sources (Harva 1938, Ohlmarks 1939, Hoffmann 1950). The idea is current among the Siberian tribes that the shaman actually flies into the sky on his drum.[519] The meaning is of course that, assisted by the rhythms of his drum, the shaman *as a shaman* (i.e. his soul) penetrates another world (that of inner spiritual vision). It is hardly surprising that we should find a similar tradition in Tibet at an early time, for Bön has many elements akin to those of the shamanism of Central and Northern Asia. What the Buddhist versions of these legends seems to be saying is that while the Bön-po takes time to rise to spiritual heights and has to use lengthy rituals to do so, the Buddhist saint can do it in the twinkling of an eye by inner realization.

"**6. Damaru (The Hand-Drum).** So much for the drum associated with Bön-po. In a fourth version of the contest, as related by Lama Anagarika Govinda, the drum is made to be a *damaru*, the intrument of Tantric Buddhism:

"*How a Drum Indented the Ice-Dome of Mount Kailas.* The magician, seeing himself defeated by Milarepa, gets such a shock that he drops his magic drum (*damaru*).

It leaped down in big bounds, and each time it bounced against the ice-dome of Kailas it emitted a loud tone and left a deep cut on the surface of the dome. 'Tang-tang-tang!' it went, to the great hilarity of the onlookers. And up to the present day a perpendicular line of star-like impressions are to be seen [sic (Ed.)], forming the vertical axis of the big swastika on the

southern face of the dome of Kailas. (Govinda 1959)

"In this account we have another element familiar in legends and folklore in many parts of the world, namely, natural features represented as having originated in legendary events; in this case it is the cut in the ice-dome of Kailas, and the line of impressions resulting from the bouncing of the drum.

"The drum, or *damaru*, referred to in this version of the tale is the one carried as an attribute by certain Buddhist deities, including the *dharmapalas* or protective deities, and the six-handed, blood-drinking, Tantric deity *Bhagavan Padma-Heruka*, who carries it in his third left hand (Evans-Wentz 1948). This is the well-known Tibetan ritual instrument shaped like an hourglass and often made of two half-crania. From the median ligature of the instrument are suspended two cords, and at the end of each hangs a hard knob. When the instrument is twirled by motion of the player's wrist, the knobs strike each of the two drumheads in turn and the resulting sound is not unlike that of a rattle.

"The same instrument turns up again in an account of a Tantric feast said to have been held by *yogins* and *yoginis* in the twelfth century, and it may be read in *The Blue Annals*.

"*The Self-Resounding Drum.* During the feast of the 400 yogins and yoginis,

there appeared several young girls attired as Brahmin girls, and holding in their hands skull-caps, mendicant staffs, and drums (*damaru*). They all became possessed (by gods), threw upwards their drums which resounded by themselves, sang the *vajra* song, assumed a cross-legged posture, and continuously drank seven measures of

---

519 According to some versions, the drum itself is made from the wood of the Cosmic or World Tree, and the flight may be towards (or around, or over) this same Tree. (Ed.)

strong wine without becoming intoxicated. (Roerich 1949)

"The preparation of the skull-drum (to which the name *höd rnga* normally refers) is, like that of the thigh-bone trumpet, of special interest. The skulls should be from persons who have been killed or who have died from an accident. A drum made from the half-skulls of two children reaching their eighth year or who have been born of incest are believed to possess strong magical properties (Nebesky-Woykowitz 1956).

"Describing the paraphernalia of the *'cham*, or ritual dance-drama (miscalled 'devil dance') as held at Tachienlou, Coombe gives some further information about the relationship of skull-drums and children. The skulls should be those of a boy and a girl, of not fewer than seven nor more than ten years of age (Coombe 1928). They represent the *Bamo* and the *Bawo*, personae in the drama, who are respectively goddesses from Lha (who carry the drums) and their consorts, of spirits of the heroes from Lha (*ibid.*). We seem also to meet with the same order of ideas in the text of an esoteric Tantric ritual known as *gChöd*. Some manuscripts pertaining to this appear in English translation in a work by Evans-Wentz (1958). It should be explained that in this rite the celebrant mystically sacrifices his body to elemental beings whom he himself evokes. Included among the instruments with magical powers required by one who would practice the rite is the *'damaru*, for overpowering apparitional beings' (Evans-Wentz 1958); this 'skull-drum, which is the best and rarest of drums, possesseth a clear sound' (*ibid.*). And in the *gChöd* text, as in

the *'cham*, we find the heroes and the heroines associated with the instrument:

When dancing in the Southern Continent, the Human World
The Heroes and Heroines move round in a triangular dancing arena;
Their feet flash upon the Head of Pride, embodied in the Lord of Death.
They drum upon the skull-drums of the Wisdom of Equality, with a peculiar sharp tapping sound."

— Crossley-Holland, pp.2-7, 10-12, 14-17, 20-21, 23-31.

TRIPARTITE FORMS.

§398A.1 "[The Clover (or Trefoil) is] an emblem of the Trinity. When it is located upon a mountain it comes to signify knowledge of the divine essence gained by hard endeavour, through sacrifice or study (equivalent to ascension).[520] Trifoliate forms, such as the Gothic three-lobed arch, bear the same significance; and, broadly speaking, so do all tripartite forms. In the Middle Ages, triple time in music was regarded in the same light, and it is so used by Scriabin in *Prometheus*." — Cirlot, pp.50-51.

TRUMPET. *(See also p.771.)*

§403.9 "Since it is a metal instrument, it corresponds to the Elements of fire and water and also to the twin-peaked Mountain of Mars. Metallic instruments pertain to nobles and warriors, whereas wooden instruments, from their associations with the valley, are more properly related to the

---

520 See Harold Bayley, *The Lost Language of Symbolism* (London, 1912; reprint 1951).

common folk and to shepherds.[521] The trumpet symbolizes the yearning for fame and glory.[522] On the other hand, the horn*, because of its shape, is connected with the symbolism of the animal-horn.[523]" — Cirlot, p.353.

§403.10 **SWAHILI (ISLAMIC) CREATION MYTH.** "Before the beginning of time there was God. He was never born nor will He ever die. If He wishes a thing, He merely says to it: 'Be!' and it exists.

"So God said: 'There be light!' And there was light. God took a fistful of this light and it shone in His hand. Then He said: 'I am pleased with you, my light, I will make out of you my prophet, I will mould you into the soul of Mohammed.'

"When he had created the soul of the prophet Mohammed (May God pray for him and give him peace), He loved it so much that He decided to create mankind so that He might send Mohammed to it as His messenger to bring His word to Earth....

"With his infinite knowledge God foresaw all the events that would happen in the centuries to follow until the last day. With His unlimited power God began to create all the things He would need for some purpose which He alone knew.

"First He created the Throne and the Carpet for Himself to sit on at the Last Judgement. The Throne has four legs supported by four strong beasts. The Carpet that covers it has all the lovely colours of the rainbow and stretches out along the skies as far as the borders of space....

"The third thing God created was the Well-preserved Tablet. It is a board so large that it can contain a complete and detailed description of all the events that ever take place anywhere in past and future.... She is called the Mother of Books, because all the Sacred Books of Mankind in which God has revealed some of His Truth contain only fragments of her contents....

"With the Tablet He created the Pen to write His commandments. The Pen is as long as the distance between Heaven and Earth. It has a thinking head and a personality, and as soon as it had come into existence, God ordered it: 'Write!' The Pen asked: 'What shall I write, my Lord?' God said: 'Destiny.' Since that moment the Pen has been busy writing on the Tablet all the deeds of men.

"Of course, if it pleases God to change His mind, He does so. If He projects a different future than was foreseen in previous plans, the writing will disappear from the Tablet and the Pen will record new facts.

"The fifth thing God created was the Trumpet, and with it the archangel Serafili [Asrafel]. The angel holds the Trumpet to his mouth, waiting patiently in the same position, century after century, until it pleases God to terminate history. Then He will give the signal, and Serafili will blow his first blast. The Trumpet has such a powerful voice that at its first sound the mountains will collapse, the stars will come plummeting down and Doomsday will begin.

"The sixth thing which God created was the Garden of Delights which was destined for the good souls....

"The seventh thing which God created, foreseeing in His wisdom that many souls would not follow the good Messenger, was the Fire. Crackling, it sprang up from the deepest bottom of shadows, in the remotest pit of space. Evil smell and smoke is its essence, roaring thunder its voice. 'My Lord,' cried the Fire, 'where are the souls of sinners, I want to see them suffer!' Who would not pray night and day that his soul may avoid this eternal torture.

---

521 See Marius Schneider, *El origen musical de los animales-simbolos en la mitologia y la escultura antiguas* (Barcelona, 1946).

522 See B. G. P., *Diccionario universal de la mitologia* (Barcelona, 1835).

523 See Schneider, *El origen musical de los animales-simbolos.*

"God went on and on creating, taking things out of non-being, for God requires no rest; neither sleep nor slumber seize Him.

"God now created the angels, a myriad of voices who proclaim His praise. [Among them are the archangels Jiburili (Gabriel) and Mikaili (Michael)]...

"Serafili [Asrafel], the angel of the Trumpet, has already been mentioned. His task is simply to wait for the signal of the end.

"Zeraili [Azrael] is the angel of death, the taker of souls, who brings each creature the last message...

"Maliki is the guardian of the Fire in which the sinful souls, the hypocrites and heathens, are punished....

"Ridhuani is the custodian of Paradise....

"Many other angels live in heaven, more than we can know. [After that God created the Universe in seven heavens, man, etc.]" — Sproul, pp.38-40.

§403.11 " 'Behold, I show you a mystery; we shall not all sleep, but we shall all be changed, in a moment, in the twinkling of an eye, at the last trump: for the trumpet shall sound, and the dead shall be raised incorruptible, and we shall be changed' (I Corinthians 15). This tremendous passage in St Paul was familiar to generations of Christians through its use in the funeral service, and the picture of the great archangel sounding the last trumpet and the dead rising from their graves in response was part of the traditional Christian picture of what would happen at the Last Judgement.

"In I Thessalonians (chapter 4) St Paul again refers to Christ descending from heaven, 'with the archangel's call, and with the sound of the trumpet of God', to judge the living and the dead. And in Matthew (chapter 24) Jesus is quoted as describing what will happen at 'the close of the age': the sun and moon will be darkened, the stars will fall from heaven, and all the people of the earth will see 'the Son of man coming on the clouds of heaven, with power and great glory; and he will send out his angels with a loud trumpet call, and they will gather his elect from the four winds, from one end of heaven to the other.'

"This Christian association of the trumpet with the judgement at the end of the world goes back directly to a verse in Isaiah (27:13) which says that in the days to come a great trumpet will be blown and all the scattered people of God will reunite to worship him in Jerusalem. More generally, it goes back to the use of trumpets in Jewish ritual and the Old Testament association of the trumpet with the voice, power and judgement of God.

"In many parts of the world the harsh, strident, carrying call of a horn* or trumpet has been regarded, on occasion, as the voice of a supernatural being and the same sound has also been used to attract the attention of supernatural beings.[524] When God descended on Mount Sinai to deliver the Ten Commandments, 'there were thunders and lightnings, and a thick cloud upon the mountain, and a very loud trumpet blast', which made all the people afraid (Exodus 19, 20). The author of Revelation heard behind him 'a loud voice like a trumpet', and turned to see that the speaker was Christ in majesty (chapter 1). It was the Jewish custom to blow trumpets at all religious feasts, on the first day of each month, and at the daily sacrifice, when the sound of the trumpet was the voice of the people calling to God. The deity himself had instructed Moses to have silver trumpets made, which were to be sounded to remind him of the people's presence and needs (Numbers 10).

---

524 See our themes 1a (Music as magical means of communication with god[s] or supreme being[s]) and T6a (Music as herald of otherworldly or supernatural being), *Introductory Remarks*, Vol I above. (Ed.)

"The Feast of Trumpets was held in the autumn, on the first day of the seventh month, which was later termed the New Year but was originally the opening of the yearly period of repentance that reached its peak on the Day of Atonement. The day of the Feast of Trumpets was said to be the day on which God judged mankind and allotted rewards and punishments, and some said that the trumpets were sounded to confuse Satan, the prosecutor in the heavenly court. This reinforced the connection between the trumpet and God as Judge, as already suggested by the trumpet blast on Sinai.

"The rabbis also connected the trumpets of Exodus and Isaiah, and the Feast of Trumpets, with the story of how Abraham obeyed God's orders to sacrifice Isaac, his son (Genesis 22). He bound Isaac and laid him on the altar but at the last moment his instructions were changed, and instead of Isaac he sacrificed a ram which he found nearby, caught by its horns in a thicket. This ram, it was said, had been specially created by God. It was the ram's left horn which would be blown in the time of the Messiah to summon the strayed sheep of Israel back to Jerusalem. The sacrifice of the ram had occurred on the first day of the seventh month, and the sounding of ram's horn trumpets on that day had been commanded by God, to remind him of Abraham's obedient binding of Isaac and as a sign that the congregation regarded themselves as bound offerings of God.

"*The Horn of Heimdall**. The use of an animal's horn as a musical instrument, like the Jewish *shofar** of ram's horn, would naturally tend to carry the associations of power, virility and aggression linked with horns. In many societies trumpets have been used to herald the accession of a king, for sounding alarms and for signalling in battle, because the sound carries well and in the hope of frightening the enemy. The fall of Jericho* was accomplished by the blast of the ram's horn trumpets, combined with the magic of the number seven, creating so formidable a battering ram of sound that the walls of the city fell down flat. The trumpets were blown by the priests who escorted the sacred ark of God, and when the ark was brought to Jerusalem by King David seven priests blew trumpets before it (Joshua 6, I Chronicles 15:24).

"These priests reappear in the book of Revelation (chapter 8) in the form of the seven angels who stand before God, who are given seven trumpets. They blow them in turn and appalling plagues and horrors strike the world.[525] When the seventh trumpet sounds (chapter 11), voices are heard in heaven proclaiming that the kingdom of the world has become the Kingdom of God.

"The association of the trumpet or horn with the end of the world appears again in Norse mythology. Heimdall, the watchman of the gods who never sleeps, lives beside Bifrost, the rainbow bridge, at the point where it reaches the sky. At the first signs of the approaching end, he will blow his great horn Gjallarhorn (ringing horn), whose note is heard through all the world. There is a rough parallel here with the Christian belief that an archangel, Gabriel or Michael, will wake the dead at the end of time with the blast of the last trump.

"In Bali spirits were summoned by blasts on horns or trumpets, which were blown again to drive them away. In some societies a medicine-man talks through a trumpet when he is speaking with the voice of a god or spirit, and the spirits of the dead played trumpets at shows staged by some 19th century mediums. In the Alps the wooden trumpet called the Alphorn, used for calling cattle and signalling over long distances, was believed to protect men and beasts from evil when sounded at dusk.

---

525 See our theme **T2b** (Music has magical effect upon orderly process of nature or life cycle), *Introductory Remarks*, Vol I above. (Ed.)

Some ceremonial trumpets are of enormous size, the lengthening of the tube deepening the note. Metal trumpets carried in funeral processions in China are so long that they can only be played when rested on the ground during a pause in the procession, and the Tibetans and Mongols used copper trumpets 16 feet long.

"Triton*, the Greek merman, who played only a very minor role in mythology, was a favourite subject in art and was frequently shown blowing a conch shell. Virgil's *Aeneid* (book 6) tells the story of how Misenus, the Trojan trumpeter, who excelled all others in his skill at 'stirring hearts with his trumpet of bronze and kindling the blaze of battle with his music', rashly challenged the gods to outdo him. The jealous Triton trapped him among rocks at the sea's edge and drowned him.

"The horn or trumpet has indeed a heart-stirring sound, connected with its use in hunting and war, and in salutes to kings and heroes. In Bunyan's *Pilgrim's Progress* the pilgrims come to the river of death, the last barrier that separates them from the Celestial City, and Mr Valiant-for-truth is summonded to cross: 'So he passed over and all the trumpets sounded for him on the other side'." — Cavendish [Man, Myth and Magic] , pp.2895, 2897.

WATER SPIRITS. *(See also p.787.)*

§416.15 "**Rusalkai.** Legendary Slavic water spirits, amphibious maidens who live half the year in water, half in the forest. They are said to be the souls of girls who died on their wedding night or, alternatively, those of unbaptized girls. Some of them are demonic, luring young men to a watery grave with their songs. Others are benevolent and bless people they meet." —

Cotterell (Macmillan Myths and Legends), p.236.[526]

§416.16 "**The Sea-Maid's Music.** In 1560 several supposed mermaids were caught by fishermen in Ceylon. They were dissected, and it was reported that they possessed organs like those of human beings. An early 17th century tale from America reported an attack on a canoe by a fierce merman whose arm had to be severed with a hatchet because he would not release his grip. The famous explorer Henry Hudson reported a sighting of mermaids in 1608, near Novaya Zemlya in the Arctic Ocean, north of Russia. He described one of them as being 'as big as one of us, her skin very white and long hair hanging down behind, of colour black. In her going down they saw her tail which was like the tail of a porpoise, speckled like a mackerel...' and 'from the navel upwards her back and breasts were like a woman's'.

"Among many curious legends one current in the British Isles is the tale of the mermaid who swam up a subterranean channel from the River Mersey at sunrise, seated herself on a church bell* and began to sing. In Cornwall, the mermaid of Zennor lured a lovelorn youth into the sea by the charm of her voice, and for years afterwards his voice could be heard singing from deep beneath the waves.

"According to John Shaw, author of *Speculum Mundi*, published in 1635, the song of the mermaid was not as tuneful as was popularly supposed. 'But above all the Mermaids and Men-fish seem to me the most strange fish in the waters. Some have supposed them to be devils or spirits in regard to their whooping noise that they make.' But this contradicts the older tradition, expressed by Shakespeare in *A Midsummer Night's Dream:*

---

526 See also pp.243, 797-99. (Ed.)

Since once I sat upon a promontory,
And heard a mermaid on a dolphin's
back
Uttering such dulcet and harmonious
breath,
That the rude sea grew civil at her
song,[527]
And certain stars shot madly from their
spheres,
To hear the sea-maid's music.

There is a tradition that the people of Machaire in Ireland are the descendents of mermaids. The Irish thought that mermaids were originally pagan women, transformed into mermaids by St Patrick and then banished from the Emerald Isle forever....

"A fierce blow against belief in mermaids was struck by the Reverend Robert Hawker of Morwenstow, a celebrated practical joker. About the year 1825 he decided to test the power of the mermaid myth by swimming to an offshore rock near Bude, on the north coast of Cornwall. Naked to the waist, and with a shining tail of oilskin wrapped about his legs, he combed his tresses of seaweed, preened himself in a mirror and began to sing, all in the light of the full moon. Large and awestruck crowds gathered to watch this remarkable phenomenon, which continued for several successive nights until finally, wearying of his performance and discovering that he had a sore throat, the Mermaid of Morwenstow suddenly burst into the strains of 'God Save the King' and, plunging from the rock, disappeared into the sea." — Maple, in Cavendish [Man, Myth and Magic], pp.1813-14.

WHISTLING.

§418A.1 "[Superstitions about whistling:]

A whistling girl and a crowing hen
Always come to no good end.

"If little girls whistle they will grow a beard.

"Whistling incites courage and is particularly helpful in the night when you follow a lonely path.

"Whistling in a house is to invite bad luck.

"Whistling aboard ship brings bad luck. This superstititon is still of vital consideration among sailors. (It has been said by one who has spent his life aboard ships that if anyone persists in whistling on board he is apt to suffer a black eye at the hands of his fellow sailors.) This superstition may have come about for a good practical reason: a whistle sounds much the same as a bosun pipe (of useful purpose) and confusion resulted. In a sailing ship a whistle is said to bring on a wind (unfavorable in its course).

"Among actors whistling back stage is unlucky." — Ferm, pp.250-51.[528]

§418A.2 "NAJARA. In the aboriginal mythology of western Australia*, a wicked spirit whose whistling tempts young boys away from their people, and who then induces them to forget their language and traditions. His whistling is heard in the grass." — Cotterell (Macmillan Myths and Legends), p.224.

---

527 See our theme **T2b** (Music has magical effect upon orderly process of nature or life cycle), *Introductory Remarks*, Vol I above. (Ed.)

528 Whistling sometimes *attracts* (evil) spirits, or bad luck, sometimes *drives them away*. Singing, dancing, and the playing of musical instruments in general can be similarly ambivalent. Perhaps the trick is to attract (or drive away) the *right* spirit (or demon). Is whistling "musical"? Well — it certainly is not speech... nor, perhaps, is it only "noise". Similar confusions present themselves with respect to e.g. the bull-roarer* and the hunting (or military) horn*. (Ed.)

WITCHCRAFT.

§419A.1 "Cone of Power. In neo-pagan witchcraft, psychic energy that is raised and directed in magic and healing.

"Raising a cone of power is done within a magic circle. It calls for coveners to focus on a desired goal, which is visualized in a symbol or image upon which everyone agrees. The power is raised usually through dancing*, chanting*, hand-clapping, drumming* or cord magic. As the coveners dance around the circle, the tempo increases, and the cone of power begins to rise over the circle, which forms the base of the cone. To those with a developed psychic ability, the energy is visible as a shimmering silver or blue-silver light. When the high priestess or priest senses that the energy is at its peak, she or he instructs the coveners to release it in a burst toward the goal. Timing is crucial; otherwise, the spell misfires. According to Gerald B. Gardner, the cone of power was one of the 'old ways' of witches. He described it as a coven dancing in a circle around a fire or candle, then linking hands and rushing toward the fire until everyone was exhausted or someone fainted, which indicated the energy had been sent off successfully. It is not certain exactly how old the cone-of-power custom is, but projection of magical energy toward a desired goal by a variety of means is an ancient, universal practice.

"The cone shape itself has symbolic significance in witchcraft. In parts of ancient Syria, the cone was the symbol of Astarte, the Phoenician goddess of motherhood, fertility and war. Tall, conical hats are traditionally associated with magicians and witches. The cone is also associated with the circle, symbol of the sun, unity, eternity and rebirth, and with the triangle, which has associations with the elements and pyramids, and represents the upward spiritual aspirations of all things." — Guiley, p.69.

ZOROASTER (ZARATHUSTRA).

§426.1 See also GATHA (Zoroastrian)*.
MITHRAIC PRACTICES
AND BELIEFS*.

§426.2 "The ancient people of Iran were related to the early invaders of India—but their high tableland bordered by mountains gave them practical problems quite different from those confronting the Aryans in India. Weather extremes of heat and cold, combined with lack of enough moisture, taxed all the husbandman's resources. Irrigation was necessary. Care of both crops and cattle required alertness and industry. And plundering nomadic hordes—from Turkestan in particular—were a constant danger. Life was a struggle against hostile powers....

"The prophet Zarathustra, or Zoroaster, concerning whose life many legends have accumulated, [was] born about 600 BC. Tradition is that he was about thirty years old when he first experienced the revelation in which he was admitted to the presence of Ahura Mazda (Wise Lord). From that time on he brought to men the message that rejoiced all creation, causing even the cattle to dance—if we may believe one account. For the religion that was revealed to him was especially a religion of joy, health, and strong will against evil. Ahura Mazda, the one Lord, would at last win the battle against evil, through enough good works done by those on his side....

"How the Whole Creation Danced to the Revelation of Zarathustra. One marvel is this which is declared, that when Zarathustra chanted revelation in the abode of Vistasp, it was danced to with joyfulness, both by the cattle and beasts of burden, and by the spirit of the fires which are in the abode.

"There seemed a righteous joyfulness of all the cattle, beasts of burden, and fires of the place, when they fully heard those words which were spoken by the righteous Zarathustra of the Spitamas." — Smith (Tree of Life), pp.309, 316.[529]

§426.3"The devout feel the presence of the yazatas everywhere [*Yazatas:* beings 'worthy of worship', included among the lesser Immortals]. In Iran at *sedra-pushun* [= 'putting on the sacred shirt', Irani name for the initiation of boys and girls into the faith] a child takes one of them as its especial guardian, and individual Parsis do the same, praying often to him and lighting lamps at the fire-temple on his feast day. The Iranis have many small shrines dedicated to individual *yazatas,* offering incense and prayers. They also regularly dance and sing at the shrines, believing that gladness pleases the diving beings. There are special rites to heal the sick, to restore lost purity, or to help a woman conceive a child. When performed by priests these always include Avestan prayers [*Avesta* — collection of holy texts], in the presence of fire; but village women sometimes perform their own rites, verging on magic, without these elements. Such practices are strongly discouraged by the community elders." — Boyce, in Hinnells, p.183.

---

529 *Spitamas:* Zarathustra was born in or by the village of Pourusaspa, in the region (?) of the Spitamas. He is addressed sometimes as "O Spitama Zarathustra". The notion of all the beasts of creation dancing at the words of the prophet is to some degree paralleled by that of the prophet, seer or shaman whose music gives him power over beasts (Orpheus* story, Väimämönen in the Finnish *Kalevala**); also echoed is the notion of music as an instrument for promoting or expressing cosmic harmony (Chinese* views of music [pp. 137 *ff.*], Harmony of the spheres* etc). (Ed.)

LIST OF SOURCES FOR
TEXT READINGS IN VOLUMES I AND II

(For other publications cited throughout Volumes I and II, see General Index.
Volume III is indexed separately.)

Aarne, Antti [Folktale]. *The Types of the Folktale*, 2nd Revision. Transl. & enl. by Stith Thompson. Helsinki: Suomalainen Tiedeakatemia/ Academia Scientiarum Fennica, 1961.

Abas, Zainab Ghulam (Compiler). *Folk Tales of Pakistan*. Karachi: Pakistan Publications (Saifee Printers and Publishers), 1957.

Abrahams, Roger D. (Selected & Edited by). *Afro-American Folktales: Stories from Black Traditions in the New World*. Pantheon Fairy Tale and Folklore Library. New York: Pantheon Books, 1985.

Aesop [Medici]. *The Medici Aesop: Spencer* MS 50. From the Spencer Collection of The New York Public Library. Fables transl. from the Greek by Bernard McTigue; intr. by Everett Fahy. New York: Harry N. Abrams, Inc., 1989.

Aesopus. *Aesop's Fables: A New Translation by V.S. Vernon-Jones, with an Introduction by G.K. Chesterton and Illustrations by Arthur Rackham*. Crown Publishers (Avenel Books), 1975[1912].

Afanas'ev, Aleksandr (Collector). *Russian Fairy Tales*, 2nd Ed. Transl. by Norbert Guterman; commentary by Roman Jakobson; illus. by Alexander Alexeieff. New York: Pantheon Books, 1945.

Al-Saleh, Khairat. *Fabled Cities, Princes and Jinn from Arab Myths and Legends*. New York: Schocken Books, 1985.

Alexander, Hartley Burr [Latin-American]. *The Mythology of All Races, Vol. 11: Latin-American*. Series Ed.: John Arnott MacCulloch. New York: Marshall Jones Co., 1920; New York: Cooper Square Publishers Inc. (reprint), 1964.

Alexander, Hartley Burr [North American]. *The Mythology of All Races, Vol. 10: North American*. Series Ed.: John Arnott MacCulloch. New York: Marshall Jones Co., 1916; New York: Cooper Square Publishers Inc. (reprint), 1964.

Alexinsky, G.: see *Larousse Encyclopedia of Mythology*.

Allen, Louis A. *Time Before Morning: Art and Myth of the Australian Aborigines*. New York: Thomas Y. Crowell Company, 1975.

Allen, Warren Dwight. *Philosophies of Music History: A Study of General Histories of Music, 1600-1960*. American Book Co., 1939; Dover Publications Ed. (corrected and with a new preface by the author), 1962.

Ananikian, Mardiros H. *The Mythology of All Races: Vol. 7: Armenian*. Series Ed.: John Arnott MacCulloch. New York: Marshall Jones Co., 1925; New York: Cooper Square Publishers Inc. (reprint), 1964.

Andersen, Johannes C. *Myths and Legends of the Polynesians*. London: George G. Harrap & Company, Ltd., 1928.

Anderson, Robert: see Sadie, Stanley.

Anderson, Warner: see Sadie, Stanley.

Anesaki, Masaharu. *The Mythology of All Races, Vol. 8: Japanese.* Series Ed.: John Arnott MacCulloch. New York: Marshall Jones Co., 1928; New York: Cooper Square Publishers Inc. (reprint), 1964.

Ariosto, Ludovico. *Orlando furioso.* Transl. by Guido Waldman. Oxford: Oxford University Press, 1974.

Aristotle: see Strunk, Oliver.

Asbjørnsen, Peter Christen & Moe, Jørgen. *Norwegian Folk Tales.* Transl. by Carl Norman & Pat Shaw Iversen. Illus. by Erik Werenskiold & Theodor Kittelsen. Oslo: Dreyers Forlag, 1960.

Athenaeus: see Strunk, Oliver.

Ausubel, Nathan (Editor). *A Treasury of Jewish Folklore: Stories, Traditions, Legends, Humor, Wisdom and Folk Songs of the Jewish People.* New York: Crown Publishers, Inc., 1948. "Two Songs for Three Hundred Rubles" adapted from Shmul Lehman, *Folks Meiselach in Anekdoten mit Nigunnim,* in *Archiv far Yiddisher Sprachwissenschaft, Literaturforschung in Etnologie,* ed. by Noah Prilutzki & Shmul Lehman (Warsaw, 1926-33).

Backman, E. Louis. *Religious Dances in the Christian Church and in Popular Medicine.* Transl. by E. Classen. London: George Allen & Unwin Ltd., 1952.

Balys, Jonas: see Leach, Maria.

Bamberger, Bernard J. *The Story of Judaism.* New York: The Union of American Hebrew Congregations, 1957.

Baring-Gould, Sabine. *Curious Myths of the Middle Ages.* Ed. & intr. by Edward Hardy. New York: Oxford University Press, 1978.

Basil, Saint: see Strunk, Oliver.

Basso, Ellen B. *A Musical View of the Universe: Kalapalo Myth and Ritual Performances.* Philadelphia: University of Pennsylvania Press, 1985.

Beaumont, Cyril W. *Complete Book of Ballets: A Guide to the Principal Ballets of the Nineteenth and Twentieth Centuries.* New York: G.P. Putnam's Sons, 1938. *Supplement to Complete Book of Ballets.* London: Putnam, 1942.

Beckwith, Martha. *Hawaiian Mythology.* New Haven CT: Yale University Press, 1940.

Berndt, Catherine H.: see Cavendish, Richard.

Besmer, Fremont E. *Horses, Musicians, and Gods: The Hausa Cult of Possession Trance.* South Hadley MA: Bergin & Garvey Publishers, 1983.

Bible, The. *Holy Bible: The Washburn College Bible, Oxford Edition.* King James Text, Modern Phrased Version. New York: Oxford University Press (1-volume edition), 1980.

Bierhorst, John [North America]. *The Mythology of North America.* New York: William Morrow & Company, 1985.

Bierhorst, John [South America]. *The Mythology of South America*. New York: William Morrow & Company, 1988.

Bierhorst, John (Editor) [Red Swan]. *The Red Swan: Myths and Tales of the American Indians*. New York: Farrar, Straus and GIroux, 1976.

Binder, Pearl. *Magic Symbols of the World*. London: The Hamlyn Publishing Group, Ltd., 1972.

Binnington, Doreen: see Sadie, Stanley.

Blacker, Carmen. *The Catalpa Bow: A Study of Shamanistic Practices in Japan*. London: George Allen & Unwin Ltd., 1975.

Boas, Orlando Villas & Boas, Claudio Villas: see Villas Boas, Orlando & Villas Boas, Claudio.

Bordman, Gerald. *American Musical Theatre: A Chronicle*. New York: Oxford University Press, 1978.

Bontemps, Arna: see Hughes, Langston.

Botkin, B.A. *A Treasury of Mississippi River Folklore: Stories, Ballads, Traditions and Folkways of the Mid-American River Country*. New York: Crown Publishers, 1955.

Bowers, Faubion. *The Dance in India*. New York: Columbia University Press, 1953; New York: AMS Press, Inc. (reprint), 1967.

Boyce, Mary: see Hinnells, John R.

Brakeley, Theresa C.: see Leach, Maria.

Brandel, Rose: see Reese, Gustave.

Brewer, J. Mason. *American Negro Folklore*. New York: Quadrangle/The New York Times Book Company, 1968.

Briggs, Katharine. *British Folktales*. Pantheon Fairy Tale and Folklore Library. New York: Pantheon Books, 1977.

Briggs, Katherine [Dictionary]. *A Dictionary of British Folk-Tales in the English Language; Incorporating the F. J. Norton Collection*. Bloomington: Indiana University Press (4 volumes), 1971.

Briggs, Katharine. *An Encyclopedia of Fairies: Hobgoblins, Brownies, Bogies, and Other Supernatural Creatures*. Pantheon Fairy Tale and Folklore Library. New York: Pantheon Books, 1976.

Brincard, Marie-Thérèse (Editor). *Sounding Forms: African Musical Instruments*. New York: The American Federation of Arts, 1989. Includes article by Sue Carole De Vale.

Browman, David L. & Schwarz, Ronald A. (Editors). *Spirits, Shamans, and Stars: Perspectives from South America*. New York: Moulton Publishers, 1979. Includes "*Yagé* Among the Siona: Cultural Patterns in Visions" by E. Jean Langdon.

Brown, George Mackay. *The Two Fiddlers*. Tales from the Isles of Orkney. United Kingdom: Piccolo Editions.

Brown, J. Mason. *American Negro Folklore*. Chicago: Quadrangle Books, 1968.

Brown, Peter. *The World of Late Antiquity:* AD 150-750. New York: Harcourt Brace Jovanovich, 1973.

Brundage, Burr Cartwright. *The Fifth Sun: Aztec Gods, Aztec World.* Illus. by Roy E. Anderson. Austin: University of Texas Press, 1979.

Bulfinch, Thomas. *Bulfinch's Mythology: The Age of Fable, The Age of Chivalry, Legends of Charlemagne.* New York: Thomas Y. Crowell Company, 1970.

Burney, Charles. *A General History of Music: From the Earliest Ages to the Present Period (1789).* Critical & historical notes by Frank Mercer. G.T. Foulis & Company, Ltd., 1935; New York: Dover Publications, Inc. (2v reprint), 1957.

Calvin, Jean: see Strunk, Oliver.

Campbell, Joseph. *The Hero with a Thousand Faces.* New York: Pantheon Books, 1949.

Campbell, Joseph. *The Masks of God. Vol. II: Oriental Mythology. Vol. III: Occidental Mythology. Vol. IV: Creative Mythology.* New York: The Viking Press, 1962, 1964, 1968; New York: Penguin Books, 1976.

Cardinall, A. W. *Tales Told in Togoland; To which is added the Mythical and Traditional History of Dagomba, by E. F. Tamakloe.* Oxford: Oxford University Press, 1931.

Carey, Margret. *Myths and Legends of Africa.* Illus. by Ron Geary. Feltham, Middlesex, England: The Hamlyn Publishing Group Ltd., 1970.

Carlyon, Richard. *A Guide to the Gods: An Essential Guide to World Mythology.* New York: William Morrow, 1981.

Caso, Alfonso. *The Aztecs: People of the Sun.* Transl. by Lowell Dunham; illus. by Miguel Covarrubias. Norman: University of Oklahoma Press, 1958.

Cassiodorus: see Strunk, Oliver.

Catlin, George. *Letters and Notes on the North American Indians* (1841). Ed. & intr. by Michael M. Mooney. New York: Clarkson N. Potter, Inc., Publisher, 1975.

Cavendish, Richard (Editor-in-Chief) [Man, Myth and Magic]. *Man, Myth and Magic: The Illustrated Encyclopedia of Mythology, Religion and the Unknown.* New edition ed. & compiled by Yvonne Deutsch. 1970; Freeport NY: Marshall Cavendish Corp. (reference ed. in 11 volumes), 1983. Includes entries by Eric Maple, Eric J. Sharpe.

Cavendish, Richard (Editor). *Mythology: An Illustrated Encyclopedia.* New York: Rizzoli International Publications, Inc., 1980. Authors include Catherine H. Berndt, Rosalie David, Emrys Evans, James H. Howard, Joanna Kaplan, Wendy O'Flaherty, Susumu Takiguchi.

Chadwick, Nora K.: see Dillon, Myles.

Chailley, Jacques. *40,000 Years of Music: Man in Search of Music.* Transl. by Rollo Myers. New York: Farrar, Straus & Giroux, Inc., 1964; New York: Da Capo Press (reprint), 1975.

Champion, Selwyn Gurney. *The Eleven Religions and Their Proverbial Lore: A Comparative Study.* New York: E.P. Dutton & Co., Inc., 1945.

Chatwin, Bruce. *The Songlines.* New York: Viking Penguin, Inc., 1987.

Christiansen, Reidar Th. (Editor). *Folktales of Norway*. Transl. by Pat Shaw Iversen. London: Routledge & Kegan Paul, Ltd., 1964.

Chrysostom, St. John: see Strunk, Oliver.

Cirlot, J. E. *A Dictionary of Symbols*, 2nd Ed. Transl. by Jack Sage. Fwd by Herbert Read. London: Routledge & Kegan Paul, Ltd., 1971; New York: Dorset Press (reprint), 1991.

Civrieux, Marc de, *Watunna: An Orinoco Creation Cycle*. Ed. & transl. by David M. Guss. San Francisco: North Point Press, 1980. Orig. publ. in a different version as *Watunna: Mitología Makiritare* (Caracas, 1970).

Clark, Ella E. *Indian Legends from the Northern Rockies*. Norman: University of Oklahoma Press, 1966.

Clarkson, Atelia & Cross, Gilbert B. (Editors). *World Folktales: A Scribner Resource Collection*. New York: Charles Scribner's Sons, 1980. Incl. selection from Cyrus Macmillan, *Canadian Wonder Tales* London: John Lane, The Bodley Head, 1920.

Coffin, Tristram Potter. *The Book of Christmas Folklore*. New York: The Seabury Press, 1973.

Coffin, Tristram Potter: see Cohen, Hennig.

Cohen, Hennig & Coffin, Tristram Potter (Editors). *The Folklore of American Holidays*. Detroit: Gale Research Company, 1987.

Cole, W. Owen: see Hinnells, John R.

Colum, Padraic. *Orpheus: Myths of the World*. Illus. by Boris Artzybasheff. New York: The Macmillan Company, 1930.

Cotterell, Arthur. *A Dictionary of World Mythology*, New Ed., Rev. & Expanded. Orig. Windward/W. H. Smith & Son Ltd., 1979; New York: Oxford University Press, 1986.

Cotterell, Arthur [Macmillan Myths and Legends]. *The Macmillan Illustrated Encyclopedia of Myths and Legends*. Conceived, ed. & designed by Marshall Editions Ltd, London. New York: Macmillan Publishing Co., 1989.

Courlander, Harold. *The Drum and the Hoe: Life and Lore of the Haitian People*. Berkeley: University of California Press, 1960.

Courlander, Harold [Folklore]. *A Treasury of Afro-American Folklore*. New York: Crown Publishers, 1976.

Cox, George W. *The Mythology of the Aryan Nations*, Rev. Ed. London: Kegan Paul, Trench & Co., 1887.

Craigie, William A. (Selected & Translated by). *Scandinavian Folk-Lore: Illustrations of the Traditional Beliefs of the Northern Peoples*. London: Alexander Gardner, 1896; Detroit, Michigan: Singing Tree Press (reprint), 1970.

Croker, T. Crofton: see Yeats, William Butler.

Cross, Gilbert B.: see Clarkson, Atelia.

Cross, Tom Peete & Slover, Clark Harris (Editors). *Ancient Irish Tales*. New York: Henry Holt & Company, 1936.

Crossley-Holland, Peter. *Musical Instruments in Tibetan Legend and Folklore.* Monograph Series in Ethnomusicology 3, ed. by Peter Crossley-Holland. Los Angeles CA: University of California Department of Music, 1982.

Crossley-Holland, Peter: see Robertson, Alec; Sadie, Stanley.

Cumont, Franz. *The Mysteries of Mithra,* 2nd Rev. Ed. Transl. by Thomas J. McCormack. New York: Dover Publications, 1956.

Cushing, Frank Hamilton (Collector & Translator). *Zuñi Folk Tales* (1901). Foreword by Major J. W. Powell; intr. by Mary Austin. New York: Alfred A. Knopf, 1931.

Dasent, George Webbe. *Popular Tales from the Norse, with an Introductory Essay on the Origin and Diffusion of Popular Tales,* 3rd Ed. Transl. from the c.1850s collection by Peter Christen Asbjørnsen and Moe]. New York: G. P. Putnam's Sons, 1888; New York: Johnson Reprint Corp., 1970.

David, Rosalie: see Cavendish, Richard.

Davidson, Hilda Roderick Ellis. *Gods and Myths of Northern Europe.* New York: Penguin Books, 1964.

Davidson, Hilda Roderick Ellis [Scandinavia]. *Pagan Scandinavia.* New York: Frederick A. Praeger, 1967.

Dawkins, R. M. (Chosen & Translated by) [Greek Folktales]. *Modern Greek Folktales.* London: Oxford at the Clarendon Press, 1953.

Dawkins, R. M. (Chosen & Translated by) [More Greek Folktales]. *More Greek Folktales.* London: Oxford at the Clarendon Press, 1955.

Day, Martin S. *The Many Meanings of Myth.* New York: University Press of America, Inc., 1984.

Dégh, Linda (Editor). *Folktales of Hungary,* transl. by Judith Halász. The University of Chicago Press, 1965.

De Re, Gerard & De Re, Patricia. *The Christmas Almanack.* Garden City, New York: Doubleday & Company, Inc., 1979.

Deva, B. Chaitanya. *An Introduction to Indian Music.* New Delhi: Government of India Ministry of Information and Broadcasting (Publications Division), 1973; Thompson CT: InterCulture Associates, 1973.

De Vale, Sue Carole: see Brincard, Marie-Thérèse; Sadie, Stanley.

Dieterlen, G.: see Fortes, M.

Dillon, Myles & Chadwick, Nora K. *The Celtic Realms.* New York: The New American Library, 1976.

Dixon, Roland B. *The Mythology of All Races, Vol. 9: Oceanic.* Series Ed.: John Arnott MacCulloch. New York: Marshall Jones Co., 1916; New York: Cooper Square Publishers Inc. (reprint), 1964.

DjeDje, Jacqueline Cogdell: see Jackson, Irene V.

Domotor, Tekla. *Hungarian Folk Beliefs.* Transl. by Christopher M. Hann. 1981; Bloomington: Indiana University Press, 1982.

Drummond, John D. *Opera in Perspective*. Minneapolis: University of Minnesota Press, 1980.

Drury, Nevill. *Dictionary of Mysticism and the Occult*. New York: Harper & Row, Publishers, 1985.

Eberhard, Wolfram (Collected & Translated by). *Chinese Fairy Tales and Folk Tales*. New York: E.P. Dutton & Company, 1938.

Eliade, Mircea (Editor in Chief). *The Encyclopedia of Religion*. New York: Macmillan Publishing Co. (16 volumes), 1987. Includes essays by Ter Ellingson, Judith Lynne Hanna, Isabel Wong.

Eliade, Mircea [Myths, Dreams]. *Myths, Dreams and Mysteries: The Encounter Between Contemporary Faiths and Archaic Realities*. Transl. by Philip Mairet. New York: Harper & Row, Publishers, 1960; Harper Torchbooks Ed., 1967.

Eliade, Mircea [Shamanism]. *Shamanism: Archaic Techniques of Ecstasy* (1951). New & enl. ed. transl. by Willard R. Trask. New York: Pantheon Books, 1964.

Ellingson, Ter: see Eliade, Mircea.

Ellis, Havelock: see Steinberg, Cobbett.

Erdoes, Richard & Ortiz, Alfonso (Selected & Edited by). *American Indian Myths and Legends*. Pantheon Fairy Tale and Folklore Library. New York: Pantheon Books, 1984.

Errington, Frederick Karl. *Karavar: Masks and Power in a Melanesian Ritual*. Ithaca NY: Cornell University Press, 1974.

Evans, Emrys: see Cavendish, Richard.

Ewen, David. *The New Encyclopedia of the Opera*. New York: Hill & Wang, 1971.

Ferguson, John C. *The Mythology of All Races, Vol. 8: Chinese*. Series Ed.: John Arnott MacCulloch. New York: Marshall Jones Co., 1928; New York: Cooper Square Publishers Inc. (reprint), 1964.

Ferm, Vergilius. *A Brief Dictionary of American Superstitions*. New York: Philosophical Library, 1959.

Fleischmann, Aloys: see Sadie, Stanley.

Fortes, M. & Dieterlen, G. (Editors). *African Systems of Thought*. New York: Oxford University Press, 1965. Authors include M. Gelfand, Robert F. Gray.

Foster, James R. (Arranged & Edited by) [Wit and Humor]. *Great Folktales of Wit and Humor*. New York: Harper & Brothers, 1955.

Foster, James R. (Arranged & Edited by) [Folktales]. *The World's Great Folktales: A Collection of 90 of the Best Stories from the Folklore of All Countries*. New York: Harper & Brothers, 1953.

Fox, William Sherwood. *The Mythology of All Races, Vol. 1: Greek and Roman*. Series Ed.: John Arnott MacCulloch. New York: Marshall Jones Co., 1916; New York: Cooper Square Publishers Inc. (reprint), 1964.

Frazer, James George [Golden]. *The Golden Bough: A Study in Magic and Religion*. New York: The Macmillan Company (1-volume abridged ed.), 1958.

Frazer, James George [Totemism]. *Totemism and Exogamy: A Treatise on Certain Forms of Superstitition and Society.* 1910, 1934; London: Dawsons of Pall Mall (4v reprint), 1968.

Frazer, James George: see Gaster, Theodor H. [Old Testament].

Garfias, Robert: see Sadie, Stanley.

Gaster, Theodor H. *The Oldest Stories in the World.* New York: The Viking Press, 1952.

Gaster, Theodor H. [Old Testament]. *Myth, Legend, and Custom in the Old Testament: A Comparative Study with Chapters from Sir James G. Frazer's* Folklore in the Old Testament. New York: Harper & Row, Publishers, Inc. (2 volumes), 1969. Incl. reprinted material from James G. Frazer, *Folklore in the Old Testament.* London: Macmillan & Company (3 volumes), 1918.

Gaster, Theodor H.: see Leach, Maria.

Geertz, Clifford. *The Religion of Java.* New York: The Free Press of Glencoe, 1960.

Gelfand, M.: see Fortes, M.

Gilfond, Henry. *Voodoo: Its Origins and Practices.* New York: Franklin Watts, 1976.

Godwin, Joscelyn. *Harmonies of Heaven and Earth: The Spiritual Dimensions of Music from Antiquity to the Avant-Garde.* Rochester VT: Inner Traditions International Ltd., 1987.

Goldsmith, Elisabeth. *Ancient Pagan Symbols.* New York: G.P. Putnam's Sons, 1929; New York: AMS Press, Inc. (reprint), 1973).

Graves, Robert. *The Greek Myths.* Orig. 1955 (2 volumes); New York: George Braziller, Inc., 1959.

Gray, Robert F.: see Fortes, M.

Grimm, Jacob & Grimm, Wilhelm. *The Complete Grimm's Fairy Tales.* Transl. by Margaret Hunt, rev., corrected & completed by James Stern. Intr. by Padraic Colum. Folkloristic commentary by Joseph Campbell. 212 illus. by Josef Scharl. New York: Pantheon Books, 1944 [1980 reprint].

Guerber, H. A. *Legends of the Middle Ages: Narrated with Special Reference to Literature and Art.* New York: American Book Company, 1896.

Guerber, H. A. [Norsemen]. *The Norsemen.* Myths and Legends Series. George G. Harrup & Co.; London: The Mystic Press (reprint), 1987.

Guiley, Rosemary Ellen. *The Encyclopedia of Witches and Witchcraft.* New York: Facts on File Inc., 1989.

Guirand, Felix: see *Larousse Encyclopedia of Mythology.*

Guirma, Frederic. *Tales of Mogho: African Stories from the Upper Volta.* New York: Macmillan Publishing Co., 1971.

Guthrie, W. K. C. *The Greeks and Their Gods.* Boston: The Beacon Press, 1950.

Guthrie, W. K. C. [Orpheus]. *Orpheus and Greek Religion: A Study of the Orphic Movement,* 2nd Ed. Methuen & Co., Ltd., 1952; New York: W. W. Norton & Co., Inc., 1966.

Hackin, J. et al. *Asiatic Mythology: A Detailed Description and Explanation of the Mythologies of All the Great Nations of Asia.* Transl. by F. M. Atkinson; intr. by Paul-Louis Couchod.

New York: Crown Publishers (Crescent Books); orig. publ. Thomas Y. Crowell Company, 1963. Authors include J. Hackin, Clément Huart, C. -H. Marchal, Henri Maspero.

Haefer, Richard: see Sadie, Stanley.

Hall, James. *Dictionary of Subjects and Symbols in Art*. New York: Harper & Row, Publishers, 1974.

Halpert, Herbert: see Hand, Wayland D.

Hamilton, Edith. *Mythology*. Orig. c.1940; New York: The New American Library (reprint), c.1969.

Hand, Wayland D. (Editor). *American Folk Legend: A Symposium*. Berkeley: University of California Press, 1971. Authors include Herbert Halpert.

Handy, E.S. Craighill & Winne, Jane Lathrop. *Music in the Marquesas Islands*. Honolulu: Bernice P. Bishop Museum Bulletin 17, 1925; New York: Kraus Reprint Co., 1971.

Hanna, Judith Lynne: see Eliade, Mircea.

Hannick, Christian: see Sadie, Stanley.

Harmon, Mamie: see Leach, Maria.

Harrison, Daphne D.: see Jackson, Irene V.

Hart, George. *A Dictionary of Egyptian Gods and Goddesses*. London: Routledge & Kegan Paul, 1986.

Hart, Mickey & Lieberman, Fredric, with Sonneborn, D. A. *Planet Drum: A Celebration of Percussion and Rhythm*. Designed and produced by Howard Jacobsen. New York: HarperCollins Publishers, 1991.

Hartland, Edwin Sidney. *The Science of Fairy Tales: An Inquiry into Fairy Mythology*. 1890; 2nd Ed. Intr. by A.A. Milne. London: Methuen & Co. Ltd., 1925.

Henderson, Joseph L. & Oakes, Maud. *The Wisdom of the Serpent: The Myths of Death, Rebirth and Resurrection*. New York: George Braziller, 1963.

Herdt, Gilbert H. (Editor). *Rituals of Manhood: Male Initiation in Papua New Guinea*. Intr. by Roger M. Keesing. Berkeley CA: University of California Press, 1982. Authors include the editor.

Herskovits, Melville Jean: see Leach, Maria.

Hickmann, Hans: see Reese, Gustave.

Higgins, Godfrey. *Anacalypsis: An Attempt to Draw Aside the Veil of the Saitic Isis; or an Inquiry into the Origin of Languages, Nations and Religions* Orig. 1836; New Hyde Park NY: University Books (reprint), 1965.

Hinnells, John R. (Editor). *A Handbook of Living Religions*. New York: Viking Penguin Inc., 1984. Includes chapters on "Zoroastrianism" by Mary Boyce, "Sikhism" by W. Owen Cole, and "Islam" by Alfred T. Welch.

Hollander, John. *The Untuning of the Sky: Ideas of Music in English Poetry, 1500-1700*. Princeton NJ: Princeton University Press, 1961.

Holmberg, Uno. *The Mythology of All Races, Vol. 4: Finno-Ugric, Siberian.* Series Ed.: John Arnott MacCulloch. New York: Marshall Jones Co., c.1915; New York: Cooper Square Publishers Inc. (reprint), 1964.

Holroyde, Peggy. *The Music of India.* Fwd. by Ravi Shankar. New York: Praeger Publishers, Inc., 1972.

Honey, James A. *South-African Folk-Tales.* The Baker & Taylor Co., 1910; New York: Negro Universities Press (reprint), 1969.

Horizon Magazine, Editors of. *The Horizon Book of Lost Worlds.* Ed. by Marshall B. Davidson. New York: The American Heritage Publishing Company, 1962.

Howard, James H.: see Cavendish, Richard.

Htin Aung, Maung (Collected & Translated by). *Burmese Monk's Tales.* New York: Columbia University Press, 1960.

Huart, Clément: see Hackin, J.

Hughes, Langston & Bontemps, Arna (Editors). *The Book of Negro Folklore.* New York: Dodd, Mead & Company, 1966.

Hummel, David. *The Collector's Guide to the American Musical Theatre.* Metuchen NJ: The Scarecrow Press (2v), 1984.

Hyde, Douglas: see Yeats, William Butler.

Idelsohn, Abraham Zvi. *Jewish Music in Its Historical Development.* 1929; New York: Shocken Books (reprint), 1967.

Inayat Khan, Pir Vilayat. *The Message in Our Time: The Life and Teaching of the Sufi Master Pir-O-Murshid Inayat Khan.* San Francisco: Harper & Row, 1979.

In-Sob, Zong (Collected, Translated & Introduced by). *Folk Tales from Korea.* New York: The Grove Press, 1953.

Irwin, Eleanor: see Warden, John.

Ivanits, Linda J. *Russian Folk Belief.* Fwd by Felix J. Olinas; illus. by Sophie Schiller. Armonk NY: M. E. Sharpe, Inc., 1989.

Jackson, Irene V. (Editor). *More than Drumming: Essays on African and Afro-Latin American Music and Musicians.* Prepared under the auspices of the Center for Ethnic Music, Howard University. Westport CT: Greenwood Press, 1985. Authors include Jacqueline Cogdell DjeDje, Daphne D. Harrison, Bennetta Jules-Rosette, Robert W. Nichols.

James, Grace. *Green Willow and Other Japanese Fairy Tales.* Early 1900s; New York: Crown Publishers (Avenel Books)(reprint), 1987.

James, William. *The Varieties of Religious Experience: A Study in Human Nature. Being the Gifford Lectures on Natural Religion Delivered at Edinburgh in 1901-1902.* Orig. 1902, 1929; New York: Random House (The Modern Library).

Jones, Charles C., Jr. *Negro Myths from the Georgia Coast: Told in the Vernacular.* Boston: Houghton, Mifflin & Company, 1888.

Jules-Rosette, Bennetta: see Jackson, Irene V.

Kalevala: The Land of Heroes. Transl. by W.F. Kirby. Intr. by J.B. Grundy. Everyman's Library No.260. London: J.M. Dent & Sons Ltd. (2v), 1907; New York: E.P. Dutton (2v), 1970.

Kaplan, Joanna: see Cavendish, Richard.

Kaufmann, Walter. *Musical References in the Chinese Classics*. Detroit: Information Coordinators, Inc., 1976.

Keesing, Roger M.: see Herdt, Gilbert H.

Keil, Charles. *Tiv Song*. Chicago: The University of Chicago Press, 1979.

Keith, Arthur Berriedale [Indian]. *The Mythology of All Races, Vol. 6: Indian*. Series Ed.: John Arnott MacCulloch. New York: Marshall Jones Co., 1917; New York: Cooper Square Publishers Inc. (reprint), 1964.

Keith, Arthur Berriedale. *The Religion and Philosophy of the Veda and Upanishads*. Delhi: Motilal Banarsidass, Publishers & Booksellers (2 volumes), 1925 (reprinted 1970, 1976); by arrangement with the Harvard University Press.

Kennedy, Patrick (Collected & Narrated by). *Legendary Fictions of the Irish Celts*. 1866; New York: Benjamin Blom, Inc. (reprint), 1969.

Kirk, G.S. [Myth]. *Myth: Its Meaning and Functions in Ancient and Other Cultures*. Cambridge: Cambridge University Press, 1970.

Kirk, G.S. *The Nature of Greek Myths*. New York: Viking Penguin, 1974.

Kirk, James A. *Stories of the Hindus: An Introduction Through Texts and Interpretation*. New York: The Macmillan Company, 1972.

Kishibe, Shigeo: see Sadie, Stanley.

Kolinski, Mieczyslaw: see Sadie, Stanley.

Kravitz, David. *Who's Who in Greek and Roman Mythology*. New York: Clarkson N. Potter, Inc., Publishers, 1975.

Krokover, Rosalyn. *The New Borzoi Book of Ballets*. New York: Alfred A. Knopf, 1956.

Kurath, Gertrude Prokosch: see Leach, Maria; Sadie, Stanley.

Lang, Andrew. *Custom and Myth*. London, 1885; New York: AMS Press, Inc. (reprint), 1968.

Lang, Andrew [Green]. *Green Fairy Book*, ed. by Brian Alderson. Illus. by Antony Maitland. Longmans, Green & Company Ltd., 1892; New York: The Viking Press, 1978.

Langdon, E. Jean: see Browman, David L. & Schwarz, Ronald A.

Lange, Roderyk. *The Nature of Dance: An Anthropological Perspective*. New York: International Publications Service, 1976.

Larousse Encyclopedia of Mythology. General editor, Felix Guirand; trans. by Richard Aldington & Delano Ames, rev. by a panel of editorial advisors; intr. by Robert Graves. New York: Prometheus Press, 1960. Authors include G. Alexinsky, Felix Guirand, P. Masson-Oursel, Louise Morin, E. Tonnelat.

Leach, Maria (Editor). *Funk & Wagnalls Standard Dictionary of Folklore, Mythology and Legend*. Jerome Fried, Associate Editor. New York: Funk & Wagnalls, 1972. Authors include Jonas Balys, Theresa C. Brakeley, Theodor H. Gaster, Mamie Harmon, Melville Jean Herskovits, Gertrude Prokosch Kurath, Alfred Métraux, John Leon Mish, Erminie W. Voegelin.

Lehman, Shmul: see Ausubel, Nathan.

Leland, Charles G. *The Algonquin Legends of New England, or Myths and Folk Lore of the Micmac, Passamaquoddy, and Penobscot Tribes*. Boston: Houghton, Mifflin & Co., 1884; Detroit: Singing Tree Press (reprint), 1968.

Lévi-Strauss, Claude. *The Naked Man (Introduction to a Science of Mythology: 4)*. Transl. by John & Doreen Weightman. New York: Harper & Row, Publishers, 1981.

Lewis, Richard. *All of You Was Singing*. Illus. by Ed Young. New York: Atheneum Publishers, 1991.

Lieberman, Fredric: see Hart, Mickey.

Life, The Editors of. *The Life Treasury of American Folklore*. New York: Time Inc., 1961.

Loewenberg, Alfred. *Annals of Opera: 1597-1940, 3rd Ed*. Totowa NY: Rowman & Littlefield, 1978.

Lüthi, Max. *The Fairytale as Art Form and Portrait of Man* (1975). Transl. by Jon Erickson. Bloomington: Indiana University Press, 1984.

MacCulloch, John Arnott [Celtic]. *The Mythology of All Races, Vol. 3: Celtic*. Series Ed.: John Arnott MacCulloch. New York: Marshall Jones Co., 1918; New York: Cooper Square Publishers Inc. (reprint), 1964.

MacCulloch, John Arnott [Eddic]. *The Mythology of All Races, Vol. 2: Eddic*. Series Ed.: John Arnott MacCulloch. 1930; New York: Cooper Square Publishers Inc. (reprint), 1964.

MacCulloch, John Arnott [Medieval]. *Medieval Faith and Fable*. 1932.

Máchal, Jan. *The Mythology of All Races, Vol. 3: Slavic*. Series Ed.: John Arnott MacCulloch. New York: Marshall Jones Co., 1918; New York: Cooper Square Publishers Inc. (reprint), 1964.

Macmillan, Cyrus: see Clarkson, Atelia.

Malm, William P. *Japanese Music and Musical Instruments*. Rutland VT: Charles E. Tuttle Company, 1959.

Manguel, Alberto & Guadalupi, Gianni. *The Dictionary of Imaginary Places, Expanded Ed*. San Diego/New York: Harcourt Brace Jovanovich, 1987.

Maple, Erich: see Cavendish, Richard.

Marchand, James W. "The Old Icelandic Allegory of the Church Modes", in *The Musical Quarterly*, LXI/4 (G. Schirmer, 1975).

Marchal, C. -H.: see Hackin, J.

Maspero, Henri: see Hackin, J.

Massey, Reginald & Massey, Jamila. *The Music of India*. Fwd. by Ravi Shankar. New York: Crescendo Publishing, 1977.

Masson-Oursel, P.: see *Larousse Encyclopedia of Mythology*.

Matthews, John & Matthews, Caitlín. *The Aquarian Guide to British and Irish Mythology*. Wellingborough, Northamptonshire (England): The Aquarian Press (Thorsons Publishing Group), 1988.

McDonagh, Don. *The Complete Guide to Modern Dance*. Garden City NY: Doubleday & Company, Inc., 1976.

McKinnon, James W.: see Sadie, Stanley.

Mehta, R. C. (Editor). *Music and Mythology: A Collection of Essays*. Bombay & Baroda: Indian Musicological Society, 1989. Includes chapters by Lewis Rowell, R. Sathyanarayana.

Mélançon, Claude. *Indian Legends of Canada*. Transl. by David Ellis. Toronto: Gage Publishing Ltd., 1974.

Merriam, Alan P. *The Anthropology of Music*. Evanston: Northwestern University Press, 1964.

Metayer, Maurice (Editor & Translator). *Tales from the Igloo*. Illus. by Agnes Nanogak. New York: St. Martin's Press, 1972.

Métraux, Alfred: see Leach, Maria.

Meyer-Baer, Kathi. *Music of the Spheres and the Dance of Death: Studies in Musical Iconology*. Princeton NJ: Princeton University Press, 1971.

Mezzanote, Riccardo (Editor-in-Chief) [Ballet]. *The Simon & Schuster Book of the Ballet: A Complete Reference Guide—1581 to the Present*. Transl. by Olive Ordish. New York: Simon & Schuster, 1979.

Mezzanote, Riccardo (Editor-in-chief) [Opera]. *The Simon & Schuster Book of the Opera*. Transl. by Catherine Atthill & others. New York: Simon & Schuster, 1977.

Michaelides, Solon. *The Music of Ancient Greece: An Encyclopedia*. London: Faber & Faber Ltd, 1978.

Milton, John. *Paradise Lost*. The World's Great Classics. Danbury CT: Grolier Enterprises Corp., 1978.

Ming-Yüeh, Liang: see Sadie, Stanley.

Mish, John Leon: see Leach, Maria.

Morin, Louise: see *Larousse Encyclopedia of Mythology*.

Müller, W. Max. *The Mythology of All Races, Vol. 12: Egyptian*. Series Ed.: John Arnott MacCulloch. New York: Marshall Jones Co., 1918; New York: Cooper Square Publishers Inc. (reprint), 1964.

Mutwa, Vusamazulu Credo. *Indaba My Children: African Tribal History, Legends, Customs and Religious Beliefs*. London: Kahn & Averill, 1985.

Myerhoff, Barbara G. *Peyote Hunt: The Sacred Journey of the Huichol Indians*. Ithaca NY: Cornell University Press, 1974.

Nagishkin, Dmitri. *Folktales of the Amur: Stories from the Russian Far East.* Transl. by Emily Lehrman; illus. by Gennady Pavlishin. New York: Harry N. Abrams, Publishers, 1980.

Nettl, Bruno: see Sadie, Stanley.

Neubauer, Eckhard: see Sadie, Stanley.

Neuman, Daniel M. *The Life of Music in North India: The Organization of an Artistic Tradition.* Detroit: Wayne State University Press, 1980.

Nichols, Robert W.: see Jackson, Irene V.

Nicholson, Irene. *Mexican and Central American Mythology,* New Rev. Ed. Library of the World's Myths and Legends. 1983; New York: Peter Betrick Books, 1985.

Norman, Howard (Selected & Edited by). *Northern Tales: Traditional Stories of Eskimo and Indian Peoples.* Pantheon Fairy Tale and Folklore Library. New York: Pantheon Books, 1990.

Norton, Dan S. & Rushton, Peters. *Classical Myths in English Literature.* New York: Holt, Rinehart & Winston, Inc., 1952.

Noy, Dov (Compilor, with Introduction & Notes by). *Moroccan Jewish Folktales.* Foreword by Raphael Patai. New York: Herzl Press, 1966.

Nulman, Macy. *Concise Encyclopedia of Jewish Music.* New York: McGraw-Hill Book Company, 1975.

Oakes, Maud: see Henderson, Joseph L.

O'Connell, Charles. *The Victor Book of Overtures, Tone Poems and Other Orchestral Works.* New York: Simon & Schuster, 1950.

O'Flaherty, Wendy Doniger. *Hindu Myths: A Sourcebook Translated from the Sanskrit, with an Introduction [etc. by the editor/translator].* Harmondsworth, Middlesex (England): Penguin Books Ltd., 1975.

O'Flaherty, Wendy Doniger: see Cavendish, Richard.

Ornstein, Ruby: see Sadie, Stanley.

Orrey, Leslie (Editor). *The Encyclopedia of Opera.* New York: Charles Scribner's Sons, 1976.

Ortiz, Alfonso: see Erdoes, Richard

O'Sullivan, Sean. *Legends from Ireland.* Drawings by John Skelton. Totowa NJ: Rowman & Littlefield, 1977.

Palmer, Roy. *The Folklore of Warwickshire.* The Folklore of the British Isles, ed. by Venetia J. Newall. Totowa NJ: Rowman & Littlefield, 1976.

Paredes, Américo (Editor & Translator). *Folktales of Mexico.* Folktales of the World; Richard M. Dorson, Gen. Ed. Chicago: The University of Chicago Press, 1970.

Peck, Harry Thurston (Editor). *Harper's Dictionary of Classical Literature and Antiquities.* Orig. 1897 (2nd Edition); New York: Cooper Square Publishers, 1963.

Petrovic, Radmila: see Sadie, Stanley.

Picard, Barbara Leonie (Retold by). *Celtic Tales: Legends of Tall Warriors and Old Enchantments.* London: Edmund Ward, 1964.

Piggott, Francis. *The Music and Musical Instruments of Japan, 2nd Edition.* Orig. 1909; New York: Da Capo Press, 1971.

Piggott, Juliet [Japanese]. *Japanese Mythology,* New Rev. Ed. Library of the World's Myths and Legends. New York: Peter Bedrick Books, 1983.

Poignant, Roslyn. *Oceanic Mythology: The Myths of Polynesia, Micronesia, Melanesia, Australia.* London: The Hamlyn Publishing Group Ltd., 1967.

Polin, Claire C. J. *Music of the Ancient Near East.* Orig. 1954; Westport CT: Greenwood Press, 1974.

Porteous, Alexander. *Forest Folklore, Mythology, and Romance.* London: George Allen & Unwin Ltd., 1928.

Portnoy, Julius. *Music in the Life of Man.* New York: Holt, Rinehart & Winston, 1963.

Price, Percival. *Bells and Man.* Oxford: Oxford University Press, 1983.

Ranke, Kurt (Editor). *Folktales of Germany.* Transl. by Lotte Baumann. Folktales of the World; Richard M. Dorson, Gen. Ed. Chicago: The University of Chicago Press, 1966.

Reed, Alexander Wyclif. *Myths and Legends of Australia.* Orig. 1965; New York: Taplinger Publishing Company, 1973.

Rees, Alwyn & Rees, Brinley. *Celtic Heritage: Ancient Tradition in Ireland and Wales.* New York: Grove Press, 1961.

Rees, Brinley: see Rees, Alwyn.

Reese, Gustave. *Music in the Middle Ages, with an Introduction on the Music of Ancient Times.* New York: W.W. Norton & Company, 1940.

Reese, Gustave & Brandel, Rose (Editors). *The Commonwealth of Music: Writings on Music in History, Art, and Culture in Honor of Curt Sachs.* New York: The Free Press, 1965. Authors include Hans Hickmann.

Reichel-Dolmatoff, Gerardo. *Amazonian Cosmos: The Sexual and Relgigious Symbolism of the Tukano Indians.* Chicago: University of Chicago Press, 1971.

Rice, Edward. *Eastern Definitions: A Short Encyclopedia of Religions of the Orient.* Garden City NY: Doubleday & Company, 1978.

Robertson, Alec & Stevens, Denis (Editors). *The Pelican History of Music. I: Ancient Forms to Polyphony.* New York: Penguin Books, 1960. Authors include Peter Crossley-Holland, Alex Robertson.

Robertson, R. Macdonald (gathered orally by). *Selected Highland Folk Tales.* Ed. by Jeremy Bruce-Watt. Edinburgh: Oliver & Boyd, 1961.

Rothmüller, Aron Marko. *The Music of the Jews: An Historical Appreciation, New & Revised Edition.* Orig. 1967; Cranbury NJ: A. S. Barnes & Company, Inc., 1975.

Rouget, Gilbert. *Music and Trance: A Theory of the Relations Between Music and Possession* (1980). Transl. & rev. by Brunhilde Biebuyck & the author. Chicago: University of Chicago Press, 1985.

Rowell, Lewis: see Mehta, R. C.

Rowling, Marjorie. *The Folklore of the Lake District.* The Folklore of the British Isles, ed. by Venetia J. Newall. Totowa NJ: Rowman & Littlefield, 1976.

Rubinstein, Michael. *Music to My Ear: Reflections on Music and Digressions on Metaphysics.* London: Quartet Books, 1985.

Rushton, Peters: see Norton, Dan S.

Rycroft, David K.: see Sadie, Stanley

Sachs, Curt [Instruments]. *The History of Musical Instruments.* New York: W. W. Norton & Company, Inc., 1940.

Sachs, Curt [Ancient World]. *The Rise of Music in the Ancient World: East and West.* New York: W.W. Norton & Company, Inc., 1943.

Sachs, Curt [Dance]. *World History of the Dance.* Transl. by Bessie Schönberg. New York: W.W. Norton & Company, Inc., 1937.

Sadie, Stanley (Editor). *The New Grove Dictionary of Music and Musicians.* London: Macmillan Publishers Ltd. (20 volumes), 1980. Authors include Robert Anderson, Warner Anderson, Doreen Binnington, Peter Crossley-Holland, Sue Carole De Vale, Aloys Fleischmann, Robert Garfias, Richard Haefer, Christian Hannick, Shigeo Kishibe, Mieczyslaw Kolinski, Gertrude Prokosch Kurath, James W. McKinnon, Liang Ming-Yüeh, Bruno Nettl, Eckhard Neubauer, Ruby Ornstein, Radmila Petrovic, David K. Rycroft, Robert Simon, Wilhelm Stauder, Robert Stevenson, Kazuyuki Tanimoto, J.M. Thomson, D.B. Waterhouse, Eric Werner.

Santillana, Giorgio de & Dechend, Hertha von. *Hamlet's Mill: An Essay on Myth and the Frame of Time.* Boston: Gambit, Inc., 1969.

Sathyanarayana, R.: see Mehta, R. C.

Schafer, R. Murray. *The Tuning of the World.* Toronto: McClelland & Stewart Ltd., 1977.

Schneider, Marius: see Wellesz, Egon.

Schwartz, Howard (Selected & Retold by). *Elijah's Violin and Other Jewish Fairy Tales.* New York: Harper & Row, Publishers, Inc./The Jewish Publication Society of America, 1983.

Schwartz, Howard (Selected & Retold by)[Miriam]. *Miriam's Tambourine: Jewish Folktales from Around the World.* Foreword by Dov Noy; illus. by Lloyd Bloom. New York: Seth Press, 1986.

Schwarz, Ronald A.: see Browman, David L.

Scott, James George. *The Mythology of All Races, Vol. 12: Indo-Chinese.* Series Ed.: John Arnott MacCulloch. New York: Marshall Jones Co., 1918; New York: Cooper Square Publishers Inc. (reprint), 1964.

Sendrey, Alfred. *Music in Ancient Israel.* New York: Philosophical Library, 1969.

Sharpe, Eric J.: see Cavendish, Richard.

Sian-tek, Lim. *Folk Tales from China.* Illus. by William Arthur Smith. New York: The John Day Co., 1944.

Simon, Henry W. *The Victor Book of the Opera*, 13th Ed. New York: Simon & Schuster, 1968.

Simon, Robert: see Sadie, Stanley.

Simpson, Jacqueline [European]. *European Mythology*. New York: Peter Bedrick Books (reprint), 1987.

Simpson, Jacqueline. *Icelandic Folktales and Legends*. Berkely: University of California Press, 1972.

Siniscalchi, Marina Maymone. "Myth and Esoterism of the Sacred Grove", in *Italian Journal* (Vol V No. 5/6), 1991.

Skinner, Charles M. [Myths and Legends]. *Myths and Legends of Our Own Land*. Philadelphia: J.B. Lippincott & Company, 1896.

Skinner, Elliott P. (Editor). *Peoples and Cultures of Africa*. Garden City, New York: The American Museum of Natural History/The Doubleday-Natural History Press, 1973. Authors include M.G. Smith.

Smith, M.G.: see Skinner, Elliott P.

Smith, Ruth (Editor) [Tree of Life]. *The Tree of Life: Selections from the Literature of the World's Religions*. Intr. by Robert O.. Ballou, illus. by Boris Artzybasheff. New York: The Viking Press, 1952.

Smither, Howard E. *A History of the Oratorio*. Chapel Hill: The University of North Carolina Press (2v), 1977.

Sonneborn, D. A.: see Hart, Mickey.

Spence, Lewis. *Myth and Ritual in Dance, Game, and Rhyme*. London: Watts & Company, 1947.

Spence, Lewis [North American]. *The Myths of the North American Indians*. London: George G. Harrap & Co., Ltd., 1914; New York: Kraus Reprint Co., 1972.

Spence, Lewis [Occultism]. *An Encyclopedia of Occultism: A Compendium of Information on the Occult Sciences, Occult Personalities, Psychic Science, Magic, Demonology, Spiritism, Mysticism and Metaphysics*. 1920; Secaucus NJ: University Books, 1960.

Sproul, Barbara C. *Primal Myths: Creating the World*. New York: Harper & Row, Publishers, 1979.

Stauder, Wilhelm: see Sadie, Stanley.

Steinberg, Cobbett (Editor). *The Dance Anthology*. New York: The New American Library, 1963. Incl. selections from Havelock Ellis, *The Dance of Life* (Boston: Houghton Mifflin, 1923) and Arthur Symons, *Studies in Seven Arts* (New York: E.P. Dutton, 1907).

Stevens, Denis: see Robertson, Alec.

Stevenson, Robert: see Sadie, Stanley.

Strunk, Oliver (Editor). *Source Readings in Music History: From Classical Antiquity through the Romantic Era*. New York: W.W. Norton & Company, 1950. Authors include Aristotle, Athenaeus, St. Basil, Cassiodorus, St. John Chrysostom.

Stutley, Margaret & Stutley, James. *Harper's Dictionary of Hinduism: Its Mythology, Folklore, Philosophy, Literature, and History*. New York: Harper & Row, Publishers, 1977.

Symons, Arthur: see Steinberg, Cobbett.

Takiguchi, Susumu: see Cavendish, Richard.

Tanimoto, Kazuyuki: see Sadie, Stanley.

Tedlock, Dennis (Translated with Commentary). *Popol Vuh: The Definitive Edition of the Mayan Book of the Dawn of Life and the Glories of Gods and Kings*. New York: Simon & Schuster, 1985.

Terry, Walter. *Ballet Guide*. New York: Dodd, Mead & Company, 1976.

Thomson, J.M.: see Sadie, Stanley.

Thompson, J. Eric S. [History/Religion]. *Maya History and Religion*. Norman: University of Oklahoma Press, 1970.

Thompson, J. Eric S. [Maya Civilization]. *The Rise and Fall of Maya Civilization*. Norman: University of Oklahoma Press, 1954.

Thompson, Stith [Motif-Index]. *Motif-Index of Folk-Literature: A Classification of Narrative Elements in Folktales, Ballads, Myths, Fables, Mediæval Romances, Exempla, Fabliaux, Jest-Books and Local Legends*, Rev. & Enl. Ed. Bloomington: Indiana University Press (6 volumes), 1955.

Thompson, Stith [Favorite Folktales]. *One Hundred Favorite Folktales*. Bloomington: Indiana University Press, 1968.

Thompson, Stith: see Aarne, Antti.

Tong, Diane. *Gypsy Folktales*. New York/San Diego CA: Harcourt Brace Jovanovich, Publishers, 1989.

Tonnelat, E.: see *Larousse Encyclopedia of Mythology*.

Tyler, Hamilton A. *Pueblo Gods and Myths*. Norman: University of Oklahoma Press, 1964.

Tyler, Royall (Selected, Edited & Translated by). *Japanese Tales*. Pantheon Fairy Tale and Folklore Library. New York: Pantheon Books, 1987.

Urlin, Ethel L. *Festivals, Holy Days, and Saints' Days: A Study in Origins and Survivals in Church Ceremonies and Secular Customs*. London: Simpkin, Marshall, Hamilton, Kent & Co., Ltd., 1915; Ann Arbor MI: Gryphon Books (reprint), 1971.

Van Gulik, R.H. *The Lore of the Chinese Lute: An Essay in the Ideology of the* Ch'in, New Edition. Tokyo: Sophia University / Rutland VT: The Charles E. Tuttle Company, 1969.

Verrill, A. Hyatt. *Strange Customs, Manners and Beliefs*. New York: L.C. Page & Company; New York:Farrar, Straus & Cudahy, Inc., 1946.

Viladesau, Richard. "Music as an Approach to God: A Theology of Aesthetic Experience", *The Catholic World*, January/February 1989.

Villas Boas, Claudio: see Villas Boas, Orlando.

Villas Boas, Orlando & Villas Boas, Claudio. *Xingu: The Indians, Their Myths* (1970), transl. by Susana Hertelendy Rudge. Drawings by Wacupiá. Fwd & ed. by Kenneth S. Brecher. New York: Farrar, Straus & Giroux, 1973.

Voegelin, Erminie W.: see Leach, Maria.

Wade, Bonnie C. *Music in India: The Classical Traditions*. Englewood Cliffs NJ: Prentice-Hall, Inc., 1979.

Walker, Barbara G. *The Woman's Encyclopedia of Myths and Secrets*. New York: Harper & Row, Publishers, 1983.

Wallis, Wilson D. *Religion in Primitive Society*. New York: F. S. Crofts & Co., 1939.

Warden, John (Editor). *Orpheus: The Metamorphoses of a Myth*. Toronto: University of Toronto Press, 1982. Includes essay by Eleanor Irwin, "The Songs of Orpheus and the New Song of Christ".

Waterhouse, D. B.: see Sadie, Stanley.

Weaver, Muriel Porter. *The Aztecs, Maya, and Their Predecessors: Archaeology of Mesoamerica*. New York: Seminar Press Inc., 1972.

Weiss, Piero (Editor). *Letters of Composers Through Six Centuries*. Philadelphia: Chilton Book Company, 1967.

Welch, Alfred T.: see Hinnells, John R.

Wellesz, Egon (Editor). *The New Oxford History of Music. Volume I: Ancient and Oriental Music*. New York: Oxford University Press, 1957. Authors include Marius Schneider.

Werner, Alice [African]. *The Mythology of All Races, Vol. 7: African*. Series Ed.: John Arnott MacCulloch. New York: Marshall Jones Co., 1925; New York: Cooper Square Publishers Inc. (reprint), 1964.

Werner, E.T.C. [China]. *Myths and Legends of China*. Singapore: Graham Brash (Pte) Ltd, 1984.

Werner, Eric: see Sadie, Stanley.

White, Emmons E. *Appreciating India's Music: An Introduction, with an Emphasis on the Music of South India*. Boston: Crescendo Publishing Company, 1971.

Williams, C.A.S. *Outlines of Chinese Symbolism and Art Motives, 3rd Rev. Ed.* Orig. 3rd Rev. Ed., 1941; Rutland VT: Charles E. Tuttle Company (reprint), 1974.

Willoughby, W. C. *The Soul of the Bantu: A Sympathetic Study of the Magico-Religious Practices and Beliefs of the Bantu Tribes of Africa*. Garden City NY: Doubleday, Doran & Co., 1928.

Winne, Jane Lathrop: see Handy, E.S. Craighill.

Wong, Isabel: see Eliade, Mircea.

Yeats, William Bulter (Editor). *Irish Fairy and Folk Tales*. New York: The Modern Library. Includes contributions by T. Crofton Croker ("The Legend of Knockgrafton") and Douglas Hyde ("The Piper and the Puca").

Zimmer, Heinrich. *Myths and Symbols in Indian Art and Civilization*, ed. by Joseph Campbell. Princeton NJ: Princeton University Press, 1946.

Zimmer, Heinrich [Philosophies]. *Philosophies of India,* ed. by Joseph Campbell. Bollingen Series XXVI. Princeton NJ: Princeton University Press, 1951.

Zimmerman, J.E. *Dictionary of Classical Mythology.* New York: Harper & Row, Publishers, 1964.

Zuckerkandl, Victor. *Sound and Symbol.* Bolingen Series XLIV. Volume 1: *Music and the External World.* Transl. by Willard R. Trask. New York: Pantheon Books, 1956. Volume 2: *Man the Musician.* Transl. by Norbert Guterman. Princeton NJ: Princeton University Press, 1973.

GENERAL INDEX TO VOLS. I & II

Note: Many entries are cross-referenced. For example, entries for the Greek god APOLLO are listed under "Apollo", "Gods" and "Greece" — with additional trails leading to "Helios", "Phoebus" and "Sun". Page numbers in **bold face type** indicate featured articles.

GODS, SPIRITS, ETC. (continued)

Hell (Greek), 793

Hephaestus (Greek)(see also VULCAN, 60, 64, 105, 180, 467

Hera (Here)(Greek)(see also JUNO), 69, 363, 422, 688, 791, 809, 1310

Heracles (Herakles)(Greek hero)(see also HERCULES): see main entry

Hercules (Roman)(see also HERACLES): see main entry

Here: see Hera

Hermes (Greek)(see also MERCURY): see main entry

Hermes Trismegistus)(Egyptian/Greek), 363, 847ff.

Hestia (Greek), 688

Heveidd Hen (Celtic), 126

Hiiaka-i-ka-pali-o-Pele (Hiiaka, Pele)(Hawaiian) — Pele (Hawaiian), 343ff.

Hiiaka-i-ka-pali-o-Pele (Hiiaka, Pele) (Hawaiian) — Pele-i-ke-ahi, 356

Hiiaka-i-ka-pali-o-Pele (Hiiaka, Pele)(Hawaiian), 344, 348, 352

Hiisi (Finno-Ugric), 256

Himalaya (Hindu), 702

Hina (Polynesian), 346, 349

Hiriadeva (Hindu bell-god), 965

Ho Hsien-ku (Chinese), 214,215

Hoa-tabu-i-tera'i (Polynesian), 346

Horagalles (Lappish), 499

Horus (Orus)(Egyptian), 101, 212, 841, 1017

Hotherus (Hod)(Eddic), 207-08

Hsi Wang Mu (Chinese), 215

Hsien (Chinese spirit), 438

Huang-ti (Chinese), 1012

Huehuecoyotl (Aztec), 749

Huehueteotl (Aztec), 747

Huitzilopochtli (Aztec), 74, 746-47, 752-53, 946

Huixtocihuatl (Aztec), 752

Huldra (Eddic nymph), 206

Hunahpu (Mayan), 533ff.

Huruing Wuhti (Hopi spirit), 678-79

Hypate (Greek Muse), 60

GODS, SPIRITS, ETC., (continued)

Iambe (Greek), 373

Ibeji (African), 105

Ifa (African), 105

Ihy (Egyptian), 208, 1017

Ilhuicamina (Aztec), 71

Ilmatar (Finno-Ugric), 1028

Inanna (Babylonian/Sumerian), 419, 766, 1040-41

Indra (Hindu god): see main entry

Indrani (Hindu), 386

Innus (Roman), 644

Io (Greek), 221, 360

Ioulo (Demeter)(Greek), 416

Ira (Hindu spirit), 324

Iringelo (Eskimo spirit), 217

Iris (Greek), 730

Ishtar (Babylonian/Assyrian): see main entry

Isis (Egyptian): see main entry

Israfil (Arabian), 62

Itsukushima in Aki, 698

Izanagi (Japanese), 437

Jakui (Brazilian water spirit), 412, 1175

Jambhala (Tibetan), 1329

Jehovah: see main entry

Jenniyah (demon), 474

Jesus Christ (Christian): see main entry

Messiah, 21

Jibril (Arabian), 62

Jinns (Arabian/Indian spirits), 246, 381,382

Jizo-bosatsu (Japanese Buddhist spirit being), 1209-10

Judy (Macedonian spirits), 244

Jumala (Finnish), 477, 481

Juno (Iuno)(Roman)(see also HERA), 508, 542, 538, 748, 848

Jupiter (Iupiter, Jove): see main entry (see also ZEUS)

Jupiter Capitolinus, 612

Jurupari (Yurupari) (Brazilian spirits), 411-14, 1173-74

Kaang (African), 912

Kachimana (Makiratare plant spirit), 1161

Kadaklan (Tinguian), 1272

Kai Yum (Mayan), 531

Kali (Hindu), 80, 102, 356, 701, 709, 1120, 1123

Kallikantzaroi (Greek), 81

GODS, SPIRITS, ETC. (continued)

Kama (Hindu), 705

Kamadhenu (Hindu), 780

Kamisama (Shinto spirits), 427

Kanaloa (Polynesian), 349-52

Kane (Polynesian/Hawaiian), 347, 349-52

Kangaroo-god, 657

Kannon (Buddhist), 428,429

Karttikeya (Hindu), 325

Kasyapa (Hindu), 323

Katajalina (Australian/New Guinea spirit), 108, 114

Katches (Armenian spirits), 241-242

Kesava (Hindu), 1131

Khambageu (African), 48

Kin-kang-li-shi (Vajrabalin)(Buddhist), 974

Kinnaras (Kimpurushas) (Hindu heavenly musicians), 324, **491-92**

Kod (primitive spirit ancestor), 664

Kojin (Japanese), 432

Komu-honua (Polynesian), 351

Kratu (Hindu spirit), 325

Krcanu (Hindu), 327

Krishna (Hindu): see main entry

Ksitigarbha (Buddhist bodhisattva), 1209

Ku (Polynesian), 349-51

K'uei (Chung K'uei, Kuei Hsing)(Chinese mythical being), 1012-16

Kullervo (Finno-Ugric), 255

Kumarbi (Babylonian/Assyrian), 420-21

Kuretes (Curetes)(Greek demigods), 98, **497**, 614, 648, 689, 811, 813-14, 854

Kwannon (Japanese), 440

Kwewele (Zuni), 1160

La'a (Polynesian), 353-54

La'a-mai-kahiki (Polynesian), 350

Lady of Beasts (Cretan), 822

Laka (Polynesian/Hawaiian), 347, 349-51, 353, 356

Laka-kane (Hawaiian), 345

Lakshmi (Hindu), 774, 942, 943, 1101

Lalo-honua (Polynesian), 351

Lamia (Egyptian), 612

Lan Ts'ai-ho (Chinese Immortal), 214-15, 265

Lar (Roman), 646

Tsonga people: see Thonga people

Tsunukwa (North American Indian spirit), 390

Tsuri daiko (Japanese drum), 189, 431

Tsuzumi (Japanese drum), 194

Tu-huru-huru, 521

Tu-kane-kai, 355

Tuareg people (African), 26

Tuatha dé Danann (Danaan)(Celtic gods), 129-30, 223, 231, 235, 509ff., 762, 1084-85, 1208-09

Tuba, 573, 612

Tubae: see Trumpet

Tubal (Tubal [Tuval] Cain)(Biblical), 467, 474, 617, 697

Tubu' (Arabian modes), 64

Tubuan, 1215

Tucano people, 264, 413

Tudor period, 123

Tudors, 1081

Tufara-pai-rai,346

Tufara-painu'u, 346

Tugeri (Kaya-Kaya) people, 115

Tukano people, 1164, 1173

Tul Tuinde (place), 1205

Tula (place), 750

Tullus Hostilius, 692

Tumbuka people, 915

Tumbuka society, 991

Tumbura, 1122

TUMBURU (Viradha)(Hindu deity), 323-24, 491, 778, 1122-23, 1132
    Tumburu gandharva, 1123

Tunava (Hindu flute?), 778

Tungu people, 714

Tungus people, 999, 1001

Tuning of the World, The (Schafer), 1045-48, 1356

Tunisia, 839

Tunyuam caves, 1095

Tuonela, 478ff.

Tuonela, swan of, 478

Tuoni, 478

Tupi Indians, 774

Tupinamba people, 686, 1003

Turco-Tatar language, 715

Turipati (place), 966

Turkestan (place), 164, 1339

Turkey (bird), 1145ff.

Turkey (place), 167, 424, 807, 830, 992, 1320

Turkic tribes, 1001

Turndun (Australian bull-roarer), 109

Turner, 1035, 1198

Turner, Victor, The Forest of Symbols, 25

Turney-High, 397

Turpin, Bishop, 1287

Turtle, 686, 1164, 1174

Turtle shell, 1167

Turville-Petre, E. O. G., Myth and Religion of the North, 187, 357, 370

Tusayan people, 109

Tuscan dancers, 853

Tuscany, 179

Tuscany, Duke of, 1081

Tusculum (place), 1220

Tut-ankh-amen, 101

Tuttle Co., Charles E., 1352, 1358-59

Tuulikki, 479

Tuval Cain: see Tubal Cain

Tuvish, 178

Tuyuca people, 713

Twa Sisters, The, 341, 720

Twanyirika (Australian spirit), 114

Twelfth Night, 90

Twelfth Night (Shakespeare), 340

Twinleaf (flute), 447

Two Bells, The, 820

Two Fiddlers, The, 250-55

Two Fiddlers, The (Brown), 1343

Tyack, G. S., A Book About Bells, 87

Tyagara, Saint and Sinner (Raghavan), 380

Tyagaraja, 1125

Tyler, Hamilton A., 678-79, 1358

Tyler, Royall, 441-47, 1358

Tylwyth Teg, 223

Tympana, 811

Tympanon (Tympanum, Typanon)(Greek percussion), 189, 333, 491, 497, 615, 622, 689, 778-79

Types of the Folk Tale, The (Aarne & Thompson), 275, 308ff., 631, 719-21, 723, 781, 800, 950, 952-53, 1023, 1212, 1320, 1341

Typhon (Greek giant), 101, 209, 724

Tyrbasia (Greek dance), 779

Tyrbe (Greek festival), 779

Tyre (city), 460, 502, 648

Tyro, 1308

Tyrol, 82

Tyrrenian (Tyrrhenian) people: see Etruscan people

Tyrrenus: see Torebus

Tyrrhenians: see Etruscan people

Tzetzes, On Lycophron, 505, 792-93

Tziltzelim (Hebrew cymbals), 160

Tzitzimitl (Aztec god), 72

Tzotzil people, 192

Tzu-ch'i, 978-79

Uacu tree, 1174

Uaitne, 1085

Ualaroi people, 114

Uanano people, 1173

Uapes people, 1173-74

Uaupe people, 771,773

Ubakala people, 987, 989

Ubar-drum (Australian aboriginal drum), 195ff.

Uber die judische Angelologie (Kohut), 1049

Ucchista (Hindu sacrifice), 1102

Uchinarashi (Kin) (Japanese bell), 429

Uchiwa-daiko (Japanese fan drum), 430

Udgatar (Udgatr) priests, 364, 694-95

Udibwa, emperor, 415

Uemac, chief, 746

Uffer, Leza, 1024

Ugab (pipe, water organ), 474

Uganda (place), 93, 667, 956, 987, 991

Ugaritic people, 118

Ugav (Hebrew flute), 648

Ugrian peoples, 201

Uitoto people, 169, 191, 662, 664, 669-70

Uji (place), 447

Ukaz (Arabian town), 63

Ukerewe (place), 100

Ukko (Finnish god), 477,478

Ukraine, 165, 545

Ulejalu, 1197

Ulemitpahot Sefarim, 79

Ullagone (Irish mourning song), 546

Ullikummi (Babylonian/Assyrian god), 421

Ulster (place), 1084, 1204-05

Ulysses (see also ODYSSEUS), 179, 574, 615, 647, 651, 827, 1220

Ulysses and the Siren (Daniel), 794

Uma (Hindu), 708

Uma: see Parvati

Umall, 130

Umbria (place), 121

Umeda people, 986

Umeko, Mrs. Hiroshima, 437

Una, 375-76

Undine, 1302

Undufe, 1194-95

Undufe ritual, 1191, 1196

Union of American Hebrew Congregations, The, 1342

United Society of Believers in Christ's Second Appearing: see Shakers

United States of America, 86, 839

Universal History, 825

Universal Lord, 997

Universe (Kamtchatka figure), 194

University Books, 1349, 1357

Other Music Titles Available from Pro/Am Music Resources

BIOGRAPHIES & COMPOSER STUDIES

ALKAN, REISSUE *by Ronald Smith*. Vol. 1: The Enigma. Vol. 2: The Music.

BEETHOVEN'S EMPIRE OF THE MIND *by John Crabbe*.

BÉLA BARTÓK: An Analysis of His Music *by Erno Lendvai*.

BÉLA BARTÓK: His Life in Pictures and Documents *by Ferenc Bónis*.

BERNARD STEVENS AND HIS MUSIC: A Symposium *edited by Bertha Stevens*.

JANÁCEK: Leaves from His Life *by Leos Janácek. Edited & transl. by Vilem & Margaret Tausky*.

JOHN FOULDS AND HIS MUSIC: An Introduction *by Malcolm MacDonald*.

LIPATTI *(Tanasescu & Bargauanu):* see PIANO, below.

LISZT AND HIS COUNTRY, 1869-1873 *by Deszo Legány*.

MASCAGNI: An Autobiography Compiled, Edited and Translated from Original Sources *by David Stivender*.

MICHAEL TIPPETT, O.M.: A Celebration *edited by Geraint Lewis. Fwd. by Peter Maxwell Davies*.

THE MUSIC OF SYZMANOWSKI *by Jim Samson*.

THE OPRICHNIK: An Opera in Four Acts by Peter Il'ich Tchaikovsky. *Transl. & notes by Philip Taylor*.

PERCY GRAINGER: The Man Behind the Music *by Eileen Dorum*.

PERCY GRAINGER: The Pictorial Biography *by Robert Simon. Fwd. by Frederick Fennell*.

RAVEL ACCORDING TO RAVEL *(Perlemuter & Jourdan-Morhange):* see PIANO, below.

RONALD STEVENSON: A Musical Biography *by Malcolm MacDonald*.

SCHUBERT'S MUSIC FOR PIANO FOUR-HANDS *(Weekly & Arganbright):* see PIANO, below.

SOMETHING ABOUT THE MUSIC 1: Landmarks of Twentieth-Century Music *by Nick Rossi*.

SOMETHING ABOUT THE MUSIC 2: Anthology of Critical Opinions *edited by Thomas P. Lewis*.

A SOURCE GUIDE TO THE MUSIC OF PERCY GRAINGER *edited by Thomas P. Lewis*.

THE SYMPHONIES OF HAVERGAL BRIAN *by Malcolm MacDonald*. Vol. 2: Symphonies 13-29. Vol. 3: Symphonies 30-32, Survey, and Summing-Up.

VERDI AND WAGNER *by Erno Lendvai*.

VILLA-LOBOS: The Music *by Lisa M. Peppercorn*.

THE WORKS OF ALAN HOVHANESS: A Catalog, Opus 1 – Opus 360 *by Richard Howard*.

XENAKIS *by Nouritza Matossian*.

ZOLTAN KODALY: His Life in Pictures and Documents *by László Eosze*.

GENERAL SUBJECTS

ACOUSTICS AND THE PERFORMANCE OF MUSIC *by Jürgen Meyer*.

AMERICAN MINIMAL MUSIC, REISSUE *by Wim Mertens. Transl. by J. Hautekiet*.

CLARINET, REISSUE *by Jack Brymer*.

A CONCISE HISTORY OF HUNGARIAN MUSIC, 2ND ENL. EDITION *by Bence Szabolozi*.

EARLY MUSIC *by Denis Stevens*. Orig. title: Musicology (reissue).

FLUTE, REISSUE *by James Galway*.

GOGOLIAN INTERLUDE:; Gogol's Story "Christmas Eve" as the Subject of the Operas by Tchaikovsky and Rimsky-Korsakov *by Philip Taylor*.

Other Music Titles Available from Pro/Am Music Resources

THE MUSICAL INSTRUMENT COLLECTOR, REVISED EDITION *by J. Robert Willcutt & Kenneth R. Ball.*

A MUSICIAN'S GUIDE TO COPYRIGHT AND PUBLISHING, ENL. EDITION *by Willis Wager.*

MUSICOLOGY IN PRACTICE: Collected Essays by Denis Stevens *edited by Thomas P. Lewis. Vol. 1: 1948-1970. Vol. 2: 1971-1990.*

MY VIOLA AND I, REISSUE *by Lionel Tertis.*

THE NUTLEY PAPERS: A Fresh Look at the Titans of Music (humor) *by James Billings.*

PEACE SONGS *compiled & edited by John Jordan.*

PERCUSSION INSTRUMENTS AND THEIR HISTORY, REV. EDITION *by James Blade.*

THE PRO/AM BOOK OF MUSIC AND MYTHOLOGY *compiled, edited & with commentaries by Thomas P. Lewis.*

THE PRO/AM GUIDE TO U. S. BOOKS ABOUT MUSIC: Annotated Guide to Current & Back-list Titles *edited by Thomas P. Lewis. 2 vols.*

SKETCHES FROM MY LIFE *by Natalia Sats.*

VIOLIN AND VIOLA, REISSUE *by Yehudi Menuhin & William Primrose, with Denis Stevens.*

GUITAR

THE AMP BOOK: A Guitarist's Inroductory Guide to Tube Amplifiers *by Donald Brosnac.*

ANIMAL MAGNETISM FOR MUSICIANS: Making a Bass Guitar and Pickup from Scratch *by Erno Zwaan.*

ANTHOLOGY OF FLAMENCO FALSETAS *collected by Ray Mitchell.*

ANTONIO DE TORRES: Guitar Maker—His Life and Work *by José Romanillos. Fwd. by Julian Bream.*

THE ART OF FLAMENCO *by D. E. Pohren.*

THE ART OF PRACTICING *by Alice Arzt.*

CLASSIC GUITAR CONSTRUCTION *by Irving Sloane.*

THE DEVELOPMENT OF THE MODERN GUITAR *by John Huber.*

THE FENDER GUITAR *by Ken Achard.*

THE GIBSON GUITAR *by Ian C. Bishop. 2 vols.*

THE GUITAR: From the Renaissance to the Present Day, REISSUE *by Harvey Turnbull.*

GUITAR HISTORY: Volume 1—Guitars Made by the Fender Company *by Donald Brosnac.*

GUITAR HISTORY: Volume 2—Gibson SGs *by John Bulli.*

GUITAR HISTORY: Volume 3—Gibson Catalogs of the Sixties *edited by Richard Hetrick.*

GUITAR REPAIR: A Manual of Repair for Guitars and Fretted Instruments *by Irving Sloane.*

GUITAR TRADER'S VINTAGE GUITAR BULLETIN. *6 vols.*

THE HISTORY AND DEVELOPMENT OF THE AMERICAN GUITAR *by Ken Achard.*

AN INTRODUCTION TO SCIENTIFIC GUITAR DESIGN *by Donald Brosnac.*

LEFT HANDED GUITAR *by Nicholas Clarke.*

LIVES AND LEGENDS OF FLAMENCO, 2ND EDITION *by D. E. Pohren.*

MANUAL OF GUITAR TECHNOLOGY: The History and Technology of Plucked String Instruments *by Franz Jahnel. English vers. by Dr. J. C. Harvey*

MAKING MUSIC SERIES: THE GURU'S GUITAR GUIDE *by Tony Bacon & Paul Day.* MAKING 4-TRACK MUSIC *by John Peel.* WHAT BASS, 2ND EDITION *by Tony Bacon & Laurence Canty.* WHAT DRUM, 2ND EDITION *by Geoff Nicholls & Andy Duncan.* WHAT GUITAR: The

Other Music Titles Available from Pro/Am Music Resources

Making Music Guide to Buying Your Electric Six String, 3RD EDITION. WHAT'S MIDI, 2ND EDITION *by Andy Honeybone et al.*

THE NATURAL CLASSICAL GUITAR, REISSUE *by Lee F. Ryan.*

THE SEGOVIA TECHNIQUE, REISSUE *by Vladimir Bobri.*

THE SOUND OF ROCK: A History of Marshall Valve Guitar Amplifiers *by Mike Doyle.*

THE STEEL STRING GUITAR: Construction and Repair, UPDATED EDITION *by David Russell Young.*

STEEL STRING GUITAR CONSTRUCTION *by Irving Sloane.*

A WAY OF LIFE, REISSUE *by D. E. Pohren.*

PERFORMANCE PRACTICE / "HOW-TO" INSTRUCTIONAL

GUIDE TO THE PRACTICAL STUDY OF HARMONY *by Peter Il'ich Tchaikovsky.*

HOW TO SELECT A BOW FOR VIOLIN FAMILY INSTRUMENTS *by Balthasar Planta.*

IMAGINATIONS: Tuneful Fun and Recital Pieces to Expand Early Grade Harp Skills *by Doris Davidson.*

THE JOY OF ORNAMENTATION: Being Giovanni Luca Conforto's *Treatise on Ornamentation* (Rome, 1593) *with a Preface by Sir Yehudi Menuhin and an Introduction by Denis Stevens.*

MAKING MUSICAL INSTRUMENTS *by Irving Sloane.*

THE MUSICIAN'S GUIDE TO MAPPING: A New Way to Learn Music *by Rebecca P. Shockley.*

THE MUSICIANS' THEORY BOOK: Reference to Fundamentals, Harmony, Counterpoint, Fugue and Form *by Asger Hamerik.*

ON BEYOND C *(Davidson):* see PIANO, below.

THE STUDENT'S DICTIONARY OF MUSICAL TERMS.

TENSIONS IN THE PERFORMANCE OF MUSIC: A Symposium, REVISED & EXTENDED EDITION *edited by Carola Grindea. Fwd. by Yehudi Menuhin.*

THE VIOLIN: Precepts and Observations *by Sourene Arakelian.*

PIANO/HARPSICHORD

THE ANATOMY OF A NEW YORK DEBUT RECITAL *by Carol Montparker.*

AT THE PIANO WITH FAURÉ, REISSUE *by Marguerite Long.*

EUROPEAN PIANO ATLAS *by H. K. Herzog.*

FRENCH PIANISM: An Historical Perspective *by Charles Timbrell.*

GLOSSARY OF HARPSICHORD TERMS *by Susanne Costa.*

KENTNER: A Symposium *edited by Harold Taylor. Fwd. by Yehudi Menuhin.*

LIPATTI *by Dragos Tanasescu & Grigore Bargauanu.*

ON BEYOND C: Tuneful Fun in Many Keys to Expand Early Grade Piano Skills *by Doris Davidson.*

THE PIANIST'S TALENT *by Harold Taylor. Fwd. by John Ogdon.*

PIANO, REISSUE *by Louis Kentner.*

THE PIANO AND HOW TO CARE FOR IT *by Otto Funke.*

THE PIANO HAMMER *by Walter Pfeifer.*

Other Music Titles Available from Pro/Am Music Resources

PIANO NOMENCLATURE, 2ND EDITION *by Nikolaus Schimmel & H. K. Herzog.*
RAVEL ACCORDING TO RAVEL *by Vlado Perlemuter & Hélène Jouran-Morhange.*
SCHUBERT'S MUSIC FOR PIANO FOUR-HANDS *by Dallas Weekly & Nancy Arganbright.*
TECHNIQUE OF PIANO PLAYING, 5TH EDITION *by József gát.*
THE TUNING OF MY HARPSICHORD *by Herbert Anton Kellner.*

See also:

ALKAN (2 volumes)*(Smith).*
LISZT AND HIS COUNTRY, 1869-1873*(Legány).*
PERCY GRAINGER: The Man Behind the Music *(Dorum).*
PERCY GRAINGER: The Pictorial Biography *(Simon).*
RONALD STEVENSON: A Musical Biography *(MacDonald).*
A SOURCE GUIDE TO THE MUSIC OF PERCY GRAINGER *(Lewis).*
TENSIONS IN THE PERFORMANCE OF MUSIC: A Symposium *(Grindea).*